The Complete
Instant Pot
Recipe Book

1500 Easy, Affordable & Tasty Instant Pot Recipes for Beginners and Advanced Users to Create Holiday & Everyday Cuisines

Martha Romero

Contents

Introduction

Instant Pot is a versatile multi-use pressure cooker. You can call it with another name, "genius or miracle pot." It is a secret weapon in your kitchen. Instant Pot is a great kitchen appliance for busy people and helps them to save time, energy, and money. No doubt, Instant Pot can change the way of life.

Cooking with Instant Pot is super easy and fun. Everyone is excited and enjoys the versatility and ease of getting mouthwatering and creative meals on the dining table in a hurry. It is a great cooking appliance that saves you many hours every week.

With this Instant Pot cooking appliance, you can cook flavorful, healthy, and quick meals with little effort. It comes with various cooking functions, cooking accessories, and user-friendly operating buttons. In this cookbook, you will get delicious and healthy recipes. You can prepare them at any time or on any occasion.

The Instant Pot makes our life easier. It cooks food in very less time. You can spend many hours with your family. You can prepare any meal like chicken, beef, lamb, pork, vegetables, appetizer, soup, stews, dips, sauces, grains, beans, rice, yogurt, fish/seafood, dessert, snacks, and many more. You don't need any other appliance because it offers all cooking functions.

It is safe to use and easy to understand. It provides the families and households with everything they need from the Instant pot, but at the accurate settings and possible size. Let's find out more about this wonderful Instant Pot cooking appliance that can make you fall in love with cooking all over again!

HAPPY COOKING!!!

Fundamentals of Instant Pot

What Is Instant Pot

The Instant Pot is a wonderful kitchen appliance. It comes with two smart programs: Pressure cooking includes steam, pressure cook, porridge, soup/broth, rice, meat/stew, bean/chili, etc. No pressure cooking includes slow cook, sauté, yogurt, and keep warm, etc. It comes with useful accessories, including the top lid, bottom lid, inner pot, cooker base, steam rack, condensation collector, and control panel. It has user-friendly operating buttons. Using Instant Pot cooking appliance, prepare chicken, beef, lamb, pork, seafood, vegetables, dessert, appetizer/snacks, soups/broth, yogurt, beans, rice meals. It

makes life comfortable.

The Instant Pot is wonderful for the family budget. You didn't need to bring a complex shopping list. In this cookbook, you will find simple and common ingredients for each recipe. You can create different meals using your favorite ingredients and spices.

Benefits of Using Instant Pot

Here are some benefits of using the Instant Pot:

Time, Money, and Energy Saving Pot
Pressure cooking is one of the most affordable ways to cook large budget-friendly foods. It saves your time and takes some hours in the week. It doesn't allow you to bring complex shopping for cooking meals. You will spend 4 to 5 hours with your family and cook food within 1 hour. You didn't need to purchase separate kitchen appliances such as pans/skillet, rice cooker, steamer, or slow cooker. It is the best pot for busy people. In the morning, you can prepare breakfast in very little time. Then, you can go on your work.

Multi-Functions
The Instant Pot offers many useful functions such as steam, pressure cook, porridge, soup/broth, rice, meat/stew, bean/chili, slow cook, sauté, yogurt, and keep warm, etc. Now, you can prepare any meal using these cooking functions. Using this cooking appliance, you will get tender, healthy, and delicious meals.

Cool Accessories
When you purchase this appliance, you will have some cool accessories, which you can use in everyday cooking. The accessories include a steam rack, inner pot, cooker base, condensation collector, top lid, etc. It is an excellent way to get started cooking. You don't need to purchase additional accessories before you start cooking. The cleaning process of these accessories is super easy.

Safe to Use
High pressure or high temperature can make you afraid of using this appliance, especially children. However, Instant Pot has created a safety mechanism, which almost certainly guarantees that the appliance will

continue to cook without any problems. There is nothing that kids and adults should be afraid of. The best way is to read about this appliance before cooking. I added all information, including safety tips, in my cookbook. You can read it before cooking food.

First Use

When you purchase an Instant Pot appliance, remove all the cooker and accessories packaging.

Cleaning before First Use
Remove the inner pot from the cooker base and rinse it with hot and soapy water. Wash with warm and clean water and use a soft cloth or dry the exterior of the pot or you can put the inner pot in the dishwasher.

Wipe the heating element with a soft cloth before returning the inner pot to the cooker base. Make sure that there are no dust and package particles present. The inner pot is a main part of the Instant Pot. The food is placed into the inner pot, not directly in the cooker base.

If you see the deformed or damaged inner pot, return it because it will cause personal injury or damage the appliance.

Install Condensation Collector
Dry the inner pot, cooker base, and accessories before returning to the main unit. When all parts are inserted in the main pot, install the condensation collector at the rear of the cooker by aligning the top of the collector and press in. When done, place the steam release handle on the lid.

Before Using Instant Pot
If you want to remove the lid, hold the handle, turn the lid counterclockwise, and lift the lid.

Remove the inner pot from the main unit. Place food and liquid into the inner pot according to the recipe instructions. Place the steam rack if using the steam cooking function onto the bottom of the inner pot first. Wipe outside of the unit and make sure that there is no food debris on the bottom side of the inner pot.

Return the inner pot to the unit and rotate slightly. Check and make sure that the sealing ring rack is completely set on the inner side of the

sealing ring. Check and make sure that there is no deformation on the sealing ring rack. Close the lid.

Ensure that the steam release valve, float valve, and anti-block shield are dust-free and debris-free. After putting a lid on, ensure that the float valve drops down. Do not put the lid on if you use a Sauté cooking function.

Initial Test
Add three cups of water into the inner pot. Close the lid.
After that, turn the steam release handle to the sealing position. Then,

press the "steam" button onto the control panel. Adjust the time for two minutes. It will take ten seconds to preheat. The display shows "ON" on the screen. The steam will release until the float valve pops up. The steam cooking function will start when pressure is reached. The instant pot will beep when cooking time is completed and turn to the "Keep Warm" button.

Introduction to Pressure Cooking

Pressure cooking is a versatile method to cook any meal. It is an efficient way to cook food quickly. You can cook your favorite meals using pressure cooking.
The pressure cooker has three stages when pressure cooking:

Preheating and Pressurization

Select desired cooking program in pressure cooking. The main unit will take ten seconds to ensure you have selected the cooking function. The display shows "ON" onto the screen to signify it has started preheating. When the Instant pot is preheated, the liquid is vaporized in the inner pot to build steam. When the steam has built up, the float valve pops up. It would be best if you locked the lid for safe cooking. When the float valve pops up, the silicone cap attached to the bottom of the float valve seals the steam inner side of the cooking chamber. Allow the pressure to rise. If pressure is high, then it means that the cooking temperature is high.
High pressure = High temperature

Cooking

When the float valve pops up, the main unit needs a few minutes to build pressure. When desired pressure level is reached, cooking starts. The display shows "ON" onto the screen in HH: MM (hours: mins) Smart program settings – pressure level (HI or Lo), Temperature, Cooking time, and Keeping warm will automatically be on or off. You can adjust at any time during cooking.

Depressurization

When pressure cooking is completed, read the recipe instructions for depressurization of the main unit. If automatic keep warm is on, the display shows counting automatically. If not, adjust the cooking time. When cooking time is completed, the display shows "END."
There are two methods for the venting process:

Natural Release Method

Some recipes call the natural release method to release steam or pressure. Leave the steam releases to handle in the sealing position. If the cooking temperature is dropped, the unit depressurizes naturally. The depressurization time increases vary based on the quantity of food and liquid. When the cooker has depressurized, the float valve drops in the lid of the main unit.

Quick-Release Method

Some recipes call the quick release method to release steam or pressure. Turn the steam releases handle from the sealing position to the venting position. Use the natural release method to vent the remaining pressure/steam.

10-minute Natural Release

Leave the steam releases to handle in the sealing position for ten minutes after cooking is completed, then turn the steam release handle to the venting position.

Main Functions of Instant Pot

There are two programs in the Instant Pot cooking appliance: Pressure cooking and Non-pressure cooking.
Pressure cooking has the following cooking functions:
• Pressure cook, Soup/Broth, Meat/Stew, Bean/Chili, Rice, Porridge, and Steam, etc.
The non-pressure cooking has the following cooking functions:
• Slow cook, Sauté, Yogurt, and Keep warm, etc.

Pressure Cooking Programs

1. Pressure Cook

Pressure cooking is the most used cooking function. It cooks food under high pressure. It takes 30 minutes to prepare a meal.

Cooking Method of Using Pressure Cook

• Place steam rack in the bottom of the inner pot.
• Add liquid to the inner pot. Place ingredients onto the steam rack.
• Insert the inner pot in the cooker base. Close lid.
• Select "Pressure Cook" cooking function.
• Select "High" or "Low" pressure level. Press "Keep warm" to turn the automatic "Keep Warm" setting on or off.
• Press the start button to begin cooking.
• Follow the direction of the recipe to choose the exact venting method.

Cooking function	Setting	Suggested use	Imp note
Pressure cook	Less/ normal/ more	Manual programming	Press pressure level to toggle between high and low pressure Press +/- button to select cooking time Adjust according to the recipe instruction

Note: You can use the following liquids using the pressure cooking method: Stock, soup, broth, juice, water, filter water, etc.

2. Steam

The steam cooking method is mostly used for vegetables. You can steam any vegetable. Insert steam rack in the bottom of the inner pot.

Cooking Method of Using Steam

• Place steam rack in the bottom of the inner pot.
• Add liquid/broth/water/stock in the inner pot. Place ingredients onto the steam rack.
• Insert the inner pot in the cooker base. Close lid.
• Select "Steam" cooking function.
• Select "High" or "Low" pressure level. Press "Keep Warm" to turn automatic keep the warm setting on or off.
• Press the start button to begin cooking.
• Follow the direction of the recipe to choose the exact venting method.

Cooking function	Setting	Suggested use	Imp note
Steam	Less/ normal/ more	Vegetables/ Fish and Seafood/ Meat	Insert steam rack in the bottom of the inner pot to elevate food from cooking liquid Use quick-release method to prevent food from burning/ overcooking

3. Rice
You can cook white rice, basmati rice, short-grain, and jasmine rice using the rice cooking method. It prefers high pressure to cook rice.

Cooking Method of Using Rice
• Add liquid/broth/water/stock in the inner pot. Place rice into the pot.
• Insert the inner pot in the cooker base. Close lid.
• Select "Rice" cooking function.
• Select "High" or "Low" pressure level. Press "Keep Warm" to turn automatic keep the warm setting on or off.
• Press the start button to begin cooking.
• Follow the direction of the recipe to choose the exact venting method.

Cooking function	Setting	Suggested use	Imp note
Rice	Less/ Normal/ More	Tender/ Normal texture/ Soft texture	Automated cooking smart program. Depending upon the quantity of rice, adjust the cooking time – the cooking range is 8-15 minutes. When cooking time is done, wait for ten minutes. Use quick method to release pressure or release remaining pressure using natural release method

4. Bean/Chili
Using the bean/chili cooking method, you can cook various beans, including black-eyed peas, kidney beans, and white beans. It prefers high pressure to cook bean/chili.

Cooking Method of Using Bean/Chili
• Add liquid/broth/water/stock in the inner pot. Place bean/chili into the pot.
• Insert the inner pot in the cooker base. Close lid.
• Select the "Bean/Chili" cooking function.
• Select "High" or "Low" pressure level. Press "Keep Warm" to turn the automatic "Keep Warm" setting on or off.
• Press the start button to begin cooking.
• Follow the direction of the recipe to choose the exact venting method.

Cooking function	Setting	Suggested use	Imp note
Bean/ chili	Less/ Normal/ More	Firm texture/Soft texture/ Very soft texture	Insert steam rack in the bottom of the inner pot to elevate food from cooking liquid Use a quick-release method to prevent food from burning/ overcooking

5. Soup/Broth
Using the soup/broth cooking method, you can prepare soup, stock, or broth. You need to select the "Soup" cooking function.

Cooking Method of Using Soup/Broth
• Add liquid to the inner pot. Place ingredients into the pot.
• Insert the inner pot in the cooker base. Close lid.
• Select "Soup/Broth" cooking function.
• Select "High" or "Low" pressure level. Press "Keep Warm" to turn the automatic "Keep Warm" setting on or off.
• Press the start button to begin cooking.
• Follow the direction of the recipe to choose the exact venting method.

Cooking function	Setting	Suggested use	Imp note
Soup/ Broth	Less/ Normal/ More	Soup without meat/soup with meat/ bone broth	The Liquid remains clear because there is less boiling motion Use natural release method always when coup has a high starch content

6. Porridge
Using the porridge cooking method, you can cook different kinds of grains. This cooking method prefers high pressure.

Cooking Method of Using Porridge
• Add liquid to the inner pot. Place ingredients into the pot.
• Insert the inner pot in the cooker base. Close lid.
• Select "porridge" cooking function.
• Select "High" or "Low" pressure level. Press "Keep Warm" to turn the automatic "Keep Warm" setting on or off.
• Press the start button to begin cooking.
• Follow the direction of the recipe to choose the exact venting method.

Cooking function	Setting	Suggested use	Imp note
Porridge	Less/ Normal/ More	Rice porridge/ White rice, porridge/ Oatmeal, rolled, steel-cut	Adjust cooking time according to the recipe's instructions. Use natural release method to release pressure when foods expand

7. Meat/Stew
Using the meat/stew cooking method, you can cook chicken, beef,

lamb, pork, and seafood and make different stews, including chicken stews, beef stew, vegetable stew, lamb stew, and sausage stew, and fish stew, etc.

Cooking Method of Using Meat/Stew
• Add liquid to the inner pot. Place ingredients into the pot.
• Insert the inner pot in the cooker base. Close lid.
• Select the "meat/stew" cooking function.
• Select "High" or "Low" pressure level. Press "Keep Warm" to turn the automatic "Keep Warm" setting on or off.
• Press the start button to begin cooking.
• Follow the direction of the recipe to choose the exact venting method.

Cooking function	Setting	Suggested use	Imp note
Meat/ Stew	Less/ Normal/ More	Soft texture/ Very soft texture/Fall off bone	Choose a setting on meat texture as you want. Adjust cooking time manually Let rest the meat for 5 to 30 minutes until tender or succulent

Non-Pressure Cooking Programs

1. Slow Cook
Slow cook is a non-pressure cooking method. It takes a lot of time to cook food but gives tender and delicious meals. This cooking method is best for meats including chicken, beef, lamb, seafood, pork, etc.

Cooking Method of Using Slow Cook
• Remove inner pot from cooker base.
• Place liquid and ingredients into the inner pot. Insert it into the cooker base. Close the lid or use a glass lid with a venting hole.
• After that, turn the steam release handle to the venting position.
• Select the "slow cook" cooking function.
• Press the cooking function again to adjust the temperature according to the recipe's instructions.
• Press +/- button to adjust the cooking time according to the recipe's instructions.
• Press "Keep Warm" to toggle the keep warm setting on or off.
• The display shows time in counting while cooking.
• When cooking time is completed, the display shows "END" onto the screen.

Cooking function	Setting	Suggested use	Imp note
Slow cook	Less/ Normal/ More	Low setting/ Medium setting/ High setting	Follow the recipe's instructions for slow cooking Cooking time should be set for a minimum of ten hours for best results

2. Sauté
Sauté cooking method is used for sautéing meats, vegetables, and many more. You don't need to use water for this setting. Pour oil into the inner pot.

Cooking Method of Using Sauté
• Insert the inner pot into the cooker base. But, don't put the lid.
• Select "sauté" cooking function.
• Press sauté mode again to adjust the cooking temperature.
• Wait for ten seconds; then display shows "ON" to indicate that it has started preheating.
• Place food in the inner pot when the display shows "HOT" onto the screen.
• When cooking time is completed, the display shows "END" onto the screen.

Cooking function	Setting	Suggested use	Imp note
Sauté	Less/ Normal/ More	Simmering/ sautéing or searing/ stir-frying	The display shows "Hot" to "ON" indicates the main unit is maintaining the cooking temp 30 minutes is perfect cooking time for safety

Deglaze the Inner Pot (Turn Pressure Cooking to Sauté Mode)
You should sauté the meat and vegetables before pressure cooking because it is the perfect way to boost the flavor. If you are using sauté cooking mode after pressure cooking, deglaze the inner pot to ensure meal ingredients do not burn. Remove the ingredients from the inner pot and add water to the hot bottom surface to deglaze.

3.Yogurt
Using yogurt function, you can make yogurt at home. You can add it to different dishes.

Cooking Method of Using Yogurt
• Select "yogurt" cooking function.
• Press yogurt cooking mode again to select cooking time.
• Press +/- button to select the fermentation time if you want.
• Wait for ten seconds the unit begins preheating.
• The display shows cooking time in counting.
• When fermentation is completed, the unit beeps, and the display shows "END."

Cooking function	Setting	Suggested use	Imp note
Yogurt	Less/ Normal/ More	For low temperature fermentation/ Fermenting milk after cultured has been included/ Pasteurizing milk	Fermentation time is 24 hours Adjust the fermentation time according to the recipe's instructions. Pasteurizing time cannot be preset. When yogurt program is running, the display shows "BOIL." If you want extra thick yogurt, do pasteurize two times.

Buttons and User Guide of Instant Pot

The Instant Pot series has user-friendly operating buttons.

Pressure cooking temperature
Select the cooking function and press "Pressure level" to toggle between HI and Lo pressure levels.

Pressure Co1 oking Time
Select the cooking function, and then press the smart program button again to adjust the Less, Normal, and More cooking time options. Press +/- button to increase or decrease the time if you want.

Non-Pressure Cooking Temperature
Select the non-pressure cooking functions, and then presses the smart program button again to Less, Normal and More cooking temperature levels if you want.

Non-Pressure Cooking Time
Select the non-pressure cooking functions, and then presses +/- button to adjust the cooking time. The cooking time can be changed during cooking.

Cancel and Standby Mode
When the unit is plugged in, the display shows "OFF" to indicate "Standby mode."
Press the "Cancel" button to stop the cooking function at any time. The main unit returns to standby mode.

Turn Sound ON/OFF
Sound ON: When the main unit is in standby mode, press the + button until the displays show "ON" onto the screen.
Sound OFF: When the main unit is in standby mode, press and hold – button until the display shows "OFF" onto the screen.

Keep Warm
The "Keep Warm" mode automatically turns on all cooking functions except Yogurt and Sauté.

Reset
When the main unit is in standby mode, press the "cancel" button to reset cooking functions, temperature, pressure level, cooking time, etc.

Cooking Lid
When the display shows "lid", it indicates that the pressure lid is not

adequately secured or missing.

Preheat
When the display shows "ON", it indicates that the main unit is preheating.

Display Timer
The display shows "Time" onto the screen in the following:
• When the cooking function is running, the display timer is a countdown to indicate the cooking time remaining in the cooking function.
• The display timer countdown until the cooking function begins when the delay starts.
• When keep warm is running, the display timer counts to indicate how long food has been warming.

Auto
The display shows "Auto" to indicate that the rice cooking function is running.

Boil
The display shows "Boil" to indicate that the Yogurt function is pasteurizing.

Hot
The display shows "Hot" to indicate that food should be placed in the inner pot – (In sauté cooking function).

End
The display shows "End" to indicate that cooking time is completed.

Food Burn
Thc display shows "Food burn" to indicate overheating in the cooking chamber.

Accessories of Instant Pot

The Instant Pot comes with different accessories.

1. Pressure Cooking Lid
The pressure cooking lid is made with stainless steel. The pressure cooking lid is used in many cooking methods.
Open and remove the pressure lid:
• Grip the upper lid handle, turn it counterclockwise, and lift it.
Close the pressure lid:
• Turn the lid clockwise until the symbol present on the lid aligns with the symbol of the cooker base.

2. Steam Release Handle

Turn the steam release handle from sealing to venting and vice versa, open and close the valve, venting, sealing the cooker as you want. When the unit releases pressure, steam is removed from the top of the steam release handle. It is the main accessory for your safety and pressure cooking. It must be installed before cooking.

Remove the steam release valve:
• Lift the steam release valve and wait until all steam is removed.
• Install the steam release handle
• Put steam release handle on steam release pipe and press down tightly.

3. Anti-Block Shield
The anti-block shield should be installed because it is necessary to prevent food particles from the steam release pipe. It is an essential accessory for your safety.
Remove the anti-block shield:
• Lift the lid tightly and press firmly against the side of the anti-block shield with your thumbs.
• Install the anti-block shield:
• Put anti-block shield over prongs and press it down.

4. Sealing Ring
You should install a sealing ring to create a tight sealing between the lid and cooker base. You should install a sealing ring before cooking. It should be cleaned after every use. You should install 1 sealing ring while using the unit.
Remove the sealing ring:
• Lift the edges of the silicone rubber and pull the sealing ring out. When the sealing ring is removed, check the rack to ensure it is secured.
Install the sealing rings:
• Put sealing ring over the sealing ring rack and press it firmly.

5. Float Valve
The float valve shows that pressure is built up within the inner pot and appears in two positions.
Pressurized:
• The float valve is appeared and pops up with the lid.
Depressurized:
• The float valve is pinched into the lid.

6. Inner Pot
The inner pot is an essential accessory in the Instant Pot appliance. Place food in the inner pot. Close the lid.

7. Cooker Base
The cooker base is present at the bottom of the main unit. The inner pot is inserted into the cooker base. Don't place food directly in the cooker base.

Cleaning and Maintenance of Instant Pot

The cleaning process of Instant Pot is super easy. You should clean it after every use.

• Remove all accessories from the main unit, including the cooker base.

• Don't use chemical detergents, scouring pads or powdered on accessories.
• Rinse condensation collector after every use.
• Rinse sealing ring, anti-block shield, silicone cap, steam release valve, and float valve under hot and soapy water. You can put them in the dishwasher.
• Remove all small parts from the lid before cleaning.
• When the steam release valve is removed, clean the inner part of the steam release pipe to prevent clogging.
• Hold it vertically and turn it 360 degrees to remove water from the lid.
• If there is tough food residue stuck at the bottom, soak it in hot water for a few hours.
• If there is an odor present in the pot, combine 1 cup of white vinegar and 1 cup of water, run pressure cook for 5 to 10 minutes, and then use a quick method to release pressure.
• When all parts get dried, return to the main unit.
• Don't put the main unit in the dishwasher. Wipe the main unit with a soft cloth.
• Wipe the exterior part of the main unit with a moist and soft cloth.

Troubleshooting

Problem – 1
If you face difficulty in closing the lid

Possible reason
The sealing ring is not installed correctly.
May be contents in the Instant pot is still hot.

Solution
Again install the sealing ring properly
Turn the steam release handle to the venting position and slowly lower the lid on the cooker base.

Problem – 2
If you face difficulty in opening the lid
Possible reason
Pressure is present inside the unit

Solution

Release pressure according to the recipe's instructions.

Problem – 3
Steam is leaked from the side of the pressure lid
Possible reason
The lid is closed properly
The sealing ring is not installed
The sealing ring is damaged

Solution
Install the sealing ring
Replace the sealing ring
Open and then close the lid

4 - Week Diet Plan

Week 1

Day 1:
Breakfast: Quiche with Kalamata Olives and No Crust
Lunch: Bok Choy with Sesame Seeds
Snack: Deviled Eggs
Dinner: Sweet Potato and Beef chili
Dessert: Cheesecake and Cookies

Day 2:
Breakfast: Yummy Gravy
Lunch: Delicious Cauliflower Queso
Snack: Sesame-Soy Frozen Pot Stickers
Dinner: Hungarian Chicken Stew
Dessert: Filled Apples

Day 3:
Breakfast: Hard bowl egg
Lunch: Honey Cayenne Carrots
Snack: Garlic White Bean Hummus
Dinner: Fresh Mixed Seafood Soup
Dessert: Crisp Pear and Cranberry

Day 4:
Breakfast: Granola Bars with Peanut Butter
Lunch: Butter Mashed Potatoes
Snack: Plant-Based Hummus
Dinner: Steamed Lemon Shrimp with Asparagus
Dessert: Yummy Pudding

Day 5:
Breakfast: Pecan and Apple Oatmeal
Lunch: Creamy Parmesan Polenta
Snack: Herbed Artichokes
Dinner: Homemade Beef Borscht Soup
Dessert: Pears in Buttery Caramel

Day 6:
Breakfast: Yummy Strawberry Jam
Lunch: Simple Zucchini Ratatouille
Snack: Fresh Tomato Chutney
Dinner: Tasty Satay Pork with Rice Noodles
Dessert: Baked Kugel

Day 7:
Breakfast: Cozy Fruit with Spice
Lunch: Delicious Scalloped Potatoes
Snack: Classic Black Beans
Dinner: Baby Back Pork Ribs
Dessert: Apple Maple Cake

Week 2

Day 1:
Breakfast: Squash Frittata Casserole
Lunch: Roasted Spaghetti Squash
Snack: Spicy Salsa
Dinner: Yummy meatballs
Dessert: Bread Pudding with Blueberries

Day 2:
Breakfast: Cozy Fruit with Spice
Lunch: Braised Eggplant
Snack: Greek Eggplant Dip
Dinner: Beef Stew
Dessert: Easy Maple-Sweetened Applesauce

Day 3:
Breakfast: Buckwheat Porridge
Lunch: Butter Potatoes Mash
Snack: Savory Cocktail Sausages
Dinner: Curry chicken with Honey
Dessert: Fresh Mango-Coconut Custard

Day 4:
Breakfast: Nutty Bread with Zucchini
Lunch: Butternut Squash and Parsnips
Snack: Lentil Balls
Dinner: Wraps with Carnitas Lettuce
Dessert: Chocolate Cheesecake with Coconut

Day 5:
Breakfast: Corn Muffins with Bananas
Lunch: Steamed Garlic Edamame
Snack: Cinnamon Almonds
Dinner: Biryani De Beef
Dessert: Creamy Rum Cheesecake

Day 6:
Breakfast: Frittata with Sausage and Cheese
Lunch: Parmesan Spaghetti Squash
Snack: Hearty Sausage Dip
Dinner: Spinach Fish Rice
Dessert: Traditional Apple Cake

Day 7:
Breakfast: Frittata with Leeks and Asparagus
Lunch: Savory Mushroom Polenta
Snack: Deviled Eggs with Jalapeno
Dinner: Mongolian beef
Dessert: Creamy Carrot Soufflé

Week 3

Day 1:
Breakfast: Yummy Gravy
Lunch: Green Beans with Tomatoes and Potatoes
Snack: Tasty Sun-Dried Tomato Cheesecake
Dinner: Mediterranean Fish Stew with Hot Sauce
Dessert: Glazed Doughnut and Apple Crisp

Day 2:
Breakfast: Yummy Shakshuka
Lunch: Gingered Sweet Potatoes
Snack: Lemony Shrimp with Cocktail Sauce
Dinner: Beef and Potato Stew
Dessert: Cake Made of Bananas

Day 3:
Breakfast: Berries Coconut Porridge with Chia Seeds
Lunch: Stuffed Acorn Squash
Snack: Smoky Roasted Red Pepper Hummus
Dinner: Delicious Chicken Noodle Soup
Dessert: Cake with Blueberries

Day 4:
Breakfast: Oatmeal Pumpkin Pie Bites
Lunch: Herbed Potato Salad
Snack: Luscious Baba Ghanoush
Dinner: Baked Fish with Parmesan
Dessert: Honey Stewed Dried Fruits

Day 5:
Breakfast: Boiled Eggs in Tomato Sauce
Lunch: Steamed Broccoli
Snack: Quinoa Energy Balls
Dinner: Greek-Shrimp with Feta Cheese
Dessert: Chocolate Pudding with Apricots

Day 6:
Breakfast: Maple Polenta with Nut
Lunch: Boiled Cabbage
Snack: Potato Pea Salad
Dinner: Sole Fillets with Vegetables
Dessert: Classical German Pancake

Day 7:
Breakfast: Creamy Oatmeal
Lunch: Saucy Brussels Sprouts and Carrots
Snack: Hot Cauliflower Bites
Dinner: Coconut Rice in Chicken Broth
Dessert: Spiced Apple Cider

Week 4

Day 1:
Breakfast: Bacon-Cheddar Egg Bites
Lunch: Ginger Broccoli and Carrots
Snack: Fresh Tomato Chutney
Dinner: Shrimp Scampi with Lemon Wedges
Dessert: Chai White Hot Chocolate

Day 2:
Breakfast: Brown Sugar Quinoa
Lunch: Garlic Green Beans
Snack: Refried Beans
Dinner: Halibut Steaks with Tomatoes
Dessert: Yummy Arroz Con Leche

Day 3:
Breakfast: Quinoa Greek Yogurt with Blueberries
Lunch: Maple Dill Carrots
Snack: Luscious Baba Ghanoush
Dinner: Drunken Chuck Roast
Dessert: Traditional Chewy Brownies

Day 4:
Breakfast: Maple Polenta with Nut
Lunch: Purple Cabbage Salad
Snack: Herbed Chickpea, Parsley, and Dill Dip
Dinner: Pork with Apple and Curry
Dessert: A Chocolate Cake without Flour

Day 5:
Breakfast: Baked Ham, Kale and Eggs
Lunch: Lemon Garlic Red Chard
Snack: Bacon-Chive Deviled Eggs
Dinner: Seamed Cod with Vegetables
Dessert: Crisp Pear and Cranberry

Day 6:
Breakfast: Feta Crustless Quiche with Spinach
Lunch: Eggplant Caponata
Snack: Plant-Based Hummus
Dinner: Butter dipped Lobster Tails
Dessert: Cake with Orange and Pecans

Day 7:
Breakfast: Oatmeal Diced Apple
Lunch: Burgundy Mushrooms
Snack: Black Bean Dip with Bacon
Dinner: Chicken Cajun with Rice
Dessert: Cups of Pumpkin Pie

Chapter 1 Breakfast Recipes

Frittata with Mushrooms and Goat Cheese

Prep Time: 10 minutes | Cook Time: 13 minutes | Serves: 4

6 large eggs
¼ cup chopped fresh basil leaves
½ cup crumbled goat cheese
½ teaspoon salt
¼ teaspoon ground black pepper

1 tablespoon olive oil
2 cups sliced baby bella mushrooms
1 small yellow onion, peeled and diced
1 cup water

1. Combine eggs, basil, goat cheese, salt, and pepper in a medium bowl. Place aside. 2. Heat oil in a pan for 30 sec and stir fry mushrooms and onions in it for 5 minutes, or until onions are transparent. 3. Place the cooked mushroom mixture in a glass bowl measuring 7 cups, coat it with cooking spray or oil, allow it to cool for 5 minutes. Add whisked eggs to the cooked mixture, and then toss everything together. 4. Add water to instant pot inner pot and insert the steam rack. Put the glass dish with the egg mixture on the steam rack. Lock the lid. 5. Press Pressure Cook button and set time to 8 minutes and level to high. 6. When the timer sounds, open the lid after allowing the steam to release on the seal position. 7. Take the dish out of the pot and let it for 10 minutes so the eggs can set. Slice and warmly serve.
Per Serving: Calories 182; Fat: 15.17g; Sodium 404mg; Carbs: 2.87g; Sugars: 1.03g; Protein 8.39g

Quiche with Kalamata Olives and No Crust

Prep Time: 10 minutes | Cook Time: 8 minutes | Serves: 6

6 large eggs
¼ cup whole milk
2 teaspoons chopped fresh dill
½ teaspoon salt
¼ teaspoon ground black pepper
1 Roma tomato, seeded and diced

¼ cup diced jarred artichokes, drained
¼ cup sliced pitted Kalamata olives
¼ cup crumbled feta cheese
¼ cup peeled and diced red onion
2 cups water

1. Whisk the eggs, salt, milk, dill, and pepper in a medium bowl. Add onion, feta cheese, tomato, artichokes, and olives. Place aside. 2. Fill a 7-cup glass dish with the egg mixture after greasing it with oil or cooking spray. 3. Fill the Instant Pot with water. Put in the steam rack. Place the egg mixture dish on the steam rack. Lid locked. 4. Press Pressure Cook button. Input 8 minutes for the cook time and select level high. After the timer beeps, let pressure to naturally release for 10 minutes on seal position, then quick-release any remaining pressure on vent position. Then open the lid. 5. After removing the dish from the pot, wait 10 minutes. Slice and warmly serve.
Per Serving: Calories 98; Fat: 6.91g; Sodium 314mg; Carbs: 4.94g; Sugars: 2.47g; Protein 4.51g

Squash Frittata Casserole

Prep Time: 10 minutes | Cook Time: 8 minutes | Serves: 4

6 large eggs
2 tablespoons whole milk
2 slices gluten-free bread, cubed
1 teaspoon salt
½ teaspoon ground black pepper

¼ cup shredded Cheddar cheese
3 cups shredded yellow squash (approximately 1 large)
¼ cup peeled and diced sweet onion
1 cup water

1. Eggs and milk should be whisked together in a medium bowl. Let the bread absorb some of the liquid. Add cheese, squash, onion, salt, and pepper. 2. Place egg mixture in a 7-cup glass bowl that has been coated with cooking oil or cooking spray. 3. Insert the steam rack and add water to the Instant Pot. Put the glass dish with the egg mixture on the steam rack. Lock lid. 4. Press Pressure Cook button and set 8 minutes for the cook time and level to High. When the timer beeps, open the lid after allowing the pressure to naturally dissipate on seal position. 5. Dish should be taken out of the pot, and the eggs should be given ten minutes to set. Slice and warmly serve.
Per Serving: Calories 170; Fat: 8.9g; Sodium 860mg; Carbs: 14.33g; Sugars: 4.95g; Protein 8.61g

Swiss Egg Muffins with Ham

Prep Time: 10 minutes | Cook Time: 8 minutes | Serves: 6

4 large eggs
½ cup small-diced cooked ham
½ cup grated Swiss cheese
2 teaspoons Dijon mustard

½ teaspoon salt
½ teaspoon ground black pepper
1 cup water

1. Mix the eggs, ham, cheese, Dijon mustard, salt, and pepper in a medium bowl. Spread the egg mixture evenly among the six silicone cupcake liners that have been gently oiled or sprayed with cooking oil. 2. Add water to the inner pot of instant pot. Insert the steam rack. Place the muffin cups in the steam rack with care. Lock lid. 3. Press Pressure Cook button and set 8 minutes for the cook time and level to High. Quickly release pressure steam on vent position when the timer sounds, and then open the lid. 4. Remove egg muffins, then warmly serve.
Per Serving: Calories 101; Fat: 6.84g; Sodium 493mg; Carbs: 1.46g; Sugars: 0.23g; Protein 8.37g

Apple Cinnamon Crumb Muffins

Prep Time: 10 minutes | Cook Time: 9 minutes | Serves: 6

Muffins
1¼ cups gluten-free all-purpose flour
2 teaspoons gluten-free baking powder
½ teaspoon baking soda
1 teaspoon ground cinnamon
⅛ teaspoon salt

½ teaspoon vanilla extract
3 tablespoons unsalted butter, melted
2 large eggs
¼ cup granulated sugar
¼ cup grated, peeled red apple
1 cup water

Crumb Topping
2 tablespoons gluten-free all-purpose flour
¼ cup light brown sugar
⅛ teaspoon ground cinnamon

⅛ teaspoon salt
2 tablespoons unsalted butter, softened

1. Flour, baking soda, cinnamon, salt, and baking powder should all be combined in a big bowl. 2. Combine apple, butter, eggs, sugar, and vanilla in a medium bowl. 3. Add the wet ingredients from the medium bowl to the dry ingredients in the big bowl. Mix the ingredients gently. Avoid overmixing. Fill six silicone cupcake liners with the mixture and gently coat with oil or cooking spray. 4. Use a fork to stir the ingredients for the crumb topping in a small bowl, working the butter into the dry ingredients to produce a crumbly consistency. Sprinkle the mixture on top after evenly distributing this among the cupcakes. 5. Add water to the Instant Pot and insert steam rack. On top, place cupcake liners. Lock lid. 6. Select the Pressure Cook option, then set the level to High and timer for the 9-minute. Quickly release steam on vent position when the timer beeps, and then open the lid. 7. Take the muffins out of the saucepan and let them cool for five minutes before serving.
Per Serving: Calories 352; Fat: 8.54g; Sodium 114mg; Carbs: 60.91g; Sugars: 13.69g; Protein 7.52g

Creamy Oatmeal

Prep time: 10 minutes | Cook time: 2 minutes | Serve: 1

½ cup rolled oats
1 cup water
1/16 teaspoon salt
½ tablespoon butter

3 teaspoons brown sugar
⅛ teaspoon vanilla extract
⅛ teaspoon ground cinnamon
½ tablespoon heavy cream

1. Mix oats with water, and salt in the Inner Pot. 2. Select Pressure Cook mode, and then press the "Pressure Cook" button again to select "Less" time option. 3. Use the "-" key to set the cooking time to 2 minutes. 4. Press the Pressure Level button to adjust the pressure to "Low Pressure." 5. When the time is up, quickly and carefully turn the steam release handle from Sealing position to the Venting position. 6. Stir oats, and then add the remaining ingredients. 7. Scoop the meal into a bowl and enjoy.
Per Serving: Calories 224; Fat 11.84g; Sodium 49mg; Carbs 39.12g; Fiber 7.4g; Sugar 8.3g; Protein 8.36g

Oatmeal with Peanut Butter and Jelly

Prep Time: 5 minutes | Cook Time: 7 minutes | Serves: 2

1 cup old-fashioned oats
1¼ cups water
⅛ teaspoon salt

2 teaspoons smooth peanut butter
2 tablespoons strawberry jelly
¼ cup whole milk

1. To the Instant Pot, add salt, water, and oats. Lock lid. 2. Press Pressure Cook button and set level to Low and time to 7 minutes. 3. Allow steam to naturally release on seal position after the timer beeps. Then open the lid. 4. Divide the oatmeal into two dishes. Add peanut butter and jelly and stir. Add milk. Serve hot.
Per Serving: Calories 173; Fat: 5.24g; Sodium 258mg; Carbs: 40.12g; Sugars: 9.09g; Protein 9.5g

Egg Muffins with Cheese and Sausage

Prep Time: 10 minutes | Cook Time: 13 minutes | Serves: 6

1 tablespoon olive oil
½ small yellow onion, peeled and diced
¼-pound ground pork sausage
4 large eggs
¼ cup grated mozzarella cheese
⅛ teaspoon salt
½ teaspoon ground black pepper
1 cup water

1. Heat oil in the Instant Pot for 30 seconds by pressing the Sauté button. Add sausage and onion. Stir-fry the sausage and onions for five minutes, or until they begin to brown. Transfer mixture to a small bowl to cool while egg mixture is being prepared. 2. Whisk the eggs, cheese, salt, and pepper in a medium bowl. Egg mixture is added to the cooled onion mixture. Spread the egg mixture evenly among the six silicone cupcake liners that have been gently oiled or sprayed with cooking oil. 3. Add water to the inner pot and insert the steam rack. Place the cupcake liners in the steam rack with care. Lock lid. 4. Press Pressure Cook button and set 8 minutes for the cook time and level to High. 5. Quickly release pressure on vent position when the timer beeps, and then open the lid. 6. Remove egg muffins, then warmly serve.
Per Serving: Calories 122; Fat: 9.2g; Sodium 107mg; Carbs: 1.28g; Sugars: 0.38g; Protein 8.24g

Savory Buckwheat Muffins with Goat Cheese and Bacon

Prep Time: 5 minutes | Cook Time: 15 minutes | Serves: 6

4 slices bacon, diced
½ small yellow onion, peeled and diced
1 cup buckwheat flour
2 teaspoons gluten-free baking powder
½ teaspoon baking soda
½ teaspoon ground black pepper
3 tablespoons unsalted butter, melted
2 large eggs, whisked
½ cup crumbled goat cheese
1 cup water

1. On the Instant Pot, click the Sauté button. To the pot, add bacon and onion. Stir-fry for 5 minutes, or until bacon is crisp and onions begin to brown. Mixture should be transferred to a small bowl lined with paper towels to cool before using. 2. Combine the flour, butter, eggs, baking soda, pepper, and baking powder in a medium bowl. Combine the cooled bacon mixture with the goat cheese. Spread the mixture evenly into six silicone cupcake liners that have been gently oiled or sprayed with cooking spray. 3. Add water to the inner pot and insert the steam rack. Place the cupcake liners in the steam rack with care. Lock lid. 4. Press Pressure Cook button and set 8 minutes for the cook time and level to High. 5. Quickly release pressure on vent position when the timer beeps, and then open the lid. 6. Remove egg muffins, and then warmly serve.
Per Serving: Calories 236; Fat: 16.14g; Sodium 157mg; Carbs: 16.03g; Sugars: 1g; Protein 8.61g

Yummy Grits

Prep Time: 5 minutes | Cook Time: 15 minutes | Serves: 6

4 slices bacon, diced
5 cups water
1 cup coarse corn grits
2 tablespoons unsalted butter
½ teaspoon salt
½ cup shredded sharp Cheddar cheese

1. On the Instant Pot, click the Sauté button. Add bacon to pot. Stir 5 minutes to crisp the bacon. Then place the bacon on a small dish lined with paper towels to cool. 2. Salt, butter, water, and grits are combined in an Instant Pot inner pot. Lock lid. 3. Press Pressure Cook button and set level to High and timer to 10 minutes. Allow steam to naturally release on seal position after the timer beeps. Then open the lid. 4. Whisk grits in pot 5 minutes until they thicken. Add cheese and fried bacon. 5. Spoon the grits into the dishes.
Per Serving: Calories 171; Fat: 13.18g; Sodium 652mg; Carbs: 7.8g; Sugars: 1.77g; Protein 5.74g

Yummy Gravy

Prep Time: 5 minutes | Cook Time: 17 minutes | Serves: 10

2 tablespoons unsalted butter
1-pound ground pork sausage
1 small sweet onion, peeled and diced
¼ cup chicken broth
¼ cup gluten-free all-purpose flour
1 tablespoon cornmeal
1½ cups whole milk
½ teaspoon salt
1 tablespoon ground black pepper

1. On the Instant Pot, click the Sauté button. Melt the butter in the pot by heating it for 1 minute. Add onion and sausage. Stir-fry for 5 minutes or until onions are transparent. There will still be some pinkness in the pork. 2. Add chicken broth to the Instant Pot. Lock lid. 3. Press Pressure Cook button and set level to high and time to 1 minute. 4. Quickly release pressure steam on vent position when the timer beeps, and then open the lid. 5. Add milk, cornmeal, flour, salt, and pepper while whisking. Press the Keep 6. Warm button, and after 10 minutes, stir the gravy once or twice to help the sauce thicken. 7. Remove gravy from heat and serve warm.
Per Serving: Calories 307; Fat: 15.6g; Sodium 237mg; Carbs: 23.48g; Sugars: 18.92g; Protein 17.76g

Yummy Muffins

Prep Time: 10 minutes | Cook Time: 9 minutes | Serves: 6

¾ cup gluten-free all-purpose flour
¼ cup old-fashioned oats
¼ cup raisins
2 tablespoons chopped pecans
1 tablespoon salted sunflower seeds
1 tablespoon peanut butter chips
¼ cup granulated sugar
2 teaspoons gluten-free baking powder
½ teaspoon baking soda
¼ teaspoon ground cinnamon
⅛ teaspoon salt
1 teaspoon vanilla extract
4 tablespoons unsalted butter, melted and cooled
2 large eggs, whisked
1 cup water

1. Mix the flour, oats, raisins, pecans, sunflower seeds, peanut butter chips, sugar, baking soda, cinnamon, and salt in a large bowl. 2. Combine eggs, butter, and vanilla in a medium bowl. 3. Add the wet ingredients from the medium bowl to the dry ingredients in the large bowl. Mix the ingredients gently. Avoid overmixing. Fill six silicone cupcake liners with the mixture and gently coat with oil or cooking spray. 4. Add water to the Instant Pot and insert steam rack. Place the muffin cups on the steam rack with care. Lid locked. 5. Select the Pressure Cook option, then set the level to High and timer for the 9-minute. Quickly release steam on vent position when the timer beeps, and then open the lid. 6. Take the muffins out of the pot and let them cool for five minutes before serving.
Per Serving: Calories 192; Fat: 10.77g; Sodium 119mg; Carbs: 21.44g; Sugars: 5.13g; Protein 4.37g

Pecan and Apple Oatmeal

Prep Time: 5 minutes | Cook Time: 7 minutes | Serves: 2

1 cup old-fashioned oats
1¼ cups water
1 peeled and cored Granny Smith apple, diced
¼ teaspoon ground cinnamon
⅛ teaspoon salt
2 tablespoons light brown sugar
¼ teaspoon vanilla extract
¼ cup chopped pecans
4 tablespoons whole milk

1. To the Instant Pot inner pot, add the oats, water, apple, cinnamon, and salt. Lock lid. 2. Press Pressure Cook button and set level to Low and time to 7 minutes. Allow steam to naturally release on seal position after the timer beeps. Then open the lid. Add vanilla and brown sugar and stir. 3. Divide the oatmeal into two dishes. Pecans are a good garnish. Over the oats, pour milk. Serve hot.
Per Serving: Calories 336; Fat: 13.29g; Sodium 181mg; Carbs: 63.05g; Sugars: 27.57g; Protein 10.54g

Creamy Berry Oats

Prep Time: 5 minutes | Cook Time: 7 minutes | Serves: 2

1 cup old-fashioned oats
1 cup water
½ cup whole milk
2 cups diced fresh strawberries, hulled
2 tablespoons granulated sugar
¼ teaspoon vanilla extract
¼ teaspoon ground cinnamon
⅛ teaspoon salt

1. Fill Instant Pot with oats, water, milk, strawberries, sugar, vanilla, cinnamon, and salt. To mix, stir. Lock lid. 2. Press Pressure Cook button. Set level to High and timer to 7 minutes. Quickly release steam on vent position when the timer beeps, and then open the lid. 3. Pour oatmeal into two dishes after stirring. Serve hot.
Per Serving: Calories 250; Fat: 5.6g; Sodium 188mg; Carbs: 58.3g; Sugars: 23.4g; Protein 10.92g

Quinoa Nutty Chocolate Bowl with Bananas

Prep Time: 5 minutes | Cook Time: 20 minutes | Serves: 4

1 cup quinoa
1¼ cups water
1½ cups whole milk, divided
2 tablespoons unsalted butter
1 teaspoon unsweetened cocoa
1 tablespoon light brown sugar
½ teaspoon salt
2 tablespoons semisweet chocolate chips
2 medium bananas, diced
¼ cup chopped pecans

1. To the Instant Pot, add quinoa, water, half a cup of milk, butter, chocolate, sugar, and salt. Stir well. Lock lid. 2. Select the Pressure Cook option, then set the level to High and timer for the 20-minute. Quickly release steam on vent position when the timer beeps, and then open the lid. 3. Fluff the quinoa with a fork after transferring it to a serving dish. Toss three times after adding chocolate chips. Garnish with diced bananas and chopped pecans. Over the quinoa, pour the remaining 1 cup of milk. Serve right away.
Per Serving: Calories 596; Fat: 23.18g; Sodium 447mg; Carbs: 82.03g; Sugars: 50.1g; Protein 17.43g

Corn Muffins with Bananas

Prep Time: 10 minutes | Cook Time: 9 minutes | Serves: 6

¾ cup gluten-free all-purpose flour
½ cup self-rising cornmeal
2 tablespoons granulated sugar
2 teaspoons gluten-free baking powder
½ teaspoon baking soda
⅛ teaspoon salt
½ teaspoon vanilla extract
3 tablespoons unsalted butter, melted
2 large eggs
2 ripe medium bananas, mashed with fork
1 cup water

1. Combine the flour, cornmeal, sugar, baking soda, baking powder, and salt in a large bowl. 2. Combine vanilla, butter, eggs, and bananas in a medium bowl. 3. Add the wet ingredients from the medium bowl to the dry ingredients in the big bowl. Mix the ingredients gently. Avoid overmixing. Fill six silicone cupcake liners with the mixture and gently coat with oil or cooking spray. 4. Add water to the Instant Pot and insert steam rack. Place the muffin cups in the steam rack with care. Lock lid. 5. Select the Pressure Cook option, then set the level to High and timer for the 9-minute. Quickly release steam on vent position when the timer beeps, and then open the lid. 6. Take the muffins out of the pot and let them cool for five minutes before serving.
Per Serving: Calories 199; Fat: 5.85g; Sodium 215mg; Carbs: 33.2g; Sugars: 7.54g; Protein 4.14g

Eggs Ranchero

Prep Time: 5 minutes | Cook Time: 6 minutes | Serves: 6

1 tablespoon extra-virgin olive oil
½ red onion, chopped
1 green bell pepper, seeded and chopped
1 teaspoon ground cumin
⅛ teaspoon cayenne pepper (optional)
1½ cups cooked black beans, or one 15-ounce can black beans, drained and rinsed
1½ cups prepared salsa, plus more
for serving
½ cup water
6 eggs
Fine sea salt and freshly ground black pepper
6 corn tortillas
Chopped green onions, crumbled feta cheese, sliced avocado, and chopped fresh cilantro, for garnish (optional)

1. Add the olive oil to the Instant Pot and select Sauté. The onion and bell pepper should be added to the heated but not smoking oil and sauté for about 6 minutes, or until soft. Press the Cancel button, then, while the pot is still hot, mix in the cumin and cayenne. 2. Fill the pot with water, add the beans, and stir thoroughly, scraping the bottom to make sure nothing sticks. Keeping the eggs at least an inch apart, carefully cracks them into the salsa. Every egg should be topped with salt and black pepper. 3. Secure the lid and move the steam release valve to seal position. Select Pressure Cook and cook on high pressure for 2 minutes. Quickly release the pressure by immediately moving the steam release valve to vent position. 4. Use a slotted spoon to scoop the eggs and portion of the salsa mixture onto a tortilla after timer beeps. Serve immediately after adding more salsa and your preferred toppings.
Per Serving: Calories 171; Fat: 11g; Sodium 583mg; Carbs: 7.87g; Sugars: 3.03g; Protein 10.39g

French Toast-Cinnamon Roll Casserole

Prep Time: 10 minutes | Cook Time: 25 minutes | Serves: 4

Casserole
4 cups cubed gluten-free bread, dried out overnight
2 cups whole milk
3 large eggs
1 teaspoon vanilla extract
2 tablespoons pure maple syrup
1 teaspoon ground cinnamon
⅛ teaspoon salt
¼ cup raisins
2 tablespoons chopped pecans
2 tablespoons unsalted butter, melted and cooled
1 cup water

Cream Cheese Drizzle
1 tablespoon whole milk
1 tablespoon powdered sugar
2 tablespoons cream cheese

1. Add bread to a 7-cup glass dish greased with either oil or cooking spray. Place aside. 2. Mix the milk, eggs, vanilla, maple syrup, cinnamon, and salt in a medium bowl. Pour onto the bread in the glass bowl. Spread the bread with the raisins, pecans, and butter equally distributed. 3. To the Instant Pot, add water. Put in the steam rack. On top of the steam rack, place the glass dish. Lock lid. 4. Press the Pressure Cook button and adjust cook time to 25 minutes and level to high. When timer beeps, quick-release steam on vent position and then unlock lid. 5. From the Instant Pot, remove the glass bowl. Place on a rack and cool for ten minutes. 6. In a small bowl, mix the cream cheese, milk, and sugar. Pour over the casserole. Serve dish by portioning it into four bowls.
Per Serving: Calories 516; Fat: 17.59g; Sodium 593mg; Carbs: 70.09g; Sugars: 25.74g; Protein 18.86g

French Toast Casserole with Chocolate and Hazelnuts

Prep Time: 10 minutes | Cook Time: 25 minutes | Serves: 4

4 cups cubed gluten-free bread, dried out overnight
4 tablespoons chocolate hazelnut spread
2 cups whole milk
3 large eggs
1 teaspoon vanilla extract
2 tablespoons granulated sugar
⅛ teaspoon salt
3 tablespoons unsalted butter, cut into 6 pats
1 cup water
2 tablespoons powdered sugar

1. Add bread to a 7-cup glass dish greased with either oil or cooking spray. Place aside. 2. Mix the chocolate hazelnut spread, milk, eggs, vanilla, sugar, and salt in a medium bowl. Pour onto the bread in the glass bowl. Add butter pats on top. 3. To the Instant Pot, add water. Put in the steam rack. On the steam rack, place the glass dish. Lock lid. 4. Select the Pressure Cook option, then set the level to High and timer for the 25-minute. Quickly release steam on vent position when the timer beeps, and then open the lid. 5. Take the glass bowl out of the pot. Place on a rack and cool for ten minutes. 6. Serve the dish with a dusting of powdered sugar.
Per Serving: Calories 683; Fat: 26.12g; Sodium 564mg; Carbs: 91.12g; Sugars: 45.13g; Protein 20.1g

Veggie Frittatas

Prep Time: 10 minutes | Cook Time: 20 minutes | Serves: 4

6 eggs
½ teaspoon fine sea salt
1 red bell pepper, seeded and chopped
3 green onions, tender white and
green parts only, chopped
1 cup chopped spinach
¼ cup crumbled feta cheese
Freshly ground black pepper

1. In a mixing dish, combine the eggs, salt, feta, bell pepper, green onions, spinach, and a few grinds of black pepper. Stir thoroughly. 2. Divide the mixture equally among the four 8-ounce Mason jars that have been lightly greased with olive oil. 3. Place the steam rack on the bottom of the Instant Pot after adding 1 cup of water. On the rack, arrange the four jars in a single layer and close the lids. Select Pressure Cook and turn the steam release valve to the seal position. Set time to 8 minutes, cook under high pressure. Allow the pressure to drop naturally for ten minutes on seal position before switching the steam release valve to vent position to let out any leftover steam. 4. Use oven mitts to remove the jars. Tip the frittatas out of the jars and onto plates to serve warm, or cover the jars and store them in the fridge for 5 days. Enjoy these frittatas chilled or reheat them, if desired.
Per Serving: Calories 240; Fat 16.78g; Sodium 554mg; Carbs: 6g; Sugars: 4.03g; Protein 15.39g

Nutty Bread with Zucchini

Prep Time: 10 minutes | Cook Time: 30 minutes | Serves: 6

2 large eggs
4 tablespoons whole milk
4 tablespoons unsalted butter, melted and cooled
½ cup grated zucchini (approximately 1 medium)
1⅓ cups gluten-free all-purpose flour

1½ teaspoons gluten-free baking powder
½ teaspoon baking soda
½ cup granulated sugar
½ teaspoon ground cinnamon
⅛ teaspoon salt
¼ cup chopped pecans
1 cup water

1. Set aside a 7"springform pan that has been lightly greased with cooking spray or oil. 2. Mix the eggs, milk, and butter in a medium bowl before adding the zucchini. 3. Combine the flour, baking powder, baking soda, sugar, cinnamon, and salt in a large basin. 4. Do not overmix as some lumps are OK. Add the wet ingredients from the medium bowl to the dry ingredients in the big bowl and stir until incorporated. Fold in the pecans. 5. Put the mixture in a springform pan that has been oiled. 6. To the Instant Pot, add water. Put in the steam rack. On the steam rack, place the springform pan. Lock lid. 7. Select the Pressure Cook option, then set the level to High and timer for the 30-minute. Quickly release steam on vent position when the timer beeps, and then open the lid. 8. Unlock springform pan and let cool 10 minutes. Slice and serve.
Per Serving: Calories 409; Fat: 10.4g; Sodium 64mg; Carbs: 69.8g; Sugars: 8.56g; Protein 9.52g

Buttermilk Corn Bread with Creamed Corn

Prep Time: 10 minutes | Cook Time: 30 minutes | Serves: 4

1 large egg
1½ cups self-rising buttermilk cornmeal mix
½ cup creamed corn
⅓ cup peeled and diced sweet onion

½ cup whole milk
1 tablespoon unsalted butter, melted
½ teaspoon granulated sugar
⅛ teaspoon salt
⅛ teaspoon ground pepper
1 cup water

1. Set aside a 7"springform pan that has been lightly greased with cooking spray or oil. 2. Egg, cornmeal, creamed corn, onion, milk, butter, sugar, salt, and pepper should all be combined in a big bowl. 3. Put the mixture in a springform pan that has been oiled. 4. To the Instant Pot, add water. Put in the steam rack. On the steam rack, place the springform pan. Lock lid. 5. Select the Pressure Cook option, then set the level to High and timer for the 30-minute. Quickly release steam on vent position when the timer beeps, and then open the lid. 6. Unlock springform pan. Slice and serve.
Per Serving: Calories 819; Fat: 8.27g; Sodium 2663mg; Carbs: 164g; Sugars: 5.8g; Protein 16.86g

Mixed-Berry Breakfast Syrup Made at Home

Prep Time: 5 minutes | Cook Time: 3 minutes | Serves: 1

1 pound frozen mixed berries
1 tablespoon unsalted butter
½ cup pure maple syrup
¼ cup freshly squeezed orange

juice
1 tablespoon orange zest
¼ teaspoon vanilla extract
⅛ teaspoon salt

1. To the Instant Pot, add all the ingredients. Lock lid. 2. Press the Pressure Cook button and set level to high and adjust cook time to 3 minutes. Quickly release steam on vent position when the timer beeps, and then open the lid. 3. Blend or process the ingredients in a food processor to get the desired consistency. Serve hot or cold.
Per Serving: Calories 1097; Fat: 24.23g; Sodium 621mg; Carbs: 213g; Sugars: 192g; Protein 14.66g

Hard bowl egg

Prep Time: 4 minutes | Cook Time: 10 minutes | Serves: 6

6 eggs   Ice

1. Add 1 cup water to the Instant Pot. Put the eggs in a single layer in inner pot. Move the steam release valve to seal position and secure the lid. Choose Pressure Cook and level to high pressure for either 4 or 5 minutes, depending on whether you want runny or fully cooked yolks. 2. Fill a large dish with ice and water to create an ice water bath for the eggs while they are cooking. 3. Move the steam release valve to vent position right away after the cooking cycle is over if you want

runny yolks. To halt the cooking process, take off the lid and slide the eggs with tongs into the ice water bath. Don't immediately open the lid if you want entirely hard-cooked yolks. Release the pressure naturally on seal position for 5 minutes, then move the steam release valve to vent position and release the remaining pressure. Transfer the eggs to the ice water bath. 4. The eggs can be kept in the refrigerator for a week in an airtight container after being let to cool in ice water bath for 5 minutes. Even if you want to save some of the eggs in the refrigerator for later, they are easier to peel right soon after being taken out of the cold water bath, so you might choose to peel them all at once.
Per Serving: Calories 130; Fat: 9.64g; Sodium 102mg; Carbs: 1.02g; Sugars: 0.65g; Protein 8.97g

Yummy Strawberry Jam

Prep Time: 5 minutes | Cook Time: 20 minutes | Serves: 15

1 pound frozen strawberries
¼ cup pure maple syrup

Pinch of fine sea salt
2 tablespoons chia seeds

1. Salt, maple syrup, and frozen strawberries should all be combined in the Instant Pot before the lid is closed. Select Pressure Cook and turn the steam release valve to the seal position. Set time to 1 minute and level to high pressure. 2. After the cooking cycle is over, release the pressure naturally on seal position for 10 minutes, then switch the steam release valve to vent position to allow any residual pressure out. Remove the lid and click Cancel to end the cooking cycle when the floating valve descends. 3. Add the chia seeds and then press the Sauté button. For about 5 minutes, simmer the jam, stirring often to prevent it from sticking to the bottom of pan. 4. Press Cancel to halt the cooking process after the mixture has somewhat thickened or if the jam begins to adhere to the pan. Put the jam in a 16-ounce glass jar with a lid and then place it in the refrigerator so that it may chill and thicken. The jam should keep in the fridge for 2 weeks.
Per Serving: Calories 1202; Fat: 107g; Sodium 1994mg; Carbs: 50g; Sugars: 11.73g; Protein 17.13g

Soft-Boiled Eggs with Salsa Verde and Kale

Prep Time: 5 minutes | Cook Time: 5 minutes | Serves: 4

4 large eggs
4 cups shredded kale
Juice of 1 lemon

Extra-virgin olive oil, for serving
Pinch flaky sea salt
Salsa Verde, for serving (optional)

1. Put the steam rack into the Instant Pot after adding 1 cup of water. 2. Place the eggs in a row on the rack. Lock the lid by closing it. 3. Choose Pressure Cook and cook for a total of 5 minutes at low pressure for a hard-boiled egg or 3 minutes at low pressure for a soft-boiled egg with a runny yolk. 4. In a mixing dish, combine the kale with the lemon juice, olive oil, and sea salt while the eggs are cooking. 5. After cooking is finished, carefully remove the lid after releasing the steam from the vent position. Peel the eggs after giving them a thorough rinse in cold water. 6. Place the dressed kale, two halves of an egg, and salsa verde on each platter.
Per Serving: Calories 65; Fat 4.6g; Sodium 14mg; Carbs: 2.87g; Sugars: 1.03g; Protein 3.39g

Yummy Eggs

Prep Time: 1 minutes | Cook Time: 10 minutes | Serves: 1

1 or more large eggs

1. Pour 1 cup of water into the Instant Pot. Insert a steam rack inside. On the rack, put the eggs. They can even be stacked and it's fine if they touch. 2. Close the lid. Choose Pressure Cook for 2 minutes for soft-boiled eggs or 5 minutes for hard-boiled eggs, and cook on high pressure. If making soft-boiled eggs, give the pressure a natural release for one minute; if making hard-boiled eggs, give it five minutes on seal position. Then, quickly release any remaining steam in the pot on vent position and take off the lid. 3. In the meantime, prepare a large dish of ice and water. 4. The eggs should be moved to the ice bath with a slotted spoon. Cooking will cease as a result. 5. Peel, eat, and enjoy!
Per Serving: Calories 64; Fat: 1.17g; Sodium 117mg; Carbs: 2.87g; Sugars: 1.03g; Protein 3.39g

Peaches & Cream Steel-Cut Oats

Prep Time: 5 minutes | Cook Time: 4 minutes | Serves: 4

2 cups steel-cut oats
4 cups water
1 pound frozen sliced peaches
½ teaspoon ground cinnamon, plus

more for serving (optional)
¼ cup pure maple syrup
½ cup full-fat coconut milk, plus
more for serving (optional)

1. Stir the water and steel-cut oats together in Instant Pot before adding the peaches, cinnamon, and maple syrup. Move the steam release valve to seal position and close the lid. Choose Pressure Cook for 4 minutes, cook under high pressure. 2. Allow the pressure to naturally relax for 15 minutes after the cooking cycle is over to finish cooking the oats. To discharge any leftover steam pressure, turn the steam release valve to the vent position. Remove the lid after the floating valve drops. 3. Stir in the coconut milk, then taste and adjust any seasonings. If preferred, top with more cinnamon or coconut milk and serve warm. Oats may be kept in the refrigerator for five days in an airtight container. You can serve them chilled, or quickly reheat them using the Sauté function of your Instant Pot. (You may need to add a splash of water as you reheat, since oats tend to thicken when chilled.)
Per Serving: Calories 343; Fat10.6g; Sodium 20mg; Carbs: 74g; Sugars: 39g; Protein 9g

Granola Bars with Peanut Butter

Prep Time: 5 minutes | Cook Time: 20 minutes | Serves: 10

1 cup quick-cooking oats
⅓ cup pure maple syrup
½ cup all-natural peanut butter
1 tablespoon extra-virgin olive oil

¼ teaspoon fine sea salt
⅓ cup dried cranberries or raisins
½ cup raw pumpkin seeds (pepitas)

1. Using parchment paper, line a 7-inch round pan. 2. In a large bowl, combine the oats, maple syrup, peanut butter, olive oil, and salt and stir well. Before pouring the batter into the ready pan and pressing the mixture into the bottom of the pan with a spatula, fold in the dried fruit and pumpkin seeds. 3. Place the Steam rack on the bottom of the Instant Pot after adding 1 cup of water. Put the pan on top of the rack. To shield the granola bars from condensation, place another piece of parchment or an upside-down plate over the pan. Moving the steam release valve to seal position, tighten the lid. Choose Pressure Cook and set timer to 20 minutes at high pressure. 4. After allowing the pressure to drop naturally for ten minutes on seal position, switch the steam release valve to vent position. Remove the lid after the floating valve has drops. Lift the rack and the pan from the pot using oven mitts. Allow at least an hour for the granola to cool fully in the pan. 5. Ten pieces of the chilled granola should be cut. The bars will have various sizes because to the circular pan, but if you'd like, you may cut them into consistent wedges. They may be kept in the refrigerator for two weeks by individually wrapping them in plastic wrap or putting them in an airtight container.
Per Serving: Calories 154; Fat: 8.7g; Sodium 166mg; Carbs: 16.6g; Sugar 8.73g; Protein 7g

Banana Oat Cake Made without Flour

Prep Time: 10 minutes | Cook Time: 40 minutes | Serves: 8

½ cup mashed ripe banana (1 large banana)
½ cup almond butter
½ cup coconut sugar
2 eggs

½ teaspoon baking soda
½ teaspoon cinnamon
¼ teaspoon fine sea salt
1 cup quick-cooking oats

1. Put a piece of parchment paper into a 7-inch circular pan and put it aside. 2. Banana, almond butter, coconut sugar, eggs, baking soda, cinnamon, and salt should all be combined in a big basin. After thoroughly stirring to remove any lumps, add the oats. With a spatula, level the top after pouring the batter into the prepared pan. 3. Place the steam rack on the bottom of the Instant Pot after adding 1 cup of water. Place the pan on top of the rack. Cover the cake with an upside-down dish or some more parchment paper to prevent condensation. 4. Close the lid, then switch the pressure valve to seal position. Choose Pressure Cook for 40 minutes at high pressure, then allow the pressure drop naturally for 10 minutes. To vent any residual steam, turn the steam release valve to vent position. Remove the lid after the floating valve drops. 5. Lift the rack and the pan from the pot using oven mitts. After the cake has firmed up fully in the pan, which should take around 30 minutes, remove it from the pan. Slice and serve refrigerated or at room temperature. For a week, keep leftovers in the refrigerator in an airtight container.

Per Serving: Calories 172; Fat: 11.17g; Sodium 213mg; Carbs: 14g; Sugars: 8.03g; Protein 6.39g

Cozy Fruit with Spice

Prep Time: 5 minutes | Cook Time: 1 minutes | Serves: 6

1 pound sliced frozen peaches
1 pound frozen pineapple chunks
1 cup frozen and pitted dark sweet cherries
2 ripe pears, sliced

¼ cup pure maple syrup
1 teaspoon curry powder, plus more as needed
Steel-cut oatmeal, for serving (optional)

1. In the Instant Pot, combine the peaches, pineapple, cherries, pears, maple syrup, and curry powder. Cover the pot. Select Pressure Cook and turn the steam release valve to the seal position. Set time to one minute, and level to high pressure. 2. Move the steam release valve to vent position as soon as the cooking cycle is over to swiftly remove the steam pressure. Remove the lid when the floating valve drops and thoroughly stir the mixture. If you like your food spicy, add more curry powder. 3. Warm fruit can be added to oatmeal or served as a side dish. When this meal is finished, the fruit should still be submerged in liquid. Scoop it with a slotted spoon and let the juices drain back into the pot before serving. Store leftovers in an airtight container in the fridge for 5 days.
Per Serving: Calories 217; Fat 0.32g; Sodium 8mg; Carbs: 55g; Sugars: 50g; Protein 1.41g

Yummy Rancheros Casserole

Prep Time: 10 minutes | Cook Time: 10 minutes | Serves: 4

Cooking spray
2 corn tortillas
1 (15-ounce) can black beans, drained or 1¾ cups cooked black beans
4 large eggs
Salt
Freshly ground black pepper

Salsa Roja or store-bought salsa, for serving
Fresh cilantro leaves, chopped, for serving
Herby Queso Fresco, crema, or sour cream for serving (optional)

1. Place the steam rack inside the Instant pot with 1 cup of water added. 2. Place the tortillas on the bottom of a 7-inch circular baking dish that has been sprayed with cooking spray. 3. On top of the tortillas, pour the black beans. Create four holes in the beans with a spoon, and then carefully crack the eggs into the holes. Add salt and pepper to taste. 4. Place aluminum foil over the dish before carefully setting it down on the rack. Lock the lid by closing it. 5. Choose the Pressure Cook mode, and cook at high pressure for 7 minutes. Once the food has finished cooking, quickly remove the steam on seal position. Carefully unlock and remove the lid. 6. Remove the foil before carefully removing the dish from the pot. Serve, topped with salsa roja, chopped cilantro, and queso fresco (if using).
Per Serving: Calories 207; Fat: 6g; Sodium 24mg; Carbs: 31.87g; Sugar0.89g; Protein 7.39g

Cereal Bowls with Maple and Cinnamon

Prep Time: 5 minutes | Cook Time: 1 minutes | Serves: 6

2 cups buckwheat groats, soaked for at least 20 minutes and up to overnight
3 cups water
1 teaspoon ground cinnamon
¼ cup pure maple syrup

1 teaspoon vanilla extract
¼ teaspoon fine sea salt
Almond milk, for serving
Chopped or sliced fresh fruit, for serving

1. Buckwheat should be rinsed and drained before being added to the Instant Pot along with water, salt, cinnamon, maple syrup, vanilla, and vanilla extract. Select Pressure Cook and turn the steam release valve to the Seal position. Set time to one minute and level to high pressure. 2. Before switching the steam release valve to vent position, let the pressure to naturally dissipate for 10 minutes on seal position. Carefully remove the lid and stir the cooked grains when the floating valve descends. 3. You may either immediately serve the buckwheat with almond milk and fruit, or you can store approximately 1 cup of the cooked grains in each of several airtight containers and keep them in the refrigerator for a week, serving them cold or warm for a quick weekday breakfast.
Per Serving: Calories 89; Fat: 0.3g; Sodium 103mg; Carbs: 20g; Sugar 8.5g; Protein 1.9g

Yummy Shakshuka

Prep Time: 10 minutes | Cook Time: 5 minutes | Serves: 4

1 tablespoon extra-virgin olive oil	4 eggs
½ yellow onion, chopped	Freshly ground black pepper
2 cloves garlic, minced	Crumbled feta or grated Parmesan
Fine sea salt	cheese, for garnish (optional)
¼ cup water	Chopped fresh flat-leaf parsley or
2½ cups marinara sauce	basil, for garnish (optional)
1 cup chopped kale, stems removed	Toast slices, for serving (optional)

1. Add the olive oil to the Instant Pot and select Sauté. Add the onion, garlic, and a bit of salt but not smoking oil and sauté for approximately 5 minutes, or until the vegetables are tender. A wooden spoon should be used to thoroughly mix after adding the water, marinara sauce, and kale to scraping the pot's bottom to prevent anything from sticking. 2. Select Cancel. Create four perfectly spaced little wells in the marinara sauce using the spoon, and then delicately crack an egg into each one of them. Add salt and pepper to the eggs as desired. 3. Move the steam release valve to seal position and fasten the lid. Choose Pressure Cook for two minutes under high pressure. When the timer beeps quickly release the pressure by immediately moving the steam release valve to vent position. 4. Take off the lid until the floating valve drops, then scoop the eggs, sauce, and a good amount of the cooked vegetables into a small serving dish. Serve immediately as is or with a couple slices of bread, garnished with cheese and chopped parsley.
Per Serving: Calories 244; Fat: 14.17g; Sodium 184mg; Carbs: 15.87g; Sugars: 10.3g; Protein 11.39g

Spanish Omelet

Prep Time: 10 minutes | Cook Time: 30 minutes | Serves: 6

Cooking spray	potatoes or fingerling potatoes),
2 tablespoons extra-virgin olive oil	cut into thin rounds
2 cups julienned onions	8 large eggs
2 medium waxy potatoes (like red	Salt

1. Spray cooking oil in a 7-inch baking dish. 2. Add the potatoes, onions, and olive oil, then choose the Sauté option. Add a bit of salt to help the onions release their moisture and start cooking. When the potatoes and onions are tender and transparent, add a little extra oil if they become too dry. Reduce the heat if they begin to turn brown and cover them for a while so they can release more moisture. You don't want them to get caramelized or brown. 3. For about 15 minutes, until the mixture is soft, keep stirring and moving it with a wooden spoon so it doesn't stick to the bottom of the pan. When finished, take the potatoes and onions out of the pot and place them aside to cool. 4. Whip the eggs in a medium bowl in the meanwhile. 5. The eggs should be combined with the potato and onion mixture before being added and poured into the prepared baking dish. Use aluminum foil to protect. 6. Place the steam rack into the Instant pot with 1½ cups of water added. Place the baking pan very gently on the rack. Close the lid. 7. Choose the Pressure Cook mode, and cook at high pressure for 15 minutes. After cooking is finished, let the steam out naturally on seal position. Carefully remove the cover after unlocking. 8. Remove the dish from the pot with care. Unmold the frittata onto a platter after removing the foil. Serve.
Per Serving: Calories 132; Fat: 8.17g; Sodium 58mg; Carbs: 10.87g; Sugars: 3.03g; Protein 4.39g

Frittata with Leeks and Asparagus

Prep Time: 10 minutes | Cook Time: 10 minutes | Serves: 4

6 eggs	pieces
¼ teaspoon fine sea salt	1 cup thinly sliced leeks
Freshly ground black pepper	¼ cup grated Parmesan cheese
8 ounces asparagus spears, woody	Chopped green onions, for garnish
stems removed, cut into 1-inch	Fresh flat-leaf parsley, for garnish

1. To avoid sticking, thoroughly grease a 7-inch circular pan with olive oil. Beat the eggs thoroughly with a fork in a large mixing basin after adding the salt, a few pinches of black pepper, and the eggs. Pour the mixture into the prepared pan after including the Parmesan, leeks, and asparagus. 2. Place the steam rack on the bottom of the Instant Pot after adding 1 cup of water. Put the pan on the top of rack. Move the steam release valve to seal and fasten the lid. Choose Pressure Cook for 10 minutes at high pressure. After 10 minutes of natural pressure release, switch the steam release valve to vent position to let off any leftover pressure. Take the lid off when the floating valve drops. 3. Use

oven mitts to lift the rack and the pan out of the pot. Before cutting and serving, allow the frittata to cool in the pan for five minutes. For five days, keep leftovers in the refrigerator in an airtight container.
Per Serving: Calories 322; Fat: 21g; Sodium 755mg; Carbs: 10.7g; Sugars: 2.03g; Protein 22.39g

Yummy Muesli

Prep Time: 5 minutes | Cook Time: 5 minutes | Serves: 2

1 cup old-fashioned rolled oats	Dried fruit, such as raisins or
2 cups apple juice	apricots, for serving
Yogurt or milk, for serving	

1. Put the steam rack into the Instant Pot after adding 1 cup of water. 2. Oats and apple juice should be combined in a 7-inch baking dish. Wrap with foil. On the rack, put the baking pan. Put the lid on. 3. Apply Pressure Cook at high pressure for 2 minutes. Once the food has finished cooking, quickly remove the steam on vent position. Remove the lid. 4. Remove the baking dish with care. Allow to cool for approximately 10 minutes. Take the foil off. 5. Add yoghurt and/or milk to get the appropriate consistency before serving. Add dried fruit on top.
Per Serving: Calories 422; Fat: 9.17g; Sodium 15mg; Carbs: 111.87g; Sugars: 25.86g; Protein 21.39g

Mini Quiches with Cheese and Mushrooms

Prep Time: 10 minutes | Cook Time: 15 minutes | Serves: 4

2 tablespoons extra-virgin olive oil	1 cup shredded Cheddar cheese
3 cups sliced button mushrooms	Freshly ground black pepper
Salt	Cooking spray
8 large eggs	Fresh spinach, torn, for garnish

1. Choose the Sauté option. 2. Add the mushrooms and olive oil. Add salt, stir, and simmer for two minutes to release moisture. 3. Till the mushrooms are cooked through, continue sautéing for an additional three minutes while stirring often. 4. Remove the mushrooms from the pot and set aside. 5. Beat the eggs just a little bit in a medium bowl. Add the cheese and mushrooms to the same bowl and mix. Add salt and pepper to taste. 6. Apply cooking spray to four 6-ounce ramekins, then fill each with a quarter cup of the egg mixture. Aluminum foil should be placed over each ramekin. 7. Place the steam rack into the Instant Pot after adding 1 cup of water to the pot. Place the ramekins on the rack with care. Close the lid. 8. Choose the Pressure Cook option and give it seven minutes at high pressure. Once the food has finished cooking, quickly remove the steam on vent position. Carefully remove the cover. 9. Remove the foil before carefully removing the ramekins from the pot. Serve with spinach for garnish.
Per Serving: Calories 274; Fat: 18.17g; Sodium 774mg; Carbs: 11.87g; Sugars: 7.03g; Protein 17.39g

Salmon, Avocado, and Poached Eggs Breakfast Bowl

Prep Time: 10 minutes | Cook Time: 5 minutes | Serves: 4

4 large eggs	6 ounces watercress
Salt	8 ounces smoked salmon, sliced
1 avocado	Extra-virgin olive oil
Juice of 1 lemon	Flaky sea salt
Freshly ground black pepper	Sesame seeds for garnish (optional)

1. Put the steam rack into the Instant Pot after adding 1 cup of water. 2. Salt each poach pod after cracking an egg inside. Place the poach pods on the rack with care. Close the lid. 3. Choose Pressure Cook and cook the eggs for one minute under low pressure using the cook setting. 4. Cut the avocado in half, remove the pit, skin it, and cut it into thin wedges while the eggs are cooking. Add some lemon juice to the dish and season with salt and pepper to suit. 5. When cooking is complete, quickly release the steam on vent position. Carefully remove the lid. Take out eggs from the the pot and put aside. 6. Four bowls should be filled with the watercress, which should be topped with a little lemon juice, olive oil, and flaky sea salt. Place the salmon and avocado slices on the sides of each bowl, with one egg slid into the center. Serve with sesame seeds as a garnish, if desired.
Per Serving: Calories 229; Fat: 16.17g; Sodium 274mg; Carbs: 6.87g; Sugars: 1.03g; Protein 16.39g

Healthy and Nutritious Veggies Breakfast

Prep Time: 15 minutes | Cook Time: 10 minutes | Serves: 4

1 tablespoon olive oil
1 small sweet onion, peeled and diced
2 large carrots, peeled and diced
2 medium potatoes, peeled and diced
1 stalk celery, diced
1 large red bell pepper, seeded and diced
1 tablespoon low-sodium soy sauce
¼ cup water
1 cup diced peeled zucchini or summer squash
2 medium tomatoes, peeled and diced
2 cups cooked brown rice
½ teaspoon ground black pepper

1. Insert the Inner Pot into the Cooker Base without the lid. 2. Select Sauté mode and then press the same button again and then adjust the cooking temperature to Normal. 3. When the display switches On to Hot, add and heat the oil; add onion and cook for 2 minutes or until just tender; add the bell pepper, carrots, potatoes and cook for another 2 minutes or until just tender; lastly, add the soy sauce and water. 4. Press the Cancel button to stop this cooking program. 5. Place and close the lid in right way. 6. Press Pressure Cook button to select the program, press it again to adjust the cooking time to 2 minutes; press Pressure Level to choose High Pressure. 7. When the time is up, quickly and carefully turn the steam release handle from the Sealing position to the Venting position; when the float valve drops, press Cancel button to stop this cooking program. 8. Open lid and then add squash, tomatoes and stir well; close the lid again. 9. Press Pressure Cook button to select the program, press it again to adjust the cooking time to 1 minutes; press Pressure Level to choose High Pressure. 10. When the time is up, quickly and carefully turn the steam release handle from the Sealing position to the Venting position; when the float valve drops, press Cancel to end this cooking program. 11. Sprinkle with black pepper and serve over rice.
Per Serving: Calories 498; Fat: 6.5g; Sodium 264mg; Carbs: 100.7g; Fiber 1g; Sugars: 8.3g; Protein 10.9g

Baked Eggs in the Shakshuka Style

Prep Time: 10 minutes | Cook Time: 10 minutes | Serves: 6

2 cups Sofrito Base Sauce
6 large eggs
Salt
Freshly ground black pepper
1 teaspoon sumac
Fresh cilantro leaves, chopped, for garnish

1. Place the steam rack into the Instant Pot after adding 1 cup of water to the pot. 2. Add the sofrito sauce to a 7-inch baking dish. Make six indentations in the sofrito using a wooden spoon. Be cautious not to crack the yolks when you crack each egg into one of the indentations. 3. Add salt and pepper to the eggs as desired. Place the dish on the steam rack with the foil covering it. Put the lid on. 4. Choose the Pressure Cook, for a set egg, cook continuously for 7 minutes at low pressure. For a runnier yolk, cook continuously for 2 minutes at low pressure. Once the food has finished cooking, quickly remove the steam on vent position. Take off the lid. 5. Remove the foil before carefully removing the dish from the pot. Sprinkle the sumac and chopped cilantro on top, and serve.
Per Serving: Calories 217; Fat: 17g; Sodium 794mg; Carbs: 4.87g; Sugars: 0.1g; Protein 11.39g

Buckwheat Porridge

Prep Time: 5 minutes | Cook Time: 10 minutes | Serves: 4

1 cup cream of buckwheat
4 cups whole milk
½ cup sweetened condensed milk (optional)
2 whole cinnamon sticks
6 whole cloves
¼ cup chopped dried fruit, toasted coconut flakes, or cocoa nibs (optional)

1. Place the steam rack inside the Instant pot with 1 cup of water added. 2. Buckwheat, whole milk, condensed milk (if using), cinnamon sticks, and cloves should all be combined in a 7-inch baking dish. Place on the rack and cover with aluminum foil. Close the lid. 3. Cook for 7 minutes using the Pressure Cook setting on Low. Once the food has finished cooking, quickly remove the steam on vent position. Carefully remove the cover. 4. Remove the baking pan with care from the stove. Remove the foil, cinnamon sticks, and cloves after they have cooled enough to handle. Mix thoroughly, then serve with toasted coconut flakes, dried fruit, or cocoa nibs on top (if using).

Per Serving: Calories 296; Fat: 8.17g; Sodium 123mg; Carbs: 45.87g; Sugars: 33.03g; Protein 10.09g

Porridge with Butternut Squash and Coconut

Prep Time: 5 minutes | Cook Time: 10 minutes | Serves: 4

4 cups cubed butternut squash
1 (13.5-ounce) can coconut milk
1 teaspoon grated fresh ginger or ¼ teaspoon ground ginger
¼ teaspoon ground nutmeg
1 cinnamon stick or ¼ teaspoon ground cinnamon
Pumpkin seeds (optional)
Maple syrup (optional)
Banana, chopped (optional)
Blueberries (optional)
Peanut butter or almond butter (optional)

1. Butternut squash, coconut milk, ginger, nutmeg, and cinnamon stick should all be added to the Instant Pot along with ¼ cup of water. Close the lid. 2. Choose the Pressure Cook setting, cook at high pressure for 6 minutes. Once the food has finished cooking, quickly remove the steam on vent position. Carefully open the lid and take it off. 3. Remove the butternut squash pieces with a slotted spoon and place them in a mixing bowl. To get the required consistency, mash with a fork or immersion blender and gradually add cooking liquid. 4. Finish the meal as desired by sprinkling it with pumpkin seeds, drizzling it with maple syrup, or adding some bananas, berries, almond butter, or peanut butter on top.
Per Serving: Calories 118; Fat: 0.17g; Sodium 108mg; Carbs: 29g; Sugars: 2.5g; Protein 2.66g

Frittata with Sausage and Cheese

Prep Time: 10 minutes | Cook Time: 20 minutes | Serves: 4

1 tablespoon butter
6 large eggs
½ cup whole milk
Salt
Freshly ground black pepper
⅛ teaspoon ground nutmeg (optional)
2 cups ½-inch slices of ready-to-eat breakfast-sausage links
1 cup shredded sharp Cheddar cheese
2 tablespoons chopped fresh parsley, scallions, tarragon, and/or chives

1. Place the steam rack into the Instant Pot after adding 1 cup of water to the pot. 2. Cut a parchment round and place it in the bottom of a 7-inch baking dish. Apply the butter to the top of the parchment and the dish's sides. 3. Whisk the eggs, milk, salt, pepper, and nutmeg (if using) vigorously in a medium bowl. Whisk in the herbs, Cheddar cheese, and sausage after adding them. 4. Fill the baking dish with the mixture. Place the object inside the Instant Pot and lightly cover with foil. Lock the lid. 5. Choose Pressure Cook and cook on high pressure for 15 minutes. Once the food has finished cooking, quickly release the steam on vent position. Take off the lid. 6. Take care when removing the baking dish, and then give it five minutes to rest. When the baking dish is cold enough to handle, remove the foil, set a big plate over it, and flip it onto a serving platter. Serve right away.
Per Serving: Calories 742; Fat: 38.17g; Sodium 966mg; Carbs: 90.87g; Sugars: 80.99g; Protein 14.39g

Herby Yummy Fresco

Prep Time: 3 minutes | Cook Time: 30 minutes | Serves: 1

8 cups whole milk
¼ cup white vinegar
1 tablespoon salt
¼ cup chopped fresh cilantro

1. Add milk to the Instant Pot. While keeping the steam vent open, close and lock the lid. 2. Choose the 30-minute option for the Yogurt. Cook on boil. 3. When everything is finished, shut off the Instant Pot, take off the cover, and gently remove the contents. Stir in the vinegar, then place it on a heat-resistant surface. For about 3 minutes, or until curds start to form, let rest. 4. Add salt when the curds have hardened. 5. Pour the mixture into a cheesecloth-lined colander. Drain for about 5 minutes, or until the curds appear drier. Add the chopped cilantro and thoroughly combine. 6. Place the curds and cheesecloth in a small bowl. Cheesecloth should be folded in half and placed over the curds before being wrapped in plastic. 7. A plate should be placed on top, followed by a weight (such as a sauce jar or a can of beans). Refrigerate overnight; the cheese will become firm. 8. Transfer the cheese to an airtight container after removing the cheesecloth. In the refrigerator, it lasts up to three days.
Per Serving: Calories 357; Fat: 12.17g; Sodium 3661mg; Carbs: 50.87g; Sugars: 50.03g; Protein 11.6g

Yummy Bread Pudding

Prep Time: 10 minutes | Cook Time: 30 minutes | Serves: 4

1 tablespoon butter
8 slices challah bread, cut into 1-inch cubes
3 large eggs
1 cup whole milk
⅓ cup pure maple syrup

2 teaspoons pure vanilla extract
1 tablespoon ground cinnamon (optional)
¼ teaspoon ground nutmeg (optional)
Pinch salt

1. Place the steam rack inside the Instant pot with 1 cup of water added. 2. A 7-inch baking dish should have the bottom and sides coated with butter. Bread cubes should completely fill the plate. 3. Whisk the eggs, milk, syrup, vanilla, cinnamon, and nutmeg together briefly in a small bowl. Use salt to season. 4. When the bread is completely submerged, about 5 minutes, pour the egg mixture over it and let it set. Place the pan on the rack and cover with aluminum foil. Lock the lid by closing it. 5. Choose the Pressure Cook setting, and cook at low pressure for 20 minutes. Once the food has finished cooking, let the steam escape naturally on the seal position for 10 minutes before quickly releasing any leftover steam on the vent position. 6. Carefully unlock and remove the lid. Carefully remove the baking dish and foil. Serve warm.
Per Serving: Calories 306; Fat: 9.57g; Sodium mg; Carbs: 46.77g; Sugars: 25.6g; Protein 7.5g

Vegetable Frittata

Prep Time: 10 minutes | Cook Time: 30 minutes | Serves: 4

1 tablespoon coconut oil or ghee
8 eggs
⅓ cup coconut cream or full-fat coconut milk
½ teaspoon sea salt
½ teaspoon freshly ground black pepper

½ teaspoon chili powder
¼ cup green bell pepper, diced
3 scallions, both white and green parts, chopped
½ cup packed fresh baby spinach
1 large avocado, sliced

1. Oil the inside of a 7-inch heatproof dish that fits inside the Instant Pot. Place aside. 2. Whisk the eggs, coconut cream, salt, pepper, and chili powder until fluffy in a medium bowl or food processor. Add the spinach, bell pepper, and scallions. To blend, stir. Place the prepared dish with the contents inside, then wrap it with foil. 3. 1½ cups of water should be poured into the Instant Pot. Insert steam rack into the pot. Place the dish containing the frittata on the rack. 4. Secure the lid. Choose Pressure Cook for 12 minutes at high pressure and cook then, release steam naturally for 15 minutes on seal position. 5. Quickly release the remaining steam in the pot on vent position and remove the lid. Cook for a further five minutes at high pressure, followed by a fast release, if you don't think it's done enough. 6. Serve with avocado slices on top after it is safe to handle.
Per Serving: Calories 426; Fat: 34.17g; Sodium 544mg; Carbs: 10.87g; Sugars: 3.03g; Protein 20.39g

Purgatory Eggs

Prep Time: 5 minutes | Cook Time: 20 minutes | Serves: 4

2 tablespoons extra-virgin olive oil
1 small eggplant, cut into ½-inch pieces
3 large garlic cloves, minced
1 (28-ounce) can diced tomatoes, with most of the liquid drained out
1 tablespoon harissa or 1 teaspoon smoked paprika

¼ teaspoon red pepper flakes
½ teaspoon sea salt
¼ teaspoon freshly ground black pepper
4 to 6 eggs
1 tablespoon chopped fresh parsley (optional)
Hot sauce (optional)

1. In Instant Pot, choose Sauté option. Oil must be heated until it shimmers. 2. For about 4 minutes, sauté the eggplant until it begins to soften. Cook for another minute after adding the garlic. 3. Add the salt, black pepper, harissa, red pepper flakes, and tomatoes. 4. Close the lid. Choose Pressure Cook, cook for 10 minutes at high pressure, and then quickly release the steam in the pot on vent position. Click Cancel, then take off the lid. 5. Choose Sauté, then whisk the sauce. One egg at a time, crack into a small bowl. Each egg should be carefully poured out of the bowl into the pot and over the sauce. 6. Simmer for 4 to 6 minutes, or until the eggs are set but the yolks are still runny. Covering with a lid will speed up the process. 7. Top with the parsley and hot sauce (if using).
Per Serving: Calories 229; Fat: 13.17g; Sodium 685mg; Carbs: 17.27g; Sugars: 10.7g; Protein 12.19g

Vanilla Banana Loaves

Prep Time: 15 minutes | Cook Time: 50 minutes | Serves: 4

1 tablespoon ground flaxseed
2½ tablespoons water, plus 1 cup
1¼ cups gluten-free oat flour
1½ teaspoons baking powder
½ teaspoon baking soda
½ teaspoon ground cinnamon
⅛ teaspoon salt

1 very ripe banana, peeled
⅓ cup maple syrup
3 tablespoons simple applesauce or no-sugar-added store-bought
1 teaspoon pure vanilla extract
Nonstick cooking spray

1. Spray 2 mini suitable bake pan with the non-stick spray. 2. In a small bowl, thoroughly mix up the flaxseed and 2½ tablespoons of water. 3. In a medium-size bowl, mash the banana, then mix up with the maple syrup, applesauce, vanilla, and flaxseed mixture. 4. In a large-sized bowl, whisk together the oat flour, baking powder, baking soda, cinnamon, and salt, then add the mixture in the medium bowl. 5. Divide the final mixture in two and arrange them to the sprayed bake pan separately; cover them with a few layers of paper towels and then tightly wrap them with aluminum foil. 6. In the Inner Pot, add the remaining 1 cup of water and place the Steam Rack in it, then transfer the bake pans to the pot. 7. Place and close the lid in right way. 8. Press Pressure Cook to select the program, press it again to adjust the cooking time to 50 minutes; press Pressure Level to choose High Pressure. 9. When the time is up, leave the steam release handle in the Sealing position for 10 minutes, then turn it to the Venting position. 10. When released, take out the bake pans, discard the covers and cool for 5 minutes. 11. Turn the bread out onto a cooling rack to cool for 10 more minutes before slicing. 12. Serve and enjoy.
Per Serving: Calories 224; Fat: 2.8g; Sodium 169mg; Carbs: 46.3g; Fiber 1g; Sugars: 19.4g; Protein 5.5g

Chickpea Breakfast Hash

Prep Time: 15 minutes | Cook Time: 35 minutes | Serves: 4

1 cup dried chickpeas
4 cups water
2 tablespoons extra-virgin olive oil, divided
1 medium onion, peeled and chopped
1 medium zucchini, trimmed and sliced
1 large red bell pepper, seeded and

chopped
1 teaspoon minced garlic
½ teaspoon ground cumin
½ teaspoon ground black pepper
¼ teaspoon salt
4 large hard-cooked eggs, peeled and halved
½ teaspoon smoked paprika

1. In the Inner Pot, add the water, chickpeas and 1 tablespoon of oil, then close the lid in right way. 2. Press Pressure Cook button to select the program, press it again to adjust the cooking time to 30 minutes; press Pressure Level to choose High Pressure. 3. When the time is up, quickly and carefully turn the steam release handle from the Sealing position to the Venting position. 4. When released, open the lid; drain the chickpeas well, set aside after transferring to a suitable bowl. 5. Press Cancel button to stop this cooking program. 6. After cleaning and drying the Inner Pot, insert it into the Cooker Base. 7. Press Sauté button and press it again to choose the Normal cooking temperature. 8. When the display switches On to Hot, add and heat the remaining 1 tablespoon of oil; add onion, bell pepper and zucchini and cook for 5 minutes until tender; add garlic, cumin, salt and bell pepper and cook for 30 seconds; lastly, add the cooked chickpeas and make them coated with the mixture evenly. 9. Arrange the food on a plate, top with eggs and paprika. 10. Serve and enjoy.
Per Serving: Calories 274; Fat: 10.3g; Sodium 174mg; Carbs: 37.5g; Fiber 1g; Sugars: 8.9g; Protein 11g

Maple Steel-Cut Oats

Prep time: 5 minutes | Cook time: 15 minutes | Serve: 1

⅓ cup steel-cut oats
1 cup water

3 tablespoons maple syrup
3 tablespoons vanilla almond milk

1. Add the oats and water to the Inner Pot. 2. Select Pressure Cook mode, and then press the "Pressure Cook" button again to select "Less" time option. 3. Use the "-" key on the control panel to set the cooking time to 15 minutes. 4. Press the Pressure Level button to adjust the pressure to "Low Pressure." 5. When cooked, allow the steam to release naturally. 6. Stir oats, and add maple syrup and almond milk. Ladle the food into a bowl and serve immediately.
Per Serving: Calories 249; Fat 2.68g; Sodium 42mg; Carbs 63.72g; Fiber 5g; Sugar 39.54g; Protein 5.58g

Vanilla Honey Buckwheat Porridge

Prep Time: 15 minutes | Cook Time: 6 minutes | Serves: 6

1 cup buckwheat groats
2 cups canned coconut milk
1 cup water
1 teaspoon kosher salt

½ teaspoon vanilla extract
2 teaspoons honey
1 cup peeled, chopped citrus fruit of choice

1. In the Inner Pot, add the buckwheat, coconut milk, water, salt, and vanilla in. Stir until the buckwheat is submerged and the coconut milk is smooth. 2. Insert the pot into the Cooker Base and then lock the lid in place. 3. Select the Pressure Cook mode. 4. Press the Pressure Cook button again and adjust the cooking time to 6 minutes; press 5. Press Level button to choose High Pressure. 6. When the time is up, leave the steam release handle in the Sealing position. 7. Carefully remove the lid and stir in the honey and fruit. Serve warm.
Per Serving: Calories 268; Fat: 19.7g; Sodium 403mg; Carbs: 22.9g; Fiber 1g; Sugars: 7g; Protein 4.4g

Berries Coconut Porridge with Chia Seeds

Prep Time: 5 minutes | Cook Time: 5 minutes | Serves: 4

1 (14-ounce) can full-fat coconut milk
½ cup chia seeds
½ cup any type of nut, or a mix
¼ cup pumpkin seeds

¼ cup pure maple syrup or raw honey
½ teaspoon ground cinnamon
½ teaspoon pure vanilla extract
2 cups fresh blueberries

1. ½ cups of water should be poured into the Instant Pot. In the pot, put a steam rack. 2. In a heatproof bowl or dish that fits your Instant Pot, combine the coconut milk, chia seeds, nuts, pumpkin seeds, maple syrup, cinnamon, vanilla, and ½ cup of water. Place the dish on the rack after adding the blueberries. 3. Close the lid. Choose Pressure Cook and cook for 5 minutes at high pressure before letting the steam release naturally for 5 minutes on seal position. Quickly release any remaining steam in the pot on vent position and remove the lid. As it cools, the porridge will get thicker.
Per Serving: Calories 613; Fat: 47g; Sodium 53mg; Carbs: 47.4g; Sugars: 37.3g; Protein 10g

Breakfast sweet potatoes

Prep Time: 5 minutes | Cook Time: 6 minutes | Serves: 2

1 sweet potato, peeled and chopped
1 apple or pear, cored and chopped
½ cup nondairy milk

2 tablespoons nut or seed butter (almond, cashew, sunflower)
¼ teaspoon ground cinnamon
Pinch ground nutmeg

1. Combine the sweet potatoes and apples in a 6- or 7-inch heatproof dish that fits inside the Instant Pot. 2. 1½ cups of water should be added to the pot along with steam rack. On the rack, place the dish. Close the lid. Choose Pressure Cook on high pressure for 6 minutes, then let the pressure release naturally for 10 minutes on seal. After that quickly release any leftover pressure in the pot on vent position and open it. 3. To the bowl, add the milk, nut butter, cinnamon, and nutmeg. Combine using an immersion blender or a standard blender, or leave chunky. If necessary, add extra milk. In bowls, serve hot food.
Per Serving: Calories 80; Fat: 5.17g; Sodium 35mg; Carbs: 4.87g; Sugars: 2.03g; Protein 3.39g

Bircher Yogurt Bowls with No Grains

Prep Time: 5 minutes | Cook Time: 15 minutes | Serves: 4

¼ cup unsalted pumpkin seeds
¼ cup unsalted sunflower seeds
¼ cup chia seeds
2 apples, cored and cut into bite-size pieces
1 cup unsweetened almond or

coconut milk
1 teaspoon pure vanilla extract
½ teaspoon ground cinnamon
¼ cup pure maple syrup (optional)
1 (32-o unce) container nondairy yogurt

1. The pumpkin seeds, sunflower seeds, chia seeds, apples, almond milk, vanilla, and cinnamon should all be combined in the Instant Pot. 2. Close the lid. Choose Pressure Cook and cook for three minutes of high pressure, quickly release the steam in the pot on vent position and remove the lid. Add the maple syrup and mix (if using). 3. In individual bowls, top the non-dairy yoghurt with the heated seed mixture.
Per Serving: Calories 571; Fat: 32g; Sodium 98mg; Carbs: 43g; Sugars: 28g; Protein 32.2g

Yummy Hash and Sausages

Prep Time: 10 minutes | Cook Time: 40 minutes | Serves: 4

1 tablespoon extra-virgin olive oil
16 ounces uncooked chorizo
2 garlic cloves, minced
1 yellow onion, diced
½ teaspoon dried rosemary
1 cup chicken broth

3 medium sweet potatoes, peeled and cut into bite-size pieces
½ teaspoon freshly ground black pepper
1 tablespoon balsamic vinegar

1. Select Sauté on the Instant Pot. Oil must be heated until it shimmers. 2. The chorizo, garlic, onion, and rosemary should be cooked for 3 to 5 minutes, stirring occasionally, until browned. Select Cancel. 3. Fill the pot with the broth. Scrape up any food particles that have fallen to the bottom using a wooden spoon. Stir in the sweet potatoes after adding them to the pot. 4. Close the lid. Choose Pressure Cook, cook for 10 minutes at high pressure, then wait 10 minutes for the pressure to naturally release on seal position. Quickly release any remaining steam on vent position in the pot and remove the lid. 5. Enjoy after adding the pepper and vinegar.
Per Serving: Calories 716; Fat: 50g; Sodium 1707mg; Carbs: 23.9g; Sugars: 7.11g; Protein 42g

Cheesy Eggs and Bacon

Prep Time: 5 minutes | Cook Time: 35 minutes | Serves: 4

1 tablespoon coconut oil or ghee
6 slices bacon, diced
6 large eggs
¼ cup full-fat coconut milk
2 cups fresh kale leaves, chopped

¼ cup nutritional yeast
¼ teaspoon sea salt
¼ teaspoon freshly ground black pepper

1. Use the ghee to coat the bottom and sides of a 6- or 7-inch heatproof bowl that fits inside your Instant Pot. Place aside. 2. Select Sauté on the Instant Pot. Cook the bacon for 5 to 8 minutes, until it is crispy. 3. In the meantime, mix the eggs with the coconut milk, nutritional yeast, salt, and pepper in a medium bowl. Place aside. 4. The kale and bacon are combined. Select Cancel. 5. Using a slotted spoon, add the bacon and greens after pouring the egg mixture into the baking dish that has been prepared. Wrap with foil. 6. Place a steam rack into the pot and add 1½ cups of water. Place the dish containing the egg mixture onto the rack. Secure the lid. Choose Pressure Cook and cook for 20 minutes of high pressure then, quickly release the steam in the pot on vent position and remove the lid. You can require an extra 5 or more minutes to cook your meal, depending on its depth. 7. Remove the egg from the Instant Pot. Serve after slicing into pieces.
Per Serving: Calories 424; Fat: 33g; Sodium 763mg; Carbs: 16.3g; Sugars: 4.49g; Protein 18g

Spanish Vegetable Tortilla

Prep Time: 15 minutes | Cook Time: 30 minutes | Serves: 6

Nonstick cooking spray
1 tablespoon olive oil
½ cup thinly sliced Yukon Gold potato
½ cup thinly sliced zucchini

½ cup thinly sliced yellow onion
6 large eggs, beaten
¼ cup kosher salt
¼ teaspoon freshly ground black pepper

1. Insert the Inner Pot into the Cooker Base without the lid. 2. Select Sauté mode and then press the same button again and then adjust the cooking temperature to Normal. 3. When the display switches On to Hot, add the olive oil and heat the oil. 4. After heating the oil, add in the potato slices, onion slices and zucchini slices. Stir occasionally for 6 minutes or until the onion slices begin to brown and the potato slices crisp. 5. Press Cancel button to stop the program, then transfer the mixture to the sprayed 6-inch cake pan. 6. Whisk together the eggs, salt and pepper in a suitable bowl, then pour the egg mixture over the vegetable mixture. 7. In the Inner Pot, add 1 cup of water and place the Steam Rack in. Arrange the cake pan to the rack and cover it with aluminum foil. 8. Insert the pot into the Cooker Base and then close the lid rightly. 9. Select Pressure Cook mode. Press Pressure Cook button again to adjust the cooking time to 30 minutes. Press Pressure Level to choose High Pressure. 10. When the time is up, leave the steam release handle in the Sealing position for 10 minutes, then turn the steam release handle to the Venting position. 11. Carefully remove the lid and lift out the cake pan. Uncover the tortilla and let it cool for 10 minutes on the rack, then cut it into 6 wedges. 12. Serve warm.
Per Serving: Calories 105; Fat: 7.3g; Sodium 168mg; Carbs: 3.7g; Sugars: 1.1g; Protein 6.7g

Banana Oatmeal with Walnuts

Prep Time: 15 minutes | Cook Time: 7 minutes | Serves: 2

1 cup rolled oats
1 cup water
1 cup whole milk
2 ripe bananas, peeled and sliced
2 tablespoons pure maple syrup
2 teaspoons ground cinnamon
¼ teaspoon vanilla extract
2 tablespoons chopped walnuts
⅛ teaspoon salt

1. In the Inner Pot, add and mix up all of the ingredients, then close the lid in right way. 2. Press Pressure Cook button to select the program, press it again to adjust the cooking time to 7 minutes; press Pressure Level to choose High Pressure. 3. When the time is up, leave the steam release handle in the Sealing position. 4. When released, open the lid and stir well. 5. Serve and enjoy.
Per Serving: Calories 441; Fat: 11.7g; Sodium 58mg; Carbs: 76.3g; Fiber 1g; Sugars: 33.4g; Protein 12.6g

Whole-Grain Vanilla Blueberry Muffins

Prep Time: 15 minutes | Cook Time: 10 minutes | Serves: 6

Nonstick cooking spray
1 cup spelt flour
1 teaspoon baking powder
¼ teaspoon baking soda
⅛ teaspoon kosher salt
1 egg, beaten
3 tablespoons nondairy milk
2 tablespoons coconut oil, melted
2 tablespoons honey
1 teaspoon vanilla extract
½ cup fresh or frozen blueberries

1. Use the non-stick cooking spray to oil the outer 6 wells of a 7-well silicone egg bite mold. 2. Combine and stir well the flour, salt, baking powder and baking soda in a medium-size bowl. 3. In another small-size bowl, crack the egg in and add the coconut oil, milk, honey and vanilla. Whisk well. 4. Add the egg mixture to the flour mixture and stir until combined into a thick batter. 5. Divide the batter between the prepared egg bite mold, filling each well about halfway. Gently press the blueberries into the top of each muffin. Place the lid on the mold. 6. In the Inner Pot, pour 1 cup of water and place the Steam Rack. Place the egg bite mold on top of the Steam Rack and then insert the pot into the Cooker Base. 7. Place the lid on the Instant Pot and lock it in place. 8. Select the Pressure Cook mode. 9. Press the Pressure Cook button again and adjust the cooking time to 10 minutes; press Level button to choose High Pressure. 10. When the time is up, leave the steam release handle in the Sealing position. 11. When done, carefully remove the lid and lift out the mold. 12. Uncover the muffins and let them cool for 3 to 5 minutes or until the mold is cool to the touch, then pop the muffins out. 13. Serve warm or store at room temperature in an airtight container for up to 3 days.
Per Serving: Calories 148; Fat: 5.7g; Sodium 64mg; Carbs: 22.6g; Sugars: 7.2g; Protein 3.8g

Flavor Spinach Feta Frittata

Prep Time: 15 minutes | Cook Time: 11-15 minutes | Serves: 4

1 tablespoon olive oil
½ medium onion, peeled and chopped
½ medium red bell pepper, seeded and chopped
2 cups chopped fresh baby spinach
1 cup water
1 cup crumbled feta cheese
6 large eggs, beaten
¼ cup low-fat plain Greek yogurt
½ teaspoon salt
½ teaspoon ground black pepper

1. Spray a 1.5-liter baking dish with the non-stick cooking spray. 2. Select Sauté mode and then press the same button again and then adjust the cooking temperature to Normal. 3. When the display switches On to Hot, add and heat the onion and bell pepper for 8 minutes or until tender; add spinach and resume cooking for 3 minutes or until wilted. 4. Press Cancel button to stop the cooking program and then transfer the food to a medium-sized bowl. 5. Drain excess liquid from spinach mixture, then add them and cheese to the prepared baking dish. 6. In another bowl, thoroughly mix up the eggs, yogurt, salt and black pepper, then also pour the mixture over the dish. Tightly cover the dish with foil. 7. In the wiped Inner Pot, place the Steam Rack in it and add 1 cup of water, then transfer the dish to the rack. 8. Select Pressure Cook mode. Press Pressure Cook button again to adjust the cooking time to 15 minutes. Press Pressure Level to choose High Pressure. 9. When the time is up, leave the steam release handle in the Sealing position until the float valve drops. 10. Wait for 10 to 15 minutes before removing the dish out of the pot. 11. Turning the frittata out onto a serving plate by running a thin knife around the edge is suggested. 12. Serve and enjoy.
Per Serving: Calories 173; Fat: 12.7g; Sodium 557mg; Carbs: 3.9g; Fiber 1g; Sugars: 2.7g; Protein 11.4g

Vanilla Blueberry Muffins

Prep Time: 15 minutes | Cook Time: 9 minutes | Serves: 6

1 cup gluten-free flour blend
¼ cup gluten-free old-fashioned rolled oats
2 teaspoons baking powder
Pinch of salt
¼ cup maple syrup
¼ cup Simple Applesauce or no-
sugar-added store-bought
2 tablespoons milk
1 tablespoon chia seeds
1 teaspoon pure vanilla extract
½ cup blueberries
1 cup water

1. In a small bowl, thoroughly mix up the chia seeds, applesauce, vanilla and milk. 2. In another medium-sized bowl, mix up the flour, baking powder, oats and salt, then add in the milk mixture and stir until just moistened. 3. After folding in the blueberries, evenly distribute the batter among 6 suitable silicone bake pans or cups. 4. In the Inner Pot, add the water and place the Steam Rack in it, then arrange the bake pans to the rack. 5. Place and close the lid in right way. 6. Press Pressure Cook button to select the program, press it again to adjust the cooking time to 9 minutes; press Pressure Level to choose High Pressure. 7. When the time is up, quickly and carefully turn the steam release handle from the Sealing position to the Venting position. 8. When released, take out the pans and remove the muffins to a cooling rack to cool for at least 10 minutes before serving.
Per Serving: Calories 134; Fat: 0.8g; Sodium 33mg; Carbs: 29.8g; Sugars: 10.4g; Protein 2.7g

Easy-to-Cook Sweet Potato Hash

Prep Time: 15 minutes | Cook Time: 13 minutes | Serves: 4

1 tablespoon olive oil
1½ pounds sweet potatoes, peeled and diced
1 yellow onion, chopped
1 red bell pepper, seeded and chopped
2 garlic cloves, minced
1 teaspoon dried oregano
½ teaspoon cayenne pepper
½ teaspoon kosher salt
¼ teaspoon freshly ground black pepper
½ cup Vegetable Broth or store-bought low-sodium vegetable broth
4 large eggs

1. Insert the Inner Pot into the Cooker Base without the lid. 2. Select Sauté mode and then press the same button again and then adjust the cooking temperature to Normal. 3. When the display switches On to Hot, add the olive oil and heat the oil, then add the sweet potatoes and stir occasionally for 10 minutes or until the sweet potatoes begin to brown and soften. 4. Add in the onion, bell pepper, oregano, garlic, cayenne pepper, salt and black pepper and resume stirring for a few minutes until well combined. 5. Press Cancel to stop this cooking program. 6. Pour in the broth and stir well, then beat in the eggs. 7. Close the lid rightly. 8. Select Pressure Cook mode and press the same button again to adjust the cooking time to 3 minutes. 9. Press Pressure Level button to choose High Pressure. 10. When the time is up, to release the steam, quickly and carefully turn the steam release handle from the Sealing position to the Venting position. 11. When done, serve and enjoy.
Per Serving: Calories 332; Fat: 9.1g; Sodium 474mg; Carbs: 53.7g; Fiber 1g; Sugars: 4.1g; Protein 10.3g

Tasty Red Pepper and Feta Egg Rolls

Prep Time: 15 minutes | Cook Time: 8 minutes | Serves: 6

1 tablespoon olive oil
½ cup crumbled feta cheese
¼ cup chopped roasted red peppers
6 large eggs, beaten
¼ teaspoon ground black pepper
1 cup water

1. In a suitable bowl which has an inverted spout, beat the eggs with the black pepper. 2. Oil the silicone muffin molds, then divide feta and roasted red peppers among the molds. 3. Insert the Inner Pot into the Cooker Base, add 1 cup of water and then place the Steam Rack in the pot; place and close the lid in right way. 4. Press Pressure Cook button to select the program and then press it again to set the cooking time to 8 minutes; press Pressure Level button to choose High Level. 5. When the time is up, quickly and carefully turn the steam release handle from Sealing position to the Venting position. 6. When the float valve drops, open the lid and take out the molds carefully. 7. Serve the food on plates.
Per Serving: Calories 127; Fat: 10g; Sodium 229mg; Carbs: 1.4g; Fiber 1g; Sugars: 1.2g; Protein 8.2g

Baked Ham, Kale and Eggs

Prep Time: 15 minutes | Cook Time: 10 minutes | Serves: 6

1 tablespoon olive oil	1 (8-ounce) package cream cheese
2 cups diced ham	¼ teaspoon salt
1 medium yellow onion, peeled and chopped	¼ teaspoon ground black pepper
2 pounds chopped kale	⅛ teaspoon ground nutmeg
½ cup heavy cream	6 large eggs
	1 cup water

1. Prepare an 8-inch round baking dish and spray it with the non-stick cooking spray. 2. Insert the Inner Pot into the Cooker Base without the lid. 3. Press the Sauté button to select the program and then press it again to adjust the cooking temperature to Normal. 4. When the display switches On to Hot, add and heat the oil. 5. When the oil heated, add ham and cook for 5 minutes or until the ham starts to brown; add the onion and resume cooking for another 5 minutes until tender, then add kale and cook for 5 minutes more or until wilted. 6. Add the nutmeg, cream, cream cheese, salt and pepper, stir for 5 minutes or until thickened. 7. Press Cancel to stop this cooking program and then transfer thickened mixture to the 8-inch sprayed baking dish. Spoon the mixture to press 6 indentations. 8. Clean the pot and then place in the Steam Rack; fold a long piece of aluminum foil in half lengthwise and then lay it over rack to form a sling. 9. Arrange the dish to the foil sling and use another piece aluminum foil to cover the dish loosely. 10. Place and close the lid rightly. 11. Press Pressure Cook button to select the program and then press it again to adjust the cooking time to 5 minutes; press Pressure Level button to choose Low Pressure. 12. When the time is up, quickly and carefully turn the steam release handle from Sealing position to the Venting position. 13. Wait for 5 minutes before removing the dish from pot. 14. Serve and enjoy.
Per Serving: Calories 413; Fat: 28.1g; Sodium 937mg; Carbs: 21g; Sugars: 1.3g; Protein 21.5g

Cinnamon Fruit Steel-Cut Oatmeal

Prep Time: 15 minutes | Cook Time: 5-10 minutes | Serves: 2

3 cups water, divided	1 tablespoon snipped dried apricots
1 cup toasted steel-cut oats	
2 teaspoons unsalted butter	1 tablespoon maple syrup
1 cup apple juice	¼ teaspoon ground cinnamon
1 tablespoon dried cranberries	⅛ teaspoon salt
1 tablespoon golden raisins	

1. In a suitable bowl, add 2-½ cups of water and the other ingredients and combine well. 2. In the Inner Pot, add the remaining ½ cup of water and then place the Steam Rack in. 3. Fold a long piece of aluminum foil in half lengthwise and then lay it over the rack to form a sling. Let the bowl rest on the foil sling. 4. Place and close the lid in right way. 5. Press Pressure Cook button to select the program; press it again to adjust the cooking time to 5 minutes for chewy oatmeal, or 8 minutes for creamy oatmeal. 6. Press Pressure Level to choose High Pressure. 7. When the time is up, to release steam, leave the steam release handle in the Sealing position. 8. Remove the bowl out of the pot carefully with the help of the foil sling. 9. Serve and enjoy.
Per Serving: Calories 218; Fat: 5.8g; Sodium 49mg; Carbs: 39.4g; Sugars: 21.5g; Protein 3.3g

Simple Boiled Eggs

Prep Time: 15 minutes | Cook Time: 5-6 minutes | Serves: 6

6 large eggs	advance.
Prepare a bowl of ice water in	

For Hard-boiled Eggs: 1. In the Inner Pot, add 1 cup of water and place the Steam Rack in. Arrange the eggs to the rack. 2. Insert the pot into the Cooker Base and then close the lid rightly. 3. Select Pressure Cook mode. Press Pressure Cook button again to adjust the cooking time to 5 minutes. Press Pressure Level to choose High Pressure. 4. When the time is up, leave the steam release handle in the Sealing position. 5. Remove the eggs to the ice water and set aside for 5 minutes. 6. Serve and enjoy.
For Soft-boiled Eggs: 1. In the Inner Pot, add 1 cup of water and place the Steam Rack in. Arrange the eggs to the rack. 2. Insert the pot into the Cooker Base and then close the lid rightly. 3. Select Pressure Cook mode. Press Pressure Cook button again to adjust the cooking time to 6 minutes. Press Pressure Level to choose Low Pressure. 4. When the time is up, to release the steam, quickly and carefully turn the steam release handle from the Sealing position to the Venting position. 5. Remove the eggs to the ice water and wait for 5 minutes. 6. Serve and enjoy.
Per Serving: Calories 72; Fat: 5g; Sodium 70mg; Carbs: 0.4g; Fiber 1g; Sugars: 0.4g; Protein 6.3g

Oatmeal Diced Apple

Prep Time: 15 minutes | Cook Time: 4 minutes | Serves: 4

2 cups water	1 teaspoon vanilla extract
1 cup gluten-free steel cut oats	½ teaspoon kosher salt
2 apples, peeled and diced	¼ cup pure maple syrup
1 teaspoon ground cinnamon	

1. In the Inner Pot, mix up the oats, apples, cinnamon, vanilla, salt and water, then insert the pot into the Cooker Base and lock the lid in place. 2. Select the Pressure Cook mode. 3. Press the Pressure Cook button again and then adjust the cooking time to 4 minutes; press Level button to choose High Pressure. 4. When the time is up, let the pressure release naturally. 5. When done, carefully remove the lid and stir in the maple syrup. Serve warm.
Per Serving: Calories 284; Fat: 3.3g; Sodium 297mg; Carbs: 58.2g; Fiber 1g; Sugars: 23.5g; Protein 7.3g

Oatmeal Pumpkin Pie Bites

Prep Time: 15 minutes | Cook Time: 10 minutes | Serves: 6

Nonstick cooking spray	¼ cup spelt flour or white whole-wheat flour
1 egg, beaten	
¾ cup pumpkin puree	1 teaspoon baking powder
3 tablespoons honey	1 teaspoon pumpkin pie spice
¾ cup gluten-free rolled oats	¼ teaspoon kosher salt

1. Spray the outer 6 wells of a 7-well silicone egg bite mold with nonstick cooking spray. 2. Prepare a suitable bowl, beat the egg in, add the honey, pumpkin puree and whisk well. 3. Continue adding the oats, flour, salt, baking powder, pumpkin pie spice and mix completely. 4. Fill each well about halfway after dividing the mixture between the prepared mold, then cover the mold with lid or aluminum foil. 5. In the Inner Pot, pour in 1 cup of water and then place in the Steam Rack. Arrange the mold to the Steam Rack. 6. Insert the pot into the Cooker Base and then close the lid rightly. 7. Select the Pressure Cook mode. 8. Press the Pressure Cook button again and adjust the cooking time to 10 minutes; press Level button to choose High Pressure. 9. When the time is up, leave the steam release handle in the Sealing position. 10. When done, carefully remove the lid and lift out the mold. Uncover the oatmeal bites and let them cool for 4 to 5 minutes before unmolding them. 11. Serve warm or at room temperature.
Per Serving: Calories 117; Fat: 1.8g; Sodium 110mg; Carbs: 23.4g; Fiber 1g; Sugars: 9.7g; Protein 3.8g

Ham Swiss Egg Rolls

Prep Time: 15 minutes | Cook Time: 12 minutes | Serves: 8

Nonstick cooking spray	¼ cup diced uncured ham
8 large eggs, beaten	½ teaspoon kosher salt
½ cup milk of choice	½ teaspoon freshly ground black pepper
½ cup shredded Swiss cheese	
½ cup finely diced red bell pepper	

1. Prepare a suitable bowl, after whisking the milk and eggs until frothy, add in the cheese, ham, bell pepper, salt and black pepper and stir thoroughly. 2. Spray the outer 6 wells of two 7-well silicone egg bite molds with nonstick cooking spray. 3. Fill each sprayed well about 3-quarter full after dividing the egg mixture between the prepared egg bite wells, filling each well about three-quarters full. Cover the molds with their lids or aluminum foil. 4. In the Inner Pot, add 1 cup of water and place the Steam Rack in. Arrange the mold to the rack. 5. Insert the pot into the Cooker Base and then close the lid rightly. 6. Select Pressure Cook mode. Press Pressure Cook button again to adjust the cooking time to 12 minutes. Press Pressure Level to choose High Pressure. 7. When the time is up, leave the steam release handle in the Sealing position for 10 minutes, then turn the steam release handle to the Venting position. 8. Carefully remove the lid and let the food cool for a minute or two minutes before releasing them from the molds. 9. Serve and enjoy.
Per Serving: Calories 114; Fat: 7.5g; Sodium 293mg; Carbs: 2.3g; Sugars: 1.6g; Protein 9.4g

Feta Crustless Quiche with Spinach

Prep Time: 15 minutes | Cook Time: 30 minutes | Serves: 4

Nonstick cooking spray
6 large eggs, beaten
¼ cup skim milk
¼ cup crumbled feta
1 shallot, finely chopped
¼ teaspoon kosher salt
¼ teaspoon freshly ground black pepper
2 cups frozen chopped spinach

1. Arrange the spinach to the sprayed 6-inch cake pan. 2. In a large-size bowl, crack in the eggs and whisk them with the milk until frothy, then add in the feta, shallot, salt, pepper and stir thoroughly. 3. Pour the egg mixture over the pan. 4. In the Inner Pot, add 1 cup of water and place the Steam Rack in. Arrange the cake pan to the rack. 5. Insert the pot into the Cooker Base and then close the lid rightly. 6. Select Pressure Cook mode. Press Pressure Cook button again to adjust the cooking time to 30 minutes. Press Pressure Level to choose High Pressure. 7. When the time is up, leave the steam release handle in the Sealing position for 10 minutes, then turn the steam release handle to the Venting position. 8. Carefully remove the lid and lift out the cake pan. Cut the quiche into 4 slices and serve.
Per Serving: Calories 141; Fat: 9.5g; Sodium 377mg; Carbs: 2.3g; Sugars: 1.8g; Protein 11.7g

Nuts Farro with Dried Fruit

Prep Time: 15 minutes | Cook Time: 20 minutes | Serves: 8

16 ounces farro, rinsed and drained
4½ cups water
¼ cup maple syrup
¼ teaspoon salt
1 cup dried mixed fruit
½ cup chopped toasted mixed nuts
2 cups almond milk

1. In the Inner Pot, add and mix up the farro, water, salt and maple syrup, then close the lid in right way. 2. Press Multigrain button to select the program, press it again to adjust the cooking time to 20 minutes; press Pressure Level to choose High Pressure. 3. When the time is up, leave the steam release handle in the Sealing position. 4. When released, open the lid and add the dried fruit; close the lid again and Keep Warm for 20 minutes. 5. With nuts and almond milk, serve and enjoy.
Per Serving: Calories 346; Fat: 23.6g; Sodium 299mg; Carbs: 31.9g; Fiber 1g; Sugars: 9.6g; Protein 7.3g

Simple Almond Date Oatmeal

Prep Time: 15 minutes | Cook Time: 12 minutes | Serves: 4

1 cup sliced almonds
4 cups water
2 cups rolled oats
1 tablespoon extra-virgin olive oil
¼ teaspoon salt
½ cup chopped pitted dates

1. Insert the Inner Pot into the Cooker Base without the lid. 2. Select Sauté mode and then press the same button again and then adjust the cooking temperature to Normal. 3. When the display switches On to Hot, add almonds. Stir constantly for 8 minutes or until the almonds are golden brown. 4. Press Cancel button to stop this cooking program, then add oil, oats, salt, dates and water in and stir well. 5. Place and close the lid in right way. 6. Press Pressure Cook button to select the program and then press it again to adjust the cooking time to 4 minutes; press Pressure Level to choose High Pressure. 7. When cooked, to release the pressure in short time, quickly and carefully turn the steam release handle from Sealing position to the Venting position. 8. When done, serve and enjoy.
Per Serving: Calories 385; Fat: 18.1g; Sodium 158mg; Carbs: 49.5g; Fiber 1g; Sugars: 15.5g; Protein 11g

Dill Egg Salad with Low-Fat Yogurt

Prep Time: 15 minutes | Cook Time: 5 minutes | Serves: 6

6 large eggs
1 cup water
1 tablespoon olive oil
1 medium red bell pepper, seeded and chopped
¼ teaspoon salt
¼ teaspoon ground black pepper
½ cup low-fat plain Greek yogurt
2 tablespoons chopped fresh dill

1. Prepare a large bowl of ice water in advance. 2. In the Inner Pot, add 1 cup of water, place in the Steam Rack and then arrange the eggs to it. 3. Select Pressure Cook mode. Press Pressure Cook button again to adjust the cooking time to 5 minutes. Press Pressure Level to choose Low Pressure. 4.

When the time is up, leave the steam release handle in the Sealing position until the float valve drops. 5. Transfer the eggs to the prepared ice water and let them stand for 10 minutes, then place the peeled and chopped egg pieces on a medium-sized bowl. 6. Clean the Inner Pot and dry it well before inserting it into the Cooker Base. 7. Without the lid, select Sauté mode and then press the same button again and then adjust the cooking temperature to Normal. 8. When the display switches On to Hot, add and heat the bell pepper, salt and black pepper for 5 minutes or until the pepper is tender. 9. When cooked, transfer the food to the bowl with egg pieces, then add yogurt and dill, fold to combine; cover with lid and chill for 1 hour before serving.
Per Serving: Calories 112; Fat: 7.4g; Sodium 180mg; Carbs: 3.4g; Sugars: 2.1g; Protein 8.7g

Quinoa with Berries

Prep Time: 15 minutes | Cook Time: 2 minutes | Serves: 4

1 cup white quinoa, rinsed
1¾ cups milk
½ cup frozen blueberries
½ cup frozen strawberries
½ cup frozen raspberries
¼ cup maple syrup
2 teaspoons pure vanilla extract
1 cup water

1. In the Inner Pot, add the water and place the Steam Rack in it. 2. Prepare a heatproof bowl, mix up the quinoa, milk, blueberries, strawberries, raspberries, maple syrup, and vanilla; arrange the bowl to the rack in the pot. 3. Place and close the lid in right way. 4. Press Pressure Cook button to select the program, press it again to adjust the cooking time to 2 minutes; press Pressure Level to choose High Pressure. 5. When the time is up, leave the steam release handle in the Sealing position. 6. When released, take out the bowl. 7. After stirring well, serve and enjoy. 8. Store in the fridge for up to 4 days in a covered container. Reheat in the microwave, adding a bit more milk, as the quinoa will thicken in the fridge.
Per Serving: Calories 297; Fat: 1.6g; Sodium 9mg; Carbs: 66.3g; Fiber 1g; Sugars: 43.4g; Protein 3.7g

Quinoa Greek Yogurt with Blueberries

Prep Time: 15 minutes | Cook Time: 12 minutes | Serves: 8

2 cups quinoa, rinsed and drained
4 cups water
1 teaspoon vanilla extract
¼ teaspoon salt
2 cups low-; Fat plain Greek
yogurt
2 cups blueberries
1 cup toasted almonds
½ cup pure maple syrup

1. In the Inner Pot, add the quinoa, vanilla, salt and water, then close the lid in right way. 2. Press Rice button to select the program, press it again to choose Normal cooking time (12 minutes); press Pressure Level to choose High Pressure. 3. When the time is up, leave the steam release handle in the Sealing position. 4. When released, open the lid and use a fork to fluff the quinoa. 5. Add yogurt and stir well, top with the blueberries, almonds and maple syrup. 6. Serve and enjoy.
Per Serving: Calories 334; Fat: 8.8g; Sodium 110mg; Carbs: 50.9g; Fiber 1g; Sugars: 18.1g; Protein 14.8g

Apple Cardamom Oatmeal

Prep Time: 15 minutes | Cook Time: 7 minutes | Serves: 4

1 tablespoon light olive oil
1 large apple, peeled, cored, and diced
½ teaspoon ground cardamom
1 cup steel-cut oats
3 cups water
¼ cup maple syrup
½ teaspoon salt

1. Insert the Inner Pot into the Cooker Base without the lid. 2. Select Sauté mode and then press the same button again and then adjust the cooking temperature to Normal. 3. When the display switches On to Hot, add the apple and cardamom in the pot and cook for 2 minutes or until the apple is just softened. 4. Press Cancel button to stop this cooking program. 5. Add oats, maple syrup, salt and water in the pot and stir well. 6. Place and close the lid in right way. 7. Select Pressure Cook mode. Press Pressure Cook button again to adjust the cooking time to 5 minutes. Press Pressure Level to choose High Pressure. 8. When the time is up, leave the steam release handle in the Sealing position for 10 minutes, then turn the steam release handle to the Venting position to quick-release the remaining pressure. 9. Stir well after removing out and serve hot.
Per Serving: Calories 153; Fat: 4.6g; Sodium 301mg; Carbs: 28.1g; Fiber 1g; Sugars: 17.7g; Protein 1.7g

Peach Pecan Oatmeal

Prep Time: 15 minutes | Cook Time: 4 minutes | Serves: 4

4 cups water	diced
2 cups rolled oats	¼ teaspoon salt
1 tablespoon light olive oil	½ cup toasted pecans
1 large peach, peeled, pitted, and	2 tablespoons maple syrup

1. In the inner pot, stir the oats, oil, peach, salt and water well, then insert the pot into the Cooker Base. 2. Place and close the lid in right way. 3. Select Pressure Cook mode. Press Pressure Cook button again to adjust the cooking time to 4 minutes. Press Pressure Level to choose Low Pressure. 4. When the time is up, quickly and carefully turn the steam release handle from Sealing position to the Venting position until the float valve drops. 5. Take out the food and stir well, then top with the pecans and maple syrup. 6. Serve and enjoy.
Per Serving: Calories 421; Fat: 26.3g; Sodium 158mg; Carbs: 41.9g; Fiber 1g; Sugars: 10.9g; Protein 8.7g

Low-Fat Greek Yogurt

Prep Time: 15 minutes | Cook Time: 10 hrs. | Serves: 6

8 cups whole or 2% milk	yogurt with live active cultures
2 tablespoons plain low-; Fat	

1. To cook successfully, you should sterilize all equipment. 2. Add the milk in the clean Inner Pot and insert the pot into the Cooker Base. Place and close the lid rightly. 3. Press Yogurt to select the program and press it again to cycle to the More option. The display indicates boil. 4. When boiled, the display indicates End. 5. When done, use the sterilized thermometer to check if the milk has reach 180°F/80°C. 6. After removing skin from milk, place the Inner Pot in an ice water bath, whisk occasionally for 5 to 7 minutes without scraping its bottom or sides. When the milk reaches 110°F/45°C, remove the pot away and dry thoroughly. 7. In a suitable bowl, whisk 1 cup of heated milk and yogurt, then pour the mixture into the Inner Pot. 8. Insert the pot into the Cooker Base and then close the lid rightly. 9. Press Yogurt to select the cooking program and then press it again to cycle to the Normal option. Use the -/+ buttons to adjust the fermentation time to 10 hours. 10. When the cooker beeps and displays End, open lid and transfer yogurt to a storage container. Refrigerate the yogurt for at least 2 hours. 11. When refrigerated, take the yogurt out of the refrigerator and use a spoon to put it into a fine mesh filter lined with 3 layers of cheesecloth or a coffee filter. 12. Place the filter on a medium-sized bowl, cover with plastic wrap and refrigerate overnight. 13. When finished, transfer the thickened yogurt to an airtight container and discard the water and cheesecloth. 14. Serve and enjoy,
Per Serving: Calories 166; Fat: 6.7g; Sodium 157mg; Carbs: 16.4g; Fiber 1g; Sugars: 15g; Protein 11g

Delicious Oatmeal with Nuts and Fruit

Prep Time: 15 minutes | Cook Time: 7 minutes | Serves: 2

1 cup rolled oats	¼ cup chopped walnuts
1¼ cups water	1 tablespoon honey
¼ cup orange juice	¼ teaspoon ground ginger
1 medium pear, peeled, cored, and cubed	¼ teaspoon ground cinnamon
¼ cup dried cherries	⅛ teaspoon salt

1. In the Inner Pot, mix up the oats, water, orange juice, pear, cherries, walnuts, honey, ginger, cinnamon, and salt, then close the lid in right way. 2. Press Pressure Cook button to select the program, press it again to adjust the cooking time to 7 minutes; press Pressure Level to choose Low Pressure. 3. When the time is up, leave the steam release handle in the Sealing position. 4. When done, serve on a plate, stir well and enjoy.
Per Serving: Calories 357; Fat: 12.1g; Sodium 15mg; Carbs: 56.2g; Fiber 1g; Sugars: 20.9g; Protein 9.8g

Fresh Fruit Buckwheat Porridge

Prep Time: 15 minutes | Cook Time: 6 minutes | Serves: 4

1 cup buckwheat groats, rinsed and drained	1 tablespoon light olive oil
3 cups water	¼ teaspoon ground cinnamon
½ cup chopped pitted dates	¼ teaspoon salt
	½ teaspoon vanilla extract

1 cup blueberries	1 cup hulled and quartered strawberries
1 cup raspberries	2 tablespoons balsamic vinegar

1. In the inner pot, stir the buckwheat, water, dates, oil, cinnamon, and salt well, then insert the pot into the Cooker Base. 2. Select Pressure Cook mode. Press Pressure Cook button again to adjust the cooking time to 6 minutes. Press Pressure Level to choose Low Pressure. 3. While cooking, in a medium-sized bowl, thoroughly mix up the blueberries, raspberries, strawberries, and vinegar. 4. When the time is up, leave the steam release handle in the Sealing position until the float valve drops. Open lid and stir in vanilla. 5. Top porridge with berry mixture. 6. Serve and enjoy.
Per Serving: Calories 246; Fat: 5g; Sodium 158mg; Carbs: 50g; Fiber 1g; Sugars: 21.8g; Protein 5.3g

Boiled Eggs in Tomato Sauce

Prep Time: 15 minutes | Cook Time: 10 minutes | Serves: 6

2 tablespoons olive oil	2 tablespoons chopped fresh oregano
1 medium onion, peeled and chopped	½ teaspoon ground fennel
1 clove garlic, peeled and minced	¼ teaspoon salt
1 (15-ounce) can tomato purée	¼ teaspoon ground black pepper
2 medium tomatoes, seeded and diced	¼ teaspoon crushed red pepper flakes
	6 large eggs

1. Insert the Inner Pot into the Cooker Base without the lid. 2. Select Sauté mode and then press the same button again and then adjust the cooking temperature to Normal. 3. When the display switches On to Hot, add and heat the oil. 4. Add onion and cook for 5 minutes until tender; add garlic and cook for 30 seconds until fragrant; add tomato purée, diced tomatoes, oregano, fennel, salt, black pepper, and crushed red pepper, stir and resume cooking for 3 minutes or until the mixture starts to bubble. 5. Press Cancel button to stop this cooking program. 6. Carefully crack eggs one at a time into a small ramekin and carefully turn out into sauce, making sure eggs are evenly distributed. 7. Select Pressure Cook mode. Press Pressure Cook button again to adjust the cooking time to 10 minutes. Press Pressure Level to choose Low Pressure. 8. When the time is up, quickly and carefully turn the steam release handle from the Sealing position to Venting position. 9. When done, serve and enjoy.
Per Serving: Calories 133; Fat: 9.9g; Sodium 170mg; Carbs: 5g; Fiber 1g; Sugars: 2.3g; Protein 7.1g

Apricots Quinoa Porridge

Prep Time: 15 minutes | Cook Time: 12 minutes | Serves: 4

1½ cups quinoa, rinsed and drained	1 cup almond milk
1 cup chopped dried apricots	1 tablespoon rose water
2½ cups water	½ teaspoon cardamom
	¼ teaspoon salt

1. In the Inner Pot, add all of the ingredients, then close the lid in right way. 2. Press Rice button to select the program, press it again to choose Normal cooking time (12 minutes); press Pressure Level to choose High Pressure. 3. When the time is up, leave the steam release handle in the Sealing position. 4. When released, open the lid and use a fork to fluff the quinoa. 5. Serve and enjoy.
Per Serving: Calories 269; Fat: 4.8g; Sodium 205mg; Carbs: 47.3g; Fiber 1g; Sugars: 5g; Protein 9.8g

Soy Yogurt

Prep Time: 15 minutes | Cook Time: 15 hours| Serves: 4

1 (32-ounce) carton unsweetened plain soy milk (containing only	soybeans and water)
	12 billion CFU probiotics

1. Mix up the soy milk in the clean Inner Pot and empty the powder in the probiotic capsule into the milk; insert the pot into the Cooker Base, place and close the lid rightly. 2. Press Yogurt to select the program and press it again to cycle to the Normal option; use the -/+ buttons to set the cooking time to 15 hours. 3. When cooked, remove and lid carefully. 4. Use a large spoon to remove and discard any excess liquid on the top of the yogurt, then transfer the yogurt to a suitable container and let it chill in the fridge. When it cools, it will thicken further. 5. For thicker Greek-style yogurt, us a clean muslin cloth to strain it for 15 to 20 minutes. 6. Serve and enjoy.
Per Serving: Calories 132; Fat: 4.3g; Sodium 125mg; Carbs: 15.4g; Fiber 1g; Sugars: 9.8g; Protein 8g

Nutritious Banana Walnut Millet Porridge

Prep Time: 15 minutes | Cook Time: 6 minutes | Serves: 4

½ cup millet
½ cup rolled oats
2½ cups almond milk
2 tablespoons maple syrup
1 tablespoon unsalted butter
½ teaspoon ground cinnamon

¼ teaspoon salt
½ teaspoon vanilla extract
1 cup toasted walnuts
2 medium bananas, peeled and sliced

1. In the Inner Pot, add the millet, oats, almond milk, maple syrup, butter, cinnamon, and salt, then close the lid in right way. 2. Press Pressure Cook button to select the program, press it again to adjust the cooking time to 6 minutes; press Pressure Level to choose High Pressure. 3. When the time is up, leave the steam release handle in the Sealing position. 4. When released, open lid and stir in vanilla. 5. Serve on a plate, top with walnuts and bananas and enjoy.
Per Serving: Calories 448; Fat: 23.9g; Sodium 207mg; Carbs: 50.7g; Fiber 1g; Sugars: 15.2g; Protein 12.6g

Peanut Butter Oatmeal with Jelly

Prep Time: 15 minutes | Cook Time: 5 minutes | Serves: 4

2 cups gluten-free old-fashioned rolled oats
2 cups milk
1 tablespoon ground flaxseed

3 cups water, divided
½ cup peanut butter
½ cup Strawberry Compote or no-sugar-added fruit preserves

1. Prepare a heatproof bowl, mix up the oats, flaxseed, milk and 2 cups of water. 2. In the Inner Pot, add the remaining 1 cup of water and place the Steam Rack in it, then transfer the bowl to the rack. 3. Place and close the lid in right way. 4. Press Pressure Cook button to select the program, press it again to adjust the cooking time to 3 minutes; press Pressure Level to choose High Pressure. 5. When the time is up, leave the steam release handle in the Sealing position for 10 minutes, then turn it to the Venting position. 6. When released, there may be some liquid on the top of the oatmeal. 7. Add he peanut butter and stir well to incorporate; top each serving with 2 tablespoons of the compote. 8. Serve and enjoy.
Per Serving: Calories 344; Fat: 20.8g; Sodium 211mg; Carbs: 28.4g; Fiber 1g; Sugars: 9.1g; Protein 14.9g

Maple Polenta with Nut

Prep Time: 15 minutes | Cook Time: 15 minutes | Serves: 4

3 cups water
2 cups milk
1 cup polenta

½ cup pecan or walnut pieces
¼ cup maple syrup

1. Insert the Inner Pot into the Cooker Base without the lid. 2. Select Sauté mode and then press the same button again and then adjust the cooking temperature to Normal. 3. When the display switches On to Hot, add water, milk and polenta in the Inner Pot, stir constantly for 5 minute or until the polenta reaches a simmer. 4. Press Cancel button to stop this cooking program. 5. Place and close the lid in right way. 6. Press Pressure Cook button to select the program, press it again to adjust the cooking time to 10 minutes; press Pressure Level to choose High Pressure. 7. When the time is up, quickly and carefully turn the steam release handle from the Sealing position to the Venting position. 8. When the float valve drops, open the lid and add the nuts, maple syrup and stir well. 9. Serve and enjoy.
Per Serving: Calories 397; Fat: 17.9g; Sodium 66mg; Carbs: 52.6g; Fiber 1g; Sugars: 18.4g; Protein 9.1g

Steel-Cut Oatmeal with Date and Walnut

Prep Time: 15 minutes | Cook Time: 5 minutes | Serves: 4

1 tablespoon light olive oil
1 cup steel-cut oats
3 cups water
⅓ cup chopped pitted dates

¼ cup ground flax
¼ teaspoon salt
½ cup toasted chopped walnuts

1. In the Inner Pot, add the oil, water, dates, flax and salt, then close the lid in right way. 2. Press Pressure Cook button to select the program, press it again to adjust the cooking time to 5 minutes; press Pressure Level to choose High Pressure. 3. When the time is up, leave the steam release handle in the Sealing position for 10 minutes, then turn the steam release handle to the Venting position. 4. When released, open lid and stir in walnuts. 5. Serve and enjoy.

Per Serving: Calories 214; Fat: 14g; Sodium 156mg; Carbs: 20g; Fiber 1g; Sugars: 9.7g; Protein 5.8g

Steamed Potatoes with Onions and Peppers

Prep Time: 15 minutes | Cook Time: 8 minutes | Serves: 4

1 cup water
2 pounds red or yellow potatoes, cubed into 1½-inch chunks
1 medium onion, diced
1 bell pepper, diced

1 teaspoon garlic powder
¾ teaspoon paprika
Freshly ground black pepper
Salt (optional)

1. In the Inner Pot, add the water and place the Steam Rack in it, then transfer the potato chunks to the rack. 2. Place and close the lid in right way. 3. Press Pressure Cook button to select the program, press it again to adjust the cooking time to 5 minutes; press Pressure Level to choose High Pressure. 4. When the time is up, leave the steam release handle in the Sealing position. 5. After removing out the rack and steamed potato chunks, dry the Inner Pot and insert it into the Cooker Base again. 6. Without closing the lid, select Sauté mode and then press the same button again and then adjust the cooking temperature to Normal. 7. When the display switches On to Hot, add the onion, pepper and sauté for 3 minutes; slowly add the water if them begin to stick, 1 tablespoon a time; add the steamed potato chunks, garlic powder, paprika, salt and black pepper, cook until they are done to your liking. 8. Serve and enjoy.
Per Serving: Calories 34; Fat: 0.2g; Sodium 43mg; Carbs: 7.8g; Fiber 1g; Sugars: 4.4g; Protein 1.1g

Steamed Eggs with Feta and Spinach

Prep Time: 15 minutes | Cook Time: 5 minutes | Serves: 2

2 tablespoons olive oil, divided
2 cups chopped baby spinach
1 scallion, chopped
1 clove garlic, peeled and minced
¼ teaspoon salt
¼ teaspoon ground black pepper

2 tablespoons low-; Fat plain Greek yogurt
2 tablespoons crumbled feta cheese
2 large eggs
1 cup water

1. Insert the Inner Pot into the Cooker Base without the lid. 2. Select Sauté mode and then press the same button again and then adjust the cooking temperature to Normal. 3. When the display switches On to Hot, add and heat 1 tablespoon of oil; add spinach, scallion and cook for 3 minutes until the spinach wilts, then add garlic and cook for about 30 seconds or until fragrant. 4. Press Cancel button to stop this cooking program. 5. Brush two 4-ounce ramekins with the remaining oil, add the spinach mixture into them separately and season with salt and pepper, then spread yogurt over them and top each ramekin with feta and egg. 6. After cleaning and drying the Inner Pot, add in water and place in the Steam Rack, then arrange the ramekins to the rack. 7. Select Pressure Cook mode. Press Pressure Cook button again to adjust the cooking time to 2 minutes. Press Pressure Level to choose Low Pressure. 8. When the time is up, quickly and carefully turn the steam release handle from Sealing position to the Venting position. 9. When done, transfer the ramekins to plate and enjoy.
Per Serving: Calories 368; Fat: 21.6g; Sodium 609mg; Carbs: 13.1g; Fiber 1g; Sugars: 10.1g; Protein 32.8g

Tomato Asparagus Frittata with Parmesan Cheese

Prep Time: 15 minutes | Cook Time: 15 minutes | Serves: 4

1 cup water
1 teaspoon olive oil
1 cup halved cherry tomatoes
1 cup cooked asparagus tips
¼ cup grated Parmesan cheese

6 large eggs
¼ cup low-; Fat plain Greek yogurt
½ teaspoon salt
½ teaspoon ground black pepper

1. Oil a 1.5-liter baking dish, then add tomatoes, asparagus and cheese to it. 2. In the Inner Pot, place in the Steam Rack and add in the water, then transfer the dish to the rack and tightly cover it with a piece of aluminum foil. 3. Select Pressure Cook mode. Press Pressure Cook button again to adjust the cooking time to 15 minutes. Press Pressure Level to choose Low Pressure. 4. When the time is up, leave the steam release handle in the Sealing position until the float valve drops. 5. Wait for 10 to 15 minutes before removing the dish out of the pot. 6. Turning the frittata out onto a serving plate by running a thin knife around the edge is suggested. 7. Serve and enjoy.
Per Serving: Calories 151; Fat: 9g; Sodium 520mg; Carbs: 4.9g; Fiber 1g; Sugars: 2.9g; Protein 12.8g

Tofu Scramble with Vegetables

Prep Time: 15 minutes | Cook Time: 10 minutes | Serves: 4

1 medium onion, diced
1 medium red bell pepper, diced
2 tablespoons no-salt-added veggie broth or water, divided
1 garlic clove, minced
1 (14-ounce) package firm tofu, drained and crumbled

2 teaspoons ground turmeric
½ teaspoon garlic powder
½ teaspoon paprika
3 ounces' fresh baby spinach
Salt (optional)
Freshly ground black pepper

1. Insert the Inner Pot into the Cooker Base without the lid. 2. Select Sauté mode and then press the same button again and then adjust the cooking temperature to Normal. 3. When the display switches On to Hot, add 1 tablespoon of the broth, onion, bell pepper and sauté for 5 minutes or until the onion begins to brown and the bell pepper is soft. 4. To prevent sticking, add a teaspoon of broth more at a time. 5. Stir in the minced garlic; add in the tofu, turmeric, garlic powder, paprika and stir until the tofu is yellow, similar to scrambled eggs; add the spinach and cook for 5 minutes more or until the spinach is just wilted. 6. Season with salt and black pepper. 7. When done, serve and enjoy.
Per Serving: Calories 127; Fat: 4.4g; Sodium 173mg; Carbs: 15.4g; Fiber 1g; Sugars: 3.4g; Protein 10.5g

Chocolate and Almonds Amaranth Breakfast Bowl

Prep Time: 15 minutes | Cook Time: 6 minutes | Serves: 6

2 cups amaranth, rinsed and drained
2 cups almond milk
2 cups water
¼ cup maple syrup
3 tablespoons cocoa powder

1 teaspoon vanilla extract
¼ teaspoon salt
½ cup toasted sliced almonds
⅓ cup miniature semisweet chocolate chips

1. In the Inner Pot, place and mix up the amaranth, water, almond mild, vanilla, maple syrup, cocoa powder and salt, then close the lid in right way. 2. Press Rice button to select the program, press it again to adjust the cooking time to 6 minutes; press Pressure Level to choose High Pressure. 3. When the time is up, quickly and carefully turn the steam release handle from the Sealing position to the Venting position. 4. When released, open the lid and stir well. 5. Top with chocolate chips and almonds and enjoy!
Per Serving: Calories 401; Fat: 12.2g; Sodium 169mg; Carbs: 63.3g; Fiber 1g; Sugars: 16.2g; Protein 12.6g

Onion Sweet Potato Hash

Prep Time: 15 minutes | Cook Time: 15 minutes | Serves: 4

1 cup water
4 medium sweet potatoes, peeled and diced
1 medium red onion, diced
1 medium red or green bell pepper, diced
1 teaspoon garlic powder

1 teaspoon smoked paprika
Freshly ground black pepper
Salt (optional)
4 to 6 leaves Swiss chard, woody stems removed and discarded, greens chopped
¼ cup milk

1. In the Inner Pot, add the water and place the Steam Rack in it, then arrange the sweet potatoes to the rack. 2. Place and close the lid in right way. 3. Press Pressure Cook button to select the program, press it again to adjust the cooking time to 6 minutes; press Pressure Level to choose High Pressure. 4. When the time is up, quickly and carefully turn the steam release handle from the Sealing position to the Venting position. 5. When the float valve drops, remove out sweet potatoes and the rack. 6. After drying the Inner Pot, insert it back into the Cooker Base. 7. Without the lid, select Sauté mode and then press the same button again and then adjust the cooking temperature to Normal. 8. When the display switches On to Hot, add the bell pepper, onion and cook for 3 to 5 minutes; to prevent sticking, add water as needed during the cooking. 9. After 5 minutes, add the sweet potatoes, garlic powder, paprika, black pepper, salt and cook for 1 to 2 minutes; add the Swiss chard and cook for 3 more minutes or until wilted; lastly, add the milk and stir to scrap the bottom of the pot. 10. When done, serve and enjoy.
Per Serving: Calories 211; Fat: 0.6g; Sodium 159mg; Carbs: 49.3g; Fiber 1g; Sugars: 4.2g; Protein 4g

Healthy Quinoa with Yogurt and Walnuts

Prep Time: 15 minutes | Cook Time: 12 minutes | Serves: 6

1½ cups quinoa, rinsed and drained
2½ cups water
1 cup almond milk
2 tablespoons honey
1 teaspoon vanilla extract

½ teaspoon ground cinnamon
¼ teaspoon salt
½ cup low-; Fat plain Greek yogurt
8 fresh figs, quartered
1 cup chopped toasted walnuts

1. In the Inner Pot, add the quinoa, almond milk, honey, vanilla, cinnamon, salt and water, then close the lid in right way. 2. Press Rice button to select the program, press it again to choose the Normal cooking time (12 minutes); press Pressure Level to choose High Pressure. 3. When the time is up, leave the steam release handle in the Sealing position. 4. When released, open lid and use a fork to fluff the quinoa. 5. With the yogurt, figs and walnuts, serve and enjoy.
Per Serving: Calories 394; Fat: 15.6g; Sodium 148mg; Carbs: 53.7g; Fiber 1g; Sugars: 20g; Protein 14.1g

Ham and Hash

Prep time: 10 minutes | Cook time: 20 minutes | Serves: 1-2

2 large eggs
½ tablespoon butter, melted
¼ cup frozen hash browns or potatoes
2 tablespoons diced ham
½ tablespoon chopped pickled

jalapeño peppers
2 tablespoons shredded Cheddar cheese
⅛ teaspoon salt
1 cup water
1 tablespoon salsa

1. Grease an 8-ounce ramekin with oil or cooking spray. 2. Whisk together eggs and butter in a bowl. 3. Add potatoes, ham, jalapeños, Cheddar cheese, and salt to the bowl, and thoroughly combine them. 4. Transfer the mixture to the prepared ramekin, and cover with foil. 5. Pour water into Inner Pot and place the Steam Rack in it. Put the ramekin on the Steam Rack. 6. Select Pressure Cook mode, and then press the "Pressure Cook" button again to select "Less" time option (20 minutes). 7. Press the Pressure Level button to adjust the pressure to "Low Pressure." 8. When cooked, allow the steam to release naturally. 9. When released, carefully remove ramekin from the Inner Pot and remove the foil. 10. Top the food with salsa and enjoy.
Per Serving: Calories 160; Fat 11.68g; Sodium 593mg; Carbs 7.61g; Fiber 0.7g; Sugar 1.58g; Protein 6.22g

Cheddar Egg Puff

Prep time: 10 minutes | Cook time: 20 minutes | Serve: 1

2 large eggs
½ tablespoon butter, melted
2 tablespoons cottage cheese
1 tablespoon chopped green chilies
2 tablespoons shredded Cheddar cheese
½ tablespoon all-purpose flour

⅛ teaspoon salt
1/16 teaspoon black pepper
1/16 teaspoon garlic powder
1/16 teaspoon ground cayenne pepper
1 cup water

1. Grease an 8-ounce ramekin with oil or cooking spray. 2. Beat eggs and butter in a small bowl. 3. Add cottage cheese, green chilies, Cheddar cheese, all-purpose flour, salt, black pepper, garlic powder, and cayenne pepper to the bowl, and combine them well. 4. Pour mixture into prepared ramekin and cover with foil. 5. Pour water into Inner Pot, and place the Steam Rack in the pot; put the ramekin on the rack. 6. Select Pressure Cook mode, and then press the "Pressure Cook" button again to select "Less" time option. 7. Use the "-" button on the control panel to adjust the cooking time to 15 minutes. 8. Press the Pressure Level button to choose "Low Pressure." 9. When cooked, allow the steam to release naturally. Then, carefully remove ramekin from Inner Pot and remove foil. 10. Serve immediately.
Per Serving: Calories 293; Fat 18.75g; Sodium 1045mg; Carbs 11.24g; Fiber 3.1g; Sugar 3.35g; Protein 20.71g

Brown Sugar Quinoa

Prep time: 10 minutes | Cook time: 2 minutes | Serves: 2

½ cup uncooked quinoa, rinsed
1 cup vanilla almond milk
1 tablespoon butter
1/16 teaspoon salt

2 tablespoons brown sugar
½ cup whole milk
¼ cup heavy cream

1. Add quinoa, almond milk, butter, and salt to the Inner Pot. 2. Select Pressure Cook mode, and then press the "Pressure Cook" button again to select "Less" time option. 3. Use the "-" key to set the cooking time to 2 minutes. 4. Press the Pressure Level button to adjust the pressure to "Low Pressure." 5. When cooked, allow the steam to release naturally. Then, carefully remove the lid and transfer the food to the serving plate. 6. Stir in brown sugar and milk, and scoop into a bowl. 7. Serve with whipped cream.
Per Serving: Calories 455; Fat 18.99g; Sodium 163mg; Carbs 59.68g; Fiber 3g; Sugar 32.24g; Protein 12.7g

Steel-Cut Oatmeal with Apple and Cinnamon

Prep Time: 15 minutes | Cook Time: 10 minutes | Serves: 4

5 cups water
2 cups gluten-free steel-cut oats
1 apple, cored and diced

3 tablespoons maple syrup
1 teaspoon ground cinnamon

1. In the Inner Pot, add and mix up the oats, apple, cinnamon, maple syrup and water, then place and close the lid in right way. 2. Press Pressure Cook button to select the program, press it again to adjust the cooking time to 10 minutes; press Pressure Level to choose High Pressure. 3. When the time is up, leave the steam release handle in the Sealing position for 10 minutes, then turn it to the Venting position; when the float valve drops, open the lid carefully. 4. There will be some liquid on the top of the oatmeal, stir well to incorporate it. 5. Serve warm and enjoy.
Per Serving: Calories 410; Fat: 6.1g; Sodium 11mg; Carbs: 76.2g; Fiber 1g; Sugars: 14.7g; Protein 14.2g

Avocado Toast with Boiled Egg

Prep time: 10 minutes | Cook time: 5 minutes | Serves: 2

1 cup water
1 large egg
½ medium avocado, peeled, pitted, and sliced
1 (1-ounce) slice sourdough bread, toasted

⅛ teaspoon salt
⅛ teaspoon black pepper
⅛ teaspoon crushed red pepper flakes
½ tablespoon roasted pepitas
½ teaspoon olive oil

1. Pour water into Inner Pot and place the Steam Rack in it. 2. Put the egg on Steam Rack. 3. Select Pressure Cook mode, and then press the "Pressure Cook" button again to select "Less" time option. 4. Use the "-" key to adjust the cooking time to 5 minutes. 5. Press the Pressure Level button to adjust the pressure to "Low Pressure." 6. When the time is up, quickly and carefully turn the steam release handle from Sealing position to the Venting position. 7. Spread avocado slices evenly over toast. 8. Carefully peel soft-boiled egg and place it on top of avocado. 9. Sprinkle salt, black pepper, red pepper flakes, pepitas, and oil over avocado. 10. Serve immediately.
Per Serving: Calories 328; Fat 13.5g; Sodium 620mg; Carbs 41.2g; Fiber 5.1g; Sugar 3.81g; Protein 12.25g

Bacon-Cheddar Egg Bites

Prep time: 10 minutes | Cook time: 8 minutes | Serves: 2

5 large eggs
¼ cup cottage cheese
⅛ teaspoon salt
1 tablespoon butter, melted

7 teaspoons crumbled bacon bits
7 tablespoons shredded Cheddar cheese
1 cup water

1. Add eggs, cottage cheese, salt, and butter to the blender, and blend them until smooth. 2. Spray a silicone egg-bite mold with cooking spray. 3. Into each cup of the mold, add 1 teaspoon bacon bits. 4. Divided the egg mixture among the cups of the mold, top each of them with 1 tablespoon Cheddar cheese, and then cover the mold with foil. 5. Pour water into Inner Pot, and place the Steam Rack in it. Put the mold on Steam Rack. 6. Select Pressure Cook mode, and then press the "Pressure Cook" button again to select "Less" time option.

7. Use the "-" key to set the cooking time to 8 minutes. 8. Press the Pressure Level button to adjust the pressure to "High Pressure." 9. When cooked, allow the steam to release naturally. Then, remove the pressure lid carefully. 10. Invert mold onto a plate and squeeze egg bites out. 11. Serve immediately.
Per Serving: Calories 339; Fat 23.15g; Sodium 856mg; Carbs 6.85g; Fiber 0.8g; Sugar 2.97g; Protein 24.71g

Feta Frittata

Prep time: 10 minutes | Cook time: 10 minutes | Serve: 1

2 large eggs
½ tablespoon heavy cream
2 tablespoons chopped spinach
2 tablespoons crumbled feta cheese

½ tablespoon chopped kalamata olives
1 cup water
¼ teaspoon balsamic glaze
⅛ teaspoon salt

1. Prepare an 8-ounce ramekin, and grease it with cooking spray. 2. Mix eggs, cream, spinach, fata, and olives in a bowl until thoroughly combined. 3. Transfer the mixture to the greased ramekin and cover with foil. 4. Pour water into Inner Pot, and place in the Steam Rack; put the ramekin on Steam Rack. 5. Select Pressure Cook mode, and then press the "Pressure Cook" button again to select "Less" time option. 6. Press the "-" button to set the cooking time to 10 minutes. 7. Press the Pressure Level button to adjust the pressure to "Low Pressure." 8. When the time is up, allow the steam to release naturally. Then, remove the pressure lid from the top carefully. 9. Drizzle the frittata with balsamic glaze and salt, and serve immediately.
Per Serving: Calories 268; Fat 19.28g; Sodium 991mg; Carbs 5.14g; Fiber 1.1g; Sugar 2.83g; Protein 18.17g

Gluten-free Banana Bread

Prep Time: 15 minutes | Cook Time: 55 minutes | Serves: 6

Nonstick cooking spray
1 ripe banana, peeled
1 large egg, beaten
2 tablespoons honey
1 tablespoon coconut oil, melted

½ teaspoon vanilla extract
1 cup gluten-free oat flour
½ teaspoon baking powder
¼ teaspoon kosher salt

1. Mash the banana until it is smooth in a large-size bowl, then add the honey, coconut oil, vanilla in and whisk well. 2. Pour the mixture onto the sprayed 6-inch cake pan lined with aluminum foil, then also cover the pan with aluminum foil. 3. In the Inner Pot, pour in 1 cup of water and then place in the Steam Rack. Arrange the cake pan to the Steam Rack. 4. Insert the pot into the Cooker Base and then close the lid rightly. 5. Select the Pressure Cook mode. 6. Press the Pressure Cook button again and adjust the cooking time to 55 minutes; press Level button to choose High Pressure. 7. When the time is up, leave the steam release handle in the Sealing position. 8. Carefully remove the lid and lift out the pan. Remove the foil cover and let the banana bread cool for 10 minutes on the rack. 9. Lift the bread from the pan and cut it into six wedges. Serve warm or at room temperature.
Per Serving: Calories 99; Fat: 3.8g; Sodium 109mg; Carbs: 14.9g; Fiber 1g; Sugars: 8.3g; Protein 2.5g

Chapter 2 Egg and Dairy Recipes

Broccoli Frittata with Ham

Prep Time: 10 minutes | Cook Time: 20 minutes | Serves: 4

Vegetable oil or unsalted butter, for greasing the pan
1 cup sliced bell peppers
8 ounces ham, cubed
2 cups frozen broccoli florets
4 eggs
1 cup half-and-half
1 teaspoon salt
2 teaspoons freshly ground black pepper
1 cup grated Cheddar cheese

1. Arrange the pepper slices to the suitable baking pan that has been oiled in advance; top with the cubed ham and cover with the frozen broccoli. 2. Thoroughly mix up the eggs, half-n-half, salt and pepper in a suitable bowl, then stir in the cheese; pour the cheese mixture over the vegetables and ham in the pan and then cover the pan with foil. 3. In the Inner Pot, add 2 cups of water and place the Steam Rack; transfer the baking pan to the rack. 4. Place and lock the lid. 5. Select Pressure Cook mode. Press Pressure Cook button again to adjust the cooking time to 20 minutes; press Pressure Level to choose High Pressure. 6. When the time is up, leave the steam release handle in the Sealing position for 10 minutes, then turn it to the Venting position. 7. Uncover the lid, carefully take out the pan and let the food stand for 5 to 10 minutes. 8. Gently loosen the sides of the frittata; place a plate on top of the pan and hold in place, then invert the frittata onto the plate. 9. Serve immediately or broil the frittata 3 to 4 minutes more to brown its top.
Per Serving: Calories: 396; Fat: 27g; Carbs: 9g; Sodium: 326mg; Fiber: 3g; Sugar: 3g; Protein: 30g

Simple Egg Loaf

Prep Time: 5 minutes | Cook Time: 4 minutes | Serves: 6

Unsalted butter, for greasing the bowl
6 eggs
2 cups water, for steaming

1. Oil a heatproof bowl with the butter and then crack in the eggs, keeping the yolks intact. 2. Use the aluminum foil to cover the bowl and set aside for later use. 3. In the Inner Pot, add the water and place the Steam Rack; transfer the bowl to the rack. 4. Place and lock the lid. 5. Select Pressure Cook mode. Press Pressure Cook button again to adjust the cooking time to 4 minutes; press Pressure Level to choose High Pressure. 6. When the time is up, quickly turn the steam release handle from the Sealing position to the Venting position. 7. Uncover the lid and carefully take out the bowl; pop out the egg loaf from the bowl. 8. Chop the egg loaf as you like. 9. You can mix the egg loaf with a little mayonnaise for egg salad, or stir with a little butter, salt and pepper for a quick snack or meal.
Per Serving: Calories: 74; Fat: 5g; Carbs: 0g; Sodium: 230mg; Fiber: 0g; Sugar: 0g; Protein: 6g

Tasty Egg Cups

Prep Time: 10 minutes | Cook Time: 7 minutes | Serves: 4

Unsalted butter or vegetable oil, for greasing the jars
4 eggs
1 cup diced vegetables, such as onions, bell peppers, mushrooms, or tomatoes
½ cup grated sharp Cheddar cheese
¼ cup half-and-half
1 teaspoon salt
1 teaspoon freshly ground black pepper
2 tablespoons chopped fresh cilantro or other herb of choice (optional)
½ cup shredded cheese of choice, for garnish

1. Prepare 4 half-pint wide-mouth, heatproof glass jars and use a brush to oil each jar into every crevice. 2. In a suitable bowl, thoroughly mix up the eggs, vegetables, cheese, half-and-half, salt, pepper and cilantro (if using); divide the mixture among the jars. 3. Place the lids on the top of the jars but do not tighten. 4. In the Inner Pot, add 2 cups of water and place the Steam Rack; transfer the jars to the rack. 5. Place and lock the lid. 6. Select Pressure Cook mode. Press Pressure Cook button again to adjust the cooking time to 5 minutes; press Pressure Level to choose High Pressure. 7. When the time is up, quickly turn the steam release handle from the Sealing position to the Venting position. 8. Uncover the lid and take out the jars carefully; top each jar with the cheese as you like. 9. Broil the jar in your oven for 2 to 3 minutes to melt the cheese until lightly browned. 10. Serve and enjoy.
Per Serving: Calories: 239; Fat: 17g; Carbs: 7g; Sodium: 235mg; Fiber: 2g; Sugar: 2g; Protein: 15g

Cream Cheese Egg Frittatas

Prep Time: 10 minutes | Cook Time: 5 minutes | Serves: 3

6 eggs
¼ cup milk
½ teaspoon cayenne pepper
Sea salt and ground black pepper, to taste
½ cup cream cheese

1. In a suitable bowl, mix up all of the ingredients and then divide the mixture into 3 molds. 2. In the Inner Pot, add 1 cup of water and place the Steam Rack; transfer the molds to the rack. 3. Place and lock the lid. 4. Select Pressure Cook mode. Press Pressure Cook button again to adjust the cooking time to 5 minutes; press Pressure Level to choose High Pressure. 5. When the time is up, quickly turn the steam release handle from the Sealing position to the Venting position. 6. Uncover the lid, serve and enjoy.
Per Serving: Calories 249; Fat 13g; Sodium 556mg; Carbs 10g; Sugar 1.1g; Fiber 0.7g; Protein 31g

Stuffed Egg White Halves

Prep Time: 10 minutes | Cook Time: 5 minutes | Serves: 5

10 eggs
½ teaspoon coarse sea salt
¼ teaspoon black pepper, to taste
½ teaspoon turmeric powder
2 teaspoons balsamic vinegar
2 tablespoons Greek-style yogurt
4 tablespoons mayonnaise
1 teaspoon fresh dill, chopped

1. In the Inner Pot, add 1 cup of water and place the Steam Rack; transfer the eggs to the rack. 2. Place and lock the lid. 3. Select Pressure Cook mode. Press Pressure Cook button again to adjust the cooking time to 5 minutes; press Pressure Level to choose High Pressure. 4. When the time is up, quickly turn the steam release handle from the Sealing position to the Venting position. 5. Uncover the lid and take out the eggs; peel the eggs and slice them into halves. 6. In a suitable bowl, thoroughly mix up the turmeric powder, vinegar, yogurt, mayonnaise, sea salt and black pepper, and then stir in the eggs yolks. 7. Fill the egg white halves with a piping bag and garnish with the fresh dill, enjoy!
Per Serving: Calories 336; Fat 17.3g; Sodium 281mg; Carbs 8.1g; Fiber 5.3g; Sugars 17.7g; Protein 32.3g

Simple Spanish Dip de Queso

Prep Time: 10 minutes | Cook Time: 10 minutes | Serves: 10

3 tablespoons butter
3 tablespoons all-purpose flour
1 cup whole milk
8 ounces Monterey Jack, shredded
Kosher salt, to taste
½ teaspoon hot sauce

1. Insert the Inner Pot into the Cooker Base without the lid. 2. Press the Sauté button to select the cooking mode and press it again to adjust the cooking temperature to Normal. 3. When the display switches On to Hot, add and melt the butter; add the flour and stir until well combined; gradually pour in the milk and stir constantly to avoid clumps. 4. When boiled, press the Cancel button to stop this cooking program. 5. Add the Monterey Jack cheese and stir until cheese melted; add the salt and hot sauce. 6. Serve warm; you can also serve with the tortilla chips.
Per Serving: Calories 272; Fat 19g; Sodium 389mg; Carbs 10.4g; Fiber 0.7g; Sugars 1.1g; Protein 15.6g

Delightful Soft Eggs with Ham and Chives

Prep Time: 5 minutes | Cook Time: 4 minutes | Serves: 3

3 eggs
1 tsp. salt
½ tsp. ground white pepper
1 tsp. paprika
1 cup water
6 oz. ham
2 tbsp. chives
¼ tsp. ground ginger

1. Prepare 3 small ramekins and crack one egg in each; season the eggs with the salt, pepper and paprika. 2. In the Inner Pot, add the water and place the Steam Rack; transfer the ramekins to the rack. 3. Place and lock the lid. 4. Select Steam mode. Press Pressure Cook button again to adjust the cooking time to 4 minutes; press Pressure Level to choose High Pressure. 5. While cooking, chop the chives, ham and combine them well in a bowl; add the ground ginger and stir well; transfer the mixture to the prepared plate. 6. When the time is up, quickly turn the steam release handle from the Sealing position to the Venting position. 7. Uncover the lid and take out the ramekins and place them on the plate. 8. Serve with the ham mixture.
Per Serving: Calories 344; Fat 14.9g; Sodium 227mg; Carbs 14g; Fiber 1g; Sugars 1.4g; Protein 25.7g

Baked Cheesy Hash Brown with Eggs

Prep Time: 30 minutes | Cook Time: 25 minutes | Serves: 3

3 ounces bacon, chopped	⅓ cup Swiss cheese, shredded
1 onion, chopped	1 teaspoon garlic powder
1 cup frozen hash browns	¼ teaspoon turmeric powder
5 eggs	Kosher salt and ground black
¼ cup milk	pepper, to taste

1. Insert the Inner Pot into the Cooker Base without the lid. 2. Press the Sauté button to select the cooking mode and press it again to adjust the cooking temperature to Normal. 3. When the display switches On to Hot, add the bacon and cook until it is crisp and browned; add the onions and stir constantly for 3 to 4 minutes; stir in the frozen hash browns and cook until slightly thawed. 4. In a suitable bowl, mix up the eggs, milk, shredded cheese, garlic powder, turmeric powder, salt, black pepper and then add in the onion mixture. 5. Oil the oven-proof dish and then spoon the egg mixture into it. 6. In the Inner Pot, add 1 cup of water and place the Steam Rack; transfer the dish to the rack. 7. Place and lock the lid. 8. Select Pressure Cook mode. Press Pressure Cook button again to adjust the cooking time to 20 minutes; press Pressure Level to choose High Pressure. 9. When the time is up, quickly turn the steam release handle from the Sealing position to the Venting position. 10. Uncover the lid, serve and enjoy!
Per Serving: Calories 312; Fat 15g; Sodium 548mg; Carbs 12g; Sugar 1.2g; Fiber 0.7g; Protein 29g

Cheese Frittata

Prep Time: 10 minutes | Cook Time: 20 minutes | Serves: 4

Vegetable oil or unsalted butter,	1½ teaspoons salt
for greasing the pan	½ teaspoon ground cumin
4 eggs	1 cup Mexican blend shredded
1 cup half-and-half	cheese, divided
1 (10-ounce) can chopped green	¼ cup chopped fresh cilantro
chilies, drained	

1. Oil a suitable baking pan in advance. 2. In a suitable bowl, combine the eggs, half-and-half, chilies, salt, cumin and ½ cup of cheese; pour the mixture into the oiled pan and the cover with foil. 3. In the Inner Pot, add 2 cups of water and place the Steam Rack; transfer the jars to the rack. 4. Place and lock the lid. 5. Select Pressure Cook mode. Press Pressure Cook button again to adjust the cooking time to 20 minutes; press Pressure Level to choose High Pressure. 6. When the time is up, leave the steam release handle in the Sealing position for 10 minutes, then turn it to the Venting position. 7. Uncover the lid and carefully take out the pan. 8. Top each frittata with the remaining cheese and then broil them in your preheated oven for 2 to 5 minutes, or until the cheese is bubbling and brown. 9. When done, let the frittata stand for 5 to 10 minutes and then gently loosen the sides from the pan with a knife; place a plate on top of the pan and hold in place, then invert the frittata onto the plate. 10. Enjoy.
Per Serving: Calories: 283; Fat: 22g; Carbs: 7g; Sodium: 326mg; Fiber: 1g; Sugar: 1g; Protein: 16g

Flavored Spanish Tortilla with Manchego Cheese

Prep Time: 30 minutes | Cook Time: 20 minutes | Serves: 4

8 eggs	or to taste
8 ounces hash browns	1 teaspoon taco seasoning mix
1 ½ tablespoons olive oil	1 teaspoon fresh garlic, minced
1 onion, sliced	⅓ cup milk
Sea salt and ground black pepper,	4 ounces Manchego cheese, grated

1. Except for the Manchego cheese, thoroughly mix up the other ingredients in a suitable bowl until well incorporated. 2. Oil a soufflé dish with the non-stick cooking oil and then scrape the mixture into it. 3. In the Inner Pot, add 1 cup of water and place the Steam Rack; transfer the dish to the rack. 4. Place and lock the lid. 5. Select Pressure Cook mode. Press Pressure Cook button again to adjust the cooking time to 17 minutes; press Pressure Level to choose High Pressure. 6. When the time is up, leave the steam release handle in the Sealing position. 7. Uncover the lid, top with the Manchego cheese and lock the lid again; let the food sit for a few minutes until the cheese melts. 8. When done, serve and enjoy.
Per Serving: Calories 272; Fat 19g; Sodium 389mg; Carbs 10.4g; Fiber 0.7g; Sugars 1.1g; Protein 15.6g

Jalapeño Pepper Omelet Cups

Prep Time: 20 minutes | Cook Time 5 minutes | Serves: 2

½ tsp. olive oil	pepper to taste
3 eggs, beaten	1 onion, chopped
1 cup water	1 jalapeño pepper, chopped
Salt and freshly ground black	

1. Rub two ramekins with a drop of olive oil. 2. In a suitable bowl, mix up the eggs, water, salt and black pepper until well combined; stir in the onion and jalapeño pepper. 3. Transfer the mixture to the ramekins. 4. In the Inner Pot, add the water and place the Steam Rack; transfer the ramekins to the rack. 5. Place and close the lid. 6. Select Pressure Cook mode. Press Pressure Cook button again to adjust the cooking time to 5 minutes; press Pressure Level to choose High Pressure. 7. When the time is up, quickly and carefully turn the steam release handle from the Sealing to Venting position. 8. Uncover the lid and serve warm.
Per Serving: Calories 344; Fat 14.9g; Sodium 227mg; Carbs 14g; Fiber 1g; Sugars 1.4g; Protein 25.7g

Hard-Boiled Eggs Ever

Prep Time: 15 minutes | Cook Time: 5 minutes | Serves: 3

5 eggs	crushed
½ teaspoon salt	2 tablespoons fresh chives,
¼ teaspoon red pepper flakes,	chopped

1. In the Inner Pot, add 1 cup of water and place the Steam Rack; transfer the eggs to the rack. 2. Place and lock the lid. 3. Select Pressure Cook mode. Press Pressure Cook button again to adjust the cooking time to 5 minutes; press Pressure Level to choose High Pressure. 4. When the time is up, quickly turn the steam release handle from the Sealing position to the Venting position. 5. Uncover the lid and transfer the eggs to icy-cold water to cool for a few minutes. 6. Peel the eggs and season with the salt and pepper. 7. Garnish with the freshly chopped chives and enjoy.
Per Serving: Calories 336; Fat 17.3g; Sodium 281mg; Carbs 8.1g; Fiber 5.3g; Sugars 17.7g; Protein 32.3g

Eggs with Bacon and Chives

Prep Time: 10 minutes | Cook Time: 8 minutes | Serves: 4

½ tsp. olive oil	Salt to taste
4 eggs	4 tbsp. chives, chopped
4 slices bacon	1 cup water

1. Oil four small ramekins and then crack one egg in each; top with one bacon slice, chives and season with the salt. 2. In the Inner Pot, add the water and place the Steam Rack; transfer the ramekins to the rack. 3. Place and lock the lid. 4. Select Pressure Cook mode. Press Pressure Cook button again to adjust the cooking time to 8 minutes; press Pressure Level to choose High Pressure. 5. When the time is up, quickly turn the steam release handle from the Sealing position to the Venting position. 6. Uncover the lid, serve and enjoy.
Per Serving: Calories 344; Fat 14.9g; Sodium 227mg; Carbs 14g; Fiber 1g; Sugars 1.4g; Protein 25.7g

Homemade Yogurt

Prep Time: 9 hours | Cook Time: 8 hours 5 minutes | Serves: 12

68-ounce milk	with cultures
2 tablespoons prepared yogurt	A pinch of salt

1. In the Inner Pot, add the milk. 2. Press Yogurt to select the program and press it again to cycle to the More option. The display indicates boil. 3. When boiled, the display indicates End; let the milk sit for 5 minutes and remove the Inner Pot. 4. When the milk cools to about 115°F/45°C, stir in the prepared yogurt with the cultures, add a pinch of salt. 5. Insert the Inner Pot back to the Cooker Base and lock the lid. 6. Press Yogurt to select the program and press it again to cycle to the Normal option. The screen displays 8:00. 7. Uncover the lid and transfer the yogurt to the refrigerator. 8. When done, serve and enjoy.
Per Serving: Calories 285; Fat 9.8g; Sodium 639mg; Carbs 11.1g; Fiber 1.2g; Sugars 5.1g; Protein 27.8g

Tomato Spinach Quiche with Parmesan Cheese

Prep Time: 15 minutes | Cook Time: 20 minutes | Serves: 4-6

10-12 large eggs, beaten
½ cup milk
½ teaspoon kosher salt
Ground black pepper to taste
2½ cups baby spinach, diced
1 cup tomato, deseeded and

roughly chopped
4 medium green onions, chopped
3 tomato slices
⅓ cup parmesan cheese, shredded
2 cups water

1. In a suitable bowl, mix up the eggs, milk, salt, and pepper until well-combined. 2. In the suitable baking dish, mix up the spinach, tomato and green onions; stir in the egg mixture and top with 3 tomato slices. 3. In the Inner Pot, add the water and place the Steam Rack; transfer the dish to the rack. 4. Place and close the lid. 5. Select Pressure Cook mode. Press Pressure Cook button again to adjust the cooking time to 20 minutes; press Pressure Level to choose High Pressure. 6. When the time is up, leave the steam release handle in the Sealing position for 5 minutes, then turn it to Venting position. 7. Uncover the lid and take out the dish. 8. Serve warm; you can also broil the dish in your broiler for a few minutes more if you want a browned top.
Per Serving: Calories 254; Fat 28 g; Sodium 346mg; Carbs 12.3 g; Sugar 1g; Fiber 0.7g; Protein 24.3 g

Cheesy Bacon Hash Brown

Prep Time: 10 minutes | Cook Time: 10 minutes | Serves: 4

6 slices bacon, chopped
2 cups frozen hash browns
8 beaten eggs
1 cup shredded cheddar cheese

½ cup milk
½ tsp salt
½ tsp ground black pepper

1. In a bowl, mix up the eggs, cheese, milk, salt and pepper. 2. Insert the Inner Pot into the Cooker Base without the lid. 3. Press the Sauté button to select the cooking mode and press it again to adjust the cooking temperature to Normal. 4. When the display switches On to Hot, add the bacon and cook until lightly crispy; add the hash brown and stir occasionally for 2 minutes until they start to thaw. 5. Press the Cancel button to stop the cooking program and pour in the egg mixture; place and lock the lid. 6. Select Pressure Cook mode. Press Pressure Cook button again to adjust the cooking time to 7 minutes; press Pressure Level to choose High Pressure. 7. When the time is up, quickly and carefully turn the steam release handle from the Sealing to Venting position. 8. Uncover the lid, slice and enjoy.
Per Serving: Calories 272; Fat 19g; Sodium 389mg; Carbs 10.4g; Fiber 0.7g; Sugars 1.1g; Protein 15.6g

Mexican-Style Omelet

Prep Time: 30 minutes | Cook Time: 11 minutes | Serves: 4

1 tablespoon olive oil
1 medium onion, chopped
2 cloves garlic, minced
1 cup Mexica cheese blend, crumbled
1 cup Chanterelle mushrooms, chopped

1 bell pepper, sliced
1 Poblano pepper, seeded and minced
5 eggs
4 ounces cream cheese
Sea salt and ground black pepper, to taste

1. In a suitable, mix up all of the ingredients. 2. Oil a soufflé dish and then scrape the mixture into it. 3. In the Inner Pot, add 1 cup of water and place the Steam Rack; transfer the dish to the rack. 4. Place and lock the lid. 5. Select Pressure Cook mode. Press Pressure Cook button again to adjust the cooking time to 11 minutes; press Pressure Level to choose High Pressure. 6. When the time is up, leave the steam release handle in the Sealing position. 7. Uncover the lid and serve; you can enjoy with the salsa.
Per Serving: Calories 344; Fat 14.9g; Sodium 227mg; Carbs 14g; Fiber 1g; Sugars 1.4g; Protein 25.7g

Egg Halves with Cottage Cheese

Prep Time: 10 minutes | Cook Time: 5 minutes | Serves: 6

6 eggs
¼ cup Cottage cheese, crumbled
1 tablespoon butter, softened
2 tablespoons fresh parsley,

minced
1 teaspoon paprika
Sea salt and ground black pepper, to taste

1. In the Inner Pot, add 1 cup of water and place the Steam Rack; transfer the eggs to the rack. 2. Place and lock the lid. 3. Select Pressure Cook mode. Press Pressure Cook button again to adjust the cooking time to 5 minutes; press Pressure Level to choose High Pressure. 4. When the time is up, quickly turn the steam release handle from the Sealing position to the Venting position. 5. Uncover the lid and take out the eggs; peel the eggs and slice them into halves after cooling them a few minutes. 6. In a suitable bowl, thoroughly mix up the Cottage cheese, butter, parsley, paprika, sea salt and black pepper, then stir in the eggs yolks. 7. Fill the egg white halves with a piping bag, then serve and enjoy.
Per Serving: Calories 344; Fat 14.9g; Sodium 227mg; Carbs 14g; Fiber 1g; Sugars 1.4g; Protein 25.7g

Mac and Cheese with Cauliflower Florets

Prep Time: 15 minutes | Cook Time: 5 minutes | Serves: 4

1-pound cauliflower florets
1 cup heavy cream
4 ounces Ricotta cheese
1 ½ cups Cheddar cheese, shredded
Sea salt and ground white pepper,

to taste
½ teaspoon garlic powder
½ teaspoon shallot powder
½ teaspoon celery seeds
½ teaspoon red pepper flakes
¼ cup Parmesan cheese

1. In the Inner Pot, add 1 cup of water and place the Steam Rack; transfer the cauliflower florets to the rack. 2. Place and lock the lid. 3. Select Pressure Cook mode. Press Pressure Cook button again to adjust the cooking time to 2 minutes; press Pressure Level to choose High Pressure. 4. When the time is up, quickly and carefully turn the steam release handle from the Sealing position to the Venting position. 5. Uncover the lid, drain the cauliflower florets and reserve. 6. Press the Cancel button and remove the lid. 7. Select the Sauté button to select the cooking mode and press it again to adjust the cooking temperature to Less. 8. When the display switches On to Hot, add the heavy cream, Ricotta cheese, Cheddar cheese, spices and let simmer until the cheese melted; add the cauliflower florets and lightly stir to combine; scatter the Parmesan cheese over the cauliflower and cheese. 9. Serve and enjoy!
Per Serving: Calories 249; Fat 13g; Sodium 556mg; Carbs 10g; Sugar 1.1g; Fiber 0.7g; Protein 31g

Delicious Ham Egg Casserole

Prep Time: 15 minutes | Cook Time: 20 minutes | Serves: 2-4

6 beaten eggs
½ cup plain Greek yogurt
1 cup cheddar cheese, shredded
1 cup ham, diced

¼ cup chives, chopped
½ teaspoon black pepper
1 cup water

1. In a heatproof bowl, mix up the eggs and yogurt until well-combined, then stir in the cheese, ham, chives and pepper. 2. In the Inner Pot, add the water and place the Steam Rack; transfer the bowl to the rack. 3. Place and close the lid. 4. Select Pressure Cook mode. Press Pressure Cook button again to adjust the cooking time to 20 minutes; press Pressure Level to choose High Pressure. 5. When the time is up, quickly and carefully turn the steam release handle from the Sealing to Venting position. 6. Uncover the lid and serve warm.
Per Serving: Calories 272; Fat 19g; Sodium 389mg; Carbs 10.4g; Fiber 0.7g; Sugars 1.1g; Protein 15.6g

Homemade Cheese Dip

Prep Time: 15 minutes | Cook Time: 10 minutes | Serves: 10

½ stick butter
½ teaspoon onion powder
½ teaspoon garlic powder
¼ teaspoon dried dill weed
Sea salt and ground black pepper,

to taste
2 tablespoons tapioca starch
1 ½ cups whole milk
1 ½ cups Swiss cheese, grated

1. Insert the Inner Pot into the Cooker Base without the lid. 2. Press the Sauté button to select the cooking mode and press it again to adjust the cooking temperature to Normal. 3. When the display switches On to Hot, add and melt the butter; add the onion powder, garlic powder, dill, salt, black pepper and stir in the tapioca starch until well combined; gradually pour in the milk and then stir constantly to avoid clumps. 4. When the mixture boiled, press the Cancel to stop this cooking program. 5. Add the Swiss cheese and stir until the cheese melted. 6. Serve warm with breadsticks or veggie sticks.
Per Serving: Calories 305; Fat 15g; Sodium 548mg; Carbs 12g; Sugar 1.2g; Fiber 0.7g; Protein 29g

Tomato Spinach Stew with Parmesan Cheese

Prep Time: 15 minutes | Cook Time: 20 minutes | Serves: 4-6

1½ cups water
12 beaten eggs
Salt and ground black pepper to the taste
½ cup milk

1 cup tomato, diced
3 cups baby spinach, chopped
3 green onions, sliced
4 tomatoes, sliced
¼ cup parmesan, grated

1. Crack the eggs in a bowl, add the salt, pepper and milk and stir until well combined. 2. In a suitable baking dish, mix up the diced tomato, spinach and green onions; pour the egg mixture and then top with the tomato slices; sprinkle with the Parmesan cheese. 3. In the Inner Pot, add the water and place the Steam Rack; transfer the dish to the rack. 4. Place and lock the lid. 5. Select Pressure Cook mode. Press Pressure Cook button again to adjust the cooking time to 20 minutes; press Pressure Level to choose High Pressure. 6. When the time is up, quickly turn the steam release handle from the Sealing position to the Venting position. 7. Uncover the lid, serve and enjoy. 8. You can slide under the oven for a few minutes more if you want a crisp top.
Per Serving: Calories 336; Fat 17.3g; Sodium 281mg; Carbs 8.1g; Fiber 5.3g; Sugars 17.7g; Protein 32.3g

Mini Raisin Almond Pancakes

Prep Time: 15 minutes | Cook Time: 8 minutes | Serves: 4

1 cup all-purpose flour
2 teaspoons baking powder
1 teaspoon salt
¼ cup milk

2 eggs, whisked
2 tablespoons maple syrup
½ cup raisins
2 tablespoons almonds, chopped

1. Thoroughly mix up the other ingredients in a suitable bowl until well incorporated. 2. Spray a muffin tin with the cooking spray and then pour the mixture into it. 3. In the Inner Pot, add 1 cup of water and place the Steam Rack; transfer the dish to the rack. 4. Place and lock the lid. 5. Select Pressure Cook mode. Press Pressure Cook button again to adjust the cooking time to 8 minutes; press Pressure Level to choose High Pressure. 6. When the time is up, leave the steam release handle in the Sealing position. 7. Uncover the lid, serve and enjoy!
Per Serving: Calories 307; Fat 11g; Sodium 477mg; Carbs 12g; Fiber 1.2g; Sugars 1g; Protein 27g

Spinach and Mushroom Frittata

Prep Time: 15 minutes | Cook Time: 5 minutes | Serves: 4

6 eggs
¼ cup double cream
1 cup Asiago cheese, shredded
Sea salt and freshly ground black pepper, to taste
1 teaspoon cayenne pepper
2 tablespoons olive oil

1 yellow onion, finely chopped
2 cloves garlic, minced
6 ounces Italian brown mushrooms, sliced
4 cups spinach, torn into pieces
1 tablespoon Italian seasoning mix

1. Thoroughly mix up the eggs, double cream, Asiago cheese, salt, black pepper and cayenne pepper, then add the remaining ingredients. 2. Spray a baking dish with the olive oil and then spoon the mixture into it. 3. In the Inner Pot, add 1 cup of water and place the Steam Rack; transfer the dish to the rack. 4. Place and lock the lid. 5. Select Pressure Cook mode. Press Pressure Cook button again to adjust the cooking time to 5 minutes; press Pressure Level to choose High Pressure. 6. When the time is up, quickly and carefully turn the steam release handle from the Sealing position to the Venting position. 7. Uncover the lid, serve and enjoy.
Per Serving: Calories 336; Fat 17.3g; Sodium 281mg; Carbs 8.1g; Fiber 5.3g; Sugars 17.7g; Protein 32.3g

Sausage Frittata with Cheddar Cheese

Prep Time: 15 minutes | Cook Time: 20 minutes | Serves: 2-4

1½ cups water
1 tablespoon butter
4 beaten eggs
2 tablespoons sour cream

¼ cup cheddar cheese, grated
½ cup cooked ground sausage
Salt and ground black pepper to taste

1. Oil a suitable soufflé dish (about 6-7 inches) with the butter. 2. In a bowl, mix up the eggs and sour cream until well combined; add the cheese,

sausage, salt and pepper and stir well. 3. Pour the mixture into the oiled dish and wrap tightly with foil all over. 4. In the Inner Pot, add the water and place the Steam Rack; arrange the dish to the rack. 5. Select Pressure Cook mode. Press Pressure Cook button again to adjust the cooking time to 17 minutes; press Pressure Level to choose Low Pressure. 6. When the time is up, quickly turn the steam release handle from the Sealing position to the Venting position. 7. Uncover the lid, serve and enjoy.
Per Serving: Calories 285; Fat 9.8g; Sodium 639mg; Carbs 11.1g; Fiber 1.2g; Sugars 5.1g; Protein 27.8g

Mayo Eggs Dish

Prep Time: 15 minutes | Cook Time 5 minutes | Serves: 4-6

1 cup water
8 eggs
¼ cup cream
1 teaspoon mayo sauce
1 tablespoon mustard

1 teaspoon ground white pepper
1 teaspoon minced garlic
½ teaspoon sea salt
¼ cup dill, chopped

1. In the Inner Pot, add the water and place the Steam Rack; transfer the eggs to the rack. 2. Place and close the lid. 3. Select Pressure Cook mode. Press Pressure Cook button again to adjust the cooking time to 5 minutes; press Pressure Level to choose High Pressure. 4. When the time is up, quickly and carefully turn the steam release handle from the Sealing to Venting position. 5. Uncover the lid and cool the eggs in the bowl of cold water for 2 to 3 minutes. 6. Peel the eggs, remove the egg yolks and mash them. 7. In a bowl, mix up the cream, mayo sauce, mustard, pepper, garlic, salt and mashed egg yolks; sprinkle the mixture with the dill and stir well. 8. Transfer the egg yolk mixture to the pastry bag; fill the egg whites with the yolk mixture. 9. Enjoy!
Per Serving: Calories 249; Fat 13g; Sodium 556mg; Carbs 10g; Sugar 1.1g; Fiber 0.7g; Protein 31g

Ham, Cheese and Egg Muffins

Prep Time: 15 minutes | Cook Time: 6 minutes | Serves: 4

8 eggs
¼ teaspoon ground black pepper, or more to taste
1 teaspoon paprika
Sea salt, to taste
1 cup green peppers, seeded and chopped

8 ounces ham, chopped
½ cup sour cream
½ cup Swiss cheese, shredded
2 tablespoons parsley, chopped
2 tablespoons cilantro, chopped
2 tablespoons scallions, chopped

1. Thoroughly mix up the other ingredients in a suitable bowl until well combined. 2. Spoon the mixture into the prepared silicone molds. 3. In the Inner Pot, add 1 cup of water and place the Steam Rack; transfer the molds to the rack. 4. Place and lock the lid. 5. Select Pressure Cook mode. Press Pressure Cook button again to adjust the cooking time to 6 minutes; press Pressure Level to choose High Pressure. 6. When the time is up, quickly and carefully turn the steam release handle from the Sealing position to the Venting position. 7. Uncover the lid, serve and enjoy.
Per Serving: Calories 336; Fat 17.3g; Sodium 281mg; Carbs 8.1g; Fiber 5.3g; Sugars 17.7g; Protein 32.3g

Egg Bacon Muffins

Prep Time: 5 minutes | Cook Time: 10 minutes | Serves: 2

4 beaten eggs
4 bacon slices, cooked and crumbled
4 tablespoons cheddar cheese, shredded

1 green onion, chopped
A pinch of salt
1½ cups water
Prepare 2 muffin cups.

1. In a suitable bowl, mix up the eggs, bacon, cheese, onion and salt until combined, then divide the mixture into the cups. 2. In the Inner Pot, add the water and place the Steam Rack; transfer the cups to the rack. 3. Place and close the lid. 4. Select Pressure Cook mode. Press Pressure Cook button again to adjust the cooking time to 8 minutes; press Pressure Level to choose High Pressure. 5. When the time is up, leave the steam release handle in the Sealing position for 2 minutes, then turn it to Venting position. 6. Uncover the lid, serve and enjoy.
Per Serving: Calories 254; Fat 28 g; Sodium 346mg; Carbs 12.3 g; Sugar 1g; Fiber 0.7g; Protein 24.3 g

Bacon and Sausage Omelet

Prep Time: 20 minutes | **Cook Time:** 30 minutes | **Serves:** 6

6-12 beaten eggs
½ cup milk
6 sausage links, sliced
1 onion, diced
Garlic powder
Salt and ground black pepper to taste

Olive oil cooking spray
2 cups water
6 bacon slices, cooked
Dried oregano, optional
Equipment:
1½-quart ceramic baking dish

1. In a bowl, beat the eggs and then pour in the milk, stir to combine well; add the sausages, onion and season with the garlic powder, salt and pepper, stir well. 2. Spray the baking dish with the cooking spray; pour the egg mixture into it and wrap tightly with the foil all over. 3. In the Inner Pot, add the water and place the Steam Rack; transfer the dish to the rack. 4. Place and close the lid. 5. Select Pressure Cook mode. Press Pressure Cook button again to adjust the cooking time to 25 minutes; press Pressure Level to choose High Pressure. 6. When the time is up, leave the steam release handle in the Sealing position. 7. Uncover the lid and remove the foil carefully; top with the cooked bacon and the shredded cheese. 8. Place and close the lid. 9. Select Pressure Cook mode. Press Pressure Cook button again to adjust the cooking time to 5 minutes; press Pressure Level to choose High Pressure. 10. When the time is up, quickly turn the steam release handle from the Sealing position to the Venting position. 11. Uncover the lid, serve and you can enjoy with the dried oregano.
Per Serving: Calories 344; Fat 14.9g; Sodium 227mg; Carbs 14g; Fiber 1g; Sugars 1.4g; Protein 25.7g

Cheesy Tomato Egg Cups

Prep Time: 10 minutes | **Cook Time:** 8 minutes | **Serves:** 4

1 cup water
1 cup chopped baby spinach
6 beaten eggs
1 chopped tomato

½ cup mozzarella cheese, shredded
¼ cup feta cheese, cubed
1 tsp black pepper
½ tsp salt

1. In a bowl, mix up the eggs, mozzarella cheese, feta cheese, chopped tomato, salt and pepper until well-combined. 2. Prepare 2 heatproof cups and add the spinach in them, then pour in the egg mixture, leaving ¼-inch of head room. 3. In the Inner Pot, add the water and place the Steam Rack; transfer the cups to the rack. 4. Place and close the lid. 5. Select Pressure Cook mode. Press Pressure Cook button again to adjust the cooking time to 8 minutes; press Pressure Level to choose High Pressure. 6. When the time is up, quickly and carefully turn the steam release handle from the Sealing to Venting position. 7. Uncover the lid and serve warm.
Per Serving: Calories 305; Fat 15g; Sodium 548mg; Carbs 12g; Sugar 1.2g; Fiber 0.7g; Protein 29g

Egg Casserole with Red Onion

Prep Time: 15 minutes | **Cook Time:** 25 minutes | **Serves:** 4-6

½ teaspoon olive oil
1 large red onion, chopped
1-pound mild sausages, ground
8 large eggs, beaten
½ cup flour
1 can black beans, rinsed
1 cup Cotija cheese (or any semi-

hard cheese)
1 cup mozzarella cheese
1 cup water
Sour cream, optional to garnish
Cilantro, optional to garnish
½ cup green onions

1. Insert the Inner Pot into the Cooker Base without the lid. 2. Press the Sauté button to select the cooking mode and press it again to adjust the cooking temperature to Normal. 3. When the display switches On to Hot, add and heat the oil; add the onion and cook for 2 to 3 minutes; add the sausages and cook until all sides start to brown. 4. Press the Cancel button to stop the cooking program. 5. In a suitable bowl, mix up the eggs and flour until well-combined; add the beans, Cotija cheese, mozzarella cheese and sausages, then pour the mixture to the heatproof round baking dish. 6. In the Inner Pot, add the water and place the Steam Rack; transfer the bowl to the rack. 7. Place and close the lid. 8. Select Pressure Cook mode. Press Pressure Cook button again to adjust the cooking time to 20 minutes; press Pressure Level to choose High Pressure. 9. When the time is up, leave the steam release handle in the Sealing position for 10 minutes, then turn it to Venting position. 10. Uncover the lid, top the dish with sour cream, green onion and cilantro. 11. Chill for a few minutes before serving.
Per Serving: Calories 336; Fat 17.3g; Sodium 281mg; Carbs 8.1g; Fiber 5.3g; Sugars 17.7g; Protein 32.3g

Cheesy Egg Bake with Turkey Bacon

Prep Time: 10 minutes | **Cook Time:** 10 minutes | **Serves:** 4

1 teaspoon olive oil
6 slices of turkey bacon, cubed
2 cups frozen hash browns
1 cup cheddar cheese, shredded

8 beaten eggs
½ cup half and half or milk
Salt to taste

1. Insert the Inner Pot into the Cooker Base without the lid. 2. Press the Sauté button to select the cooking mode and press it again to adjust the cooking temperature to Normal. 3. When the display switches On to Hot, add and heat the oil; add the turkey bacon slices and cook for 1 to 2 minutes until browned. 4. Press the Cancel button and then top the bacon with the hash brown potatoes; sprinkle half of the Cheddar cheese. 5. Place and close the lid. 6. Select Pressure Cook mode. Press Pressure Cook button again to adjust the cooking time to 7 minutes; press Pressure Level to choose High Pressure. 7. When the time is up, quickly and carefully turn the steam release handle from the Sealing to Venting position. 8. Uncover the lid, serve and enjoy.
Per Serving: Calories 285; Fat 9.8g; Sodium 639mg; Carbs 11.1g; Fiber 1.2g; Sugars 5.1g; Protein 27.8g

Egg and Potato Salad with Mayonnaise

Prep Time: 15 minutes | **Cook Time:** 5 minutes | **Serves:** 2-4

1½ cups water
6 russet potatoes, peeled and diced
4 large eggs
1 cup mayonnaise
2 tablespoons fresh parsley, chopped

¼ cup onion, chopped
1 tablespoon dill pickle juice
1 tablespoon mustard
Pinch of salt
Pinch of ground black pepper

1. In the Inner Pot, add the water and place the Steam Rack; transfer the eggs and potatoes to the rack. 2. Place and close the lid. 3. Select Pressure Cook mode. Press Pressure Cook button again to adjust the cooking time to 5 minutes; press Pressure Level to choose High Pressure. 4. While cooking, in a bowl, mix up the mayonnaise, parsley, onion, dill pickle juice, mustard, salt and pepper. 5. When the time is up, quickly and carefully turn the steam release handle from the Sealing to Venting position. 6. Uncover the lid and transfer the eggs to the bowl of cold water to cool for 2 to 3 minutes. 7. Peel and slice the eggs; toss the potatoes and eggs in the bowl and stir with the mixture. 8. Enjoy.
Per Serving: Calories 336; Fat 17.3g; Sodium 281mg; Carbs 8.1g; Fiber 5.3g; Sugars 17.7g; Protein 32.3g

Bacon Cheese Quiche with Sausage

Prep Time: 20 minutes | **Cook Time:** 30 minutes | **Serves:** 4

1 cup water
6 large eggs, beaten
½ cup almond or coconut milk
¼ teaspoon salt
⅛ teaspoon black pepper, ground
½ cup diced ham

1 cup ground sausage, cooked
4 slices cooked and crumbled bacon
1 cup parmesan Cheese
2 large green onions, chopped

1. In a heatproof round baking dish, mix up the eggs, milk, salt and pepper until combined; stir in the ham, sausage, bacon, cheese and green onion. 2. Cover the dish with foil. 3. In the Inner Pot, add the water and place the Steam Rack; transfer the dish to the rack. 4. Place and close the lid. 5. Select Pressure Cook mode. Press Pressure Cook button again to adjust the cooking time to 30 minutes; press Pressure Level to choose High Pressure. 6. When the time is up, leave the steam release handle in the Sealing position for 10 minutes, then turn it to Venting position. 7. Uncover the lid and remove the foil. 8. Serve immediately; you can sprinkle more cheese and broil the dish in the broiler for a few minutes if you want a crisp top.
Per Serving: Calories 344; Fat 14.9g; Sodium 227mg; Carbs 14g; Fiber 1g; Sugars 1.4g; Protein 25.7g

Delectable Mac and Cheese

Prep Time: 15 minutes | Cook Time: 5 minutes | Serves: 6

12 ounces elbow macaroni	3 cups water
2 tablespoons butter	4 ounces milk
½ teaspoon celery seeds	2 ½ cups cheddar cheese, shredded
Kosher salt, to taste	1 cup Parmesan cheese, shredded

1. In the Inner Pot, add the elbow macaroni, butter, celery seeds, water and salt. 2. Place and lock the lid. 3. Select Pressure Cook mode. Press Pressure Cook button again to adjust the cooking time to 5 minutes; press Pressure Level to choose Low Pressure. 4. When the time is up, quickly and carefully turn the steam release handle from the Sealing position to the Venting position. 5. Uncover the lid, add the milk and half of the cheeses and stir until the cheeses are melted; add the remaining cheeses and stir until well combined. 6. When the sauce cools, it will be thickening. 7. Bon appétit!
Per Serving: Calories 254; Fat 28 g; Sodium 346mg; Carbs 12.3 g; Sugar 1g; Fiber 0.7g; Protein 24.3 g

Easy Hard-Boiled Eggs

Prep Time: 10 minutes | Cook Time: 5 minutes | Serves: 4-8

5-15 eggs	1 cup water

1. In the Inner Pot, add the water and place the Steam Rack; transfer the eggs to the rack. 2. Place and lock the lid. 3. Select Pressure Cook mode. Press Pressure Cook button again to adjust the cooking time to 5 minutes; press Pressure Level to choose High Pressure. 4. When the time is up, leave the steam release handle in the Sealing position for 5 minutes, then turn it to the Venting position. 5. Uncover the lid; cool the eggs in the bowl of cold water for 2 to 3 minutes. 6. Serve.
Per Serving: Calories 336; Fat 17.3g; Sodium 281mg; Carbs 8.1g; Fiber 5.3g; Sugars 17.7g; Protein 32.3g

Mushroom Frittata with Cheddar Cheese

Prep Time: 15 minutes | Cook Time: 5 minutes | Serves: 2-4

4 beaten eggs	pepper to taste
1 cup fresh mushrooms, chopped	1 cup sharp cheddar cheese, shredded
¼ cup half-and-half	and divided
Salt and freshly ground black	1 cup water

1. In a suitable bowl, mix up the eggs, mushrooms, half-and-half, salt and pepper, and ½ cup of cheese. 2. Divide the mixture into ½-pint wide mouth jars evenly and sprinkle with the remaining cheese; place the lids on the top of the jars but do not tighten. 3. In the Inner Pot, add the water and place the Steam Rack; arrange the jars to the rack. 4. Select Pressure Cook mode. Press Pressure Cook button again to adjust the cooking time to 3 minutes; press Pressure Level to choose High Pressure. 5. When the time is up, quickly turn the steam release handle from the Sealing position to the Venting position. 6. Uncover the lid, serve and enjoy.
Per Serving: Calories 305; Fat 15g; Sodium 548mg; Carbs 12g; Sugar 1.2g; Fiber 0.7g; Protein 29g

Simple Soft-Boiled Eggs

Prep Time: 5 minutes | Cook Time: 4 minutes | Serves: 2

4 eggs	Salt and ground black pepper to
1 cup water	taste
2 English muffins, toasted	

1. In the Inner Pot, add the water and place the Steam Rack; transfer the eggs to the rack. 2. Place and lock the lid. 3. Select Steam mode. Press Pressure Cook button again to adjust the cooking time to 4 minutes; press Pressure Level to choose High Pressure. 4. When the time is up, quickly turn the steam release handle from the Sealing position to the Venting position. 5. Uncover the lid and transfer the eggs to the bowl of cold water to cool for 2 to 3 minutes. 6. When cooled, peel each egg into 2 slices; serve one egg per half of toasted English muffin. 7. Season with the salt and pepper, enjoy.
Per Serving: Calories 285; Fat 9.8g; Sodium 639mg; Carbs 11.1g; Fiber 1.2g; Sugars 5.1g; Protein 27.8g

Homemade Fresh Cream Cheese

Prep Time: 20 minutes | Cook Time: 5 minutes | Serves: 10

3 ½ cups whole milk	1 teaspoon kosher salt
1 cup double cream	2 tablespoons lemon juice

1. In the Inner Pot, stir in the milk, double cream and salt. 2. Place and lock the lid. 3. Select Pressure Cook mode. Press Pressure Cook button again to adjust the cooking time to 5 minutes; press Pressure Level to choose Low Pressure. 4. When the time is up, leave the steam release handle in the Sealing position. 5. Uncover the lid and stir in the lemon juice. 6. Prepare a strainer and line with cheesecloth, then pour the mixture into the cheesecloth; allow the curds to continue to drain in the strainer for about 1 hour. 7. Discard the whey. 8. Form your cheese into ball and remove from the cheesecloth. 9. The cheese balls can be refrigerated for a week. 10. Bon appétit!
Per Serving: Calories 351; Fat 22g; Sodium 502mg; Carbs 15.2g; Sugar 1.1g; Fiber 0.7g; Protein 26.4g

Herbed Egg Cups

Prep Time: 15 minutes | Cook Time: 4 minutes | Serves: 4

4 bell peppers	⅔ cup water
4 eggs	2 tablespoons mozzarella cheese,
Salt and ground black pepper to	grated freshly
taste	Chopped fresh herbs

1. Cut the bell peppers ends to form about 1½-inch high cup and discard the seeds. 2. Crack one egg into each pepper, season with the salt and black pepper and cover each pepper with foil. 3. In the Inner Pot, add the water and place the Steam Rack; transfer the bell peppers to the rack. 4. Place and close the lid. 5. Select Pressure Cook mode. Press Pressure Cook button again to adjust the cooking time to 4 minutes; press Pressure Level to choose High Pressure. 6. When the time is up, quickly and carefully turn the steam release handle from the Sealing to Venting position. 7. Uncover the lid and serve the pepper on a plate; sprinkle with the mozzarella cheese and chopped fresh herbs as you like.
Per Serving: Calories 285; Fat 9.8g; Sodium 639mg; Carbs 11.1g; Fiber 1.2g; Sugars 5.1g; Protein 27.8g

Chapter 3 Rice Recipes

Simple Homemade Brown Rice

Prep Time: 1 minutes | Cook Time: 22 minutes | Serves: 4

1 cup brown rice	1 cup chicken stock

1. In the Inner Pot, add the rice and chicken stock. 2. Place and close the lid rightly. 3. Select Pressure Cook mode. Press Pressure Cook button again to adjust the cooking time to 22 minutes; press Pressure Level to choose High Pressure. 4. When the time is up, leave the steam release handle in the Sealing position. 5. When done, use a fork to fluff the rice and serve.
Per Serving: Calories: 130; Fat: 1g; Sodium: 86mg; Carbs: 25g; Sugar: 1g; Protein: 4g

Tasty Jasmine Rice

Prep Time: 1 minutes | Cook Time: 3 minutes | Serves: 4

1 cup jasmine rice	1 cup water

1. Rinse the rice well in a fine-mesh strainer. 2. In the Inner Pot, add the rice and water. 3. Place and close the lid rightly. 4. Select Pressure Cook mode. Press Pressure Cook button again to adjust the cooking time to 3 minutes; press Pressure Level to choose High Pressure. 5. When the time is up, leave the steam release handle in the Sealing position. 6. When done, use a fork to fluff the rice and serve.
Per Serving: Calories: 154; Fat: 0g; Sodium: 1mg; Carbs: 33g; Sugar: 0g; Protein: 3g

Lime Cilantro Brown Rice

Prep Time: 5 minutes | Cook Time: 22 minutes | Serves: 4

1 cup brown rice	2 tablespoons extra-virgin olive oil
1 cup water	2 tablespoons fresh lime juice
1 teaspoon salt	1 cup chopped fresh cilantro

1. In the Inner Pot, add the rice, salt and water. 2. Place and close the lid rightly. 3. Select Pressure Cook mode. Press Pressure Cook button again to adjust the cooking time to 22 minutes; press Pressure Level to choose High Pressure. 4. When the time is up, leave the steam release handle in the Sealing position. 5. When done, use a fork to fluff the rice and transfer to a large bowl. 6. Cool the rice for a few minutes, then combine the rice with the olive oil, lime juice and cilantro. 7. Enjoy.
Per Serving: Calories: 171; Fat: 7g; Sodium: 583mg; Carbs: 23g; Sugar: 0g; Protein: 2g

Turmeric Jasmine Rice

Prep Time: 5 minutes | Cook Time: 5 minutes | Serves: 4

1 cup jasmine rice	¼ teaspoon ground cumin
1 tablespoon avocado oil	⅛ teaspoon ground cinnamon
2 cloves garlic, minced	1 cup chicken stock
1 tablespoon peeled and grated fresh turmeric	½ cup chopped fresh cilantro

1. Rinse the rice in a fine-mesh strainer. 2. Insert the Inner Pot into the Cooker Base without the lid. 3. Press the Sauté button to select the cooking mode and press it again to adjust the cooking temperature to Normal. 4. When the display switches On to Hot, add and heat the oil for 1 minutes; add the turmeric, garlic, cumin and cinnamon and stir constantly for 1 to 2 minutes. 5. Press Cancel button to stop this cooking program. 6. Still in the Inner Pot, add and combine the clean rice and stock; scrape any brown bits stuck to the bottom of the pot with a spoon. 7. Place and close the lid in right way. 8. Select Pressure Cook mode. Press Pressure Cook button again to adjust the cooking time to 3 minutes; press Pressure Level to choose High Pressure. 9. When the time is up, leave the steam release handle in the Sealing position. 10. When released, use a fork to fluff the rice. 11. With the fresh cilantro, serve and enjoy.
Per Serving: Calories: 216; Fat: 4g; Sodium: 88mg; Carbs: 38g; Sugar: 1g; Protein: 5g

Flavorful Forbidden Rice

Prep Time: 15 minutes | Cook Time: 30 minutes | Serves: 4

1 cup forbidden rice	⅛ teaspoon salt
1 cup water	1 medium just-ripe mango, peeled, pitted, and cut into ½" dice
⅛ cup fresh lime juice	
⅛ cup fresh orange juice	½ cup finely chopped red onion
2 tablespoons extra-virgin olive oil	½ cup unsalted almond slices

3 scallions, thinly sliced	minced
1 medium jalapeño, seeded and	½ cup fresh cilantro leaves

1. In the Inner Pot, add the rice and water. 2. Place and close the lid rightly. 3. Select the Pressure Cook and press the button again to adjust the cooking time to 30 minutes; press the Pressure Level button to choose High Pressure. 4. While cooking the rice, to make the dressing, mix up the lime juice, oil, orange juice and salt in a small bowl. 5. When the time is up, leave the steam release handle in the Sealing position. 6. When done, use a fork to fluff the rice and then transfer to a suitable bowl. 7. Toss the rice with the mango, onion, almond slices, scallions and jalapeño, then add the dressing and cilantro and coat well. 8. You can serve the rice cold or at room temperature.
Per Serving: Calories: 304; Fat: 14g; Sodium: 79mg; Carbs: 42g; Sugar: 15g; Protein: 7g

Jasmine Rice with Mushrooms

Prep Time: 5 minutes | Cook Time: 15 minutes | Serves: 4

1 cup jasmine rice	mushrooms
1 tablespoon avocado oil	3 cloves garlic, minced
1 small yellow onion, peeled and chopped	¼ teaspoon salt
	1 cup vegetable broth
10 ounces sliced baby bella	

1. Rinse the rice in a fine-mesh strainer. 2. Insert the pot into the Cooker Base without the lid. 3. Select Sauté mode and then press the same button again and then adjust the cooking temperature to Normal. 4. When the display switches On to Hot, add and heat the oil for 1 minute; add the garlic, onion, mushrooms and salt and cook for 5 minutes. 5. Press the Cancel button to stop this cooking program. 6. Stir in the clean rice and vegetable broth, then lock the lid in right way. 7. Select the Pressure Cook and press the button again to adjust the cooking time to 10 minutes; press the Pressure Level button to choose High Pressure. 8. When the time is up, leave the steam release handle in the Sealing position. 9. When done, serve and enjoy.
Per Serving: Calories: 229; Fat: 4g; Sodium: 287mg; Carbs: 43g; Sugar: 2g; Protein: 5g

Wild Rice Blend in Chicken Stock

Prep Time: 1 minutes | Cook Time: 28 minutes | Serves: 4

1 cup wild rice blend	1 cup chicken stock

1. In the Inner Pot, add the wild rice blend and chicken stock. 2. Place and close the lid rightly. 3. Select the Pressure Cook and press the button again to adjust the cooking time to 28 minutes; press the Pressure Level button to choose High Pressure. 4. When the time is up, leave the steam release handle in the Sealing position. 5. When done, use a fork to fluff the rice and enjoy.
Per Serving: Calories: 164; Fat: 1g; Sodium: 88mg; Carbs: 32g; Sugar: 2g; Protein: 7g

Spanish-Style Rice

Prep Time: 15 minutes | Cook Time: 4 minutes | Serves: 6

2 tablespoons vegetable oil	bought or homemade (here)
2 tablespoons finely chopped onion	1 (10-ounce) can diced tomatoes with green chilies (such as Ro-Tel)
2 cups long-grain white rice, rinsed until the water runs clear	1 teaspoon seasoning salt
	½ teaspoon chili powder
1½ cups chicken broth, store-	¼ teaspoon garlic powder

1. Insert the Inner Pot into the Cooker Base without the lid. 2. Select Sauté mode and then press the same button again and then adjust the cooking temperature to Normal. 3. When the display switches On to Hot, add and heat the vegetable oil; add the onion and cook for 1-2 minutes until soft; add the rice and cook for 2 minutes more. 4. Press the Cancel button to stop this cooking program. 5. Still in the Inner Pot, add the chicken broth, diced tomatoes with green chilies with their juices, seasoning salt, chili powder and garlic powder. 6. Lock the lid. Select the Pressure Cook mode and press the button again to adjust the cooking time to 3 minutes; press the Pressure Level to choose High Pressure. 7. When the time is up, leave the steam release handle in the Sealing position for 10 minutes, then turn the handle to the Venting position. 8. When released, use a fork to fluff the rice and serve.
Per Serving: Calories: 283; Fat: 9g; Sodium: 615mg; Carbs: 52g; Fiber: 1g; Protein: 6g

Risotto with Cheeses

Prep Time: 15 minutes | Cook Time: 6 minutes | Serves: 6

3 tablespoons unsalted butter
1 cup finely chopped onion
2 garlic cloves, minced
1½ cups arborio rice
½ cup dry white wine
3 cups chicken broth, store-bought or homemade (here)

1 cup heavy cream
½ teaspoon salt
¼ teaspoon freshly ground black pepper
½ cup shredded fontina cheese
½ cup shredded mozzarella cheese
½ cup shredded Parmesan cheese

1. Insert the Inner Pot into the Cooker Base without the lid. 2. Select Sauté mode and then press the same button again and then adjust the cooking temperature to Normal. 3. When the display switches On to Hot, add and melt the butter; add the garlic and onion and cook for 2 minutes; add the rice and wine and stir for 2-½ minutes; stir in the chicken broth, heavy cream, salt and pepper. 4. Press the Cancel button to stop this cooking program. 5. Lock the lid. Select the Pressure Cook mode and press the button again to adjust the cooking time to 6 minutes; press the Pressure Level to choose High Pressure. 6. When the time is up, quickly and carefully turn the steam release handle from the Sealing position to the Venting position. 7. Open the lid, regularly stir in the cheeses until they are melted. 8. Without the lid, let the food sit in the pot for 3 to 4 minutes until thickened. 9. When done, serve and enjoy.
Per Serving: Calories: 464; Fat: 35g; Sodium: 539mg; Carbs: 43g; Fiber: 2g; Protein: 14g

Tasty White Basmati Rice

Prep Time: 10 minutes | Cook Time: 6 minutes | Serves: 4

1 cup white basmati rice
1¼ cups water

¼ tsp. salt
Butter to taste, optional

1. Rinse the basmati rice in a fine-mesh strainer. 2. In the Inner Pot, add the rice and stir in the salt and water. 3. Select the Pressure Cook mode and press the button again to adjust the cooking time to 6 minutes; press the Pressure Level button to choose High Pressure. 4. When the time is up, leave the steam release handle from the Sealing position for 10 minutes, then turn it to the Venting position. 5. Uncover the lid when released and then use a fork to fluff the rice. 6. Serve and you can enjoy with the butter as you like.
Per Serving: Calories 336; Fat 17.3g; Sodium 281mg; Carbs 8.1g; Fiber 5.3g; Sugars 17.7g; Protein 32.3g

Basmati Rice in Beef Broth

Prep Time: 20 minutes | Cook Time: 25 minutes | Serves: 4-6

1 tbsp. olive oil
2 cups basmati rice
3 oz. butter
1 tbsp. minced garlic
1 cup spinach

1 tsp. salt
1 tsp. dried oregano
1 cup dill
2½ cups beef broth

1. Rinse the spinach and dill carefully, then chop them. 2. Blend the chopped spinach and dill in a blender, set aside for later use. 3. Insert the Inner Pot into the Cooker Base without the lid. 4. Select Sauté mode and then press the same button again and then adjust the cooking temperature to Normal. 5. When the display switches On to Hot, add and heat the oil; add the garlic, butter and rice and sauté for 5 minutes; stir in the beef broth, the blended spinach and dill. 6. Press the Cancel button to stop this cooking program. 7. Still in the Inner Pot, add the salt and dried oregano, then lock the lid. 8. Select the Rice mode and press the button again to adjust the cooking time to 20 minutes; press the Pressure Level button to choose High Pressure. 9. When the time is up, quickly and carefully turn the steam release handle from the Sealing to the Venting position. 10. Uncover the lid, serve the rice in a prepared bowl and enjoy.
Per Serving: Calories 272; Fat 19g; Sodium 389mg; Carbs 10.4g; Fiber 0.7g; Sugars 1.1g; Protein 15.6g

Lime Long-Grain White Rice

Prep Time: 15 minutes | Cook Time: 4 minutes | Serves: 4

1 cup long-grain white rice, rinsed until the water runs clear
1 cup water
½ teaspoon salt
1 tablespoon finely chopped fresh

cilantro
1 teaspoon grated lime zest
1 tablespoon fresh lime juice
1 teaspoon vegetable oil

1. In the Inner Pot, add the rice, water and salt, stir well. 2. Place and close the lid rightly. 3. Select Pressure Cook mode. Press Pressure Cook button again to adjust the cooking time to 4 minutes; press Pressure Level to choose High Pressure. 4. When the time is up, leave the steam release handle in the Sealing position for 10 minutes, then turn the steam release handle to the Venting position. 5. When released, stir in the oil, cilantro, lime zest and juice, then use a fork to fluff the rice. 6. Serve and enjoy.
Per Serving: Calories: 182; Fat: 2g; Sodium: 293mg; Carbs: 38g; Fiber: 1g; Protein: 3g

Long Grain White Rice with Onion

Prep Time: 10 minutes | Cook Time: 15 minutes | Serves: 4-6

1 tbsp. olive oil
¼ cup onion, diced
2 cups long grain white rice

2 cups chicken stock
1 cup salsa
1 tsp salt

1. Insert the Inner Pot into the Cooker Base without the lid. 2. Select Sauté mode and then press the same button again and then adjust the cooking temperature to Normal. 3. When the display switches On to Hot, add and heat the oil; add the onion and cook for 2 minutes or until translucent; add the rice and cook for 2 to 3 minutes. 4. Press the Cancel button to stop this cooking program. 5. Stir in the salt, salsa and chicken stock, then lock the lid. 6. Select the Pressure Cook mode and press the button again to adjust the cooking time to 10 minutes; press the Pressure Level button to choose High Pressure. 7. When the time is up, leave the steam release handle from the Sealing position for 10 minutes, then turn it to the Venting position. 8. Uncover the lid and then use a fork to fluff the rice. 9. Serve and enjoy.
Per Serving: Calories 285; Fat 9.8g; Sodium 639mg; Carbs 11.1g; Fiber 1.2g; Sugars 5.1g; Protein 27.8g

Delicious Risotto in Chicken Stock

Prep Time: 20 minutes | Cook Time: 20 minutes | Serves: 4-6

1½ tbsp. olive oil
1 finely chopped medium onion
1½ cups Arborio rice
2½ cups chicken stock

Salt and ground black pepper to taste
3 tbsp. Romano or Parmesan cheese

1. Insert the Inner Pot into the Cooker Base without the lid. 2. Select Sauté mode and then press the same button again and then adjust the cooking temperature to Normal. 3. When the display switches On to Hot, add and heat the oil; add the onion and cook for a few minutes until translucent, then add the rice and chicken stock. 4. Press the Cancel button to stop this cooking program and then lock the lid in right way. 5. Select the Rice mode and press the button again to adjust the cooking time to 15 minutes; press the Pressure Level button to choose High Pressure. 6. When the time is up, leave the steam release handle in the Sealing position for 10 minutes, then turn it to the Venting position. 7. When released, carefully remove the lid. 8. Season with the salt and black pepper. 9. With the Romano or Parmesan cheese, enjoy.
Per Serving: Calories: 285; Fat 9.8g; Sodium: 639mg; Carbs 11.1g; Fiber 1.2g; Sugars 5.1g; Protein 27.8g

Mushroom Risotto with Parmesan Cheese

Prep Time: 15 minutes | Cook Time: 15 minutes | Serves: 4

2 oz. olive oil
2 cloves garlic, crushed
1 yellow onion, chopped
8 oz. mushrooms, sliced
2 cups Arborio rice
3 cups chicken stock

4 oz. sherry vinegar
4 oz. heavy cream
2 tbsp. Parmesan cheese, grated
1 oz. basil, fincly chopped
Salt to taste

1. Insert the Inner Pot into the Cooker Base without the lid. 2. Select Sauté mode and then press the same button again and then adjust the cooking temperature to Normal. 3. When the display switches On to Hot, add and heat the oil; add the garlic, mushrooms and onion and cook for 3 minutes. 4. Stir in the rice, vinegar and chicken stock, then lock the lid in right way. 5. Select the Pressure Cook mode and press the button again to adjust the cooking time to 10 minutes; press the Pressure Level button to choose High Pressure. 6. When the time is up, quickly and carefully turn the steam release handle from the Sealing position to the Venting position. 7. Uncover the lid and stir in the Parmesan and heavy cream. 8. Sprinkle salt and top with basil, serve and enjoy.
Per Serving: Calories 249; Fat 13g; Sodium 556mg; Carbs 10g; Sugar 1.1g; Fiber 0.7g; Protein 31g

Homemade Risotto

Prep Time: 20 minutes | Cook Time: 11 minutes | Serves: 4-6

2 tbsp. butter	1 cup milk
1½ cups Arborio rice	Salt to taste
⅓ cup brown sugar	1½ tsp cinnamon powder
2 apples, cored and sliced	½ cup cherries, dried
1 cup apple juice	

1. Insert the Inner Pot into the Cooker Base without the lid. 2. Select Sauté mode and then press the same button again and then adjust the cooking temperature to Normal. 3. When the display switches On to Hot, add and melt the butter; add the rice and stir for 5 minutes; stir in the cinnamon, sugar, apple juice, apple slices, milk and a pinch of salt. 4. Press the Cancel button to stop this cooking program and then lock the lid in right way. 5. Select the Pressure Cook and press the button again to adjust the cooking time to 6 minutes; press the Pressure Level button to choose High Pressure. 6. When the time is up, leave the steam release handle in the Sealing position. 7. When released, carefully remove the lid and add the cherries; stir well and close the lid, let the food sit in the pot for 5 minutes. 8. When done, serve and enjoy.
Per Serving: Calories 307; Fat 11g; Sodium 477mg; Carbs 14g; Fiber 1g; Sugars 1.4g; Protein 25.7g

Brown Rice with Black Beans

Prep Time: 10 minutes | Cook Time: 28 minutes | Serves: 4-6

2 cups uncooked brown rice	1 tsp garlic
1 cup soaked black beans	2 tsp onion powder
5 cups water	2 tsp chili powder
6 oz. tomato paste	1 tsp salt

1. In a suitable bowl, add the beans and pour in enough water to cover them, let the beans soak for at least 2 hours. 2. Rinse and drain the beans. 3. In the Inner Pot, add the soaked beans and the remaining ingredients. 4. Place and lock the lid. 5. Select the Rice mode and press the button again to adjust the cooking time to 28 minutes; press the Pressure Level button to choose High Pressure. 6. When the time is up, quickly and carefully turn the steam release handle from the Sealing to the Venting position. 7. Uncover the lid and serve the rice in a prepared bowl. 8. Enjoy.
Per Serving: Calories 272; Fat 19g; Sodium 389mg; Carbs 10.4g; Fiber 0.7g; Sugars 1.1g; Protein 15.6g

Thai Sweet Rice with Coconut Milk

Prep Time: 20 minutes | Cook Time: 3 minutes | Serves: 2-4

1 cup Thai sweet rice	2 tbsp. sugar
1½ cups water	½ tsp. salt
½ can full-; Fat coconut milk	

1. In the Inner Pot, add the rice and stir in water. 2. Place and lock the lid in right way. 3. Select the Pressure Cook mode and press the button again to adjust the cooking time to 3 minutes; press the Pressure Level button to choose High Pressure. 4. While cooking the rice, heat the sugar, salt and coconut milk in a saucepan, until the sugar has melted. 5. When the time is up, leave the steam release handle from the Sealing position for 10 minutes, then turn it to the Venting position. 6. Uncover the lid and stir in the coconut milk mixture. 7. Close the lid again and wait for 5 to 10 minutes before serving.
Per Serving: Calories 344; Fat 14.9g; Sodium 227mg; Carbs 14g; Fiber 1g; Sugars 1.4g; Protein 25.7g

Rice Bowl with Maple Syrup

Prep Time: 15 minutes | Cook Time: 20 minutes | Serves: 4

1 cup brown rice	¼ cup raisins
1 cup water	Salt to taste
1 cup coconut milk	A pinch of cinnamon powder
½ cup coconut chips	½ cup maple syrup
¼ cup almonds	

1. In the Inner Pot, add the rice and chicken stock. 2. Place and close the lid rightly. 3. Select Pressure Cook mode. Press Pressure Cook button again to adjust the cooking time to 15 minutes; press Pressure Level to choose High Pressure. 4. When the time is up, quickly and carefully turn the steam release handle from the Sealing position to the Venting position. 5. Open the lid, stir in the milk, coconut chips, almonds, raisins, maple syrup, salt and cinnamon. 6. Continue to cook for 5 minutes more on Pressure Cook mode at High Pressure. 7. When cooked, quickly and carefully release the pressure by turning the steam release handle from the Sealing position to the Venting position. 8. When done, serve and enjoy.
Per Serving: Calories 336; Fat 17.3g; Sodium 281mg; Carbs 8.1g; Fiber 5.3g; Sugars 17.7g; Protein 32.3g

Beef Rice Porridge with Onion Dice

Prep Time: 15 minutes | Cook Time: 6 minutes | Serves: 4

1 tbsp. olive oil	1½ cups basmati rice, rinsed
5 cloves garlic, minced	1½ cups water (chicken or
1 cup onion, diced	vegetable stock)
1 lb. ground beef	Salt to taste

1. Insert the Inner Pot into the Cooker Base without the lid. 2. Select Sauté mode and then press the same button again and then adjust the cooking temperature to Normal. 3. When the display switches On to Hot, add and heat the oil; add the garlic and cook for 30 seconds; add the onion and ground beef, stir regularly until the onion start to brown. 4. Add the rice, salt and stir in the water. 5. Press the Cancel button to stop this cooking program and then lock the lid. 6. Select the Pressure Cook mode and press the button again to adjust the cooking time to 5 minutes; press the Pressure Level button to choose High Pressure. 7. When the time is up, leave the steam release handle from the Sealing position. 8. When released, carefully remove the lid and serve.
Per Serving: Calories: 254; Fat: 14.2 g; Sodium 345g; Fiber 1.2g; Sugar 1.1g; Carbs: 5.7 g; Protein: 39.1 g

Basmati Rice with Carrot Dice

Prep Time: 15 minutes | Cook Time: 20 minutes | Serves: 4-6

1 tbsp. olive oil	2 tsp curry powder
1 clove garlic, minced	1½ cups chicken broth
¼ cup shallots, chopped	1 cup frozen peas
1½ cups basmati rice	Salt and ground black pepper to
½ cup carrots, chopped	taste

1. Rinse the basmati rice in a fine-mesh strainer. 2. Insert the Inner Pot into the Cooker Base without the lid. 3. Select Sauté mode and then press the same button again and then adjust the cooking temperature to Normal. 4. When the display switches On to Hot, add and heat the oil; add the shallots and garlic until fragrant; add the rice, peas, carrots and stir in chicken broth, then sprinkle the curry powder, salt and pepper. 5. Press the Cancel button to stop this cooking program and then lock the lid. 6. Select the Rice mode and press the button again to adjust the cooking time to 20 minutes; press the Pressure Level button to choose High Pressure. 7. When the time is up, leave the steam release handle from the Sealing position for 10 minutes, then turn it to the Venting position. 8. Uncover the lid and then use a fork to fluff the rice. 9. Serve and enjoy.
Per Serving: Calories 312; Fat 15g; Sodium 548mg; Carbs 12g; Sugar 1.2g; Fiber 0.7g; Protein 29g

Cheese Long Grain Rice with Chicken Breasts

Prep Time: 15 minutes | Cook Time: 25 minutes | Serves: 4-6

2 tbsp. butter	taste
1½ lbs. boneless chicken breasts, sliced	1 and ⅓ cups long grain rice
1 onion, chopped	1 and ⅓ cups chicken broth
2 cloves garlic, minced	½ cup milk
Salt and ground black pepper to	1 cup broccoli florets
	½ cup cheddar cheese, grated

1. Insert the Inner Pot into the Cooker Base without the lid. 2. Select Sauté mode and then press the same button again and then adjust the cooking temperature to Normal. 3. When the display switches On to Hot, add and melt the butter; add the garlic, onion, chicken pieces, salt and pepper and cook for 5 minutes, until the chicken pieces have slightly browned. 4. Press the Cancel button to stop this cooking program. 5. Add the rice, broccoli florets, cheddar cheese and stir in the milk and chicken broth, then lock the lid. 6. Select the Pressure Cook mode and press the button again to adjust the cooking time to 15 minutes; press the Pressure Level button to choose High Pressure. 7. When the time is up, leave the steam release handle from the Sealing position for 10 minutes, then turn it to the Venting position. 8. Uncover the lid and serve.
Per Serving: Calories 336; Fat 17.3g; Sodium 281mg; Carbs 8.1g; Fiber 5.3g; Sugars 17.7g; Protein 32.3g

Parmesan Risotto with Peas

Prep Time: 15 minutes | Cook Time: 15 minutes | Serves: 4

1 tbsp. extra-virgin olive oil	1½ cups frozen peas, thawed
2 tbsp. butter	2 tbsp. parmesan, finely grated
1 yellow onion, chopped	2 tbsp. parsley, finely chopped
1½ cups Arborio rice	1 tsp lemon zest, grated
3 cups chicken stock	Salt and ground black pepper to
2 tbsp. lemon juice	taste

1. Insert the Inner Pot into the Cooker Base without the lid. 2. Select Sauté mode and then press the same button again and then adjust the cooking temperature to Normal. 3. When the display switches On to Hot, heat the oil and 1 tablespoon of butter; add the onion and cook for 5 minutes; add the rice and stir for 3 minutes. 4. Stir in the lemon juice and 3 cups of stock, then press the Cancel button to stop this cooking program and lock the lid. 5. Select the Pressure Cook mode and press the button again to adjust the cooking time to 5 minutes; press the Pressure Level button to choose High Pressure. 6. When the time is up, quickly and carefully turn the steam release handle from the Sealing position to the Venting position. 7. When released, remove the lid, add the peas and the remaining stock, then cook for 2 minutes more on Sauté mode at Less cooking temperature. 8. Stir in the parmesan, parsley, lemon zest, salt, pepper and the remaining butter. 9. Serve and enjoy.
Per Serving: Calories 305; Fat 15g; Sodium 548mg; Carbs 12g; Sugar 1.2g; Fiber 0.7g; Protein 29g

Turmeric Basmati Rice with Sweet Corn

Prep Time: 10 minutes | Cook Time: 10 minutes | Serves: 6-8

3 tbsp. olive oil	1 cup garden peas, frozen
1 large onion, finely chopped	¼ tsp. salt
3 cloves garlic, minced	1 tsp. turmeric powder
3 tbsp. cilantro stalks, chopped	3 cups chicken stock
2 cups basmati rice	2 tbsp. butter, optional
1 cup sweet corn, frozen	

1. Rinse the basmati rice well in a fine-mesh strainer. 2. Insert the Inner Pot into the Cooker Base without the lid. 3. Select Sauté mode and then press the same button again and then adjust the cooking temperature to Normal. 4. When the display switches On to Hot, add and heat the oil; add the garlic, onion and cilantro and cook for 5 to 6 minutes until the onion is translucent. 5. Add the rice, peas and sweet corn, stir in the salt, turmeric and chicken stock. 6. Press the Cancel button to stop this cooking program and then lock the lid in right way. 7. Select the Pressure Cook mode and press the button again to adjust the cooking time to 4 minutes; press the Pressure Level button to choose High Pressure. 8. When the time is up, quickly and carefully turn the steam release handle from the Sealing to the Venting position. 9. Uncover the lid, serve and you can enjoy with the butter as you like.
Per Serving: Calories 344; Fat 14.9g; Sodium 227mg; Carbs 14g; Fiber 1g; Sugars 1.4g; Protein 25.7g

Rice in Vegetable Stock

Prep Time: 2 minutes | Cook Time: 30 minutes | Serves: 4

1 cup rice	1 cup vegetable stock

1. In the Inner Pot, add the forbidden rice and vegetable stock. 2. Place and close the lid rightly. 3. Select the Pressure Cook and press the button again to adjust the cooking time to 30 minutes; press the Pressure Level button to choose High Pressure. 4. When the time is up, leave the steam release handle in the Sealing position. 5. When done, use a fork to fluff the rice and enjoy.
Per Serving: Calories: 114; Fat: 1g; Sodium: 218mg; Carbs: 22g; Sugar: 1g; Protein: 4g

Butter Brown Rice in Vegetable Stock

Prep Time: 20 minutes | Cook Time: 22 minutes | Serves: 4-6

1 stick (½ cup) butter	1 cups vegetable stock
2 cups brown rice	1½ cups French onion soup

1. Insert the Inner Pot into the Cooker Base without the lid. 2. Select Sauté mode and then press the same button again and then adjust the cooking temperature to Normal. 3. When the display switches On to Hot, add and melt the butter; add the rice and stir in the vegetable stock and onion soup. 4. Press the Cancel button to stop this cooking program and then lock the lid. 5. Select the Pressure Cook mode and press the button again to adjust the cooking time to 22 minutes; press the Pressure Level button to choose High Pressure. 6. When the time is up, leave the steam release handle from the Sealing position for 10 minutes, then turn it to the Venting position. 7. Uncover the lid and serve, you can enjoy with the fresh parsley.
Per Serving: Calories 344; Fat 14.9g; Sodium 227mg; Carbs 14g; Fiber 1g; Sugars 1.4g; Protein 25.7g

Brown Rice and Wild Rice

Prep Time: 15 minutes | Cook Time: 25 minutes | Serves: 4

3-4 tbsp. red, wild or black rice	¼ tsp. sea salt
¾ cup (or more) short grain brown rice	1½ cups water

1. Rinse the rice in a fine-mesh strainer. 2. In the Inner Pot, add the rice and stir in the salt and water. 3. Select the Multigrain mode and press the button again to adjust the cooking time to 23 minutes; press the Pressure Level button to choose High Pressure. 4. When the time is up, leave the steam release handle from the Sealing position for 10 minutes, then turn it to the Venting position. 5. Uncover the lid and then use a fork to fluff the rice. 6. Serve and enjoy.
Per Serving: Calories 336; Fat 17.3g; Sodium 281mg; Carbs 8.1g; Fiber 5.3g; Sugars 17.7g; Protein 32.3g

White Jasmine Rice with Chicken Thighs

Prep Time: 30 minutes | Cook Time: 20 minutes | Serves: 4-6

1 tbsp. olive oil	3 carrots, diced
3 small shallots, diced	1½ cups white jasmine rice, rinsed and drained
2 cloves garlic, minced	
1 lb. boneless chicken thighs	1½ cups chicken stock
Salt and ground black pepper to taste	2 tbsp. thyme leaves

1. Insert the Inner Pot into the Cooker Base without the lid. 2. Select Sauté mode and then press the same button again and then adjust the cooking temperature to Normal. 3. When the display switches On to Hot, add and heat the oil; add the chicken thighs, salt, pepper and stir regularly for 5 minutes, until the chicken meat starts to brown; stir in the carrots, rice, thyme leaves and chicken stock. 4. Press the Cancel button to stop this cooking program and then lock the lid. 5. Select the Pressure Cook mode and press the button again to adjust the cooking time to 10 minutes; press the Pressure Level button to choose High Pressure. 6. When the time is up, leave the steam release handle from the Sealing position for 10 minutes, then turn it to the Venting position. 7. Uncover the lid and then use a fork to fluff the rice. 8. Serve and enjoy.
Per Serving: Calories 254; Fat 28 g; Sodium 346mg; Carbs 12.3 g; Sugar 1g; Fiber 0.7g; Protein 24.3 g

Ginger Pumpkin Risotto

Prep Time: 10 minutes | Cook Time: 12 minutes | Serves: 4-6

2 oz. extra virgin olive oil	1 tsp thyme, chopped
2 cloves garlic, minced	½ tsp nutmeg
1 small yellow onion, chopped	½ tsp ginger, grated
2 cups Arborio rice	½ tsp cinnamon
3 cups chicken stock	½ cup heavy cream
¾ cup pumpkin puree	Salt to taste

1. Insert the Inner Pot into the Cooker Base without the lid. 2. Select Sauté mode and then press the same button again and then adjust the cooking temperature to Normal. 3. When the display switches On to Hot, add and heat the oil; add the garlic and onion and cook for 1-2 minutes. 4. Press the Cancel button to stop this cooking program. 5. Stir in the rice, cinnamon, pumpkin puree, thyme, nutmeg, ginger and chicken stock, then lock the lid in right way. 6. Select the Pressure Cook mode and press the button again to adjust the cooking time to 10 minutes; press the Pressure Level button to choose High Pressure. 7. When the time is up, quickly and carefully turn the steam release handle from the Sealing position to the Venting position. 8. Uncover the lid and stir in the heavy cream. 9. Serve and enjoy.
Per Serving: Calories 272; Fat 19g; Sodium 389mg; Carbs 10.4g; Fiber 0.7g; Sugars 1.1g; Protein 15.6g

Long Grain Rice in Tomato Sauce

Prep Time: 20 minutes | Cook Time: 15 minutes | Serves: 4-6

2 tbsp. butter
2 cups long grain rice
1½ cups chicken stock or water
8 oz. tomato sauce
1 tsp. cumin

1 tsp. chili powder
½ tsp. garlic powder
½ tsp. onion powder
½ tsp. salt

1. Insert the Inner Pot into the Cooker Base without the lid. 2. Select Sauté mode and then press the same button again and then adjust the cooking temperature to Normal. 3. When the display switches On to Hot, add and melt the butter; add the rice and stir regularly for 4 minutes. 4. Press the Cancel button to stop this cooking program. 5. Add the cumin, chili powder, garlic powder, onion powder, salt and stir in the chicken stock and tomato sauce, then lock the lid. 6. Select the Pressure Cook mode and press the button again to adjust the cooking time to 10 minutes; press the Pressure Level button to choose High Pressure. 7. When the time is up, leave the steam release handle from the Sealing position for 10 minutes, then turn it to the Venting position. 8. Uncover the lid and use a fork to fluff the rice. 9. Serve and enjoy.
Per Serving: Calories 272; Fat 19g; Sodium 389mg; Carbs 10.4g; Fiber 0.7g; Sugars 1.1g; Protein 15.6g

Wild Rice in Chicken Stock

Prep Time: 1 minutes | Cook Time: 30 minutes | Serves: 4

1 cup wild rice

1 cup chicken stock

1. In the Inner Pot, add the wild rice and chicken stock. 2. Place and close the lid rightly. 3. Select the Pressure Cook and press the button again to adjust the cooking time to 30 minutes; press the Pressure Level button to choose High Pressure. 4. When the time is up, leave the steam release handle in the Sealing position. 5. When done, use a fork to fluff the rice and serve.
Per Serving: Calories: 164; Fat: 1g; Sodium: 88mg; Carbs: 32g; Sugar: 2g; Protein: 7g

Brown Rice with Chopped Cilantro

Prep Time: 15 minutes | Cook Time: 12 minutes | Serves: 4-6

2 cups brown rice, rinsed
2¾ cups water
4 small bay leaves
½ cup chopped cilantro

1½ tbsp. olive oil
1 lime, juiced
1 tsp. salt

1. In the Inner Pot, add the rice, bay leaves and water. 2. Place and lock the lid. 3. Select the Rice mode and press the button again to adjust the cooking time to 12 minutes; press the Pressure Level button to choose High Pressure. 4. When the time is up, leave the steam release handle from the Sealing position for 10 minutes, then turn it to the Venting position. 5. Uncover the lid and mix the rice with the oil, lime juice, salt and cilantro. 6. Serve and enjoy.
Per Serving: Calories 307; Fat 11g; Sodium 477mg; Carbs 14g; Fiber 1g; Sugars 1.4g; Protein 25.7g

Brown Rice in Vegetable Broth

Prep Time: 10 minutes | Cook Time: 21 minutes | Serves: 4-6

2 cups brown rice
2 cups vegetable broth or water

½ tsp. salt

1. In the Inner Pot, add the rice and stir in the salt and vegetable broth (or water). 2. Select the Pressure Cook mode and press the button again to adjust the cooking time to 21 minutes; press the Pressure Level button to choose High Pressure. 3. When the time is up, leave the steam release handle from the Sealing position for 10 minutes, then turn it to the Venting position. 4. Uncover the lid and then use a fork to fluff the rice. 5. Serve and enjoy.
Per Serving: Calories 351; Fat 22g; Sodium 502mg; Carbs 15.2g; Sugar 1.1g; Fiber 0.7g; Protein 26.4g

Rice and Millet

Prep Time: 5 minutes | Cook Time: 10 minutes | Serves: 4-6

2 cups jasmine rice or long-grain white rice
½ cup millet

3¼ cups water
1 tsp. salt

1. In the Inner Pot, add the rice, millet, salt and stir in the water. 2. Select the Rice mode and press the button again to adjust the cooking time to 10 minutes; press the Pressure Level button to choose Low Pressure. 3. When the time is up, quickly and carefully turn the steam release handle from the Sealing to the Venting position. 4. Uncover the lid and then use a fork to fluff the rice. 5. Serve and enjoy.
Per Serving: Calories 336; Fat 17.3g; Sodium 281mg; Carbs 8.1g; Fiber 5.3g; Sugars 17.7g; Protein 32.3g

Simple Jasmine Rice

Prep Time: 15 minutes | Cook Time: 5 minutes | Serves: 4-6

2 cups jasmine rice
2 cups water

2 tsp. olive oil
½ tsp. salt

1. Rinse the jasmine rice in a fine-mesh strainer. 2. In the Inner Pot, add the rice and stir in the oil, salt and water. 3. Select the Pressure Cook mode and press the button again to adjust the cooking time to 4 minutes; press the Pressure Level button to choose High Pressure. 4. When the time is up, leave the steam release handle from the Sealing position for 10 minutes, then turn it to the Venting position. 5. Uncover the lid when released and then use a fork to fluff the rice. 6. Serve and enjoy.
Per Serving: Calories 344; Fat 14.9g; Sodium 227mg; Carbs 12g; Fiber 1.2g; Sugars 1g; Protein 27g

Cauliflower and Pineapple Rice

Prep Time: 20 minutes | Cook Time: 20 minutes | Serves: 4-6

2 tsp. extra virgin olive oil
2½ cups water
2 cups jasmine rice
1 cauliflower, florets separated and

chopped
½ pineapple, peeled and chopped
Salt and ground black pepper to taste

1. In the Inner Pot, add all of the ingredients and mix well. 2. Place and lock the lid in right way. 3. Select the Pressure Cook mode and press the button again to adjust the cooking time to 20 minutes; press the Pressure Level button to choose Low Pressure. 4. When the time is up, leave the steam release handle from the Sealing position for 10 minutes, then turn it to the Venting position. 5. Uncover the lid and then use a fork to fluff the rice. 6. Serve and enjoy.
Per Serving: Calories 249; Fat 13g; Sodium 556mg; Carbs 10g; Sugar 1.1g; Fiber 0.7g; Protein 31g

Shawarma Rice with Ground Beef

Prep Time: 20 minutes | Cook Time: 15 minutes | Serves: 6-8

1½ cups basmati rice, rinsed and drained
1 lb. ground beef (chicken, fish, pork, etc. optional), cooked
1½ cups water
4 cups cabbage, shredded

1 tbsp. olive oil
5 cloves garlic, minced
1 cup onion, chopped
3 tbsp. shawarma spice
1 tsp. salt
¼ cup cilantro, chopped

1. In the Inner Pot, add the clean basmati rice, ground beef, cabbage, olive oil, garlic, onion, shawarma spice and salt, stir well to mix. 2. Place and lock the lid in right way. 3. Select the Pressure Cook mode and press the button again to adjust the cooking time to 15 minutes; press the Pressure Level button to choose High Pressure. 4. When the time is up, leave the steam release handle from the Sealing position for 10 minutes, then turn it to the Venting position. 5. Uncover the lid and stir in the cilantro. 6. Serve and enjoy.
Per Serving: Calories 285; Fat 9.8g; Sodium 639mg; Carbs 11.1g; Fiber 1.2g; Sugars 5.1g; Protein 27.8g

Simple-Cooked Pink Rice

Prep Time: 15 minutes | Cook Time: 5 minutes | Serves: 2-4

1 cup pink rice
1 cup water

½ tsp salt

1. Rinse the pink rice in a fine-mesh strainer. 2. In the Inner Pot, add the rice and stir in the salt and water. 3. Select the Pressure Cook mode and press the button again to adjust the cooking time to 5 minutes; press the Pressure Level button to choose High Pressure. 4. When the time is up, leave the steam release handle from the Sealing position for 10 minutes, then turn it to the Venting position. 5. Uncover the lid and then use a fork to fluff the rice. 6. Serve and enjoy.
Per Serving: Calories 344; Fat 14.9g; Sodium 227mg; Carbs 14g; Fiber 1g; Sugars 1.4g; Protein 25.7g

Chapter 4 Snack and Appetizer Recipes

Sesame-Soy Frozen Pot Stickers

Prep Time: 5 minutes | Cook Time: 3 minutes | Serves: 5

Pot Stickers
1 cup water
5 frozen pot stickers
1 teaspoon chopped green onion
½ tablespoon sesame seeds
Sesame-Soy Dipping Sauce
1 tablespoon soy sauce
1 tablespoon rice wine vinegar
1 teaspoon sesame oil
⅛ teaspoon grated fresh ginger
⅛ teaspoon minced garlic
¼ teaspoon chopped green onion
1/16 teaspoon crushed red pepper flakes
⅛ teaspoon chili oil

1. In the inner pot, pour water and the pot sticks. 2. Close the lid and turn the steam release handle to Sealing position. 3. Set the Instant Pot on Pressure Cook at High and adjust time to 3 minutes. 4. While cooking, mix all the Sesame-Soy Dipping Sauce ingredients in a small bowl. 5. When cooked, turn the handle from Sealing to Venting to release the pressure and then remove the lid carefully. 6. Transfer carefully the pot stickers onto a serving plate. 7. Add chopped green onion and sesame seeds to garnish. 8. Serve with Sesame-Soy Dipping Sauce. Enjoy!
Per Serving: Calories 346; Fat: 10.5g; Sodium 977mg; Carbs: 49.4g; Fiber 1g; Sugars: 5.1g; Protein 15.5g

Green Sauce

Prep Time: 10 minutes | Cook Time: 2 minutes | Serves: 8

1-pound tomatillos, outer husks removed and cut into halves
2 small jalapeño peppers, seeded and chopped
1 small onion, peeled and diced
½ cup chopped fresh cilantro
1 teaspoon ground coriander
1 teaspoon sea salt
1½ cups water

1. Place the tomatillo halves in the inner pot and then pour water to cover. 2. Close the lid and turn the steam release handle to Sealing position. 3. Set the Instant Pot on Pressure Cook at High and adjust time to 2 minutes. 4. When cooked, naturally release the pressure about 20 minutes. Turn off the heat and carefully open the lid. 5. Drain excess water off the tomatillos and transfer to a food processor. Add onion, cilantro, salt, water, coriander, and jalapeno and pulse to combine well. 6. Chill in a serving dish in the refrigerator for at least 2 hours.
Per Serving: Calories 22; Fat: 0.6g; Sodium 240mg; Carbs: 4.2g; Fiber 1g; Sugars: 0.4g; Protein 0.7g

Deviled Eggs

Prep Time: 5 minutes | Cook Time: 16 minutes | Serves: 1

1 cup water
2 large eggs
1 tablespoon mayonnaise
⅛ teaspoon yellow mustard
1/16 teaspoon salt
1/16 teaspoon ground black pepper
1/16 teaspoon smoked paprika

1. In the inner pot, pour water and place the trivet at the bottom. Place the eggs onto the trivet. 2. Close the lid and turn the steam release handle to Sealing. 3. Set the Instant Pot on Pressure Cook at High and adjust time to 2 minutes. 4. When cooked, naturally release pressure about 14 minutes and then remove the lid carefully. 5. Place the eggs in an ice bath about 10 minutes. Peel and cut lengthwise in half, then remove the egg yolks in a small bowl and egg white halves in a small plate. 6. Break up egg yolks with a fork until crumbly. 7. Add in mayonnaise, salt, mustard, and pepper and mix well. 8. Stuff the egg white halves with the whisked egg yolks and sprinkle paprika on the top. 9. Serve in a serving plate and enjoy!
Per Serving: Calories 201; Fat: 14.9g; Sodium 399mg; Carbs: 4.4g; Fiber 1g; Sugars: 1.7g; Protein 12.7g

Hearty Sausage Dip

Prep Time: 10 minutes | Cook Time: 25 minutes | Serves: 4

2 ounces cream cheese, softened
3 tablespoons Rotel Diced Tomatoes and Green Chilies
½ cup cooked and crumbled
Italian sausage
3 tablespoons shredded Cheddar cheese, divided
1 cup water

1. Prepare an 8-ounce ramekin and grease. Set it aside. 2. Add tomatoes, chilies, 2 tablespoons Cheddar, sausage, and cream cheese in a small bowl and combine well. Then spoon into the greased ramekin and use foil to cover. 3. In the inner pot, pour water and place the trivet at the bottom. 4. Close the lid and turn the steam release handle to Sealing position. 5. Set the Instant Pot on Pressure Cook at High and adjust time to 20 minutes. 6. When cooked, release the pressure by turn the handle from Sealing to Venting and then carefully remove the lid, transfer the ramekin to an ovenproof plate. 7. Remove the foil from the dip and top with the remaining Cheddar. 8. Preheat your air fryer to high heat. 9. Then broil in the air fryer for 3 to 5 minutes or until brown. Serve and enjoy!
Per Serving: Calories 122; Fat: 9.5g; Sodium 592mg; Carbs: 3.9g; Fiber 1g; Sugars: 2.4g; Protein 5.1g

Spicy Salsa

Prep Time: 10 minutes | Cook Time: 20 minutes | Serves: 12

12 cups seeded diced tomatoes
6 ounces tomato paste
2 medium yellow onions, peeled and diced
6 small jalapeño peppers, seeded and minced
4 cloves garlic, peeled and minced
¼ cup white vinegar
¼ cup lime juice
2 tablespoons granulated sugar
2 teaspoons salt
¼ cup chopped fresh cilantro

1. In the inner pot, add tomato paste, jalapeno, garlic, salt, sugar, lime juice, vinegar, onions, and tomatoes and stir well. 2. Close the lid and turn the steam release handle to Sealing. 3. Set the Instant Pot on Pressure Cook at High and adjust time to 20 minutes. 4. When cooked, quick-release the pressure and open the lid carefully. 5. Stir in cilantro and then turn off the heat. Cool the salsa to room temperature. 6. Transfer to a storage container and chill in the refrigerator overnight.
Per Serving: Calories 32; Fat: 0.2g; Sodium 587mg; Carbs: 7.4g; Fiber 1g; Sugars: 4.8g; Protein 1g

Traditional Applesauce

Prep Time: 5 minutes | Cook Time: 10 minutes | Serves: 4

1 medium Granny Smith apple, peeled, cored, and sliced
1 medium honey-crisp apple, peeled, cored, and sliced
½ tablespoon lemon juice
¼ teaspoon ground cinnamon
½ cup water
1 tablespoon sugar

1. In the inner pot, add lemon juice, cinnamon, water, and apples. 2. Close the lid and turn the steam release handle to Sealing position. 3. Set the Instant Pot on Pressure Cook at High and adjust time to 10 minutes. 4. When cooked, naturally release the pressure about 15 minutes and then remove the lid carefully. 5. Stir in applesauce to combine well and then taste to season with 1 tablespoon of sugar or more as you like. 6. Serve in a bowl and enjoy!
Per Serving: Calories 61; Fat: 0.1g; Sodium 2mg; Carbs: 16.4g; Fiber 1g; Sugars: 13.1g; Protein 0.2g

Mediterranean Stuffed Grape Leaves

Prep Time: 10 minutes | Cook Time: 15 minutes | Serves: 16

⅓ cup extra-virgin olive oil
½ medium onion, peeled and diced
¼ cup minced fresh mint
¼ cup minced fresh dill
3 cloves garlic, peeled and minced
1 cup long-grain white rice
2 cups vegetable broth
½ teaspoon salt
¼ teaspoon ground black pepper
½ teaspoon grated lemon zest
1 (16-ounce) jar grape leaves
2 cups water
½ cup lemon juice

1. Set the Instant Pot on Sauté at Normal and add oil to heat in the inner pot. 2. Cook the onion, dill, and mint about 4 minutes or until tender. Then add garlic and cook about 30 seconds or until fragrant. 3. Add rice to coat and then the broth, salt, pepper, and lemon zest to stir together. 4. Close the lid and turn the steam release handle to Sealing position. 5. Set the Instant Pot on Pressure Cook at High and adjust time to 8 minutes. 6. When cooked, quick-release the pressure and then turn off the heat. Carefully open the lid and transfer the rice mixture into a medium bowl. 7. Drain grape leaves and rinse with warm water. With leave rib side up. spoon about 2 teaspoons of rice mixture for each. Roll the leave and arrange the stuffed leaves with seam side down. Lay onto the steamer basket. 8. In the inner pot, pour water and place the steamer basket inside. Pour lemon juice over the stuffed leaves. 9. Close the lid and turn the steam release handle to Sealing position. 10. Set the Instant Pot on Pressure Cook at High and adjust time to 10 minutes. 11. When cooked, quick-release the pressure and carefully open the lid. Remove from the pot and sit for 5 minutes. 12. Serve and enjoy!
Per Serving: Calories 109; Fat: 4.7g; Sodium 175mg; Carbs: 15.5g; Fiber 1g; Sugars: 5g; Protein 2g

Spiced Vanilla-Pear Sauce

Prep Time: 5 minutes | Cook Time: 10 minutes | Serves: 6

3 medium ripe pears, peeled, cored, and diced	1/16 teaspoon ground cloves
1/8 teaspoon ground cinnamon	1/16 teaspoon ground nutmeg
1/16 teaspoon ground ginger	1/3 cup apple juice
	1/2 teaspoon vanilla extract

1. Combine pears, gingers, nutmeg, cloves, apple juice, and cinnamon in the inner pot. 2. Close the lid and turn the steam release handle to Sealing position. 3. Set the Instant Pot on Pressure Cook at High and adjust time to 10 minutes. 4. When cooked, release the pressure by turn the handle from Sealing to Venting and then remove the lid carefully. 5. Stir in the pear sauce with a whisk or potato masher until all the pears are broken up and smooth. 6. Add vanilla and stir well. Then transfer to a bowl. 7. Serve warm or chill in the refrigerator until ready to serve.
Per Serving: Calories 56; Fat: 0.2g; Sodium 2mg; Carbs: 14.3g; Fiber 1g; Sugars: 9.5g; Protein 0.3g

Lemony Shrimp with Cocktail Sauce

Prep Time: 5 minutes | Cook Time: 10 minutes | Serves: 4

1 cup water	jumbo shrimp
1/2 teaspoon salt	2 tablespoons cocktail sauce
2 cups frozen peeled and deveined	
1/2 medium lemon	

1. Add salt, shrimp, and water in the inner pot. 2. Close the lid and turn the steam release handle to Sealing position. 3. Set the Instant Pot on Pressure Cook at High and adjust time to 10 minutes. 4. When cooked, release the pressure by turning the handle from Sealing to Venting and then remove the lid carefully. 5. Drain the shrimp and soak in icy water 5 minutes. 6. Serve with the cocktail sauce and lemon. Enjoy!
Per Serving: Calories 113; Fat: 1.1g; Sodium 929mg; Carbs: 9.5g; Fiber 1g; Sugars: 6.5g; Protein 15g

Deviled Eggs with Jalapeno

Prep Time: 5 minutes | Cook Time: 16 minutes | Serves: 1

1 cup water	1/16 teaspoon ground black pepper
2 large eggs	4 slices pickled jalapeño pepper
1 tablespoon ranch dressing	4 small potato chips
1/16 teaspoon salt	

1. In the inner pot, pour the water and place the trivet. 2. Close the lid and turn the steam release handle to Sealing position. 3. Set the Instant Pot on Pressure Cook at High and adjust time to 2 minutes. 4. When cooked, naturally release the pressure for 14 minutes and then remove the lid carefully. 5. Soak the eggs in an ice bath about 10 minutes. Peel and cut lengthwise half. Remove the yolks to a small bowl and the egg white halves on a small plate. 6. Mash the egg yolks with a fork until crumbly. Then add ranch, pepper, and salt, and mix well until smooth. 7. Stuff the egg white halves with egg yolk mixture. Sprinkle a jalapeno slice and potato chip on the top. 8. Serve in a serving plate.
Per Serving: Calories 326; Fat: 21.4g; Sodium 1998mg; Carbs: 19.9g; Fiber 3.6g; Sugars: 3.2g; Protein 15.5g

Bacon-Chive Deviled Eggs

Prep Time: 5 minutes | Cook Time: 16 minutes | Serves: 2

1 cup water	1/8 teaspoon dried chives
2 large eggs	1/16 teaspoon salt
1 tablespoon mayonnaise	1/16 teaspoon ground black pepper
1 teaspoon bacon bits	

1. In the inner pot, pour the water and place the trivet. 2. Close the lid and turn the steam release handle to Sealing position. 3. Set the Instant Pot on Pressure Cook at High and adjust time to 2 minutes. 4. When cooked, naturally release the pressure for 14 minutes and then remove the lid carefully. 5. Soak the eggs in an ice bath about 10 minutes. Peel and cut lengthwise half. Remove the yolks to a small bowl and the egg white halves on a small plate. 6. Mash the egg yolks with a fork until crumbly. Then add bacon bits, salt, chives, pepper, and mayonnaise and mix well until smooth. 7. Stuff the egg white halves with egg yolk mixture. 8. Serve in a serving plate.
Per Serving: Calories 152; Fat: 11.4g; Sodium 419mg; Carbs: 2.3g; Fiber 1g; Sugars: 0.9g; Protein 9.9g

Parmesan Stuffed Artichoke

Prep Time: 5 minutes | Cook Time: 45 minutes | Serves: 6

1 cup water	2 tablespoons grated Parmesan cheese
1 large (over 1-pound) artichoke	1 tablespoon lemon juice
2 tablespoons panko bread crumbs	3 tablespoons butter, melted, divided
1/2 teaspoon Italian seasoning	
1/2 teaspoon minced garlic	

1. In the inner pot, pour water and place the trivet. 2. Remove the bottom stem off the artichoke and then discard the 1/4 top off the artichoke. Trim the tips of the outer leaves. 3. Then spread the leaves to leave gaps among leaves. 4. Add the bread crumbs, Parmesan, Italian seasoning, and garlic in a small bowl and toss well. 5. Then sprinkle over the artichoke and press down to spread evenly among the leaves. Transfer the artichoke onto the trivet. 6. Close the lid and turn the steam release handle to Sealing. 7. Set the Instant Pot on Pressure Cook at High and adjust time to 45 minutes. 8. When cooked, release the handle by turning the handle from Sealing to Venting and then remove the lid carefully. 9. Transfer the artichoke onto a serving plate. Pour lemon juice and 1 tablespoon of butter on the top. Leave the 2 tablespoons of butter for dipping. 10. Serve and enjoy!
Per Serving: Calories 102; Fat: 8.1g; Sodium 166mg; Carbs: 4.4g; Fiber 1g; Sugars: 0.4g; Protein 4.1g

Savory Chili-Cheese Dip

Prep Time: 10 minutes | Cook Time: 25 minutes | Serves: 4

3 ounces cream cheese, softened	cheese, divided
1/2 cup chili (any kind)	1 cup water
4 tablespoons shredded Cheddar	

1. Prepare an 8-ounce ramekin and grease. Set it aside. 2. Add chili, 3 tablespoons of Cheddar, and cream cheese in a small bowl and combine well. Then use a spoon to transfer the mixture into the greased ramekin and use a piece of foil to cover. 3. In the inner pot, pour water and place the trivet at the bottom. Transfer ramekin onto the trivet. 4. Close the lid and turn the steam release handle to Sealing position. 5. Set the Instant Pot on Pressure Cook at High and adjust time to 20 minutes. 6. When cooked, quick-release the pressure and then remove the lid carefully. Transfer the ramekin onto an ovenproof plate. 7. Preheat your air fryer to high heat. 8. Remove the foil from the dip and then top with the remaining Cheddar cheese. 9. Broil in the air fryer until browned about 3 to 5 minutes. 10. Serve and enjoy!
Per Serving: Calories 138; Fat: 11.5g; Sodium 276mg; Carbs: 4.5g; Fiber 1g; Sugars: 0.5g; Protein 5.2g

White Bean Soup with Dandelion

Prep Time: 10 minutes | Cook Time: 30 minutes | Serves: 6

1 tablespoon olive oil	2 teaspoons fresh thyme leaves
2 medium onions, peeled and chopped	1 teaspoon salt
3 medium carrots, peeled and chopped	1/2 teaspoon ground black pepper
3 stalks celery, chopped	8 cups vegetable stock
4 cloves garlic, peeled and minced	2 cups fresh dandelion greens, steamed until wilted
1 bay leaf	1 (15-ounce) can cannellini beans, drained and rinsed
1/4 cup chopped fresh parsley	1/4 cup grated Parmesan cheese

1. Set the Instant Pot on Sauté at Normal and add oil to heat. 2. Cook onion, celery, carrots, and garlic in the inner pot until soften. Then add parsley, thyme, pepper, salt, and bay leaf and cook until fragrant about 5 minutes. Turn off the heat. 3. Stir in stock. Close the lid and turn the steam release handle to Sealing. 4. Set the Instant Pot on Soup at High and adjust time to 20 minutes. 5. When cooked, quick-release the pressure and then turn off the heat. 6. Carefully open the lid and mix in beans and dandelion greens. 7. Close the lid and turn the steam release handle to Sealing position. 8. Set the Instant Pot on Pressure Cook at High and adjust time to 1 minute. 9. When cooked, quick-release the pressure and then turn off the heat. 10. Carefully open the lid and remove. Give away bay leaf. 11. Sprinkle cheese on the top to serve.
Per Serving: Calories 233; Fat: 2.7g; Sodium 396mg; Carbs: 40g; Sugars: 4.4g; Protein 14.3g

Black Bean Dip with Bacon

Prep Time: 10 minutes | Cook Time: 35 minutes | Serves: 16

1 tablespoon olive oil
2 slices bacon, finely diced
1 small onion, peeled and diced
3 cloves garlic, peeled and minced
1 cup low-sodium chicken broth
1 cup dried black beans, soaked
overnight and drained
1 (14.5-ounce) can diced tomatoes,
including juice

1 small jalapeño pepper, seeded
and minced
1 teaspoon ground cumin
½ teaspoon smoked paprika
1 tablespoon lime juice
½ teaspoon dried oregano
¼ cup minced fresh cilantro
¼ teaspoon sea salt

1. Set the Instant Pot on Sauté at More and heat the oil. 2. Add onion and bacon and cook until the onion is just transparent about 5 minutes. 3. Then add garlic and cook about 30 seconds or until fragrant. 4. Pour broth and scrape all the browned bits off the pot. 5. Place tomatoes, jalapeno, paprika, cumin cilantro, salt, oregano, beans, and lime juice. Turn off the heat. 6. Close the lid and turn the steam release handle to Sealing position. 7. Set the Instant Pot on Bean at More and adjust time to 30 minutes. 8. When cooked, naturally release the pressure about 10 minutes and quick-release the rest pressure. Turn off the heat and carefully open the lid. 9. Blend the ingredients in a blender until smooth. 10. Serve and enjoy!
Per Serving: Calories 71; Fat: 2.2g; Sodium 93mg; Carbs: 9.4g; Fiber 1g; Sugars: 1.2g; Protein 4g

Garlic White Bean Hummus

Prep Time: 10 minutes | Cook Time: 30 minutes | Serves: 10

⅔ cup dried white beans, rinsed
and drained
3 cloves garlic, peeled and crushed

¼ cup olive oil
1 tablespoon lemon juice
½ teaspoon salt

1. In the inner pot, stir in beans and garlic. Pour cold water until the mixture is covered. 2. Close the lid and turn the steam release handle to Sealing position. 3. Set the Instant Pot on Pressure Cook at High and adjust time to 30 minutes. 4. When cooked, naturally release about 20 minutes. Turn off the heat and carefully open the lid. 5. Drain the beans and transfer to a food processor and add in lemon juice, salt, and oil. Process until it is smooth with little chunks. 6. Transfer into a storage container and chill in the refrigerator for at least 4 hours and up to 7 days. 7. Serve and enjoy!
Per Serving: Calories 90; Fat: 5.2g; Sodium 119mg; Carbs: 8.5g; Fiber 1g; Sugars: 0.3g; Protein 3.2g

Savory Cocktail Sausages

Prep Time: 3 minutes | Cook Time: 15 minutes | Serves: 4

1 cup water
½ (14-ounce) package cocktail
sausages

2 tablespoons barbecue sauce
¼ cup grape jelly

1. In the inner pot, pour water and place the trivet. 2. In a suitable cake pan, add the cocktail sausages, barbecue sauce, and the grape jelly and then use foil sheet to cover. Transfer onto the trivet. 3. Close the lid and turn the steam release handle to Sealing. 4. Set the Instant Pot on Pressure Cook at High and adjust time to 15 minutes. 5. When cooked, release the pressure by turning the handle from Sealing to Venting and then remove the lid carefully. 6. Transfer the sausages to a serving plate. Enjoy!
Per Serving: Calories 88; Fat: 1.4g; Sodium 129mg; Carbs: 17.6g; Fiber 1g; Sugars: 11.7g; Protein 1g

Greek Eggplant Dip

Prep Time: 10 minutes | Cook Time: 3 minutes | Serves: 8

1 cup water
1 large eggplant, peeled and
chopped
1 clove garlic, peeled

½ teaspoon salt
1 tablespoon red wine vinegar
½ cup extra-virgin olive oil
2 tablespoons minced fresh parsley

1. In the inner pot, pour water and place the rack. Place the steamer basket on the rack. 2. Spread eggplant onto the steamer basket. 3. Close the lid and set the steam release handle to Sealing position. 4. Set the Instant Pot on Pressure Cook at High and adjust time to 3 minutes. 5. When cooked, quick-release the pressure and turn off the heat. Open the lid carefully and transfer the eggplant to a food

processor. 6. Add salt, garlic, and vinegar and pulse until smooth. 7. Add oil and stir until well incorporated. 8. Sprinkle with the chopped parsley. 9. Serve and enjoy!
Per Serving: Calories 124; Fat: 12.7g; Sodium 150mg; Carbs: 3.6g; Fiber 1g; Sugars: 1.7g; Protein 0.6g

Cheddar Jalapeño Popper Dip

Prep Time: 10 minutes | Cook Time: 20 minutes | Serves: 4

2 ounces cream cheese, softened
4 tablespoons shredded Cheddar
cheese, divided
2 tablespoons minced pickled
jalapeño peppers
1 tablespoon sour cream

4 teaspoons bacon bits
1/16 teaspoon salt
1/16 teaspoon garlic powder
3 slices pickled jalapeño peppers
1 cup water

1. Prepare an 8-ounce ramekin and grease. Set aside. 2. Add 3 tablespoons Cheddar, sour cream, bacon bits, garlic powder, salt, and cream cheese in a small bowl. Then spoon into the greased ramekin and sprinkle the jalapeno slices on the top and use a piece of foil to cover. 3. In the inner pot, pour water and place the trivet. Transfer the ramekin onto the trivet. 4. Close the lid and turn the steam release handle to Sealing. 5. Set the Instant Pot on Pressure Cook at High and adjust time to 15 minutes. 6. When cooked, release the pressure by turn the handle from Sealing to Venting and then carefully remove the ramekin onto an ovenproof plate. 7. Preheat your air fryer to a high heat. 8. Uncover the foil and top the dip with the remaining Cheddar. 9. Broil in the air fryer about 3 to 5 minutes. Serve and enjoy!
Per Serving: Calories 188; Fat: 15.9g; Sodium 619mg; Carbs: 1.1g; Fiber 1g; Sugars: 0.2g; Protein 10g

Plant-Based Hummus

Prep Time: 10 minutes | Cook Time: 30 minutes | Serves: 6

1 cup dried chickpeas
4 cups water
1 tablespoon plus ¼ cup extra-
virgin olive oil, divided
⅓ cup tahini
1½ teaspoons ground cumin

¾ teaspoon salt
½ teaspoon ground black pepper
½ teaspoon ground coriander
⅓ cup lemon juice
1 teaspoon minced garlic

1. In the inner pot, add water, chickpeas, and 1 tablespoon of oil. 2. Close the lid and turn the steam release handle to Sealing. 3. Set the Instant Pot on Pressure Cook at High and then adjust time to 30 minutes. 4. When cooked, quick-release the pressure and then carefully open the lid. Turn off heat. Reserve the cooking liquid. 5. In a food processor, add the remaining oil, cumin, tahini, pepper, salt, garlic, lemon juice, coriander, and chickpeas and process until creamy. 6. If hummus is too thick, add reserved cooking liquid 1 tablespoon at a time until it reaches desired consistency. 7. Serve at room temperature.
Per Serving: Calories 212; Fat: 9.7g; Sodium 325mg; Carbs: 24.4g; Fiber 1g; Sugars: 4g; Protein 9.2g

Garlic Hummus with Tahini

Prep Time: 10 minutes | Cook Time: 30 minutes | Serves: 8

1 cup dried chickpeas
4 cups water
1 tablespoon plus ¼ cup extra-
virgin olive oil, divided
⅓ cup tahini
1 teaspoon ground cumin
½ teaspoon onion powder

¾ teaspoon salt
½ teaspoon ground black pepper
⅓ cup lemon juice
3 tablespoons mashed roasted
garlic
2 tablespoons chopped fresh
parsley

1. In the inner pot, add water, 1 tablespoon of oil, and chickpea. 2. Close the lid and turn the steam release handle to Sealing. 3. Set the Instant Pot on Pressure Cook at High and adjust time to 30 minutes. 4. When cooked, quick-release the pressure and then turn off the heat. Open the lid and drain. Reserve the cooking liquid. 5. In a food processor, add the remaining ¼ cup oil, cumin, tahini, salt, onion powder, lemon juice, roasted garlic, pepper, and the chickpeas and process until creamy. 6. If hummus is too thick, add reserved cooking liquid 1 tablespoon at a time until it reaches desired consistency. 7. Then sprinkle the chopped parsley on the top. Serve and enjoy!
Per Serving: Calories 155; Fat: 7g; Sodium 241mg; Carbs: 17.9g; Fiber 1g; Sugars: 3g; Protein 6.7g

Tasty Sun-Dried Tomato Cheesecake

Prep Time: 10 minutes | Cook Time: 20 minutes | Serves: 12

3 tablespoons unsalted butter, melted
⅓ cup bread crumbs
½ cup sun-dried tomatoes in oil, drained, leaving 1 tablespoon oil
6 cloves garlic, peeled and minced
1 teaspoon dried oregano
3 large eggs
3 tablespoons all-purpose flour
2 (8-ounce) packages cream cheese
¾ cup sour cream, divided
½ cup diced scallions
2 cups hot water

1. Brush butter inside ta suitable spring-form pan. Then arrange bread crumbs at the bottom and sides of the pan. 2. Put the pan in the center of a piece of plastic wrap and then form and crimp an equal-sized aluminum foil to seal. 3. In a food processor, add tomatoes, garlic, oregano, flour, eggs, cream cheese, and ¼ cup sour cream. Puree until smooth. Add scallions and stir well. 4. Pour into prepared pan. Cover with foil; crimp to seal. 5. In the inner pot, place a rack and then pour in water. 6. Fold a long piece of foil in half lengthwise and lay over rack to form a sling. Place pan in the pot so it rests on the sling. 7. Close the lid and then turn the steam release handle to Sealing position. 8. Set the Instant Pot on Pressure Cook at High and adjust time to 20 minutes. 9. When cooked, naturally release the pressure about 10 minutes and then quick-release the remaining pressure. Then open the lid carefully and allow it to cool until all the steam has dissipated. 10. Lift the pan from pot with sling. Remove foil lid and use a paper towel to dab away any accumulated moisture. Cool cheesecake completely. 11. Top the cheesecake with the remaining sour cream. Serve at room temperature or chill at least 4 hours in the refrigerator.
Per Serving: Calories 229; Fat: 20.5g; Sodium 182mg; Carbs: 6.3g; Fiber 1g; Sugars: 0.5g; Protein 5.7g

Mayonnaise Spinach-Artichoke Dip

Prep Time: 10 minutes | Cook Time: 25 minutes | Serves: 6

4 ounces cream cheese, softened
2 tablespoons mayonnaise
2 tablespoons sautéed spinach
2 tablespoons finely minced artichoke hearts
1 tablespoon chopped green chilies
½ cup shredded mozzarella cheese
2 tablespoons shredded Parmesan cheese, divided
⅛ teaspoon salt
⅛ teaspoon crushed red pepper flakes
1 cup water

1. Prepare an 8-ounce ramekin and grease inside. Set aside. 2. Add cream cheese, mayonnaise, spinach, artichokes, chilies, mozzarella, 1 tablespoon Parmesan, salt, and red pepper flakes in a small bowl. 3. Spoon the mixture into prepared the greased ramekin and use a piece of foil to cover. 4. In the inner pot, pour water and place the trivet at the bottom. Then transfer the greased ramekin onto the trivet. 5. Close the lid and turn the steam release handle to Sealing position. 6. Set the Instant Pot on Pressure Cook at High and adjust time to 20 minutes. 7. When cooked, release the pressure by turning the handle from Sealing to Venting and then remove the ramekin to an oven-proof plate. 8. Preheat your air fryer to high heat. 9. Remove the foil from the dip and top with the remaining Parmesan. 10. Broil until the top is browned about 3 to 5 minutes. Serve and enjoy!
Per Serving: Calories 143; Fat: 10.7g; Sodium 233mg; Carbs: 6.8g; Fiber 1g; Sugars: 0.9g; Protein 6.6g

Savory Deviled Eggs

Prep Time: 10 minutes | Cook Time: 18 minutes | Serves: 6

6 large eggs
1 cup water
2 tablespoons olive oil mayonnaise
½ teaspoon Dijon mustard
2 tablespoons chopped fresh dill
1 tablespoon chopped capers
1 tablespoon minced Kalamata olives
¼ teaspoon ground black pepper

1. Prepare a large bowl of ice water. In the inner pot, place a rack at the bottom. 2. Place the eggs on the rack and then pour water. 3. Close the lid and turn the steam release handle to Sealing position. 4. Set the Instant Pot on Pressure Cook at High and adjust time to 8 minutes. 5. When cooked, naturally release the pressure about 10 minutes and then quick-release the remaining pressure. 6. Turn off the heat and carefully open the lid. Remove eggs into ice water. Let it stand for 10 minutes. Remove shells. 7. Slice the eggs into halves and remove the yolks. In a medium bowl, place the yolks. Mash the yolks until crumbled and add mayonnaise and mustard. 8. Fold in dill, olives,

capers, and pepper. 9. Fill egg whites with yolk mixture, then chill for at least 2 hours before serving.
Per Serving: Calories 77; Fat: 5.2g; Sodium 133mg; Carbs: 1.2g; Fiber 1g; Sugars: 0.4g; Protein 6.6g

Herbed Artichokes

Prep Time: 10 minutes | Cook Time: 10 minutes | Serves: 6

3 medium artichokes with stems cut off
1 medium lemon, halved
1 cup water
¼ cup lemon juice
⅓ cup extra-virgin olive oil
1 clove garlic, peeled and minced
¼ teaspoon salt
1 teaspoon chopped fresh oregano
1 teaspoon chopped fresh rosemary
1 teaspoon chopped fresh flat-leaf parsley
1 teaspoon fresh thyme leaves
Clean and rinse completely the artichokes.

1. Slice off top ⅓ of artichoke and discard any tough outer leaves. Rub lemon over the cut surfaces. 2. In the inner pot, pour together lemon juice and water and place a rack. 3. Arrange artichokes upside down on the rack. 4. Close the lid and turn the steam release handle to Sealing position. 5. Set the Instant Pot on Pressure Cook at High and adjust time to 10 minutes. 6. When cooked, naturally release the pressure about 20 minutes. 7. Turn off the heat and carefully open the lid. Transfer the artichoke onto a cutting board and slice in half. Transfer onto a serving plate. 8. Combine garlic, oregano, parsley, thyme, rosemary, salt, and oil in a small bowl. Add half the mixture over the artichokes. 9. Serve with the remaining mixture as a dipping.
Per Serving: Calories 153; Fat: 11.5g; Sodium 206mg; Carbs: 12.2g; Fiber 1g; Sugars: 1.4g; Protein 3.8g

Flavorful Black-Eyed Pea "Caviar"

Prep Time: 10 minutes | Cook Time: 30 minutes | Serves: 10

1 cup dried black-eyed peas
4 cups water
1-pound cooked corn kernels
½ medium red onion, peeled and diced
½ medium green bell pepper, seeded and diced
2 tablespoons minced pickled jalapeño pepper
1 medium tomato, diced
2 tablespoons chopped fresh cilantro
¼ cup red wine vinegar
2 tablespoons extra-virgin olive oil
1 teaspoon salt
½ teaspoon ground black pepper
½ teaspoon ground cumin

1. In the inner pot, pour water and add black-eyed peas. 2. Close the lid and turn the stream release handle to Sealing. 3. Set the Instant Pot on Pressure Cook at High and adjust time to 30 minutes. 4. When cooked, naturally release the pressure about 25 minutes and then open the lid carefully. 5. Drain the peas and place into a large mixing bowl. 6. Stir in all the remaining ingredients in the bowl until well combined. 7. Cover and chill in the refrigerator about 2 hours before serving.
Per Serving: Calories 64; Fat: 3.3g; Sodium 266mg; Carbs: 7.8g; Fiber 1g; Sugars: 1.4g; Protein 2g

Herbed White Bean Dip

Prep Time: 10 minutes | Cook Time: 30 minutes | Serves: 16

1 cup dried white beans, rinsed and drained
3 cloves garlic, peeled and crushed
8 cups water
¼ cup extra-virgin olive oil
¼ cup chopped fresh flat-leaf parsley
1 tablespoon chopped fresh
oregano
1 tablespoon chopped fresh tarragon
1 teaspoon chopped fresh thyme leaves
1 teaspoon grated lemon zest
¼ teaspoon salt
¼ teaspoon ground black pepper

1. In the inner pot, add garlic and beans and stir well. 2. Then pour water and place the trivet in the inner pot. 3. Set the Instant Pot on Pressure Cook at High and adjust time to 30 minutes. 4. When cooked, naturally release the pressure about 20 minutes. Turn off the heat and open the lid carefully. Drain the beans and transfer the beans and garlic to a food processor. 5. Mix in pepper, parsley, tarragon, thyme, salt, lemon zest, oregano, and thyme. Pulse 3 to 5 times. 6. Store in a container and chill in a refrigerator for 4 hours or overnight. 7. Serve and enjoy!
Per Serving: Calories 72; Fat: 3.3g; Sodium 41mg; Carbs: 8.2g; Fiber 1g; Sugars: 0.3g; Protein 3.1g

Marinated Balsamic Mushrooms and Pearl Onions

Prep Time: 10 minutes | Cook Time: 4 minutes | Serves: 10

3 pounds button mushrooms, trimmed
1 (15-ounce) bag frozen pearl onions, thawed
3 cloves garlic, peeled and minced
1 cup vegetable broth
¼ cup balsamic vinegar
¼ cup red wine
2 tablespoons olive oil
2 sprigs fresh thyme
½ teaspoon ground black pepper
¼ teaspoon crushed red pepper flakes

1. In the inner pot, add all the ingredients and mix well. 2. Close the lid and turn the steam release handle to Sealing. 3. Set the Instant Pot on Pressure Cook at High and adjust time to 4 minutes. 4. When cooked, quick-release the pressure and carefully open the lid. 5. Serve on a bowl and enjoy!
Per Serving: Calories 65; Fat: 3.3g; Sodium 85mg; Carbs: 5.2g; Fiber 1g; Sugars: 2.5g; Protein 4.8g

Tasty Buffalo Chicken Dip

Prep Time: 8 minutes | Cook Time: 20 minutes | Serves: 6

1 (8-ounce) boneless, skinless chicken breast
1 cup water
1/16 teaspoon salt
1/16 teaspoon ground black pepper
2 ounces cream cheese, softened
2 tablespoons buffalo sauce
1 teaspoon dry ranch seasoning
1 ½ tablespoons shredded Cheddar cheese
1 tablespoon chopped green onion

1. Add chicken and water in the inner pot and then add salt and pepper to season. 2. Close the lid and turn the steam release handle to Sealing position. 3. Set the Instant Pot on Pressure Cook at High and adjust time to 20 minutes. 4. When cooked, naturally release the pressure about 10 minutes and then carefully remove the lid. 5. Transfer the chicken to a small bowl and then pour in the 1 tablespoon cooking liquid. Shred the chicken with 2 forks. 6. Mix in the remaining ingredients thoroughly. 7. Serve in a serving bowl and enjoy!
Per Serving: Calories 88; Fat: 4.8g; Sodium 403mg; Carbs: 1g; Fiber 1g; Sugars: 0.1g; Protein 9.2g

Greek Egg Dish

Prep Time: 10 minutes | Cook Time: 8 minutes | Serves: 4

½ cup crumbled feta cheese
¼ cup bread crumbs
1 medium onion, peeled and minced
4 tablespoons all-purpose flour
2 tablespoons minced fresh mint
½ teaspoon salt
½ teaspoon ground black pepper
1 tablespoon dried thyme
6 large eggs, beaten
1 cup water

1. Add bread crumbs, onion, mint, flour, pepper, salt, thyme, and cheese in a medium bowl and then whisk in the eggs. 2. Spritz nonstick cooking spray over a suitable round baking dish. Then pour the egg mixture into dish. 3. In the inner pot, pour water and place rack at the bottom. 4. Fold a long piece of foil in half lengthwise. Lay foil over rack to form a sling and top with dish. Cover loosely with foil. 5. Close the lid and turn the steam release handle to Sealing position. 6. Set the Instant Pot on Pressure Cook at High and adjust time to 8 minutes. 7. When cooked, quick-release the pressure and then open the lid carefully. Let it stand for 5 minutes. 8. Serve and enjoy!
Per Serving: Calories 227; Fat: 12g; Sodium 659mg; Carbs: 15.6g; Sugars: 3g; Protein 14.3g

Creamy Corn Dip

Prep Time: 10 minutes | Cook Time: 20 minutes | Serves: 6

2 ounces cream cheese, softened
3 tablespoons shredded Cheddar cheese
1 tablespoon minced pickled jalapeño peppers
½ cup corn
1 tablespoon bacon bits
1/16 teaspoon salt
1/16 teaspoon ground black pepper
1 cup water
1 tablespoon shredded Parmesan cheese

1. Lightly grease an 8-ounce ramekin and set it aside. 2. Add Cheddar, corn, salt, bacon bits, pepper, cream cheese, and jalapeños in a small bowl. Then use a spoon to transfer the mixture into the greased ramekin and use foil to cover. 3. In the inner pot, pour water and place

the trivet. Transfer the ramekin onto the trivet. 4. Close the lid and turn the steam release handle to Sealing position. 5. Set the Instant Pot on Pressure Cook at High and adjust time to 15 minutes. 6. When cooked, release the pressure by turning the handle from Sealing to Venting and then remove the lid carefully. 7. Transfer the ramekin onto an oven-proof plate. 8. Preheat your air fryer to high heat. 9. Remove the foil from the dip and then top with Parmesan. 10. Broil in the air fryer until brown about 3 to 5 minutes. 11. Serve and enjoy!
Per Serving: Calories 91; Fat: 7g; Sodium 211mg; Carbs: 3g; Fiber 1g; Sugars: 0.5g; Protein 4.7g

Smoky Roasted Red Pepper Hummus

Prep Time: 10 minutes | Cook Time: 30 minutes | Serves: 12

1 cup dried chickpeas
4 cups water
1 tablespoon plus ¼ cup extra-virgin olive oil, divided
½ cup chopped roasted red pepper, divided
⅓ cup tahini
1 teaspoon ground cumin
¾ teaspoon salt
½ teaspoon ground black pepper
¼ teaspoon smoked paprika
⅓ cup lemon juice
½ teaspoon minced garlic

1. In the inner pot, add water, 1 tablespoon of oil, and chickpeas. 2. Close the lid and turn the steam release handle to Sealing position. 3. Set the Instant Pot on Pressure Cook at High and adjust time to 30 minutes. 4. When cooked, quick-release the pressure. Turn off the heat and open the lid carefully. 5. Drain and reserve the cooking liquid. 6. In a food processor, add ⅓ cup roasted red pepper, cumin, tahini, paprika, lemon juice, salt, garlic, the remaining oil, black pepper, and chickpeas and process until creamy. 7. If hummus is too thick, add reserved cooking liquid 1 tablespoon at a time until it reaches desired consistency. 8. Sprinkle the reserve roasted red pepper on the top to garnish. Serve and enjoy!
Per Serving: Calories 105; Fat: 4.7g; Sodium 181mg; Carbs: 12.3g; Fiber 1g; Sugars: 2.3g; Protein 4.5g

Herbed Chickpea, Parsley, and Dill Dip

Prep Time: 10 minutes | Cook Time: 21 minutes | Serves: 12

8 cups 2 tablespoons water, divided
1 cup dried chickpeas
3 tablespoons olive oil, divided
2 garlic cloves, peeled and minced
2 tablespoons chopped fresh
parsley
2 tablespoons chopped fresh dill
1 tablespoon lemon juice
¼ teaspoon salt

1. In the inner pot, pour 4 cups of water. 2. Close the lid and turn the steam release handle to Sealing position. 3. Set the Instant Pot on Pressure Cook at High and adjust time to 1 minute. 4. When cooked, quick-release the pressure and turn off the heat. Open the lid carefully. 5. Add water and the chickpeas to the pot. Soak for 1 hour. 6. Add 1 tablespoon of oil in the pot. Close the lid and then turn the steam release handle to Sealing position. 7. Set the Instant Pot on Pressure Cook at High and adjust time to 20 minutes. 8. When cooked, naturally release the pressure about 20 minutes. 9. Turn off the heat and carefully open the lid. Drain the beans and transfer to a blender. Add garlic, dill, lemon juice, the remaining water, and parsley and blend for about 30 seconds. 10. Add the remaining oil slowly and blend. Then add salt to season. 11. Serve and enjoy!
Per Serving: Calories 93; Fat: 4.5g; Sodium 56mg; Carbs: 10.6g; Fiber 1g; Sugars: 1.8g; Protein 3.4g

Unsweetened Applesauce

Prep time: 10 minutes | Cook time: 8 minutes | Serves: 6

6 apples (about 1½-pound)
¼ cup water
¼ teaspoon ground cinnamon

1. Peel and core the apples. Cut each apple into roughly eight large chunks. 2. Combine the apples, water, and cinnamon in the Inner Pot. 3. Select Pressure Cook mode, and then press the "Pressure Cook" button again to select "Less" time option. 4. Use the "-" key to set the cooking time to 8 minutes. 5. Press the Pressure Level button to adjust the pressure to "High Pressure." 6. Once the cooking cycle is completed, allow the steam to release naturally for 10 minutes, then turn the steam release handle to the Venting position. 7. Gently mash the apples into applesauce. 8. Serve warm or refrigerate in an airtight container for up to 10 days.
Per Serving: Calories 95; Fat 0.31g; Sodium 2mg; Carbs 25.23g; Fiber 4.4g; Sugar 18.91g; Protein 0.48g

Greek-style Garlic Dip

Prep Time: 10 minutes | Cook Time: 10 minutes | Serves: 16

1-pound russet potatoes, peeled and quartered
3 cups plus ¼ cup water, divided
2 teaspoons salt, divided
8 cloves garlic, peeled and minced
¾ cup blanched almonds
½ cup extra-virgin olive oil
2 tablespoons lemon juice
2 tablespoons white wine vinegar
½ teaspoon ground black pepper

1. In the inner pot, add 3 cups of water, 1 teaspoon salt, and potatoes and stir well. 2. Close the lid and turn the steam release handle to Sealing position. 3. Set the Instant Pot on Pressure Cook at High and adjust time to 10 minutes. 4. Meanwhile, spread the remaining salt and garlic on a cutting board. Press the garlic and salt to make a paste with a side of a knife. 5. Transfer into a food processor and add in the olive oil and almonds. 6. Purée into a paste. Set aside. 7. When cooked, quick-release the pressure and then turn off the heat. Open the lid carefully. Drain the potatoes and then place in a medium bowl. 8. Mash the garlic mixture with a potato masher until smooth. 9. Add lemon juice, pepper, and vinegar and stir well. 10. Then Stir in ¼ cup water a little at a time until mixture is thin enough for dipping. 11. Serve and enjoy!
Per Serving: Calories 103; Fat: 8.6g; Sodium 293mg; Carbs: 6g; Fiber 1g; Sugars: 0.6g; Protein 1.6g

Avocado Pinto Bean Dip

Prep Time: 10 minutes | Cook Time: 30 minutes | Serves: 16

1 cup dried pinto beans, soaked overnight and drained
4 cups water
4 tablespoons roughly chopped cilantro, divided
3 tablespoons extra-virgin olive oil
1 teaspoon ground cumin
1 clove garlic, peeled and minced
½ teaspoon salt
1 medium avocado, peeled, pitted, and diced
1 large ripe tomato, seeded and diced
1 small jalapeño pepper, seeded and minced
½ medium white onion, peeled and chopped
2 teaspoons lime juice

1. In the inner pot, add water, 2 tablespoons cilantro, and beans 2. Close the lid and turn the steam release handle to Sealing position. 3. Set the Instant Pot on Bean at High and adjust time to 30 minutes. 4. When cooked, naturally release the pressure about 20 minutes. Then carefully open the lid. 5. Drain off water from the beans and transfer to a medium bowl. Mash the beans until chunky. 6. Mix in oil, garlic, salt, and cumin. 7. In a separate bowl, add the remaining cilantro, avocado, tomato, jalapeno, lime juice, and onion and toss well. 8. Spoon topping over bean dip in a serving bowl. Serve and enjoy!
Per Serving: Calories 94; Fat: 5.3g; Sodium 79mg; Carbs: 9.5g; Fiber 1g; Sugars: 0.8g; Protein 3g

Simple Hard-Boiled Eggs

Prep Time: 1 minutes | Cook Time: 15 minutes | Serves: 1

1 cup water
2 large eggs
⅛ teaspoon salt

1. In the inner pot, pour water and place the trivet at the bottom. 2. Add the eggs onto the trivet. 3. Close the lid and turn the steam release handle to Sealing position. 4. Set the Instant Pot on Pressure Cook at High and adjust time to 2 minutes. 5. When cooked, naturally release the pressure and then remove the lid carefully. 6. Soak the eggs in an ice bath about 10 minutes. Peel the eggs and transfer into a serving bowl. 7. Add salt to season. Serve and enjoy!
Per Serving: Calories 143; Fat: 9.9g; Sodium 147mg; Carbs: 0.8g; Fiber 1g; Sugars: 0.8g; Protein 12.6g

Kidney Bean Dip

Prep Time: 10 minutes | Cook Time: 30 minutes | Serves: 16

1 cup dried kidney beans, soaked overnight and drained
4 cups water
3 cloves garlic, peeled and crushed
¼ cup roughly chopped cilantro, divided
¼ cup extra-virgin olive oil
1 tablespoon lime juice
2 teaspoons grated lime zest
1 teaspoon ground cumin
½ teaspoon salt

1. In the inner pot, add water, 2 tablespoons cilantro, garlic, and beans. 2. Close the lid and turn the steam release handle to Sealing position. 3. Set the Instant Pot on Bean at Normal and adjust time to 30 minutes.

4. When cooked, naturally release the pressure about 20 minutes. Turn off the heat and then carefully open the lid. 5. Drain off the excess water from the beans and transfer to a medium bowl. Mash beans until chunky. 6. Stir in lime juice, lime zest, salt, cumin, and remaining 2 tablespoons of cilantro and combine well. 7. Serve and enjoy!
Per Serving: Calories 67; Fat: 3.3g; Sodium 77mg; Carbs: 7.3g; Fiber 1g; Sugars: 0.3g; Protein 2.7g

Luscious Baba Ghanoush

Prep Time: 10 minutes | Cook Time: 6 minutes | Serves: 8

2 tablespoons extra-virgin olive oil, divided
1 large eggplant, peeled and diced
3 cloves garlic, peeled and minced
½ cup water
3 tablespoons chopped fresh flat-
leaf parsley
½ teaspoon salt
¼ teaspoon smoked paprika
2 tablespoons lemon juice
2 tablespoons tahini

1. Set the Instant Pot on Sauté at Normal and heat 1 tablespoon of oil. 2. Cook eggplant until soft about 5 minutes. Add in garlic and cook about 30 seconds or until fragrant. 3. In the inner pot, pour water. Close the lid and turn the steam release handle to Sealing. 4. Set the Instant Pot on Pressure Cook at High and adjust time to 6 minutes. 5. When cooked, quick-release the pressure and turn off the heat. Open the lid carefully. 6. Strain the cooked eggplant and garlic and transfer into a food processor. Then add salt, smoked paprika, tahini, lemon juice, and parsley. Scrape off the browned bits from the blender. 7. Add the remaining oil and process until smooth. 8. Serve and enjoy!
Per Serving: Calories 70; Fat: 5.7g; Sodium 155mg; Carbs: 4.7g; Fiber 1g; Sugars: 1.9g; Protein 1.4g

Unique Pepperoni Pizza Dip

Prep Time: 10 minutes | Cook Time: 20 minutes | Serves: 6

2 ounces cream cheese, softened
3 tablespoons shredded mozzarella cheese, divided
⅛ teaspoon garlic powder
⅛ teaspoon plus 1/16 teaspoon Italian seasoning, divided
⅛ teaspoon salt
3 tablespoons marinara sauce
1 tablespoon diced pepperoni
1 teaspoon shredded Parmesan cheese
1 cup water

1. Prepare an 8-ounce ramekin and grease. Set it aside. 2. Add salt, garlic powder, cream cheese, 2 tablespoons mozzarella, and ⅛ teaspoon Italian seasoning. Use a spoon to transfer onto the greased ramekin. 3. Sprinkle the remaining 1 tablespoon of mozzarella, Parmesan, peperoni, marinara, and the remaining 1/16 teaspoon Italian seasoning. Cover with foil. 4. In the inner pot, pour water and place the trivet at the bottom. Transfer the ramekin on the trivet. 5. Close the lid and turn the steam release handle to Sealing position. 6. Set the Instant Pot on Pressure Cook at High and adjust time to 15 minutes. 7. When cooked, release the pressure by turning the handle from Sealing to Venting and then carefully remove the lid. 8. Transfer the ramekin to an ovenproof plate. 9. Preheat your air fryer to high heat. Remove the foil from the dip and then broil in the air fryer until browned about 3 to 5 minutes. 10. Serve and enjoy!
Per Serving: Calories 301; Fat: 25.4g; Sodium 881mg; Carbs: 2g; Fiber 1g; Sugars: 0.7g; Protein 15.8g

Fresh Tomato Chutney

Prep Time: 10 minutes | Cook Time: 10 minutes | Serves: 12

4 pounds ripe tomatoes, peeled
1 (1") piece fresh ginger, peeled
3 cloves garlic, peeled and chopped
1¾ cups sugar
1 cup red wine vinegar
2 medium onions, peeled and diced
¼ cup golden raisins
¾ teaspoon ground cinnamon
½ teaspoon ground coriander
¼ teaspoon ground cloves
¼ teaspoon ground nutmeg
¼ teaspoon ground ginger
1 teaspoon chili powder
⅛ teaspoon paprika
1 tablespoon curry paste

1. In a blender, add tomatoes and fresh ginger to puree. 2. In the inner pot, pour the tomato mixture and then add the remaining ingredients. Stir well. 3. Close the lid and turn the steam release handle to Sealing position. 4. Set the Instant Pot on Pressure Cook at Low and adjust time to 10 minutes. 5. When cooked, naturally release the pressure about 25 minutes and then carefully release the pressure. Stir well. 6. Store in a storage container and chill in the refrigerator. Serve at room temperature or chilled.
Per Serving: Calories 262; Fat: 1.1g; Sodium 12mg; Carbs: 65.2g; Fiber 1g; Sugars: 60.8g; Protein 1.8g

Garlic Lentil Dip

Prep Time: 10 minutes | Cook Time: 30 minutes | Serves: 16

2 tablespoons olive oil
½ medium yellow onion, peeled and diced
3 cloves garlic, peeled and minced
2 cups dried red lentils, rinsed and drained

4 cups water
1 teaspoon salt
¼ teaspoon ground black pepper
2 tablespoons minced fresh flat-leaf parsley

1. Set the Instant Pot on Sauté at Normal and add oil in the inner pot. Cook the onion in the inner pot for about 2 to 3 minutes. Then add garlic and cook about 30 seconds. 2. Add in water, salt, and beans in the pot and stir well. 3. Close the lid and turn the steam release handle to Sealing position. 4. Set the Instant Pot on Bean at High and adjust time to 30 minutes. 5. When cooked, naturally release the pressure about 10 minutes and quick-release the remaining pressure. 6. In a food processor, add the lentil mixture and blend until smoke. 7. Add pepper and parsley. Serve and enjoy!
Per Serving: Calories 102; Fat: 2g; Sodium 151mg; Carbs: 15g; Fiber 1g; Sugars: 0.7g; Protein 6.3g

Classic Hummus

Prep time: 10 minutes | Cook time: 60 minutes | Serves: 2

¾ cup dried chickpeas
1½ cups water
4 garlic cloves
½ teaspoon baking soda

2 tablespoons tahini
1 tablespoon lemon juice
¼ teaspoon kosher salt
¼ teaspoon ground cumin

1. Combine the chickpeas, water, garlic, and baking soda in the Inner Pot. 2. Select Pressure Cook mode, and then press the "Pressure Cook" button again to select "More" time option. 3. Use the "+" key to set the cooking time to 60 minutes. 4. Press the Pressure Level button to adjust the pressure to "High Pressure." 5. Once the cooking cycle is completed, quickly and carefully turn the steam release handle from Sealing position to the Venting position. 6. Add the tahini and lemon juice to the pot, and stir them well. 7. Use an immersion blender to puree the hummus into a smooth paste. 8. Season with salt and cumin. 9. Serve warm or chilled.
Per Serving: Calories 384; Fat 12.7g; Sodium 646mg; Carbs 53.01g; Fiber 10.7g; Sugar 8.36g; Protein 18.36g

Refried Beans

Prep time: 10 minutes | Cook time: 60 minutes | Serves: 6

6 cups homemade chicken stock or store-bought chicken stock
3 cups dried pinto beans
1 yellow onion, diced

1 tablespoon apple cider vinegar
2 teaspoons ground cumin
½ teaspoon kosher salt

1. Combine the stock, beans, onion, vinegar, cumin, and salt in the Inner Pot. 2. Select Pressure Cook mode, and then press the "Pressure Cook" button again to select "More" time option. 3. Use the "+" key to set the cooking time to 60 minutes. 4. Press the Pressure Level button to adjust the pressure to "High Pressure." 5. Once the cooking cycle is completed, allow the steam to release naturally for 10 minutes, then turn the steam release handle to the Venting position. 6. Carefully remove the lid. 7. Reserve ½ cup of the bean cooking liquid, then drain the beans. 8. Return the beans to the pot and use an immersion blender to blend them to your desired consistency. 9. Serve.
Per Serving: Calories 432; Fat 4.24g; Sodium 551mg; Carbs 70.88g; Fiber 15.3g; Sugar 6.63g; Protein 27.04g

Classic Black Beans

Prep time: 10 minutes | Cook time: 40 minutes | Serves: 4

2 tablespoons olive oil
1 yellow onion, diced
1 green bell pepper, seeded and diced
1 jalapeño pepper, seeded and minced
2 garlic cloves, minced

1 teaspoon dried oregano
1 teaspoon ground cumin
1 cup dried black beans
1 tablespoon apple cider vinegar
½ teaspoon kosher salt
1½ cups water

1. Heat the olive oil in the Inner Pot on Sauté mode at Normal cooking temperature. 2. When the oil is hot, add the onion, bell pepper, jalapeño, and garlic, and sauté them for 3 to 5 minutes until softened.

3. Press the Cancel button. 4. Add the oregano and cumin to the pot and stir well, then add the beans, vinegar, salt, and water. 5. Select Pressure Cook mode, and then press the "Pressure Cook" button again to select "Normal" time option. 6. Use the "+" key to set the cooking time to 40 minutes. 7. Press the Pressure Level button to adjust the pressure to "High Pressure." 8. Once the cooking cycle is completed, allow the steam to release naturally for 10 minutes, then turn the steam release handle to the Venting position. 9. Serve directly.
Per Serving: Calories 251; Fat 7.65g; Sodium 299mg; Carbs 35.88g; Fiber 8.5g; Sugar 3.39g; Protein 11.44g

Cilantro-Lime Brown Rice

Prep time: 10 minutes | Cook time: 15 minutes | Serves: 4

1 cup long-grain brown rice, rinsed
1¼ cups water

Zest and juice of 1 lime
¼ cup freshly chopped cilantro
1 teaspoon kosher salt

1. Combine the rice and water in the Inner Pot. 2. Select Pressure Cook mode, and then press the "Pressure Cook" button again to select "Less" time option. 3. Use the "-" key to set the cooking time to 15 minutes. 4. Press the Pressure Level button to adjust the pressure to "High Pressure." 5. Once the cooking cycle is completed, allow the steam to release naturally for 10 minutes, then turn the steam release handle to the Venting position. 6. Add the lime zest, lime juice, cilantro, and salt to the pot, and stir them well. 7. Serve and enjoy.
Per Serving: Calories 334; Fat 7.9g; Sodium 704mg; Carbs 6g; Fiber 3.6g; Sugar 6g; Protein 18g

Coconut Brown Rice

Prep time: 10 minutes | Cook time: 15 minutes | Serves: 6

2 tablespoons unsweetened shredded coconut
1½ cups long-grain brown rice, rinsed

1 (14-ounce) can light coconut milk
½ cup water
¼ teaspoon kosher salt

1. Cook the shredded coconut in the Inner Pot on Sauté mode at Normal cooking temperature, for 2 to 3 minutes. 2. Press the Cancel button to stop this cooking program. 3. Transfer the toasted coconut to a small dish, and set aside for later use. 4. Combine the rice, light coconut milk, water, and salt in the Inner Pot. 5. Select Pressure Cook mode, and then press the "Pressure Cook" button again to select "Less" time option. 6. Use the "-" key to set the cooking time to 15 minutes. 7. Press the Pressure Level button to adjust the pressure to "High Pressure." 8. Once the cooking cycle is completed, allow the steam to release naturally for 10 minutes, then turn the steam release handle to the Venting position. 9. Remove the lid and stir in the toasted coconut before serving.
Per Serving: Calories 324; Fat 17.13g; Sodium 116mg; Carbs 39.57g; Fiber 3.1g; Sugar 2.73g; Protein 5.22g

Feta Chickpea Salad

Prep time: 10 minutes | Cook time: 15 minutes | Serves: 4

2 tablespoons olive oil, plus ¼ cup
1 red onion, diced
1 red bell pepper, seeded and diced
1 zucchini, diced
1 cup dried chickpeas, soaked overnight
3 cups water

1 cup baby spinach
3 tablespoons lemon juice
¼ teaspoon kosher salt
¼ teaspoon black pepper
¼ cup crumbled feta cheese
1 teaspoon dried oregano

1. Heat 2 tablespoons of olive oil in the Inner Pot on Sauté mode at Normal cooking temperature. 2. When the oil is hot, add the onion, bell pepper, and zucchini, and sauté them for 4 to 5 minutes until softened. 3. Press the Cancel button to stop this cooking program. 4. Add the chickpeas and water to the Inner Pot. 5. Select Pressure Cook mode, and then press the "Pressure Cook" button again to select "Less" time option. 6. Use the "-" key to set the cooking time to 15 minutes. 7. Press the Pressure Level button to adjust the pressure to "High Pressure." 8. Once the cooking cycle is completed, allow the steam to release naturally for 10 minutes, then turn the steam release handle to the Venting position. 9. Add the remaining ¼ cup of olive oil, the spinach, lemon juice, salt, and black pepper to the pot, and stir well. 10. Top this dish with the feta and oregano, and enjoy.
Per Serving: Calories 221; Fat 7.9g; Sodium 704mg; Carbs 6g; Fiber 3.6g; Sugar 6g; Protein 18g

Potato Pea Salad

Prep time: 10 minutes | Cook time: 4 minutes | Serves: 6

1½-pound (4 or 5) yellow potatoes
1 shallot, finely chopped
¼ cup apple cider vinegar
¼ cup olive oil

1 teaspoon Dijon mustard
½ teaspoon kosher salt
4-ounce sugar snap peas, halved lengthwise

1. Cut each potato into 12 pieces. 2. Whisk the shallot, vinegar, olive oil, mustard, and salt in a bowl. Set the dressing aside for later use. 3. Pour 2 cups of water into the Inner Pot and place the Steam Rack in the pot. 4. Put the potatoes on the rack. 5. Select Pressure Cook mode, and then press the "Pressure Cook" button again to select "Less" time option. 6. Use the "-" key to set the cooking time to 4 minutes. 7. Press the Pressure Level button to adjust the pressure to "High Pressure." 8. Once the cooking cycle is completed, quickly and carefully turn the steam release handle from Sealing position to the Venting position. 9. Transfer the cooked potatoes to the bowl of dressing, and then stir in the peas. 10. Enjoy this salad warm or chilled.
Per Serving: Calories 182; Fat 9.18g; Sodium 212mg; Carbs 23.01g; Fiber 3.1g; Sugar 2.9g; Protein 2.94g

Cider Collard Greens

Prep time: 10 minutes | Cook time: 12 minutes | Serves: 6

6 no-sugar-added uncured bacon slices, diced
1 yellow onion, diced
16-ounce frozen chopped collard

greens
1 tablespoon apple cider vinegar
¼ teaspoon kosher salt
¼ teaspoon garlic powder

1. Select Sauté mode and Normal setting. 2. Add the bacon to the Inner Pot, and sauté for 3 minutes until the fat renders. 3. Add the onion and sauté for 3 minutes until soft. 4. Press the Cancel button to stop Sauté program. 5. Add the collard greens, vinegar, salt, and garlic powder to the pot, and stir well. 6. Use your spoon to scrape up anything that's stuck to the bottom of the pot. 7. Cover the pot with lid. 8. Select Pressure Cook mode, and then press the "Pressure Cook" button again to select "Less" time option. 9. Use the "-" key to set the cooking time to 12 minutes. 10. Press the Pressure Level button to adjust the pressure to "High Pressure." 11. Once the cooking cycle is completed, quickly and carefully turn the steam release handle from Sealing position to the Venting position. 12. Carefully remove the lid, stir, and serve.
Per Serving: Calories 139; Fat 10.51g; Sodium 256mg; Carbs 6.93g; Fiber 3g; Sugar 1.01g; Protein 5.52g

Garlicky Brussels Sprouts

Prep time: 10 minutes | Cook time: 2 minutes | Serves: 6

1 tablespoon olive oil
1 pound Brussels sprouts, bottoms trimmed
½ cup Vegetable Broth or store-bought low-sodium vegetable

broth
5 garlic cloves, minced
¼ teaspoon kosher salt
¼ teaspoon black pepper

1. Heat the oil on Sauté mode at Normal cooking temperature. 2. When the oil is hot, add the Brussels sprouts, and cook undisturbed for 3 to 4 minutes until lightly browned. 3. Press the Cancel button to stop this cooking program. 4. Add the broth, garlic, salt and black pepper to the pot, and then cover the pot. 5. Select Pressure Cook mode, and then press the "Pressure Cook" button again to select "Less" time option. 6. Use the "-" key to set the cooking time to 2 minutes. 7. Press the Pressure Level button to adjust the pressure to "High Pressure." 8. Once the cooking cycle is completed, quickly and carefully turn the steam release handle from Sealing position to the Venting position. 9. Serve.
Per Serving: Calories 60; Fat 2.56g; Sodium 128mg; Carbs 8.48g; Fiber 3.1g; Sugar 2.28g; Protein 2.92g

Cinnamon Acorn Squash

Prep time: 10 minutes | Cook time: 5 minutes | Serves: 4

2 acorn squash
4 teaspoons coconut oil
4 teaspoons pure maple syrup

¼ teaspoon ground cinnamon
¼ teaspoon kosher salt

1. Cut the squash in half through the root, then scoop out and discard the seeds. 2. Divide the coconut oil, maple syrup, cinnamon, and salt evenly between the centers of each squash half. 3. Pour 1 cup of water into the Inner Pot and insert the Steam Rack. 4. Stack the squash, cut-

side up, on top of the Steam Rack. 5. Put on the pressure cooker's lid and turn the steam valve to "Sealing" position. 6. Press the "Pressure Cook" button three times to select "Less" option. 7. Use the "+/-" keys on the control panel to set the cooking time to 5 minutes. 8. Press the Pressure Level button to adjust the pressure to "High Pressure." 9. Once the cooking cycle is completed, allow the steam to release naturally for 10 minutes, then turn the steam release handle to the Venting position. 10. When all the steam is released, remove the pressure lid from the top carefully. 11. Serve.
Per Serving: Calories 184; Fat 5g; Sodium 441mg; Carbs 17g; Fiber 4.6g; Sugar 5g; Protein 9g

Mashed Potato and Cauliflower

Prep time: 10 minutes | Cook time: 8 minutes | Serves: 6

1 pound potatoes, peeled and cubed
2 cups fresh or frozen cauliflower florets
4 garlic cloves

¼ cup unsweetened nondairy milk, such as almond or coconut
¼ teaspoon kosher salt
½ teaspoon black pepper

1. Pour 2 cups of water into the Inner Pot, and add the potatoes, cauliflower, and garlic. 2. Select Pressure Cook mode, and then press the "Pressure Cook" button again to select "Less" time option. 3. Use the "-" key to set the cooking time to 8 minutes. 4. Press the Pressure Level button to adjust the pressure to "High Pressure." 5. Once the cooking cycle is completed, quickly and carefully turn the steam release handle from Sealing position to the Venting position. 6. Drain the water. 7. Return the vegetables to the pot, and add the milk, salt, and pepper. 8. Use a potato masher to mash the potatoes and cauliflower to your desired consistency, and then serve.
Per Serving: Calories 77; Fat 0.41g; Sodium 117mg; Carbs 16.58g; Fiber 2.8g; Sugar 2.1g; Protein 2.9g

Honey Sweet Potatoes

Prep time: 15 minutes | Cook time: 7 minutes | Serves: 4

1 pound sweet potatoes (about 2 medium potatoes), cut into ½-inch rounds
2 teaspoons coconut oil

1 teaspoon honey
1 teaspoon chili powder
¼ teaspoon smoked paprika
¼ teaspoon kosher salt

1. Pour ½ cup of water into the Inner Pot, then add the potato rounds. 2. Put on the pressure cooker's lid and turn the steam valve to "Sealing" position. 3. Select Pressure Cook mode, and then press the "Pressure Cook" button again to select "Less" time option. 4. Use the "-" key to set the cooking time to 4 minutes. 5. Press the Pressure Level button to adjust the pressure to "High Pressure." 6. Once the cooking cycle is completed, quickly and carefully turn the steam release handle from Sealing position to the Venting position. 7. Press Cancel to stop this cooking program. 8. Add the coconut oil, honey, chili powder, paprika, and salt to the pot, and stir well. 9. Press the "Sauté" button two times to select "Normal" mode and cook for 2 to 3 minutes, until the potatoes are coated with a thick glaze. 10. Serve warm.
Per Serving: Calories 113; Fat 2.52g; Sodium 195mg; Carbs 21.97g; Fiber 3.1g; Sugar 8.03g; Protein 1.67g

Cinnamon Raisin Granola Bars

Prep time: 15 minutes | Cook time: 10 minutes | Serves: 10

2 cups quick-cooking oats
⅓ cup date syrup
⅓ cup avocado oil
⅓ cup monk fruit sweetener

⅓ cup almond butter
⅓ cup raisins
½ teaspoon ground cinnamon

1. Combine the oats, date syrup, oil, fruit sweetener, almond butter, raisins, and cinnamon in a medium bowl. 2. Spray a suitable baking dish with cooking spray. Press the oat mixture firmly into the pan. 3. Add 1 cup water to the Inner Pot and place the Steam Rack inside. 4. Put the baking dish on the Steam Rack. 5. Select Pressure Cook mode, and then press the "Pressure Cook" button again to select "Less" time option. 6. Use the "-" key to set the cooking time to 10 minutes. 7. Press the Pressure Level button to adjust the pressure to "High Pressure." 8. Once the cooking cycle is completed, quickly and carefully turn the steam release handle from Sealing position to the Venting position. 9. Once completely cooled, turn the pan upside down onto a cutting board to remove the granola from the pan. 10. Cut into ten bars and serve.
Per Serving: Calories 186; Fat 12.2g; Sodium 8mg; Carbs 20.87g; Fiber 2.1g; Sugar 14.06g; Protein 3.15g

Almond Butter Chocolate Chip Granola Bars

Prep time: 15 minutes | Cook time: 10 minutes | Serves: 10

2 cups quick-cooking oats
⅔ cup almond butter
⅓ cup avocado oil
⅓ cup monk fruit sweetener

⅓ cup stevia-sweetened dark chocolate chips
¼ teaspoon salt

1. Combine the oats, almond butter, oil, sweetener, chocolate chips, and salt in a medium bowl. 2. Spray a suitable baking dish with cooking spray. Press the oat mixture firmly into the pan. 3. Add 1 cup water to the Inner Pot and place the steam rack inside. 4. Put the baking dish on the steam rack. 5. Select Pressure Cook button, and then press the "Pressure Cook" button again to select "Less" time option. 6. Use the "-" key to set the cooking time to 10 minutes. 7. Press the Pressure Level button to adjust the pressure to "Low Pressure." 8. Once the cooking cycle is completed, quickly and carefully turn the steam release handle from Sealing position to the Venting position. 9. Carefully remove the pan from the Inner Pot and place it on a baking rack to cool completely. 10. Once completely cooled, turn the pan upside down onto a cutting board to remove the granola from the pan. 11. Cut into ten bars and serve.
Per Serving: Calories 232; Fat 17.91g; Sodium 84mg; Carbs 17.53g; Fiber 3g; Sugar 7.65g; Protein 5.26g

Buffalo Chicken Dip

Prep time: 10 minutes | Cook time: 7 minutes | Serves: 10

2 cups cooked, shredded chicken
1 cup vegan nondairy blue cheese-style dressing

8-ounce nondairy cream cheese
½ cup buffalo hot sauce

1. In a 7" glass bowl, add the chicken, blue cheese dressing, cream cheese, and hot sauce. Mix. 2. Add 1 cup water to the Inner Pot and place the steam rack inside. Place the bowl on top of the steam rack. 3. Put on the pressure cooker's lid and turn the steam valve to "Sealing" position. 4. Select Pressure Cook mode, and then press the "Pressure Cook" button again to select "Less" time option. 5. Use the "+/-" keys on the control panel to set the cooking time to 7 minutes. 6. Press the Pressure Level button to adjust the pressure to "High Pressure." 7. Once the cooking cycle is completed, allow the steam to release naturally. 8. When all the steam is released, remove the pressure lid from the top carefully. 9. Stir the dip and then serve warm.
Per Serving: Calories 129; Fat 8.15g; Sodium 295mg; Carbs 3g; Fiber 0.3g; Sugar 2.45g; Protein 10.64g

Hot Cauliflower Bites

Prep time: 15 minutes | Cook time: 2 minutes | Serves: 4

1 large head cauliflower, cut into large pieces

½ cup buffalo hot sauce

1. Pour 1 cup water into the Inner Pot and place the Steam Rack inside. 2. Place the cauliflower in a 7-cup glass bowl, and add the buffalo hot sauce. 3. Toss to evenly coat. Put the bowl on the steam rack. 4. Select Pressure Cook mode, and then press the "Pressure Cook" button again to select "Less" time option. 5. Use the "-" key to set the cooking time to 2 minutes. 6. Press the Pressure Level button to adjust the pressure to "High Pressure." 7. Once the cooking cycle is completed, quickly and carefully turn the steam release handle from Sealing position to the Venting position. 8. Transfer to a plate and serve with toothpicks.
Per Serving: Calories 62; Fat 0.64g; Sodium 292mg; Carbs 12.62g; Fiber 4.8g; Sugar 5.29g; Protein 4.53g

Spinach Artichoke Dip

Prep time: 10 minutes | Cook time: 6 minutes | Serves: 10

½ cup vegetable stock
1 (10-ounce) package frozen, cut spinach
1 (14-ounce) can artichoke quarters, drained
8-ounce nondairy cream cheese

¾ cup nondairy Greek yogurt
¼ cup vegan mayonnaise
1 teaspoon onion powder
¼ teaspoon garlic salt
¼ teaspoon black pepper
1 cup nutritional yeast

1. Add all of the ingredients to the Inner Pot. 2. Select Pressure Cook mode, and then press the "Pressure Cook" button again to select "Less" time option. 3. Use the "-" key to set the cooking time to 6 minutes. 4. Press the Pressure Level button to adjust the pressure to

"High Pressure." 5. Once the cooking cycle is completed, quickly and carefully turn the steam release handle from Sealing position to the Venting position. 6. Stir well, and then transfer the dip to a serving bowl. The dip will thicken as it sits.
Per Serving: Calories 167; Fat 9.39g; Sodium 1072mg; Carbs 10.85g; Fiber 3.5g; Sugar 2.56g; Protein 10.86g

Sweet Potato Hummus

Prep time: 10 minutes | Cook time: 10 minutes | Serves: 10

2 tablespoons avocado oil
1 large sweet potato, peeled and cut into cubes
½ teaspoon salt
3 cloves garlic, minced

Juice from 1 large lemon
1 (15-ounce) can cooked chickpeas
¼ cup tahini
1 teaspoon ground cumin

1. Select Sauté mode and press the "Sauté" button again to select "Normal" setting. 2. Add the oil to the Inner Pot, and heat the oil for 2 minutes. 3. Add the sweet potato and salt, and sauté for 2 minutes; add the garlic, and sauté for 30 seconds. 4. Press the Cancel button to stop this cooking program, and then add the lemon juice to the pot. 5. Select Pressure Cook mode, and then press the "Pressure Cook" button again to select "Less" time option. 6. Use the "-" key to set the cooking time to 2 minutes. 7. Press the Pressure Level button to adjust the pressure to "High Pressure." 8. Once the cooking cycle is completed, quickly and carefully turn the steam release handle from Sealing position to the Venting position. 9. Transfer the food to a large food processor. 10. Add the chickpeas, tahini, and cumin to the processor, and process them until smooth. 11. Allow the hummus to chill in the refrigerator at least 30 minutes before serving.
Per Serving: Calories 115; Fat 6.82g; Sodium 192mg; Carbs 11.42g; Fiber 2.8g; Sugar 2.35g; Protein 3.28g

Nacho Cheese Sauce

Prep time: 5 minutes | Cook time: 10 minutes | Serves: 4

1¼ cups vegetable broth
1 cup plain nondairy yogurt
3 tablespoons oat flour
¼ teaspoon salt
¼ teaspoon garlic salt

½ teaspoon cumin
1 teaspoon chili powder
¼ teaspoon paprika
⅛ teaspoon cayenne powder

1. Mix the yogurt and flour in a bowl. 2. Select Sauté mode and press the "Sauté" button again to select "Normal" setting. 3. Add the broth to the Inner Pot and bring to a boil. 4. When boiled, add the yogurt mixture, salt, and spices to the pot; cook and stir them for 5 minutes until thick and bubbly. 5. Transfer to a bowl and serve.
Per Serving: Calories 65; Fat 2.62g; Sodium 366mg; Carbs 7.62g; Fiber 0.7g; Sugar 3.59g; Protein 3.02g

Cauliflower Hummus

Prep time: 15 minutes | Cook time: 15 minutes | Serves: 10

1 tablespoon avocado oil
1 small yellow onion, chopped
3 cloves garlic, minced
1 small head cauliflower, cut into florets
¾ cup water

½ teaspoon salt
Juice from 1 large lemon
1 (15-ounce) can cooked chickpeas
¼ cup tahini
1 teaspoon ground cumin

1. Select Sauté mode and press the "Sauté" button again to select "Normal" setting. 2. Add the oil to the Inner Pot, and heat it for 1 minute. 3. Add the onion, and sauté for 7 minutes until softened. 4. Add the garlic, and sauté for 30 seconds. 5. Press the Cancel button, and add the cauliflower and water to the pot. 6. Select Pressure Cook mode, and then press the "Pressure Cook" button again to select "Less" time option. 7. Use the "+/-" keys on the control panel to set the cooking time to 5 minutes. 8. Press the Pressure Level button to adjust the pressure to "Low Pressure." 9. Once the cooking cycle is completed, quickly and carefully turn the steam release handle from Sealing position to the Venting position. 10. Transfer the food to a large food processor, leaving the liquid in the pot. 11. Add the salt, lemon juice, chickpeas, tahini, and cumin to the processor, and process them until you have a smooth mixture. 12. If the mixture is too thick, add some of the liquid in the Inner Pot. 13. Allow the hummus to chill in the refrigerator at least 30 minutes before serving.
Per Serving: Calories 96; Fat 5.47g; Sodium 195mg; Carbs 9.66g; Fiber 2.9g; Sugar 1.98g; Protein 3.5g

Black Bean Dip

Prep time: 10 minutes | Cook time: 7 minutes | Serves: 10

1 tablespoon avocado oil
1 medium yellow onion, peeled and chopped
2 (15-ounce) cans black beans, drained
1 teaspoon ground cumin
½ teaspoon chili powder
½ teaspoon smoked paprika
½ teaspoon salt
Juice from ½ medium lime
¼ cup nutritional yeast

1. Select Sauté mode and press the "Sauté" button again to select "Normal" setting. 2. Add the oil to the pot and heat for 1 minute; add the onion and sauté for 3 minutes until softened. 3. Press the Cancel button. 4. Add the beans, cumin, chili powder, paprika, and salt to the pot. 5. Select Pressure Cook mode, and then press the "Pressure Cook" button again to select "Less" time option. 6. Use the "-" key to set the cooking time to 3 minutes. 7. Press the Pressure Level button to adjust the pressure to "Low Pressure." 8. Once the cooking cycle is completed, quickly and carefully turn the steam release handle from Sealing position to the Venting position. 9. Add the lime juice and nutritional yeast and use an immersion blender to blend the dip. 10. Serve warm.
Per Serving: Calories 42; Fat 1.76g; Sodium 335mg; Carbs 4.75g; Fiber 1.6g; Sugar 0.98g; Protein 2.4g

White Bean Dip

Prep time: 5 minutes | Cook time: 8 minutes | Serves: 10

1 tablespoon avocado oil
1 medium yellow onion, peeled and chopped
2 cloves garlic, minced
2 (15-ounce) cans cannellini beans, drained
1 (15-ounce) can diced tomatoes, drained
½ teaspoon salt
¼ teaspoon black pepper
½ cup chopped fresh basil
1 tablespoon fresh lemon juice

1. Select Sauté mode and press the "Sauté" button again to select "Normal" setting. and add the oil to the Inner Pot. 2. Add the oil to the Inner Pot and heat for 1 minute; add the onion and sauté the onion for 3 minutes until softened. 3. Add the garlic, and sauté for 30 seconds. 4. Press the Cancel button. Add the beans, tomatoes, salt, and pepper to the pot, and stir well. 5. Select Pressure Cook mode, and then press the "Pressure Cook" button again to select "Less" time option. 6. Use the "-" key to set the cooking time to 3 minutes. 7. Press the Pressure Level button to adjust the pressure to "High Pressure." 8. Once the cooking cycle is completed, quickly and carefully turn the steam release handle from Sealing position to the Venting position. 9. Stir in the basil and lemon juice, and then use an immersion blender to blend to a chunky consistency. 10. Serve warm or cold.
Per Serving: Calories 35; Fat 1.74g; Sodium 169mg; Carbs 4.81g; Fiber 1.9g; Sugar 1.99g; Protein 1.04g

Lentil Balls

Prep time: 40 minutes | Cook time: 15 minutes | Serves: 4

For the Lentil Balls
⅓ cup cooked black beans, drained
½ cup old fashioned rolled oats
1¼ cups cooked lentils
¼ cup unsweetened almond milk
¼ teaspoon coarse salt
For the Sauce
¾ cup tomato sauce
1 tablespoon tomato paste
¼ cup maple syrup
2 tablespoons cup coconut aminos
¼ teaspoon ground ginger
⅛ teaspoon garlic powder
⅛ teaspoon black pepper
2 tablespoons avocado oil
2 tablespoons oat flour
1 tablespoon apple cider vinegar
½ teaspoon ground ginger
¼ teaspoon crushed red pepper flakes

1. Partially mash the black beans in a bowl. 2. Pulse the oats a few times in a food processor; add the lentils and pulse again. 3. Add the milk, salt, ginger, garlic powder, and black pepper, and pulse. Do not over mix. 4. Combine the lentil mixture and black beans. 5. Form the mixture into tablespoon-sized balls and refrigerate for 30 minutes. 6. Mix all of the sauce ingredients together in a medium bowl. 7. Pour the oat flour into a shallow bowl, and coat the lentil balls with the flour. 8. Select Sauté mode and press the "Sauté" button again to select "More" setting. 9. Add the avocado oil to the Inner Pot and heat for 2 minutes. 10. Add the lentil balls to the oil, and carefully move them around to brown, for about 1 minute per side. 11. Remove the balls and place them in a suitable cake pan. 12. Mix all the sauce ingredients in a bowl. 13. Top the lentil balls with the sauce and cover

with a paper towel, then tightly cover the pan with foil. 14. Add ½ cup water to Inner Pot and scrape up any brown bits from the bottom. 15. Place the Steam Rack in the pot, and put the pan on the rack. 16. Select Pressure Cook mode, and then press the "Pressure Cook" button again to select "Less" time option. 17. Use the "-" key to set the cooking time to 5 minutes. 18. Press the Pressure Level button to adjust the pressure to "Low Pressure." 19. Once the cooking cycle is completed, quickly and carefully turn the steam release handle from Sealing position to the Venting position. 20. Serve directly.
Per Serving: Calories 336; Fat 9.07g; Sodium 975mg; Carbs 56.38g; Fiber 12.8g; Sugar 23.72g; Protein 11.88g

Quinoa Energy Balls

Prep time: 15 minutes | Cook time: 5 minutes | Serves: 5

½ cup quinoa
1 cup water
¼ cup almond butter
2 teaspoons raw honey
½ teaspoon ground cinnamon
½ teaspoon blackstrap molasses
⅛ teaspoon fine sea salt

1. Place the quinoa in a fine-mesh strainer and rinse under water until the water runs clear. 2. Add the quinoa and water to the Inner Pot. 3. Select Pressure Cook mode, and then press the "Pressure Cook" button again to select "Less" time option. 4. Use the "-" key to set the cooking time to 5 minutes. 5. Press the Pressure Level button to adjust the pressure to "High Pressure." 6. Once the cooking cycle is completed, quickly and carefully turn the steam release handle from Sealing position to the Venting position. 7. Transfer the cooked quinoa to a medium bowl and allow it to cool. 8. Once it is cooled, add the rest of the ingredients to the bowl and stir to combine. 9. Form the mixture into 1" balls and place them onto a tray or plate. 10. Place them in the freezer about 30 minutes to firm. 11. Keep stored in the refrigerator.
Per Serving: Calories 151; Fat 7.97g; Sodium 93mg; Carbs 16.32g; Fiber 2.6g; Sugar 3.63g; Protein 5.04g

Cinnamon Almonds

Prep time: 5 minutes | Cook time: 2 minutes | Serves: 8

2 cups raw unsalted almonds
1 teaspoon ground cinnamon
2 tablespoons water
40 drops pure liquid stevia
½ teaspoon pure vanilla extract
¼ teaspoon coarse salt

1. Mix all the ingredients in a 7-cup glass bowl. 2. Pour ½ cup hot water into the Inner Pot and place the steam rack inside. 3. Put the glass bowl on the rack. 4. Select Pressure Cook mode, and then press the "Pressure Cook" button again to select "Less" time option. 5. Use the "-" key to set the cooking time to 2 minutes. 6. Press the Pressure Level button to adjust the pressure to "High Pressure." 7. Once the cooking cycle is completed, quickly and carefully turn the steam release handle from Sealing position to the Venting position. 8. Serve warm.
Per Serving: Calories 208; Fat 18.13g; Sodium 74mg; Carbs 8.04g; Fiber 3.9g; Sugar 1.72g; Protein 7.24g

Broccoli Bites

Prep time: 10 minutes | Cook time: 1 minute | Serves: 4

1 large crown broccoli, cut into large pieces
2 tablespoons toasted sesame oil
½ teaspoon salt
¼ teaspoon ground ginger
⅛ teaspoon garlic powder
2 tablespoons sesame seeds

1. Place the broccoli pieces into a suitable cake pan. 2. In a small bowl, whisk together the sesame oil, salt, ginger, and garlic powder. 3. Add it to the broccoli and toss to coat. 4. Pour 1 cup water into the Inner Pot and place the Steam Rack inside. 5. Put the pan on the rack. 6. Select Pressure Cook mode, and then press the "Pressure Cook" button again to select "Less" time option. 7. Use the "-" key to set the cooking time to 1 minute. 8. Press the Pressure Level button to adjust the pressure to "High Pressure." 9. Once the cooking cycle is completed, quickly and carefully turn the steam release handle from Sealing position to the Venting position. 10. Carefully remove the pan from the Inner Pot. 11. Toss the broccoli pieces with sesame seeds. Transfer the food to a plate and enjoy.
Per Serving: Calories 94; Fat 9.35g; Sodium 300mg; Carbs 2.12g; Fiber 0.5g; Sugar 0.03g; Protein 1.7g

Avocado Hummus

Prep time: 15 minutes | Cook time: 10 minutes | Serves: 8

¾ cup dry chickpeas
3 cups water
1 teaspoon salt
1 large avocado, peeled, pitted, and sliced

2 tablespoons olive oil plus ⅛ teaspoon for drizzling
2 tablespoons fresh lemon juice
½ teaspoon crushed red pepper flakes

1. Put the chickpeas in a bowl, and cover with 3" water. 2. Allow to soak 4–8 hours, and then drain them. 3. Add the soaked chickpeas, 3 cups water, and salt to the Inner Pot. 4. Select Pressure Cook mode, and then press the "Pressure Cook" button again to select "Less" time option. 5. Use the "-" key to set the cooking time to 10 minutes. 6. Press the Pressure Level button to adjust the pressure to "High Pressure." 7. Once the cooking cycle is completed, allow the steam to release naturally for 10 minutes, then turn the steam release handle to the Venting position. 8. Transfer the chickpeas to your food processor, and add the avocado, oil, and lemon juice. 9. Process until super smooth. 10. If the mixture is too thick, add water, 1 teaspoon at a time until desired consistency is reached. 11. Refrigerate until completely cooled and then sprinkle with crushed red pepper flakes and drizzle with the remaining ⅛ teaspoon olive oil before serving.
Per Serving: Calories 74; Fat 4.64g; Sodium 342mg; Carbs 7.28g; Fiber 3.1g; Sugar 1.22g; Protein 2.04g

Jalapeño Peppers with Cashews

Prep time: 10 minutes | Cook time: 30 minutes | Serves: 4-6

2 jalapeño peppers
½ pound dried great northern beans, rinsed and sorted
½ medium onion, roughly chopped
4 cups water
½ cup cashews

¼ cup unsweetened plant-based milk
2 garlic cloves, crushed
2 tablespoons nutritional yeast
1 tablespoon chickpea miso paste
1 tablespoon apple cider vinegar

1. Slice one jalapeños pepper in half lengthwise and remove the seeds. 2. Combine the halved pepper, beans, onion, and 3 cups of the water in the Inner Pot. 3. Select Pressure Cook mode, and then press the "Pressure Cook" button again to select "Normal" time option. 4. Use the "-" key to set the cooking time to 30 minutes. 5. Press the Pressure Level button to adjust the pressure to "High Pressure." 6. While cooking, boil the remaining 1 cup of water and, using a large bowl, pour it over the cashews; let soak for at least 30 minutes. 7. Drain and discard the soaking liquid before using the cashews. 8. Once the cooking cycle is completed, allow the steam to release naturally for 10 minutes, then turn the steam release handle to the Venting position. 9. Remove the jalapeño pepper from the pot, and finely chop it. 10. Finely chop another raw jalapeño pepper, removing the seeds if you prefer a milder dish. 11. Set both peppers aside. 12. Drain the beans and onion, then combine them in a blender with the cashews, milk, garlic, nutritional yeast, miso paste, and vinegar. 13. Blend them until creamy. 14. Spoon the mixture into a medium mixing bowl, and stir in the jalapeños. 15. Enjoy.
Per Serving: Calories 295; Fat 10.9g; Sodium 354mg; Carbs 20.5g; Fiber 4.1g; Sugar 8.2g; Protein 06g

Avocado Deviled Eggs

Prep time: 15 minutes | Cook time: 7 minutes | Serves: 12

6 large eggs
1 medium avocado, peeled, pitted, and diced
2½ tablespoons mayonnaise
2 teaspoons lime juice

1 clove garlic, crushed
⅛ teaspoon cayenne pepper
⅛ teaspoon salt
1 medium jalapeño pepper, sliced
12 dashes hot sauce

1. Pour 1 cup water into the Inner Pot and place the Steam Rack inside. 2. Carefully place the eggs directly onto the steam rack. 3. Put on the pressure cooker's lid and turn the steam valve to "Sealing" position. 4. Select Pressure Cook mode, and then press the "Steam" button again to select "Normal" option. 5. Use the "+/-" keys on the control panel to set the cooking time to 7 minutes. 6. Press the Pressure Level button to adjust the pressure to "Low Pressure." 7. Once the cooking cycle is completed, quickly and carefully turn the steam release handle from Sealing position to the Venting position. 8. Transfer the eggs to a bowl filled with iced water and let them sit 15 minutes. 9. Remove the eggs from the water and peel the shells away from the eggs. 10. Slice the eggs in half. 11. Scoop egg yolks into a medium bowl, and add the avocado, mayonnaise, lime juice, garlic, cayenne pepper, and salt. 12.

Mash the egg yolk mixture until filling is evenly combined. 13. Spoon the filling into a piping bag and pipe filling into each egg white. 14. Top each with a jalapeño slice and a dash of hot sauce.
Per Serving: Calories 75; Fat 5.86g; Sodium 214mg; Carbs 2.31g; Fiber 1.2g; Sugar 0.5g; Protein 3.78g

Cauliflower Queso with Bell Pepper

Prep time: 5 minutes | Cook time: 5 minutes | Serves: 5

1 head cauliflower, cut into about 4 cups florets
2 cups water
1½ cups carrots, chopped into ½-inch-thick round pieces
½ cup raw cashews
1 (15-ounce) can no-salt-added diced tomatoes

½ cup nutritional yeast
1 tablespoon white miso paste
2 teaspoons gluten-free chili powder
1 red bell pepper, diced
4 scallions, white and green parts, diced

1. Combine the cauliflower, water, carrots, and cashews in the Inner Pot. 2. Select Pressure Cook mode, and then press the "Pressure Cook" button again to select "Less" time option. 3. Use the "-" key to set the cooking time to 5 minutes. 4. Press the Pressure Level button to adjust the pressure to "High Pressure." 5. Once the cooking cycle is completed, quickly and carefully turn the steam release handle from Sealing position to the Venting position. 6. Drain the water, then transfer the mixture to a blender. 7. Add the liquid from the can of tomatoes and set the drained tomatoes aside. 8. Add the nutritional yeast, miso, and chili powder, and blend until very smooth. 9. Transfer the mixture to a medium bowl and stir in the drained tomatoes, bell pepper, and scallions. 10. Enjoy.
Per Serving: Calories 268; Fat 14.71g; Sodium 1139mg; Carbs 25.67g; Fiber 7.3g; Sugar 8.7g; Protein 12.95g

Tamari Edamame

Prep time: 5 minutes | Cook time: 1 minute | Serves: 4

1 (10-ounce) bag frozen edamame in pods
2 tablespoons reduced sodium

tamari
¼ teaspoon kosher salt

1. Pour 1 cup water in the Inner Pot, and place a Steam Rack in the pot. 2. Place the edamame in a steamer basket and place basket on the steam rack. 3. Select Steam mode and press the "Steam" button again to select "Less" setting. 4. Use the "-" key to set the cooking time to 1 minutes. 5. Press the Pressure Level button to adjust the pressure to "Low Pressure." 6. Once the cooking cycle is completed, quickly and carefully turn the steam release handle from Sealing position to the Venting position. 7. Transfer the edamame to a medium bowl and top with the tamari and salt, and enjoy.
Per Serving: Calories 134; Fat 7.68g; Sodium 166mg; Carbs 8.79g; Fiber 4.2g; Sugar 2.29g; Protein 9.63g

Simple Lentil-Walnut Dip

Prep time: 10 minutes | Cook time: 10 minutes | Serves: 4-6

¾ cup walnuts
2 cups water
1 cup green or brown lentils
½ medium onion, roughly chopped
1 bay leaf

2 garlic cloves, minced
2 tablespoons lemon juice
1 tablespoon white miso paste
1 tablespoon apple cider vinegar
Black pepper

1. Select Sauté mode and press the "Sauté" button again to select "Normal" setting. Let the machine heat for 2 minutes. 2. Add walnuts to the Inner Pot, and sauté for 3 to 5 minutes until slightly darker in color and the oils begin to release. Transfer the walnuts to a bowl and set aside for later use. 3. Combine the water, lentils, onion, and bay leaf in the Inner Pot. 4. Select Pressure Cook mode, and then press the "Pressure Cook" button again to select "Less" time option. 5. Use the "+/-" keys on the control panel to set the cooking time to 10 minutes. 6. Press the Pressure Level button to adjust the pressure to "High Pressure." 7. Once the cooking cycle is completed, allow the steam to release naturally for 10 minutes, then turn the steam release handle to the Venting position. 8. Remove and discard the bay leaf. 9. Add the lentils, onion, garlic, lemon juice, miso paste, vinegar, and black pepper to the blender. Blend them until creamy. 10. Serve either immediately as a warm dip or chill.
Per Serving: Calories 282; Fat 7.9g; Sodium 704mg; Carbs 6g; Fiber 3.6g; Sugar 6g; Protein 18g

Hard-Boiled Eggs

Prep time: 5 minutes | Cook time: 10 minutes | Serves: 6

6 large eggs

1. Pour 1 cup water into the Inner Pot and place the Steam Rack inside. 2. Carefully place the eggs directly onto the rack. 3. Select Pressure Cook mode, and then press the "Steam" button again to select "Normal" time option. 4. Use the "-" key to set the cooking time to 7 minutes. 5. Press the Pressure Level button to adjust the pressure to "High Pressure." 6. Once the cooking cycle is completed, quickly and carefully turn the steam release handle from Sealing position to the Venting position. 7. Immediately transfer the eggs to a bowl filled with iced water and let them sit 15 minutes. 8. Remove the eggs from the water and peel the shells away from the eggs. 9. Store in the refrigerator.
Per Serving: Calories 72; Fat 4.76g; Sodium 71mg; Carbs 0.36g; Fiber 0g; Sugar 0.19g; Protein 6.28g

Sweet Potatoes with Maple Syrup

Prep time: 10 minutes | Cook time: 9 minutes | Serves:4-6

4 sweet potatoes (about 2 pounds), peeled and cut into 1-inch chunks
1 cup orange juice
2 garlic cloves, minced
1 (1-inch) knob fresh ginger, peeled and grated, or 1 teaspoon
ground ginger
1 (1-inch) knob fresh turmeric, peeled and grated, or 1 teaspoon ground turmeric
½ teaspoon ground cinnamon
1 tablespoon maple syrup

1. Combine the sweet potatoes, orange juice, garlic, ginger, turmeric, and cinnamon in the Inner Pot. 2. Select Pressure Cook mode, and then press the "Pressure Cook" button again to select "Less" time option. 3. Use the "+/-" keys on the control panel to set the cooking time to 9 minutes. 4. Press the Pressure Level button to adjust the pressure to "High Pressure." 5. Once the cooking cycle is completed, quickly and carefully turn the steam release handle from Sealing position to the Venting position. 6. Add the maple syrup to the sweet potatoes, and mash the potatoes with a handheld potato masher or a large fork. 7. Stir well and serve immediately.
Per Serving: Calories 184; Fat 5g; Sodium 441mg; Carbs 17g; Fiber 4.6g; Sugar 5g; Protein 9g

Dijon Brussels Sprouts

Prep time: 10 minutes | Cook time: 1 minutes | Serves: 4-6

1 pound fresh Brussels sprouts
1 cup water
2 garlic cloves, smashed
3 tablespoons apple cider vinegar
2 tablespoons Dijon mustard
1 tablespoon maple syrup
Black pepper

1. Combine the Brussels sprouts, water, and garlic in the Inner Pot. 2. Select Pressure Cook mode, and then press the "Pressure Cook" button again to select "Less" time option. 3. Use the "-" key to set the cooking time to 1 minute. 4. Press the Pressure Level button to adjust the pressure to "High Pressure." 5. Once the cooking cycle is completed, quickly and carefully turn the steam release handle from Sealing position to the Venting position. 6. Whisk the vinegar, mustard, and maple syrup in a small bowl. 7. When the cook time is complete, quick-release the pressure and carefully remove the lid. 8. Drain the water and mince the garlic. Add the mustard dressing to the sprouts and garlic, and toss to coat. 9. Season the Brussels sprouts with pepper and enjoy.
Per Serving: Calories 122; Fat 7.9g; Sodium 704mg; Carbs 6g; Fiber 3.6g; Sugar 6g; Protein 18g

Lemon Eggplant in Vegetable Broth

Prep time: 5 minutes | Cook time: 15 minutes | Serves: 2

¼ to ½ cup vegetable broth
1 medium eggplant, peeled and sliced
1 cup water
3 garlic cloves, unpeeled
2 tablespoons lemon juice
2 tablespoons tahini
1 tablespoon white miso paste
½ teaspoon ground cumin, plus more for garnish

1. Select Sauté mode and press the "Sauté" button again to select "Normal" setting. 2. Pour 2 tablespoons of broth in the Inner Pot. 3. Arrange as many slices of eggplant as possible in one layer on the bottom of the pot. 4. Cook the eggplant slices for 2 minutes, then flip, adding more of the broth as needed, and cook for another 2 minutes.

5. After another 2 minutes, pile the first batch of eggplant on one side of the Inner Pot and add the remaining eggplant. 6. Cook them for 2 minutes on each side, adding broth as needed. 7. Press the Cancel button, and add the water and garlic. 8. Select Pressure Cook mode, and then press the "Pressure Cook" button again to select "Less" time option. 9. Use the "-" key to set the cooking time to 3 minutes. 10. Press the Pressure Level button to adjust the pressure to "High Pressure." 11. Once the cooking cycle is completed, quickly and carefully turn the steam release handle from Sealing position to the Venting position. 12. Remove the garlic and take off the outer peel. 13. Blend the garlic, eggplant, lemon juice, tahini, miso, and cumin in the blender until smooth, then transfer the dish to the serving plate and enjoy. 14. You can also cover the plate and refrigerate this meal, and serve cold.
Per Serving: Calories 207; Fat 10.64g; Sodium 488mg; Carbs 24.46g; Fiber 10.2g; Sugar 10.95g; Protein 8.17g

Spiced Potatoes Dip

Prep time: 15 minutes | Cook time: 27 minutes | Serves: 4-6

1 cup unsweetened plant-based milk
½ cup vegetable broth
2 scallions, white and green parts, chopped
2 tablespoons nutritional yeast
1 tablespoon arrowroot powder
1 teaspoon garlic powder
1 teaspoon minced fresh rosemary
1 teaspoon mustard powder
Black pepper
Salt
1½-pound russet potatoes (4 or 5 medium), peeled
1 cup water

1. Whisk the milk, broth, scallions, nutritional yeast, arrowroot powder, garlic powder, rosemary, and mustard powder in a large bowl. 2. Season the milk mixture with pepper and salt. 3. Slice the potatoes very thinly. 4. Arrange a 1-inch layer of potatoes on a suitable ovenproof baking dish, followed by enough of the sauce to just cover the potatoes. 5. Continue layering until all the potatoes are submerged under the sauce. 6. Pour the water into your Inner Pot and insert the Steam Rack. Place the baking dish on the Steam Rack. 7. Select Pressure Cook mode, and then press the "Pressure Cook" button again to select "Less" time option. 8. Use the "+" key to set the cooking time to 27 minutes. 9. Press the Pressure Level button to adjust the pressure to "High Pressure." 10. Once the cooking cycle is completed, quickly and carefully turn the steam release handle from Sealing position to the Venting position. 11. Serve immediately.
Per Serving: Calories 361; Fat 10.9g; Sodium 454mg; Carbs 10g; Fiber 3.1g; Sugar 5.2g; Protein 10g

Polenta with Mushroom Ragù

Prep time: 10 minutes | Cook time: 30 minutes | Serves: 4-6

1 medium onion, diced
1⅓ cups Easy Vegetable Broth
2 garlic cloves, minced
8-ounce white button mushrooms, sliced
8-ounce cremini mushrooms, sliced
3 tablespoons tomato paste
2 teaspoons dried thyme
1 teaspoon balsamic vinegar
Black pepper
3 cups water
1 cup polenta or ground cornmeal
1 cup unsweetened plant-based milk

1. Select Sauté mode and press the "Sauté" button again to select "Normal" setting. Let the machine heat for 2 minutes. 2. Sauté the onion for 3 to 5 minutes until translucent, adding broth as needed to prevent it from sticking. 3. Add the garlic and sauté for 30 seconds; add the mushrooms and sauté for about 5 minutes until softened. 4. Stir in the tomato paste, thyme, vinegar, and pepper to taste. 5. Add ⅓ cup of the broth and scrape up any browned bits from the bottom of the pot. 6. Bring to a simmer and cook for 3 minutes. 7. Cancel the Sauté function and remove the mushroom mixture to a small bowl. 8. Rinse and dry the Inner Pot. 9. Add the water, polenta, milk, and the remaining 1 cup of broth to the Inner Pot, then cook them for 5 minutes on Sauté mode at Normal cooking temperature. 10. Press Cancel button to stop this cooking program. 11. Select Pressure Cook mode, and then press the "Pressure Cook" button again to select "Less" time option. 12. Use the "-" key to set the cooking time to 10 minutes. 13. Press the Pressure Level button to adjust the pressure to "High Pressure." 14. Once the cooking cycle is completed, allow the steam to release naturally. 15. Stir, then transfer to a serving bowl and top with the mushroom ragù. 16. Serve immediately.
Per Serving: Calories 295; Fat 12.9g; Sodium 414mg; Carbs 11g; Fiber 5g; Sugar 9g; Protein 11g

Corn with Tofu Crema

Prep time: 10 minutes | Cook time: 6 minutes | Serves: 4-6

1 cup water
4 to 6 frozen mini corncobs
1 (14-ounce) package silken tofu, drained
1 tablespoon lemon juice
1 tablespoon apple cider vinegar
1 teaspoon ground cumin
Salt
1 lime, cut into wedges
1 tablespoon no-salt-added gluten-free chili powder

1. Pour the water into the Inner Pot and place the Steam Rack inside. Put the corncobs on the Steam Rack. 2. Select Pressure Cook mode, and then press the "Pressure Cook" button again to select "Less" time option. 3. Use the "+/-" keys on the control panel to set the cooking time to 6 minutes. 4. Press the Pressure Level button to adjust the pressure to "High Pressure." 5. Once the cooking cycle is completed, quickly and carefully turn the steam release handle from Sealing position to the Venting position. 6. Add the tofu, lemon juice, vinegar, cumin, and salt to a blender, blend them well and set aside for later use. 7. Rub each cob with a lime wedge and then slather it with a generous amount of crema. 8. Sprinkle ¼ to ½ teaspoon chili powder on each. 9. Serve immediately.
Per Serving: Calories 334; Fat 7.9g; Sodium 704mg; Carbs 6g; Fiber 3.6g; Sugar 6g; Protein 18g

Garlic Baby Potatoes

Prep time: 10 minutes | Cook time: 7 minutes | Serves: 4-6

2-pound baby red-skinned potatoes
1 cup water
3 tablespoons plant-based butter, melted, or olive oil
1 teaspoon garlic powder
1 teaspoon dried thyme
1 teaspoon dried rosemary, crushed
1 teaspoon salt
Black pepper

1. Pierce the potatoes with a fork and slice any larger potatoes in half. 2. Combine the potatoes and water in the Inner Pot. 3. Select Pressure Cook mode, and then press the "Pressure Cook" button again to select "Less" time option. 4. Use the "+/-" keys on the control panel to set the cooking time to 7 minutes. 5. Press the Pressure Level button to adjust the pressure to "High Pressure." 6. Once the cooking cycle is completed, quickly and carefully turn the steam release handle from Sealing position to the Venting position. 7. Drain the water, select the Sauté function and Normal setting. 8. Add the butter or olive oil, garlic powder, thyme, rosemary, salt, and black pepper to taste. 9. Stir to combine and allow the potatoes to brown slightly for 3 to 4 minutes.
Per Serving: Calories 184; Fat 5g; Sodium 441mg; Carbs 17g; Fiber 4.6g; Sugar 5g; Protein 9g

Creamed Spinach with Cashews

Prep time: 10 minutes | Cook time: 12 minutes | Serves: 4-6

½ medium onion, diced
4 garlic cloves, minced
1 (16-ounce) package frozen chopped spinach
1¾ cups unsweetened plant-based milk
1 cup water
¾ cup raw cashews
1 tablespoon lemon juice
1 teaspoon chickpea miso paste
½ teaspoon ground or freshly grated nutmeg
Black pepper

1. Select Sauté mode and press the "Sauté" button again to select "Normal" setting. Let the machine heat for 2 minutes. 2. Sauté the onion in the pot for 3 to 5 minutes until translucent, adding water as needed to prevent sticking. 3. Add the garlic and sauté for 30 seconds. 4. Cancel the Sauté function, then add the spinach and 1¼ cups of the milk. 5. Select Pressure Cook mode, and then press the "Pressure Cook" button again to select "Less" time option. 6. Use the "-" key to set the cooking time to 5 minutes. 7. Press the Pressure Level button to adjust the pressure to "High Pressure." 8. Once the cooking cycle is completed, allow the steam to release naturally. 9. Boil the water, then pour it over the cashews; let the cashews soak for at least 30 minutes before draining. 10. Add the drained cashews, the remaining milk, the lemon juice, miso paste, nutmeg, and black pepper to a blender, blend them until smooth. 11. Combine the sauce with the spinach. 12. Serve immediately.
Per Serving: Calories 372; Fat 20g; Sodium 891mg; Carbs 29g; Fiber 3g; Sugar 8g; Protein 7g

Garlic Collard Greens in Vegetable Broth

Prep time: 10 minutes | Cook time: 10 minutes | Serves: 4-6

1½-pound collard greens, stems removed, leaves chopped
1½ cups no-salt-added vegetable broth
3 tablespoons rice vinegar
3 garlic cloves, minced
1 (2-inch) knob fresh ginger, grated

1. Mix the collard greens, vegetable broth, vinegar, garlic, and ginger in the Inner Pot. 2. Select Pressure Cook mode, and then press the "Pressure Cook" button again to select "Less" time option. 3. Use the "-" key to set the cooking time to 10 minutes. 4. Press the Pressure Level button to adjust the pressure to "High Pressure." 5. Once the cooking cycle is completed, quickly and carefully turn the steam release handle from Sealing position to the Venting position. 6. Serve and enjoy.
Per Serving: Calories 289; Fat 14g; Sodium 791mg; Carbs 18.9g; Fiber 4.6g; Sugar 8g; Protein 6g

Beet Hummus

Prep time: 10 minutes | Cook time: 45 minutes | Serves: 4-6

3 cups water
1 cup dried chickpeas, rinsed and sorted
1 medium beet, peeled and quartered
½ cup tahini
2 tablespoons lemon juice
4 garlic cloves, crushed
Salt

1. Combine the water, chickpeas, and beets in the Inner Pot. 2. Select Pressure Cook mode, and then press the "Pressure Cook" button again to select "More" time option (45 minutes). 3. Press the Pressure Level button to adjust the pressure to "High Pressure." 4. Once the cooking cycle is completed, allow the steam to release naturally for 10 minutes, then turn the steam release handle to the Venting position. 5. Using a slotted spoon, transfer the chickpeas and beets to a blender, leaving the liquid in the pot. 6. Add the tahini, lemon juice, garlic, and salt to the blender---blend them well, adding one tablespoon of the liquid at a time. 7. Serve.
Per Serving: Calories 382; Fat 7.9g; Sodium 704mg; Carbs 6g; Fiber 3.6g; Sugar 6g; Protein 18g

Chapter 5 Soup, Stew, and Chili Recipes

Creamy onion soup

Prep Time: 35 minutes | Cook Time: 45 minutes | Serves: 8

6 tablespoons salted butter, divided	1 bay leaf
3 pounds sweet onions, peeled and sliced	½ teaspoon dried thyme
1 tablespoon light brown sugar	¼ teaspoon ground black pepper
¼ cup white wine	4 cups Beef Stock
2 cloves garlic, peeled and smashed	4 cups Beef Broth
1 tablespoon balsamic vinegar	8 (1"-thick) slices French baguette
	1 cup grated Gruyère cheese

1. Melt 3 tablespoons of butter in the Instant Pot by pressing the Sauté button. Add brown sugar and onions. Cook for about 5 minutes, or until onions are barely soft. Press the Cancel button. Close the lid, set the steam release to seal position, select Pressure Cook, and set the timer for 15 minutes. Quickly release the steam on vent position when the timer beeps, then click Cancel. 2. Drain the inner pot of any extra liquid. Put the inner pot back in the pot and choose Sauté. Adding the remaining butter, sauté the onions for 15 to 20 minutes, turning regularly, until they are caramelized and browned. 3. Add wine to the pot after scraping out any browned pieces. Press the Cancel button. Pepper, stock, vinegar, bay leaf, thyme, garlic, and vinegar to the pot. Close the lid, set the steam release to seal position, select Pressure Cook, and set the timer for 20 minutes. Allow pressure to naturally relax for around 20 minutes on seal position after the timer chimes. Open the lid, press the Cancel button, and mix well. Get rid of the bay leaf. 4. To thicken the soup, select the Sauté option and boil it for 10 minutes while stirring often. 5. Put the soup in heat-resistant bowls. Each bowl should have a slice of bread on it before the cheese is distributed. Broil for 3-5 minutes, or until bubbling and browned, cook the cheese on low pressure by selection Pressure Cook after adding 1 cup water and placing steam rack. Serve warm.
Per Serving: Calories 147; Fat: 10.17g; Sodium 97mg; Carbs: 13.87g; Sugars: 8.9g; Protein 1.56g

Yummy Soup

Prep Time: 15 minutes | Cook Time: 24 minutes | Serves: 8

1 (3½-pound) chicken, cut into pieces	1 bay leaf
3 stalks celery, chopped	1 teaspoon poultry seasoning
2 medium carrots, peeled and chopped	½ teaspoon dried thyme
1 medium yellow onion, peeled and chopped	1 teaspoon salt
1 clove garlic, peeled and smashed	¼ teaspoon ground black pepper
	4 cups low-sodium chicken broth
	4 ounces dried egg noodles

1. In the Instant Pot, combine the chicken, celery, carrots, onion, garlic, bay leaf, poultry seasoning, thyme, salt, and pepper. Press the Soup button, close the lid, set the steam release to seal position, and cook the soup for the preset 20 minutes. 2. Allow the pressure to naturally for 20 to 25 minutes after the timer beeps on seal. Press the Cancel button and open lid. 3. Get rid of the bay leaf. Chicken should be moved to a cutting board using tongs or a slotted spoon. Chicken should be delicately shredded, skin and bones removed. Stir the chicken back into the pot. Add the noodles, secure the cover, set the steam release to seal position, select Pressure Cook, and set the timer for 4 minutes. 4. Quickly release the pressure on vent position, take off the lid, and thoroughly stir after the timer sounds. Serve warm.
Per Serving: Calories 560; Fat: 16g; Sodium 1023mg; Carbs: 9g; Sugars: 3g; Protein 89g

Yummy Veggies Beef Soup

Prep Time: 20 minutes | Cook Time: 20 minutes | Serves: 8

2 pounds boneless chuck roast, cut into 1" pieces	chopped
¼ cup all-purpose flour	2 stalks celery, chopped
1 teaspoon salt, divided	2 cloves garlic, peeled and minced
1 teaspoon ground black pepper, divided	¼ teaspoon dried thyme
2 tablespoons vegetable oil, divided	1 russet potato, peeled and cut into ½" cubes
2 medium yellow onions, peeled and chopped	1 (14-ounce) can diced tomatoes, undrained
2 medium carrots, peeled and	4 cups Vegetable Broth
	2 cups water

1. A big zip-top plastic bag should be filled with meat, flour, and ½ teaspoon of salt and pepper each. Make sure the steak is uniformly covered and shake thoroughly. 2. Heat 1 tablespoon of oil in the Instant Pot by pressing the Sauté button. Make sure there is enough space between each piece of meat before adding the first half to the saucepan. each side for two to three minutes. Repeat with the remaining oil and meat after transferring the hamburger to a dish. 3. Add celery, onions, and carrots to the pot. Cook for approximately 5 minutes, or until barely tender. Cook for approximately 30 seconds, or until the garlic and thyme are aromatic. Press the Cancel button. 4. Return beef to pot. To the broth, water, tomato sauce, and potato, add. Stir well, being sure to scrape off any food remnants from the pot's bottom. Close lid, set steam release to seal position, press the Soup button, and cook for the default time of 20 minutes. 5. When the timer beeps, let pressure release naturally on seal position, about 15 minutes. Open lid and stir in remaining ½ teaspoon each salt and pepper. Serve hot.
Per Serving: Calories 1394; Fat: 138g; Sodium 456mg; Carbs: 18g; Sugars: 3.4g; Protein 32.39g

Noodle Soup with Beef

Prep Time: 30 minutes | Cook Time: 24 minutes | Serves: 8

2 pounds boneless chuck roast, cut into 1" pieces	chopped
¼ cup all-purpose flour	2 stalks celery, chopped
1 teaspoon salt, divided	2 cloves garlic, peeled and minced
1 teaspoon ground black pepper, divided	1 tablespoon tomato paste
2 tablespoons vegetable oil, divided	¼ teaspoon dried thyme
2 medium yellow onions, peeled and chopped	1 (14-ounce) can diced tomatoes, undrained
2 medium carrots, peeled and	4 cups Beef Broth
	2 cups water
	4 ounces elbow macaroni

1. A big zip-top plastic bag should be filled with beef, flour, and ½ teaspoon of salt and pepper each. Make sure the beef is uniformly covered and shake thoroughly. 2. Heat 1 tablespoon of oil in the Instant Pot by pressing the Sauté button. Making ensuring there is enough room between each piece, add half the meat to the saucepan. each side for two to three minutes. Repeat with the remaining oil and meat after transferring the hamburger to a dish. 3. Add celery, onions, and carrots to the saucepan. Cook for approximately 5 minutes, or until the vegetables are soft. Cook the garlic, tomato paste, and thyme for about a minute, or until aromatic. Press the Cancel button. 4. Return beef to pot. Add tomatoes, broth, and water. Stir well, being sure to scrape off any food remnants from the pot's bottom. Close lid, set steam release to seal position, press the Pressure Cook button, and cook for 20 minutes on high level. 5. Allow pressure to naturally relax for around 15 minutes after the timer beeps. Remove lid, then add the final ½ teaspoon of each salt and pepper. Press the Cancel button. 6. Stir thoroughly after adding macaroni to the pot. Close the lid, set the steam release to seal position, hit the Pressure Cook button, and select 4 minutes for the time. Release the pressure immediately once the timer beeps on vent position. Open lid, then thoroughly stir. Serve hot.
Per Serving: Calories 467; Fat: 19.1g; Sodium 546mg; Carbs: 20.7g; Sugars: 3.9g; Protein 54g

Black Bean and Quinoa Chili

Prep Time: 10 minutes | Cook Time: 10 minutes | Serves: 6

1 tablespoon vegetable oil	½ teaspoon salt
1 medium onion, peeled and chopped	½ teaspoon ground black pepper
1 medium red bell pepper, seeded and chopped	2 cups Vegetable Broth
2 cloves garlic, peeled and minced	1 cup water
3 tablespoons chili powder	¾ cup quinoa
1 teaspoon ground cumin	2 (15-ounce) cans black beans, drained and rinsed

1. Heat oil in the Instant Pot by pressing the Sauté button. Include bell pepper and onion. Cook for approximately 5 minutes, or until veggies are tender. Cook the garlic, chili powder, cumin, salt, and black pepper for about a minute, or until fragrant. 2. After thoroughly stirring in the broth and water, add the quinoa and beans. Close the lid, turn the steam release valve to the vent position, click the Pressure Cook button, and set the timer to 10 minutes. 3. Quickly remove the steam when the timer beeps then open the lid and thoroughly stir. Serve hot.
Per Serving: Calories 867; Fat: 88g; Sodium 315mg; Carbs: 23g; Sugars: 2.03g; Protein 5.39g

Vegan Three-Bean Chili

Prep Time: 5 minutes | Cook Time: 30 minutes | Serves: 8

1 cup dried pinto beans, soaked
1 cup dried red beans, soaked
1 cup dried black beans, soaked
2 medium white onions, peeled and chopped
2 medium red bell peppers, seeded and chopped
2 stalks celery, chopped
1 (28-ounce) can diced tomatoes

1 (15-ounce) can tomato sauce
¼ cup chili powder
2 tablespoons smoked paprika
1 teaspoon ground cumin
1 teaspoon ground coriander
½ teaspoon salt
½ teaspoon ground black pepper
3 cups Vegetable Broth
1 cup water

1. All ingredients should be added to the Instant Pot. Put the lid on, choose vent for the steam release, select Pressure Cook, and cook for the 30 minutes on Low. 2. Quickly remove the steam on vent position, then open the lid and thoroughly stir when the timer beeps. If the chili is too thin, click the Cancel and Sauté buttons, then let the chill simmer, covered, until the appropriate thickness is achieved. Serve warm.
Per Serving: Calories 955; Fat: 77g; Sodium 460mg; Carbs: 58.7g; Sugars: 8.03g; Protein 18.39g

Yummy Italian Soup

Prep Time: 30 minutes | Cook Time: 25 minutes | Serves: 8

½ medium yellow onion, peeled and minced
1 large egg, beaten
1 clove garlic, peeled and minced
¼ cup bread crumbs
½ teaspoon Italian seasoning
1 teaspoon salt, divided
¼ teaspoon crushed red pepper flakes
8 ounces ground pork
4 ounces 90% lean ground beef
1 tablespoon vegetable oil

1 medium yellow onion, peeled and roughly chopped
1 medium carrot, peeled and chopped
1 stalk celery, chopped
2 cloves garlic, chopped
½ teaspoon dried thyme
½ teaspoon ground black pepper
⅓cup white wine
4 cups Vegetable Broth
2 cups water
8 ounces baby spinach

1. Combine the ground beef, ground pork, and red pepper flakes in a large bowl along with the chopped onion, minced garlic, bread crumbs, Italian seasoning, and ½ teaspoon salt. Mix gently until well blended. Meatballs of 1 ½" in diameter should be formed. Place on a tray, then chill until prepared to cook. 2. Heat oil in the Instant Pot by pressing the Sauté button. Add the onion, carrot, and celery, and simmer for approximately 5 minutes, or until just soft. Add pepper, thyme, and minced garlic. For 30 seconds, cook. Keep scraping the pot's bottom, add the wine and simmer for 30 seconds. Click Cancel. 3. Add the remaining ½ teaspoon of salt, water, and vegetable broth. Insert the meatballs slowly. Press the Soup button, close the lid, set the steam release to seal position, and cook the soup for the 20 minutes. 4. When the timer beeps, let pressure release naturally on seal position, about 15 minutes. Open lid and stir in spinach. Replace the lid, press the Keep Warm button, and simmer for 5 minutes. Serve hot.
Per Serving: Calories 1230; Fat: 134g; Sodium 354mg; Carbs: 3.87g; Sugars: 1.4g; Protein 12g

Cheesy Green Soup

Prep Time: 20 minutes | Cook Time: 5 minutes | Serves: 8

3 tablespoons unsalted butter
2 medium carrots, peeled and finely chopped
2 stalks celery, finely chopped
1 medium yellow onion, peeled and finely chopped
1 clove garlic, peeled and minced
½ teaspoon dried thyme
3 cups chopped broccoli florets,

divided
¼ cup all-purpose flour
3 cups Chicken Broth
1 tablespoon water
½ cup heavy cream
2 cups shredded mild Cheddar cheese
1 cup shredded Gruyère cheese

1. Melt butter in the Instant Pot by using the Sauté button. Add the onion, celery, and carrots. Cook for approximately 5 minutes, stirring frequently, until softened. About 30 seconds after adding the garlic, mix in the thyme and 2 cups of the broccoli. 2. Cook for one minute after adding the flour and thoroughly combining. Add the broth gradually, scraping the bottom of the pot as you go. Click the Cancel button. 3. Close the lid, set the steam release to seal position, hit the Pressure Cook button, and select a 5-minute timer. Allow pressure to naturally release for around 15 minutes after the timer beeps on seal

position. Open the lid and use an immersion blender to puree the soup. 4. In a medium bowl that can be microwaved, add the remaining 1 cup of broccoli and water. When broccoli is tender, microwave it for 4 minutes with the cover on. Drain, then add broccoli to pot. 5. Stir in cream, then add cheeses 1 cup at a time, whisking each addition until completely melted before adding another. Serve hot.
Per Serving: Calories 406; Fat: 23g; Sodium 1404mg; Carbs: 18.87g; Sugars: 8.03g; Protein 32.39g

Chicken and Rice Soup with Cream

Prep Time: 20 minutes | Cook Time: 24 minutes | Serves: 8

3 tablespoons unsalted butter
3 stalks celery, chopped
2 medium carrots, peeled and chopped
1 medium yellow onion, peeled and chopped
2 cloves garlic, peeled and smashed
2 tablespoons all-purpose flour
4 cups Chicken Broth, divided

1 bay leaf
1 teaspoon poultry seasoning
½ teaspoon dried thyme
1 teaspoon salt
¼ teaspoon ground black pepper
1 (3-pound) chicken, cut into pieces
½ cup uncooked white rice
½ cup heavy whipping cream

1. Melt butter in the Instant Pot by using the Sauté button. Add the onion, carrots, and celery. Cook, often stirring, for approximately 5 minutes or until veggies soften. Add garlic and cook for 30 seconds, then add flour and cook for 1 minute. 2 cups of broth should be added and well mixed up, being sure to stir bottom. Click the Cancel button. 2. Add salt, pepper, thyme, poultry seasoning, and bay leaf to the pot. Stir thoroughly, add the chicken, and then pour the remaining liquid up to the Max Fill line. Press the Pressure Cook button, close the lid, set the steam release to seal position, and cook the soup for the 20 minutes. 3. Allow pressure to naturally relax for 20 to 25 minutes after the timer beeps. Open lid and press the Cancel button. 4. Get rid of the bay leaf. Chicken should be moved to a chopping board using tongs or a slotted spoon. Using care, shred the meat, removing the skin and bones. Stir the chicken back into the pot. Add the rice, close the lid, set the steam release to seal position, select Pressure Cook, and set the timer for 4 minutes. 5. Quickly release the steam on vent position, take off the lid, and thoroughly stir once the timer beeps. Add cream and serve hot.
Per Serving: Calories 394; Fat: 16.17g; Sodium 866mg; Carbs: 15.87g; Sugars: 1.63g; Protein 43.19g

Healthy Barley Soup

Prep Time: 10 minutes | Cook Time: 30 minutes | Serves: 8

2 tablespoons vegetable oil
½ medium yellow onion, peeled and chopped
1 medium carrot, peeled and chopped
1 stalk celery, chopped
2 cups sliced mushrooms
2 cloves garlic, peeled and minced
½ teaspoon dried thyme
½ teaspoon ground black pepper
1 large russet potato, peeled and cut into ½" cubes

1 (14-ounce) can fire-roasted diced tomatoes, undrained
½ cup medium pearled barley
4 cups Vegetable Broth
2 cups water
1 (15-ounce) can corn, drained
1 (15-ounce) can cut green beans, drained
1 (15-ounce) can Great Northern beans, drained and rinsed
½ teaspoon salt

1. Heat oil in the Instant Pot by pressing the Sauté button. Add the mushrooms, onion, carrot, and celery. Cook for approximately 5 minutes, or until barely tender. Add pepper, garlic, and thyme. For 30 seconds, cook. Press the Cancel button. 2. Barley, potatoes, tomatoes, broth, and water should be added. Press the Soup button, close the lid, set the steam release to seal position, and cook the soup for the preset 20 minutes. 3. Allow pressure to naturally release for around 15 minutes after the timer beeps on seal position. Add corn, green beans, and Great Northern beans after lifting the top and stirring the soup. Replace the lid, choose "Keep Warm," and wait 10 minutes. Remove the lid, then sprinkle with salt. Serve warm.
Per Serving: Calories 1172; Fat: 113g; Sodium 234mg; Carbs: 42g; Sugars: 4.03g; Protein 8g

Vegan Green Soup

Prep Time: 10 minutes | Cook Time: 6 minutes | Serves: 8

3 tablespoons vegetable oil	½ teaspoon dried thyme
3 medium carrots, peeled and finely chopped	¼ teaspoon smoked paprika
1 stalk celery, chopped	½ cup nutritional yeast
1 medium yellow onion, peeled and diced	½ cup whole raw cashews
1 medium russet potato, peeled and chopped	4 cups Vegetable Broth
	1 tablespoon lemon juice
2 cloves garlic, peeled and minced	3 cups chopped broccoli
	½ teaspoon salt

1. Heat oil in the Instant Pot by pressing the Sauté button. Add the onion, celery, and carrots. Cook for approximately 5 minutes, stirring frequently, until softened. 2. Cook the potato, garlic, thyme, and paprika for approximately 30 seconds, or until the garlic and spices are aromatic. Don't hesitate to click Cancel. Add the lemon juice, cashews, broth, and nutritional yeast. Mix thoroughly. 3. Close the lid, set the steam release to seal position, hit the Pressure Cook button, and select a 5-minute timer. Allow pressure to naturally relax for around 15 minutes after the timer chimes. Open the lid and combine the contents in batches or with an immersion blender. 4. Stir thoroughly after adding broccoli to the saucepan. Close the lid, set the steam release to seal position, hit the Pressure Cook button, and set the timer to 1 before pressing the Cancel button. When the timer beeps, quick-release the pressure on vent position. Remove lid, add salt, and stir well. Serve hot.
Per Serving: Calories 1069; Fat: 111.17g; Sodium 404mg; Carbs: 20.7g; Sugars: 3g; Protein 8.39g

Cincinnati Style Chili

Prep Time: 15 minutes | Cook Time: 10 minutes | Serves: 8

2 pounds 90% lean ground beef	2 tablespoons red wine vinegar
3 large yellow onions, peeled and diced, divided	2 tablespoons honey
3 cloves garlic, peeled and minced	1 tablespoon pumpkin pie spice
2 (16-ounce) cans kidney beans, rinsed and drained	1 teaspoon ground cumin
	½ teaspoon ground cardamom
1 (15-ounce) can tomato sauce	¼ teaspoon ground cloves
1 cup Beef Broth	½ teaspoon salt
2 tablespoons chili powder	½ teaspoon freshly cracked black pepper
2 tablespoons semisweet chocolate chips	1 pound cooked spaghetti
	4 cups shredded Cheddar cheese

1. Add the ground beef and ¾ of the diced onion, then press the Sauté button on the Instant Pot. Cook for approximately 8 minutes, turning often, or until the meat is browned and the onion is translucent. Extra fat should be drained and thrown away. For 30 seconds, add the garlic and sauté it. 2. When everything is thoroughly combined, add beans, tomato sauce, broth, chili powder, chocolate chips, vinegar, honey, pumpkin pie spice, cumin, cardamom, cloves, salt, and pepper. Cook for 1 minute, or until the spices are aromatic. 3. To alter the cook time to 10 minutes, click the Pressure Cook button, close the lid, set the steam release to vent, and hit the Cancel button. Quickly remove the pressure on vent position when the timer sounds and open the lid. Good stirring. Add cheese and onions that were set aside to serve over pasta.
Per Serving: Calories 645; Fat: 30.17g; Sodium 1704mg; Carbs: 42.87g; Sugars: 17.03g; Protein 53.39g

Yummiest Soup

Prep Time: 10 minutes | Cook Time: 15 minutes | Serves: 8

2 tablespoons vegetable oil	4 cups Chicken Broth or water
1 medium yellow onion, peeled and chopped	4 cups shredded cooked chicken breast
2 cloves garlic, peeled and minced	1 (15-ounce) can pinto beans, drained and rinsed
2 jalapeño peppers, seeded and minced	1 teaspoon salt
½ teaspoon ground cumin	¼ teaspoon ground black pepper
¼ teaspoon smoked paprika	¼ cup lime juice
1 (15-ounce) can fire-roasted tomatoes, undrained	1 cup shredded Cheddar cheese
½ cup roughly chopped cilantro	3 ounces tortilla chips, roughly crushed

1. Heat oil in the Instant Pot by using the Sauté button. Add the onion and simmer for 5 minutes or until soft. Cook the garlic, jalapenos, cumin, and paprika for approximately a minute, or until fragrant.

Press the Cancel button. 2. Stir in tomatoes, cilantro, and broth. Stir thoroughly, then cover pot, set the steam release to seal position, push the Pressure Cook button, and choose a 5-minute timer on high. 3. Allow pressure to release normally for 15 minutes after the timer beeps, then quickly remove any leftover pressure. Chicken, beans, salt, pepper, and lime juice are added after lifting the lid. Press the Keep Warm button and let soup stand. 4. Divide soup among bowls and garnish with cheese and tortilla chips. Serve hot.
Per Serving: Calories 429; Fat: 15.7g; Sodium 1004mg; Carbs: 18.87g; Sugars: 3.3g; Protein 51.9g

Tomato and Kale Tortellini Soup

Prep Time: 30 minutes | Cook Time: 5 minutes | Serves: 8

1 tablespoon vegetable oil	½ teaspoon black pepper
1 medium yellow onion, peeled and chopped	1 (15-ounce) can diced tomatoes, drained
2 stalks celery, chopped	4 cups Vegetable Broth
1 medium carrot, peeled and chopped	9 ounces cheese tortellini
	½ teaspoon salt
3 cups chopped kale	¼ cup chopped fresh flat-leaf parsley
2 cloves garlic, chopped	
1 teaspoon Italian seasoning	

1. Heat oil in the Instant Pot by pressing the Sauté button. Add kale, onion, celery, and carrot. Cook for approximately 5 minutes, or until barely tender. Add pepper, garlic, and Italian seasoning. For 30 seconds, cook. Cook for 30 seconds after adding the tomatoes. Press the Cancel button. 2. Add 1 cup of water and broth. Stir well. Close the lid, set the steam release to seal position, select Pressure Cook, and set the timer to 5 minutes on high. 3. Allow pressure to naturally release for around 15 minutes after the timer beeps on seal position. Remove lid, add salt and pasta. Press the Cancel button, close lid, set steam release to seal position, press the Pressure Cook button, and set time to 0 minutes. When the timer beeps, quick-release the pressure on vent position. Open lid and stir well. 4. Divide soup into bowls. Top each with parsley and serve hot.
Per Serving: Calories 1029; Fat: 109g; Sodium 797mg; Carbs: 14g; Sugars: 6.55g; Protein 9.45g

Yummy Red Chili

Prep Time: 25 minutes | Cook Time: 30 minutes | Serves: 8

2 dried Anaheim chilies, halved and seeded	1 medium onion, peeled and chopped
2 dried New Mexico chilies, halved and seeded	2 cloves garlic, peeled and minced
1 tablespoon chili powder	1 tablespoon light brown sugar
1 teaspoon ground cumin	½ teaspoon salt
1 (12-ounce) can lager- or bock-style beer, divided	½ teaspoon ground black pepper
1 tablespoon vegetable oil	2 cups Beef Broth
	1½ cups water, divided
2 pounds chili meat made from chuck roast	¼ cup corn masa
	1 tablespoon lime juice
	1 teaspoon hot sauce

1. Place chilies on a baking sheet and cook for 8 minutes on Pressure Cook function High. Place chilies in a large heatproof bowl and cover with hot water. Let chilies soak until tender, about 30 minutes. 2. Chilies should be drained before being blended with cumin, chili powder, and half the beer. Purée for approximately a minute, or until smooth. Place aside. 3. Heat oil in the Instant Pot by using the Sauté button. Add the chili meat, and cook it for 8 minutes while stirring often. Cook for about 10 minutes, or until onions are just soft, before adding the onion, garlic, brown sugar, salt, and pepper. 4. Add the remaining beer, broth, 1 cup water, and chili paste. Stir thoroughly, scraping any crumbs from the pot's bottom. Click the Cancel button. Cook for 30 minutes, then close the lid, set the steam release to seal position, and click the Pressure Cook button on high. 5. Allow pressure to naturally relax on seal position for around 20 minutes after the timer chimes. Lift lid, then thoroughly stir. Press the Sauté button after pressing the Cancel button. 6. In a small bowl mix masa with reserved water. Whisk mixture into the chili, then add lime juice and hot sauce. Bring chili to a boil to thicken, about 5 minutes. Serve hot.
Per Serving: Calories 334; Fat: 10g; Sodium 304mg; Carbs: 8.89g; Sugars: 1.03g; Protein 46.9g

Yummy Baked Potato Soup

Prep Time: 15 minutes | Cook Time: 10 minutes | Serves: 8

4 tablespoons unsalted butter
1 medium yellow onion, peeled and chopped
3 tablespoons all-purpose flour
1 teaspoon salt
½ teaspoon ground black pepper
6 cups Chicken Broth
5 pounds russet potatoes, peeled and cubed
4 ounces cream cheese
1 cup heavy cream
8 slices thick-cut bacon, cooked crisp and chopped
4 scallions, sliced
1 cup shredded Cheddar cheese
1 cup sour cream

1. Melt butter in the Instant Pot by using the Sauté button. Add the onion and simmer for 3 minutes, or until it is soft. Cook the flour, salt, and pepper for about a minute, or until the flour is moistened. Add potatoes after whisking in the broth gradually. Press the Cancel button. 2. Close the lid, set the steam release to seal position, push the Pressure Cook button, and select 10 minutes for the time on high. Allow pressure to naturally release on seal position for around 15 minutes after the timer beeps. 3. Lift lid, then thoroughly stir. Purée the soup using an immersion blender until it is largely smooth with some noticeable potato bits. Cream should be added after the cream cheese has been added and well mixed. Garnish with sour cream, bacon, onions, and Cheddar cheese while still hot.
Per Serving: Calories 795; Fat: 35g; Sodium 1664mg; Carbs: 63g; Sugars: 5.8g; Protein 55g

Ham and Split Pea Soup

Prep Time: 10 minutes | Cook Time: 20 minutes | Serves: 8

4 tablespoons unsalted butter
1 medium yellow onion, peeled and finely diced
2 stalks celery, finely diced
2 cups diced ham steak
2 cloves garlic, peeled and minced
1 pound dried green split peas
6 cups Ham Stock or Chicken Stock
1 bay leaf
½ teaspoon salt
½ teaspoon ground black pepper

1. Melt butter in the Instant Pot by pressing the Sauté button. Add the ham, onion, and celery. three minutes for sautéing. Add the garlic and heat for 30 seconds or until fragrant. Press the Cancel button. 2. To the pot, add the peas, stock, bay leaf, salt, and pepper. Close the lid, select Pressure Cook, and set the timer for 20 minutes. Release the pressure quickly on vent position once the timer beeps. Open the lid, press the Cancel button, then throw out the bay leaf. 3. Blend one-third of the soup until smooth, then add it back to the pot and thoroughly mix. Serve warm.
Per Serving: Calories 968; Fat: 25.17g; Sodium 1662mg; Carbs: 15.7g; Sugars: 2.43g; Protein 161g

Bacon and Cabbage Soup

Prep Time: 20 minutes | Cook Time: 3 minutes | Serves: 8

2 tablespoons vegetable oil
8 slices thick-cut bacon, chopped
2 medium yellow onions, peeled and chopped
1 large head cabbage, cored and chopped
2 cloves garlic, peeled and minced
4 cups Vegetable Broth
1 cup Bone Broth
¼ teaspoon crushed red pepper flakes
½ teaspoon salt
½ teaspoon ground black pepper

1. Heat oil in the Instant Pot by pressing the Sauté button. Add the bacon and cook for approximately 8 minutes, or until the edges are just beginning to brown. Add the onions and simmer for 5 minutes or until they are soft. Cook the garlic and cabbage together for approximately a minute, or until aromatic. Press the Cancel button. 2. Mix in the broths and the red pepper flakes. Stir thoroughly, fasten the lid, select Pressure Cook, and set the timer for 3 minutes on high. 3. Allow the pressure to naturally release on seal position for 20 to 25 minutes after the timer sounds. Add salt and pepper after opening the lid. Serve hot.
Per Serving: Calories 1072; Fat: 117g; Sodium 294mg; Carbs: 8.72g; Sugars: 4.03g; Protein 9.39g

Chicken and Rice Soup with Lemon

Prep Time: 10 minutes | Cook Time: 5 minutes | Serves: 8

2 tablespoons vegetable oil
2 stalks celery, sliced
1 medium carrot, peeled and chopped
1 medium yellow onion, peeled and chopped
2 cloves garlic, peeled and minced
½ teaspoon dried thyme
1 bay leaf
4 cups Chicken Broth or water
3 cups shredded cooked chicken breast
½ cup uncooked white rice
¼ cup lemon juice
2 tablespoons chopped fresh flat-leaf parsley
1 teaspoon salt
¼ teaspoon ground black pepper

1. Heat oil in the Instant Pot by pressing the Sauté button. Cook the celery, carrot, and onion for approximately 5 minutes or until they are soft. Cook the garlic and thyme for about a minute, or until fragrant. Press the Cancel button. 2. Rice, chicken, and broth should all be added. Stir thoroughly, then cover container, set the steam release to seal position, push the Pressure Cook button, and choose a 5-minute timer on high. 3. Allow pressure to release normally for 15 minutes after the timer beeps on seal, then quickly remove any leftover pressure on vent position. Remove lid, add salt, pepper, parsley, and lemon juice. Remove and discard bay leaf. Serve hot.
Per Serving: Calories 366; Fat: 13.57g; Sodium 834mg; Carbs: 13.87g; Sugars: 1.43g; Protein 43.39g

Basil Tomato Fresh Soup

Prep Time: 20 minutes | Cook Time: 5 minutes | Serves: 4

¼ cup olive oil
1 medium yellow onion, peeled and chopped
4 cloves garlic, minced
8 large tomatoes, peeled and cut into big chunks
1 bay leaf
1 tablespoon sugar
¼ cup chopped basil
1 teaspoon dried oregano
1 teaspoon dried fennel
1 teaspoon salt
½ teaspoon black pepper
2 cups Vegetable Broth or Chicken Broth
2 tablespoons unsalted butter
½ cup heavy cream

1. Heat olive oil in the Instant Pot by pressing the Sauté button. After approximately 5 minutes of cooking the onion until it is tender, add the garlic and sauté it for about 30 seconds until it is fragrant. 2. Cook for 4-5 minutes, or until tomatoes begin to release juice, after adding the bay leaf and tomatoes. 3. Add honey, basil, oregano, fennel, salt, pepper, and broth after pressing the Cancel button. Stir thoroughly, then cover. Press the Pressure Cook button, set the steam release to seal position, then set the timer for 5 minutes on high. 4. Quickly remove the pressure when the timer beeps on vent, then click Cancel. Open the lid, add the melted butter, and then mix in the cream. Discard bay leaf. 5. Purée soup with an immersion blender or transfer to a blender and purée until smooth. If you prefer a slightly chunky soup, only purée half or three-quarters of the soup. Serve hot.
Per Serving: Calories 255; Fat: 17g; Sodium 1101mg; Carbs: 23g; Sugars: 14g; Protein 4.8g

Fast Tomato Lentil Soup

Prep Time: 5 minutes | Cook Time: 30 minutes | Serves: 4

2 teaspoons cornstarch
6 cups plus 4 teaspoons cold water, divided
1 cup dried lentils
1 (28-ounce) can diced tomatoes, drained
1 chicken or vegetable bouillon
cube (optional)
1 tablespoon onion powder
2 teaspoons brown sugar (optional)
1 teaspoon fine sea salt
¼ teaspoon ground black pepper
Chopped fresh basil, for garnish

1. Make a slurry in a small bowl by thoroughly combining the cornstarch with the 4 teaspoons of cold water. The inner cooking pot should be filled with the lentils, tomatoes, 6 cups of water, slurry, bouillon (if used), onion powder, brown sugar (if using), salt, and pepper. 2. Turn the valve to seal position and secure the lid in place. Select Pressure Cook and set the pressure to High when cooking. A 12-minute timer should be set. After cooking is finished, flip the valve to vent position to quickly remove any leftover steam. After 10 minutes, let the pressure dissipate naturally. 3. Remove lid. Stir the soup, taste it, and make any necessary flavor adjustments. Stir in the basil.
Per Serving: Calories 75; Fat: 1g; Sodium 784mg; Carbs: 16g; Sugars: 7g; Protein 3g

Soup with Broccoli and Cheese

Prep Time: 5 minutes | Cook Time: 30 minutes | Serves: 4

2 tablespoons unsalted butter
1 small onion, chopped
1 cup sliced carrots
2 (14-ounce) cans low-sodium chicken or vegetable broth
1 tablespoon all-purpose flour
1 cup milk

1 (16-ounce) package frozen chopped broccoli, thawed
1 cup half-and-half
2 cups shredded Cheddar cheese
1 teaspoon fine sea salt
½ teaspoon ground black pepper

1. Choose Sauté and set the temperature to Medium. Butter should be added to the inner cooking kettle. Add the onion and carrots to the foaming butter and cook for 3 minutes. Put the broth in. 2. Turn the valve to seal position and secure the lid in place. Choose Pressure Cook. Set the pressure to High when cooking. A 12-minute timer should be set. After cooking is finished, set the valve to vent position to quickly remove any leftover pressure. After 5 minutes, let the pressure dissipate naturally. 3. Mix the milk and flour together in a small bowl. Broccoli should be added to the heated soup after unlocking and removing the pot's lid. Combine the milk and flour; add the half-and-half; and whisk. Stir in the cheese until melted. Season with salt and pepper.
Per Serving: Calories 717; Fat: 22g; Sodium 2304mg; Carbs: 95g; Sugars: 38g; Protein 58.39g

Soup Lasagna

Prep Time: 5 minutes | Cook Time: 30 minutes | Serves: 4

1 tablespoon unsalted butter
1 small onion, chopped
1 tablespoon minced garlic
1 green bell pepper, seeded and chopped (optional)
1 pound Italian sausage, casings removed
2 (24-ounce) jars pasta sauce

4 cups low-sodium beef broth
1 tablespoon Italian seasoning
8 ounces lasagna noodles, broken up
1 cup ricotta cheese, for serving (optional)
1 cup shredded mozzarella cheese, for serving

1. Choose Sauté. Butter should be added to the inner cooking kettle. When it begins to froth, add the sausage, onion, garlic, bell pepper (if using), and continue to sauté for an additional 5 minutes while breaking up the meat. 2. Pasta sauce, stock, and Italian spice should all be added at this point. Add the broken lasagna noodles and give them a good toss to coat them. 3. Turn the valve to seal position and secure the lid in place. Choose Pressure Cook. Set the pressure to High when cooking. A 4-minute timer should be set. When cooking ends, let the pressure release naturally for 10 minutes, then turn the valve to vent position to quickly release the remaining pressure. 4. Remove the lid. Stir the soup and add into bowls. Garnish each bowl with a dollop of ricotta cheese (if using) and a sprinkle of mozzarella.
Per Serving: Calories 740; Fat: 35.17g; Sodium 1800mg; Carbs: 74.87g; Sugars: 4.03g; Protein 59.39g

Cheddar and Bratwurst Soup Wisconsin

Prep Time: 5 minutes | Cook Time: 25 minutes | Serves: 8

4 tablespoons (½ stick) unsalted butter
1 (28-ounce) bag frozen potatoes O'Brien
1 celery stalk, chopped (optional)
2 carrots, chopped
¼ cup all-purpose flour
2 (14-ounce) cans low-sodium chicken broth

1 tablespoon Dijon mustard
½ small head cabbage, shredded (optional)
1 pound smoked sausage, cut into bite-size pieces
2 cups milk or half-and-half
2 cups shredded sharp Cheddar cheese

1. Choose Sauté. The butter should be heated in the inner cooking pot until it foams. For five minutes, add the potatoes, carrots, and celery (if using). 2. When the veggies are evenly covered, add the flour and stir the mixture constantly. Add the broth gradually while swirling frequently to incorporate the roux into the liquid. Stir the mustard to remove any lumps before adding it. Add the sausage and cabbage, if using. 3. Turn the valve to seal position and secure the lid in place. Choose Pressure Cook. Adjust the heat to High. Set the time for 5 minutes. When cooking ends, carefully turn the valve to vent position to quick-release. 4. Unlock and remove the lid and stir the milk into the soup. Add the cheese and stir until it melts.

Per Serving: Calories 375; Fat: 21g; Sodium 1404mg; Carbs: 26g; Sugars: 9g; Protein 23g

Bean Soup

Prep Time: 5 minutes | Cook Time: 50 minutes | Serves: 4

2 tablespoons olive oil
1 cup finely chopped onion
1 cup finely chopped celery (optional)
2 medium carrots, finely chopped
2 garlic cloves, minced

1 pound dried navy beans
8 cups low-sodium chicken broth or water
2 ham hocks (optional)
1 teaspoon fine sea salt

1. Choose Sauté. When the oil is added, heat it until shimmering. For five minutes, add the onion, carrots, garlic, and celery (if using). 2. Wash the beans, then throw away any that float. Stir in the beans, broth, salt, and ham hocks (if using). 3. Turn the valve to seal position and secure the lid in place. Choose Pressure Cook. Set the pressure to High when cooking. Time for 25 minutes. When you're done cooking, switch the valve to vent position to quickly relieve the pressure after letting it naturally dissipate for 20 minutes. 4. Open the lid, take it off, and check the beans for doneness. To thicken the soup, mash some of the beans against the Instant Pot side with a fork.
Per Serving: Calories 147; Fat: 8g; Sodium 636mg; Carbs: 15g; Sugars: 4g; Protein 6.39g

Soup with Chicken Enchilada

Prep Time: 5 minutes | Cook Time: 25 minutes | Serves: 4

2 boneless, skinless chicken breasts
1 (15-ounce) can kidney beans, rinsed and drained
1 (14-ounce) can diced tomatoes, drained
1 (14-ounce) can sweet corn kernels, drained
1 small onion, chopped

1 green bell pepper, seeded, and diced (optional)
1 jalapeño, seeded and diced (optional)
1 (10-ounce) can enchilada sauce
½ cup low-sodium chicken broth
1½ cups milk
3 tablespoons cornstarch
3 tablespoons cold water

1. In the inner cooking pot, combine the chicken, beans, tomatoes, corn, onion, peppers, enchilada sauce, and stock. 2. Turn the valve to seal position and secure the lid in place. Choose Pressure Cook, then choose High. Set the time for 5 minutes. After 10 minutes, let the steam dissipate naturally. After cooking is finished, flip the valve to vent positio to quickly remove any leftover steam. 3. Unlock and remove the lid. Place the chicken on a plate or chopping board. Use two forks to shred, or slice into bite-sized pieces. Add the milk and the chicken back to the saucepan, stirring. In a small bowl, combine the cornstarch and cold water and whisk until the mixture is smooth. The soup will begin to gently thicken as you whisk in the slurry.
Per Serving: Calories 670; Fat: 37g; Sodium 1004mg; Carbs: 35g; Sugars: 13g; Protein 61g

Espresso Chili

Prep Time: 5 minutes | Cook Time: 20 minutes | Serves: 6

1 tablespoon vegetable oil
1-pound lean ground beef
2 onions, chopped
2 garlic cloves, minced
2 (16-ounce) cans kidney beans, rinsed and drained

1 (14-ounce) can tomato purée
1 (14-ounce) can stewed tomatoes, drained
2 tablespoons chili powder
½ teaspoon fine sea salt

1. Choose Sauté. The inner cooking pot should contain oil. When it is heated, add the onions, garlic, and ground beef. Cook, turning periodically, for approximately 5 minutes, or until the meat is browned. 2. Salt, chili powder, tomato purée, stewed tomatoes, and beans should all be added. Stir and slowly bring to a boil. 3. Turn the valve to seal position and secure the lid in place. Choose Pressure Cook. Set the pressure to High when cooking. Set the time for 15 minutes. Turn the valve carefully to vent position when cooking is finished to quickly release pressure. 4. Unlock and remove the lid. To mash the beans and thicken the soup, press them against the side of the Instant Pot with a fork.
Per Serving: Calories 455; Fat: 21g; Sodium 704mg; Carbs: 24g; Sugars: 8g; Protein 35g

Chili Beer Chipotle

Prep Time: 25 minutes | Cook Time: 35 minutes | Serves: 8

2 pounds chili meat made from chuck roast
1 medium onion, peeled and chopped
3 cloves garlic, peeled and minced
3 tablespoons minced chipotle in adobo
2 tablespoons chili powder
1 teaspoon ground cumin
½ teaspoon ground coriander

2 tablespoons light brown sugar
½ teaspoon salt
½ teaspoon ground black pepper
2 cups Beef Broth
1 (12-ounce) bottle lager-style beer
½ cup water
¼ cup corn masa
1 tablespoon lime juice

1. Use the Instant Pot Sauté function to thoroughly brown the chili meat for around 10 minutes. Cook for approximately 10 minutes, or until the onions are just soft, adding the onion, garlic, chipotle, chili powder, cumin, coriander, brown sugar, salt, and pepper as needed. 2. Combine the beer and broth. Press the Cancel button, secure the lid, choose vent for the steam release, select Pressure Cook, and cook for the 30 minutes on high. 3. Quickly remove the steam on vent position, then open the lid and thoroughly stir when the timer sounds. Press the Sauté button after you've pressed the Cancel button. Water, masa, and chili are all whisked together. Stirring regularly, bring to a boil for 5 minutes or until it begins to thicken. Add the lime juice after pressing the Cancel button. Serve hot.
Per Serving: Calories 294; Fat: 9g; Sodium 374mg; Carbs: 6g; Sugars: 1.03g; Protein 45.39g

Heart Healthy Soup

Prep Time: 20 minutes | Cook Time: 25 minutes | Serves: 8

1 tablespoon vegetable oil
½ pound 90% lean ground beef
½ medium yellow onion, peeled and chopped
1 medium carrot, peeled and chopped
1 stalk celery, chopped
1 medium green bell pepper, seeded and chopped
1 (15-ounce) can diced tomatoes, undrained

1 large russet potato, peeled and cut into ½" cubes
½ cup medium pearled barley
2 cloves garlic, peeled and minced
½ teaspoon dried thyme
½ teaspoon ground black pepper
4 cups Beef Broth
2 cups water
1 (15-ounce) can cut green beans, drained
½ teaspoon salt

1. Heat oil in the Instant Pot by pressing the Sauté button. Add the beef and brown it well for 8 minutes. Add the bell pepper, onion, carrot, and celery. Cook for approximately 5 minutes, or until barely tender. Include tomatoes, potatoes, barley, black pepper, thyme, garlic, broth, and water. Press the Cancel button. 2. Press the Soup button, close the lid, set the steam release to seal position, and cook the soup for the 20 minutes. Allow pressure to naturally release for around 15 minutes after the timer beeps. Remove the lid, give soup a stir, then add salt and green beans. Replace the lid, press the Keep Warm button, and simmer for 5 minutes. Serve warm.
Per Serving: Calories 321; Fat: 12.17g; Sodium 182mg; Carbs: 24g; Sugars: 3g; Protein 31.39g

Yummy Beany Pasta

Prep Time: 20 minutes | Cook Time: 23 minutes | Serves: 8

1-pound bulk Italian sausage
1 medium yellow onion, peeled and chopped
2 stalks celery, chopped
1 large carrot, peeled and chopped
2 cloves garlic, peeled and chopped
½ teaspoon dried thyme
1 teaspoon Italian seasoning
½ teaspoon ground black pepper
1 (15-ounce) can diced tomatoes,

undrained
4 cups Chicken Broth
1 cup water
1 cup dried cannellini beans, soaked overnight and drained
1 cup ditalini pasta
1 cup grated Parmesan cheese
2 tablespoons chopped fresh flat-leaf parsley
2 tablespoons chopped fresh basil

1. On the Instant Pot, click the Sauté button. Add the sausage and cook it for approximately 8 minutes, breaking it up into bite-sized pieces as it browns. Cook the carrot, celery, and onion for approximately 5 minutes, or until they are barely soft. Pepper, Italian spice, garlic, and thyme should be added. 30 second cook time. After scraping the pot's bottom, add the tomatoes and heat for 30 seconds. Press the Cancel button. 2. Add the beans, water, and broth. Good stirring. Press the Soup button, close the lid, set the steam release to seal position, and

cook the soup for the preset 20 minutes. 3. Allow pressure to naturally release on seal position for about 15 minutes after the timer beeps. Add pasta and shake off the lid. Close the lid, set the steam release to seal position, hit the Pressure Cook button, and set the timer for 3 minutes before pressing the Cancel button. 4. Divide soup into bowls. Top each with cheese, parsley, and basil. Serve hot.
Per Serving: Calories 571; Fat: 32g; Sodium 1004mg; Carbs: 26g; Sugars: 4.03g; Protein 4 6.39g

Classic Beef Chili

Prep Time: 25 minutes | Cook Time: 35 minutes | Serves: 8

2 pounds chili meat made from chuck roast
1 medium onion, peeled and chopped
3 cloves garlic, peeled and minced
¼ cup chili powder
1 teaspoon ground cumin

2 tablespoons light brown sugar
½ teaspoon salt
½ teaspoon ground black pepper
2 cups Beef Broth
2½ cups water, divided
¼ cup corn masa
1 tablespoon lime juice

1. Use the Instant Pot Sauté function to thoroughly brown the meat for 10 minutes. Cook for approximately 10 minutes, until the onions are just starting to get soft, adding the onion, garlic, chili powder, cumin, brown sugar, salt, and pepper. 2. Stir thoroughly after adding 2 cups of water and broth. Press the Cancel button, secure the lid, choose vent position for the steam release, select Pressure Cook, and cook for the 30 minutes on high. 3. Quickly remove the pressure on vent position, open the lid, and stir well when the timer sounds. Press the Sauté button after you've pressed the Cancel button. Masa and any reserved water are whisked together, then the chili is added. Stirring regularly, bring to a boil for 5 minutes or until it begins to thicken. Then add lime juice after pressing the Cancel button. Serve hot.
Per Serving: Calories 299; Fat: 9g; Sodium 385mg; Carbs: 7g; Sugars: 1.03g; Protein 46.9g

Chili with Beans and Beef

Prep Time: 20 minutes | Cook Time: 20 minutes | Serves: 8

1 pound 80% lean ground beef
1 medium onion, peeled and chopped
2 cloves garlic, peeled and minced
¼ cup chili powder
1 teaspoon ground cumin
½ teaspoon ground coriander
2 tablespoons brown sugar

½ teaspoon salt
½ teaspoon ground black pepper
1 (14.5-ounce) can diced tomatoes
2 cups dried pinto beans, soaked overnight in water to cover and drained
2 cups Beef Broth
1 tablespoon lime juice

1. Use the Instant Pot Sauté function to brown the meat for 10 minutes or until no pink is visible. Cook for approximately 10 minutes, or until the onions are barely soft, adding the brown sugar, salt, pepper, chili powder, cumin, and coriander. 2. Stir thoroughly before adding tomatoes, soaking beans, and broth. Close the lid, set the steam release to seal position, click the Pressure Cook button, and set the timer for 20 minutes before pressing the Cancel button. 3. Allow pressure to naturally release on seal position for around 20 minutes after the timer chimes. Open lid and press the Cancel button. Add the lime juice, then thoroughly whisk. Serve hot.
Per Serving: Calories 409; Fat: 11g; Sodium 418mg; Carbs: 38.7g; Sugars: 5.03g; Protein 39g

Ham and Black-Eyed Peas

Prep Time: 10 minutes | Cook Time: 20 minutes | Serves: 10

1 pkg. (16 oz.) dried black-eyed peas
4 cups water
1 cup cubed fully cooked ham
1 medium onion, finely chopped

3 garlic cloves, minced
2 tsp. seasoned salt
1 tsp. pepper
Thinly sliced green onions, optional

1. Black-eyed peas should be sorted and rinsed. Transfer them to the Instant pot. Ham, onion, garlic, seasoned salt, water and pepper are all stirred in. Close the pressure-release valve and lock the lid. Adjust to Pressure Cook on high for 18 minutes. Allow any leftover pressure to naturally release for ten minutes on seal position before quick-releasing it on vent position. 2. Serve with a slotted spoon. Add some thinly sliced green onions if desired.
Per Serving: Calories 40; Fat: 1g; Sodium 788mg; Carbs: 2.87g; Sugars: 1g; Protein 4g

Sweet Potato and Beef chili

Prep Time: 20 minutes | Cook Time: 15 minutes | Serves: 6

2 pounds 80% lean ground beef
1 medium onion, peeled and finely chopped
1 (14.5-ounce) can diced tomatoes, drained
3 cloves garlic, peeled and minced
¼ cup chili powder
½ teaspoon ground cumin

½ teaspoon dried oregano
½ teaspoon smoked paprika
½ teaspoon salt
½ teaspoon ground black pepper
1 (28-ounce) can crushed tomatoes
2 cups Chicken Broth
2 medium sweet potatoes, peeled and diced

1. Utilizing the Sauté function on the Instant Pot, brown the meat for 10 minutes while thoroughly crushing it. Add the onion and simmer for 5 minutes or until soft. Cook for 2 minutes or until aromatic after adding the tomatoes, garlic, chili powder, cumin, oregano, paprika, salt, and pepper. 2. Stir thoroughly after adding the broth, tomatoes, and sweet potatoes. Close the lid, set the steam release to seal position, click the Pressure Cook button, and set the timer to 15 minutes. Then press the Cancel button. 3. Allow pressure to naturally release on seal position for around 20 minutes after the timer beeps. Lift lid, then thoroughly stir. Serve hot.
Per Serving: Calories 516; Fat: 20g; Sodium 761mg; Carbs: 21g; Sugars: 9.73g; Protein 60.7g

Chili with Buffalo Chicken

Prep Time: 15 minutes | Cook Time: 32 minutes | Serves: 6

1 tablespoon vegetable oil
1 medium onion, peeled and chopped
1 stalk celery, finely chopped
2 cloves garlic, peeled and minced
½ cup Buffalo-style hot sauce
½ teaspoon salt
½ teaspoon ground black pepper
1 (15-ounce) can fire-roasted tomatoes, drained

2 (15-ounce) cans cannellini beans, drained and rinsed
2 cups Chicken Broth
3 (6-ounce) bone-in chicken breasts, skin removed
8 ounces cream cheese, cubed, at room temperature
1 cup shredded Monterey jack cheese
¼ cup sliced scallions

1. Heat oil in the Instant Pot by pressing the Sauté button. Cook the onion, celery, and garlic for approximately 5 minutes, or until the onions are just starting to soften. 2. Stir in the spicy sauce, salt, pepper, tomatoes, and beans. Add chicken breasts and broth. Close the lid, set the steam release to seal position, click the Pressure Cook button, and set the timer for 30 minutes on high. 3. Allow pressure to naturally release on seal position for around 20 minutes after the timer beeps. Open lid and press the Cancel button. With two forks, carefully remove the chicken, pull the flesh from the bones, and shred. Place aside. 4. Select Sauté. Cream cheese should be added and properly mixed up. Cook the chicken and cheese shreds for approximately two minutes, or until the cheese is smooth and melted. Press the Cancel button. Serve hot with scallions for garnish.
Per Serving: Calories 688; Fat: 42g; Sodium 1002mg; Carbs: 13g; Sugars: 6.2g; Protein 62g

Garlic with Broccoli

Prep Time: 5 minutes | Cook Time: 9 minutes | Serves: 4

3 tablespoons olive oil
2 medium heads broccoli, cut into florets

½ teaspoon salt
½ teaspoon black pepper
4 cloves garlic, crushed

1. Click the Sauté button. Add oil, heat for one minute. 2. Add the broccoli, seasonings, and stir. With the lid on, heat for 4 minutes while stirring now and then. 3. Add garlic and cover the lid. Allow it simmer for a further 4 minutes while stirring periodically. 4. Remove from heat and serve hot.
Per Serving: Calories 95; Fat: 10g; Sodium 291mg; Carbs: 2g; Sugars: 0.03g; Protein 0.39g

Chili Macaroni with Cheese

Prep Time: 25 minutes | Cook Time: 34 minutes | Serves: 8

1-pound chili meat made from chuck roast
1 medium onion, peeled and finely chopped

1 medium red bell pepper, seeded and finely chopped
1 medium carrot, peeled and finely chopped

1 (15-ounce) can fire-roasted tomatoes, drained
3 cloves garlic, peeled and minced
2 tablespoons chili powder
1 teaspoon ground cumin
½ teaspoon dried oregano
½ teaspoon salt

½ teaspoon ground black pepper
2 cups Beef Broth
6 ounces elbow macaroni
4 ounces cream cheese
¼ cup heavy cream
1½ cups shredded mild Cheddar cheese

1. Use the Instant Pot's Sauté function to thoroughly brown the chili meat for around 10 minutes. Add onion, bell pepper, and carrot once it has browned. Cook for approximately 8 minutes, or until the veggies are soft. Cook the tomatoes, garlic, cumin, oregano, chili powder, salt, and black pepper for approximately two minutes, or until aromatic. 2. Stir thoroughly after adding broth. Press the Cancel button, secure the lid, choose vent for the steam release, select Pressure Cook, and cook for the 30 minutes on low. 3. Quickly remove the steam on vent position when the timer sounds, then open the lid and thoroughly stir. Then add macaroni after pressing the Cancel button. Close the lid, set the steam release to seal position, select Pressure Cook, and set the timer for 4 minutes. When the timer beeps, quick-release the pressure. Open lid and stir well. Add cream cheese and stir until melted. Add cream and Cheddar cheese and stir until cheese is completely melted. Serve hot.
Per Serving: Calories 348; Fat: 13g; Sodium 424mg; Carbs: 23g; Sugars: 4.03g; Protein 34.39g

Easy Veggie Chili

Prep Time: 10 minutes | Cook Time: 30 minutes | Serves: 8

1 tablespoon olive oil
2 medium white onions, peeled and finely chopped
1 medium red bell pepper, seeded and finely chopped
1 medium carrot, peeled and finely chopped
2 small jalapeño peppers, seeded and finely chopped
2 cloves garlic, minced
1 (28-ounce) can diced tomatoes
1 (15-ounce) can tomato sauce
¼ cup chili powder

¼ cup chopped cilantro
1 tablespoon smoked paprika
1½ teaspoons ground cumin
1 teaspoon ground coriander
½ teaspoon salt
½ teaspoon black pepper
2 cups dried kidney beans, soaked overnight in water to cover and drained
½ cup bulgur wheat
3 cups Vegetable Broth
1 cup water

1. Heat oil in the Instant Pot by pressing the Sauté button. Add the onions, bell pepper, and carrot and sauté for about 8 minutes, or until the veggies are soft. Garlic and jalapenos should be cooked for approximately a minute, or until aromatic. Don't hesitate to click Cancel. 2. In a pot, combine the beans, bulgur, tomatoes, tomato sauce, chili powder, cilantro, paprika, cumin, coriander, salt, and black pepper. Put the cover on, choose vent for the steam release, select Pressure Cook, and cook for the 30 minutes. 3. Quickly remove the pressure on vent position, then open the lid and thoroughly stir when the timer sounds. If the chili is too thin, click the Cancel and Sauté buttons, then let the chill simmer, covered, until the appropriate thickness is achieved. Serve warm.
Per Serving: Calories 766; Fat: 80g; Sodium 457mg; Carbs: 17g; Sugars: 7.03g; Protein 4.39g

Tomato-Based Spaghetti Squash

Prep Time: 15 minutes | Cook Time: 10 minutes | Serves: 10

1 medium spaghetti squash, halved lengthwise, seeds removed
1 can (14 oz.) diced tomatoes, drained
¼ cup sliced green olives with pimientos

1 tsp. dried oregano
½ tsp. salt
½ tsp. pepper
½ cup shredded cheddar cheese
¼ cup minced fresh basil

1. In the Instant Pot, add a steam rack and 1 cup of water. Overlap the squash as necessary to fit it on the rack. Close the lid. Adjust to Pressure Cook for 7 minutes on high. Quickly release pressure on vent position. Select Cancel. 2. Drain cooking liquid from pot after removing squash and rack. Squash skin should be discarded after cutting the squash into spaghetti-like strands. Return squash to pot. Add salt, pepper, oregano, tomatoes, and olives to the mixture. Choose the sauté option. For approximately 3 minutes, stir and cook until well cooked. Add cheese and basil on top.
Per Serving: Calories 40; Fat: 1g; Sodium 304mg; Carbs: 4g; Sugars: 2.03g; Protein 2.39g

Chili De Veau

Prep Time: 20 minutes | Cook Time: 30 minutes | Serves: 8

2 pounds ground venison
1 medium yellow onion, peeled and chopped
1 medium poblano pepper, seeded and chopped
2 cloves garlic, peeled and minced
1 (28-ounce) can diced tomatoes
¼ cup chili powder
1 teaspoon ground cumin

1 teaspoon smoked paprika
½ teaspoon dried oregano
½ teaspoon salt
½ teaspoon ground black pepper
1 cup dried kidney beans, soaked overnight in water to cover and drained
4 cups Beef Broth
1 teaspoon Worcestershire sauce

1. Use the Instant Pot Sauté function to thoroughly brown the venison for around 10 minutes. Cook the ingredients for about 10 minutes, until the onions are just tender: onion, poblano pepper, garlic, tomatoes, chili powder, cumin, paprika, oregano, salt, and black pepper. 2. Stir thoroughly after adding the beans, stock, and Worcestershire sauce to the saucepan. Press the Cancel button, secure the lid, choose vent for the steam release, select Pressure Cook, and cook for the 30 minutes on low. 3. Quickly remove the steam on vent position when the timer beeps, then open the lid and thoroughly stir. Serve hot.
Per Serving: Calories 356; Fat: 16.17g; Sodium 542mg; Carbs: 9.7g; Sugars: 4g; Protein 45g

Turkish Chili

Prep Time: 15 minutes | Cook Time: 30 minutes | Serves: 8

2 pounds ground turkey
1 medium onion, peeled and chopped
1 medium carrot, peeled and finely chopped
3 cloves garlic, peeled and minced
1 small jalapeño pepper, seeded and minced
¼ cup chili powder
1 teaspoon ground cumin

½ teaspoon smoked paprika
1 tablespoon light brown sugar
½ teaspoon salt
½ teaspoon ground black pepper
2 cups Chicken Broth
1 cup water
1 (15-ounce) can kidney beans, drained and rinsed
1 tablespoon lime juice

1. Use the Instant Pot Sauté function to thoroughly brown the turkey for 10 minutes. It takes around 3 minutes to sauté the onion, carrot, garlic, jalapeño, chili powder, cumin, and paprika until they are aromatic. Cook for 30 seconds after adding salt, pepper, and brown sugar. 2. Add water and broth. Stir thoroughly, click the Cancel button, close the lid, choose Vent for the steam release, select Pressure Cook, and cook on Low for 30 minutes. 3. Quickly remove the steam, then open the lid and thoroughly stir when the timer sounds. Beans will heat up after 10 minutes of standing after being stirred in with lime juice. If the chili is too thin, click the Cancel and Sauté buttons, then let the chill simmer, covered, until the appropriate thickness is achieved. Serve warm.
Per Serving: Calories 670; Fat: 54g; Sodium 366mg; Carbs: 7g; Sugars: 1.3g; Protein 36.9g

Lamb and Chili

Prep Time: 15 minutes | Cook Time: 30 minutes | Serves: 6

3 tablespoons extra-virgin olive oil
2 pounds ground lamb
1 large yellow onion, peeled and diced
4 cloves garlic, peeled and minced
2 tablespoons chili powder
1 tablespoon ground cumin
½ teaspoon oregano
2 small jalapeño peppers, seeded and minced
2 medium green bell peppers,

seeded and diced
1 (28-ounce) can diced tomatoes
1 (8-ounce) can tomato sauce
1 teaspoon Worcestershire sauce
1 cup dried white beans, soaked overnight in water to cover and drained
½ teaspoon salt
½ teaspoon freshly cracked black pepper

1. Heat oil in the Instant Pot by pressing the Sauté button. Cumin, chili powder, onion, and lamb should all be added to the pot. For about 8 minutes, cook the lamb while crumbling it until the meat is browned and the onion is translucent. Cook the bell peppers, jalapenos, and oregano for approximately 5 minutes, or until the bell peppers are just soft. Press the Cancel button. 2. Beans, salt, black pepper, tomato sauce, Worcestershire sauce, and tomatoes should be added. Stir thoroughly, cover, set the steam release to seal position, select Pressure Cook, and cook for the 30 minutes. Allow pressure to naturally release for around 20 minutes after the timer beeps. Open lid, then thoroughly stir. Serve hot.
Per Serving: Calories 490; Fat: 23g; Sodium 643mg; Carbs: 32g;

Sugars: 7g; Protein 41g

Chili with Chicken and White Beans

Prep Time: 20 minutes | Cook Time: 30 minutes | Serves: 6

1 tablespoon vegetable oil
1 medium onion, peeled and chopped
2 cloves garlic, peeled and minced
1 tablespoon ground cumin
1 teaspoon ground coriander
½ teaspoon salt
½ teaspoon ground black pepper

2 (6-ounce) cans diced green chilies
2 cups dried white beans, soaked overnight in water to cover and drained
2 cups Chicken Broth
3 (6-ounce) bone-in chicken breasts, skin removed

1. Heat oil in the Instant Pot by pressing the Sauté button. Cook for approximately 10 minutes, or until the onions are just soft, adding the onion, garlic, cumin, coriander, salt, and pepper. 2. Stir thoroughly after adding the green chilies, beans, and broth. Insert chicken breasts. Close the lid, set the steam release to seal position, click the Pressure Cook button, and set the timer for 30 minutes. 3. Allow pressure to naturally release for around 20 minutes after the timer beeps. Open lid. With two forks, carefully remove the chicken, pull the flesh from the bones, and shred. Place aside. 4. One cup of the liquid-bean mixture should be taken out of the pot and mashed with a fork or puréed in a food processor. Stir chicken and mashed beans into pot. Serve hot.
Per Serving: Calories 724; Fat: 26g; Sodium 1504mg; Carbs: 60g; Sugars: 4.03g; Protein 68.39g

Pork with Black-Eyed Pea Chili

Prep Time: 30 minutes | Cook Time: 30 minutes | Serves: 6

2 tablespoons vegetable oil
2 pounds boneless pork shoulder, cut into 1" pieces
1 medium onion, peeled and finely chopped
1 (14.5-ounce) can diced tomatoes, drained
3 cloves garlic, peeled and minced
3 tablespoons chili powder

1 teaspoon ground cumin
½ teaspoon ground coriander
½ teaspoon salt
½ teaspoon ground black pepper
4 cups Chicken Broth
2 cups dried black-eyed peas, soaked overnight in water to cover and drained
1 tablespoon lime juice

1. Heat oil in the Instant Pot by pressing the Sauté button. Working in batches will help to avoid the pork from steaming. Add half the pork to the saucepan in an equal layer. Cook for three minutes on each side. Repeat with the remaining pork after transferring it to a platter and setting it aside. 2. Add the onion to the saucepan and simmer for 5 minutes or until it is soft. Cook the tomatoes, garlic, chili powder, cumin, coriander, salt, and pepper for approximately two minutes, or until the mixture is aromatic. 3. Stir thoroughly after adding the broth, black-eyed peas, and cooked pork. Close the lid, set the steam release to seal position, click the Pressure Cook button, and set the timer to 30 minutes. 4. Allow pressure to naturally release for around 20 minutes after the timer chimes. Add lime juice after lifting the top. Serve hot.
Per Serving: Calories 521; Fat: 21g; Sodium 1704mg; Carbs: 8g; Sugars: 3g; Protein 70g

Yummy Dressing

Prep Time: 15 minutes | Cook Time: 10 minutes | Serves: 8

2 Tbsp. olive oil
1 medium celery rib, chopped
1 small onion, chopped
2 cups reduced-sodium chicken broth

1 tsp. poultry seasoning
¼ tsp. salt
¼ tsp. pepper
8 cups unseasoned stuffing cubes

1. Choose the Instant Pot's sauté setting. Add oil. Celery and onion should be cooked and stirred in heated oil for 3 to 4 minutes, or until crisp-tender. Select "Cancel." Seasonings and broth are stirred in. Add the stuffing cubes and mix just until combined. Transfer to a 1½ qt. oiled baking pan. 2. In the instant pot, add a steam rack and one cup of water. Cover baking dish with foil. An 18x12-inch strip of foil is folded into thirds along its length to create a sling. Lower the dish onto the rack using the sling. 3. Close lid. Adjust to Pressure Cook on high for 15 minutes. Allow any leftover pressure to naturally release for ten minutes on seal position before quick-releasing it on vent position. Carefully remove baking dish using foil sling. Let stand 10 minutes.
Per Serving: Calories 270; Fat: 10g; Sodium 344mg; Carbs: 2g; Sugars: 1.03g; Protein 38.39g

Yummy Beefy stew

Prep Time: 10 minutes | Cook Time: 50 minutes | Serves: 4

1½ pounds beef stew meat
¼ cup all-purpose flour
2 tablespoons vegetable oil
6 cups low-sodium beef broth
1 large onion, cut into 8 wedges
8 carrots, cut into 1-inch pieces

4 potatoes, scrubbed or peeled, cut into 1-inch chunks
3 celery stalks, cut into 1-inch pieces
½ teaspoon fine sea salt
¼ teaspoon ground black pepper

1. Toss the stew meat with the flour in a medium mixing basin until evenly covered. 2. Choose Sauté. The inner cooking pot should contain oil. Brown roughly half of the meat after adding it to the oil (the longer you brown the meat, the darker your sauce will be). Repeat with the remaining meat after transferring the browned beef to a platter. Returning the first batch of meat to the pot after adding the onion and stock. 3. Turn the valve to seal position and secure the lid in place. Choose Pressure Cook. Set the pressure to High when cooking. Set the time for 30 minutes. When cooking ends, turn the valve to vent position to quickly release the pressure. 4. Unlock and remove the lid. Add the salt, pepper, and the carrots, potatoes, and celery. 5. Turn the valve to seal position and secure the lid in place. Choose Pressure Cook. Set the pressure to High when cooking. Schedule 8 minutes in the timer. Turn the valve carefully to vent position when cooking is finished to quickly release pressure. Unlock and remove the lid.
Per Serving: Calories 822; Fat: 30g; Sodium 920mg; Carbs: 120g; Sugars: 12g; Protein 26g

Yummy Tuscany soup

Prep Time: 5 minutes | Cook Time: 30 minutes | Serves: 4

1 tablespoon olive oil
1 cup chopped onion
1 pound Italian sausage, casings removed
2 garlic cloves, minced
¼ to ½ teaspoon red pepper flakes
1 (14-ounce) can low-sodium chicken broth
2 large russet potatoes, halved and

cut into ¼-inch-thick slices
4 cups water
2 cups chopped kale
Fine sea salt
Ground black pepper
1 cup heavy cream
6 bacon slices, cooked and cut into bite-size pieces

1. Choose Sauté and set the temperature to Medium. The inner cooking pot should contain oil. When it's heated, add the onion and sausage, breaking up the meat as you sauté for 5 minutes. Stir in the red pepper flakes and garlic. 2. Stir to remove any onion bits that may have settled to the bottom before adding the chicken broth. Add the potatoes and water and stir. On top of the liquid in the saucepan, scatter the kale. Add salt and pepper to taste. 3. Turn the valve to seal position and secure the lid in place. Choose Pressure Cook. Set the pressure to High when cooking. Decide on a 15-minute time frame. Turn the valve carefully to vent position when cooking is finished to quickly release pressure. 4. Unlock and remove the lid and stir in the cream. Heat through, then stir in the bacon.
Per Serving: Calories 1024; Fat: 77g; Sodium 1404mg; Carbs: 52g; Sugars: 5g; Protein 38.39g

Chili Tex-Mex

Prep Time: 10 minutes | Cook Time: 38 minutes | Serves: 6

1½ pounds lean ground beef
2 tablespoons vegetable oil
3 garlic cloves, minced
2 onions, finely chopped
3 tablespoons chili powder
1 teaspoon ground cumin
½ teaspoon dried oregano
1 teaspoon fine sea salt
½ teaspoon ground black pepper

⅛teaspoon cayenne pepper (optional)
1½ cups low-sodium beef broth
1 (14-ounce) can tomato purée
1 (15-ounce) can pinto beans, rinsed and drained
2 tablespoons cornmeal
½ cup shredded Cheddar cheese (optional)

1. Choose Sauté. For about 5 minutes, add the ground beef to the inner heating pot and brown it. Get rid of any fat. 2. Add the garlic, onions, chili powder, cumin, oregano, salt, pepper, and cayenne to the saucepan along with the vegetable oil (if using). Cook for five minutes. Scrape off any browned pieces from the pot's bottom before adding the broth and tomato purée and stirring to mix. 3. Turn the valve to seal position and secure the lid in place. Choose Pressure Cook. Set the pressure to High when cooking. Set the time for 15 minutes. Turn the valve carefully to vent position when cooking is finished to quickly release pressure. 4. Unlock and remove the lid.

Choose Sauté. When the pinto beans are added, bring the mixture to a simmer and cook for 3 minutes, or until the beans are warm. After adding the cornmeal, mix the beans until they are thick. Add shredded cheese as a garnish after ladling into dishes (if using).
Per Serving: Calories 455; Fat: 20g; Sodium 788mg; Carbs: 32g; Sugars: 8g; Protein 38.39g

Spring Squash

Prep Time: 20 minutes | Cook Time: 5 minutes | Serves: 8

1 lb. medium yellow summer squash
1 lb. medium zucchini
2 medium tomatoes, chopped
1 cup vegetable broth
¼ cup thinly sliced green onions
½ tsp. salt

¼ tsp. pepper
1 ½ cups Caesar salad croutons, coarsely crushed
½ cup shredded cheddar cheese
4 bacon strips, cooked and crumbled

1. Place the squash in Instant pot after slicing it into 14-inch-thick pieces. Include the broth, green onions, tomatoes, salt, and pepper. Close the lid. Adjust to Pressure Cook for one minute on high. Rapidly release pressure on valve to vent and unlock the lid. Use a slotted spoon to remove the squash. 2. Add cheese, bacon, and croutons to serve.
Per Serving: Calories 307; Fat: 30g; Sodium 384mg; Carbs: 7g; Sugars: 3g; Protein 5g

Steamed Leeks

Prep Time: 10 minutes | Cook Time: 5 minutes | Serves: 6

1 large tomato, chopped
1 small navel orange, peeled, sectioned and chopped
2 Tbsp. minced fresh parsley
2 Tbsp. sliced Greek olives
1 tsp. capers, drained
1 tsp. red wine vinegar

1 tsp. olive oil
½ tsp. grated orange zest
½ tsp. pepper
6 medium leeks (white portion only), halved lengthwise, cleaned
Crumbled feta cheese

1. Set aside after combining the first nine ingredients. In Instant pot, add steam rack and one cup of water. Place leeks on the rack. Close the lid. Set to Pressure Cook for 2 minutes on high. Quickly release pressure on vent position. 2. Leeks should be moved to a serving plate. Top with tomato mixture and cheese, then spoon it on.
Per Serving: Calories 82; Fat: 1g; Sodium 74mg; Carbs: 16.87g; Sugars: 6.03g; Protein 2.39g

Cob-Styled Corn

Prep Time: 5 minutes | Cook Time: 5 minutes | Serves: 4

1 cup water
¼ teaspoon salt

4 ears corn

1. Add steam rack to the Instant Pot after adding water and salt. Put corn on the rack's top. 2. Set the pressure release to seal position and close the lid. 3. Press Pressure Cook button and adjust time to 5 minutes. 4. Quickly release the pressure on vent position when the timer beeps, then open the lid and take it off. Serve corn.
Per Serving: Calories 282; Fat: 2.17g; Sodium 222mg; Carbs: 15.87g; Sugars: 1.03g; Protein 1.39g

Yummy Wing Potatoes

Prep Time: 15 minutes | Cook Time: 5 minutes | Serves: 6

2 lbs. Yukon Gold potatoes, cut into 1-in. cubes
1 small sweet yellow pepper, chopped
½ small red onion, chopped

¼ cup Buffalo wing sauce
½ cup shredded cheddar cheese
Optional toppings: Crumbled cooked bacon, sliced green onions and sour cream

1. In the Instant Pot, add the steam rack and one cup of water. Put the potatoes, onion, and yellow pepper in the rack. Close the pressure-release valve and lock the lid. Adjust to Pressure Cook on high for 3 minutes. Quickly release the pressure on vent position. Select Cancel. 2. Take out the veggies and pour the cooking liquid away. Stir the veggies in the Buffalo wing sauce until evenly coated. grate some cheese on top. For 1-2 minutes, while the cheese melts, cover and leave out. Add bacon, green onions, and sour cream as desired.
Per Serving: Calories 187; Fat: 3g; Sodium 290mg; Carbs: 32g; Sugars: 2.03g; Protein 7g

Yummy Beets

Prep Time: 20 minutes | Cook Time: 20 minutes | Serves: 8

5 large fresh beets (about 3½ lbs.)	1 Tbsp. minced fresh rosemary or
1 Tbsp. olive oil	1 tsp. dried rosemary, crushed
1 medium red onion, chopped	2 tsp. minced fresh thyme or ¾
2 garlic cloves, minced	tsp. dried thyme
1 medium orange, peeled and	¾ tsp. salt
chopped	½ tsp. Chinese five-spice powder
⅓ cup honey	½ tsp. coarsely ground pepper
¼ cup white balsamic vinegar	1 cup crumbled feta cheese

1. In the Instant Pot, add the steam rack and one cup of water. Beets should be scrubbed and their tops should be cut off at 1 inch. Close the pressure-release valve and lock the lid. Adjust to Pressure Cook on high for 20 minutes. Allow the pressure to release naturally. Select Cancel. 2. When cool enough to handle, remove the beets. Eliminate steam rack and throw away cooking fluids. Wipe the pot dry. Beets are peeled and sliced into wedges. 3. Choose the sauté option. Oil and red onion should be cooked and stirred for 4-5 minutes after the oil is heated. For a further minute, add the garlic. Heat through the addition of the orange, honey, vinegar, rosemary, thyme, salt, Chinese five-spice, and beets. Select Cancel. Serve hot, or cool and store in the fridge. Cheese should be added before serving with a slotted spoon.
Per Serving: Calories 138; Fat: 5g; Sodium 432mg; Carbs: 18.87g; Sugars: 16g; Protein 3g

Tagine Du Chickpea

Prep Time: 30 minutes | Cook Time: 5 minutes | Serves: 12

2 Tbsp. olive oil	1 can (15 oz.) chickpeas or
2 garlic cloves, minced	garbanzo beans, rinsed and drained
2 tsp. paprika	1 medium sweet red pepper,
1 tsp. ground ginger	coarsely chopped
1 tsp. ground cumin	1 medium onion, coarsely chopped
½ tsp. salt	12 dried apricots, halved
¼ tsp. pepper	½ cup water
¼ tsp. ground cinnamon	2 to 3 tsp. harissa chili paste
1 small butternut squash (about	2 tsp. honey
2 lbs.), peeled and cut into ½-in.	1 can (14.5 oz.) crushed tomatoes,
cubes	undrained
2 medium zucchini, cut into ½-in.	¼ cup chopped fresh mint leaves
pieces	Plain Greek yogurt, optional

1. Choose the Instant Pot's sauté setting. Add oil, garlic, paprika, ginger, cumin, salt, pepper, and cinnamon when the oil is heated. Cook and stir for approximately a minute, or until fragrant. Select Cancel. 2. Add the water, harissa, honey, onion, red pepper, zucchini, squash, chickpeas, and apricot halves. Close the pressure-release valve and lock the lid. Adjust to Pressure Cook on high for 3 minutes. Rapidly release pressure on vent position. Select Cancel. Add tomatoes and mint, stirring gently, and heat through. 3. If desired, top with yogurt and additional mint, olive oil and honey.
Per Serving: Calories 386; Fat: 3g; Sodium 283mg; Carbs: 91g; Sugars: 73g; Protein 8.39g

Chili with Black Beans and Corn

Prep Time: 10 minutes | Cook Time: 30 minutes | Serves: 8

1 tablespoon vegetable oil	1 cup frozen corn kernels
1 medium white onion, peeled and	1 (28-ounce) can diced tomatoes
chopped	3 tablespoons chili powder
1 medium red bell pepper, seeded	1 tablespoon smoked paprika
and chopped	2 teaspoons ground cumin
1 medium carrot, peeled and	1 teaspoon ground coriander
chopped	½ teaspoon salt
½ pound ground turkey	½ teaspoon ground black pepper
1½ cups dried black beans, soaked	3 cups Vegetable Broth
overnight in water to cover and	1 cup water
drained	

1. Heat oil in the Instant Pot by pressing the Sauté button. For approximately 5 minutes, add the onion, bell pepper, and carrot and simmer until tender. Add the ground turkey and simmer for about 6 minutes, or until the meat is no longer pink. Don't hesitate to click Cancel. 2. the pot with the remaining ingredients. Put the cover on, choose vent for the steam release, select Pressure Cook, and cook for the predetermined 30 minutes. 3. Quickly remove the steam on vent position, then open the lid and thoroughly stir when the timer sounds.

If the chili is too thin, click the Cancel and press Sauté buttons, then let the chili simmer, covered, until the appropriate thickness is achieved. Serve warm.
Per Serving: Calories 895; Fat: 80g; Sodium 380mg; Carbs: 36g; Sugars: 6g; Protein 16g

Ham & White Beans Smoked

Prep Time: 15 minutes | Cook Time: 30 minutes | Serves: 10

1 lb. dried great northern beans	1 large onion, chopped
3 smoked ham hocks (about 1½	1 Tbsp. onion powder
lbs.)	1 Tbsp. garlic powder
3 cans (14½ oz. each) reduced-	2 tsp. pepper
sodium chicken or beef broth	Thinly sliced green onions,
2 cups water	optional

1. Sort and rinse the beans. Add to the Instant Pot. Toss in the ham hocks. Add the spices, water, onion, and broth. Close the pressure-release valve and lock the lid. Adjust to Pressure Cook on high for 30 minutes. Ten minutes after allowing the pressure to naturally dissipate, quickly release any lingering pressure. Select Cancel. 2. Remove meat from bones once it is cold enough to handle; chop up ham into bite-sized pieces; and put back in Pressure Cook. Use a slotted spoon before serving. If desired, garnish with green onions.
Per Serving: Calories 500; Fat: 12.17g; Sodium 2884mg; Carbs: 36g; Sugars: 2g; Protein 63g

Yummy Potatoes

Prep Time: 5 minutes | Cook Time: 15 minutes | Serves: 4

1 cup water	4 medium sweet potatoes

1. Add steam rack and fill the Instant Pot with water. 2. On the top and bottom, pierce sweet potatoes with a fork on both sides. The rack should be covered with sweet potatoes. 3. Set the pressure release to seal position and close the lid. 4. Set the timer to 15 minutes and press the Pressure Cook button. 5. Quickly release the pressure on vent position when the timer beeps, then open the lid and take it off. 6. Serve.
Per Serving: Calories 115; Fat: 1g; Sodium 40mg; Carbs: 26g; Sugars: 8.03g; Protein 2.39g

Yummy Baked Potatoes

Prep Time: 5 minutes | Cook Time: 20 minutes | Serves: 4

1 cup water	4 medium russet potatoes
½ teaspoon salt	

1. Add steam rack to the Instant Pot after adding water and salt. 2. On the top and bottom, pierce potatoes with a fork on all sides. Put potatoes on the rack's top. 3. Set the pressure release to seal position and close the lid. 4. Set the timer to 20 minutes and press the Pressure Cook button. 5. Quickly release the pressure on vent position when the timer beeps, then open the lid and take it off. 6. Serve potatoes.
Per Serving: Calories 110; Fat: 1.17g; Sodium 404mg; Carbs: 12.87g; Sugars: 7.3g; Protein 2.39g

Potato Salad in Red

Prep Time: 24 minutes | Cook Time: 4 minutes | Serves: 6

1 cup water	1 tablespoon apple cider vinegar
2½ pounds medium red potatoes,	½ teaspoon salt
peeled and cut into 1" cubes	½ teaspoon black pepper
½ cup mayonnaise	½ teaspoon paprika
2 tablespoons yellow mustard	4 medium green onions, sliced

1. Fill the Instant Pot with water. Put the steam rack into the Instant pot. 2. Potato cubes should be arranged in the steam rack. 3. Set the pressure release to seal position and close the lid. 4. Set the timer to 4 minutes and press the Pressure Cook button. 5. Quickly release the pressure on vent position when the timer beeps, then open the lid and take it off. 6. Place potatoes in a dish of cold water after removing them from the Instant Pot. Wait for ten minutes. 7. Mayonnaise, mustard, vinegar, salt, pepper, and paprika should all be combined in a small basin. 8. Place potatoes in a big, dry dish after removing them from the cold bath. 9. Add the sauce to the potatoes and toss to cover well. Add green onions in slices to the potato salad. 10. Chill until ready to serve.
Per Serving: Calories 204; Fat: 6g; Sodium 440mg; Carbs: 32g; Sugars: 3g; Protein 5g

Fritters of Zucchini

Prep Time: 15 minutes | Cook Time: 24 minutes | Serves: 4

4 cups shredded zucchini	⅓ cup shredded Parmesan cheese
1 teaspoon salt	2 cloves garlic, minced
1 large egg, beaten	½ teaspoon black pepper
⅓ cup all-purpose flour	6 tablespoons olive oil

1. Salt the zucchini and place it in a colander. Wait for ten minutes. 2. Take the zucchini out of the colander and cover it in a fresh kitchen towel. wring and squeeze the water out of the zucchini. 3. Combine zucchini with the egg, flour, Parmesan, garlic, and pepper in a large bowl. Blend well. 4. Press the Instant Pot's Sauté button. Fill the Instant Pot with 2 tablespoons of oil. 5. Put heaping teaspoons of zucchini in the Pressure Cook. Using the back of a spoon, flatten into 2½" rounds. Make three fritters at a time while working in batches. 6. After 4 minutes, turn the food. Cook the second side for a further 4 minutes. 7. Using a slotted spatula, remove the zucchini fritters. Cook the zucchini in batches, using more oil as needed, until all are consumed. 8. Serve hot.
Per Serving: Calories 296; Fat: 12g; Sodium 810mg; Carbs: 26g; Sugars: 0.03g; Protein 6g

Mashed Potatoes with Garlic

Prep Time: 10 minutes | Cook Time: 8 minutes | Serves: 4

2½ pounds russet potatoes, peeled	¾ cup whole milk, warm
1 cup chicken broth	2 tablespoons butter
½ teaspoon salt	5 cloves garlic, minced

1. Add salt, stock, and potatoes to the Instant Pot. 2. Set the pressure release to seal position and close the lid. 3. Set the timer to 8 minutes and press the Pressure Cook button. 4. Quickly release the pressure on vent position when the timer beeps, then open the lid and take it off. 5. Spit out the broth. 6. Mash the potatoes in the pot with a potato masher. Add warm milk and stir. 7. Melt the butter before adding it. Add garlic and fold. 8. Serve warm.
Per Serving: Calories 417; Fat: 12g; Sodium 618mg; Carbs: 60g; Sugars: 7g; Protein 20g

Baked Sweet Potatoes

Prep Time: 10 minutes | Cook Time: 23 minutes | Serves: 6

1 cup water	¼ cup butter, melted
3 (15-ounce) cans sweet potatoes, drained	3 tablespoons orange juice
½ cup packed brown sugar	⅛ teaspoon ground cinnamon
	1 (10-ounce) bag mini marshmallows

1. Add steam rack and fill the Instant Pot with water. Organize a 7-inch cake pan with grease. 2. Sweet potatoes, brown sugar, butter, orange juice, and cinnamon should all be combined in a big basin. Completely mix by blending. 3. Fill the cake pan with the sweet potato mixture. Add the remaining bag of small marshmallows on top. 4. Cake pan should be covered with foil and a dry paper towel. To prevent the paper towel from slipping, secure foil over the pan. 5. Make a foil sling, gently place the covered cake pan inside the Instant Pot, and cover the cake pan with the ends of the sling. 6. Set the pressure release to seal position and close the lid. 7. Set the timer to 20 minutes and press the Pressure Cook button. 8. Quickly release the pressure on vent position when the timer beeps, then open the lid and take it off. 9. Utilizing a foil sling, carefully remove the cake pan. Remove the paper towel and foil. 10. Top the dish with the remaining half of the small marshmallows. 11. Casserole in the oven for 2 to 3 minutes, or until marshmallows start to turn golden. To prevent marshmallows from burning, keep a close eye on them. Serve.
Per Serving: Calories 495; Fat: 14.17g; Sodium 280mg; Carbs: 116g; Sugars: 66g; Protein 3g

Dipping Sauce Artichokes

Prep Time: 10 minutes | Cook Time: 15 minutes | Serves: 4

2 large artichokes	¾ teaspoon salt, divided
1 medium lemon	3 tablespoons mayonnaise
1 cup water	¼ teaspoon chili powder
3 cloves garlic, crushed	⅛ teaspoon black pepper

1. Slice the top half an inch off of each artichoke after rinsing them. 2. Half a lemon, please. Set aside one half. wedge-cut the remaining half.

3. Add water, garlic, lemon wedges, and ½ teaspoon salt to the Instant Pot. 4. Arrange artichokes on the steam rack before placing it in the Instant Pot. If necessary, cut the artichoke stems so the lid will shut. 5. Set the pressure release to seal position and close the lid. 6. Set the timer to 15 minutes and press the Pressure Cook button. 7. Quickly release the pressure when the timer beeps, then open the lid and take it off. Remove artichokes. 8. Mix the remaining juice from ½ a lemon, ¼ teaspoon of salt, chili powder, and pepper in a small dish with the mayonnaise. 9. Cut artichokes in half and serve with sauce.
Per Serving: Calories 81; Fat: 3g; Sodium 606mg; Carbs: 11g; Sugars: 1g; Protein 3g

Shallot-Topped Green Beans

Prep Time: 5 minutes | Cook Time: 6 minutes | Serves: 4

1 cup water	1 medium shallot, peeled and
¾ teaspoon salt, divided	minced
1 pound green beans, trimmed	½ teaspoon black pepper
2 tablespoons olive oil	

1. Place steam rack to the Instant Pot after adding water and ½ teaspoon salt. Place green beans on top of steam rack. 2. Set the pressure release to seal position and close the lid. 3. Set the time to 0 minutes, press the Pressure Cook button on low. 4. Quickly release the pressure when the timer beeps, then open the lid and take it off. Remove green beans. Drain water. 5. Add oil to the pot and press the Sauté button. 6. Add green beans and shallot. Cook for 6 minutes while periodically stirring. 7. Add the final ¼ teaspoon of salt and pepper to taste. Remove from heat and serve.
Per Serving: Calories 86; Fat: 7g; Sodium 440mg; Carbs: 5g; Sugars: 1g; Protein 1g

Curry-Style Cauliflower

Prep Time: 5 minutes | Cook Time: 13 minutes | Serves: 4

2 tablespoons olive oil	½ teaspoon curry powder
1 medium head cauliflower, cut	⅛ teaspoon salt
into florets	⅛ teaspoon black pepper

1. Click the Sauté button. Add in oil and heat for 1 minute. 2. Stir in the cauliflower, curry powder, salt, and pepper. Now cook for 12 minutes under cover with occasional stirring. 3. Remove from heat and serve hot.
Per Serving: Calories 77; Fat: 7g; Sodium 93mg; Carbs: 3g; Sugars: 1.03g; Protein 1g

Apple Strawberry Sauce

Prep Time: 10 minutes | Cook Time: 5 minutes | Serves: 6

6 cups roughly chopped Gala	½ cup granulated sugar
apples	½ cup water
4 cups frozen strawberries	¼ teaspoon salt

1. In the Instant Pot, add strawberries and apples. 2. Add salt, water, and sugar. Blend well. 3. Set the pressure release to seal position and close the lid. 4. Press Pressure Cook button and adjust time to 5 minutes on low. 5. Allow the pressure to naturally dissipate once the timer beeps, then open the lid and take it off. 6. Blend the ingredients with an immersion blender until it's smooth. 7. Chill in the refrigerator 2 hours. Serve cold.
Per Serving: Calories 146; Fat: 1g; Sodium 5mg; Carbs: 36g; Sugars: 26g; Protein 1g

Honed Yummy Carrots

Prep Time: 10 minutes | Cook Time: 16 minutes | Serves: 4

⅓ cup olive oil	½ teaspoon salt
1 pound carrots, cut into ½" slices	¼ teaspoon black pepper
1 teaspoon cumin	¼ cup honey

1. Click the Sauté button. Add in oil and heat it for 1 minute. 2. Cumin, salt, pepper, and carrots should be added. Stirring periodically, cook for 10 minutes with lid on. 3. Add honey, then combine before capping. Allow it simmer for a further five minutes while stirring periodically. 4. Remove from heat and serve hot.
Per Serving: Calories 288; Fat: 18g; Sodium 373mg; Carbs: 28g; Sugars: 22g; Protein 1.23g

Yummy Cauliflower

Prep Time: 10 minutes | Cook Time: 2 minutes | Serves: 4

1 cup water
1 medium head cauliflower, cut into florets

1 cup whole milk, warm
1 tablespoon unsalted butter
¼ teaspoon salt

1. Fill the Instant Pot with water. Place the steam rack into the Instant Pot. 2. On top of the steam rack, arrange the cauliflower. 3. Set the pressure release to seal position and close the lid. 4. Press Pressure Cook button and adjust time to 2 minutes on high. 5. Quickly release the pressure when the timer beeps, then open the lid and take it off. 6. Drain the water, then take the steam rack off. 7. In the Instant Pot bottom put the cauliflower. Use a potato masher to thoroughly mash the cauliflower. 8. Mix in warm milk and stir until cauliflower absorbs milk. 9. Fold in butter and salt. Mix until butter is melted. Serve warm.
Per Serving: Calories 90; Fat: 4g; Sodium 48mg; Carbs: 12g; Sugars: 9.1g; Protein 3.2g

Tamalito Sweet Corn

Prep Time: 15 minutes | Cook Time: 50 minutes | Serves: 6

5 tablespoons butter, melted
¼ cup masa harina
½ cup granulated sugar
2½ cups water, divided
2 cups frozen corn kernels,

thawed, divided
½ cup cornmeal
4 teaspoons whole milk
1 teaspoon baking powder
½ teaspoon salt

1. Mix sugar, masa harina, and butter in a large basin until well-combined. 2. Combine ½ cup water, 1 cup corn, and ¼ cup cornmeal in a blender. Until smooth, blend. 3. Combine the masa mixture with the pureed corn. 4. Add the remaining 1 cup of corn, milk, baking soda, and salt while whisking. Stir well to mix. 5. Into a 7-cup metal basin, pour the batter. The bowl should have a paper towel on top, and the foil should be well sealed. 6. Add the final 2 cups of water to the Instant Pot. Place steam rack inside. To carefully put the bowl into the Instant Pot, use a foil sling. 7. Set to seal position and close the lid. 8. Click the Steam button, then set the timer to 50 minutes. 9. Quickly release the pressure when the timer beeps, then open the lid and take it off. 10. Using a foil sling, remove the bowl. Remove the foil and paper towels. 11. Stir before serving.
Per Serving: Calories 227; Fat: 10g; Sodium 81mg; Carbs: 30g; Sugars: 9g; Protein 2g

Bread with Corn

Prep Time: 10 minutes | Cook Time: 25 minutes | Serves: 6

1 cup water
1½ cups all-purpose flour
¾ cup cornmeal
2 cups granulated sugar
2 teaspoons baking powder

½ teaspoon salt
1 large egg, beaten
1 cup whole milk
½ cup vegetable oil
½ cup frozen corn kernels, thawed

1. Add steam rack and water to the Instant Pot. A 6-cup Bundt pan should be greased and set aside. 2. Mix the flour, cornmeal, sugar, baking soda, and salt in a large basin. 3. Create a well in the center of the dry ingredients, then add the milk, oil, and egg. Just mix the dry components with the wet ones by folding. 4. Mix in the corn until it is spread evenly. 5. Fill the Bundt pan with the corn bread batter. Pan should first be securely covered with a paper towel before foil. 6. The Bundt pan should be delicately lowered into the Instant Pot using a foil sling. 7. Set the pressure release to seal position and close the lid. 8. Press Pressure Cook button and set the timer for 25 minutes on high. 9. Allow pressure to naturally relax on seal position for 10 minutes after the timer beeps, then quickly remove any leftover pressure on vent position. Remove the lid by unlocking it. Using a foil sling, remove the pan from the Instant Pot. 10. Let cool on a wire rack before serving.
Per Serving: Calories 534; Fat: 20g; Sodium 217mg; Carbs: 81g; Sugars: 38g; Protein 6g

Corn Zucchini Casserole

Prep Time: 15 minutes | Cook Time: 65 minutes | Serves: 6

1½ cups water
1½ cups all-purpose flour
¾ cup cornmeal
2 teaspoons baking powder
1 teaspoon salt

¼ teaspoon black pepper
2 large eggs, beaten
1 cup whole milk
¼ cup vegetable oil
4 cups shredded zucchini

1½ cups Monterey jack cheese

1. Add steam rack and fill the Instant Pot with water. Organize a 7-inch cake pan with grease. 2. Mix the flour, cornmeal, baking powder, salt, and pepper in a big basin. 3. The egg, milk, and oil should be added after making a well in the dry ingredients. Mix thoroughly. 4. Add the zucchini and blend well. Add the cheese after that. 5. Fill the cake pan with the casserole batter. Add a paper towel on top and carefully wrap the foil around the pan's top. Cake pan should be delicately lowered into Instant Pot using a foil sling. 6. Set the pressure release to seal position and close the lid. 7. Set the timer to 65 minutes and press the Pressure Cook button on high. 8. When the timer beeps, quickly release pressure and then unlock lid and remove it. Remove pan from Instant Pot using foil sling. 9. Serve hot.
Per Serving: Calories 508; Fat: 27g; Sodium 712mg; Carbs: 45g; Sugars: 6g; Protein 19g

Tian Vegetable

Prep Time: 10 minutes | Cook Time: 30 minutes | Serves: 4

1 tablespoon olive oil
½ medium yellow onion, peeled and diced
2 cloves garlic, minced
1 cup water
1 medium yellow squash, cut into ½"-thick slices
1 medium zucchini, cut into ½"-thick slices

2 Roma tomatoes, cut into ½"-thick slices
1 large russet potato, cut into ½"-thick slices
¼ teaspoon salt
⅛ teaspoon black pepper
½ cup shredded mozzarella cheese
¼ cup grated Parmesan cheese

1. Press the Instant Pot's Sauté button. 2. Add onion and oil. Cook for 4 minutes, or until softened. 3. Add the garlic and cook for 30 seconds or until fragrant. 4. Spread the onion and garlic on the bottom of a 7-inch cake pan after removing them. 5. Place the cleaned inner pot inside the Instant Pot once again. Pot with steam rack and water added. 6. Around the perimeter of the cake pan, arrange the sliced veggies in a pattern of squash, zucchini, tomato, and potato. Once all of the veggies have been utilized, continue in the middle of the pan. 7. Add a paper towel on top and carefully wrap the foil around the pan's top. Cake pan should be delicately lowered into Instant Pot using a foil sling. 8. Set the pressure release to seal position and close the lid. 9. Press Pressure Cook button and adjust time to 30 minutes. 10. Allow 10 minutes for the pressure to naturally release on seal position once the timer beeps. Release any residual pressure quickly on vent position, then open the lid and take it off. 11. Using a foil sling, remove the pan from the Instant Pot. On top, grate mozzarella, Parmesan, salt, and pepper. Serve warm.
Per Serving: Calories 135; Fat: 4g; Sodium 400mg; Carbs: 13g; Sugars: 1g; Protein 10g

Yummy Spaghetti Squash

Prep Time: 5 minutes | Cook Time: 30 minutes | Serves: 4

1 spaghetti squash
2 or 3 garlic cloves, minced
1 to 2 tablespoons olive oil or vegan margarine, plus more as needed
1 cup peas

2 to 3 tablespoons nutritional yeast, plus more as needed
Salt
1 cup cherry tomatoes, halved
Freshly ground black pepper

1. Put the spaghetti squash Instant pot inner pot. If the squash won't fit, split it in half, remove the seeds with a big spoon, and stack the halves cut-side down in the pot. Add one or two cups of water. Select Pressure Cook and high pressure, close the lid, check that the pressure valve is shut, and set the timer for 10 to 15 minutes. 2. Allow the pressure to naturally release for 10 minutes on seal position after the cook time is over. 3. Carefully unlock and remove the lid once all the pressure has been removed. Carefully remove the squash using tongs or a big fork and spoon, then place it somewhere to cool. 4. After draining the pot of its water, put it back into the Instant pot. Choose Sauté. Garlic should be nicely browned after adding it to the oil and cooking for about 2 minutes while stirring periodically. For one to two minutes, add the peas and stir to soften. 5. Slice the squash in half and remove the seeds if it is whole. Scrape the flesh of the squash into strands with a fork, then add them back to the saucepan. Salt should be added before adding the nutritional yeast to the strands. Toss to evenly coat in oil. 6. Add the cherry tomatoes, plus more nutritional yeast, olive oil, salt, and pepper, if needed.
Per Serving: Calories 80; Fat: 3g; Sodium 304mg; Carbs: 10g; Sugars: 5g; Protein 3g

Artichokes Steamed in Lemon

Prep Time: 2 minutes | Cook Time: 30 minutes | Serves: 2

2 medium to large artichokes, tops
and stems trimmed
1 lemon
½ teaspoon garlic salt

1. Add a steam rack to the bottom of the Instant Pot and add 1 ½ cups of water. 2. Place the artichokes stem-side down and standing up on the rack. 3. Sprinkle garlic salt over each artichoke after squeezing the juice from half a lemon over them. Try to get some of the spice under the leaves. 4. Seal the valve and lock the lid. Choose Pressure Cook. Cook for 25 minutes at high pressure, then quickly reduce the pressure in the pot on vent position when the timer beeps, then remove the lid. 5. The artichokes should be taken out of the pot with tongs and served.
Per Serving: Calories 104; Fat: 3g; Sodium 445mg; Carbs: 18g; Sugars: 1g; Protein 4g

Spicy Asparagus

Prep Time: 2 minutes | Cook Time: 10 minutes | Serves: 6

1-pound asparagus spears, woody
ends trimmed
1 tablespoon extra-virgin olive oil
½ teaspoon Italian seasoning
½ teaspoon sea salt
¼ teaspoon freshly ground black
pepper

1. Put a steam rack in the bottom of Instant Pot and add 1 ½ cups of water. 2. Add the oil and arrange the asparagus in the rack. Add some salt, pepper, and Italian seasoning. 3. Close the lid. Choose Pressure Cook on high pressure for 1 minute, then quickly release the pressure in the pot on vent position when the timer beeps and remove the lid. 4. Using tongs, remove the asparagus and serve.
Per Serving: Calories 25; Fat: 1g; Sodium 232mg; Carbs: 3g; Sugars: 2.03g; Protein 1.6g

Balsamic-Maple Parsnips

Prep Time: 5 minutes | Cook Time: 10 minutes | Serves: 4

2 or 3 parsnips, peeled and cut into
½-inch pieces
2 garlic cloves, minced
½ cup applesauce
¼ cup maple syrup
2 tablespoons balsamic vinegar
2 tablespoons extra-virgin olive oil
½ teaspoon dried thyme
¼ teaspoon sea salt

1. Combine the parsnips, garlic, applesauce, maple syrup, vinegar, oil, thyme, and salt in the Instant Pot. 2. Close the lid. Select Pressure Cook on high pressure for 2 minutes, then quickly release the pressure in the pot on vent position when the timer beeps and remove the lid. 3. Cook the parsnips for an additional minute under high pressure if they are too hard for your tastes.
Per Serving: Calories 100; Fat: 3g; Sodium 210mg; Carbs: 18g; Sugars: 16g; Protein 1g

Coconut Creamed Kale

Prep Time: 5 minutes | Cook Time: 15 minutes | Serves: 4

1 tablespoon extra-virgin olive oil
3 garlic cloves, minced
1 bunch kale, stemmed and torn
into bite-size pieces
¼ teaspoon sea salt
⅛ teaspoon freshly ground black
pepper
1 cup full-fat coconut milk

1. Select Instant Pot Sauté option. Oil must be heated until it shimmers. 2. Stirring continuously, add the garlic and sauté for 30 seconds. Stir in the greens after adding the salt and pepper. Over the top, pour the coconut milk. Select Cancel. 3. Seal the valve and lock the lid. Select Pressure Cook on high pressure for 5 minutes, then quickly release the pressure in the pot on vent position when the timer beeps and remove the lid. 4. After stirring the kale, transfer it to a serving bowl with tongs or a slotted spoon. Serve and enjoy!
Per Serving: Calories 157; Fat: 16g; Sodium 186mg; Carbs: 4g; Sugars: 2g; Protein 2g

Braised Brussels sprouts in cider

Prep Time: 5 minutes | Cook Time: 15 minutes | Serves: 6

1 tablespoon extra-virgin olive oil
1 shallot, diced
1 cup apple cider or juice
1 tablespoon Dijon mustard
1 teaspoon dried thyme
½ teaspoon sea salt
¼ teaspoon freshly ground black
pepper

1 pound Brussels sprouts, trimmed   and halved

1. Select Instant Pot Sauté option. Oil must be heated until it shimmers. 2. Add the shallot and cook it for 2 to 3 minutes, stirring often, until it is tender and translucent. Add the salt, pepper, mustard, thyme, and apple cider. To blend, stir. Stir in the Brussels sprouts after adding them. Select Cancel. 3. Seal the valve and lock the lid. Choose Pressure Cook on high pressure for 10 minute, then quickly release the pressure in the pot on vent position when the timer beeps and remove the lid. 4. Place the Brussels sprouts to a serving bowl using a slotted spoon.
Per Serving: Calories 62; Fat: 2g; Sodium 263mg; Carbs: 12g; Sugars: 5g; Protein 2g

Yummiest Sweet Potatoes

Prep Time: 5 minutes | Cook Time: 30 minutes | Serves: 4

4 medium sweet potatoes
Ghee (optional)
Chopped chives or scallions, both
white and green parts (optional)
Avocado slices (optional)
Chopped, cooked bacon (optional)

1. ½ cups of water should be added to the Instant Pot bowl along with a steam rack. 2. After washing, make vents by poking each sweet potato numerous times. They should be put on the rack, stacked as necessary. 3. Seal the vent and lock the lid. Choose Pressure Cook on high pressure for 20 minutes, then release the pressure naturally for 10 minutes on seal position when the timer beeps. Remove the lid after quickly release any leftover pressure in the pot on vent position. If some of the cooked sweet potatoes aren't soft enough for you, add additional 3 to 5 minutes of cooking time with at least 1 cup of water, depending on how soft you want them. 4. When cool enough to handle, slice open the potatoes. If using, top with the ghee, chives, avocado slices, and bacon.
Per Serving: Calories 140; Fat: 5g; Sodium 70mg; Carbs: 20g; Sugars: 6g; Protein 2g

Dill and Lemon Baby Potatoes

Prep Time: 5 minutes | Cook Time: 20 minutes | Serves: 4

2 pounds baby potatoes, scrubbed
2 tablespoons olive oil
2 tablespoons freshly squeezed
lemon juice
1 teaspoon dried dill
2 tablespoons nutritional yeast
(optional)
Salt

1. The potatoes should be added to the Instant pot after adding a cup or two of water. Select Pressure Cook and high pressure, set the timer for 10 minutes, secure the lid and make sure the pressure valve is sealed. 2. Allow the pressure to naturally release for 10 minutes on seal position after the cook time is over. 3. Carefully unlock and remove the lid once all the pressure has been removed. Let the potatoes drain. 4. Mix the olive oil, lemon juice, dill, and nutritional yeast in a small bowl (if using). Add to the saucepan and stir to coat the potatoes.
Per Serving: Calories 254; Fat: 7g; Sodium 281mg; Carbs: 42g; Sugars: 5g; Protein 6g

Rice with Cauliflower

Prep Time: 5 minutes | Cook Time: 10 minutes | Serves: 4

1 head cauliflower, cut into small
florets
½ teaspoon sea salt
¼ teaspoon freshly ground black
pepper
1 tablespoon seasonings: garlic
powder, ground ginger, curry
powder, herbs, etc. (optional)
2 tablespoons coconut oil or ghee

1. The cauliflower florets should be added to a food processor and pulsed several times to resemble rice-like grains. Add optional spices, salt and pepper to taste (if using). Place aside. 2. Select Instant Pot Sauté option. Oil must be heated until it shimmers. Cook the riced cauliflower for 1 to 2 minutes, or until it begins to soften, after adding it. Select Cancel. 3. Transfer the rice to an Instant Pot-compatible 6 to 7-inch ceramic or heatproof bowl. 4. There is no need to wash the residual cauliflower parts out of the Instant Pot bowl before adding 1½ cups of water and setting a rack at the bottom. Set the dish on top of the rack of cauliflower rice. 5. Secure the lid and seal the valve. Select Pressure Cook and cook on high pressure for 5 minutes, then quickly release the pressure in the pot on vent position when the timer beeps and remove the lid to serve.
Per Serving: Calories 83; Fat: 7g; Sodium 312mg; Carbs: 5g; Sugars: 1.3g; Protein 1.6g

Tasty Mashed "No-Taters"

Prep Time: 5 minutes | Cook Time: 20 minutes | Serves: 4

1 head cauliflower, cut into large florets
2 tablespoons coconut oil or ghee
½ teaspoon sea salt
¼ teaspoon freshly ground black

pepper
¼ teaspoon garlic powder
1 tablespoon chopped fresh chives (optional)

1. Add 1 ½ cups of water to the bowl of the Instant Pot along with a steam rack. 2. Place the rack and cauliflower in the Instant Pot. 3. Close the lid and seal the valve. Choose Pressure Cook and cook for 4 minutes on high pressure, then quickly release the pressure in the pot on vent position when the timer beeps and remove the lid. 4. Drain the water from the pot after removing the rack and cauliflower. Return just the cauliflower to the bowl. 5. Garlic powder, salt, and ghee should all be added. Use an immersion blender or a potato masher to puree the ingredients in the pot. 6. Garnish with chives (if using) and serve.
Per Serving: Calories 76; Fat: 7g; Sodium 311mg; Carbs: 3g; Sugars: 1.03g; Protein 1.39g

Easy Bok Choy Sesame

Prep Time: 5 minutes | Cook Time: 10 minutes | Serves: 4

1 medium head bok choy, chopped
1 tablespoon coconut aminos
1 tablespoon toasted sesame oil
2 teaspoons sesame seeds

¼ teaspoon sea salt
¼ teaspoon freshly ground black pepper

1. One and a half cups of water should be added to the Instant Pot's along with a steam rack. 2. Fill the rack with the bok choy. 3. Close the lid and seal the valve. Choose Pressure Cook and cook on high pressure for 1 minute, then quickly release the pressure in the pot on vent position when the timer beeps and remove the lid. 4. Bok choy should be placed in a bowl and mixed with the sesame seeds, oil, coconut aminos, salt, and pepper.
Per Serving: Calories 102; Fat: 5.17g; Sodium 200mg; Carbs: 2.87g; Sugars: 1.03g; Protein 1.39g

Spicy Cauliflower

Prep Time: 5 minutes | Cook Time: 10 minutes | Serves: 4

1 tablespoon ghee or extra-virgin olive oil
1 teaspoon cumin seeds
1 white onion, diced
1 garlic clove, minced

1 head cauliflower, cut into florets
1 tablespoon ground coriander
1 teaspoon ground cumin
½ teaspoon sea salt
½ teaspoon garam masala

1. Select Instant Pot Sauté option. Till the ghee melts, heat the oil. 2. Stirring continuously, add the cumin seeds and cook for 30 seconds. The onion should be added and sautéed for 1 to 2 minutes, or until tender. Add the garlic and continue to sauté for 30 seconds later while stirring constantly. Select Cancel. 3. Add 1 cup of water and mix in the salt, cumin, coriander, and cauliflower. 4. Close the lid and seal the valve. Choose Pressure Cook on low pressure for one minute, then quickly release the pressure in the pot on vent position when the timer beeps and take the lid off. Garam masala is next added and served.
Per Serving: Calories 46; Fat: 2g; Sodium 344mg; Carbs: 6g; Sugars: 2g; Protein 1.8g

Spicy korma

Prep Time: 15 minutes | Cook Time: 20 minutes | Serves:6

1 (14-ounce) can diced tomatoes
1 cup full-fat coconut milk
1 small onion, chopped
2 jalapeño peppers, seeded and sliced
6 garlic cloves, smashed
2 teaspoons garam masala
1 teaspoon sea salt
1 teaspoon ground turmeric
½ teaspoon cumin
1 teaspoon red pepper flakes

2 tablespoons cashew butter or almond butter (optional)
2 small sweet potatoes, peeled and cut into 1-inch chunks
2 medium carrots, cut into 1-inch chunks
2 cups cauliflower florets
1 cup frozen green peas
½ cup chopped fresh cilantro
½ cup roasted cashews or almonds

1. Combine the tomatoes, tomato juice, and coconut milk in the Instant Pot. Add the garlic, onion, jalapenos, salt, turmeric, cumin, red pepper flakes, and cashew butter along with the other ingredients. Stir to combine. 2. Sweet potatoes and carrots should be placed into a steam rack and placed on top of the sauce components in the bowl. Seal the valve and lock the lid. Choose Pressure Cook. After two minutes of continuous high pressure cooking, quickly reduce the pressure in the pot on vent position when the timer beeps and remove the lid. Select Cancel. Remove and lay away the steam rack. 3. Puree the sauce in an immersion blender until it's smooth. Add the carrots and sweet potatoes to the bowl. Stir in the cauliflower and peas after adding them. 4. Close the lid and seal the valve. Select Pressure Cook and cook on low pressure for 2 minutes, then quickly release the pressure in the pot on vent position when the timer beeps and remove the lid. 5. Garnish with the cilantro and cashews and serve.
Per Serving: Calories 268; Fat: 18g; Sodium 582mg; Carbs: 24g; Sugars: 9g; Protein 7g

Soft Potatoes

Prep Time: 10 minutes | Cook Time: 10 minutes | Serves: 6

4 to 6 medium russet potatoes, scrubbed or peeled and uniformly chopped (about 5 cups)
1 cup unsalted vegetable broth or water
Salt

2 to 4 tablespoons olive oil, coconut oil, or vegan margarine
2 to 4 tablespoons unsweetened nondairy milk
½ teaspoon garlic powder (optional)

1. Combine the potatoes, vegetable broth, and a dash of salt in your Instant Pot. Select Pressure Cook and high pressure, set the timer for 5 minutes, lock the lid and check that the pressure valve is sealed. 2. Quickly release the pressure on vent position when the cooking period is through, taking cautious not to touch your face or fingers to the steam release. 3. Carefully unlock and remove the lid once all the pressure has been removed. Lift the saucepan out using oven mitts. 4. Garlic powder, milk, and olive oil should all be added to the pot. Mash the potatoes using a potato masher. Alternately, purée the potatoes in the saucepan using an immersion blender to get the desired consistency. If necessary, add extra salt after tasting.
Per Serving: Calories 255; Fat: 4g; Sodium 23mg; Carbs: 48g; Sugars: 2.8g; Protein 6g

Rice Pilaf with Mushrooms

Prep Time: 20 minutes | Cook Time: 5 minutes | Serves: 6

¼ cup butter
1 cup medium grain rice
½ lb. sliced baby portobello mushrooms

6 green onions, chopped
2 garlic cloves, minced
1 cup water
4 tsp. beef base

1. Choose the Instant Pot's sauté setting. Put butter in. Cook and stir rice for 3 to 5 minutes while butter is still hot. Select Cancel. Include the garlic, green onions, and mushrooms. In a small bowl, whisk water and beef base; pour over rice mixture. 2. Close the pressure-release valve and lock the lid. Adjust to Pressure Cook on high for 4 minutes. Allow the pressure to release naturally on seal position. Serve with more green onions if desired.
Per Serving: Calories 218; Fat: 9.17g; Sodium 73mg; Carbs: 29.87g; Sugars: 4.03g; Protein 4.39g

Beets Pickled with Balsamic and Allspice

Prep Time: 5 minutes | Cook Time: 15 minutes | Serves: 8

½ cup balsamic vinegar
¼ cup apple cider vinegar
3 tablespoons unrefined sugar
1 teaspoon salt
½ teaspoon ground coriander or 1 teaspoon coriander seeds

½ teaspoon ground allspice or 1 teaspoon allspice berries
½ cup water
3 or 4 large beets, peeled and sliced

1. Stir the vinegars, sugar, salt, coriander, allspice, and water together in the Instant pot. Put the beets in. Once the pressure valve is sealed and the lid is closed and locked, choose Pressure Cook and high pressure and set the timer for 8 minutes. 2. Quickly release the pressure on vent position when the cooking period is through, taking cautious not to touch your face or fingers to the steam release. 3. Carefully unlock and remove the lid once all the pressure has been removed. Scoop out the beets and serve after allowing to cool for a few minutes with the cover open to let the vinegar steam escape.
Per Serving: Calories 43; Fat: 1g; Sodium 319mg; Carbs: 9g; Sugars: 8g; Protein 1g

Salad of Potatoes

Prep Time: 5 minutes | Cook Time: 20 minutes | Serves: 4

4 to 6 medium russet potatoes, scrubbed and cut in large uniform cubes (4 to 5 cups)
½ cup unsweetened nondairy yogurt
2 teaspoons Dijon mustard

1½ teaspoons apple cider vinegar
½ teaspoon onion powder (optional)
¼ teaspoon salt
3 or 4 celery stalks, chopped
2 scallions, chopped
Freshly ground black pepper

1. Place a steam rack in the Instant pot, add one or two cups of water, and then place potatoes on rack. (Alternatively, you may just boil potatoes in water; however, this will result in much softer potatoes.) Select Pressure Cook and high pressure, set the timer for 6 minutes, secure the lid and check that the pressure valve is shut. 2. Allow the pressure to naturally relax for 10 minutes on seal position after the cook time is over. 3. In the meantime, combine the yoghurt, mustard, vinegar, onion powder (if using), and salt in a large bowl. Stir in the celery and scallions after adding them. 4. After releasing all the pressure, carefully unlock and remove the lid. Carefully remove the steam rack from the pot while using oven mitts (or drain the potatoes if you cooked them directly in the water). Stir the potatoes into the bowl with the veggies and dressing after allowing them to cool for a few minutes. After tasting, add pepper to taste.
Per Serving: Calories 318; Fat: 1g; Sodium 217mg; Carbs: 70g; Sugars: 4g; Protein 9g

Avocado Dip with Spicy Potato Bites

Prep Time: 5 minutes | Cook Time: 20 minutes | Serves: 4

4 to 6 medium russet potatoes, scrubbed and cut in large uniform cubes (4 to 5 cups)
1 avocado, peeled and pitted
2 tablespoons freshly squeezed lime juice
2 teaspoons onion powder, divided

1 teaspoon garlic powder, divided
Pinch salt
1 to 2 tablespoons water, if needed
1 tablespoon olive oil
½ teaspoon smoked paprika
¼ teaspoon ground chipotle pepper

1. In your Instant Pot, place a steam rack, add a cup or two of water, and add the potatoes to the rack. Make sure the pressure valve is shut, then close and lock the lid. Set the timer for 6 minutes and choose high pressure. 2. Allow the pressure to naturally relax for 10 minutes on seal position after the cook time is over. 3. Blend the avocado with the lime juice, salt, 1 teaspoon of onion powder, ½ teaspoon of garlic powder, and 1 teaspoon of garlic powder. Purée, adding water as necessary to reach the desired consistency. Put in a serving dish. 4. Carefully unlock and remove the lid once all the pressure has been removed. Lift the steam rack from the saucepan using oven mitts. 5. Then choose Sauté. Add the olive oil, paprika, chipotle pepper, remaining ½ teaspoon of garlic powder, remaining 1 teaspoon of onion powder, and the potatoes back to the saucepan. Stirring occasionally, cook for about 2 minutes or until any liquid has evaporated. Serve the avocado dipping sauce beside the potatoes.
Per Serving: Calories 412; Fat: 11g; Sodium 24mg; Carbs: 73g; Sugars: 3g; Protein 9g

Sweet Potato Bowls for Breakfast

Prep Time: 10 minutes | Cook Time: 20 minutes | Serves: 2

1 sweet potato, peeled and chopped
1 apple or pear, cored and quartered
½ cup nondairy milk, plus more as needed
2 tablespoons nut or seed butter

(almond, cashew, sunflower)
¼ teaspoon ground cinnamon (optional)
Pinch ground nutmeg (optional)
Unrefined sugar or pure maple syrup, for serving (optional)

1. Combine the sweet potato and apple in an Instant Pot-compatible heat-resistant dish. 2. Add a cup or two of water to the pot, insert the steam rack, and place the dish on the rack. Use a foil sling or silicone helping handles if necessary to lower the dish onto the steam rack if it won't fit otherwise. Select high pressure and set the timer for 6 minutes after sealing the pressure valve and closing the lid. 3. Allow the pressure to naturally relax for 10 minutes on seal position after the cook time is over. 4. Carefully unlock and remove the lid once all the pressure has been removed. Before gently removing the dish with oven gloves or tongs, let cool for a few minutes. Transfer the sweet potatoes and apples to a blender. 5. Add the milk, nut butter, cinnamon (if using), and nutmeg (if using). Purée. Add more milk if needed, plus

sugar or maple syrup, if you like.
Per Serving: Calories 214; Fat: 9g; Sodium 42mg; Carbs: 32g; Sugars: 26g; Protein 3.9g

Red Wine with Balsamic Mushrooms

Prep Time: 5 minutes | Cook Time: 10 minutes | Serves: 4

¼ cup dry red wine
¼ cup water
2 tablespoons balsamic vinegar
1 tablespoon olive oil
1 teaspoon cornstarch or arrowroot powder
½ teaspoon dried basil or mixed

herbs
¼ teaspoon salt, plus more as needed
Freshly ground black pepper
1 pound white mushrooms, quartered

1. Stir together the red wine, water, vinegar, olive oil, cornstarch, basil, and salt in the Instant pot. Use pepper to season. Mushrooms should be added to the sauce. Once the pressure valve is sealed and the lid is closed and locked, choose Pressure Cook and set the timer for 2 minutes on high. 2. Quickly release the pressure on vent position when the cooking period is through, taking cautious not to touch your face or fingers to the steam release. 3. Carefully unlock and remove the lid once all the pressure has been removed. If necessary, taste and add additional salt and pepper.
Per Serving: Calories 76; Fat: 3g; Sodium 155mg; Carbs: 8g; Sugars: 3g; Protein 2.1g

Yummy Ratatouille

Prep Time: 10 minutes | Cook Time: 35 minutes | Serves: 6

1 onion, diced
4 garlic cloves, minced
1 to 2 teaspoons olive oil
1 cup water
3 or 4 tomatoes, diced
1 eggplant, cubed
1 or 2 bell peppers, any color,

seeded and chopped
1½ tablespoons dried herbes de Provence (or any mixture of dried basil, oregano, thyme, marjoram, and rosemary)
½ teaspoon salt
Freshly ground black pepper

1. Choose Sauté on your Instant pot. Olive oil, onion, and garlic are added. The onion should soften after 4 to 5 minutes of cooking while being stirred occasionally. Tomatoes, eggplant, bell peppers, water, and Provence herbs should all be added. Stop Sauté. 2. Select Pressure Cook and high pressure, set the timer for 6 minutes, secure the lid and check that the pressure valve is shut. 3. Allow the pressure to naturally release on seal position for 20 minutes after the cook time is over. 4. Carefully unlock and remove the lid once all the pressure has been removed. After a brief cooling period, season with salt and pepper.
Per Serving: Calories 54; Fat: 1g; Sodium 201mg; Carbs: 11g; Sugars: 6g; Protein 2g

Pineapple with Butternut Squash

Prep Time: 5 minutes | Cook Time: 30 minutes | Serves: 4

1 butternut squash
4 cups chopped bok choy
1 scallion, chopped
1 to 2 teaspoons toasted sesame oil

10 ounces bite-size pineapple chunks (about 1½ cups)
1 to 2 tablespoons tamari or soy sauce

1. Butternut squash should be placed in the Instant pot. If the squash won't fit, slice it in half lengthwise, remove the seeds with a big spoon, and stack the halves cut-side down in the saucepan. Add one or two cups of water. Select Pressure Cook High Pressure, lock the lid, check that the pressure valve is shut, and set the timer for 10 to 15 minutes. (Depending on the size, set the timer for 5 to 7 minutes if you've chopped the squash in half.) 2. Allow the pressure to naturally release for 10 minutes on seal position after the cook time is over. 3. Carefully unlock and remove the lid once all the pressure has been removed. Carefully remove the squash from the pot with tongs or a big fork and spoon. Allow to cool for a few minutes. 4. Empty the water from the pot and return the pot to the pot. Choose Sauté. Add the sesame oil, bok choy, and scallion. The veggies should be cooked for 1 minute, stirring once or twice, until tender. 5. If the squash is entire, split it lengthwise, remove the skin, and scoop out the seeds. The squash should be chopped into bite-sized pieces and added to the saucepan with the pineapple and tamari. Mix everything together and heat well.
Per Serving: Calories 497; Fat: 18g; Sodium 349mg; Carbs: 40g; Sugars: 16g; Protein 4 3.9g

Curry with Green Peas And Cauliflower

Prep Time: 5 minutes | Cook Time: 15 minutes | Serves: 4

1 (1-inch) piece fresh ginger, peeled and minced (optional)	2 cups frozen peas
1 tablespoon coconut oil or olive oil	1 cup water
1 head cauliflower, chopped	2 tablespoons tomato paste
1 (28-ounce) can crushed tomatoes	1 tablespoon curry powder
	Salt
	Freshly ground black pepper

1. Choose Sauté on Instant pot. When the ginger is softened, add it together with the coconut oil and simmer for 2 to 3 minutes, stirring periodically. 2. Stir in the cauliflower, tomatoes, peas, tomato paste, water, and curry powder. Stop Sauté. 3. Depending on how soft you prefer your cauliflower, choose Pressure Cook and low pressure, shut the cover, check that the pressure valve is sealed, and set the timer for 1 to 2 minutes. 4. Quickly release the pressure on vent position when the cooking period is through, taking cautious not to touch your face or fingers to the steam release. 5. Carefully unlock and remove the lid once all the pressure has been removed. Add salt and pepper after tasting.
Per Serving: Calories 122; Fat: 4g; Sodium 271mg; Carbs: 18.7g; Sugars: 7g; Protein 5g

Thai Curry Stew

Prep time: 20 minutes | Cook time: 44 minutes | Serves: 4-6

2 tablespoons sesame oil	½ teaspoons ground cloves
2-pound beef chuck, cubed	½ teaspoons cardamom
2 onions, thinly sliced	½ teaspoons cumin
2 cloves garlic, pressed	1 cinnamon quill
1 (2-inch) galangal piece, peeled and sliced	Sea salt and ground white pepper, to taste
1 Bird's eye chili pepper, seeded and minced	½ (15-ounce) can full-fat coconut milk
½ cup tomato paste	2 cups cauliflower florets
4 cups chicken bone broth	2 tablespoons fresh cilantro, roughly chopped
¼ cup Thai red curry paste	
1 tablespoon soy sauce	

1. Press the "Sauté" button twice to select "Normal" settings and heat the sesame oil. 2. When the oil starts to sizzle, cook the meat until browned on all sides. 3. Add a splash of broth and use a spoon to scrape the brown bits from the bottom of the pot. 4. Next, stir in the onion, garlic, galangal, chili pepper, tomato paste, broth, curry paste, soy sauce, and spices. 5. Put on the pressure cooker's lid and turn the steam valve to "Sealing" position. 6. Set the Instant Pot on "Soup/Broth". 7. Use the "+/-" keys on the control panel to set the cooking time to 40 minutes. 8. Press the Pressure Level button to adjust the pressure to "High". 9. Once the cooking cycle is completed, quick-release the steam. 10. When all the steam is released, remove the pressure lid from the top carefully. 11. After that, add the coconut milk and cauliflower to the inner pot. 12. Set the Instant Pot on Pressure Cook again and cook for 4 minutes at High pressure. 13. Once cooking is complete, use a quick pressure release; carefully remove the lid. 14. Serve garnished with fresh cilantro. 15. Enjoy!
Per Serving: Calories 479; Fat 10g; Sodium 891mg; Carbs 22.9g; Fiber 4g; Sugar 4g; Protein 33g

Primavera Spaghetti Squash

Prep Time: 5 minutes | Cook Time: 20 minutes | Serves: 4

1 spaghetti squash	3 tablespoons nutritional yeast
2 tablespoons extra-virgin olive oil, divided	½ teaspoon sea salt
2 garlic cloves, minced	¼ teaspoon freshly ground black pepper
1 cup peas	1 cup cherry tomatoes, halved

1. ½ cups of water should be added to the Instant Pot bowl along with a steam rack. Scoop out the seeds after cutting the spaghetti squash in half crosswise. Place both halves, stacking if necessary, on the rack. 2. Close the lid. Choose Pressure Cook and cook on high pressure for 7 minutes, then quickly release the pressure in the pot on vent position when the timer beeps and remove the lid. Select Cancel. Cook the squash under high pressure for a further one to three minutes if you want it more tender. 3. Squash should be removed and put aside to cool. Remove the bowl's water and empty it. 4. Choose Sauté. 1 teaspoon of oil should be heated till shimmering. Cook the garlic for 30 seconds after adding it. The peas should be added and cooked for one to two minutes, stirring regularly, until tender. 5. Scrape the

squash threads off the skin with a fork, then add them back to the saucepan. Throw away the skin. Add the remaining 1 tablespoon of oil, salt, and pepper, along with the nutritional yeast. Add the cherry tomatoes and stir gently. Serve and enjoy!
Per Serving: Calories 154; Fat: 4g; Sodium 800mg; Carbs: 26g; Sugars: 12g; Protein 5g

Carrot Marinara Sauce

Prep Time: 10 minutes | Cook Time: 15 minutes | Serves: 6

1 tablespoon extra-virgin olive oil	needed
1 onion, diced	1 cup water
2 garlic cloves, minced	¼ teaspoon freshly ground black pepper, plus more as needed
6 to 8 carrots, peeled or scrubbed and chopped (about 5 cups)	1 tablespoon dried basil
2 medium beets, scrubbed and chopped (about 2 cups)	2 tablespoons freshly squeezed lemon juice
1 teaspoon sea salt, plus more as	

1. Select Instant Pot Sauté option. Oil must be heated until it shimmers. 2. Add the garlic and onion. Stirring periodically, sauté for 2 to 3 minutes until softened. Select Cancel. 3. Add the salt, pepper, 1 cup of water, carrots, and beets. 4. Seal the valve and lock the lid. Choose Pressure Cook under high pressure for 10 minutes, then release the pressure naturally for 15 minutes on seal position when the timer beeps. Remove the lid and quickly release any leftover pressure in the pot on vent position. 5. Basil and lemon juice should be combined. After allowing to cool for a few minutes, purée the beet and carrot combination using a standup blender or an immersion blender directly in the pot. Add more water if necessary. Taste and season with more salt and pepper, if desired.
Per Serving: Calories 50; Fat: 2g; Sodium 385mg; Carbs: 8g; Sugars: 3g; Protein 1g

Maple Parsnips

Prep Time: 5 minutes | Cook Time: 17 minutes | Serves: 4

2 or 3 parsnips, peeled and chopped	1 tablespoon olive oil
1 garlic clove, minced	½ teaspoon dried thyme leaves or ¼ teaspoon ground thyme
2 tablespoons balsamic vinegar	Pinch salt
1 tablespoon pure maple syrup	

1. Combine the parsnips, garlic, vinegar, maple syrup, olive oil, thyme, and salt in a heat-resistant dish that will fit inside the Instant pot. 2. After adding a cup or two of water to the saucepan and the steam rack, place the dish on the steam rack. Use a foil sling or silicone helping handles if necessary to lower the dish onto the steam rack if it won't fit otherwise. Select Pressure Cook and high pressure and set the timer for 6 minutes after sealing the pressure valve and closing the lid. 3. Allow the pressure to naturally release for 10 minutes on seal position after the cook time is over. 4. Carefully unlock and remove the lid once all the pressure has been removed. Lift the dish out of the oven with oven mitts and serve.
Per Serving: Calories 90; Fat: 3g; Sodium 8mg; Carbs: 14g; Sugars: 6g; Protein 1g

Miso Eggplant

Prep Time: 5 minutes | Cook Time: 17 minutes | Serves: 4

¼ cup white or red miso paste	1 tablespoon tomato paste
3 tablespoons water	1 teaspoon toasted sesame oil
1 tablespoon unrefined sugar	1 eggplant, cubed

1. Miso, water, sugar, tomato paste, and sesame oil should be thoroughly mixed and creamy in a big bowl. Toss the eggplant with the dressing after adding it. Transfer the eggplant to a heat-resistant plate that will fit inside the cooking pot of your Instant pot. 2. Place the dish on the rack, add a cup or two of water to the pot, and add a steam rack. Use a foil sling or silicone helping handles if necessary to lower the dish onto the steam rack if it won't fit otherwise. Select Pressure Cook and high pressure, set the timer for 6 minutes, close the lid and check that the pressure valve is shut. 3. Allow the pressure to naturally release for 10 minutes on seal position after the cook time is over. 4. Once all the pressure has released, carefully unlock and remove the lid. Using oven mitts, lift the dish out of the pot and serve.
Per Serving: Calories 89; Fat: 2g; Sodium 647mg; Carbs: 16g; Sugars: 8g; Protein 3g

Pork Chile Verde

Prep time: 20 minutes | Cook time: 20 minutes | Serves: 4-6

1 pound tomatillos, halved
4 garlic cloves, sliced
2 chili peppers, minced
2 heaping tablespoons cilantro, chopped
2 tablespoons olive oil
3-pound pork stew meat, cut into

2-inch cubes
1 onion, chopped
1 bell pepper, deveined and sliced
Salt and black pepper, to taste
2 cups vegetable broth

1. Place the tomatillos under a preheated broiler for about 6 minutes. Let cool enough to handle. 2. Purée the tomatillos with the garlic, chili peppers, and cilantro in your blender; process until chopped. 3. Press the "Sauté" button twice to select "Normal" settings and heat the oil. 4. Once hot, cook the pork until no longer pink. 5. Add the onion and cook for a few minutes more or until it is tender and translucent. 6. Add the remaining ingredients, including tomatillo sauce, to the inner pot. 7. Put on the pressure cooker's lid and turn the steam valve to "Sealing" position. 8. Set the Instant Pot to "Meat/Stew". 9. Use the "+/-" keys on the control panel to set the cooking time to 20 minutes. 10. Press the Pressure Level button to adjust the pressure to "High". 11. Once the cooking cycle is completed, quick-release the steam. 12. When all the steam is released, remove the pressure lid from the top carefully. 13. Ladle into serving bowls and garnish with tortillas if desired. 14. Bon appétit!
Per Serving: Calories 412; Fat 20g; Sodium 491mg; Carbs 9g; Fiber 3g; Sugar 8g; Protein 31g

Brunswick Stew

Prep time: 20 minutes | Cook time: 12 minutes | Serves: 4-6

2 tablespoons lard, melted
1 onion, diced
2 cloves garlic, minced
1-pound chicken breast, cut into
1-inch cubes
2 cups lima beans, soaked
1 (14½-ounce) can tomatoes, diced

2 cups chicken broth
1 tablespoon Worcestershire sauce
1 teaspoon Creole seasoning
Sea salt and black pepper, to taste
1 teaspoon hot sauce
1 cup corn kernels

1. Press the "Sauté" button twice to select "Normal" settings and melt the lard. 2. Once hot, cook the onion and garlic until just tender and aromatic. 3. Now, add the chicken and cook an additional 3 minutes, stirring frequently. 4. Add the lima beans, tomatoes, broth, Worcestershire sauce, Creole seasoning, salt, black pepper, and hot sauce to the inner pot. 5. Put on the pressure cooker's lid and turn the steam valve to "Sealing" position. 6. Set the Instant Pot to Pressure Cook. 7. Use the "+/-" keys on the control panel to set the cooking time to 12 minutes. 8. Press the Pressure Level button to adjust the pressure to "High". 9. Once the cooking cycle is completed, allow the steam to release naturally. 10. When all the steam is released, remove the pressure lid from the top carefully. 11. Stir in the corn kernels and seal the lid. Let it sit in the residual heat until heated through. 12. Enjoy!
Per Serving: Calories 419; Fat 14g; Sodium 791mg; Carbs 8.9g; Fiber 4.6g; Sugar 8g; Protein 3g

Tasty Kabocha squash

Prep Time: 5 minutes | Cook Time: 30 minutes | Serves: 4

1 kabocha squash
3 or 4 kale leaves, chopped
1 to 2 teaspoons toasted sesame oil
¼ cup tamari or soy sauce

2 tablespoons brown rice vinegar
1 tablespoon pure maple syrup or unrefined sugar
⅛ to ¼ teaspoon red pepper flakes

1. Place the whole squash in the Instant pot. (If the squash won't fit, split it in half lengthwise, scoop the seeds out with a big spoon, and then place the cut-side-down pieces in the pot.) Add one or two cups of water. Select Pressure Cook and high pressure, close the lid, check that the pressure valve is shut, and set the timer for 10 to 15 minutes. (Depending on the size, set the timer for 5 to 7 minutes if you've chopped the squash in half.) 2. After the cooking period is through, wait 10 minutes for the pressure to naturally release on seal position. 3. Take off the lid when all the pressure has been released. Lift the squash out of the pot gently using tongs or a big fork and spoon, and allow it to cool for a few minutes. 4. Empty the

water from the pot. Choose Sauté. The kale will wilt after approximately a minute of cooking when combined with the sesame oil in the pan. Add the red pepper flakes, vinegar, tamari, and maple syrup. 5. Squash should be cut in half lengthwise, the skin removed, and the seeds removed. Squash should be added to the pot after being broken up with a wooden spoon. (Alternatively, you may chop up the cooked squash before adding it to the pot.) Squash and spices are combined by stirring.
Per Serving: Calories 74; Fat: 2g; Sodium 1014mg; Carbs: 12g; Sugars: 8g; Protein 5g

Traditional Polish Stew

Prep time: 20 minutes | Cook time: 15 minutes | Serves: 4-6

2 slices smoked bacon, diced
1-pound Kielbasa, sliced
½ pound pork stew meat, cubed
1 onion, chopped
4 garlic cloves, sliced
2 carrots, trimmed and diced
1-pound sauerkraut, drained
1-pound fresh cabbage, shredded
1 teaspoon dried thyme
1 teaspoon dried basil

2 bay leaves
1 tablespoon cayenne pepper
1 teaspoon mustard seeds
1 teaspoon caraway seeds, crushed
Sea salt, to taste
½ teaspoons black peppercorns
½ cup dry red wine
2½ cups beef stock
½ cup tomato puree

1. Press the "Sauté" button twice to select "Normal" settings. 2. Now, cook the bacon, Kielbasa, and pork stew meat until the bacon is crisp; reserve. 3. Add the onion and garlic, and sauté them until they're softened and starting to brown. 4. Add the remaining ingredients to the inner pot, including the reserved meat mixture. 5. Put on the pressure cooker's lid and turn the steam valve to "Sealing" position. 6. Set the Instant Pot to Pressure Cook. 7. Use the "+/-" keys on the control panel to set the cooking time to 15 minutes. 8. Press the Pressure Level button to adjust the pressure to "High". 9. Once the cooking cycle is completed, quick-release the steam. 10. When all the steam is released, remove the pressure lid from the top carefully. 11. Ladle into individual bowls and serve warm.
Per Serving: Calories 584; Fat 15g; Sodium 441mg; Carbs 17g; Fiber 4.6g; Sugar 5g; Protein 29g

Vegetarian Ratatouille

Prep time: 20 minutes | Cook time: 15 minutes | Serves: 4-6

1-pound eggplant, cut into rounds
1 tablespoon sea salt
3 tablespoons olive oil
1 red onion, sliced
4 cloves garlic, minced
4 sweet peppers, seeded and chopped
1 red chili pepper, seeded and

minced
Sea salt and black pepper, to taste
1 teaspoon capers
½ teaspoons celery seeds
2 tomatoes, pureed
1 cup roasted vegetable broth
2 tablespoons coriander, chopped

1. Toss the eggplant with 1 tablespoon of sea salt; allow it to drain in a colander. 2. Press the "Sauté" button twice to select "Normal" settings and heat the olive oil. 3. Sauté the onion until tender and translucent, about 4 minutes. 4. Add the garlic and continue to sauté for 30 seconds more or until fragrant. 5. Add the remaining ingredients to the inner pot, including the drained eggplant. 6. Press the "Sauté" button two times to select "Normal" setting and cook for 7 minutes. 7. Bon appétit!
Per Serving: Calories 584; Fat 15g; Sodium 441mg; Carbs 17g; Fiber 4.6g; Sugar 5g; Protein 29g

Easy Beet Soup

Prep Time: 15 minutes | Cook Time: 35 minutes | Serves: 4

¾ lb. beets, peeled and chopped
4 cups chicken broth
1 onion, chopped

Salt and ground black pepper to taste
¼ cup fresh basil leaves, chopped

1. Put all the ingredients in the Inner Pot and stir to mix up. 2. Close and lock the lid. Select the Soup/Broth on the panel. 3. Press the button Again to choose Normal option; use the "+" button to adjust the cooking time to 35 minutes. 4. Press Pressure Level to choose High pressure. 5. When the timer beeps, leave the steam release handle in the Sealing position for 10 minutes, then release any remaining steam manually. 6. Uncover the lid carefully. 7. Blend with an immersion blender until smooth. 8. Season by adding some salt and pepper.
Per Serving: Calories 336; Fat 17.3g; Sodium 281mg; Carbs 8.1g; Fiber 5.3g; Sugars 17.7g; Protein 32.3g

Hungarian Beef Goulash

Prep time: 20 minutes | Cook time: 20 minutes | Serves: 4-6

2 tablespoons olive oil
2-pound beef chuck, cut into bite-sized pieces
¼ cup Hungarian red wine
2 onions, sliced
2 garlic cloves, crushed
1 red chili pepper, minced

Sea salt and black pepper, to taste
1 tablespoon Hungarian paprika
1 beef stock cube
2 cups water
2 ripe tomatoes, puréed
2 bay leaves

1. Press the "Sauté" button twice to select "Normal" settings and heat the oil. 2. Once hot, cook the beef until no longer pink. 3. Add the red wine and stir with a wooden spoon. 4. Stir in the remaining ingredients. 5. Put on the pressure cooker's lid and turn the steam valve to "Sealing" position. 6. Set the Instant Pot to Pressure Cook. 7. Use the "+/-" keys on the control panel to set the cooking time to 20 minutes. 8. Press the Pressure Level button to adjust the pressure to "High". 9. Once the cooking cycle is completed, quick-release the steam. 10. When all the steam is released, remove the pressure lid from the top carefully. 11. Serve in individual bowls and enjoy!
Per Serving: Calories 521; Fat 10.9g; Sodium 354mg; Carbs 10.5g; Fiber 4.1g; Sugar 8.2g; Protein 26g

Beef and Potato Stew

Prep time: 20 minutes | Cook time: 20 minutes | Serves: 4-6

1 tablespoon lard, melted
2-pound chuck roast, cut into 2-inch cubes
2 onions, chopped
2 cloves garlic, minced
2 tablespoons Hungarian paprika
4 bell peppers, deveined and chopped

1 chili pepper, chopped
1 cup tomato puree
4 potatoes, diced
4 cups beef broth
2 bay leaves
Seasoned salt and black pepper, to taste

1. Press the "Sauté" button twice to select "Normal" settings and melt the lard. 2. Once hot, cook the beef until no longer pink. 3. Add a splash of broth and stir with a wooden spoon, scraping up the browned bits on the bottom of the inner pot. 4. Add the onion to the inner pot; continue sautéing an additional 3 minutes. 5. Now, stir in the garlic and cook for 30 seconds more. 6. Stir in the remaining ingredients. 7. Put on the pressure cooker's lid and turn the steam valve to "Sealing" position. 8. Set the Instant Pot on "Meat/Stew". 9. Press the Pressure Level button to adjust the pressure to "High". 10. Use the "+/-" keys on the control panel to set the cooking time to 20 minutes. 11. Once the cooking cycle is completed, quick-release the steam. 12. When all the steam is released, remove the pressure lid from the top carefully. 13. Discard the bay leaves and serve in individual bowls. 14. Bon appétit!
Per Serving: Calories 492; Fat 12.9g; Sodium 414mg; Carbs 11g; Fiber 5g; Sugar 9g; Protein 31g

Hungarian Chicken Stew

Prep time: 20 minutes | Cook time: 15 minutes | Serves: 4-6

2 tablespoons lard, at room temperature
2-pound chicken, cut into pieces
2 onions, chopped
2 cloves garlic, minced
1 cup tomato puree
1 Hungarian pepper, diced

2 tablespoons Hungarian paprika
2 cups chicken stock
Kosher salt and cracked black pepper
3 tablespoons all-purpose flour
1 cup full-fat sour cream

1. Press the "Sauté" button twice to select "Normal" settings and melt the lard. 2. Once hot, cook the chicken for about 3 minutes or until no longer pink. 3. Add the onion to the inner pot; continue sautéing an additional 3 minutes. 4. Now, stir in the garlic and cook for 30 seconds more. 5. Add the tomato puree, Hungarian pepper, paprika, chicken stock, salt, and black pepper to the inner pot. 6. Put on the pressure cooker's lid and turn the steam valve to "Sealing" position. 7. Set the Instant Pot to Pressure Cook. 8. Use the "+/-" keys on the control panel to set the cooking time to 15 minutes. 9. Press the Pressure Level button to adjust the pressure to "High". 10. Once the cooking cycle is completed, quick-release the steam. 11. When all the steam is released, remove the pressure lid from the top carefully. 12. Remove the chicken from the inner pot; shred the chicken and discard the bones. 13. In a

mixing bowl, stir the flour into the sour cream. 14. Add the flour/cream mixture to the cooking liquid, stirring constantly with a wire whisk. 15. Let it simmer until the sauce is thickened. 16. Return the chicken to your paprika, stir and press the "Cancel" button. 17. Enjoy!
Per Serving: Calories 584; Fat 15g; Sodium 441mg; Carbs 17g; Fiber 4.6g; Sugar 5g; Protein 29g

Italian Beef Ragù

Prep time: 20 minutes | Cook time: 10 minutes | Serves: 4-6

2 tablespoons butter, melted
1 medium leek, diced
2 carrots, diced
1 stalk celery, diced
5-ounce bacon, diced
1-pound ground chuck
½ cup Italian red wine

¼ cup tomato puree
2 cups chicken stock
1 tablespoon Italian seasoning blend
½ teaspoons kosher salt
½ teaspoons black pepper

1. Press the "Sauté" button twice to select "Normal" settings and melt the butter. 2. Sauté the leek, carrot, celery and garlic for 2 to 3 minutes. 3. Add the bacon and ground beef to the inner pot; continue to cook an additional 3 minutes, stirring frequently. 4. Add the remaining ingredients to the inner pot. 5. Put on the pressure cooker's lid and turn the steam valve to "Sealing" position. 6. Set the Instant Pot to Pressure Cook. 7. Use the "+/-" keys on the control panel to set the cooking time to 5 minutes. 8. Press the Pressure Level button to adjust the pressure to "High". 9. Once the cooking cycle is completed, quick-release the steam. 10. When all the steam is released, remove the pressure lid from the top carefully. 11. Serve with hot pasta if desired. 12. Bon appétit!
Per Serving: Calories 449; Fat 2.9g; Sodium 511mg; Carbs 12g; Fiber 3g; Sugar 8g; Protein 28g

Spanish Olla Podrida

Prep time: 20 minutes | Cook time: 20 minutes | Serves: 4-6

2½-pound meaty pork ribs in adobo
½ pound Spanish chorizo sausage, sliced
1 tablespoon olive oil
2 onions, chopped
2 carrots, sliced

2 garlic cloves, sliced
Salt and black pepper, to taste
1 pound alubias de Ibeas beans, soaked overnight

1. Place the pork and sausage in the inner pot; cover with water. 2. Add the other ingredients and stir to combine. 3. Put on the pressure cooker's lid and turn the steam valve to "Sealing" position. 4. Set the Instant Pot to Pressure Cook. 5. Use the "+/-" keys on the control panel to set the cooking time to 20 minutes. 6. Press the Pressure Level button to adjust the pressure to "High". 7. Once the cooking cycle is completed, quick-release the pressure. 8. When all the steam is released, remove the pressure lid from the top carefully. 9. Serve hot with corn tortilla if desired. 10. Enjoy!
Per Serving: Calories 492; Fat 7.9g; Sodium 704mg; Carbs 6g; Fiber 3.6g; Sugar 6g; Protein 18g

Delicious Bean and Ham Soup

Prep Time: 20 minutes | Cook Time: 50 minutes | Serves: 6-8

1 leftover ham bone with meat
1 lb. white beans, rinsed
1 can diced tomatoes
1 clove garlic, minced

1 onion diced
1 tsp chili powder
1 lemon, juiced
8 cups chicken broth

1. Put all the ingredients in the Inner Pot and stir to mix up. 2. Close and lock the lid. Select the Bean/Chili on the panel. 3. Press the button Again to choose More option; use the "+" button to adjust the cooking time to 50 minutes. 4. Press Pressure Level to choose High pressure. 5. When the timer beeps, quickly and carefully turn the steam release handle from Sealing position to the Venting position. 6. Let the soup sit for 10 minutes. Uncover the lid carefully. 7. Serve.
Per Serving: Calories 336; Fat 17.3g; Sodium 281mg; Carbs 8.1g; Fiber 5.3g; Sugars 17.7g; Protein 32.3g

Mulligan Stew

Prep time: 20 minutes | Cook time: 20 minutes | Serves: 8

1 tablespoon lard, melted
2-pound pork butt roast, cut into
2-inch pieces
2-pound beef stew meat, cut into
2-inch pieces
2 chicken thighs, boneless
2 bell peppers, chopped
1 red chili pepper, chopped
1 onion, chopped

2 carrots, chopped
4 garlic cloves, chopped
4 cups beef bone broth
1 cup beer
1 (28-ounce) can tomatoes, crushed
Sea salt and black pepper, to taste
1 pound frozen corn kernels
3 tablespoons Worcestershire sauce

1. Press the "Sauté" button twice to select "Normal" settings and melt the lard. Once hot, brown the meat in batches. Remove the browned meats to a bowl. 2. Then, sauté the peppers, onion, carrots for about 3 minutes or until tender and fragrant. Add the garlic and continue to cook for 30 seconds more. 3. Add the meat back to the Instant Pot. Stir in the remaining ingredients, except for the corn kernels. 4. Put on the pressure cooker's lid and turn the steam valve to "Sealing" position. 5. Set the Instant Pot to "Meat/Stew". 6. Use the "+/-" keys on the control panel to set the cooking time to 20 minutes. 7. Press the Pressure Level button to adjust the pressure to "High". 8. Once the cooking cycle is completed, allow the steam to release naturally. 9. When all the steam is released, quick-release the steam. 10. Lastly, stir in the corn and continue to cook for a few minutes more on the "Sauté" function. 11. Serve immediately.
Per Serving: Calories 334; Fat 10.9g; Sodium 454mg; Carbs 10g; Fiber 3.1g; Sugar 5.2g; Protein 20g

Irish Bean Cabbage Stew

Prep time: 20 minutes | Cook time: 25 minutes | Serves: 4-6

2 cups white beans, soaked and rinsed
½ cup pearled barley
4 cups roasted vegetable broth
1 shallot, chopped
2 carrots, chopped
2 ribs celery, chopped
1 sweet pepper, chopped
1 serrano pepper, chopped

4 cloves garlic, minced
1-pound cabbage, chopped
½ pound potatoes, diced
2 bay leaves
½ teaspoons mustard seeds
½ teaspoons caraway seeds
1 teaspoon cayenne pepper
Sea salt and black pepper, to taste
1 (14½-ounce) can tomatoes, diced

1. Place the white beans, barley, and vegetable broth in the inner pot. 2. Put on the pressure cooker's lid and turn the steam valve to "Sealing" position. 3. Set the Instant Pot to "Bean/Chili". 4. Use the "+/-" keys on the control panel to set the cooking time to 25 minutes. 5. Press the Pressure Level button to adjust the pressure to "High". 6. Once the cooking cycle is completed, quick-release the steam. 7. When all the steam is released, remove the pressure lid from the top carefully. 8. Add the remaining ingredients and stir to combine. 9. Set the Instant Pot to Pressure Cook and cook for 5 minutes at High pressure. 10. Once cooking is complete, use a quick pressure release; carefully remove the lid. 11. Serve in individual bowls and enjoy!
Per Serving: Calories 449; Fat 2.9g; Sodium 511mg; Carbs 12g; Fiber 3g; Sugar 8g; Protein 28g

Rich Chicken Purloo

Prep time: 20 minutes | Cook time: 10 minutes | Serves: 8

1 tablespoon olive oil
1 onion, chopped
3-pound chicken legs, boneless and skinless
2 garlic cloves, minced
5 cups water
2 carrots, diced
2 celery ribs, diced

2 bay leaves
1 teaspoon mustard seeds
¼ teaspoon marjoram
Seasoned salt and black pepper, to taste
1 teaspoon cayenne pepper
2 cups white long-grain rice

1. Press the "Sauté" button twice to select "Normal" settings and heat the olive oil. 2. Now, add the onion and chicken legs; cook until the onion is translucent or about 4 minutes. 3. Stir in the minced garlic and continue to cook for a minute more. Add the water. 4. Put on the pressure cooker's lid and turn the steam valve to "Sealing" position. 5. Set the Instant Pot to Pressure Cook. 6. Use the "+/-" keys on the control panel to set the cooking time to 10 minutes. 7. Press the

Pressure Level button to adjust the pressure to "High". 8. Once the cooking cycle is completed, quick-release the steam. 9. When all the steam is released, remove the pressure lid from the top carefully. 10. Add the remaining ingredients. 11. Set the Instant Pot to Pressure Cook and cook for 5 minutes at High pressure. 12. Once cooking is complete, use a quick pressure release; carefully remove the lid. 13. Serve warm.
Per Serving: Calories 479; Fat 10g; Sodium 891mg; Carbs 22.9g; Fiber 4g; Sugar 4g; Protein 33g

Almond Lentil Vegetable Stew

Prep time: 20 minutes | Cook time: 10 minutes | Serves: 4-6

1 tablespoon olive oil
1 onion, chopped
1 teaspoon fresh garlic, minced
1 dried chili pepper, crushed
1 pound potatoes, cut into 1-inch pieces
1-pound cauliflower, broken into florets
1 cup green lentils
3 cups tomato juice

3 cups vegetable broth
Seasoned salt and black pepper, to taste
1 teaspoon cayenne pepper
½ cup almond butter
2 heaping tablespoons cilantro, roughly chopped
1 heaping tablespoon parsley, roughly chopped

1. Press the "Sauté" button twice to select "Normal" settings and heat the olive oil. 2. Now, sauté the onion until it is transparent. Add garlic and continue to sauté an additional minute. 3. Stir in the chili pepper, potatoes, cauliflower, lentils, tomato juice, vegetable broth, salt, black pepper, and cayenne pepper. 4. Put on the pressure cooker's lid and turn the steam valve to "Sealing" position. 5. Set the Instant Pot to Pressure Cook. 6. Use the "+/-" keys on the control panel to set the cooking time to 10 minutes. 7. Press the Pressure Level button to adjust the pressure to "High". 8. Once the cooking cycle is completed, quick-release the steam. 9. When all the steam is released, remove the pressure lid from the top carefully. 10. Stir in the almond butter. Press the "Sauté" button on "Less" settings. 11. And simmer for about 3 minutes. 12. Garnish with cilantro and parsley. 13. Bon appétit!
Per Serving: Calories 461; Fat 7.9g; Sodium 704mg; Carbs 6g; Fiber 3.6g; Sugar 6g; Protein 18g

Tasty Soup with Cheddar, Broccoli and Potato

Prep Time: 30 minutes | Cook Time: 10 minutes | Serves: 4-6

2 tbsp. butter
2 cloves garlic, crushed
2 lbs. Yukon gold potatoes, peeled and cut into small chunks
1 broccoli head, medium-sized, broken into large florets
4 cups vegetable broth

1 cup half and half
1 cup cheddar cheese, shredded
Chives or green onion, chopped, for garnish
Salt and ground black pepper to taste

1. To preheat the Inner Pot, press Sauté to select the program and then press it again to choose the Normal temperature option. Once hot, add the butter and melt it. 2. Add the garlic and sauté for 2-3 minutes, until browned. 3. Add the potato, broccoli, and broth into the Inner Pot. Add salt and pepper as you like. Stir to mix up. 4. Press the Cancel key to stop the Sauté function. 5. Close and lock the lid. Select the Pressure Cook on the panel. 6. Press the button Again to choose Less option; use the "-" button to adjust the cooking time to 5 minutes. 7. Press Pressure Level to choose High Pressure. 8. When the timer beeps, leave the steam release handle in the Sealing position for 10 minutes, then release any remaining steam manually. Uncover the lid carefully. 9. Add the half and half and ½ cup cheese into the Inner Pot. Blend with an immersion blender until smooth. 10. Season by adding some salt and pepper. 11. Add the remaining cheese and green onion on the top. 12. Serve and enjoy.
Per Serving: Calories 344; Fat 14.9g; Sodium 227mg; Carbs 14g; Fiber 1g; Sugars 1.4g; Protein 25.7g

Catalan Shellfish Stew

Prep time: 20 minutes | Cook time: 10 minutes | Serves: 4-6

4 tablespoons olive oil	4 cups clam juice
1 onion, chopped	1 laurel (bay leaf)
3 cloves garlic, minced	Sea salt and black pepper, to taste
4-ounce prosciutto, diced	1 teaspoon guindilla (cayenne pepper)
1½-pound shrimp	1 teaspoon rosemary, chopped
1½-pound clams	1 teaspoon basil, chopped
1 Chile de Árbol, minced	2 tomatoes, pureed
½ cup dry white wine	1 fresh lemon, sliced

1. Press the "Sauté" button two times to select "Normal" settings and heat the olive oil. 2. Now, sauté the onion until it is transparent. Add the garlic and continue to sauté an additional 1 minute. 3. Add the prosciutto and cook an additional 3 minutes. Add the remaining ingredients, except for the lemon. 4. Put on the pressure cooker's lid and turn the steam valve to "Sealing" position. 5. Set the Instant Pot to Pressure Cook. 6. Use the "+/-" keys on the control panel to set the cooking time to 10 minutes. 7. Press the Pressure Level button to adjust the pressure to "High". 8. Once the cooking cycle is completed, allow the steam to release naturally for 10 minutes. 9. When all the steam is released, remove the pressure lid from the top carefully. 10. Serve in individual bowls garnished with lemon slices. 11. Enjoy!
Per Serving: Calories 478; Fat 7.9g; Sodium 704mg; Carbs 6g; Fiber 3.6g; Sugar 6g; Protein 18g

Indian Bean Stew

Prep time: 20 minutes | Cook time: 26 minutes | Serves: 4-6

2 tablespoons sesame oil	5 cups vegetable broth
1 onion, sliced	1 teaspoon coriander seeds
4 cloves garlic, finely chopped	½ teaspoons cumin seeds
1 (1-inch) piece fresh ginger root, peeled and grated	¼ teaspoon ground cinnamon
2 cups red kidney beans, soaked overnight	Seasoned salt and black pepper, to taste
2 Bhut jolokia peppers, minced	2 tomatoes, pureed
1 teaspoon red curry paste	2 tablespoons fresh coriander, chopped

1. Press the "Sauté" button twice to select "Normal" settings and heat the oil. 2. Now, sauté the onion until it is transparent. 3. Add the garlic and ginger and continue to sauté an additional 1 minute. 4. Add the beans, peppers, curry paste, vegetable broth spices, and tomatoes. 5. Put on the pressure cooker's lid and turn the steam valve to "Sealing" position. 6. Set the Instant Pot to Pressure Cook. 7. Use the "+/-" keys on the control panel to set the cooking time to 25 minutes. 8. Press the Pressure Level button to adjust the pressure to "High". 9. Once the cooking cycle is completed, quick-release the pressure. 10. When all the steam is released, remove the pressure lid from the top carefully. 11. Serve in individual bowls garnished with fresh coriander. 12. Enjoy!
Per Serving: Calories 472; Fat 10.9g; Sodium 354mg; Carbs 10.5g; Fiber 4.1g; Sugar 8.2g; Protein 26g

Mediterranean Chicken Stew

Prep time: 20 minutes | Cook time: 15 minutes | Serves: 4

2 tablespoons olive oil	2 cups chicken bone broth
1 onion, chopped	2 bay leaves
1 stalk celery, chopped	Sea salt and black pepper, to taste
2 carrots, chopped	½ teaspoon dried basil
1 teaspoon garlic, minced	1 teaspoon dried oregano
4 chicken legs, boneless skinless	½ cup Kalamata olives, pitted and sliced
¼ cup dry red wine	
2 ripe tomatoes, pureed	

1. Press the "Sauté" button twice to select "Normal" settings and heat the oil. 2. Now, sauté the onion, celery, and carrot for 4 to 5 minutes or until they are tender. 3. Add the other ingredients, except for the Kalamata olives, and stir to combine. 4. Put on the pressure cooker's lid and turn the steam valve to "Sealing" position. 5. Set the Instant Pot to Pressure Cook. 6. Use the "+/-" keys on the control panel to set the cooking time to 15 minutes. 7. Press the Pressure Level button to adjust the pressure to "High". 8. Once the cooking cycle is completed, allow the steam to release naturally. 9. When all the steam is released,

remove the pressure lid from the top carefully. 10. Serve warm garnished with Kalamata olives. 11. Bon appétit!
Per Serving: Calories 479; Fat 10g; Sodium 891mg; Carbs 22.9g; Fiber 4g; Sugar 4g; Protein 33g

Seafood Vegetable Ragout

Prep time: 20 minutes | Cook time: 10 minutes | Serves: 4-6

2 tablespoons olive oil	1 bay leaf
1 shallot, diced	1-pound shrimp, deveined
2 carrots, diced	½ pound scallops
1 parsnip, diced	Seasoned salt and pepper, to taste
1 teaspoon fresh garlic, minced	1 tablespoon paprika
½ cup dry white wine	2 tablespoons fresh parsley, chopped
2 cups fish stock	1 lime, sliced
1 tomato, pureed	

1. Press the "Sauté" button twice to select "Normal" settings and heat the oil. 2. Now, sauté the shallot, carrot, and parsnip for 4 to 5 minutes or until they are tender. 3. Stir in the garlic and continue to sauté an additional 30 second or until aromatic. 4. Stir in the white wine, stock, tomato, bay leaf, shrimp, scallops, salt, black pepper, and paprika. 5. Put on the pressure cooker's lid and turn the steam valve to "Sealing" position. 6. Set the Instant Pot to Pressure Cook. 7. Use the "+/-" keys on the control panel to set the cooking time to 5 minutes. 8. Press the Pressure Level button to adjust the pressure to "High". 9. Once the cooking cycle is completed, allow the steam to release naturally for 5 minutes. 10. When all the steam is released, remove the pressure lid from the top carefully. 11. Enjoy!
Per Serving: Calories 449; Fat 2.9g; Sodium 511mg; Carbs 12g; Fiber 3g; Sugar 8g; Protein 28g

Fresh Fish Soup

Prep Time: 10 minutes | Cook Time: 10 minutes | Serves: 4-6

1 lb. white fish fillets, boneless, skinless and cubed	1 carrot, chopped
1 cup bacon, chopped	4 cups chicken stock
	2 cups heavy cream

1. In the Inner Pot, combine the fish, bacon, carrot, and stock. stir to mix up. 2. Close and lock the lid. Select the Pressure Cook on the panel. 3. Press the button Again to choose Less option; use the "-" button to adjust the cooking time to 5 minutes. 4. Press Pressure Level to choose High Pressure 5. When the timer beeps, quickly and carefully turn the steam release handle from Sealing position to the Venting position. Uncover the lid carefully. 6. Add the heavy cream and stir. 7. Press Sauté to select the program, press it again to choose the Less temperature option and then simmer for 3 minutes. 8. Serve.
Per Serving: Calories 305; Fat 15g; Sodium 548mg; Carbs 12g; Sugar 1.2g; Fiber 0.7g; Protein 29g

Vegan Pottage Stew

Prep time: 20 minutes | Cook time: 15 minutes | Serves: 4-6

2 tablespoons olive oil	2 thyme sprigs
1 onion, chopped	2 rosemary sprigs
2 garlic cloves, minced	Kosher salt and black pepper, to taste
2 carrots, diced	
2 parsnips, diced	¼ cup red wine
1 turnip, diced	1 cup porridge oats
4 cups vegetable broth	
2 bay leaves	

1. Press the "Sauté" button twice to select "Normal" settings and heat the olive oil until sizzling. 2. Now, sauté the onion and garlic until just tender and fragrant. 3. Add the remaining ingredients to the inner pot; stir to combine. 4. Put on the pressure cooker's lid and turn the steam valve to "Sealing" position. 5. Set the Instant Pot to Pressure Cook. 6. Use the "+/-" keys on the control panel to set the cooking time to 10 minutes. 7. Press the Pressure Level button to adjust the pressure to "High". 8. Once the cooking cycle is completed, quick-release the steam. 9. When all the steam is released, remove the pressure lid from the top carefully. 10. Ladle into individual bowls and serve immediately. 11. Bon appétit!
Per Serving: Calories 382; Fat 7.9g; Sodium 704mg; Carbs 6g; Fiber 3.6g; Sugar 6g; Protein 18g

Delicious Pumpkin Soup

Prep Time: 20 minutes | Cook Time: 15 minutes | Serves: 2-4

½ tbsp. butter
½ brown onion, chopped
½ butternut pumpkin, chunks
½ red potato or radishes, diced
Pinch curry powder
1½ cups chicken stock

½ apple, peeled, cored and grated
1 cup coconut milk
2 bay leaves
Salt and ground black pepper to taste

1. Insert the inner pot into the cooker base. 2. Connect the power cord to a 120 V power source. The cooker goes to Standby mode and the display indicates OFF. 3. Press Sauté to select the program and then press it again to choose the Normal temperature option. 4. Add the onion, pumpkin, potato, and curry powder. Stir and sauté for 7-9 minutes until the onion is browned. 5. Add the stock, apple, bay leaves, salt and black pepper, stir. Close and lock the lid. 6. Press the Cancel button to reset the cooking program, and then choose the Pressure Cook. 7. Press the button Again to choose Less option; use the "-" button to adjust the cooking time to 5 minutes. 8. Press Pressure Level to choose High pressure. 9. When the cooking is finished, select Cancel and leave the steam release handle in the Sealing position for 10 minutes. Uncover the lid carefully. 10. Remove the bay leaves. Add the milk and stir to mix up. 11. Blend the soup until smooth using an immersion blender. 12. Season by adding some salt and pepper. Serve.
Per Serving: Calories 336; Fat 17.3g; Sodium 281mg; Carbs 8.1g; Fiber 5.3g; Sugars 17.7g; Protein 32.3g

Basque Squid Stew

Prep time: 20 minutes | Cook time: 10 minutes | Serves: 4-6

2 tablespoons olive oil
1 onion, finely diced
2 cloves garlic, minced
1 thyme sprig, chopped
1 rosemary sprig, chopped
1 serrano pepper, deseeded and chopped
2 tomatoes, pureed
½ cup clam juice

1 cup chicken stock
½ cup cooking sherry
1-pound fresh squid, cleaned and sliced into rings
Sea salt and black pepper, to taste
1 teaspoon cayenne pepper
1 bay leaf
¼ teaspoon saffron
1 lemon, cut into wedges

1. Press the "Sauté" button twice to select "Normal" settings and heat the oil. 2. Now, sauté the onion until tender and translucent. 3. Now, add the garlic and continue to sauté an additional minute. 4. Add the remaining ingredients, except for the lemon. 5. Put on the pressure cooker's lid and turn the steam valve to "Sealing" position. 6. Set the Instant Pot to Pressure Cook. 7. Use the "+/-" keys on the control panel to set the cooking time to 10 minutes. 8. Press the Pressure Level button to adjust the pressure to "High". 9. Once the cooking cycle is completed, quick-release the pressure. 10. When all the steam is released, remove the pressure lid from the top carefully. 11. Serve garnished with lemon wedges. 12. Bon appétit!
Per Serving: Calories 493; Fat 12.9g; Sodium 414mg; Carbs 11g; Fiber 5g; Sugar 9g; Protein 31g

French Pot-Au-Feu

Prep time: 20 minutes | Cook time: 20 minutes | Serves: 4-6

2 tablespoons olive oil
2-pound beef pot roast, cut into 2-inch pieces
1 onion, chopped
2 carrots, chopped
3 garlic cloves, pressed
2 tomatoes, pureed
1 cup dry red wine

3 cups beef broth
½ teaspoons marjoram
½ teaspoons sage
Sea salt and black pepper, to taste
1 shallot, sliced
1 pound cremini mushrooms, sliced
1 cup chèvres cheese, crumbled

1. Press the "Sauté" button twice to select "Normal" settings and heat the olive oil. 2. Cook the beef in batches and transfer to a bowl. 3. Then, cook the onion in pan drippings. 4. Stir in the carrots and garlic and continue to cook an additional 3 minutes. 5. Add the tomatoes, wine, broth, marjoram, sage, salt, and black pepper. Add the browned beef. 6. Put on the pressure cooker's lid and turn the steam valve to "Sealing" position. 7. Set the Instant Pot on "Meat/Stew". 8. Use the "+/-" keys on the control panel to set the cooking time to 45 minutes. 9. Press the Pressure Level button to adjust the pressure to "High". 10. Once the cooking cycle is completed, quick-release the pressure. 11. When all the steam is released, remove the pressure lid from the top carefully. 12. Now, add the shallot and mushrooms; continue to cook on the "Sauté" function for 10 minutes. 13. Transfer your stew to a lightly greased casserole dish. 14. Top with the cheese and place under a preheated

broiler for 10 minutes or until the cheese melts. 15. Serve warm.
Per Serving: Calories 489; Fat 11g; Sodium 501mg; Carbs 8.9g; Fiber 4.6g; Sugar 8g; Protein 26g

Slumgullion Stew

Prep time: 20 minutes | Cook time: 10 minutes | Serves: 4-6

1 tablespoon canola oil
1 leek, chopped
2 garlic cloves, minced
2 carrots, chopped
½ (16-ounce) package macaroni
½ pound ground beef
½ pound pork sausage, crumbled

1½ cups tomato puree
1½ cups chicken broth
Seasoned salt and black pepper, to taste
1 (15-ounce) can stewed tomatoes
2 cups green beans, cut into thirds

1. Press the "Sauté" button twice to select "Normal" settings and heat the oil. 2. Now, sauté the leek, garlic and carrot until they have softened. 3. Then, add the macaroni, ground beef, sausage, tomato puree, chicken broth, salt, and black pepper to the inner pot. 4. Put on the pressure cooker's lid and turn the steam valve to "Sealing" position. 5. Set the Instant Pot to Pressure Cook. 6. Use the "+/-" keys on the control panel to set the cooking time to 10 minutes. 7. Press the Pressure Level button to adjust the pressure to "High". 8. Once the cooking cycle is completed, quick-release the pressure. 9. When all the steam is released, remove the pressure from the top carefully. 10. After that, add the canned tomatoes and green beans; let it simmer on the "Sauté" function for 2 to 3 minutes. 11. Bon appétit!
Per Serving: Calories 405; Fat 19g; Sodium 354mg; Carbs 15g; Fiber 5.1g; Sugar 8.2g; Protein 32g

Lentil Vegetable Hotpot

Prep time: 20 minutes | Cook time: 15 minutes | Serves: 4-6

1 tablespoon olive oil
1 onion, chopped
3 cloves garlic, minced
1 carrot, chopped
1 stalk celery, chopped
1 parsnip, chopped
2 cups brown lentils
2 tomatoes, pureed

1 sprig thyme, chopped
1 sprig rosemary, chopped
1 teaspoon basil
Kosher salt and black pepper, to taste
2 cups vegetable broth
3 cups Swiss chard, torn into pieces

1. Press the "Sauté" button twice to select "Normal" settings and heat the oil. 2. Sauté the onion until tender and translucent or about 4 minutes. 3. Then, stir in the garlic and cook an additional 30 seconds or until fragrant. 4. Now, stir in the carrot, celery, parsnip, lentils, tomatoes, spices, and broth. 5. Afterwards, add the Swiss chard to the inner pot. 6. Put on the pressure cooker's lid and turn the steam valve to "Sealing" position. 7. Set the Instant Pot to Pressure Cook. 8. Use the "+/-" keys on the control panel to set the cooking time to 10 minutes. 9. Press the Pressure Level button to adjust the pressure to "High". 10. Once the cooking cycle is completed, quick-release the pressure. 11. When all the steam is released, remove the pressure lid from the top carefully. 12. Bon appétit!
Per Serving: Calories 419; Fat 14g; Sodium 791mg; Carbs 8.9g; Fiber 4.6g; Sugar 8g; Protein 3g

Barley Pottage

Prep time: 20 minutes | Cook time: 20 minutes | Serves: 4-6

1 tablespoon olive oil
1 onion, chopped
2 cloves garlic, minced
1 red chili pepper, minced
2 sweet peppers, seeded and chopped
1½ cups pearled barley
2 cups water

4 cups vegetable broth
2 stalks celery, chopped
2 carrots, chopped
2 tomatoes, pureed
1 teaspoon red pepper flakes
Sea salt and black pepper, to taste

1. Press the "Sauté" button twice to select "Normal" settings and heat the olive oil. 2. Now, sauté the onion until tender and translucent. 3. Then, stir in the garlic and peppers and cook an additional 3 minutes. Stir in the pearled barley. 4. Pour in water and broth. 5. Add the remaining ingredients to the inner pot. 6. Put on the pressure cooker's lid and turn the steam valve to "Sealing" position. 7. Set the Instant Pot to Pressure Cook. 8. Use the "+/-" keys on the control panel to set the cooking time to 15 minutes. 9. Press the Pressure Level button to adjust the pressure to "High". 10. Once the cooking cycle is completed, quick-release the steam. 11. When all the steam is released, remove the pressure lid from the top carefully. 12. Bon appétit!
Per Serving: Calories 405; Fat 10.9g; Sodium 454mg; Carbs 10g; Fiber 3.1g; Sugar 5.2g; Protein 20g

Homemade Broccoli Cheddar Soup

Prep Time: 10 minutes | Cook Time: 15 minutes | Serves: 4-6

1 tbsp. olive oil	4 cups chicken broth
½ onion, chopped	1 tsp garlic salt
2 carrots, chopped	1½ cups cheddar cheese, grated
6 cups broccoli, chopped	¼ cup heavy cream

1. Insert the inner pot into the cooker base. 2. Connect the power cord to a 120 V power source. The cooker goes to Standby mode and the display indicates OFF. 3. Press Sauté to select the program and then press it again to choose the Normal temperature option. 4. Pour the oil into the Inner Pot and heat it. 5. Add the onion and sauté for 3-4 minutes until translucent. 6. Add the carrots and broccoli and sauté for 2 minutes more. 7. Pour in the broth. Press the Cancel key to stop the Sauté function. 8. Close and lock the lid. Select the Pressure Cook on the panel. 9. Press the button Again to choose Less option; use the "-" button to adjust the cooking time to 5 minutes. 10. Press Pressure Level to choose High Pressure. 11. When the timer beeps, quickly and carefully turn the steam release handle from Sealing position to the Venting position. Uncover the lid carefully. 12. Let the dish chill for a while. 13. Blend the soup to your desired texture using an immersion blender. 14. Season with salt and add the cheese and heavy cream. Stir to mix up for 1-2 minutes until the cheese melts. 15. Serve.
Per Serving: Calories 236; Fat 13.9g; Sodium 451mg; Carbs 13.2g; Fiber 1.2g; Sugars 1.4g; Protein 14.3g

Chicken Fricassee with Wine

Prep time: 20 minutes | Cook time: 15 minutes | Serves: 4-6

2 tablespoons canola oil	½ teaspoon mustard powder
6 chicken wings	2 carrots, chopped
1 onion, chopped	2 celery stalks, chopped
2 garlic cloves, minced	3 cups vegetable broth
Kosher salt and black pepper, to taste	½ cup cooking sherry
1 teaspoon cayenne pepper	2 tablespoons all-purpose flour
1 teaspoon celery seeds	1 cup double cream

1. Press the "Sauté" button twice to select "Normal" settings and heat 1 tablespoon of olive oil. 2. Now, cook the chicken wings for 2 to 3 minutes per side; set aside. 3. Add a splash of cooking sherry to deglaze the pot. 4. Then, heat the remaining tablespoon of olive oil; sauté the onion until just tender or about 3 minutes. 5. Stir in the garlic and continue to cook an additional minute, stirring frequently. 6. Add the reserved chicken, salt, black pepper, cayenne pepper, celery seeds, mustard powder, carrots, celery, broth, and sherry to the inner pot. 7. Put on the pressure cooker's lid and turn the steam valve to "Sealing" position. 8. Set the Instant Pot on "Poultry". 9. Use the "+/-" keys on the control panel to set the cooking time to 15 minutes. 10. Press the Pressure Level button to adjust the pressure to "High". 11. Once the cooking cycle is completed, quick-release the pressure. 12. When all the steam is released, remove the pressure lid from the top carefully. 13. Mix the flour with the double cream. 14. Add the flour mixture to the hot cooking liquid. 15. Seal the lid and let it sit in the residual heat until thoroughly warmed. 16. Ladle into individual bowls and serve. 17. Bon appétit!
Per Serving: Calories 334; Fat 7.9g; Sodium 704mg; Carbs 6g; Fiber 3.6g; Sugar 6g; Protein 18g

Hyderabadi- Lentil Stew

Prep time: 20 minutes | Cook time: 10 minutes | Serves: 4-6

2 tablespoons canola oil	½ teaspoons tamarind paste
1 teaspoon cumin seeds	½ teaspoons red chili powder
1 onion, chopped	10 curry leaves
1 teaspoon garlic paste	1 cup tomato sauce
2 cups yellow lentils, soaked for 30 minutes and rinsed	Kosher salt and white pepper, to taste

1. Press the "Sauté" button twice to select "Normal" settings and heat the oil. 2. Then, sauté the cumin seeds for 1 to 2 minutes, stirring frequently. 3. Then, add the onion and cook an additional 2 minutes. Stir in the remaining ingredients. 4. Put on the pressure cooker's lid and turn the steam valve to "Sealing" position. 5. Set the Instant Pot to Pressure Cook. 6. Use the "+/-" keys on the control panel to set the cooking time to 5 minutes. 7. Press the Pressure Level button to adjust the pressure to "High". 8. Once the cooking cycle is completed, allow the steam to release naturally for 10 minutes. 9. When all the steam is released, remove the pressure lid from the top carefully. 10. Ladle into individual bowls and serve immediately. 11. Bon appétit!

Per Serving: Calories 405; Fat 12.9g; Sodium 414mg; Carbs 11g; Fiber 5g; Sugar 9g; Protein 31g

Oyster Stew with Chorizo

Prep time: 20 minutes | Cook time: 10 minutes | Serves: 4-6

2 tablespoons olive oil	½ pound fresh oysters, cleaned
8-ounce Spanish chorizo sausage, sliced	Sea salt and black pepper, to taste
1 onion, chopped	3 cups chicken broth
1 teaspoon ginger-garlic paste	2 cups kale leaves, washed
½ teaspoons dried rosemary	1 cup heavy cream
½ teaspoons smoked paprika	

1. Press the "Sauté" button twice to select "Normal" settings and heat the sesame oil. 2. When the oil starts to sizzle, cook the sausage until no longer pink. 3. Add the onion to the inner pot and continue to sauté for a further 3 minutes or until tender and translucent. 4. Now, stir in the ginger-garlic paste, rosemary, paprika, oysters, salt, pepper, and chicken broth. 5. Put on the pressure cooker's lid and turn the steam valve to "Sealing" position. 6. Set the Instant Pot to Pressure Cook. 7. Use the "+/-" keys on the control panel to set the cooking time to 6 minutes. 8. Press the Pressure Level button to adjust the pressure to "High". 9. Once the cooking cycle is completed, quick-release the steam. 10. When all the steam is released, remove the pressure lid from the top carefully. 11. Add the kale leaves and heavy cream, seal the lid again, and let it sit in the residual heat. 12. Serve warm and enjoy!
Per Serving: Calories 412; Fat 20g; Sodium 491mg; Carbs 9g; Fiber 3g; Sugar 8g; Protein 31g

Tasty Beef Soup

Prep Time: 10 minutes | Cook Time: 20 minutes | Serves: 4-6

1 lb. beef meat, ground	½ cup white rice
1 tbsp. vegetable oil	15 oz. canned garbanzo beans, rinsed
1 celery rib, chopped	14 oz. canned tomatoes, crushed
1 yellow onion, chopped	12 oz. spicy V8 juice
3 cloves garlic, minced	28 oz. canned beef stock
1 potato, cubed	Salt and black pepper to taste
2 carrots, thinly sliced	½ cup frozen peas

1. Insert the inner pot into the cooker base. Do not use a lid. 2. Press Sauté to select the program and then press it again to choose the Normal temperature option. 3. After 10 seconds, the cooker displays On to indicate that it has begun heating. 4. When display switches from On to Hot, add the ground beef and cook, stirring, for 5 minutes, until browned. When cooking completes, transfer the meat to a bowl. 5. Add the oil, celery and onion, stirring for 5 minutes, and then add the garlic and sauté for another 1 minute. 6. Stir in the potato, carrots, rice, beans, tomatoes, spicy juice, stock, browned beef, salt and pepper. 7. Press the Cancel key to stop the Sauté function. 8. Lock the lid in right way and then resume cooking for 5 minutes on Pressure Cook mode at High Pressure. 9. When the time is up, use a quick release and then remove the lid carefully. 10. Stir in the peas and let sit for 5 minutes. 11. Serve and enjoy.
Per Serving: Calories 351; Fat 22g; Sodium 502mg; Carbs 15.2g; Sugar 1.1g; Fiber 0.7g; Protein 26.4g

Homemade Chicken Moringa Soup

Prep Time: 15 minutes | Cook Time: 20 minutes | Serves: 6-8

1½ lbs. chicken breasts	1 thumb-size ginger
5 cups water	2 cups moringa leaves or kale leaves
1 onion, chopped	
2 cloves garlic, minced	Salt and ground black pepper to taste
1 cup tomatoes, chopped	

1. Combine all of the ingredients, except moringa leaves, in the Inner Pot and stir to mix up. 2. Close and lock the lid. Select the Poultry on the panel. 3. Press the button Again to choose Normal option. 4. When the timer beeps, leave the steam release handle in the Sealing position for 15 minutes, then release any remaining steam manually. Uncover the lid carefully. 5. Add the moringa leaves and stir. Press Sauté to select the program and then press it again to choose the Less temperature option and then simmer for 3 minutes. 6. Season by adding some salt and pepper. 7. Serve and enjoy.
Per Serving: Calories 249; Fat 13g; Sodium 556mg; Carbs 10g; Sugar 1.1g; Fiber 0.7g; Protein 31g

Kentucky Burgoo

Prep time: 20 minutes | Cook time: 55 minutes | Serves: 8

2 tablespoons lard, melted	2 carrots, sliced thickly
2 onions, chopped	2 parsnips, sliced thickly
1-pound pork shank, cubed	1 celery rib, sliced thickly
2-pound beef shank, cubed	2 sweet peppers, seeded and sliced
1-pound chicken legs	1 jalapeno pepper, seeded and
½ cup Kentucky bourbon	minced
4 cups chicken broth	1 teaspoon dried sage, crushed
2 cups dry lima beans, soaked	1 teaspoon dried basil, crushed
2 cups tomato puree	Salt and black pepper, to taste
1 pound potatoes, diced	

1. Press the "Sauté" button two times to select "Normal" settings and melt 1 tablespoon of lard. 2. Once hot, sauté the onion until tender and translucent; reserve. 3. Add the remaining tablespoon of lard; brown the meat in batches until no longer pink or about 4 minutes. 4. Add a splash of Kentucky bourbon to deglaze the pot. Pour chicken broth into the inner pot. 5. Put on the pressure cooker's lid and turn the steam valve to "Sealing" position. 6. Set the Instant Pot on "Meat/Stew". 7. Use the "+/-" keys on the control panel to set the cooking time to 45 minutes. 8. Press the Pressure Level button to adjust the pressure to "High". 9. Once the cooking cycle is completed, quick-release the pressure. 10. When all the steam is released, remove the pressure lid from the top carefully. 11. Shred chicken meat and discard the bones; add the chicken back to the inner pot. 12. Next, stir in lima beans and tomato puree. 13. Set the Instant Pot on Pressure Cook. Cook for 5 minutes at High pressure. 14. Once cooking is complete, use a quick pressure release; carefully remove the lid. 15. Then, stir in the remaining ingredients, including the sautéed onion. 16. Set the Instant Pot on Pressure Cook again. Cook for 5 minutes at High pressure. 17. Once cooking is complete, use a quick pressure release; carefully remove the lid. 18. Serve with cornbread if desired.
Per Serving: Calories 382; Fat 7.9g; Sodium 704mg; Carbs 6g; Fiber 3.6g; Sugar 6g; Protein 18g

Fresh and Delicious Buffalo Chicken Soup

Prep Time: 15 minutes | Cook Time: 10 minutes | Serves: 4

2 chicken breasts, boneless, skinless, frozen or fresh	1 tbsp. ranch dressing mix
1 clove garlic, chopped	3 cups chicken broth
¼ cup onion, diced	⅓ cup hot sauce
½ cup celery, diced	2 cups cheddar cheese, shredded
2 tbsp. butter	1 cup heavy cream

1. Put the chicken breasts, garlic, onion and celery into the Inner Pot and then add the butter, ranch dressing mix, broth, and hot sauce before mixing them up. 2. Close and lock the lid and turn the steam release handle to the Sealing position. 3. Select Pressure Cook mode. Press Pressure Cook button again to adjust the cooking time to 10 minutes. Press Pressure level to choose High Pressure. 4. Leave the steam release handle in the Sealing position for 10 minutes after cooking has completed, then turn the steam release handle to the Venting position. 5. Transfer the chicken to a plate and shred the meat. Return to the pot. 6. Add the cheese and heavy cream. Stir to mix up. 7. Let sit for 5 minutes and serve.

Lentil Curry Stew

Prep time: 20 minutes | Cook time: 15 minutes | Serves: 4-6

Dahl:

2 tablespoons butter	2 tomatoes, chopped
1 brown onion, chopped	½ teaspoons ground cumin
4 garlic cloves, minced	¼ teaspoon ground cardamom
1 (1-inch) piece ginger, peeled and grated	1½ cups dried chana dal, soaked
1 red chili pepper, deseeded and minced	4 cups vegetable broth
6 fresh curry leaves	½ teaspoons turmeric powder
	Kosher salt and black pepper, to taste

Tadka (Tempering):

1 tablespoon butter	½ onion, sliced
A pinch of asafetida	1 bay leaf
½ teaspoons cumin seeds	2 dried chili peppers, seeded and
1 teaspoon mustard seeds	cut in half

1. Press the "Sauté" button twice to select "Normal" settings and melt 2 tablespoons of butter. 2. Once hot, cook the onion until tender and

78 | Chapter 5 Soup, Stew, and Chili Recipes

translucent or about 3 minutes. 3. Then, stir in the garlic and ginger; continue to cook an additional minute or until they are fragrant. 4. Add the remaining ingredients for the Dahl. 5. Put on the pressure cooker's lid and turn the steam valve to "Sealing" position. 6. Set the Instant Pot to Pressure Cook. 7. Use the "+/-" keys on the control panel to set the cooking time to 10 minutes. 8. Press the Pressure Level button to adjust the pressure to "High". 9. Once the cooking cycle is completed, quick-release the pressure. 10. When all the steam is released, remove the pressure lid from the top carefully. 11. Clean the inner pot and Press the "Sauté" button two times to select "Normal" settings again. 12. Melt 1 tablespoon of butter. 13. Now, add a pinch of asafetida, cumin seeds, mustard seeds, onion and bay leaf; sauté for a minute. 14. Stir in the dried chili peppers and cook for 30 seconds longer. 15. Pour the hot tadka over the hot dal and serve.
Per Serving: Calories 305; Fat 7.9g; Sodium 704mg; Carbs 6g; Fiber 3.6g; Sugar 6g; Protein 18g

Delicious Beef Barley Soup

Prep Time: 20 minutes | Cook Time: 50 minutes | Serves: 6-8

2 tbsp. olive oil	4 large carrots, chopped
2 lbs. beef chuck roast, cut into 1½ inch steaks	1 stalk of celery, chopped
Salt and ground black pepper to taste	1 cup pearl barley, rinsed
	1 bay leaf
2 onions, chopped	8 cups chicken stock
4 cloves of garlic, sliced	1 tbsp. fish sauce

1. Insert the inner pot into the cooker base. 2. Connect the power cord to a 120 V power source. The cooker goes to Standby mode and the display indicates OFF. 3. Press Sauté to select the program and then press it again to choose the Normal temperature option. 4. Pour the oil into the Inner Pot and heat it. Then Sprinkle the beef with salt and pepper. Put in the pot and brown for about 5 minutes. Turn and brown the other side. 5. Transfer the meat to a bowl. 6. Add the onion, garlic, carrots, and celery, stirring, for 6 minutes, and then return the beef to the pot. Add the pearl barley, bay leaf, chicken stock and fish sauce. Stir to mix up. 7. Close and lock the lid. Press the Cancel button to reset the cooking program, then select the Pressure Cook on the panel. 8. Press the Pressure Cook button Again to choose Normal option; use the "-" button to adjust the cooking time to 30 minutes. 9. Press Pressure Level to choose High Pressure. 10. Leave the steam release handle in the Sealing position for 10 minutes after cooking has completed, and then release any remaining pressure manually. Open the lid carefully. 11. Remove cloves garlic, large vegetable chunks and bay leaf. 12. Season by adding some salt and pepper.
Per Serving: Calories 285; Fat 9.8g; Sodium 639mg; Carbs 11.1g; Fiber 1.2g; Sugars 5.1g; Protein 27.8g

Homemade Beef Borscht Soup

Prep Time: 20 | Cook Time: 20 minutes | Serves: 4-6

2 lbs. ground beef	3 cups shredded cabbage
3 beets, peeled and diced	6 cups beef stock
2 large carrots, diced	½ tbsp. thyme
3 stalks of celery, diced	1 bay leaf
1 onion, diced	Salt and ground black pepper to taste
2 cloves garlic, diced	

1. Insert the inner pot into the cooker base. Connect the power cord to a 120 V power source. The cooker goes to Standby mode and the display indicates OFF. 2. Press Sauté to select the program and then press it again to choose the Normal temperature option. 3. After 10 seconds, the cooker displays on to indicate that it has begun heating. 4. When display switches from On to Hot, add the ground beef and cook, stirring, for 5 minutes, until browned. 5. Add all the rest ingredients into the Inner Pot and stir to mix up. Close and lock the lid. 6. Press the Cancel key to stop the Sauté function. 7. Select the Pressure Cook on the panel. 8. Press the button Again to choose Less option; use the" – "button to adjust the cooking time to 15 minutes. 9. Press Pressure Level to choose High Pressure. 10. When cooking completes, leave the steam release handle in the Sealing position for 10 minutes after cooking has completed, and then release any remaining pressure manually. Open the lid carefully. 11. Let the dish sit for 5-10 minutes and serve.
Per Serving: Calories 305; Fat 15g; Sodium 548mg; Carbs 12g; Sugar 1.2g; Fiber 0.7g; Protein 29g

Egg Roll Soup Easy to Make

Prep Time: 15 minutes | Cook Time: 35 minutes | Serves: 4-6

1 tbsp. olive oil
1 onion, cubed
1 lb. ground beef
½ head cabbage, chopped
2 cups carrots, shredded
1 tsp garlic powder
1 tsp onion powder

1 tsp ground ginger
⅔ cup coconut aminos or soy sauce
4 cups chicken broth
Salt and ground black pepper to taste

1. Insert the inner pot into the cooker base. 2. Connect the power cord to a 120 V power source. The cooker goes to Standby mode and the display indicates OFF. 3. Press Sauté to select the program and then press it again to choose the Normal temperature option. 4. Pour the oil into the Inner Pot and heat it. 5. Add the onion and ground beef. Cook for 4-5 minutes, stir now and then and browned all the meat. 6. Add the cabbage, carrots, garlic powder, onion powder, ginger, coconut aminos, and broth. stir to mix up. 7. Add some salt and pepper before stirring. Close and lock the lid. 8. Press the Cancel button to stop the Sauté function, then press Soup/Broth to select the program and then press it again to choose the Less temperature option, and use the "+" button to adjust the time to 25 minutes. 9. Once timer beeps, quickly and carefully turn the steam release handle from Sealing position to the Venting position. Uncover the lid carefully. 10. Let the soup sit for 5-10 minutes and serve.

Per Serving: Calories 285; Fat 9.8g; Sodium 639mg; Carbs 11.1g; Fiber 1.2g; Sugars 5.1g; Protein 27.8g

Wonderful Cauliflower Soup

Prep Time: 15 minutes | Cook Time: 10 minutes | Serves: 4

1 tbsp. butter
1 large onion, chopped
3 cups chicken broth

1 medium cauliflower, chopped
Salt and ground black pepper to taste

1. Insert the inner pot into the cooker base. 2. Connect the power cord to a 120 V power source. The cooker goes to Standby mode and the display indicates OFF. 3. Press Sauté to select the program and then press it again to choose the Normal temperature option. 4. Once hot, add the butter and melt it. 5. Add the onion and sauté for 4-5 minutes, until softened. 6. Add the broth, cauliflower, salt and pepper. Stir to mix up. Close and lock the lid. 7. Press the Cancel button to stop the Sauté function, then select the Pressure Cook on the panel. 8. Press the button Again to choose Less option; use the "–" button to adjust the cooking time to 5 minutes. 9. Press Pressure Level to choose High pressure. 10. Once timer beeps, quickly and carefully turn the steam release handle from Sealing position to the Venting position. Uncover the lid carefully. 11. Blend the soup to your desired texture using an immersion blender. 12. Serve and enjoy.

Per Serving: Calories 344; Fat 14.9g; Sodium 227mg; Carbs 14g; Fiber 1g; Sugars 1.4g; Protein 25.7g

Tasty Wild Rice and Chicken Soup

Prep Time: 15 minutes | Cook Time: 15 minutes | Serves: 4-6

2 tbsp. butter
1 cup yellow onion, chopped
1 cup celery, chopped
1 cup carrots, chopped
6 oz. wild rice
2 chicken breasts, skinless and boneless and chopped
1 tbsp. parsley, dried
28 oz. chicken stock

A pinch of red pepper flakes
Salt and ground black pepper to taste
2 tbsp. cornstarch mixed with 2 tbsp. water
4 oz. cream cheese, cubed
1 cup milk
1 cup half and half

1. Insert the inner pot into the cooker base. Do not use a lid. 2. Connect the power cord to a 120 V power source. The cooker goes to Standby mode and the display indicates OFF. 3. Press Sauté to select the program and then press it again to choose the Normal temperature option. Once hot, add the butter and melt it. 4. Add the onion, celery, and carrot. Stir and sauté for 5 minutes. 5. Add the rice, chicken breasts, parsley, stock, red pepper, salt and black pepper. Stir to mix up. 6. Close and lock the lid. Press the Cancel button to stop the Sauté function, then select the Pressure Cook on the panel. 7. Press the button Again to choose Less option; use the "-" button to adjust the cooking time to 5 minutes. 8. Press Pressure Level to choose High pressure. 9. When the timer beeps, quickly and carefully turn the steam release handle from Sealing position to the Venting position.

Uncover the lid carefully. 10. Add the cornstarch mixed with water and stir to mix up. 11. Add the cheese, milk, half and half and stir. 12. Press Sauté to select the program and then press it again to choose the Less temperature option and cook for 3 minutes. 13. Serve.

Per Serving: Calories 336; Fat 17.3g; Sodium 281mg; Carbs 8.1g; Fiber 5.3g; Sugars 17.7g; Protein 32.3g

Delicious Chicken Noodle Soup

Prep Time: 20 minutes | Cook Time: 10 minutes | Serves: 6

3 tbsps. butter
1 medium onion, diced
3 celery stalks, diced
2 large carrots, diced
5 cloves garlic, minced
1 tsp oregano
1 tsp basil, dried
1 tsp thyme, dried
2 cups skinless and boneless

chicken breasts, cooked and cubed
8 cups chicken broth or vegetable broth
8 oz. spaghetti noodles break in half
2 cups spinach, chopped
Salt and ground black pepper to taste

1. Insert the inner pot into the cooker base. Do not use a lid. 2. Connect the power cord to a 120 V power source. The cooker goes to Standby mode and the display indicates OFF. 3. Press Sauté to select the program and then press it again to choose the Normal temperature option Once hot, add the butter and melt it. 4. Add the onion, celery, carrot and a big pinch of salt. Stir and sauté for 5 minutes until they're soft. 5. Add the garlic, oregano, basil and thyme. stir to mix up and sauté for 1 minute more. 6. Add the chicken, broth and noodles. And then close and lock the lid. 7. Press the Cancel button to reset the cooking program, then select the Pressure Cook on the panel. 8. Press the button Again to choose Less option; use the "-" button to adjust the cooking time to 4 minutes. 9. Press Pressure Level to choose High Pressure. 10. When the timer beeps, quickly and carefully turn the steam release handle from Sealing position to the Venting position. Uncover the lid carefully. 11. Add the spinach and Add salt and pepper as you like. stir to mix up and enjoy it.

Per Serving: Calories 305; Fat 15g; Sodium 548mg; Carbs 12g; Sugar 1.2g; Fiber 0.7g; Protein 29g

Homemade Pork Shank Soup

Prep Time: 45 minutes Cook Time: 40 minutes | Serves: 4-6

1½ lbs. pork shank, cleaned and trimmed of excess; Fat
2 carrots, cut into chunks
1 thin slice of ginger
1 large green radish, cut into chunks

1 small piece of chenpi (dried mandarin peel)
2 jujubes, dried (optional)
4½ cups water
Sea salt to taste

1. Soak the chenpi in cold water for 20 minutes. 2. Put all the ingredients in the Inner Pot and stir to mix up. 3. Close and lock the lid. Select the Pressure Cook on the panel. 4. Press the button Again to choose Normal option. 5. Press Pressure Level to choose High Pressure. 6. When the cooking is finished, leave the steam release handle in the Sealing position for 20 minutes. Release any remaining steam manually. Open the lid carefully. 7. Press Sauté to select the program, press it again to choose the Less temperature option and then simmer for 20 minutes. 8. Season by adding some salt and pepper. 9. Serve.

Per Serving: Calories 254; Fat 28 g; Sodium 346mg; Carbs 12.3 g; Sugar 1g; Fiber 0.7g; Protein 24.3 g

Chicken Barley Soup Simple and Quick to Make

Prep Time: 15 minutes | Cook Time: 20 minutes | Serves: 6

½ cup pearl barley, rinsed and drained
2 cups chicken breasts, sliced
2 cups carrots, diced
1 cup red potatoes, peeled and diced
1 cup onion, diced

¾ cup celery
3 cups chicken stock
2 cups water
1 tbsp. oregano
1 bay leaf
Salt and ground black pepper to taste

1. Put all of the ingredients into the Inner Pot and mix them up. 2. Close and lock the lid. Press the Pressure Cook on the panel. 3. Press the button Again to choose Less option. 4. Leave the steam release handle in the Sealing position for 5 minutes when the cooking is finished. Release any remaining steam manually before uncovering the pot. 5. Serve.

Per Serving: Calories 236; Fat 13.9g; Sodium 451mg; Carbs 13.2g; Fiber 1.2g; Sugars 1.4g; Protein 14.3g

Tomato and Basil Soup Easy to Make

Prep Time: 20 minutes | Cook Time: 20 minutes | Serves: 8

2 tbsp. olive oil
1 medium yellow onion, diced
2 large stalks celery, diced
2 large carrots, diced
Salt and ground black pepper to taste
¼ tsp red pepper flakes
½ cup fresh basil leaves, chopped
2 cans whole Roma tomatoes
1 cup vegetable broth
2 bay leaves
¾ cup heavy cream

1. Insert the inner pot into the cooker base. 2. Connect the power cord to a 120 V power source. The cooker goes to Standby mode and the display indicates OFF. 3. Press Sauté to select the program and then press it again to choose the Normal temperature option. 4. Pour the oil into the Inner Pot and heat it. Add the onion, celery, and carrot. Stir and sauté for 5-6 minutes, until softened. 5. Add the salt, black pepper, red pepper flakes and basil, and sauté for 1-2 minutes more. 6. Add remaining ingredients, except for the heavy cream, in the Inner Pot and stir to mix up. 7. Close and lock the lid. Select the Pressure Cook on the panel. 8. Press the button Again to choose Less option; use the "-" button to adjust the cooking time to 10 minutes. 9. Press Pressure Level to choose High Pressure. 10. When the timer beeps, quickly and carefully turn the steam release handle from Sealing position to the Venting position. Uncover the lid carefully. 11. Press the Cancel button to stop the Pressure Cook function, then select the Sauté on the panel. 12. Press the button Again to choose Less option and simmer for 2 minutes. 13. Press the Cancel key to stop the Sauté function. 14. Serve and enjoy.
Per Serving: Calories 305; Fat 15g; Sodium 548mg; Carbs 12g; Sugar 1.2g; Fiber 0.7g; Protein 29g

Homemade Sweet Potato Soup

Prep Time: 15 minutes | Cook Time: 30 minutes | Serves: 4

2 tbsp. butter
1 whole onion, chopped
4 cloves garlic, chopped
6 carrots, peeled and diced
4 large red sweet potatoes, peeled and diced
½ tsp thyme
½ tsp ground sage
1-quart vegetarian broth
Salt and ground black pepper to taste

1. Press Sauté to select the program and then press it again to choose the Normal temperature option. 2. Once hot, add the butter and melt it. 3. Add the onion, garlic, and carrots and sauté for about 8 minutes, until the onion is translucent. 4. Add the sweet potatoes, thyme, sage and broth. Season by adding some salt and pepper. Close and lock the lid. 5. Press the Cancel button to stop the Sauté function, then select the Pressure Cook on the panel. 6. Press the button Again to choose Less option. 7. Press Pressure Level to choose High pressure. 8. Once timer beeps, quickly and carefully turn the steam release handle from Sealing position to the Venting position. Uncover the lid carefully. 9. Blend the soup to your desired texture using an immersion blender. Serve.
Per Serving: Calories 285; Fat 9.8g; Sodium 639mg; Carbs 11.1g; Fiber 1.2g; Sugars 5.1g; Protein 27.8g

Meatball Soup

Prep Time: 10 minutes | Cook Time: 30 minutes | Serves: 4-6

1 tbsp. olive oil
1 onion, chopped
2 cloves garlic, minced
1 package prepared meatballs
1 cup carrots, chopped finely
1 can diced tomatoes
4 cups beef broth
1 green bell pepper, chopped
½ tsp cumin
1 tbsp. oregano
Salt and ground black pepper to taste
1 egg, beaten

1. Insert the inner pot into the cooker base. 2. Connect the power cord to a 120 V power source. The cooker goes to Standby mode and the display indicates OFF. 3. Press Sauté to select the program and then press it again to choose the Normal temperature options. Pour the oil into the Inner Pot and heat it. 4. Add the onion and garlic, sauté for 1-2 minutes. 5. Add the meatballs and cook for 4-5 minutes and brown all the meatballs. 6. Combine the carrot, tomatoes, water, bell pepper, cumin, oregano, salt and black pepper, stir to mix up. 7. Close and lock the lid. Press the Cancel button to stop the Sauté function, then press the Soup/Broth button on the panel. 8. Press the button Again to choose Less option; use the "-" button to adjust the cooking time to 15 minutes. 9. Press Pressure Level to choose High pressure 10. When the timer beeps, quickly and carefully turn the steam release handle from Sealing position to the Venting position. Uncover the lid carefully. 11. Press the Cancel button to stop the Soup

function. 12. Cook the food for 3 to 4 minutes on Sauté mode at Less cooking temperature. 13. When done, serve and enjoy.
Per Serving: Calories 351; Fat 22g; Sodium 502mg; Carbs 15.2g; Sugar 1.1g; Fiber 0.7g; Protein 26.4g

Toscana Soup

Prep Time: 5 minutes | Cook Time: 35 minutes | Serves: 4-6

2 tbsp. olive oil
1 onion, diced
4 cloves garlic, minced
1 lb. Italian sausages, chopped
3 large russet potatoes, unpeeled and sliced thickly
¼ cup water
6 cups chicken broth
Salt and ground black pepper to taste
2 cups kale, chopped
¾ cup heavy cream

1. Insert the inner pot into the cooker base. Do not use a lid. 2. Connect the power cord to a 120 V power source. The cooker goes to Standby mode and the display indicates OFF. 3. Press Sauté to select the program and then press it again to choose the Normal temperature option. Pour the oil into the Inner Pot and heat it. 4. Add the onion, garlic, and Italian sausages. Stir and sauté for 4-5 minutes, until the sausages have turned light brown. 5. Add the potatoes, water, and chicken broth and stir to mix up. 6. Sprinkle with salt and pepper. 7. Press the Cancel key to stop the Sauté function. 8. Close and lock the lid. Select the Pressure Cook on the panel. 9. Press the button Again to choose Less option 10. Press Pressure Level to choose High Pressure 11. When the timer beeps, quickly and carefully turn the steam release handle from Sealing position to the Venting position. Uncover the lid carefully. 12. Press the Cancel button to stop the Pressure Cook function, then Select the Sauté on the panel. 13. Press the button Again to choose Less option and simmer for 3-4 minutes. 14. Press the Cancel key and let it sit for 5 minutes. 15. Serve.
Per Serving: Calories 236; Fat 13.9g; Sodium 451mg; Carbs 13.2g; Fiber 1.2g; Sugars 1.4g; Protein 14.3g

Homemade Chicken Soup

Prep Time: 20 minutes | Cook Time: 25 minutes | Serves: 4

2 frozen, boneless chicken breasts
4 medium-sized potatoes, cut into chunks
3 carrots, peeled and cut into chunks
½ big onion, diced
2 cups chicken stock
2 cups water
Salt and ground black pepper to taste

1. Put the chicken breasts, potatoes, carrots and onion into the Inner Pot and then add the stock, water, salt and pepper before mixing them up. 2. Close and lock the lid and turn the steam release handle to the Sealing position. 3. Select Pressure Cook and set the cooking time for 25 minutes at High pressure. 4. When the timer beeps, leave the steam release handle in the Sealing position for 10 minutes. Do not unlock the lid until the remaining pressure are released. 5. Serve.
Per Serving: Calories: 285; Fat: 12.8 g; Sodium 345mg; Carbs: 3.7 g; Protein: 38.1 g

Tasty Pomodoro Soup

Prep Time: 15 minutes | Cook Time: 15 minutes | Serves: 8

3 tbsp. vegan butter
1 onion, diced
3 lbs. tomatoes, peeled and quartered
3½ cups vegetable broth
1 cup coconut cream

1. Press Sauté to select the program and then press it again to choose the Normal temperature option. 2. Once hot, add the butter and melt it. 3. Add the onion and sauté for 5 minutes. 4. Add the tomatoes and sauté for another 2-3 minutes. 5. Pour in the broth, stir. Close and lock the lid. 6. Press the Cancel button to reset the cooking program, and then select the Soup/Broth on the panel. 7. Press the button Again to choose Less option; use the "-" button to adjust the cooking time to 6 minutes. 8. Press Pressure Level to choose High pressure. 9. When the timer beeps, quickly and carefully turn the steam release handle from Sealing position to the Venting position. Uncover the lid carefully. 10. Add the coconut cream and stir. 11. Press the Cancel button to reset the cooking program, and then press Sauté to select the program. 12. Press it again to choose the Less temperature option and cook for 1-2 minutes. 13. Blend the soup to your desired texture using an immersion blender. 14. Serve and enjoy.
Per Serving: Calories 285; Fat 9.8g; Sodium 639mg; Carbs 11.1g; Fiber 1.2g; Sugars 5.1g; Protein 27.8g

Tasty Ham and Potato Soup

Prep Time: 10 minutes | Cook Time: 30 minutes | Serves: 4-6

2 tbsp. butter
8 cloves garlic, minced
1 onion, diced
2 lbs. Yukon Gold potatoes, cut into small chunks
A dash of cayenne pepper

1 cup cooked ham, diced
½ cup cheddar cheese, grated
4 cups chicken broth
Salt and ground black pepper to taste
2 tbsp. fried bacon bits

1. Insert the inner pot into the cooker base. Do not use a lid. 2. Connect the power cord to a 120 V power source. The cooker goes to Standby mode and the display indicates OFF. 3. To preheat the Inner Pot, press Sauté to select the program and then press it again to choose the Normal temperature option. 4. Once hot, add the the butter and melt it. 5. Add the garlic and onion, sauté for 1-2 minutes, or until fragrant. 6. Add the potatoes and sauté for 3 minutes more. 7. Add the cayenne pepper, cooked ham, and cheese. Pour in the broth and stir. 8. Add salt and pepper as you like. Close and lock the lid. 9. Press the Cancel button to reset the cooking program. Select the Pressure Cook on the panel. 10. Press the button Again to choose Less option; use the "+" button to adjust the cooking time to 25 minutes. 11. Press Pressure Level to choose High pressure 12. Once timer beeps, quickly and carefully turn the steam release handle from Sealing position to the Venting position. Uncover the lid carefully. 13. Top with bacon bits and serve.
Per Serving: Calories 344; Fat 14.9g; Sodium 227mg; Carbs 14g; Fiber 1g; Sugars 1.4g; Protein 25.7g

Turkey Cabbage Soup Easy to Make

Prep Time: 20 minutes | Cook Time: 15 minutes | Serves: 4-6

1 tbsp. olive oil
1 lb. ground turkey
2 cloves garlic, minced
1 pack frozen onion, cubed
1 pack cauliflower florets
1 jar marinara sauce

4 cups chicken broth
2 cups water
1 head cabbage, chopped
Salt and ground black pepper to taste

1. Insert the inner pot into the cooker base. 2. Connect the power cord to a 120 V power source. The cooker goes to Standby mode and the display indicates OFF. 3. Press Sauté to select the program and then press it again to choose the Normal temperature option. Pour the oil into the Inner Pot and heat it. 4. Add the ground turkey and garlic and sauté, stir now and then, for 5-6 minutes and browned all the meat. 5. Transfer the browned turkey to a bowl. 6. Press the Cancel key to stop the Sauté function. 7. Stir in the onion, cauliflower, marinara sauce, broth and water to the pot. 8. Put the cabbage on top. 9. Close and lock the lid. Select the Pressure Cook on the panel. 10. Press the button Again to choose Less option; use the "-" button to adjust the cooking time to 6 minutes. 11. Press Pressure Level to choose High Pressure 12. When the timer beeps, leave the steam release handle in the Sealing position. 13. Open the lid carefully. Return the meat to the pot and stir to mix up. 14. Add salt and pepper as you like. 15. Serve.
Per Serving: Calories 285; Fat 9.8g; Sodium 639mg; Carbs 11.1g; Fiber 1.2g; Sugars 5.1g; Protein 27.8g

Delicious Smoked Turkey Soup

Prep Time: 15 minutes | Cook Time: 40 minutes | Serves: 8

½ tbsp. olive oil
1 medium-size onion, chopped
1 celery stalk, chopped
1 large carrot, chopped
½ cup parsley, chopped
3 cloves garlic, pressed

6 cups water
10-12 oz. smoked turkey drumstick
2 cups black beans, dried
1 tsp salt
¼ tsp ground black pepper
2 bay leaves

1. Insert the inner pot into the cooker base. 2. Connect the power cord to a 120 V power source. The cooker goes to Standby mode and the display indicates OFF. 3. Press Sauté to select the program and then press it again to choose the Less temperature option. 4. Pour the oil into the Inner Pot and heat it. 5. Put the onion, celery, carrots, and parsley in the pot. 6. Sauté for 8-10 minutes, until the veggies are softened. 7. Add the garlic and sauté for 1 minute more. 8. Pour in the water. Add the turkey, beans, salt, pepper and bay leaves, stir to mix up. 9. Bring to a boil, close and lock the lid. 10. Press the Cancel button to reset the cooking program, then select the Pressure Cook on the panel. 11. Press the button Again to choose Normal option; use the

"-" button to adjust the cooking time to 30 minutes. 12. Press Pressure Level to choose High pressure 13. When the cooking is finished, leave the steam release handle in the Sealing position for 10 minutes. Release any remaining steam manually. Open the lid carefully. 14. Remove the bay leaves. Transfer the turkey drumstick to a plate. Shred the meat. 15. Blend the soup to your desired texture using an immersion blender. Return the meat to the pot and stir. 16. Serve and enjoy the delicious soup.
Per Serving: Calories 344; Fat 14.9g; Sodium 227mg; Carbs 14g; Fiber 1g; Sugars 1.4g; Protein 25.7g

Bacon Soup with Navy Bean and Spinach

Prep Time: 20 minutes Cook Time: 30 minutes | Serves: 6

3 cans (15 oz. each) navy beans, rinsed and drained
1 cup water
4 slices bacon, chopped
1 onion, chopped
1 large carrot, chopped
1 large celery stalk, chopped

2 tbsp. tomato paste
1 sprig fresh rosemary
2 bay leaves
4 cups chicken broth
3 cups baby spinach
Salt and ground black pepper to taste

1. Combine the 1 can beans with 1 cup of water. 2. Blend the mixture with an immersion blender. 3. Insert the inner pot into the cooker base. 4. Connect the power cord to a 120 V power source. The cooker goes to Standby mode and the display indicates OFF. 5. Press Sauté to select the program and then press it again to choose the Normal temperature option. Add the bacon and sauté until crisp. 6. Transfer the bacon to a plate. 7. Add the onion, carrot, and celery to the pot and sauté for 5 minutes, until softened. 8. Add the tomato paste and stir well. 9. Add 2 cans beans, pureed beans, rosemary, bay leaves, and broth. Close and lock the lid. 10. Press the Cancel key to stop the Sauté function. 11. Close and lock the lid. Select the Pressure Cook on the panel. 12. Press the button Again to choose Less option; use the "-" button to adjust the cooking time to 15 minutes. 13. Press Pressure Level to choose High Pressure. 14. When the cooking is finished, leave the steam release handle in the Sealing position for 10 minutes. Release any remaining steam manually. Open the lid carefully. 15. Remove the rosemary and bay leaves. Add the spinach. Add some salt and pepper before stirring well. 16. Let the dish sit for 5 minutes. Serve.
Per Serving: Calories 236; Fat 13.9g; Sodium 451mg; Carbs 13.2g; Fiber 1.2g; Sugars 1.4g; Protein 14.3g

Homemade Keto Low-Carb Soup

Prep Time: 10 minutes | Cook Time: 25 minutes | Serves: 4-6

1 tbsp. olive oil
2 cloves garlic, minced
1 large yellow onion, diced
1 tbsp. onion powder
1 head cauliflower, coarsely chopped
1 green bell pepper, chopped
32 oz. chicken stock

Salt and ground black pepper
1 tbsp. Dijon mustard
4 dashes hot pepper sauce
6 slices cooked turkey bacon, diced
2 cups shredded Cheddar cheese
1 cup half and half

1. Insert the inner pot into the cooker base. 2. Connect the power cord to a 120 V power source. The cooker goes to Standby mode and the display indicates OFF. 3. Press Sauté to select the program and then press it again to choose the Normal temperature option. 4. Pour the oil into the Inner Pot and heat it. 5. Add the garlic and onion and sauté for 3-4 minutes. 6. Add the onion powder, cauliflower, bell pepper, and stock. Add salt and pepper as you like. Stir to mix up. 7. Close and lock the lid. Press the Cancel button to stop the Sauté function, then select the Soup/Broth on the panel. 8. Press the button Again to choose Less option; use the "-" button to adjust the cooking time to 15 minutes. 9. Press Pressure Level to choose High pressure. 10. When the timer beeps, quickly and carefully turn the steam release handle from Sealing position to the Venting position. 11. Wait for 5 minutes and uncover the lid carefully. 12. Add the Dijon mustard, hot sauce, turkey bacon, cheddar cheese, and half and half. Mix up well. 13. Press the Cancel button to stop the Soup function. 14. Press Sauté to select the program and then press it again to choose the Less temperature option and simmer the soup for 4-5 minutes. 15. Serve.
Per Serving: Calories 351; Fat 22g; Sodium 502mg; Carbs 15.2g; Sugar 1.1g; Fiber 0.7g; Protein 26.4g

Chicken Soup with Cannellini Beans

Prep Time: 20 minutes | Cook Time: 45 minutes | Serves: 6

1 cup cannellini beans
1 lb. chicken fillet, cut into 1½ inch strips
7 cups water
1 jalapeno pepper, chopped
1 red bell pepper, sliced
1 white onion, sliced
1 cup fresh dill, chopped
4 tbsp. salsa
⅓ cup cream
1 tsp soy sauce
2 tsp kosher salt
1 tsp ground black pepper

1. Put the cannellini beans and chicken in the Inner Pot. 2. Pour in the water and stir. Close and lock the lid. 3. Select the Pressure Cook on the panel, press the button again to adjust the cooking time to 30 minutes. 4. Press Pressure Level to choose High Pressure. 5. When the timer beeps, quickly and carefully turn the steam release handle from Sealing position to the Venting position. Uncover the lid carefully. 6. Add the jalapeno pepper, bell pepper, onion, and dill. Mix up well. 7. Close and lock the lid. Select the Soup/Broth on the panel. 8. Press the button Again to choose Less option; use the - button to adjust the cooking time to 15 minutes. 9. Press Pressure Level to choose High pressure. 10. When the timer beeps, quickly and carefully turn the steam release handle from Sealing position to the Venting position. Uncover the lid carefully. 11. Add the salsa, cream, soy sauce, salt and black pepper. Stir to mix up, close the lid and let the soup sit for 10 minutes. 12. Serve.
Per Serving: Calories 344; Fat 14.9g; Sodium 227mg; Carbs 14g; Fiber 1g; Sugars 1.4g; Protein 25.7g

Tomato Soup with Cream

Prep Time: 5 minutes | Cook Time: 25 minutes | Serves: 4

1 tablespoon unsalted butter
½ small onion, diced
2 (28-ounce) cans crushed tomatoes
2 tablespoons granulated sugar
1 cup low-sodium chicken or
vegetable broth
1 teaspoon Worcestershire sauce (optional)
½ cup heavy cream
Chopped fresh basil, for garnish

1. Choose Sauté. Butter should be added to the inner pot. Add the onion and cook for 5 minutes, or until it starts to brown and caramelize, after it starts to bubble. Stir to remove any onion bits that may have become attached to the saucepan before adding the tomatoes, sugar, stock, and Worcestershire sauce (if using). 2. Turn the valve to seal position and secure the lid in place. Choose Pressure Cook. Set the pressure to High when cooking. Schedule 7 minutes in the timer. Turn the valve carefully to vent position when cooking is finished to quickly release pressure. 3. Stir in the cream after unlocking and removing the cover. Basil should be used as a garnish after fully warming.
Per Serving: Calories 147; Fat: 9g; Sodium 336mg; Carbs: 15g; Sugars: 12g; Protein 3g

Nutritious Multi-Bean Soup

Prep Time: 15 minutes | Cook Time: 40 minutes | Serves: 8-10

1 tbsp. olive oil
1 onion, chopped
3 cloves garlic, minced
1 red bell pepper, chopped
2 carrots, peeled and chopped
2 stalks celery, chopped
1 bag of 15-bean soup blend (Hurst
Beans brand)
1 can tomatoes, crushed
3 sprigs fresh thyme
1 bay leaf
8 cups vegetable stock
Salt and ground black pepper to taste

1. Insert the inner pot into the cooker base. 2. Connect the power cord to a 120 V power source. The cooker goes to Standby mode and the display indicates OFF. 3. Press Sauté to select the program and then press it again to choose the Normal temperature option. 4. Pour the oil into the Inner Pot and heat it. 5. Add the onion and garlic and sauté for 1-2 minutes until fragrant. 6. Add the bell pepper, carrot, and celery and sauté for another 6 minutes. 7. Add the beans, tomatoes, thyme, bay leaf and stock. Mix up well. 8. Add salt and pepper as you like. Close and lock the lid. 9. Press the Cancel button to reset the cooking program, then select the Pressure Cook on the panel. 10. Press the button Again to choose Normal option; use the "-" button to adjust the cooking time to 30 minutes. 11. Press Pressure Level to choose High pressure 12. When the cooking is finished, select Cancel and leave the steam release handle in the Sealing position for 10 minutes. Release any remaining steam manually. Open the lid carefully. 13. Stir and Serve.
Per Serving: Calories 254; Fat 28 g; Sodium 346mg; Carbs 12.3 g; Sugar 1g; Fiber 0.7g; Protein 24.3 g

Delicious Lentil Soup with Sweet Potato

Prep Time: 20 minutes | Cook Time: 20 minutes | Serves: 6

2 tsp olive oil
½ yellow onion, chopped
1 large celery stalk, diced
4 cloves garlic, minced
1 tsp paprika
1 tsp ground cumin
½ tsp red pepper flakes
¾ lb. sweet potato, peeled and cut
into ½-inch dice
1 cup green lentils
1 can (14 oz.) petite diced tomatoes
1 cup water
3½ cups vegetable broth
Salt and ground black pepper to taste
4 oz. spinach leaves

1. Insert the inner pot into the cooker base. 2. Connect the power cord to a 120 V power source. The cooker goes to Standby mode and the display indicates OFF. 3. Press Sauté to select the program and then press it again to choose the Normal temperature option. 4. Pour the oil into the Inner Pot and heat it. 5. Add the onion and celery and sauté for 4-5 minutes, until softened. 6. Add the garlic, paprika, and red pepper flakes, stir to mix up. Sauté for 1 minute. 7. Add the sweet potato, lentil, tomatoes, water, and broth. Stir to mix up. 8. Add salt and pepper as you like. 9. Press the Cancel key to stop the Sauté function. 10. Close and lock the lid. Select the Pressure Cook on the panel. 11. Press the button Again to choose Less option; use the "-" button to adjust the cooking time to 12 minutes. 12. Press Pressure Level to choose High Pressure 13. Once timer beeps, wait for 10 minutes, and then quickly and carefully turn the steam release handle from Sealing position to the Venting position. Uncover the lid carefully. 14. Add the spinach and stir. Serve.
Per Serving: Calories 312; Fat 15g; Sodium 548mg; Carbs 12g; Sugar 1.2g; Fiber 0.7g; Protein 29g

Fragrant and Delicious Black Bean Soup

Prep Time: 20 minutes | Cook Time: 50 minutes | Serves: 6

2 tbsp. olive oil
5 cloves garlic, minced
1 onion, chopped
1 red bell pepper, chopped
2 tsp. ground oregano
1 tsp. ground cumin
1 bay leaf
1 lb. dried black beans, soaked overnight
4 cups water
½ cup red wine
2 tbsp. sherry vinegar
Salt and ground black pepper to taste

1. Insert the inner pot into the cooker base. 2. Connect the power cord to a 120 V power source. The cooker goes to Standby mode and the display indicates OFF. 3. Press Sauté to select the program and then press it again to choose the Normal temperature option. 4. Pour the oil into the Inner Pot and heat it. Add the garlic and onion and sauté for 2 minutes, until fragrant. 5. Add the bell pepper, oregano, cumin, and bay leaf. Stir and sauté for 1 minute more. 6. Add the beans and pour the water, wine and vinegar. Stir to mix up. 7. Sprinkle with salt and pepper. Close and lock the lid. 8. Press the Cancel button to stop the Sauté function, then select the Bean/Chili on the panel. 9. Press the button Again to choose the More option. 10. Use the "+" button to adjust the cooking time to 45 minutes. 11. Press Pressure Level to choose High pressure. 12. When the timer beeps, quickly and carefully turn the steam release handle from Sealing position to the Venting position. Uncover the lid carefully. 13. Serve.
Per Serving: Calories 285; Fat 9.8g; Sodium 639mg; Carbs 11.1g; Fiber 1.2g; Sugars 5.1g; Protein 27.8g

Chapter 6 Bean, Pasta and Grain Recipes

Garlic Risotto with Parmesan Cheese

Prep Time: 10 minutes | Cook Time: 10 minutes | Serves: 6

5 tablespoons salted butter, divided
1 medium onion, diced
3 garlic cloves, minced
2 cups Arborio rice
½ cup white wine
4 cups chicken broth

1 tablespoon dried thyme
1 teaspoon salt
½ teaspoon freshly ground black pepper
½ cup freshly grated Parmesan cheese

1. Insert the pot into the Cooker Base without the lid. 2. Select Sauté mode and then press the same button again and then adjust the cooking temperature to Normal. 3. When the display switches On to Hot, melt 2 tablespoons of butter; add diced onion and cook for 3 minutes or until just softened; add the garlic and cook for 1 minute or until fragrant; add the Arborio rice and stir constantly for 3 minutes; lastly, stir in the wine and deglaze and scrape up the browned bits from the bottom. 4. After adding the chicken broth, thyme, salt and pepper and stirring well, place and close the lid in right way. 5. Select Pressure Cook mode. Press Pressure Cook button again to adjust the cooking time to 5 minutes; press Pressure Level to choose High Pressure. 6. When the time is up, quickly and carefully turn the steam release handle from the Sealing position to the Venting position. 7. When the float valve drops, open the lid; stir in the remaining butter and cheese, then season with additional salt and pepper. 8. Serve and enjoy.
Per Serving: Calories 285; Fat 9.8g; Sodium 639mg; Carbs 11.1g; Fiber 1.2g; Sugars 5.1g; Protein 27.8g

Tasty Shrimp Paella with Peas

Prep Time: 10 minutes | Cook Time: 9 minutes | Serves: 4

4 tablespoons (½ stick) unsalted butter
1 medium red bell pepper, seeded and diced
4 garlic cloves, minced
1½ cups chicken broth
1 cup jasmine rice, rinsed
¼ cup chopped fresh flat-leaf parsley

1 teaspoon salt
¼ teaspoon freshly ground black pepper
¼ teaspoon red pepper flakes
Juice of 1 medium lemon
¼ teaspoon saffron
1-pound frozen wild shrimp (16–20 count), shells and tails on
½ cup frozen peas, thawed

1. Insert the pot into the Cooker Base without the lid. 2. Select Sauté mode and then press the same button again and then adjust the cooking temperature to Normal. 3. When the display switches On to Hot, melt the butter; add the garlic, diced bell pepper and cook for 4 minutes or until the peppers start to soften; add the right amount of broth to deglaze the pot, stir and scrap the browned bits from the bottom. 4. Add the rice, parsley, red pepper flakes, lemon juice, saffron, salt, black pepper and the remaining chicken broth without stirring them, then top with the shrimp. 5. Place and close the lid rightly. 6. Select Pressure Cook mode. Press Pressure Cook button again to adjust the cooking time to 5 minutes; press Pressure Level to choose High Pressure. 7. When the time is up, quickly and carefully turn the steam release handle from the Sealing position to the Venting position. 8. When released, carefully remove the cooked shrimp from the rice and then peel them; transfer them back to the rice and then stir in the peas. 9. Serve and enjoy.
Per Serving: Calories 254; Fat 28 g; Sodium 346mg; Carbs 12.3 g; Sugar 1g; Fiber 0.7g; Protein 24.3 g

Pinto Beans in Tomato Sauce

Prep Time: 10 minutes | Cook Time: 31 minutes | Serves: 8

2 cups (1 pound) dry pinto beans
2 tablespoons avocado oil
1 large yellow onion, peeled and diced
1 medium jalapeño, seeded and diced
2 teaspoons minced garlic
3½ cups chicken stock

1 (8-ounce) can tomato sauce
2 tablespoons chili powder
1 tablespoon yellow mustard
1 teaspoon dried oregano
1 teaspoon cumin
½ teaspoon black pepper
2 bay leaves
½ teaspoon salt

1. In a bowl, add the beans and 3" water; allow the beans soak 4 to 8 hours; drain them. 2. Insert the pot into the Cooker Base without the lid. 3. Select Sauté mode and then press the same button again and then adjust the cooking temperature to Normal. 4. When the display switches On to Hot, add and heat the oil for 1 minute; add the onion, jalapeño, garlic and cook for 5 minutes or until softened; add the soaked beans, stock, tomato sauce, chili powder, mustard, oregano,

cumin, pepper, bay leaves and salt, stir well and scrape any brown bits from the bottom of the pot. 5. Press Cancel button to stop this cooking program; place and close the lid in right way. 6. Select Pressure Cook mode. Press Pressure Cook button again to adjust the cooking time to 25 minutes; press Pressure Level to choose High Pressure. 7. When the time is up, leave the steam release handle in the Sealing position. 8. When the float valve drops, open the lid and discard the bay leaves. 9. Serve and enjoy.
Per Serving: Calories: 289; Fat: 5g; Sodium: 516mg; Fiber: 10g; Carbs: 44g; Sugar: 5g; Protein: 16g

Tuscan White Beans in Vegetable Broth

Prep Time: 5 minutes | Cook Time: 28 minutes | Serves: 6

½ pound dry cannellini beans
1 tablespoon avocado oil
3 large cloves garlic, smashed

¼ teaspoon crushed red pepper flakes
3 cups vegetable broth

1. In a bowl, add the beans and 5 cups of water; allow the beans soak 4 to 8 hours; drain them. 2. Insert the pot into the Cooker Base without the lid. 3. Select Sauté mode and then press the same button again and then adjust the cooking temperature to Normal. 4. When the display switches On to Hot, add and heat the oil for 2 minute; add the garlic, red pepper flakes and cook them for 30 seconds. 5. Add the beans and broth, press Cancel button stop this cooking program; place and close the lid in right way. 6. Select Pressure Cook mode. Press Pressure Cook button again to adjust the cooking time to 25 minutes; press Pressure Level to choose High Pressure. 7. When the time is up, quickly and carefully turn the steam release handle from the Sealing position to the Venting position. 8. When finished, serve and enjoy.
Per Serving: Calories: 156; Fat: 3g; Sodium: 276mg; Fiber: 6g; Carbs: 25g; Sugar: 1g; Protein: 9g

Ginger Chicken Porridge

Prep Time: 10 minutes | Cook Time: 15 minutes | Serves: 6

¼ cup vegetable oil
2 thumbs fresh ginger, peeled and cut into matchsticks
3 garlic cloves, minced
1 large onion, chopped
3 carrots, peeled and cubed
3 celery stalks, sliced
2 tablespoons fish sauce
2 to 3 pounds boneless, skinless chicken thighs

1¼ cups jasmine rice, rinsed
1½ tablespoons salt
1½ teaspoons freshly ground black pepper
2 bay leaves
8 cups chicken broth
6 hard-boiled eggs, peeled, for serving (optional)
Lemon slices, for serving (optional)

1. Insert the pot into the Cooker Base without the lid. 2. Select Sauté mode and then press the same button again and then adjust the cooking temperature to Normal. 3. When the display switches On to Hot, add and heat the oil; add the ginger, garlic, carrot, onion and celery and cook for 5 minutes or until the celery starts to soften; stir in the fish sauce. 4. Add the chicken thighs, bay leaves, broth, rice, salt and pepper without stirring them. 5. Place and close the lid rightly. 6. Select Pressure Cook mode. Press Pressure Cook button again to adjust the cooking time to 10 minutes; press Pressure Level to choose High Pressure. 7. When the time is up, leave the steam release handle in the Sealing position for 10 minutes, then turn it to the Venting position. 8. When released, take out the chicken thighs and shred them, then arrange them back to the pot. 9. Discard the bay leaves. 10. Serve and enjoy with an egg and a slice of lemon.
Per Serving: Calories 285; Fat 9.8g; Sodium 639mg; Carbs 11.1g; Fiber 1.2g; Sugars 5.1g; Protein 27.8g

Homemade Teff

Prep Time: 1 minutes | Cook Time: 4 minutes | Serves: 4

1 cup dry teff
½ teaspoon salt

3 cups water

1. In the Inner Pot, add the teff, salt and water. 2. Insert the pot into the Cooker Base and then close the lid rightly. 3. Select Pressure Cook mode. Press Pressure Cook button again to adjust the cooking time to 4 minutes; press Pressure Level to choose High Pressure. 4. When the time is up, leave the steam release handle in the Sealing position. 5. When done, serve and enjoy.
Per Serving: Calories: 177; Fat: 1g; Sodium: 296mg; Fiber: 4g; Carbs: 35g; Sugar: 1g; Protein: 6g

Creamy and Cheesy Elbow Macaroni

Prep Time: 10 minutes | Cook Time: 4 minutes | Serves: 6

2½ cups uncooked elbow macaroni	pepper
1 cup chicken broth	¼ teaspoon mustard powder
2 cups water	¼ teaspoon garlic powder
3 tablespoons unsalted butter, cubed	⅓ cup whole or 2 percent milk
¼ teaspoon salt	⅓ cup heavy (whipping) cream
¼ teaspoon freshly ground black	2 cups shredded sharp cheddar cheese

1. In the Inner Pot, mix up the macaroni, broth, water, butter, mustard powder, garlic powder, salt and black pepper. 2. Insert the pot into the Cooker Base and then close the lid rightly. 3. Select Pressure Cook mode. Press Pressure Cook button again to adjust the cooking time to 4 minutes; press Pressure Level to choose High Pressure. 4. When the time is up, quickly and carefully turn the steam release handle from the Sealing position to the Venting position. 5. When released, stir in the milk, cream and cheese until smooth and creamy. 6. Serve and enjoy.
Per Serving: Calories 305; Fat 15g; Sodium 548mg; Carbs 12g; Sugar 1.2g; Fiber 0.7g; Protein 29g

Simple Steamed Black Beans

Prep Time: 5 minutes | Cook Time: 25 minutes | Serves: 8

1 pound dry black beans	2 teaspoons salt
6 cups water	

1. In a bowl, add the dry black beans and 3" water; allow the beans soak 4 to 8 hours; drain them. 2. In the Inner Pot, add 6 cups of water and the soaked beans. 3. Insert the pot into the Cooker Base and then close the lid rightly. 4. Select Pressure Cook mode. Press Pressure Cook button again to adjust the cooking time to 25 minutes; press Pressure Level to choose High Pressure. 5. When the time is up, leave the steam release handle in the Sealing position for 10 minutes, then turn the steam release handle to the Venting position. 6. When the float valve drops, open the lid, add the salt and then transfer the beans to a bowl. 7. Serve and enjoy.
Per Serving: Calories: 192; Fat: 0g; Sodium: 586mg; Fiber: 9g; Carbs: 36g; Sugar: 1g; Protein: 12g

Nutritious White Bean Salad with Vegetables

Prep Time: 10 minutes | Cook Time: 25 minutes | Serves: 4

1 cup dry cannellini beans	¼ teaspoon black pepper
2 cups water	1 cup grape tomatoes, halved
3 tablespoons extra-virgin olive oil	1 large avocado, peeled, pitted, cut in half lengthwise, and sliced
1 tablespoon lemon juice	
1 clove garlic, minced	1 cup packed basil leaves, chopped
½ teaspoon coarse sea salt	

1. In a suitable bowl, add the beans and cover with 3" water; allow the beans soak 4 to 8 hours; drain them. 2. In the Inner Pot, add the beans and 2 cups of water. 3. Insert the pot into the Cooker Base and then close the lid rightly. 4. Select Pressure Cook mode. Press Pressure Cook button again to adjust the cooking time to 25 minutes; press Pressure Level to choose High Pressure. 5. While cooking, prepare an airtight container, add the oil, lemon juice, garlic, salt and pepper and shake them until they are well combined; set aside for later use. 6. When the time is up, leave the steam release handle in the Sealing position. 7. When the float valve drops, open the lid and cool the beans. 8. In a large bowl, add the beans, tomatoes, avocado and basil; drizzle them with the dressing and stir gently to coat evenly. 9. Enjoy.
Per Serving: Calories: 336; Fat: 15g; Sodium: 205mg; Fiber: 16g; Carbs: 39g; Sugar: 1g; Protein: 13g

Easy-to-Make Chickpeas

Prep Time: 10 minutes | Cook Time: 10 minutes | Serves: 8

2 cups (1 pound) dry chickpeas	2 teaspoons salt
6 cups water	

1. In a large bowl, add the chickpeas and 3" water; allow the beans soak 4 to 8 hours; drain them. 2. In the Inner Pot, add chickpeas, salt and water. 3. Insert the pot into the Cooker Base and then close the lid rightly. 4. Select Pressure Cook mode. Press Pressure Cook button again to adjust the cooking time to 10 minutes; press Pressure Level

to choose High Pressure. 5. When the time is up, leave the steam release handle in the Sealing position for 10 minutes, then turn it to the Venting position. 6. When finished, serve and enjoy.
Per Serving: Calories: 214; Fat: 3g; Sodium: 594mg; Fiber: 7g; Carbs: 36g; Sugar: 6g; Protein: 12g

Ginger Oregano Brown Lentils

Prep Time: 2 minutes | Cook Time: 20 minutes | Serves: 6

1½ cups brown lentils	2 teaspoons curry powder
2 cups vegetable broth	½ teaspoon dried ginger
2 tablespoons tomato paste	½ teaspoon dried oregano
1 (15-ounce) can unsweetened full-; Fat coconut milk	¼ teaspoon garlic salt

1. In the Inner Pot, add and mix up all of the ingredients. 2. Insert the pot into the Cooker Base and then close the lid rightly. 3. Select Pressure Cook mode. Press Pressure Cook button again to adjust the cooking time to 20 minutes; press Pressure Level to choose High Pressure. 4. When the time is up, leave the steam release handle in the Sealing position; when the float valve drops, open the lid. 5. Stir well before serving.
Per Serving: Calories: 320; Fat: 15g; Sodium: 316mg; Fiber: 6g; Carbs: 35g; Sugar: 2g; Protein: 14g

Spiced Millet with Onion

Prep Time: 5 minutes | Cook Time: 7 minutes | Serves: 6

1 tablespoon avocado oil	⅛ teaspoon ground cinnamon
1 medium yellow onion, peeled and diced	1 bay leaf
	2 cups millet
¼ teaspoon ground cumin	3 cups water
¼ teaspoon ground cardamom	

1. Insert the pot into the Cooker Base without the lid. 2. Select Sauté mode and then press the same button again and then adjust the cooking temperature to Normal. 3. When the display switches On to Hot, add and heat the oil for 1 minute; add the onion, cumin, cardamom, cinnamon, and bay leaf, stir constantly for 5 minutes. 4. Press the Cancel button to stop this cooking program. 5. Add the millet and water to the Inner Pot and combine well; scrape any brown bits that may be stuck to the bottom. 6. Insert the pot into the Cooker Base and then close the lid rightly. 7. Select Pressure Cook mode. Press Pressure Cook button again to adjust the cooking time to 1 minutes; press Pressure Level to choose High Pressure. 8. When the time is up, leave the steam release handle in the Sealing position. 9. When the float valve drops, open the lid, discard the bay leaf and the transfer the millet to a bowl. 10. Serve and enjoy.
Per Serving: Calories: 280; Fat: 5g; Sodium: 4mg; Fiber: 6g; Carbs: 50g; Sugar: 1g; Protein: 8g

Rice Pilaf in Chicken Broth

Prep Time: 10 minutes | Cook Time: 10-15 minutes | Serves: 4

4 tablespoons (½ stick) unsalted butter	¾ teaspoon salt
	¼ teaspoon freshly ground black pepper
⅓ cup vermicelli, broken into ½-inch pieces	
	½ teaspoon onion powder
1 cup long-grain white rice	¼ teaspoon paprika
1½ cups chicken broth	1 teaspoon dried parsley
1 teaspoon garlic powder	

1. Insert the pot into the Cooker Base without the lid. 2. Select Sauté mode and then press the same button again and then adjust the cooking temperature to Normal. 3. When the display switches On to Hot, melt the butter; add the vermicelli and stir for 2 to 3 minutes or until browned; add the rice and cook for 3 to 4 minutes more or until the rice starts to toast; lastly, stir in the chicken broth and the remaining ingredients, scrap up any browned bits from the bottom of the pot. 4. Place and close the lid in right way. 5. Select Pressure Cook mode. Press Pressure Cook button again to adjust the cooking time to 3 minutes; press Pressure Level to choose High Pressure. 6. When the time is up, leave the steam release handle in the Sealing position for 10 minutes, then turn it to the Venting position. 7. When done, serve and enjoy.
Per Serving: Calories 361; Fat 10g; Sodium 218mg; Carbs 16g; Sugar 1.2g; Fiber 0.7g; Protein 24g

Healthier Refried Beans with Onion

Prep Time: 11 minutes | Cook Time: 27 minutes | Serves: 12

2 cups (1 pound) dry pinto beans	7 cups water
1 tablespoon avocado oil	2 teaspoons chili powder
1 large yellow onion, peeled and diced	1 teaspoon ground cumin
4 cloves garlic, minced	2 teaspoons salt

1. In a bowl, add the beans and 2" water; allow the beans soak 4 to 8 hours at room temperature; rinse and then drain them. 2. Insert the pot into the Cooker Base without the lid. 3. Select Sauté mode and then press the same button again and then adjust the cooking temperature to Normal. 4. When the display switches On to Hot, add and heat the oil; add the onion and cook for 6 minutes or until softened; add the garlic and cook for 30 seconds more. 5. Press Cancel button to stop this cooking program. 6. Transfer the processed beans, chili powder, cumin, water and salt to the Inner Pot; place and close the lid in right way. 7. Select Pressure Cook mode. Press Pressure Cook button again to adjust the cooking time to 20 minutes; press Pressure Level to choose High Pressure. 8. When the time is up, leave the steam release handle in the Sealing position. 9. When the float valve drops, open the lid, drain the beans and reserve the liquid; place the drained beans back to the Inner Pot, then use an immersion blender or potato masher to mix or mash the beans to the consistency you want, adding any reserved liquid as needed. 10. When done, serve and enjoy. 11. Transfer the beans to a bowl for serving. Refried beans may be stored in the refrigerator for three to four days or the freezer up to three months.
Per Serving: Calories: 149; Fat: 2g; Sodium: 405mg; Fiber: 6g; Carbs: 25g; Sugar: 1g; Protein: 8g

Chicken Fried Rice with Peas

Prep Time: 10 minutes | Cook Time: 11 minutes | Serves: 4

2 teaspoons vegetable oil, divided	1 cup peeled and diced carrots
2 eggs, whisked	1½ cups jasmine rice, rinsed
3 garlic cloves, minced	3 tablespoons soy sauce
1¼ cups chicken broth	½ teaspoon toasted sesame oil
1-pound boneless, skinless chicken breasts, cubed	½ cup frozen peas, thawed
	Sesame seeds, for garnish (optional)

1. Insert the pot into the Cooker Base without the lid. 2. Select Sauté mode and then press the same button again and then adjust the cooking temperature to Normal. 3. When the display switches On to Hot, add and heat 1 teaspoon of the oil; add the eggs and use a spatula to push them around to scramble them until fully cooked, then arrange them to a plate and set aside for later use. 4. Add and heat the remaining oil; add the garlic and cook for 1 minute until fragrant. 5. Press Cancel button to stop this cooking program. 6. Still in the Inner Pot, add the chicken, carrot and rice without stirring them; press the rice down to submerge it 7. Place and close the lid rightly. 8. Select Pressure Cook mode. Press Pressure Cook button again to adjust the cooking time to 3 minutes; press Pressure Level to choose High Pressure. 9. When the time is up, leave the steam release handle in the Sealing position for 10 minutes, then turn it to the Venting position. 10. When released, open the lid; stir in the soy sauce and sesame oil until the rice is well coated; add the scrambled eggs and peas, stir well. 11. Close the lid again and Keep Warm the food for 5 minutes to warm the peas and eggs. 12. When done, toss with sesame seeds and serve.
Per Serving: Calories 285; Fat 9.8g; Sodium 639mg; Carbs 11.1g; Fiber 1.2g, Sugars 5.1g; Protein 27.8g

Quinoa with Enchilada Sauce and Cheese

Prep Time: 10 minutes | Cook Time: 1 minutes | Serves: 4

½ small onion, diced	½ teaspoon ground cumin
1 (4.3-ounce) can mild green chilies	¼ teaspoon salt
1 (10-ounce) bag frozen corn	1 cup uncooked quinoa, rinsed well
1 (15-ounce) can black beans, drained and rinsed	2 cups water
1 cup chopped fresh tomatoes	1 cup enchilada sauce
1 teaspoon chili powder	1 cup shredded Monterey Jack cheese

1. In the Inner Pot, mix up the onion, chilies, corn, beans, cumin, chopped tomatoes, quinoa, salt and water. 2. Insert the pot into the Cooker Base and then close the lid rightly. 3. Select Pressure Cook

mode. Press Pressure Cook button again to adjust the cooking time to 1 minutes; press Pressure Level to choose High Pressure. 4. When the time is up, leave the steam release handle in the Sealing position. 5. With the enchilada sauce and cheese, serve and enjoy.
Per Serving: Calories 272; Fat 19g; Sodium 389mg; Carbs 10.4g; Fiber 0.7g; Sugars 1.1g; Protein 15.6g

Black Beans in Vegetable Stock

Prep Time: 5 minutes | Cook Time: 20 minutes | Serves: 6

½ pound dry black beans	1 tablespoon chopped fresh, peeled ginger
1 (13.25-ounce) can unsweetened full-fat coconut milk	1 tablespoon red curry paste
3 cups vegetable stock	½ teaspoon kosher salt

1. In a bowl, add the dry black beans and 3" water; allow the beans soak 4 to 8 hours; drain them. 2. In the Inner Pot, add and mix up the soaked beans, coconut milk, stock, ginger, curry paste, and salt. 3. Insert the pot into the Cooker Base and then close the lid rightly. 4. Select Pressure Cook mode. Press Pressure Cook button again to adjust the cooking time to 20 minutes; press Pressure Level to choose High Pressure. 5. When the time is up, quickly and carefully turn the steam release handle from the Sealing position to the Venting position. 6. When finished, serve and enjoy.
Per Serving: Calories: 263; Fat: 13g; Sodium: 705mg; Fiber: 6g; Carbs: 27g; Sugar: 1g; Protein: 11g

Lime Black Beans with Cilantro

Prep Time: 5 minutes | Cook Time: 10 minutes | Serves: 12

2 cups (1 pound) dry black beans	¼ teaspoon salt
4 cups vegetable broth	Juice from 1 large lime
1 tablespoon chili powder	½ cup chopped cilantro
1 teaspoon smoked paprika	

1. In a bowl, add the beans and 3" water; allow the beans soak 4 to 8 hours at room temperature; rinse and then drain them. 2. In the Inner Pot, mix up the soaked beans, broth, paprika, chili powder and salt. 3. Insert the pot into the Cooker Base and then close the lid rightly. 4. Select Pressure Cook mode. Press Pressure Cook button again to adjust the cooking time to 10 minutes; press Pressure Level to choose High Pressure. 5. When the time is up, leave the steam release handle in the Sealing position. 6. When the float valve drops, open the lid, stir in the lime juice and cilantro. 7. Serve and enjoy.
Per Serving: Calories: 136; Fat: 0g; Sodium: 251mg; Fiber: 7g; Carbs: 26g; Sugar: 1g; Protein: 8g

Barley with Ham and Onion

Prep Time: 10 minutes | Cook Time: 25 minutes | Serves: 4

1 tablespoon unsalted butter	½ teaspoon salt
1 cup hulled barley	½ cup diced cooked ham
¼ cup finely chopped onion	½ cup mustard greens
4 cups water	4 eggs, cooked to your preference

1. Insert the pot into the Cooker Base without the lid. 2. Select Sauté mode and then press the same button again and then adjust the cooking temperature to Normal. 3. When the display switches On to Hot, add and melt the butter; add the barley, onion and cook for 1 to 2 minutes until the barley starts to toast; add the salt and water and stir well. 4. Press Cancel button to stop this cooking program; place and close the lid in right way. 5. Select Pressure Cook mode. Press Pressure Cook button again to adjust the cooking time to 18 minutes; press Pressure Level to choose High Pressure. 6. When the time is up, quickly and carefully turn the steam release handle from the Sealing position to the Venting position. 7. Drain the remaining liquid as needed. 8. Press Cancel button to stop this cooking program. 9. Select Sauté mode and then press the same button again and then adjust the cooking temperature to Normal. 10. Add the ham, greens and cook for 5 minutes or until the greens are just wilted. 11. When done, scoop a quarter of the barley into each bowl and put an egg of your choice on top.
Per Serving: Calories 344; Fat 14.9g; Sodium 227mg; Carbs 14g; Fiber 1g; Sugars 1.4g; Protein 25.7g

Coconut Rice in Chicken Broth

Prep Time: 10 minutes | Cook Time: 5 minutes | Serves: 6

1½ cups jasmine rice, rinsed
1 (14-ounce) can unsweetened coconut milk
½ cup chicken broth
¼ teaspoon salt

1. In the Inner Pot, mix up the rice, coconut milk, chicken broth and salt. 2. Insert the pot into the Cooker Base and then close the lid rightly. 3. Select Pressure Cook mode. Press Pressure Cook button again to adjust the cooking time to 5 minutes; press Pressure Level to choose High Pressure. 4. When the time is up, leave the steam release handle in the Sealing position. 5.When done, use a fork to fluff the rice and serve.
Per Serving: Calories 236; Fat 13.9g; Sodium 451mg; Carbs 13.2g; Fiber 1.2g; Sugars 1.4g; Protein 14.3g

Garlic Shrimp Pasta with Thai Sweet Chili Sauce

Prep Time: 10 minutes | Cook Time: 6 minutes | Serves: 4

2 tablespoons olive oil
3 garlic cloves, minced, divided
16 ounces spaghetti, broken in half
3 cups water
1-pound medium shrimp (36–40 count), shells and tails left on
1 teaspoon paprika
¾ tablespoon lime juice
½ cup mayonnaise
⅓ cup Thai sweet chili sauce
2 teaspoons sriracha
¼ teaspoon red pepper flakes

1. Insert the pot into the Cooker Base without the lid. 2. Select Sauté mode and then press the same button again and then adjust the cooking temperature to Normal. 3. When the display switches On to Hot, add and heat the oil; add the garlic and cook for 1 minute or until fragrant. 4. Layer the spaghetti in a crisscross pattern and add the water, then gently press the spaghetti down to submerge completely. 5. Prepare a piece of aluminum foil, put the shrimp in its middle and then sprinkle the paprika and lime juice over the shrimp; fold the foil into a parcel and arrange it to the top of the spaghetti. 6. Place and close the lid rightly. 7. Select Pressure Cook mode. Press Pressure Cook button again to adjust the cooking time to 5 minutes; press Pressure Level to choose High Pressure. 8. While cooking, mix up the mayonnaise, chili sauce, sriracha, and red pepper flakes in a suitable bowl. 9. When the time is up, quickly and carefully turn the steam release handle from the Sealing position to the Venting position. 10. When released, unfold the shrimp parcel and dump the juices into the pasta; peel the shrimp and place them on the pasta. 11. Break up any spaghetti clumps, then stir in the sauce until everything is well combined. 12. Serve and enjoy.
Per Serving: Calories 344; Fat 14.9g; Sodium 227mg; Carbs 14g; Fiber 1g; Sugars 1.4g; Protein 25.7g

Worcestershire Mushroom Brown Rice

Prep Time: 10 minutes | Cook Time: 35 minutes | Serves: 4

3 tablespoons unsalted butter, divided
1 small onion, diced
3 garlic cloves, minced
1-pound baby bella mushrooms, sliced
2 teaspoons Worcestershire sauce
½ teaspoon dried thyme
1 cup long-grain brown rice
1¼ cups vegetable broth
Salt
Freshly ground black pepper

1. Insert the pot into the Cooker Base without the lid. 2. Select Sauté mode and then press the same button again and then adjust the cooking temperature to Normal. 3. When the display switches On to Hot, melt 1 tablespoon of the butter; add the onion and cook for 3 minutes or until just softened; add the garlic and cook for 1 minute or until fragrant; add the mushrooms, Worcestershire sauce, thyme and stir constantly for 5 to 6 minutes until the mushrooms reduce in size; lastly, stir in rice and broth. 4. Place and close the lid in right way. 5. Select Pressure Cook mode. Press Pressure Cook button again to adjust the cooking time to 25 minutes; press Pressure Level to choose High Pressure. 6. When the time is up, quickly and carefully turn the steam release handle from the Sealing position to the Venting position. 7. When released, add the remaining butter and stir well; season with salt and black pepper. 8. Enjoy.
Per Serving: Calories 249; Fat 13g; Sodium 556mg; Carbs 10g; Sugar 1.1g; Fiber 0.7g; Protein 31g

Long-Grain White Rice with Jalapeño

Prep Time: 10 minutes | Cook Time: 17 minutes | Serves: 6

2 tablespoons olive oil
1 medium yellow onion, diced
1 medium carrot, peeled and diced
2 celery stalks, diced
1 small jalapeño, diced
3 garlic cloves, minced
1 tablespoon apple cider vinegar
6 thyme sprigs
1 bay leaf
1 cup long-grain white rice
2 teaspoons sea salt
2½ cups chicken or vegetable broth
28 ounces frozen black-eyed peas

1. Insert the pot into the Cooker Base without the lid. 2. Select Sauté mode and then press the same button again and then adjust the cooking temperature to Normal. 3. When the display switches On to Hot, add the onion, carrot, celery and jalapeño, stir constantly for 4 minutes or until they are fragrant; add the garlic, thyme, vinegar and bay leaf, cook for 1 more minute; lastly, stir in the rice, chicken broth, peas and salt. 4. Press Cancel button to stop this cooking program. 5. Place and close the lid rightly. 6. Select Pressure Cook mode. Press Pressure Cook button again to adjust the cooking time to 12 minutes; press Pressure Level to choose High Pressure. 7. When the time is up, leave the steam release handle in the Sealing position for 10 minutes, then turn it to the Venting position. 8. When done, remove the thyme sprigs and bay leaf. 9. Serve and enjoy.
Per Serving: Calories 336; Fat 17.3g; Sodium 281mg; Carbs 8.1g; Fiber 5.3g; Sugars 17.7g; Protein 32.3g

Chicken Burrito Bowls with Chunky Salsa

Prep Time: 10 minutes | Cook Time: 15 minutes | Serves: 5

2 tablespoons olive oil
1 medium onion, diced
3 garlic cloves, minced
1½ tablespoons chili powder
1½ teaspoons ground cumin
1 cup chicken broth
Salt
Freshly ground black pepper
2 pounds boneless, skinless chicken thighs, cubed
1 (15-ounce) can black beans, drained and rinsed
1 cup frozen corn
1 (16-ounce) jar chunky salsa
1 cup long-grain white rice

1. Insert the pot into the Cooker Base without the lid. 2. Select Sauté mode and then press the same button again and then adjust the cooking temperature to Normal. 3. When the display switches On to Hot, add and heat the oil; add the onion, garlic and cook for 4 minutes or until the onion is translucent; add the cumin, chili powder and cook for 1 minute until fragrant; add the broth and stir to scrape the browned bits from the bottom. 4. Sprinkle salt and pepper over the chicken evenly and arrange it to the Inner Pot, then stir well with the beans, corn, salsa; sprinkle the rice and just use a spoon to press it down gently to submerge it. 5. Place and close the lid rightly. 6. Select Pressure Cook mode. Press Pressure Cook button again to adjust the cooking time to 10 minutes; press Pressure Level to choose High Pressure. 7. When the time is up, leave the steam release handle in the Sealing position. 8. Stir everything to combine before serving.
Per Serving: Calories 307; Fat 11g; Sodium 477mg; Carbs 14g; Fiber 1g; Sugars 1.4g; Protein 25.7g

Tomato Goulash

Prep Time: 10 minutes | Cook Time: 12 minutes | Serves: 6

1 tablespoon oil
1-pound ground beef
1 large onion, chopped
3 garlic cloves, minced
2½ cups water
3 cups elbow noodles, uncooked
2 (15-ounce) cans diced tomatoes
2 (15-ounce) cans tomato sauce
3 tablespoons soy sauce
2 tablespoons Italian seasoning
3 bay leaves
Salt
Freshly ground black pepper

1. Insert the pot into the Cooker Base without the lid. 2. Sauté mode and then press the same button again and then adjust the cooking temperature to Normal. 3. When the display switches On to Hot, add and heat the oil; add the beef, onion, garlic and cook for 5 to 7 minutes until the meat is browned. 4. Drain the redundant fat, stir in water and scrape up any browned bits from the bottom; without stirring, add the noodles, diced tomatoes and their juices, tomato sauce, soy sauce, Italian seasoning, bay leaves, salt and black pepper in order. 5. Press Cancel button to stop this cooking program and close the lid in right way. 6. Select Pressure Cook mode. Press Pressure Cook button again to adjust the cooking time to 5 minutes; press Pressure Level to choose High Pressure. 7. When the time is up, still quickly and carefully turn the steam release handle from the Sealing position to the Venting position. 8. When done, stir well after discarding the bay leaves. 9. Serve and done.
Per Serving: Calories 254; Fat 28 g; Sodium 346mg; Carbs 12.3 g; Sugar 1g; Fiber 0.7g; Protein 24.3 g

"Dirty" Rice with Herbs

Prep Time: 10 minutes | Cook Time: 12-18 minutes | Serves: 4

1-pound ground beef
½ cup chopped celery
1 small onion, chopped
½ cup chopped green bell pepper
1 cup beef broth
1 tablespoon Creole seasoning

1 teaspoon dried thyme
1 teaspoon dried oregano
Salt
Freshly ground black pepper
1 cup long-grain white rice

1. Insert the pot into the Cooker Base without the lid. 2. Select Sauté mode and then press the same button again and then adjust the cooking temperature to Normal. 3. When the display switches On to Hot, add the beef and cook for 5 to 7 minutes until brown, then breaking it into small pieces as needed. 4. Add the onion, celery and bell pepper, cook with the beef pieces for 3 to 5 minutes until softened. 5. Press Cancel button to stop this cooking program. 6. Add the beef broth, thyme, oregano, Creole seasoning, salt and black pepper, stir to scrape up the brown bits from the bottom; add rice and just press it down gently to submerge it. 7. Place and close the lid rightly. 8. Select Pressure Cook mode. Press Pressure Cook button again to adjust the cooking time to 6 minutes; press Pressure Level to choose High Pressure. 9. When the time is up, leave the steam release handle in the Sealing position for 10 minutes, then turn it to the Venting position. 10. When released, use a fork to fluff the rice. 11. Serve and enjoy.
Per Serving: Calories 249; Fat 13g; Sodium 556mg; Carbs 10g; Sugar 1.1g; Fiber 0.7g; Protein 31g

Tuna Casserole with Noodles

Prep Time: 10 minutes | Cook Time: 7 minutes | Serves: 8

3 tablespoons unsalted butter
1 small onion, diced
3 cups chicken broth
½ teaspoon salt
½ teaspoon freshly ground black pepper
2 garlic cloves, minced
1 teaspoon onion powder
1 cup whole milk

2 (6-ounce) cans chunk white tuna in water, drained
1 (12-ounce) bag frozen peas
12 ounces wide egg noodles, uncooked
2 (10.5-ounce) cans condensed cream of mushroom soup
2 cups shredded mild cheddar cheese

1. Insert the pot into the Cooker Base without the lid. 2. Select Sauté mode and then press the same button again and then adjust the cooking temperature to Normal. 3. When the display switches On to Hot, melt the butter; add the onion and cook for 4 minutes or until translucent; stir in the broth, garlic, onion powder, salt and black pepper. 4. Add the tuna, peas, noodles and milk without stirring them, then spread the mushroom soup over the noodles evenly without stirring them. 5. Place and close the lid rightly. 6. Select Pressure Cook mode. Press Pressure Cook button again to adjust the cooking time to 3 minutes; press Pressure Level to choose High Pressure. 7. When the time is up, quickly and carefully turn the steam release handle from the Sealing position to the Venting position. 8. When released, stir in the cheese. 9. Serve and enjoy.
Per Serving: Calories 351; Fat 22g; Sodium 502mg; Carbs 15.2g; Sugar 1.1g; Fiber 0.7g; Protein 26.4g

Shrimp Scampi with Lemon Wedges

Prep Time: 10 minutes | Cook Time: 10 minutes | Serves: 6

2 tablespoons olive oil
3 tablespoons unsalted butter
3 garlic cloves, minced
¼ cup finely chopped flat-leaf parsley
½ cup dry white wine (such as Pinot Grigio, Sauvignon Blanc, or Chardonnay)
½ teaspoon red pepper flakes
½ teaspoon salt

½ teaspoon freshly ground black pepper
1 (15-ounce) can chicken broth
Juice of ½ lemon
2 pounds frozen medium shrimp (36–40 count), peeled and deveined
12 ounces angel hair pasta
Lemon wedges, for serving (optional)

1. Insert the pot into the Cooker Base without the lid. 2. Select Sauté mode and then press the same button again and then adjust the cooking temperature to Normal. 3. When the display switches On to Hot, add the garlic, parsley and cook for 1 to 2 minutes; add the red pepper flakes, wine, salt and black pepper and cook for 3 minutes; stir in the broth and lemon juice and scrape up the browned bits from the bottom; add the shrimp. 4. Divide the pasta into two pieces and layer them on the top of the shrimp, make sure they are completely

submerged in the liquid without stirring them. 5. Place and close the lid rightly. 6. Select Pressure Cook mode. Press Pressure Cook button again to adjust the cooking time to 5 minutes; press Pressure Level to choose High Pressure. 7. When the time is up, quickly and carefully turn the steam release handle from the Sealing position to the Venting position. 8. Stir well and serve with the lemon wedges.
Per Serving: Calories 336; Fat 17.3g; Sodium 281mg; Carbs 8.1g; Fiber 5.3g; Sugars 17.7g; Protein 32.3g

Cheesy Chicken Broccoli Rice Casserole

Prep Time: 10 minutes | Cook Time: 15 minutes | Serves: 4

2 tablespoons unsalted butter
2 pounds boneless, skinless chicken breasts, cubed
1 small onion, diced
2 garlic cloves, minced
1⅓ cups chicken broth
1 teaspoon salt
¾ teaspoon freshly ground black

pepper
1 teaspoon garlic powder
1⅓ cups long-grain rice
½ cup whole milk
2 cups shredded mild cheddar cheese
2 cups frozen broccoli florets, thawed

1. Insert the pot into the Cooker Base without the lid. 2. Select Sauté mode and then press the same button again and then adjust the cooking temperature to Normal. 3. When the display switches On to Hot, melt the butter; add chicken and onion and cook for 5 minutes or until the onion starts to turn translucent; add the garlic and cook for 1 minutes until fragrant; stir in the broth, salt, pepper and garlic powder. 4. Add the rice without stirring, just press it down to submerge it. 5. Place and close the lid rightly. 6. Select Pressure Cook mode. Press Pressure Cook button again to adjust the cooking time to 5 minutes; press Pressure Level to choose High Pressure. 7. When the time is up, leave the steam release handle in the Sealing position. 8. When released, stir in the milk, cheese and broccoli; close the lid again and Keep Warm for 2 to 3 minutes to melt the cheese and heat the broccoli. 9. Serve and enjoy.
Per Serving: Calories 272; Fat 19g; Sodium 389mg; Carbs 10.4g; Fiber 0.7g; Sugars 1.1g; Protein 15.6g

Parmesan Spaghetti Meatballs

Prep Time: 10 minutes | Cook Time: 3 minutes | Serves: 8

1 (26-ounce) bag Italian-style frozen meatballs
16 ounces' spaghetti, broken in half

1 (24-ounce) jar pasta sauce
1 cup water
½ cup finely grated Parmesan cheese

1. In the Inner Pot, add the frozen meatballs and then layer the spaghetti in a crisscross pattern over them; without stirring, add the sauce and water. 2. Place and close the lid rightly. 3. Select Pressure Cook mode. Press Pressure Cook button again to adjust the cooking time to 3 minutes; press Pressure Level to choose High Pressure. 4. When the time is up, leave the steam release handle in the Sealing position. 5. When released, open the lid and stir well. 6. With the Parmesan on the top, enjoy.
Per Serving: Calories 285; Fat 9.8g; Sodium 639mg; Carbs 11.1g; Fiber 1.2g; Sugars 5.1g; Protein 27.8g

Tomato Brown Lentils

Prep Time: 2 minutes | Cook Time: 20 minutes | Serves: 6

1½ cups brown lentils
1 (15-ounce) can tomato sauce
2 tablespoons tomato paste
1 (15-ounce) can unsweetened full-; Fat coconut milk

⅓ cup water
1 teaspoon dried basil
1 teaspoon dried oregano
¼ teaspoon garlic salt

1. In the Inner Pot, add and mix up all of the ingredients. 2. Insert the pot into the Cooker Base and then close the lid rightly. 3. Select Pressure Cook mode. Press Pressure Cook button again to adjust the cooking time to 20 minutes; press Pressure Level to choose High Pressure. 4. When the time is up, leave the steam release handle in the Sealing position; when the float valve drops, open the lid. 5. Stir well before serving.
Per Serving: Calories: 330; Fat: 15g; Sodium: 471mg; Fiber: 7g; Carbs: 37g; Sugar: 4g; Protein: 14g

Simple Quinoa

Prep Time: 1 minutes | Cook Time: 1 minutes | Serves: 4

1 cup dry quinoa	1 cup water

1. In a fine-mesh strainer, add the quinoa and rinse them until the water doesn't become turbid anymore. 2. In the Inner Pot, add the clean quinoa and water. 3. Insert the pot into the Cooker Base and then close the lid rightly. 4. Select Pressure Cook mode. Press Pressure Cook button again to adjust the cooking time to 1 minutes; press Pressure Level to choose High Pressure. 5. When the time is up, leave the steam release handle in the Sealing position. 6. When the float valve drops, open the lid; use a fork to fluff the quinoa. 7. Serve and enjoy.
Per Serving: Calories: 156; Fat: 2g; Sodium: 2mg; Fiber: 3g; Carbs: 27g; Sugar: 0g; Protein: 6g

Chicken Pasta with Monterey Jack Cheese

Prep Time: 10 minutes | Cook Time: 14 minutes | Serves: 6

1-pound boneless, skinless chicken breasts	16 ounces' penne pasta
4 tablespoons (½ stick) unsalted butter	8 ounces' cream cheese, cubed
1 cup hot sauce	1 cup prepared ranch or blue cheese dressing
4 cups water, divided	¾ cup shredded Monterey Jack cheese

1. In the Inner Pot, mix up the butter, hot sauce, chicken and 1 cup of water. 2. Insert the pot into the Cooker Base and then close the lid rightly. 3. Select Pressure Cook mode. Press Pressure Cook button again to adjust the cooking time to 10 minutes; press Pressure Level to choose High Pressure. 4. When the time is up, quickly and carefully turn the steam release handle from the Sealing position to the Venting position. 5. When released, open the lid, reserve the liquid; take out the chicken and shred it. 6. Still in the Inner Pot, add the pasta and lay the shredded chicken on the surface; add the cream cheese, dressing and the remaining water. 7. Place and close the lid again. 8. Select Pressure Cook mode. Press Pressure Cook button again to adjust the cooking time to 4 minutes; press Pressure Level to choose High Pressure. 9. When the time is up, still quickly and carefully turn the steam release handle from the Sealing position to the Venting position. 10. When done, serve and stir in the Monterey Jack cheese. Enjoy.
Per Serving: Calories 285; Fat 9.8g; Sodium 639mg; Carbs 11.1g; Fiber 1.2g; Sugars 5.1g; Protein 27.8g

Creamy Chicken Alfredo

Prep Time: 10 minutes | Cook Time: 5 minutes | Serves: 4

1½ cups chicken broth	8 ounces' linguine pasta, broken in half
1½ cups heavy (whipping) cream	
3 garlic cloves, minced	5 chicken tenderloins
Salt	1 cup shredded Parmesan cheese
Freshly ground black pepper	

1. In the Inner Pot, mix up the broth, cream, garlic, salt and pepper in order; layer in the pasta and arrange it in a crisscross pattern to prevent clumping, do not stir but push the noodles down with the back of a spoon to make them covered by the liquids. 2. Arrange the chicken to the pasta, season with salt and pepper. 3. Place and close the lid rightly. 4. Select Pressure Cook mode. Press Pressure Cook button again to adjust the cooking time to 5 minutes; press Pressure Level to choose High Pressure. 5. When the time is up, leave the steam release handle in the Sealing position. 6. When released, remove the chicken, then slowly add the Parmesan and use a tong to stir the pasta around. 7. Dice the chicken and toss into the sauce. 8. Serve and enjoy.
Per Serving: Calories 272; Fat 19g; Sodium 389mg; Carbs 10.4g; Fiber 0.7g; Sugars 1.1g; Protein 15.6g

Spanish Rice with Tomato Paste

Prep Time: 10 minutes | Cook Time: 15 minutes | Serves: 4

1 tablespoon unsalted butter	1 tablespoon ground cumin
1 small red bell pepper, seeded and chopped	1 teaspoon paprika
1 small onion, chopped	½ jalapeño pepper, seeded and diced
3 garlic cloves, minced	1½ cups water
1 cup long-grain white rice	Salt
2 tablespoons tomato paste	Freshly ground black pepper

1. Insert the pot into the Cooker Base without the lid. 2. Select Sauté mode and then press the same button again and then adjust the cooking temperature to Normal. 3. When the display switches On to Hot, melt the butter; add the onion and bell pepper and cook for 3 minutes or until they start to soften; add the garlic and cook for 1 minutes until fragrant. 4. Press the Cancel button to stop this cooking program. 5. In the Inner Pot, mix up the rice, cumin, paprika, tomato paste, jalapeño and water. 6. Place and close the lid rightly. 7. Select Pressure Cook mode. Press Pressure Cook button again to adjust the cooking time to 5 minutes; press Pressure Level to choose High Pressure. 8. When the time is up, leave the steam release handle in the Sealing position for 10 minutes, then turn it to the Venting position. 9. When done, use a fork to fluff the rice, season with salt and pepper. 10. Serve and enjoy.
Per Serving: Calories 285; Fat 9.8g; Sodium 639mg; Carbs 11.1g; Fiber 1.2g; Sugars 5.1g; Protein 27.8g

Chickpea Mushrooms

Prep time: 15 minutes | Cook time: 40 minutes | Serves: 8

2 cups dried chickpeas, soaked overnight and drained	¼ cup chopped fresh flat-leaf parsley
½ teaspoon salt	2 tablespoons chopped fresh chives
9 cups water	2 tablespoons chopped fresh tarragon
½ pound fresh green beans, trimmed and cut into 1" pieces	¼ cup olive oil
4-ounce sliced button mushrooms	2 tablespoons red wine vinegar
½ red bell pepper, seeded, thinly sliced, and cut into 1" pieces	1 teaspoon Dijon mustard
	1 teaspoon honey
½ medium red onion, peeled and diced	½ teaspoon black pepper
	¼ teaspoon salt
	¼ cup grated Parmesan cheese

1. Add chickpeas, salt, and 8 cups of water to the Inner Pot. 2. Select Pressure Cook mode, and then press the "Pressure Cook" button again to select "Normal" time option. 3. Use the "+" key to set the cooking time to 40 minutes. 4. Press the Pressure Level button to adjust the pressure to "Low Pressure." 5. Once the cooking cycle is completed, allow the steam to release naturally for 10 minutes, then turn the steam release handle to the Venting position. 6. Drain chickpeas, transfer them to a large bowl and cool to room temperature. 7. Add the remaining water to the Inner Pot. Place the Steam Rack in the Inner Pot. 8. Add the green beans to the steamer basket and put the basket on the rack. 9. Select Pressure Cook mode, and then press the "Pressure Cook" button again to select "Less" time option. 10. Use the "-" key to set the cooking time to 10 minutes. 11. Press the Pressure Level button to adjust the pressure to "High Pressure." 12. Once the cooking cycle is completed, allow the steam to release naturally. 13. Rinse the green beans with cool water and add to bowl with the chickpeas. 14. Add green bean to the mushrooms along bell pepper, red onion, parsley, chives, and tarragon, mix well. 15. In a small bowl, combine olive oil, vinegar, mustard, honey, black pepper, and salt. 16. Whisk to combine, then pour over chickpea and green bean mixture, and toss to coat. 17. Top the dish with cheese and serve immediately.
Per Serving: Calories 122; Fat 7.9g; Sodium 704mg; Carbs 6g; Fiber 3.6g; Sugar 6g; Protein 18g

Dill Black-Eyed Peas

Prep time: 10 minutes | Cook time: 20 minutes | Serves: 8

¼ cup olive oil	stems reserved
4 sprigs oregano, leaves minced and stems reserved	1 pound dried black-eyed peas, soaked overnight and drained
2 sprigs thyme, leaves stripped and stems reserved	¼ teaspoon salt
	1 teaspoon black pepper
4 sprigs dill, fronds chopped and	4 cups water

1. In a small bowl, combine oil, oregano leaves, thyme leaves, and dill fronds, and mix to combine. 2. Cover and set aside. Tie herb stems together with butcher's twine. 3. Add to the Inner Pot along with black-eyed peas, salt, pepper, and water. 4. Put on the pressure cooker's lid and turn the steam valve to "Sealing" position. 5. Select Pressure Cook mode, and then press the "Pressure Cook" button again to select "Less" time option. 6. Press the Pressure Level button to adjust the pressure to "Low Pressure." 7. Once the cooking cycle is completed, allow the steam to release naturally. 8. When all the steam is released, remove the pressure lid from the top carefully. 9. Remove and discard herb stem bundle, and drain off any excess liquid. 10. Stir in olive oil mixture. 11. Serve hot.
Per Serving: Calories 184; Fat 5g; Sodium 441mg; Carbs 17g; Fiber 4.6g; Sugar 5g; Protein 9g

Chickpea Salad

Prep time: 15 minutes | Cook time: 20 minutes | Serves: 12

1 pound dried chickpeas
1½ tablespoons plus ¼ cup olive oil
4 cups water
¾ teaspoon salt
4 scallions, sliced
1 medium red onion, peeled and diced
1 small green bell pepper, seeded and diced
1 small red bell pepper, seeded and

diced
½ cup minced fresh parsley
1 large carrot, peeled and grated
2 teaspoons lemon juice
2 teaspoons white wine vinegar
1 tablespoon olive oil mayonnaise
1 clove garlic, peeled and minced
⅛ teaspoon ground white pepper
½ teaspoon dried oregano
¼ cup grated Parmesan cheese

1. Place chickpeas in the Inner Pot along with 1½ tablespoons oil, 4 cups of water, and salt. 2. Put on the pressure cooker's lid and turn the steam valve to "Sealing" position. 3. Select Pressure Cook mode, and then press the "Pressure Cook" button again to select "Less" time option. 4. Press the Pressure Level button to adjust the pressure to "Low Pressure." 5. Once the cooking cycle is completed, allow the steam to release naturally. 6. When all the steam is released, remove the pressure lid from the top carefully. 7. Add scallions, onion, bell peppers, parsley, and carrot to chickpeas and toss to combine. 8. In a small bowl, combine remaining ¼ cup of oil, lemon juice, vinegar, mayonnaise, garlic, white pepper, and oregano, and whisk to mix. 9. Pour dressing over chickpea mixture and stir to combine. Sprinkle cheese on top. 10. Close lid and allow to stand on the Keep Warm setting for 10 minutes before serving.
Per Serving: Calories 221; Fat 19g; Sodium 354mg; Carbs 15g; Fiber 5.1g; Sugar 8.2g; Protein 12g

Salty Edamame

Prep time: 10 minutes | Cook time: 25 minutes | Serves: 4

1 cup shelled edamame
8 cups water
1 tablespoon vegetable oil

1 teaspoon coarse sea salt
2 tablespoons soy sauce

1. Add edamame and 4 cups of water to the Inner Pot. 2. Put on the pressure cooker's lid and turn the steam valve to "Sealing" position. 3. Select Pressure Cook mode, and then press the "Pressure Cook" button again to select "Less" time option. 4. Use the "+/-" keys on the control panel to set the cooking time to 1 minutes. 5. Press the Pressure Level button to adjust the pressure to "High Pressure." 6. Once the cooking cycle is completed, quickly and carefully turn the steam release handle from Sealing position to the Venting position. 7. When all the steam is released, remove the pressure lid from the top carefully. 8. Add the remaining 4 cups of water and resuming cooking on Pressure Cook mode for 11 minutes at High Pressure. 9. Once the cooking cycle is completed, allow the pressure release naturally. 10. When done, drain edamame and transfer to a serving bowl. 11. Sprinkle with salt and serve with soy sauce on the side for dipping.
Per Serving: Calories 334; Fat 7.9g; Sodium 704mg; Carbs 6g; Fiber 3.6g; Sugar 6g; Protein 18g

Homemade Three-Bean Salad

Prep time: 15 minutes | Cook time: 30 minutes | Serves: 8

¼ pound dried pinto beans, soaked overnight and drained
¼ pound dried black beans, soaked overnight and drained
¼ pound dried red beans, soaked overnight and drained
8 cups water
1 tablespoon light olive oil
1 stalk celery, chopped
½ medium red onion, peeled and

chopped
½ medium green bell pepper, seeded and chopped
¼ cup minced fresh cilantro
¼ cup minced fresh flat-leaf parsley
3 tablespoons olive oil
3 tablespoons red wine vinegar
1 tablespoon honey
½ teaspoon black pepper
½ teaspoon sea salt

1. Place beans, water, and light olive oil in the Inner Pot. 2. Put on the pressure cooker's lid and turn the steam valve to "Sealing" position. 3. Press the "Bean/Chili" button twice to select "Normal" option. 4. Press the Pressure Level button to adjust the pressure to "Low Pressure." 5. Once the cooking cycle is completed, allow the steam to release naturally. 6. When all the steam is released, remove the pressure lid from the top carefully and drain the beans, set aside to cool to room temperature. 7. Transfer cooled beans to a large bowl. Add celery, onion, bell pepper, cilantro, and parsley. 8. Mix well. In a small bowl, whisk together olive oil, vinegar, honey, black pepper, and salt. 9. Pour dressing over bean

mixture and toss to coat. Refrigerate for 4 hours before serving.
Per Serving: Calories 219; Fat 10g; Sodium 891mg; Carbs 22.9g; Fiber 4g; Sugar 4g; Protein 13g

Cannellini Bean Salads

Prep time: 15 minutes | Cook time: 40 minutes | Serves: 6

1 cup dried cannellini beans, soaked overnight and drained
4 cups water
4 cups vegetable stock
1 tablespoon olive oil

1 teaspoon salt
2 cloves garlic, peeled and minced
½ cup diced tomato
½ teaspoon dried sage
½ teaspoon black pepper

1. Add beans and water to the Inner Pot. 2. Put on the pressure cooker's lid and turn the steam valve to "Sealing" position. 3. Press the "Bean/Chili" button twice to select "Normal" option. 4. Press the Pressure Level button to adjust the pressure to "High Pressure." 5. Once the cooking cycle is completed, quickly and carefully turn the steam release handle from Sealing position to the Venting position. 6. When all the steam is released, remove the pressure lid from the top carefully. 7. Drain and rinse beans, and return to pot along with stock. Soak for 1 hour. 8. Add olive oil, salt, garlic, tomato, sage, and pepper to beans. 9. Put on the pressure cooker's lid and turn the steam valve to "Sealing" position. 10. Select Pressure Cook mode, and then press the "Pressure Cook" button again to select "Less" time option. 11. Use the "+/-" keys on the control panel to set the cooking time to 10 minutes. 12. Press the Pressure Level button to adjust the pressure to "Low Pressure." 13. Once the cooking cycle is completed, quickly and carefully turn the steam release handle from Sealing position to the Venting position. 14. When all the steam is released, remove the pressure lid from the top carefully. 15. Serve hot.
Per Serving: Calories 289; Fat 14g; Sodium 791mg; Carbs 18.9g; Fiber 4.6g; Sugar 8g; Protein 6g

Garlicky Black-Eyed Pea Soup

Prep time: 10 minutes | Cook time: 30 minutes | Serves: 8

2 tablespoons light olive oil
2 stalks celery, chopped
1 medium white onion, peeled and chopped
2 cloves garlic, peeled and minced
2 tablespoons chopped fresh oregano
1 teaspoon fresh thyme leaves

1 pound dried black-eyed peas, soaked overnight and drained
¼ teaspoon salt
1 teaspoon black pepper
4 cups water
1 (15-ounce) can diced tomatoes

1. Press the "Sauté" button two time to select "Normal" and then heat oil. 2. Add celery and onion, and cook for 5 minutes or until just tender. 3. Add garlic, oregano, and thyme, and cook until fragrant, about 30 seconds. 4. Press the Cancel button. 5. Add black-eyed peas, salt, pepper, water, and tomatoes to the Inner Pot and stir well. 6. Put on the pressure cooker's lid and turn the steam valve to "Sealing" position. 7. Select Pressure Cook mode, and then press the "Pressure Cook" button again to select "Less" time option. 8. Press the Pressure Level button to adjust the pressure to "Low Pressure." 9. Once the cooking cycle is completed, allow the steam to release naturally. 10. When all the steam is released, remove the pressure lid from the top carefully. 11. Stir well. Serve hot.
Per Serving: Calories 310; Fat 7.9g; Sodium 704mg; Carbs 6g; Fiber 3.6g; Sugar 6g; Protein 18g

Chickpea Soup

Prep time: 10 minutes | Cook time: 25 minutes | Serves: 8

1 pound dried chickpeas
4 cups water
¾ teaspoon salt
½ teaspoon black pepper
10 strands saffron
2 medium onions, peeled and

diced
1 cup olive oil
1 teaspoon dried oregano
3 tablespoons lemon juice
2 tablespoons chopped fresh parsley

1. Add chickpeas, water, salt, pepper, saffron, onions, oil, and oregano to the Inner Pot and stir well. 2. Put on the pressure cooker's lid and turn the steam valve to "Sealing" position. 3. Press the "Bean/Chili" button one time to select "Less" option. 4. Press the Pressure Level button to adjust the pressure to "Low Pressure." 5. Once the cooking cycle is completed, allow the steam to release naturally. 6. When all the steam is released, remove the pressure lid from the top carefully. 7. Serve hot or cold, sprinkled with lemon juice. 8. Garnish with chopped parsley.
Per Serving: Calories 289; Fat 14g; Sodium 791mg; Carbs 18.9g; Fiber 4.6g; Sugar 8g; Protein 6g

Black Bean Sliders

Prep time: 10 minutes | Cook time: 55 minutes | Serves: 8

1 tablespoon olive oil	¼ teaspoon coriander
1 slice bacon	½ teaspoon chili powder
1 small red bell pepper, seeded and diced	½ teaspoon ground cumin
2 cups vegetable broth	½ teaspoon sea salt
1 cup dried black beans, soaked overnight and drained	¼ cup chopped fresh cilantro
½ teaspoon garlic powder	1 large egg
	1 cup panko bread crumbs
	16 slider buns

1. Press the "Sauté" button twice to select "Normal" and then heat oil. 2. Add bacon and bell pepper. Cook until bacon is cooked through, about 5 minutes. 3. Add broth and scrape bottom of pot to release browned bits. 4. Add beans, garlic powder, coriander, chili powder, cumin, salt, and cilantro. 5. Stir well, then press the Cancel button. 6. Put on the pressure cooker's lid and turn the steam valve to "Sealing" position. 7. Press the "Pressure Cook" button one time to select "Normal" option. 8. Use the "+/-" keys on the control panel to set the cooking time to 30 minutes. 9. Press the Pressure Level button to adjust the pressure to "Low Pressure." 10. Once the cooking cycle is completed, allow the steam to release naturally. 11. When all the steam is released, remove the pressure lid from the top carefully. 12. Remove and discard bacon. 13. Without the lid, press the Sauté button, press again to change the heat to Less, and simmer bean mixture for 10 minutes to thicken. 14. Transfer mixture to a large bowl. Once cool enough to handle, quickly mix in egg and bread crumbs. 15. Form into 16 equal-sized small patties. 16. Cook on stovetop in a skillet over medium heat for approximately 2–3 minutes per side until browned. 17. Remove from heat and add each patty to a bun. 18. Serve warm.
Per Serving: Calories 314; Fat 7.9g; Sodium 704mg; Carbs 6g; Fiber 3.6g; Sugar 6g; Protein 18g

Beans with Tomato and Parsley

Prep time: 10 minutes | Cook time: 60 minutes | Serves: 4

2 tablespoons light olive oil	1 (15-ounce) can diced tomatoes, drained
1 medium white onion, peeled and chopped	1 (8-ounce) can tomato sauce
2 cloves garlic, peeled and minced	¼ cup chopped fresh flat-leaf parsley
1 pound dried giant beans, soaked overnight and drained	2 tablespoons chopped fresh oregano
2 thyme sprigs	1 tablespoon chopped fresh dill
1 bay leaf	½ cup crumbled feta cheese
5 cups water	1 small lemon, cut into 8 wedges

1. Press the "Sauté" button twice to select the cooking mode and "Normal" cooking temperature, then add and heat oil. 2. Add onion and cook until tender, about 3 minutes. 3. Add garlic and cook until fragrant, about 30 seconds. Press the Cancel button. 4. Add beans, thyme, bay leaf, and water to the Inner Pot. 5. Put on the pressure cooker's lid and turn the steam valve to "Sealing" position. 6. Press the "Pressure Cook" button one time to select "More" option. 7. Use the "+/-" keys on the control panel to set the cooking time to 50 minutes. 8. Press the Pressure Level button to adjust the pressure to "Low Pressure." 9. Once the cooking cycle is completed, quickly and carefully turn the steam release handle from Sealing position to the Venting position. 10. When all the steam is released, remove the pressure lid from the top carefully. 11. Add diced tomatoes and tomato sauce. 12. Close lid and let stand on the Keep Warm setting for 10 minutes to heat through. 13. Remove and discard bay leaf. Stir in herbs and ladle into soup bowls. 14. Garnish with feta and lemon slices, and serve hot.
Per Serving: Calories 382; Fat 10.9g; Sodium 354mg; Carbs 20.5g; Fiber 4.1g; Sugar 8.2g; Protein 06g

Black Beans with Corn and Tomato Relish

Prep time: 10 minutes | Cook time: 30 minutes | Serves: 6

½ pound dried black beans, soaked overnight and drained	8 cups water
1 medium white onion, peeled and sliced in half	1 cup corn kernels
	1 large tomato, seeded and chopped
2 cloves garlic, peeled and lightly crushed	½ medium red onion, peeled and chopped
¼ cup minced fresh cilantro	
½ teaspoon ground cumin	¼ teaspoon salt
¼ teaspoon smoked paprika	3 tablespoons olive oil
¼ teaspoon black pepper	3 tablespoons lime juice

1. Add beans, white onion, garlic, and water to the Inner Pot. 2. Put on the pressure cooker's lid and turn the steam valve to "Sealing" position. 3. Press the "Bean/Chili" button twice to select "Normal" option. 4. Press the Pressure Level button to adjust the pressure to "High Pressure." 5. Once the cooking cycle is completed, allow the steam to release naturally. 6. When all the steam is released, remove the pressure lid from the top carefully. 7. Discard onion and garlic. Drain beans well and transfer to a medium bowl. 8. Cool to room temperature, about 30 minutes. 9. In a separate small bowl, combine corn, tomato, red onion, cilantro, cumin, paprika, pepper, and salt. 10. Toss to combine. Add to black beans and gently fold to mix. 11. Whisk together olive oil and lime juice in a small bowl and pour over black bean mixture. Gently toss to coat. 12. Serve at room temperature or refrigerate for at least 2 hours.
Per Serving: Calories 372; Fat 20g; Sodium 891mg; Carbs 29g; Fiber 3g; Sugar 8g; Protein 7g

White Bean Soup

Prep time: 10 minutes | Cook time: 30 minutes | Serves: 8

4 cups water	1 tablespoon dried rosemary
1 pound dried white kidney beans, soaked overnight and drained	1 tablespoon dried thyme
	3 bay leaves
2 medium carrots, peeled and sliced	4 tablespoons minced fresh parsley
2 medium onions, peeled and diced	¼ cup olive oil
2 stalks celery, thinly sliced	4 cloves garlic, peeled
1 medium parsnip, peeled and thinly sliced	¾ teaspoon salt
	½ teaspoon black pepper
1 cup tomato sauce	

1. Place water, beans, carrots, onions, celery, parsnip, tomato sauce, rosemary, thyme, bay leaves, parsley, oil, and garlic in the Inner Pot. 2. Put on the pressure cooker's lid and turn the steam valve to "Sealing" position. 3. Press the "Bean/Chili" button twice to select "Normal" option. 4. Press the Pressure Level button to adjust the pressure to "Low Pressure." 5. Once the cooking cycle is completed, allow the steam to release naturally. 6. When all the steam is released, remove the pressure lid from the top carefully. 7. Discard bay leaves, and season with salt and pepper. 8. Serve hot.
Per Serving: Calories 349; Fat 2.9g; Sodium 511mg; Carbs 12g; Fiber 3g; Sugar 8g; Protein 7g

Vegetarian Loaf

Prep time: 10 minutes | Cook time: 50 minutes | Serves: 6

1 cup dried pinto beans, soaked overnight and drained	1 large egg, beaten
	¾ cup ketchup
8 cups water	1 teaspoon garlic powder
1 tablespoon vegetable oil	1 teaspoon dried basil
1 teaspoon salt	1 teaspoon dried parsley
1 cup diced onion	½ teaspoon salt
1 cup chopped walnuts	½ teaspoon black pepper
½ cup rolled oats	

1. Add beans and 4 cups of water to the Inner Pot. 2. Put on the pressure cooker's lid and turn the steam valve to "Sealing" position. 3. Select Pressure Cook mode, and then press the "Pressure Cook" button again to select "Less" time option. 4. Use the "+/-" keys on the control panel to set the cooking time to 1 minutes. 5. Press the Pressure Level button to adjust the pressure to "High Pressure." 6. Once the cooking cycle is completed, quickly and carefully turn the steam release handle from Sealing position to the Venting position. 7. When all the steam is released, remove the pressure lid from the top carefully; drain and rinse the beans and then return to the pot with the remaining 4 cups of water. Soak for 1 hour. 8. Still in the pot. Add the oil and salt. 9. Put on the pressure cooker's lid and turn the steam valve to "Sealing" position. 10. Select Pressure Cook mode, and then press the "Pressure Cook" button again to select "Less" time option. 11. Use the "+/-" keys on the control panel to set the cooking time to 11 minutes. 12. Press the Pressure Level button to adjust the pressure to "High Pressure." 13. Once the cooking cycle is completed, allow the pressure release naturally. 14. In a suitable bowl, stir in onion, walnuts, oats, egg, ketchup, garlic powder, basil, parsley, salt, and pepper. 15. Spread the mixture into a loaf pan and bake for 30–35 minutes in the preheated oven at 350°F/175°C. 16. Cool for 20 minutes in pan before slicing and serving.
Per Serving: Calories 221; Fat 7.9g; Sodium 704mg; Carbs 6g; Fiber 3.6g; Sugar 6g; Protein 18g

White Bean Cassoulet

Prep time: 10 minutes | Cook time: 45 minutes | Serves: 8

1 tablespoon olive oil	chopped
1 medium onion, peeled and diced	½ teaspoon fennel seed
2 cups dried cannellini beans, soaked overnight and drained	¼ teaspoon ground nutmeg
1 medium parsnip, peeled and diced	½ teaspoon garlic powder
	1 teaspoon sea salt
2 medium carrots, peeled and diced	½ teaspoon black pepper
	2 cups vegetable broth
2 stalks celery, diced	1 (15-ounce) can diced tomatoes, including juice
1 medium zucchini, trimmed and	2 sprigs rosemary

1. Press the "Sauté" button two time to select "Normal" mode on the Inner Pot and heat oil. 2. Add onion and cook until translucent, about 5 minutes. Add beans and toss. 3. Add a layer of parsnip, then a layer of carrots, and next a layer of celery. 4. Finally, add a layer of zucchini. Sprinkle in fennel seed, nutmeg, garlic powder, salt, and pepper. 5. Press Cancel button to stop this cooking program. 6. Gently pour in broth and canned tomatoes. Top with rosemary. 7. Put on the pressure cooker's lid and turn the steam valve to "Sealing" position. 8. Press the "Pressure Cook" button one time to select "Normal" option. 9. Use the "+/-" keys on the control panel to set the cooking time to 30 minutes. 10. Press the Pressure Level button to adjust the pressure to "Low Pressure." 11. Once the cooking cycle is completed, allow the steam to release naturally for 10 minutes, then turn the steam release handle to the Venting position. 12. When all the steam is released, press Cancel button to stop this cooking program and remove the pressure lid from the top carefully. 13. Press the Sauté button twice to select the cooking mode and "Less" cooking temperature, and simmer bean mixture uncovered for 10 minutes to thicken. 14. Transfer to a serving bowl and carefully toss. 15. Remove and discard rosemary and serve.

Per Serving: Calories 220; Fat 10.9g; Sodium 354mg; Carbs 20.5g; Fiber 4.1g; Sugar 8.2g; Protein 06g

Toasted Orzo Salad

Prep time: 10 minutes | Cook time: 10 minutes | Serves: 6

2 tablespoons light olive oil	1 medium red bell pepper, seeded and diced
1 clove garlic, peeled and crushed	
2 cups orzo	¼ cup crumbled feta cheese
3 cups vegetable broth	1 tablespoon olive oil
½ cup sliced black olives	1 tablespoon red wine vinegar
3 scallions, thinly sliced	½ teaspoon black pepper
1 medium Roma tomato, seeded and diced	¼ teaspoon salt

1. Press the "Sauté" button twice to select "Normal" and heat light olive oil. 2. Add garlic and orzo and cook, stirring frequently, until orzo is light golden brown, about 5 minutes. 3. Press Cancel button to stop this cooking program, add the broth and stir. 4. Put on the pressure cooker's lid and turn the steam valve to "Sealing" position. 5. Select Pressure Cook mode, and then press the "Pressure Cook" button again to select "Less" time option. 6. Use the "+/-" keys on the control panel to set the cooking time to 3 minutes. 7. Press the Pressure Level button to adjust the pressure to "Low Pressure." 8. Once the cooking cycle is completed, quickly and carefully turn the steam release handle from Sealing position to the Venting position. 9. When all the steam is released, remove the pressure lid from the top carefully. 10. Transfer orzo to a medium bowl, then set aside to cool to room temperature, about 30 minutes. 11. Add olives, scallions, tomato, bell pepper, feta, olive oil, vinegar, black pepper, and salt, and stir until combined. 12. Serve at room temperature or refrigerate for at least 2 hours.

Per Serving: Calories 282; Fat 12.9g; Sodium 414mg; Carbs 11g; Fiber 5g; Sugar 9g; Protein 11g

Three-Bean Chili

Prep time: 10 minutes | Cook time: 40 minutes | Serves: 12

1 cup dried pinto beans, soaked overnight and drained	2 stalks celery, chopped
	1 (28-ounce) can diced tomatoes
1 cup dried red beans, soaked overnight and drained	1 (15-ounce) can tomato sauce
	¼ cup chili powder
1 cup dried black beans, soaked overnight and drained	2 tablespoons smoked paprika
	1 teaspoon ground cumin
2 medium white onions, peeled and chopped	1 teaspoon ground coriander
	½ teaspoon salt
2 medium red bell peppers, seeded and chopped	½ teaspoon black pepper
	3 cups vegetable broth

1 cup water

1. Place all ingredients in the Inner Pot and stir to combine. 2. Put on the pressure cooker's lid and turn the steam valve to "Sealing" position. 3. Press the "Bean/Chili" button twice to select "Normal" option. 4. Press the Pressure Level button to adjust the pressure to "Low Pressure." 5. Once the cooking cycle is completed, quickly and carefully turn the steam release handle from Sealing position to the Venting position. 6. When all the steam is released, remove the pressure lid from the top carefully. 7. Press Cancel button to stop this cooking program. 8. Press the "Sauté" button twice to select "Less" mode and let chili simmer, uncovered, until desired thickness is reached. 9. Serve warm.

Per Serving: Calories 289; Fat 14g; Sodium 791mg; Carbs 18.9g; Fiber 4.6g; Sugar 8g; Protein 6g

White Bean Barley Soup

Prep time: 10 minutes | Cook time: 37 minutes | Serves: 8

2 tablespoons light olive oil	1 (14-ounce) can fire-roasted diced tomatoes, undrained
½ medium onion, peeled and chopped	
	½ cup medium pearl barley, rinsed and drained
1 medium carrot, peeled and chopped	
	4 cups vegetable broth
1 stalk celery, chopped	2 cups water
2 cloves garlic, peeled and minced	2 (15-ounce) cans Great Northern beans, drained
2 sprigs fresh thyme	
1 bay leaf	½ teaspoon salt
½ teaspoon black pepper	

1. Press the "Sauté" button twice to select "Normal" and heat oil. 2. Add onion, carrot, and celery. Cook until just tender, about 5 minutes. 3. Add garlic, thyme, bay leaf, and pepper, and cook until fragrant, about 30 seconds. Press the Cancel button. 4. Add the tomatoes, barley, broth, and water. 5. Put on the pressure cooker's lid and turn the steam valve to "Sealing" position. 6. Press the "Soup" button one time to select "Less" option. 7. Press the Pressure Level button to adjust the pressure to "Low Pressure." 8. Once the cooking cycle is completed, allow the steam to release naturally. 9. When all the steam is released, remove the pressure lid from the top carefully. 10. Stir soup, then add beans and salt. Close lid and let stand on the Keep Warm setting for 10 minutes. 11. Remove and discard bay leaf. 12. Serve hot.

Per Serving: Calories 382; Fat 7.9g; Sodium 704mg; Carbs 6g; Fiber 3.6g; Sugar 6g; Protein 18g

Bean and Lentil Chili

Prep time: 10 minutes | Cook time: 25 minutes | Serves: 6

2 tablespoons vegetable oil	drained
1 large Spanish onion, peeled and diced	3 tablespoons chili powder
	1 tablespoon sweet paprika
1 small jalapeño pepper, seeded and minced	1 teaspoon dried oregano
	1 teaspoon ground cumin
1 clove garlic, peeled and minced	1 (28-ounce) can diced tomatoes
1 cup dried brown or green lentils, rinsed and drained	1 chipotle pepper in adobo sauce, minced
1 (15-ounce) can black beans, drained	6 cups vegetable broth
	½ teaspoon salt
1 cup pearl barley, rinsed and	¼ teaspoon black pepper

1. Press the "Sauté" button two time to select "Normal" and heat oil. 2. Add onion and cook until just tender, about 3 minutes. Stir in jalapeño and cook for 1 minute. 3. Add garlic and cook until fragrant, about 30 seconds. 4. Stir in lentils, black beans, barley, chili powder, paprika, oregano, cumin, tomatoes, chipotle pepper, and vegetable broth. 5. Put on the pressure cooker's lid and turn the steam valve to "Sealing" position. 6. Select Pressure Cook mode, and then press the "Pressure Cook" button again to select "Less" time option. 7. Use the "+/-" keys on the control panel to set the cooking time to 10 minutes. 8. Press the Pressure Level button to adjust the pressure to "Low Pressure." 9. Once the cooking cycle is completed, quickly and carefully turn the steam release handle from Sealing position to the Venting position. 10. When all the steam is released, remove the pressure lid from the top carefully. 11. Press the Cancel button, then press the Sauté button twice to choose "Less". 12. Bring to a simmer. Season with salt and black pepper, and simmer until slightly thickened, about 10 minutes. 13. Serve immediately.

Per Serving: Calories 450; Fat 7.9g; Sodium 704mg; Carbs 6g; Fiber 3.6g; Sugar 6g; Protein 18g

Chili-Spiced Beans

Prep time: 10 minutes | Cook time: 40 minutes | Serves: 8

1 pound dried pinto beans, soaked overnight and drained
1 medium onion, peeled and chopped
¼ cup chopped fresh cilantro
1 (15-ounce) can tomato sauce
¼ cup chili powder
2 tablespoons smoked paprika
1 teaspoon ground cumin
1 teaspoon ground coriander
½ teaspoon black pepper
2 cups vegetable broth
1 cup water

1. Place all ingredients in the Inner Pot and stir to combine. 2. Put on the pressure cooker's lid and turn the steam valve to "Sealing" position. 3. Press the "Bean/Chili" button one time to select "Normal" option. 4. Press the Pressure Level button to adjust the pressure to "Low Pressure." 5. Once the cooking cycle is completed, quickly and carefully turn the steam release handle from Sealing position to the Venting position. 6. When all the steam is released, remove the pressure lid from the top carefully. 7. Press Cancel button to stop this cooking program. 8. Press the "Sauté" button two time to select "Less" mode and let beans simmer, uncovered, until desired thickness is reached. 9. Serve warm.
Per Serving: Calories 334; Fat 7.9g; Sodium 704mg; Carbs 6g; Fiber 3.6g; Sugar 6g; Protein 18g

Lima Bean Soup

Prep time: 10 minutes | Cook time: 17 minutes | Serves: 6

1 tablespoon olive oil
1 small onion, peeled and diced
1 clove garlic, peeled and minced
2 cups vegetable stock
½ cup water
2 cups dried lima beans, soaked overnight and drained
½ teaspoon salt
½ teaspoon black pepper
2 tablespoons thinly sliced chives

1. Press the "Sauté" button two time to select "Normal" mode on the Inner Pot and heat oil. 2. Add onion and cook until golden brown, about 10 minutes. 3. Add garlic and cook until fragrant, about 30 seconds. 4. Press the Cancel button. 5. Add stock, water, and lima beans. 6. Put on the pressure cooker's lid and turn the steam valve to "Sealing" position. 7. Select Pressure Cook mode, and then press the "Pressure Cook" button again to select "Less" time option. 8. Use the "+/-" keys on the control panel to set the cooking time to 6 minutes. 9. Press the Pressure Level button to adjust the pressure to "High Pressure." 10. Once the cooking cycle is completed, allow the steam to release naturally. 11. When all the steam is released, remove the pressure lid from the top carefully. 12. Purée soup with an immersion blender or in batches in a blender. 13. Season with salt and pepper, then sprinkle with chives before serving.
Per Serving: Calories 212; Fat 10.9g; Sodium 454mg; Carbs 10g; Fiber 3.1g; Sugar 5.2g; Protein 10g

White Bean Soup with Kale

Prep time: 10 minutes | Cook time: 27 minutes | Serves: 8

1 tablespoon light olive oil
2 stalks celery, chopped
1 medium yellow onion, peeled and chopped
2 cloves garlic, peeled and minced
1 tablespoon chopped fresh oregano
4 cups chopped kale
1 pound dried Great Northern beans, soaked overnight and drained
8 cups vegetable broth
¼ cup lemon juice
1 tablespoon olive oil
1 teaspoon black pepper

1. Press the "Sauté" button two time to select "Normal" mode and heat light olive oil. 2. Add celery and onion and cook 5 minutes. Add garlic and oregano and sauté 30 seconds. 3. Add kale and turn to coat, then cook until just starting to wilt, about 1 minute. 4. Press the Cancel button. 5. Add beans, broth, lemon juice, olive oil, and pepper to the Inner Pot and stir well. 6. Put on the pressure cooker's lid and turn the steam valve to "Sealing" position. 7. Select Pressure Cook mode, and then press the "Pressure Cook" button again to select "Less" time option. 8. Press the Pressure Level button to adjust the pressure to "Low Pressure." 9. Once the cooking cycle is completed, allow the steam to release naturally. 10. When all the steam is released, remove the pressure lid from the top carefully. 11. Serve hot.
Per Serving: Calories 450; Fat 7.9g; Sodium 704mg; Carbs 6g; Fiber 3.6g; Sugar 6g; Protein 18g

Beefsteak Tomatoes with Cheese

Prep time: 10 minutes | Cook time: 30 minutes | Serves: 4

½ cup orzo
4 large beefsteak tomatoes
1 cup shredded mozzarella cheese
2 cloves garlic, peeled and minced
2 tablespoons minced fresh basil
2 tablespoons minced fresh parsley
½ teaspoon salt
¼ teaspoon black pepper
2 tablespoons olive oil

1. Place orzo in the Inner Pot and add water just to cover. 2. Put on the pressure cooker's lid and turn the steam valve to "Sealing" position. 3. Select Pressure Cook mode, and then press the "Pressure Cook" button again to select "Less" time option. 4. Use the "+/-" keys on the control panel to set the cooking time to 3 minutes. 5. Press the Pressure Level button to adjust the pressure to "Low Pressure." 6. Once the cooking cycle is completed, quickly and carefully turn the steam release handle from Sealing position to the Venting position. 7. When all the steam is released, remove the pressure lid from the top carefully. 8. Drain orzo and set aside. Cut tops off tomatoes and scoop out seeds and pulp. 9. Place pulp in a medium bowl. Add orzo, cheese, garlic, basil, parsley, salt, and pepper. 10. Stuff tomatoes with orzo mixture and place on a baking sheet. 11. Drizzle oil over tomatoes and bake for 15–20 minutes at 350°F/175°C in your preheated oven. 12. Serve hot.
Per Serving: Calories 289; Fat 14g; Sodium 791mg; Carbs 18.9g; Fiber 4.6g; Sugar 8g; Protein 6g

Creamy White Bean Soup

Prep time: 10 minutes | Cook time: 27 minutes | Serves: 6

1 tablespoon olive oil
1 medium white onion, peeled and chopped
1 medium carrot, peeled and chopped
1 stalk celery, chopped
2 cloves garlic, peeled and minced
1 cup dried cannellini beans, soaked overnight and drained
4 cups vegetable broth
1 (15-ounce) can diced tomatoes
1 teaspoon minced fresh sage
½ teaspoon black pepper
½ teaspoon sea salt

1. Press the "Sauté" button two time to select "Normal" and heat oil. 2. Add onion, carrot, and celery and sauté 5 minutes. 3. Add garlic and cook 30 seconds. Stir in beans. Press the Cancel button. 4. Add broth, tomatoes, sage, pepper, and salt and stir. 5. Put on the pressure cooker's lid and turn the steam valve to "Sealing" position. 6. Select Pressure Cook mode, and then press the "Pressure Cook" button again to select "Less" time option. 7. Press the Pressure Level button to adjust the pressure to "Low Pressure." 8. Once the cooking cycle is completed, quickly and carefully turn the steam release handle from Sealing position to the Venting position. 9. When all the steam is released, remove the pressure lid from the top carefully. 10. Remove 1 cup beans and mash until smooth. Stir back into pot. 11. Serve hot.
Per Serving: Calories 372; Fat 20g; Sodium 891mg; Carbs 29g; Fiber 3g; Sugar 8g; Protein 7g

Greek Navy Bean Soup

Prep time: 10 minutes | Cook time: 30 minutes | Serves: 8

1 cup small dried navy beans, soaked overnight and drained
1 large stalk celery, halved lengthwise and sliced into ½" pieces
1 large carrot, peeled, halved, and sliced into ½" pieces
2 medium onions, peeled and chopped
½ cup tomato purée
½ cup olive oil
2 bay leaves
1 medium chili pepper, stemmed and minced
2 teaspoons smoked paprika
8 cups water
½ teaspoon salt

1. Add beans, celery, carrot, onions, tomato purée, oil, bay leaves, chili pepper, paprika, and water to the Inner Pot. 2. Put on the pressure cooker's lid and turn the steam valve to "Sealing" position. 3. Press the "Bean/Chili" button twice to select "Normal" option. 4. Press the Pressure Level button to adjust the pressure to "High Pressure." 5. Once the cooking cycle is completed, allow the steam to release naturally. 6. When all the steam is released, remove the pressure lid from the top carefully. 7. Season with salt. Remove and discard bay leaves. 8. Serve hot.
Per Serving: Calories 282; Fat 12.9g; Sodium 414mg; Carbs 11g; Fiber 5g; Sugar 9g; Protein 11g

Pasta with Marinated Artichokes

Prep time: 10 minutes | Cook time: 10 minutes | Serves: 6

1-pound whole-wheat spaghetti, broken in half	hearts
3½ cups water	2 tablespoons chopped fresh oregano
4 tablespoons olive oil	2 tablespoons chopped fresh flat-leaf parsley
¼ teaspoon salt	
2 cups baby spinach	1 teaspoon black pepper
1 cup drained marinated artichoke	½ cup grated Parmesan cheese

1. Add pasta, water, 2 tablespoons oil, and salt to the Inner Pot. 2. Put on the pressure cooker's lid and turn the steam valve to "Sealing" position. 3. Select Pressure Cook mode, and then press the "Pressure Cook" button again to select "Less" time option. 4. Use the "+/-" keys on the control panel to set the cooking time to 5 minutes. 5. Press the Pressure Level button to adjust the pressure to "High Pressure." 6. Once the cooking cycle is completed, allow the steam to release naturally. 7. When all the steam is released, press Cancel button and remove the pressure lid from the top carefully. 8. Press the "Sauté" Button, two times to select "Normal" settings. 9. Stir in remaining 2 tablespoons oil and spinach. Toss until spinach is wilted. 10. Stir in artichokes, oregano, and parsley until well mixed. 11. Sprinkle with pepper and cheese, and serve immediately.
Per Serving: Calories 302; Fat 19g; Sodium 354mg; Carbs 15g; Fiber 5.1g; Sugar 8.2g; Protein 12g

Couscous with Tomatoes

Prep time: 10 minutes | Cook time: 3 minutes | Serves: 4

1 tablespoon tomato paste	2 tablespoons minced fresh oregano
2 cups vegetable broth	
1 cup couscous	2 tablespoons minced fresh chives
1 cup halved cherry tomatoes	1 tablespoon olive oil
½ cup halved mixed olives	1 tablespoon red wine vinegar
¼ cup minced fresh flat-leaf parsley	½ teaspoon black pepper

1. Pour tomato paste and broth into the Inner Pot and stir until completely dissolved. Stir in couscous. 2. Put on the pressure cooker's lid and turn the steam valve to "Sealing" position. 3. Select Pressure Cook mode, and then press the "Pressure Cook" button again to select "Less" time option. 4. Use the "+/-" keys on the control panel to set the cooking time to 3 minutes. 5. Press the Pressure Level button to adjust the pressure to "High Pressure." 6. Once the cooking cycle is completed, allow the steam to release naturally for 10 minutes, then turn the steam release handle to the Venting position. 7. When all the steam is released, remove the pressure lid from the top carefully. 8. Fluff couscous with a fork. 9. Add tomatoes, olives, parsley, oregano, chives, oil, vinegar, and pepper, and stir until combined. 10. Serve warm or at room temperature.
Per Serving: Calories 334; Fat 7.9g; Sodium 704mg; Carbs 6g; Fiber 3.6g; Sugar 6g; Protein 18g

Pasta Primavera

Prep time: 10 minutes | Cook time: 20 minutes | Serves: 8

1-pound bowtie pasta	2 cloves garlic, peeled and chopped
4 cups water	
2 tablespoons olive oil	1 cup white wine
1½ cups chopped summer squash	2 tablespoons cold unsalted butter
1½ cups chopped zucchini	½ teaspoon salt
3 cups chopped broccoli	¾ teaspoon black pepper
½ cup sun-dried tomatoes	¼ cup chopped fresh basil

1. Place pasta, water, and 1 tablespoon oil in the Inner Pot. 2. Put on the pressure cooker's lid and turn the steam valve to "Sealing" position. 3. Select Pressure Cook mode, and then press the "Pressure Cook" button again to select "Less" time option. 4. Use the "+/-" keys on the control panel to set the cooking time to 4 minutes. 5. Press the Pressure Level button to adjust the pressure to "Low Pressure." 6. Once the cooking cycle is completed, quickly and carefully turn the steam release handle from Sealing position to the Venting position. 7. When all the steam is released, press Cancel button and remove the pressure lid from the top carefully. 8. Press the "Sauté" Button, two times to select "Normal" settings. 9. Heat remaining 1 tablespoon oil. 10. Add squash, zucchini, broccoli, and sun-dried tomatoes, and cook until very tender, about 10 minutes. 11. Add garlic and wine. Allow wine to reduce for about 2–3 minutes. 12. Add butter to pot, stirring

constantly to create an emulsion. Season with salt and pepper. 13. Pour sauce and vegetables over pasta, and stir to coat. 14. Top with basil and enjoy.
Per Serving: Calories 361; Fat 7.9g; Sodium 704mg; Carbs 6g; Fiber 3.6g; Sugar 6g; Protein 18g

Couscous with Crab

Prep time: 10 minutes | Cook time: 7 minutes | Serves: 4

1 cup couscous	1 tablespoon minced fresh dill
1 clove garlic, peeled and minced	8 oz. jumbo lump crabmeat
2 cups water	3 tablespoons lemon juice
3 tablespoons olive oil	½ teaspoon black pepper
¼ cup minced fresh flat-leaf parsley	¼ cup grated Parmesan cheese

1. Place couscous, garlic, water, and 1 tablespoon oil in the Inner Pot and stir well. 2. Put on the pressure cooker's lid and turn the steam valve to "Sealing" position. 3. Select Pressure Cook mode, and then press the "Pressure Cook" button again to select "Less" time option. 4. Use the "+/-" keys on the control panel to set the cooking time to 7 minutes. 5. Press the Pressure Level button to adjust the pressure to "Low Pressure." 6. Once the cooking cycle is completed, allow the steam to release naturally for 10 minutes, then turn the steam release handle to the Venting position. 7. When all the steam is released, remove the pressure lid from the top carefully. 8. Fluff couscous with a fork. 9. Add parsley, dill, crabmeat, lemon juice, pepper, and remaining 2 tablespoons oil, and stir until combined. 10. Top with cheese and serve immediately.
Per Serving: Calories 184; Fat 5g; Sodium 441mg; Carbs 17g; Fiber 4.6g; Sugar 5g; Protein 9g

Herbed Lima Beans

Prep time: 10 minutes | Cook time: 6 minutes | Serves: 6

1 pound frozen baby lima beans, thawed	2 tablespoons olive oil
	3 cups water
2 cloves garlic, peeled and minced	1 tablespoon chopped fresh dill
2 thyme sprigs	1 tablespoon chopped fresh tarragon
1 bay leaf	1 tablespoon chopped fresh mint

1. Add lima beans, garlic, thyme, bay leaf, oil, and water to the Inner Pot. 2. Put on the pressure cooker's lid and turn the steam valve to "Sealing" position. 3. Select Pressure Cook mode, and then press the "Pressure Cook" button again to select "Less" time option. 4. Use the "+/-" keys on the control panel to set the cooking time to 6 minutes. 5. Press the Pressure Level button to adjust the pressure to "High Pressure." 6. Once the cooking cycle is completed, quickly and carefully turn the steam release handle from Sealing position to the Venting position. 7. When all the steam is released, remove the pressure lid from the top carefully. 8. Discard thyme and bay leaf, and stir well. 9. Stir in dill, tarragon, and mint, and serve.
Per Serving: Calories 219; Fat 10g; Sodium 891mg; Carbs 22.9g; Fiber 4g; Sugar 4g; Protein 13g

Pepper Couscous Salad

Prep time: 10 minutes | Cook time: 7 minutes | Serves: 4

1 cup couscous	1 clove garlic, peeled and minced
2 cups water	1 teaspoon olive oil
⅓ cup chopped Kalamata olives	1 teaspoon red wine vinegar
1 medium red bell pepper, seeded and diced	½ teaspoon salt

1. Stir couscous and water together in the Inner Pot. 2. Put on the pressure cooker's lid and turn the steam valve to "Sealing" position. 3. Select Pressure Cook mode, and then press the "Pressure Cook" button again to select "Less" time option. 4. Use the "+/-" keys on the control panel to set the cooking time to 7 minutes. 5. Press the Pressure Level button to adjust the pressure to "High Pressure." 6. Once the cooking cycle is completed, allow the steam to release naturally. 7. When all the steam is released, remove the pressure lid from the top carefully for 10 minutes, then turn the steam release handle to the Venting position. 8. Fluff couscous with a fork. Stir in olives, bell pepper, garlic, oil, vinegar, and salt. 9. Cover and refrigerate for 2 hours before serving.
Per Serving: Calories 382; Fat 7.9g; Sodium 704mg; Carbs 6g; Fiber 3.6g; Sugar 6g; Protein 18g

Spaghetti with Meat Sauce

Prep time: 10 minutes | Cook time: 20 minutes | Serves: 6

1-pound spaghetti	¼ cup white wine
4 cups water	½ cup tomato sauce
3 tablespoons olive oil	1 (3") cinnamon stick
1 medium white onion, peeled and diced	2 bay leaves
	1 clove garlic, peeled
½ pound lean ground veal	¼ cup grated aged mizithra or
½ teaspoon salt	Parmesan cheese
¼ teaspoon black pepper	

1. Add pasta, water, and 1 tablespoon oil to the Inner Pot. 2. Put on the pressure cooker's lid and turn the steam valve to "Sealing" position. 3. Select Pressure Cook mode, and then press the "Pressure Cook" button again to select "Less" time option. 4. Use the "+/-" keys on the control panel to set the cooking time to 4 minutes. 5. Press the Pressure Level button to adjust the pressure to "High Pressure." 6. Once the cooking cycle is completed, quickly and carefully turn the steam release handle from Sealing position to the Venting position. 7. When all the steam is released, press Cancel button and remove the pressure lid from the top carefully. 8. Press the "Sauté" Button, two times to select "normal" settings and heat remaining 2 tablespoons oil. 9. Add onion and cook until soft, about 3 minutes. 10. Add veal and crumble well. Keep stirring until meat is browned, about 5 minutes. 11. Add salt, pepper, wine, and tomato sauce, and mix well. 12. 3 Stir in cinnamon stick, bay leaves, and garlic. Press the Cancel button. 13. Put on the pressure cooker's lid and turn the steam valve to "Sealing" position. 14. Select Pressure Cook mode, and then press the "Pressure Cook" button again to select "Less" time option. 15. Use the "+/-" keys on the control panel to set the cooking time to 5 minutes. 16. Press the Pressure Level button to adjust the pressure to "Low Pressure." 17. Once the cooking cycle is completed, quickly and carefully turn the steam release handle from Sealing position to the Venting position. 18. When all the steam is released, remove the pressure lid from the top carefully. 19. Remove and discard cinnamon stick and bay leaves. 20. Place pasta in a large bowl. Sprinkle with cheese and spoon meat sauce over top. 21. Serve immediately.
Per Serving: Calories 357; Fat 7.9g; Sodium 704mg; Carbs 6g; Fiber 3.6g; Sugar 6g; Protein 18g

Couscous with Olives

Prep time: 10 minutes | Cook time: 7 minutes | Serves: 4

1 tablespoon tomato paste	¼ cup minced fresh flat-leaf parsley
2 cups vegetable broth	2 tablespoons minced fresh oregano
1 cup couscous	2 tablespoons minced fresh chives
1 cup sliced cherry tomatoes	1 tablespoon olive oil
½ large English cucumber, chopped	1 tablespoon red wine vinegar
½ cup pitted and chopped mixed olives	½ teaspoon black pepper

1. Stir together tomato paste and broth until completely dissolved. 2. Add to the Inner Pot with couscous and stir well. 3. Put on the pressure cooker's lid and turn the steam valve to "Sealing" position. 4. Select Pressure Cook mode, and then press the "Pressure Cook" button again to select "Less" time option. 5. Use the "+/-" keys on the control panel to set the cooking time to 7 minutes. 6. Press the Pressure Level button to adjust the pressure to "High Pressure." 7. Once the cooking cycle is completed, allow the steam to release naturally for 10 minutes, then turn the steam release handle to the Venting position. 8. When all the steam is released, remove the pressure lid from the top carefully. 9. Fluff couscous with a fork. Add all remaining ingredients and stir until combined. 10. Serve warm or at room temperature.
Per Serving: Calories 372; Fat 20g; Sodium 891mg; Carbs 29g; Fiber 3g; Sugar 8g; Protein 7g

Israeli Pasta Salad

Prep time: 10 minutes | Cook time: 5 minutes | Serves: 6

½ pound whole-wheat penne pasta	½ medium red onion, peeled and chopped
4 cups water	
1 tablespoon plus ¼ cup olive oil	½ cup crumbled feta cheese
1 cup quartered cherry tomatoes	1 teaspoon fresh thyme leaves
½ English cucumber, chopped	1 teaspoon chopped fresh oregano
½ medium orange bell pepper, seeded and chopped	½ teaspoon black pepper
	¼ cup lemon juice

1. Add pasta, water, and 1 tablespoon oil to the Inner Pot. 2. Put on the

pressure cooker's lid and turn the steam valve to "Sealing" position. 3. Select Pressure Cook mode, and then press the "Pressure Cook" button again to select "Less" time option. 4. Use the "+/-" keys on the control panel to set the cooking time to 4 minutes. 5. Press the Pressure Level button to adjust the pressure to "High Pressure." 6. Once the cooking cycle is completed, quickly and carefully turn the steam release handle from Sealing position to the Venting position. 7. When all the steam is released, remove the pressure lid from the top carefully. 8. Drain and set aside to cool for 30 minutes. 9. Stir in tomatoes, cucumber, bell pepper, onion, feta, thyme, oregano, black pepper, lemon juice, and remaining ¼ cup oil. 10. Serve.
Per Serving: Calories 334; Fat 7.9g; Sodium 704mg; Carbs 6g; Fiber 3.6g; Sugar 6g; Protein 18g

Rotini with Walnut Pesto

Prep time: 10 minutes | Cook time: 4 minutes | Serves: 8

1 cup packed fresh basil leaves	¼ teaspoon salt
⅓ cup chopped walnuts	1-pound whole-wheat rotini pasta
¼ cup grated Parmesan cheese	4 cups water
¼ cup plus 1 tablespoon olive oil	1-pint cherry tomatoes
1 clove garlic, peeled	1 cup fresh or frozen green peas
1 tablespoon lemon juice	½ teaspoon black pepper

1. In a food processor, add basil and walnuts. 2. Pulse until finely chopped, about 12 pulses. 3. Add cheese, ¼ cup oil, garlic, lemon juice, and salt, and pulse until a rough paste forms, about 10 pulses. 4. Refrigerate until ready to use. 5. Add pasta, water, and remaining 1 tablespoon oil to the Inner Pot. 6. Put on the pressure cooker's lid and turn the steam valve to "Sealing" position. 7. Select Pressure Cook mode, and then press the "Pressure Cook" button again to select "Less" time option. 8. Use the "+/-" keys on the control panel to set the cooking time to 4 minutes. 9. Press the Pressure Level button to adjust the pressure to "High Pressure." 10. Once the cooking cycle is completed, quickly and carefully turn the steam release handle from Sealing position to the Venting position. 11. When all the steam is released, remove the pressure lid from the top carefully. 12. Drain off any excess liquid. Allow pasta to cool to room temperature, about 30 minutes. 13. Stir in basil mixture until pasta is well coated. Add tomatoes, peas, and pepper and toss to coat. 14. Refrigerate for 2 hours. Stir well before serving.
Per Serving: Calories 237; Fat 7.9g; Sodium 704mg; Carbs 6g; Fiber 3.6g; Sugar 6g; Protein 18g

Pasta with Chickpeas and Cabbage

Prep time: 10 minutes | Cook time: 30 minutes | Serves: 8

1-pound rotini pasta	⅔ cup dried chickpeas, soaked
8 cups water	overnight and drained
2 tablespoons olive oil	8 oz. button mushrooms, sliced
1 stalk celery, thinly sliced	½ teaspoon salt
1 medium red onion, peeled and sliced	¾ teaspoon black pepper
	½ cup grated Pecorino Romano
1 small head savoy cabbage, cored and shredded	cheese

1. Add pasta, 4 cups water, and 1 tablespoon oil to the Inner Pot. 2. Put on the pressure cooker's lid and turn the steam valve to "Sealing" position. 3. Select Pressure Cook mode, and then press the "Pressure Cook" button again to select "Less" time option. 4. Use the "+/-" keys on the control panel to set the cooking time to 4 minutes. 5. Press the Pressure Level button to adjust the pressure to "Low Pressure." 6. Once the cooking cycle is completed, quickly and carefully turn the steam release handle from Sealing position to the Venting position. 7. When all the steam is released, press the Cancel button and remove the pressure lid from the top carefully. 8. Press the "Sauté" Button, two times to select "normal" settings and heat remaining 1 tablespoon oil. 9. Add celery and onion, and cook until just tender, about 4 minutes. 10. Stir in cabbage and cook until wilted, about 2 minutes. 11. Add chickpeas, mushrooms, and remaining 4 cups water. Stir well, then press the Cancel button. 12. Put on the pressure cooker's lid and turn the steam valve to "Sealing" position. 13. Select Pressure Cook mode, and then press the "Pressure Cook" button again to select "Less" time option. 14. Press the Pressure Level button to adjust the pressure to "Low Pressure." 15. Once the cooking cycle is completed, allow the steam to release naturally. 16. When all the steam is released, remove the pressure lid from the top carefully. 17. Season with salt and pepper. 18. Pour sauce over pasta and top with cheese. 19. Serve hot.
Per Serving: Calories 184; Fat 5g; Sodium 441mg; Carbs 17g; Fiber 4.6g; Sugar 5g; Protein 9g

Mixed Vegetable Couscous

Prep time: 10 minutes | Cook time: 10 minutes | Serves: 8

1 tablespoon light olive oil
1 medium zucchini, trimmed and chopped
1 medium yellow squash, chopped
1 large red bell pepper, seeded and chopped
1 large orange bell pepper, seeded and chopped
2 tablespoons chopped fresh

oregano
2 cups Israeli couscous
3 cups vegetable broth
½ cup crumbled feta cheese
¼ cup red wine vinegar
¼ cup olive oil
½ teaspoon black pepper
¼ cup chopped fresh basil

1. Press the "Sauté" Button two times to select "Normal" settings and heat light olive oil. 2. Add zucchini, squash, bell peppers, and oregano, and sauté 8 minutes. 3. Press the Cancel button. Transfer to a serving bowl and set aside to cool. 4. Add couscous and broth to the Inner Pot and stir well. 5. Put on the pressure cooker's lid and turn the steam valve to "Sealing" position. 6. Select Pressure Cook mode, and then press the "Pressure Cook" button again to select "Less" time option. 7. Use the "+/-" keys on the control panel to set the cooking time to 2 minutes. 8. Press the Pressure Level button to adjust the pressure to "High Pressure." 9. Once the cooking cycle is completed, allow the steam to release naturally. 10. When all the steam is released, remove the pressure lid from the top carefully. 11. Fluff with a fork and stir in cooked vegetables, cheese, vinegar, olive oil, black pepper, and basil. 12. Serve warm.
Per Serving: Calories 226; Fat 10.9g; Sodium 354mg; Carbs 20.5g; Fiber 4.1g; Sugar 8.2g; Protein 06g

Toasted Couscous with Feta

Prep time: 10 minutes | Cook time: 10 minutes | Serves: 8

1 tablespoon plus ¼ cup light olive oil
2 cups Israeli couscous
3 cups vegetable broth
2 large tomatoes, seeded and diced
1 large English cucumber, diced
1 medium red onion, peeled and

chopped
½ cup crumbled feta cheese
¼ cup red wine vinegar
½ teaspoon black pepper
¼ cup chopped flat-leaf parsley
¼ cup chopped fresh basil

1. Press the "Sauté" Button two times to select "normal" settings and heat 1 tablespoon oil. 2. Add couscous and cook, stirring frequently, until couscous is light golden brown, about 7 minutes. 3. Press the Cancel button. Add broth and stir. 4. Put on the pressure cooker's lid and turn the steam valve to "Sealing" position. 5. Select Pressure Cook mode, and then press the "Pressure Cook" button again to select "Less" time option. 6. Use the "+/-" keys on the control panel to set the cooking time to 2 minutes. 7. Press the Pressure Level button to adjust the pressure to "Low Pressure." 8. Once the cooking cycle is completed, allow the steam to release naturally. 9. When all the steam is released, remove the pressure lid from the top carefully. 10. Fluff couscous with a fork, then transfer to a medium bowl and set aside to cool. 11. Add remaining ¼ cup oil, tomatoes, cucumber, onion, feta, vinegar, pepper, parsley, and basil, and stir until combined. 12. Serve.
Per Serving: Calories 302; Fat 12.9g; Sodium 414mg; Carbs 11g; Fiber 5g; Sugar 9g; Protein 11g

Rotini with Red Wine Marinara

Prep time: 10 minutes | Cook time: 25 minutes | Serves: 6

1-pound rotini
4 cups water
1 tablespoon olive oil
½ medium yellow onion, peeled and diced
3 cloves garlic, peeled and minced

1 (15-ounce) can crushed tomatoes
½ cup red wine
1 teaspoon sugar
2 tablespoons chopped fresh basil
½ teaspoon salt
¼ teaspoon black pepper

1. Add pasta and water to the Inner Pot. 2. Put on the pressure cooker's lid and turn the steam valve to "Sealing" position. 3. Select Pressure Cook mode, and then press the "Pressure Cook" button again to select "Less" time option. 4. Use the "+/-" keys on the control panel to set the cooking time to 4 minutes. 5. Press the Pressure Level button to adjust the pressure to "Low Pressure." 6. Once the cooking cycle is completed, quickly and carefully turn the steam release handle from Sealing position to the Venting position. 7. When all the steam is

released, press the Cancel button and remove the pressure lid from the top carefully. 8. Press the "Sauté" Button two times to select "Normal" settings and heat oil. 9. Add onion and cook until it begins to caramelize, about 10 minutes. Add garlic and cook 30 seconds. 10. Add tomatoes, red wine, and sugar, and simmer for 10 minutes. 11. Add basil, salt, pepper, and pasta. 12. Serve immediately.
Per Serving: Calories 212; Fat 7.9g; Sodium 704mg; Carbs 6g; Fiber 3.6g; Sugar 6g; Protein 18g

Zesty Couscous

Prep time: 10 minutes | Cook time: 5 minutes | Serves: 6

2 cups couscous
2½ cups water
1 cup low-sodium chicken broth
1 teaspoon salt

1 tablespoon unsalted butter
1 teaspoon grated lemon zest

1. Place all ingredients in the Inner Pot and stir to combine. 2. Put on the pressure cooker's lid and turn the steam valve to "Sealing" position. 3. Select Pressure Cook mode, and then press the "Pressure Cook" button again to select "Less" time option. 4. Use the "+/-" keys on the control panel to set the cooking time to 4 minutes. 5. Press the Pressure Level button to adjust the pressure to "High Pressure." 6. Once the cooking cycle is completed, quickly and carefully turn the steam release handle from Sealing position to the Venting position. 7. When all the steam is released, remove the pressure lid from the top carefully. 8. Stir well. Serve immediately.
Per Serving: Calories 351; Fat 10.9g; Sodium 454mg; Carbs 10g; Fiber 3.1g; Sugar 5.2g; Protein 10g

Tahini Soup

Prep time: 10 minutes | Cook time: 5 minutes | Serves: 6

2 cups orzo
8 cups water
1 tablespoon olive oil
1 teaspoon salt

½ teaspoon black pepper
½ cup tahini
¼ cup lemon juice

1. Add pasta, water, oil, salt, and pepper to the Inner Pot. 2. Put on the pressure cooker's lid and turn the steam valve to "Sealing" position. 3. Select Pressure Cook mode, and then press the "Pressure Cook" button again to select "Less" time option. 4. Use the "+/-" keys on the control panel to set the cooking time to 4 minutes. 5. Press the Pressure Level button to adjust the pressure to "High Pressure." 6. Once the cooking cycle is completed, quickly and carefully turn the steam release handle from Sealing position to the Venting position. 7. When all the steam is released, remove the pressure lid from the top carefully. 8. Add tahini to a small mixing bowl and slowly add lemon juice while whisking constantly. 9. Once lemon juice has been incorporated, take about ½ cup hot broth from the pot and slowly add to tahini mixture while whisking, until creamy smooth. 10. Pour mixture into the soup and mix well. 11. Serve immediately.
Per Serving: Calories 320; Fat 19g; Sodium 354mg; Carbs 15g; Fiber 5.1g; Sugar 8.2g; Protein 12g

Marinara Spaghetti with Mozzarella Cheese

Prep time: 10 minutes | Cook time: 5 minutes | Serves: 8

1-pound spaghetti
4 cups water
1 tablespoon olive oil
4 cups cooked pinto beans

4 cups marinara sauce
1 cup shredded mozzarella cheese
2 tablespoons chopped fresh basil

1. Add pasta, water, and olive oil to the Inner Pot. 2. Put on the pressure cooker's lid and turn the steam valve to "Sealing" position. 3. Select Pressure Cook mode, and then press the "Pressure Cook" button again to select "Less" time option. 4. Use the "+/-" keys on the control panel to set the cooking time to 4 minutes. 5. Press the Pressure Level button to adjust the pressure to "High Pressure." 6. Once the cooking cycle is completed, quickly and carefully turn the steam release handle from Sealing position to the Venting position. 7. When all the steam is released, remove the pressure lid from the top carefully. 8. Add beans and marinara sauce, and stir well. 9. Top with cheese and basil and serve hot.
Per Serving: Calories 334; Fat 7.9g; Sodium 704mg; Carbs 6g; Fiber 3.6g; Sugar 6g; Protein 18g

Angel Hair Pasta with Spinach and White Wine

Prep time: 10 minutes | Cook time: 15 minutes | Serves: 6

1-pound angel hair pasta
4¼ cups water
2 tablespoons olive oil
¼ medium yellow onion, peeled and diced
2 cloves garlic, peeled and minced
½ cup white wine
1 tablespoon unsalted butter
1 tablespoon all-purpose flour
½ teaspoon salt
¼ teaspoon black pepper
1 cup steamed spinach

1. Place pasta, 4 cups water, and 1 tablespoon oil in the Inner Pot. 2. Put on the pressure cooker's lid and turn the steam valve to "Sealing" position. 3. Select Pressure Cook mode, and then press the "Pressure Cook" button again to select "Less" time option. 4. Use the "+/-" keys on the control panel to set the cooking time to 4 minutes. 5. Press the Pressure Level button to adjust the pressure to "High Pressure." 6. Once the cooking cycle is completed, quickly and carefully turn the steam release handle from Sealing position to the Venting position. 7. When all the steam is released, press Cancel button and remove the pressure lid from the top carefully. 8. Press the "Sauté" Button two times to select "Normal" settings and heat remaining 1 tablespoon oil. 9. Add onion and garlic. Cook until onion is soft, about 5 minutes. 10. Add white wine and remaining ¼ cup water, then bring to a low simmer for about 10 minutes. 11. Add butter and flour, stirring until completely combined and sauce begins to thicken. 12. Season with salt and pepper. 13. In a large mixing bowl, combine spinach, pasta, and white wine sauce, then toss until the pasta is completely coated. 14. Serve immediately.
Per Serving: Calories 219; Fat 10g; Sodium 891mg; Carbs 22.9g; Fiber 4g; Sugar 4g; Protein 13g

Avgolemono

Prep time: 10 minutes | Cook time: 13 minutes | Serves: 6

6 cups chicken stock
½ cup orzo
1 tablespoon olive oil
12-ounce cooked chicken breast, shredded
½ teaspoon salt
½ teaspoon black pepper
¼ cup lemon juice
2 large eggs
2 tablespoons chopped fresh dill
1 tablespoon chopped fresh flat-leaf parsley

1. Add stock, orzo, and olive oil to the Inner Pot. 2. Put on the pressure cooker's lid and turn the steam valve to "Sealing" position. 3. Select Pressure Cook mode, and then press the "Pressure Cook" button again to select "Less" time option. 4. Use the "+/-" keys on the control panel to set the cooking time to 3 minutes. 5. Press the Pressure Level button to adjust the pressure to "High Pressure." 6. Once the cooking cycle is completed, quickly and carefully turn the steam release handle from Sealing position to the Venting position. 7. When all the steam is released, remove the pressure lid from the top carefully. 8. Stir in chicken, salt, and pepper. 9. In a medium bowl, combine lemon juice and eggs, then slowly whisk in hot cooking liquid. 10. Immediately add egg mixture to soup and stir well. 11. Let stand on the Keep Warm setting, stirring occasionally, for 10 minutes. 12. Add dill and parsley. Serve immediately.
Per Serving: Calories 349; Fat 2.9g; Sodium 511mg; Carbs 12g; Fiber 3g; Sugar 8g; Protein 7g

Tomato, Arugula and Feta Pasta Salad

Prep time: 10 minutes | Cook time: 5 minutes | Serves: 8

1-pound rotini
4 cups water
3 tablespoons olive oil
2 medium Roma tomatoes, diced
2 cloves garlic, peeled and minced
1 medium red bell pepper, seeded
and diced
2 tablespoons white wine vinegar
5-ounce baby arugula
1 cup crumbled feta cheese
½ teaspoon salt
½ teaspoon black pepper

1. Add pasta, water, and 1 tablespoon oil to the Inner Pot. 2. Put on the pressure cooker's lid and turn the steam valve to "Sealing" position. 3. Select Pressure Cook mode, and then press the "Pressure Cook" button again to select "Less" time option. 4. Use the "+/-" keys on the control panel to set the cooking time to 4 minutes. 5. Press the Pressure Level button to adjust the pressure to "High Pressure." 6. Once the cooking cycle is completed, quickly and carefully turn the steam release handle from Sealing position to the Venting position. 7. When all the steam is released, remove the pressure lid from the top carefully. 8. Drain pasta, then rinse with cold water. Set aside. 9. In a large bowl, mix the remaining oil, tomatoes, garlic, bell pepper, vinegar, arugula, and cheese. 10. Stir in pasta and season with salt and pepper. 11. Cover and refrigerate for 2 hours before serving.
Per Serving: Calories 289; Fat 14g; Sodium 791mg; Carbs 18.9g; Fiber 4.6g; Sugar 8g; Protein 6g

Dill Pasta Salad

Prep time: 10 minutes | Cook time: 5 minutes | Serves: 8

½ cup low-fat plain Greek yogurt
1 tablespoon apple cider vinegar
2 tablespoons chopped fresh dill
1 teaspoon honey
1-pound whole-wheat elbow macaroni
4 cups water
1 tablespoon olive oil
1 medium red bell pepper, seeded and chopped
1 medium sweet onion, peeled and diced
1 stalk celery, diced
½ teaspoon black pepper

1. In a small bowl, combine yogurt and vinegar. 2. Add dill and honey, and mix well. Refrigerate until ready to use. 3. Place pasta, water, and olive oil to the Inner Pot. 4. Put on the pressure cooker's lid and turn the steam valve to "Sealing" position. 5. Select Pressure Cook mode, and then press the "Pressure Cook" button again to select "Less" time option. 6. Use the "+/-" keys on the control panel to set the cooking time to 4 minutes. 7. Press the Pressure Level button to adjust the pressure to "Low Pressure." 8. Once the cooking cycle is completed, quickly and carefully turn the steam release handle from Sealing position to the Venting position. 9. When all the steam is released, remove the pressure lid from the top carefully. 10. Drain off any excess liquid. Cool pasta to room temperature, about 30 minutes. 11. Add prepared dressing and toss until pasta is well coated. 12. Add bell pepper, onion, celery, and black pepper, and toss to coat. 13. Refrigerate for 2 hours. Stir well before serving.
Per Serving: Calories 382; Fat 7.9g; Sodium 704mg; Carbs 6g; Fiber 3.6g; Sugar 6g; Protein 18g

Linguine Clams with Parmesan Cheese

Prep Time: 15 minutes | Cook Time: 10 minutes | Serves: 4

2 tablespoons olive oil
4 cups sliced mushrooms
1 medium yellow onion, peeled and diced
2 tablespoons chopped fresh oregano
3 cloves garlic, peeled and minced
¼ teaspoon salt
¼ teaspoon ground black pepper
½ cup white wine
1½ cups water
8 ounces' linguine, broken in half
1-pound fresh clams, rinsed and purged
3 tablespoons lemon juice
¼ cup grated Parmesan cheese
2 tablespoons chopped fresh parsley

1. Insert the pot into the Cooker Base without the lid. 2. Select Sauté mode and then press the same button again and then adjust the cooking temperature to Normal. 3. When the display switches On to Hot, add and heat the oil; add onion and mushrooms and cook for 5 minutes or until tender; add oregano, garlic, salt, and pepper and cook for 30 seconds or until very fragrant; add the water, wine and press the pasta down to submerge it. 4. Press Cancel button to stop this cooking program. 5. Top the clams over and pasta and sprinkle with lemon juice. 6. Place and close the lid rightly. 7. Select Pressure Cook mode. Press Pressure Cook button again to adjust the cooking time to 5 minutes; press Pressure Level to choose High Pressure. 8. When the time is up, quickly and carefully turn the steam release handle from the Sealing position to the Venting position. 9. When the float valve drops, open the lid, then serve the food on a suitable bowl. 10. Top with cheese and parsley before enjoying.
Per Serving: Calories:486; Fat:11g, Sodium:301mg, Fiber:5g, Carbs: 52g, Sugar: 12g, Protein:39g

Simple Steamed Onion Clams

Prep Time: 15 minutes | Cook Time: 10 minutes | Serves: 4

2 pounds' fresh clams, rinsed
1 tablespoon olive oil
1 small white onion, peeled and diced
1 clove garlic, peeled and quartered
½ cup Chardonnay
½ cup water

1. Insert the pot into the Cooker Base without the lid. 2. Select Sauté mode and then press the same button again and then adjust the cooking temperature to Normal. 3. When the display switches On to Hot, add the onion and cook for 3 minutes or until tender; add the garlic and cook for 30 seconds; pour in water and the Chardonnay. 4. Press Cancel button to stop this cooking program. 5. Place the clams on the Steam Rack and then arrange it to the Inner Pot. 6. Place and close the lid in right way. 7. Select Pressure Cook mode. Press Pressure Cook button again to adjust the cooking time to 4 minutes; press Pressure Level to choose High Pressure. 8. When the time is up, quickly and carefully turn the steam release handle from the Sealing position to the Venting position. 9. When done, place the clams in 4 bowls with a tablespoon of cooking sauce on top. 10. Enjoy.
Per Serving: Calories:205; Fat:6g, Sodium:135mg; Fiber:0g, Carbs: 7g, Sugar: 1g; Protein:30g

Steamed Calamari with Vegetables

Prep Time: 15 minutes | Cook Time: 15 minutes | Serves: 6

2 tablespoons olive oil
1 small carrot, peeled and grated
1 stalk celery, finely diced
1 small white onion, peeled and diced
3 cloves garlic, peeled and minced
2½ pounds calamari
1 (28-ounce) can diced tomatoes
½ cup white wine
⅓ cup water
1 teaspoon dried parsley
1 teaspoon dried basil
½ teaspoon salt
½ teaspoon ground black pepper

1. Insert the pot into the Cooker Base without the lid. 2. Select Sauté mode and then press the same button again and then adjust the cooking temperature to Normal. 3. When the display switches On to Hot, add and heat the oil; add the celery, carrot and cook for 2 minutes or until tender; add the onion and cook for 3 minutes or until tender; add the garlic and stir for 30 seconds or until fragrant. 4. Press Cancel button to stop this cooking program. 5. Still in the Inner Pot, add the calamari, tomatoes, wine, water, parsley, basil, salt and black pepper. 6. Place and close the lid in right way. 7. Select Pressure Cook mode. Press Pressure Cook button again to adjust the cooking time to 10 minutes; press Pressure Level to choose High Pressure. 8. When the time is up, quickly and carefully turn the steam release handle from the Sealing position to the Venting position. 9. When done, serve and enjoy.

Per Serving: Calories:394; Fat:7g, Sodium:505mg; Fiber:3g, Carbs: 12g, Sugar: 4g; Protein:62g

Rosemary Salmon with Lemon Wedges

Prep Time: 15 minutes | Cook Time: 5 minutes | Serves: 4

1 cup water
4 (4-ounce) salmon fillets
½ teaspoon salt
½ teaspoon ground black pepper
1 sprig rosemary, leaves stripped
off and minced
2 tablespoons chopped fresh thyme
2 tablespoons extra-virgin olive oil
4 lemon wedges

1. Season the fillets with salt and pepper. 2. Prepare 4 pieces of large foil, lay the fillets on them separately; top them with rosemary, thyme and drizzle each with olive oil. 3. Carefully wrap fillet loosely in foil. 4. In the Inner Pot, place the Steam Rack and then place the foil pouches on the rack. 5. Select Steam mode. Press the button again to adjust the cooking time to 5 minutes; press Pressure Level to choose High Pressure. 6. When the time is up, quickly and carefully turn the steam release handle from the Sealing position to the Venting position. 7. When done, serve and enjoy with the lemon wedges.
Per Serving: Calories:160; Fat:8g, Sodium:445mg; Fiber:0g, Carbs: 0g, Sugar: 0g; Protein:24g

Garlic Mussels with White Wine

Prep Time: 15 minutes | Cook Time: 7 minutes | Serves: 6

2 tablespoons light olive oil
2 shallots, peeled and minced
4 cloves garlic, peeled and minced
½ teaspoon ground black pepper
3 pounds' mussels, scrubbed and
beards removed
2 cups white wine
¼ cup chopped fresh chives
¼ cup chopped fresh tarragon
2 tablespoons chopped fresh dill

1. Insert the pot into the Cooker Base without the lid. 2. Select Sauté mode and then press the same button again and then adjust the cooking temperature to Normal. 3. When the display switches On to Hot, heat the oil; add the shallots and cook for 1 minute until tender; add the garlic and pepper and cook for 30 seconds until fragrant. 4. Press Cancel button to stop this cooking program. 5. Still in the Inner Pot, stir in the mussels and wine, then place and close the lid in right way. 6. Select Pressure Cook mode. Press Pressure Cook button again to adjust the cooking time to 3 minutes; press Pressure Level to choose High Pressure. 7. When the time is up, quickly and carefully turn the steam release handle from the Sealing position to the Venting position. 8. When the float valve drops, open the lid and discard the unopened mussels; transfer mussels to a serving bowl but reserve the broth in the pot. 9. Press Cancel button to stop this cooking program. 10. Without the lid, select Sauté mode and then press the same button again and then adjust the cooking temperature to Normal. 11. Bring the broth to boil, add the chives, tarragon and dill and whisk for 3 minutes or until the broth has reduced slightly. 12. When cooked, pour the broth over the mussels and serve warm.
Per Serving: Calories:146; Fat:7g, Sodium:321mg; Fiber:0g, Carbs: 6g, Sugar: 0g; Protein:14g

Garlic Shrimp with Parsley

Prep Time: 15 minutes | Cook Time: 5 minutes | Serves: 6

2 tablespoons light olive oil
1 small shallot, peeled and minced
6 cloves garlic, peeled and thinly sliced
1 tablespoon chopped fresh dill
1 tablespoon chopped fresh chives
½ teaspoon ground black pepper
¼ teaspoon salt
¼ cup white wine
¼ cup low-sodium chicken broth
2 pounds' large tail-on shrimp
2 tablespoons lemon juice
2 tablespoons chopped fresh parsley

1. Insert the pot into the Cooker Base without the lid. 2. Select Sauté mode and then press the same button again and then adjust the cooking temperature to Normal. 3. When the display switches On to Hot, heat the oil; add the shallot and garlic and cook for 1 minute; add the dill, chives, pepper and salt and cook for 3 minutes; stir in wine and broth. 4. Press Cancel button to stop this cooking program. 5. Close the lid in right way. 6. Select Pressure Cook mode. Press Pressure Cook button again to adjust the cooking time to 1 minutes; press Pressure Level to choose High Pressure. 7. When the time is up, quickly and carefully turn the steam release handle from the Sealing position to the Venting position. 8. When done, add the lemon juice and parsley. 9. Serve and enjoy.
Per Serving: Calories:151; Fat:5g, Sodium:691mg; Fiber:0g, Carbs: 0g, Sugar: 0g; Protein:25g

Oregano Mussels Saganaki with Feta Cheese

Prep Time: 15 minutes | Cook Time: 6 minutes | Serves: 2

2 tablespoons extra-virgin olive oil
1 medium banana pepper, stemmed, seeded, and thinly sliced
2 medium tomatoes, chopped
½ teaspoon salt

1-pound mussels, scrubbed and beards removed
⅓ cup white wine
⅓ cup crumbled feta cheese
2 teaspoons dried oregano

1. Insert the pot into the Cooker Base without the lid. 2. Select Sauté mode and then press the same button again and then adjust the cooking temperature to Normal. 3. When the display switches On to Hot, heat the oil; add the pepper, tomatoes and salt and cook for 3 minutes until tender. 4. Press Cancel button to stop this cooking program. 5. Still in the Inner Pot, add the mussels and wine, then place and close the lid in right way. 6. Cook the food on Pressure Cook mode at High Pressure for 3 minutes. 7. When the time is up, quickly and carefully turn the steam release handle from the Sealing position to the Venting position. 8. When done, discard the unopened mussels. 9. Add feta, oregano and stir them to combine well with the sauce. 10. Serve and enjoy.
Per Serving: Calories:250; Fat:21g, Sodium:1140mg; Fiber:1g, Carbs: 7g, Sugar: 2g; Protein:18g

Fresh Mixed Seafood Soup

Prep Time: 15 minutes | Cook Time: 21 minutes | Serves: 8

2 tablespoons light olive oil
1 medium yellow onion, peeled and diced
1 medium red bell pepper, seeded and diced
3 cloves garlic, peeled and minced
1 tablespoon chopped fresh oregano
½ teaspoon Italian seasoning
½ teaspoon ground black pepper

2 tablespoons tomato paste
½ cup white wine
2 cups seafood stock
1 bay leaf
½ pound medium shrimp, peeled and deveined
½ pound fresh scallops
½ pound fresh calamari rings
1 tablespoon lemon juice

1. Insert the pot into the Cooker Base without the lid. 2. Select Sauté mode and then press the same button again and then adjust the cooking temperature to Normal. 3. When the display switches On to Hot, heat the oil; add the onion and bell pepper and cook for 5 minutes or until just tender; add the garlic, oregano, Italian seasoning, pepper and cook for 30 seconds until fragrant; add the tomato paste and cook for 1 minute; lastly, slowly pour in wine and scrape bottom of pot. 4. Press Cancel button to stop this cooking program. 5. Still in the Inner Pot, add the stock and bay leaf and stir well. 6. Place and close the lid in right way. 7. Select Pressure Cook mode. Press Pressure Cook button again to adjust the cooking time to 5 minutes; press Pressure Level to choose High Pressure. 8. When the time is up, quickly and carefully turn the steam release handle from the Sealing position to the Venting position. 9. When the float valve drops, open the lid, add in the shrimp, scallops, calamari rings, lemon juice and stir well. 10. Press Cancel button to stop this cooking program and remove the lid. 11. Allow soup to simmer for 10 minutes until seafood is cooked through under the Sauté mode at Normal temperature. 12. When done, discard the bay leaf and serve.
Per Serving: Calories:172; Fat:7g, Sodium:481mg; Fiber:1g, Carbs: 9g, Sugar: 2g; Protein:15g

Steamed Cilantro Lime Salmon

Prep Time: 15 minutes | Cook Time: 3 minutes | Serves: 4

1 cup water
4 (4-ounce) skin-on salmon fillets, about 1 pound
¼ teaspoon ground cumin
¼ teaspoon smoked paprika

¼ teaspoon salt
¼ teaspoon ground black pepper
¼ cup chopped fresh cilantro
1 small lime, thinly sliced
2 tablespoons extra-virgin olive oil

1. Season the salmon fillets with the cumin, paprika, salt and black pepper; top each fillet with the cilantro and 2-3 lime slice. 2. In the Inner Pot, add the water and place the Steam Rack, then arrange the fillets to the rack. 3. Place and close the lid in right way. 4. Select Steam mode. Press the button again to adjust the cooking time to 3 minutes; press Pressure Level to choose High Pressure. 5. When the time is up, quickly and carefully turn the steam release handle from the Sealing position to the Venting position. 6. When released, serve and fillets on a plate and then drizzle with the olive oil. 7. Enjoy.
Per Serving: Calories:100; Fat:3g, Sodium:398mg; Fiber:0g, Carbs: 0g, Sugar: 0g; Protein:19g

Lemon Trout in Parsley Sauce

Prep Time: 15 minutes | Cook Time: 3 minutes | Serves: 4

4 (½-pound) river trout, rinsed and patted dry
¾ teaspoon salt, divided
4 cups torn lettuce leaves, divided
1 teaspoon white wine vinegar
½ cup water
½ cup minced fresh flat-leaf parsley

1 small shallot, peeled and minced
2 tablespoons olive oil mayonnaise
½ teaspoon lemon juice
¼ teaspoon sugar
2 tablespoons toasted sliced almonds

1. Season the trout inside and out with ½ teaspoon of salt. 2. In the Inner Pot, put 3 cups of lettuce leaves on the bottom, then arrange the trout to the leaves and top with the remaining lettuce; stir in vinegar and water. 3. Place and close the lid in right way. 4. Select Pressure Cook mode. Press the button again to adjust the cooking time to 3 minutes; press Pressure Level to choose High Pressure. 5. When the time is up, quickly and carefully turn the steam release handle from the Sealing position to the Venting position. 6. Transfer the trout to a plate with a spatula, peel and discard the skin and heads. 7. In a small bowl, thoroughly mix up the parsley, shallot, mayonnaise, lemon juice, sugar, and remaining salt; evenly spread the mixture over the trout. 8. Sprinkle toasted almonds over the sauce and enjoy.
Per Serving: Calories:159; Fat:9g, Sodium:860mg; Fiber:1g, Carbs: 4g, Sugar: 0g; Protein:15g

Herbed Fish Packets

Prep Time: 15 minutes | Cook Time: 5 minutes | Serves: 4

1 cup water
4 (4-ounce) halibut or other white fish fillets
½ teaspoon salt
½ teaspoon ground black pepper
1 small lemon, thinly sliced

¼ cup chopped fresh dill
¼ cup chopped fresh chives
2 tablespoons chopped fresh tarragon
2 tablespoons extra-virgin olive oil

1. Season the fillets with salt and pepper. 2. Prepare 4 pieces of large foil, lay the fillets on them separately; top the fillets with the lemon, dill, chives, and tarragon and drizzle each with olive oil. 3. Carefully wrap fillet loosely in foil. 4. In the Inner Pot, add the water and place the Steam Rack, then arrange the fillet pouches to the rack. 5. Place and close the lid rightly. 6. Select Steam mode. Press the button again to adjust the cooking time to 5 minutes; press Pressure Level to choose High Pressure. 7. When the time is up, quickly and carefully turn the steam release handle from the Sealing position to the Venting position. 8. When done, serve and enjoy.
Per Serving: Calories:185; Fat:9g, Sodium:355mg; Fiber:0g, Carbs: 0g, Sugar: 0g; Protein:23g

Lemon Shrimp Scampi in White Wine

Prep Time: 15 minutes | Cook Time: 5 minutes | Serves: 6

3 tablespoons unsalted butter
3 tablespoons olive oil
3 cloves garlic, peeled and minced
½ teaspoon salt
½ teaspoon ground black pepper
½ cup white wine

½ cup low-sodium chicken broth
2 pounds' tail-on shrimp (21/25 count)
1 tablespoon lemon juice
2 tablespoons chopped fresh flat-leaf parsley

1. Insert the pot into the Cooker Base without the lid. 2. Select Sauté mode and then press the same button again and then adjust the cooking temperature to Normal. 3. When the display switches On to Hot, heat the butter and olive oil; add the garlic, salt and black pepper and cook for 30 seconds; add the broth, white wine and stir quickly. 4. Press Cancel button to stop this cooking program. 5. Still in the Inner Pot, add the shrimp and let evenly coat with the garlic mixture. 6. Place and close the lid in right way. 7. Select Pressure Cook mode. Press Pressure Cook button again to adjust the cooking time to 1 minutes; press Pressure Level to choose High Pressure. 8. When the time is up, quickly and carefully turn the steam release handle from the Sealing position to the Venting position. 9. When done, add lemon juice and parsley. 10. Serve and enjoy.
Per Serving: Calories:326; Fat:25g, Sodium:1062mg; Fiber:0g, Carbs: 0g, Sugar: 0g; Protein:22g

Poached Garlic Octopus with Potatoes

Prep Time: 15 minutes | Cook Time: 2 minutes | Serves: 8

2 pounds' potatoes (about 6 medium)
3 teaspoons salt, divided
1 (2-pound) frozen octopus, thawed, cleaned, and rinsed
3 cloves garlic, peeled, divided

1 bay leaf
2 teaspoons whole peppercorns
½ cup olive oil
¼ cup white wine vinegar
½ teaspoon ground black pepper
½ cup chopped fresh parsley

1. In the Inner Pot, add the potatoes and salt, then pour the water to just cover the potatoes halfway. 2. Insert the pot into the Cooker Base and then close the lid rightly. 3. Select Pressure Cook mode. Press Pressure Cook button again to adjust the cooking time to 6 minutes; press Pressure Level to choose High Pressure. 4. When the time is up, quickly and carefully turn the steam release handle from the Sealing position to the Venting position. 5. Press Cancel button to stop this cooking program. 6. With reserving the cooking water, use a tong to pick out the potatoes, peel them when they are just cool, dice them and set aside for later use. 7. Still in the Inner Pot, add the octopus and more water if needed; add the bay leaf, peppercorns, and 1 garlic clove. 8. Close the lid and cook them under High Pressure for 10 minutes on Pressure Cook mode. 9. When the time is up, quickly and carefully turn the steam release handle from the Sealing position to the Venting position; when released, discard the bay leaf. 10. It is done if you can use a fork to sink the octopus easily into its thickest part; if not, you can cook 1 to 2 minutes more. 11. Drain the octopus, chop the head and tentacles into small, bite-sized chunks. 12. In a suitable container, crush the remaining garlic cloves, add olive oil, vinegar, the remaining salt and pepper, then cover lid and shake to combine well. 13. In your serving plate, mix up the potatoes and octopus, top with vinaigrette and sprinkle with parsley. Enjoy.
Per Serving: Calories:301; Fat:15g, Sodium:883mg; Fiber:2g, Carbs: 30g, Sugar: 1g; Protein:15g

Shrimp Risotto with Parmesan Cheese

Prep Time: 15 minutes | Cook Time: 22 minutes | Serves: 6

4 tablespoons olive oil, divided
1 medium yellow onion, peeled and chopped
1 clove garlic, peeled and minced
1 teaspoon fresh thyme leaves
1½ cups Arborio rice

½ cup white wine
4 cups low-sodium chicken broth
1-pound medium shrimp, peeled and deveined
½ teaspoon ground black pepper
½ cup grated Parmesan cheese

1. Insert the pot into the Cooker Base without the lid. 2. Select Sauté mode and then press the same button again and then adjust the cooking temperature to Normal. 3. When the display switches On to Hot, heat 2 tablespoons of oil; add onion and cook for 3 minutes or until tender; add the garlic and thyme and cook for 30 seconds; add the rice and cook for 3 minutes, making sure the rice is thoroughly and evenly coated in fat. 4. Still in the Inner Pot, add the wine and stir constantly for 2 minutes until completely evaporated; add the broth, bring to boil, stir constantly for 3 minutes. 5. Press Cancel button to stop this cooking program. 6. Place and close the lid in right way. 7. Select Pressure Cook mode. Press Pressure Cook button again to adjust the cooking time to 6 minutes; press Pressure Level to choose High Pressure. 8. When the time is up, leave the steam release handle from the Sealing position. 9. When the float valve drops, press Cancel button to stop this cooking program and remove the lid. 10. Select Sauté mode and then press the same button again and then adjust the cooking temperature to Normal. 11. When the display switches On to Hot, stir in shrimp, pepper and cook for 4 minutes until they are pink and curled. 12. When done, place the risotto in 6 suitable bowls, top with cheese and the remaining oil. 13. Enjoy.
Per Serving: Calories:412; Fat:16g, Sodium:670mg; Fiber:4g, Carbs: 37g, Sugar: 2g; Protein:27g

Italian Fish with Herbs

Prep Time: 15 minutes | Cook Time: 3 minutes | Serves: 4

1 (14.5-ounce) can diced tomatoes
¼ teaspoon dried minced onion
¼ teaspoon onion powder
¼ teaspoon dried minced garlic
¼ teaspoon garlic powder
¼ teaspoon dried basil
¼ teaspoon dried parsley
⅛ teaspoon dried oregano
¼ teaspoon sugar

⅛ teaspoon dried lemon granules, crushed
⅛ teaspoon chili powder
⅛ teaspoon dried red pepper flakes
1 tablespoon grated Parmesan cheese
4 (4-ounce) cod fillets, rinsed and patted dry

1. In the Inner Pot, thoroughly mix up the tomatoes, minced onion, onion powder, minced garlic, garlic powder, basil, parsley, oregano, sugar, lemon granules, chili powder, red pepper flakes and cheese; arrange the fillets to this mixture, fold the thin tail ends under to give the fillets even thickness, then spoon some of the tomato mixture over the fillets. 2. Place and close the lid in right way. 3. Select Pressure Cook mode. Press Pressure Cook button again to adjust the cooking time to 3 minutes; press Pressure Level to choose High Pressure. 4. When the time is up, quickly and carefully turn the steam release handle from the Sealing position to the Venting position. 5. When done, serve and enjoy.
Per Serving: Calories:116; Fat:3g, Sodium:400mg; Fiber:2g, Carbs: 5g, Sugar: 3g; Protein:20g

Lemon Shrimp Pasta with Feta Cheese

Prep Time: 15 minutes | Cook Time: 10 minutes | Serves: 6

3 tablespoons olive oil, divided
4 cloves garlic, peeled and minced
¼ teaspoon salt
¼ teaspoon ground black pepper
2 cups water
8 ounces' whole-wheat penne pasta

2 pounds' tail-on shrimp (3⅓5 count)
1 tablespoon lemon juice
1 teaspoon grated lemon zest
2 tablespoons chopped fresh basil
¼ cup crumbled feta cheese

1. Insert the pot into the Cooker Base without the lid. 2. Select Sauté mode and then press the same button again and then adjust the cooking temperature to Normal. 3. When the display switches On to Hot, add and heat 1 tablespoon oil; add the garlic, salt, black pepper and cook for 30 seconds or until fragrant; stir in the water and pasta. 4. Press Cancel button to stop this cooking program. 5. Place and close the lid in right way. 6. Select Pressure Cook mode. Press Pressure Cook button again to adjust the cooking time to 4 minutes; press Pressure Level to choose High Pressure. 7. When the time is up, quickly and carefully turn the steam release handle from the Sealing position to the Venting position. 8. When the float valve drops, open the lid; drain off any excess water before transferring the pasta to a serving bowl and covering with foil. 9. Press Cancel button to stop this cooking program. 10. After cleaning and drying the pot, insert it into the Cooker Base again. 11. Select Sauté mode and then press the same button again and then adjust the cooking temperature to Normal. 12. When the display switches On to Hot, heat the remaining oil; add shrimp and stir constantly for 2 minutes; add the lemon juice, lemon zest and basil and cook for 30 seconds. 13. When done, place the shrimp over the pasta and then top with feta. 14. Enjoy!
Per Serving: Calories:206; Fat:9g, Sodium:789mg; Fiber:2g, Carbs: 7g, Sugar: 0g; Protein:37g

Mediterranean Cod Fillets and Shrimp

Prep Time: 15 minutes | Cook Time: 10 minutes | Serves: 6

2 tablespoons olive oil
1 medium yellow onion, peeled and chopped
1 stalk celery, chopped
1 medium carrot, peeled and chopped
3 cloves garlic, peeled and minced
1 tablespoon tomato paste
1 teaspoon fresh thyme leaves
1 teaspoon chopped fresh oregano
¼ teaspoon crushed red pepper flakes

¼ teaspoon salt
¼ teaspoon ground black pepper
1 (28-ounce) can diced tomatoes
½ cup seafood stock
1-pound medium shrimp, peeled and deveined
8 ounces' cod fillets, cut into 1" pieces
2 cups cooked white rice
2 tablespoons chopped fresh parsley

1. Insert the pot into the Cooker Base without the lid. 2. Select Sauté mode and then press the same button again and then adjust the cooking temperature to Normal. 3. When the display switches On to Hot, add and heat the oil; add the celery, onion and carrot and cook for 5 minutes or until tender; add the garlic, tomato paste, thyme, oregano, red pepper flakes, salt and black pepper and cook for 30 seconds or until fragrant; lastly, add the tomatoes and stock and stir well. 4. Place and close the lid in right way. 5. Select Pressure Cook mode. Press Pressure Cook button again to adjust the cooking time to 5 minutes; press Pressure Level to choose High Pressure. 6. When the time is up, quickly and carefully turn the steam release handle from the Sealing position to the Venting position. 7. When released, open the lid and stir gently. 8. Serve with the rice and garnish with the parsley.
Per Serving: Calories:239; Fat:7g, Sodium:701mg; Fiber:3g, Carbs: 25g, Sugar: 5g; Protein:21g

Steamed Lemon Shrimp with Asparagus

Prep Time: 15 minutes | Cook Time: 1 minutes | Serves: 4

1 cup water
1 bunch asparagus, trimmed
½ teaspoon salt, divided
1-pound shrimp (21/25 count),
peeled and deveined
1½ tablespoons lemon juice
2 tablespoons olive oil

1. In the Inner Pot, add the water, put the Steam Rack in and place a suitable steamer basket on it. 2. Arrange the asparagus on steamer basket and sprinkle with ¼ teaspoon salt; add shrimp, drizzle with lemon juice, olive oil and sprinkle with remaining ¼ teaspoon salt. 3. Place and close the lid in right way. 4. Select Pressure Cook mode. Press Pressure Cook button again to adjust the cooking time to 1 minutes; press Pressure Level to choose High Pressure. 5. When the time is up, quickly and carefully turn the steam release handle from the Sealing position to the Venting position. 6. When the float valve drops, open the lid and serve the food on a plate. 7. Enjoy.
Per Serving: Calories:145; Fat:8g, Sodium:295mg; Fiber:0g, Carbs: 1g, Sugar: 1g; Protein:19g

Mediterranean Cod with Roma Tomato

Prep Time: 15 minutes | Cook Time: 6 minutes | Serves: 2

1 cup water
2 (5-ounce) cod fillets
2 teaspoons olive oil
½ teaspoon salt
10 Kalamata olives, pitted and
halved
1 small Roma tomato, diced
3 tablespoons chopped fresh basil leaves, divided

1. Prepare a 10" × 10" square of aluminum foil and place each cod piece on it; drizzle each fillet with 1 teaspoon of oil and sprinkle with ¼ teaspoon of salt; top them 5 olives, half of the tomatoes and 1 tablespoon of basil; lift the sides of the foil and crimp on top to form a foil pouch. 2. In the Inner Pot, add the water and place the Steam Rack, then arrange the foil pouches to the rack. 3. Place and close the lid rightly. 4. Select Pressure Cook mode. Press the button again to adjust the cooking time to 6 minutes; press Pressure Level to choose High Pressure. 5. When the time is up, quickly and carefully turn the steam release handle from the Sealing position to the Venting position. 6. When released, remove the pouches out of the pot and transfer the fillets to 2 plates. 7. Enjoy with the remaining basil.
Per Serving: Calories:148; Fat:9g, Sodium:1202mg; Fiber:0g, Carbs: 1g, Sugar: 1g; Protein:18g

Seafood Paella with Vegetables

Prep Time: 15 minutes | Cook Time: 10 minutes | Serves: 4

½ teaspoon saffron threads
2 cups vegetable broth
2 tablespoons olive oil
1 medium yellow onion, peeled and diced
1 cup diced carrot
1 medium green bell pepper, seeded and diced
1 cup fresh or frozen green peas
2 cloves garlic, peeled and minced
1 cup basmati rice
¼ cup chopped fresh flat-leaf parsley
½ pound medium shrimp, peeled and deveined
½ pound mussels, scrubbed and beards removed
½ pound clams, rinsed
¼ teaspoon ground black pepper

1. In a medium microwave-safe bowl, mix up the saffron and broth; microwave them for 30 seconds on High or the broth just starts to warm; set aside for later use. 2. Insert the pot into the Cooker Base without the lid. 3. Select Sauté mode and then press the same button again and then adjust the cooking temperature to Normal. 4. When the display switches On to Hot, heat the oil; add the onion, carrot, bell pepper, peas and cook for 5 minutes until they begin to soften; stir in the garlic and rice until well coated; add the saffron broth and parsley. 5. Press Cancel button to stop this cooking program. 6. Place and close the lid in right way. 7. Select Pressure Cook mode. Press Pressure Cook button again to adjust the cooking time to 5 minutes; press Pressure Level to choose High Pressure. 8. When the time is up, quickly and carefully turn the steam release handle from the Sealing position to the Venting position. 9. When released, stir well and top with shrimp, mussels, and clams. 10. Close the lid again and resume cook them on the Pressure Cook mode at High Pressure for 1 minutes. 11. When the time is up, leave the steam release handle in the Sealing position for 10 minutes, then turn it to the Venting position. 12. When

done, discard the unopened mussels, season with black pepper. 13. Serve and enjoy.
Per Serving: Calories:555; Fat:12g, Sodium:1266mg; Fiber:3g, Carbs: 49g, Sugar: 6g; Protein:58g

Tomato Mussels with Parsley

Prep Time: 15 minutes | Cook Time: 12 minutes | Serves: 6

2 pounds' baby Yukon Gold potatoes, cut in half
½ cup water
2 tablespoons olive oil, divided
1 medium yellow onion, peeled and diced
1 tablespoon chopped fresh oregano
½ teaspoon paprika
4 cloves garlic, peeled and minced
¼ teaspoon salt
¼ teaspoon ground black pepper
1 (15-ounce) can diced tomatoes
1½ cups water
2 pounds' mussels, scrubbed and beards removed
½ cup sliced green olives
2 tablespoons chopped fresh parsley

1. In the Inner Pot, add the potatoes, water, and 1 tablespoon oil. 2. Insert the pot into the Cooker Base and then close the lid rightly. 3. Select Pressure Cook mode. Press Pressure Cook button again to adjust the cooking time to 2 minutes; press Pressure Level to choose High Pressure. 4. When the time is up, leave the steam release handle in the Sealing position until the float valve drops. 5. Press Cancel button to stop this cooking program. 6. Without the lid, select Sauté mode and then press the same button again and then adjust the cooking temperature to Normal. 7. When the display switches On to Hot, add and heat the remaining oil; add onion and cook for 4 minutes or until tender; add the oregano, garlic, paprika, salt, black pepper and cook for 30 seconds or until very fragrant; stir in the tomatoes and water. 8. Press Cancel button to stop this cooking program, after stirring in the mussels, olives and potatoes, close the lid. 9. Select Pressure Cook mode again. Press Pressure Cook button again to adjust the cooking time to 5 minutes; press Pressure Level to choose High Pressure. 10. When the time is up, quickly and carefully turn the steam release handle from the Sealing position to the Venting position. 11. When released, discard the unopened mussels. 12. Serve with garnishing the parsley and enjoy.
Per Serving: Calories:272; Fat:8g, Sodium:560mg; Fiber:4g, Carbs: 35g, Sugar: 4g; Protein:15g

Vegetable Fish Soup

Prep Time: 15 minutes | Cook Time: 20-25 minutes | Serves: 12

8 cups water
2 medium onions, peeled and diced
2 medium potatoes, cubed
2 stalks celery, diced
2 medium carrots, peeled and chopped
1 tablespoon dried marjoram
½ teaspoon salt
½ teaspoon ground black pepper
2 pounds' fresh cod, cut into pieces
2 pounds' fresh grey mullet, deboned and cut into pieces
1-pound mussels, scrubbed and beards removed
¼ cup chopped fresh parsley
¼ cup extra-virgin olive oil
2 tablespoons lemon juice

1. In the Inner Pot, add the water, onions, potatoes, celery, carrots, marjoram, salt and pepper. 2. Insert the pot into the Cooker Base and then close the lid rightly. 3. Select Pressure Cook mode. Press Pressure Cook button again to adjust the cooking time to 10 minutes; press Pressure Level to choose High Pressure. 4. When the time is up, quickly and carefully turn the steam release handle from the Sealing position to the Venting position. 5. Press Cancel button to stop this cooking program. 6. Still in the Inner Pot, add the cod, mullet, mussels and parsley; cook them under High Pressure for 4 minutes on Pressure Cook mode. 7. When the time is up, quickly and carefully turn the steam release handle from the Sealing position to the Venting position. 8. When released, discard the unopened mussels; serve the fish and mussels on a plate with a slotted spoon. 9. Filter the ingredients through a sieve; push softened vegetables through a sieve with a wooden spoon and then put the strained stock back to the pot. 10. Without the lid, select Sauté mode and then press the button again to adjust the cooking temperature to Normal. 11. When the display switches On to Hot, add the olive oil and lemon juice and bring them to simmer; add the fish and mussels and simmer for 3–5 minutes. 12. When done, serve and enjoy.
Per Serving: Calories:163; Fat:6g, Sodium:171mg; Fiber:2g, Carbs: 10g, Sugar: 3g; Protein:18g

Steamed Cayenne Dungeness Crab

Prep Time: 15 minutes | Cook Time: 3 minutes | Serves: 2

1 tablespoon extra-virgin olive oil
½ teaspoon Old Bay seafood seasoning
½ teaspoon smoked paprika
¼ teaspoon cayenne pepper
2 cloves garlic, peeled and minced
2 (2-pound) Dungeness crabs
1 cup water

1. In a medium bowl, thoroughly mix up the oil, seafood seasoning, smoked paprika, cayenne pepper and garlic; coat the crabs with the mixture and then arrange them to the Steam Rack. 2. In the Inner Pot, add the water and place the Steam Rack, then close the lid in right way. 3. Select Pressure Cook mode. Press Pressure Cook button again to adjust the cooking time to 3 minutes; press Pressure Level to choose High Pressure. 4. When the time is up, quickly and carefully turn the steam release handle from the Sealing position to the Venting position. 5. When done, serve the crabs on a clean plate and enjoy.
Per Serving: Calories:185; Fat:8g, Sodium:434mg; Fiber:0g, Carbs: 1g, Sugar: 0g; Protein:25g

Basil Cod Kebabs with Lemon Wedges

Prep Time: 15 minutes | Cook Time: 2 minutes | Serves: 4

1 cup water
4 (4-ounce) cod or other white fish fillets, cut into 1" pieces
½ medium onion, peeled and cut into 1" pieces
½ medium red bell pepper, seeded
and cut into 1" pieces
2 tablespoons extra-virgin olive oil
2 tablespoons chopped fresh basil
½ teaspoon salt
½ teaspoon ground black pepper
1 small lemon, cut into wedges

1. Alternately thread the fish, onions, and bell peppers on four wooden skewers; brush each skewers with the olive oil, top with the basil, salt and black pepper, then place them on the Steam Rack. 2. In the Inner Pot, add water and place the Steam Rack. 3. Place and close the lid rightly. 4. Select Steam mode. Press Steam button again to adjust the cooking time to 2 minutes; press Pressure Level to choose High Pressure. 5. When the time is up, quickly and carefully turn the steam release handle from the Sealing position to the Venting position. 6. When done, serve and enjoy.
Per Serving: Calories:93; Fat:7g, Sodium:312mg; Fiber:1g, Carbs: 2g, Sugar: 1g; Protein:5g

Steamed Halibut Fillets with Tomato

Prep Time: 15 minutes | Cook Time: 7 minutes | Serves: 4

2 tablespoons olive oil
1 medium onion, peeled and chopped
2 cloves garlic, peeled and minced
1 tablespoon chopped fresh oregano
1 teaspoon fresh thyme leaves
½ teaspoon ground fennel
¼ teaspoon ground black pepper
¼ teaspoon crushed red pepper flakes
1 (14.5-ounce) can diced tomatoes
1 cup vegetable broth
1-pound halibut fillets
2 tablespoons chopped fresh parsley

1. Insert the pot into the Cooker Base without the lid. 2. Select Sauté mode and then press the same button again and then adjust the cooking temperature to Normal. 3. When the display switches On to Hot, add and heat the oil; add the onion and cook for 4 minutes until soft; add the garlic, oregano, thyme, fennel and cook for 30 seconds until fragrant; add the black pepper, red pepper flakes, tomatoes and vegetable broth. 4. Press Cancel button to stop this cooking program and then close the lid in right way. 5. Select Pressure Cook mode. Press the button again to adjust the cooking time to 3 minutes; press Pressure Level to choose High Pressure. 6. When the time is up, quickly and carefully turn the steam release handle from the Sealing position to the Venting position. 7. When released, serve the fillets on a plate and spoon sauce over them, sprinkle with the parsley and serve.
Per Serving: Calories:212; Fat:8g, Sodium:449mg; Fiber:2g, Carbs: 10g, Sugar: 7g; Protein:24g

Spiced Fish Potato Stew

Prep Time: 15 minutes | Cook Time: 10 minutes | Serves: 4

3 tablespoons olive oil
2 stalks celery, sliced
2 medium carrots, peeled and sliced
1 medium onion, peeled and chopped
½ fennel bulb, trimmed and chopped
2 cloves garlic, peeled and minced
1 tablespoon chopped fresh oregano
3 sprigs fresh thyme
1 (14.5-ounce) can diced tomatoes
1½ cups vegetable broth
2 medium russet potatoes, peeled
and diced
1-pound cod or other white fish fillets, cut into 1" pieces
¼ teaspoon ground black pepper
2 tablespoons chopped fresh parsley

1. Insert the pot into the Cooker Base without the lid. 2. Select Sauté mode and then press the same button again and then adjust the cooking temperature to Normal. 3. When the display switches On to Hot, add and heat the oil; add the celery, carrots, onion, fennel and cook for 8 minutes until vegetables are soft; add the garlic, oregano, thyme and cook for 30 seconds; lastly, stir in the tomatoes, potatoes and vegetable broth. 4. Press Cancel button to stop this cooking program and close the lid in right way. 5. Select Pressure Cook mode. Press the button again to adjust the cooking time to 4 minutes; press Pressure Level to choose High Pressure. 6. When the time is up, quickly and carefully turn the steam release handle from the Sealing position to the Venting position. 7. When released, stop this cooking mode by pressing Cancel button. 8. Still in the Inner Pot, add the fish, pepper and cook for 3 to 5 minutes on Sauté mode at Normal cooking temperature, until the fish is opaque. 9. When done, serve and sprinkle with parsley.
Per Serving: Calories:363; Fat:11g, Sodium:295mg; Fiber:6g, Carbs: 38g, Sugar: 11g; Protein:24g

Spinach Fish Rice

Prep Time: 15 minutes | Cook Time: 5 minutes | Serves: 4

1 cup water
1 cup white rice
1 tablespoon light olive oil
4 (4-ounce) cod or other white fish fillets
½ teaspoon salt
½ teaspoon ground black pepper
2 cups baby spinach
2 tablespoons extra-virgin olive oil
4 lemon wedges

1. Season the fillets with salt and pepper. 2. Prepare 4 pieces of large foil, lay the spinach and fillets on them separately; drizzle with extra-virgin olive oil and squeeze juice from lemon wedges. 3. Carefully wrap fillet loosely in foil. 4. In the Inner Pot, add the rice, light olive oil and water; place the Steam Rack in it and put the suitable steamer basket on the rack, then place the foil pouches on the basket. 5. Place and close the lid rightly. 6. Select Steam mode. Press the button again to adjust the cooking time to 5 minutes; press Pressure Level to choose High Pressure. 7. When the time is up, quickly and carefully turn the steam release handle from the Sealing position to the Venting position. 8. When released, carefully take out the pouches. 9. Divide rice into four servings, then enjoy with the fillets and spinach.
Per Serving: Calories:266; Fat:18g, Sodium:799mg; Fiber:1g, Carbs: 12g, Sugar: 0g; Protein:16g

Lobster Tails with Herbed Olive Oil

Prep Time: 15 minutes | Cook Time: 3 minutes | Serves: 4

¼ cup extra-virgin olive oil
¼ teaspoon salt
¼ teaspoon ground black pepper
1 clove garlic, peeled and minced
1 tablespoon grated lemon zest
1 teaspoon chopped fresh tarragon
1 teaspoon chopped fresh dill
1 cup low-sodium chicken broth
2 tablespoons Old Bay seafood seasoning
2 pounds fresh cold-water lobster tails

1. In a skillet or saucepan, heat the oil, garlic, lemon zest, salt and pepper over low heat until oil is warm; after stirring in tarragon and dill, turn off the heat immediately; cover and set aside for later use. 2. In the Inner Pot, stir in the broth and seafood seasoning; place the Steam Rack in and then place the lobster tails shell side down on the rack. 3. Insert the pot into the Cooker Base and then close the lid rightly. 4. Select Pressure Cook mode. Press Pressure Cook button again to adjust the cooking time to 3 minutes; press Pressure Level to choose High Pressure. 5. When the time is up, quickly and carefully turn the steam release handle from the Sealing position to the Venting position. 6. When released, serve the lobster tails on a large plate; use the kitchen shears to carefully cut the bottom of each shell and pull tail meat out in one piece; slice into ½"-thick pieces. 7. With the herbed olive oil, serve and enjoy.
Per Serving: Calories:230; Fat:15g, Sodium:534mg; Fiber:0g, Carbs: 0g, Sugar: 0g; Protein:22g

Spiced Mussels with Tomatoes

Prep Time: 15 minutes | Cook Time: 6 minutes | Serves: 6

2 tablespoons light olive oil	½ teaspoon ground fennel
1 medium white onion, peeled and chopped	½ teaspoon ground black pepper
2 cloves garlic, peeled and minced	3 pounds' mussels, scrubbed and beards removed
2 tablespoons chopped fresh dill	½ cup vegetable broth
2 tablespoons chopped fresh tarragon	1 (14.5-ounce) can diced tomatoes, drained

1. Insert the pot into the Cooker Base without the lid. 2. Select Sauté mode and then press the same button again and then adjust the cooking temperature to Normal. 3. When the display switches On to Hot, heat the oil; add the onion and cook for 3 minutes until tender; add the garlic, dill, tarragon, fennel and pepper and cook for 30 seconds until the garlic is fragrant. 4. Press Cancel button to stop this cooking program. 5. Still in the Inner Pot, stir in the mussels, tomatoes and broth, then place and close the lid in right way. 6. Select Pressure Cook mode. Press Pressure Cook button again to adjust the cooking time to 3 minutes; press Pressure Level to choose High Pressure. 7. When the time is up, quickly and carefully turn the steam release handle from the Sealing position to the Venting position. 8. When done, discard the unopened mussels. 9. Serve and enjoy.
Per Serving: Calories:162; Fat:7g, Sodium:435mg; Fiber:2g, Carbs: 10g, Sugar: 3g; Protein:14g

Citrus Fish Tacos

Prep Time: 15 minutes | Cook Time: 3 minutes | Serves: 8

½ cup grated cabbage	1-pound cod, cut into 2" pieces
1 large carrot, peeled and grated	2 tablespoons orange juice
1 small jicama, peeled and julienned	1 teaspoon garlic salt
2 tablespoons lime juice, divided	1 teaspoon ground cumin
2 tablespoons olive oil, divided	1 cup water
⅛ teaspoon hot sauce	½ cup guacamole
¼ cup chopped fresh cilantro	½ cup diced tomatoes
½ teaspoon salt	8 (6") soft corn tortillas

1. In a medium bowl, mix up the cabbage, carrot, jicama, 1 tablespoon lime juice, hot sauce, cilantro, salt and 1 tablespoon of oil, then cover and refrigerate the mixture for 30 minutes or overnight. 2. In a large bowl, mix up the cod pieces, orange juice, garlic salt, cumin, the remaining lime juice and oil, then refrigerate for 15 minutes. 3. In the Inner Pot, add the water and place the Steam Rack, then put the suitable steamer basket on the rack. 4. Arrange the cod pieces to the basket and add the remaining marinade. 5. Place and close the lid in right way. 6. Select Pressure Cook mode. Press the button again to adjust the cooking time to 3 minutes; press Pressure Level to choose High Pressure. 7. When the time is up, quickly and carefully turn the steam release handle from the Sealing position to the Venting position. 8. When released, transfer the cod pieces to the serving bowl. 9. To make the cod tacos, add equal amounts of fish, slaw, guacamole, and tomatoes to each corn tortilla. 10. Enjoy.
Per Serving: Calories:240; Fat:8g, Sodium:564mg; Fiber:5g, Carbs: 25g, Sugar: 3g; Protein:14g

Spiced Salmon with Parsley

Prep Time: 15 minutes | Cook Time: 3 minutes | Serves: 4

1 cup water	¼ cup chopped fresh dill
4 (4-ounce) skin-on salmon fillets	1 small lemon, thinly sliced
½ teaspoon salt	2 tablespoons extra-virgin olive oil
½ teaspoon ground black pepper	1 tablespoon chopped fresh parsley

1. Season the fish fillets with salt and pepper. 2. In the Inner Pot, add the water and place the Steam Rack. 3. Transfer the fish fillets to the rack, top them with the dill and 2-3 lemon slices. 4. Place and close the lid rightly. 5. Select Steam mode. Press Steam button again to adjust the cooking time to 3 minutes; press Pressure Level to choose High Pressure. 6. When the time is up, quickly and carefully turn the steam release handle from the Sealing position to the Venting position. 7. When released, serve the fillets on a plate; drizzle with the olive and garnish with the fresh parsley. 8. Enjoy.
Per Serving: Calories:160; Fat:9g, Sodium:545mg; Fiber:0g, Carbs: 0g, Sugar: 0g; Protein:19g

Spiced Salmon Poached in Red Wine

Prep Time: 15 minutes | Cook Time: 16 minutes | Serves: 6

1 medium onion, peeled and quartered	2 cups dry red wine
2 cloves garlic, peeled and smashed	2 tablespoons red wine vinegar
1 stalk celery, diced	½ teaspoon salt
1 bay leaf	½ teaspoon black peppercorns
½ teaspoon dried thyme	1 (2½-pound) center-cut salmon roast
3½ cups water	1 medium lemon, cut into wedges

1. In the Inner Pot, add all ingredients except salmon and lemon. 2. Place and close the lid in right way. 3. Select Pressure Cook mode. Press the button again to adjust the cooking time to 10 minutes; press Pressure Level to choose High Pressure. 4. When the time is up, quickly and carefully turn the steam release handle from the Sealing position to the Venting position. 5. When released, stop this cooking mode by pressing Cancel button. 6. Still in the Inner Pot, place the Steam Rack and transfer a suitable steamer basket to the rack. 7. Wrap salmon in cheesecloth so that the ends are long enough to extend about 3 inches; use two sets of tongs to hold the 3-inch cheesecloth extension and then place the salmon on the rack. 8. Place and close the lid rightly. 9. Select Pressure Cook mode. Press the button again to adjust the cooking time to 6 minutes; press Pressure Level to choose High Pressure. 10. When the time is up, leave the steam release handle in the Sealing position. 11. When released, hold on to the 3-inch cheesecloth extensions to remove the salmon out of the pot with the tongs; drain away the extra moisture by setting in a colander. 12. Unwrap the cheesecloth after the salmon is cool enough to handle, then peel away and discard the skin. 13. Serve the salmon on a plate and garnish with lemon wedges.
Per Serving: Calories:435; Fat:24g, Sodium:213mg; Fiber:0g, Carbs: 4g, Sugar: 3g; Protein:43g

Carp Pilaf

Prep time: 20 minutes | Cook time: 6 minutes | Serves: 4

1 tablespoon olive oil	½ teaspoons dried marjoram leaves
1 cup chicken stock	Sea salt and black pepper, to taste
1 cup tomato paste	½ teaspoons dried oregano leaves
1 teaspoon dried rosemary, crushed	1 cup Arborio rice
1 tablespoon dried parsley	1-pound carp, chopped

1. Simply throw all of the above ingredients into your Inner Pot. 2. Put on the pressure cooker's lid and turn the steam valve to "Sealing" position. 3. Select Pressure Cook mode, and then press the "Pressure Cook" button again to select "Less" time option. 4. Use the "+/-" keys on the control panel to set the cooking time to 6 minutes. 5. Press the Pressure Level button to adjust the pressure to "High Pressure." 6. Once the cooking cycle is completed, quickly and carefully turn the steam release handle from Sealing position to the Venting position. 7. When all the steam is released, remove the pressure lid from the top carefully. 8. Serve in individual serving bowls, garnished with fresh lemon slices.
Per Serving: Calories 421; Fat 7.9g; Sodium 704mg; Carbs 6g; Fiber 3.6g; Sugar 6g; Protein 18g

Tuna Fillets with Eschalots

Prep Time: 20 minutes | Cook time: 5 minutes | Serves: 4

2 lemons, 1 whole and 1 cutted	1 tablespoon dried parsley flakes
1-pound tuna fillets	2 tablespoons butter, melted
Sea salt and black pepper, to taste	2 eschalots, thinly sliced

1. Place 1 cup of water and lemon juice in the Inner Pot. Add a steamer basket too. 2. Place the tuna fillets in the steamer basket. 3. Sprinkle the salt, pepper, and parsley over the fish; drizzle with butter and top with thinly sliced eschalots. 4. Put on the pressure cooker's lid and turn the steam valve to "Sealing" position. 5. Press the "Steam" button one time to select "Less" option. 6. Use the "+/-" keys on the control panel to set the cooking time to 3 minutes. 7. Press the Pressure Level button to adjust the pressure to "High Pressure." 8. Once the cooking cycle is completed, quickly and carefully turn the steam release handle from Sealing position to the Venting position. 9. When all the steam is released, remove the pressure lid from the top carefully. 10. Serve immediately with lemon. Bon appétit!
Per Serving: Calories 219; Fat 10g; Sodium 891mg; Carbs 22.9g; Fiber 4g; Sugar 4g; Protein 23g

Cod Stew Vegetables

Prep Time: 15 minutes | Cook Time: 10 minutes | Serves: 4

3 tablespoons olive oil
1 medium onion, peeled and diced
1 stalk celery, diced
1 medium carrot, peeled and chopped
2 cloves garlic, peeled and minced
1 tablespoon chopped fresh oregano
½ teaspoon ground fennel
1 sprig fresh thyme
1 (14.5-ounce) can diced tomatoes
1½ cups vegetable broth
1-pound cod fillets, cut into 1"
pieces
⅓ cup sliced green olives
¼ teaspoon ground black pepper
2 tablespoons chopped fresh dill

1. Insert the pot into the Cooker Base without the lid. 2. Select Sauté mode and then press the same button again and then adjust the cooking temperature to Normal. 3. When the display switches On to Hot, heat the oil; add the onion, celery, carrot and cook for 6 minutes until tender; add the garlic, oregano, fennel, thyme and cook for 30 seconds; lastly, stir in the tomatoes and vegetable broth. 4. Press Cancel button to stop this cooking program. 5. Place and close the lid in right way. 6. Select Pressure Cook mode. Press Pressure Cook button again to adjust the cooking time to 3 minutes; press Pressure Level to choose High Pressure. 7. When the time is up, quickly and carefully turn the steam release handle from the Sealing position to the Venting position. 8. When released, press Cancel button to stop this cooking program. 9. Still in the Inner Pot, add the fish, olives, pepper and cook for 3 to 5 minutes on Sauté mode at Normal cooking temperature. 10. When done, sprinkle with dill and serve.
Per Serving: Calories:200; Fat:16g, Sodium:379mg; Fiber:3g, Carbs: 14g, Sugar: 8g; Protein:7g

Flavored Cioppino

Prep Time: 15 minutes | Cook Time: 10 minutes | Serves: 6

3 tablespoons light olive oil
1 medium yellow onion, peeled and chopped
1 medium red bell pepper, seeded and chopped
2 cloves garlic, peeled and minced
1 (28-ounce) can crushed tomatoes
1 cup red wine
1 cup seafood stock
1 tablespoon lemon juice
1 bay leaf
¼ cup chopped fresh basil
½ teaspoon ground black pepper
1-pound fresh mussels, scrubbed and beards removed
1-pound large shrimp, peeled and deveined
1-pound clams, scrubbed

1. Insert the pot into the Cooker Base without the lid. 2. Select Sauté mode and then press the same button again and then adjust the cooking temperature to Normal. 3. When the display switches On to Hot, heat the oil; add the onion and bell pepper and cook for 3 minutes until just tender; add the garlic and cook for 30 seconds until fragrant; stir in the wine, tomatoes, stock, lemon juice, bay leaf, basil and black pepper. 4. Press Cancel button to stop this cooking program. 5. Place and close the lid in right way. 6. Select Pressure Cook mode. Press Pressure Cook button again to adjust the cooking time to 5 minutes; press Pressure Level to choose High Pressure. 7. When the time is up, quickly and carefully turn the steam release handle from the Sealing position to the Venting position. 8. When done, stop this cooking mode by pressing the Cancel button. 9. Open the lid, remove the bay leaf, add the mussels, shrimp and clams and cook for 3 minutes on Sauté mode at Normal temperature, until the shrimp are pink and shellfish have opened. 10. When cooked, discard the unopened mussels and serve.
Per Serving: Calories:384; Fat:11g, Sodium:671mg; Fiber:3g, Carbs: 14g, Sugar: 6g; Protein:47g

Steamed Lemon Cod

Prep Time: 15 minutes | Cook Time: 3 minutes | Serves: 4

1 cup water
4 (4-ounce) cod fillets, rinsed and patted dry
½ teaspoon ground black pepper
1 small lemon, thinly sliced
2 tablespoons extra-virgin olive oil
¼ cup chopped fresh parsley
2 tablespoons capers
1 tablespoon chopped fresh chives

1. Season the fish fillets with pepper and top each fillet with 3 lemon slices. 2. In the Inner Pot, add the water and place the Steam Rack, then arrange the fillets to the rack. 3. Place and close the lid rightly. 4. Select Steam mode. Press Steam button again to adjust the cooking time to 3 minutes; press Pressure Level to choose High Pressure. 5. While cooking, in a small bowl, thoroughly mix up the olive oil, parsley, capers and chives. 6. When the time is up, quickly and carefully turn the steam release handle from the Sealing position to

the Venting position. 7. When done, transfer the fillets to a plate and discard the lemon slices. 8. Drizzle the fillets with the chives mixture and make sure each one is coated well. 9. Enjoy.
Per Serving: Calories:140; Fat:10g, Sodium:370mg; Fiber:0g, Carbs: 0g, Sugar: 0g; Protein:14g

Spiced Catfish with Tomatoes

Prep Time: 15 minutes | Cook Time: 5 minutes | Serves: 4

1 (1½-pound) catfish fillet, rinsed in cold water, patted dry, cut into bite-sized pieces
1 (14.5-ounce) can diced tomatoes
2 teaspoons dried minced onion
¼ teaspoon onion powder
1 teaspoon dried minced garlic
¼ teaspoon garlic powder
1 teaspoon hot paprika
¼ teaspoon dried tarragon
1 medium green bell pepper, seeded and diced
1 stalk celery, finely diced
¼ teaspoon sugar
½ cup chili sauce
½ teaspoon salt
½ teaspoon ground black pepper

1. In the Inner Pot, mix up all of the ingredients. 2. Place and close the lid in right way. 3. Select Pressure Cook mode. Press the button again to adjust the cooking time to 5 minutes; press Pressure Level to choose High Pressure. 4. When the time is up, quickly and carefully turn the steam release handle from the Sealing position to the Venting position. 5. When released, stir gently; serve and enjoy.
Per Serving: Calories:284; Fat:9g, Sodium:696mg; Fiber:3g, Carbs: 7g, Sugar: 4g; Protein:31g

Simple and Delicious Halibut Fillets

Prep Time: 15 minutes | Cook Time: 5 minutes | Serves: 2

1 cup chopped broccoli
1 large potato, peeled and diced
1 large carrot, peeled and grated
1 small zucchini, trimmed and grated
4 ounces' mushrooms, sliced
¼ teaspoon dried thyme
¼ teaspoon grated lemon zest
1 (½-pound) halibut fillet
½ cup white wine
½ cup lemon juice
1 teaspoon dried parsley
¼ teaspoon salt
¼ teaspoon ground black pepper
⅛ teaspoon ground nutmeg

1. In the Inner Pot, place the Steam Rack and then arrange the suitable steamer basket to the rack. 2. On the basket, place the broccoli, potato, carrot, zucchini, mushrooms and then sprinkle with the thyme and lemon zest. 3. Arrange the fillets over the vegetables, pour the lemon juice and wine, then sprinkle the parsley, salt and black pepper. 4. Place and close the lid rightly. 5. Select Pressure Cook mode. Press the button again to adjust the cooking time to 5 minutes; press Pressure Level to choose High Pressure. 6. When the time is up, quickly and carefully turn the steam release handle from the Sealing position to the Venting position. 7. When released, take out the food and divide them between 2 plates. 8. Sprinkle with the nutmeg and enjoy.
Per Serving: Calories:278; Fat:3g, Sodium:409mg; Fiber:5g, Carbs: 23g, Sugar: 4g; Protein:31g

Ocean Trout Fillets

Prep time: 20 minutes | Cook time: 3 minutes | Serves: 4

1-pound ocean trout fillets
Sea salt, to taste
1 teaspoon caraway seeds
½ teaspoons mustard seeds
½ teaspoons paprika
½ cup spring onions, chopped
2 garlic cloves, minced
1 teaspoon mixed peppercorns
2 tablespoons champagne vinegar
1 tablespoon fish sauce
2½ cups broth, preferably homemade

1. Place the steaming basket in your Inner Pot. 2. Sprinkle the ocean trout fillets with salt, caraway seeds, mustard seeds, and paprika. 3. Place the ocean trout fillet in the steaming basket. Add the other ingredients. 4. Put on the pressure cooker's lid and turn the steam valve to "Sealing" position. 5. Select Pressure Cook mode, and then press the "Pressure Cook" button again to select "Less" time option. 6. Use the "+/-" keys on the control panel to set the cooking time to 3 minutes. 7. Press the Pressure Level button to adjust the pressure to "Low Pressure." 8. Once the cooking cycle is completed, quickly and carefully turn the steam release handle from Sealing position to the Venting position. 9. When all the steam is released, remove the pressure lid from the top carefully. 10. Serve.
Per Serving: Calories 334; Fat 19g; Sodium 354mg; Carbs 15g; Fiber 5.1g; Sugar 8.2g; Protein 32g

Dijon Halibut with Pistachio

Prep Time: 15 minutes | Cook Time: 6 minutes | Serves: 2

1 tablespoon Dijon mustard
1 teaspoon lemon juice
2 tablespoons panko bread crumbs
¼ cup chopped unsalted pistachios
¼ teaspoon salt
2 (5-ounce) halibut fillets
1 cup water

1. Prepare a baking sheet and line a piece of parchment paper on it. 2. In a suitable bowl, thoroughly mix up the mustard, lemon juice, bread crumbs, pistachios and salt to form a thick paste. 3. Use a paper towel to pat the fillets dry; rub the paste on the top of each fillet and place and then place them on the Steam Rack. 4. In the Inner Pot, add water and transfer the rack to it; place and close the lid rightly. 5. Select Pressure Cook mode. Press Pressure Cook button again to adjust the cooking time to 5 minutes; press Pressure Level to choose High Pressure. 6. While cooking, prepare a baking sheet and line a piece of parchment paper on it; preheat your broiler. 7. When the time is up, quickly and carefully turn the steam release handle from the Sealing position to the Venting position. 8. When released, transfer the fillets to the baking sheet; broil them in the broiler for 1 to 2 minutes until the tops are browned. 9. When done, serve and enjoy.
Per Serving: Calories:235; Fat:9g, Sodium:411mg; Fiber:2g, Carbs: 4g, Sugar: 1g; Protein:35g

Thyme Cod Fillet Soup

Prep Time: 15 minutes | Cook Time: 20 minutes | Serves: 6

3 tablespoons olive oil
1 fennel bulb, white part only, chopped
1 medium onion, peeled and chopped
1 medium zucchini, trimmed and chopped
4 cloves garlic, peeled and minced
1 tablespoon tomato paste
1 (14.5-ounce) can diced tomatoes
3 sprigs fresh thyme
1 tablespoon chopped fresh oregano
2 teaspoons grated orange zest
½ cup white wine
3 cups low-sodium chicken broth
1-pound russet potatoes, peeled and chopped
1-pound cod fillets, cut into 1" pieces
¼ cup chopped Kalamata olives
3 basil leaves, roughly torn

1. Insert the pot into the Cooker Base without the lid. 2. Select Sauté mode and then press the same button again and then adjust the cooking temperature to Normal. 3. When the display switches On to Hot, add and heat the oil; add the fennel and onion and cook for 8 minutes or until soft; add the zucchini, garlic and tomato paste and cook for 1 minute until fragrant; lastly, stir in the tomatoes, thyme, oregano and orange zest. 4. Press the Cancel button to stop this cooking program. 5. Still in the Inner Pot, add the potatoes, wine and broth, the close the lid in right way. 6. Select Pressure Cook mode. Press the button again to adjust the cooking time to 5 minutes; press Pressure Level to choose High Pressure. 7. When the time is up, quickly and carefully turn the steam release handle from the Sealing position to the Venting position. 8. When released, stop this cooking mode by pressing the Cancel button. 9. Add the fish and olives and cook for 3 to 5 minutes at Normal cooking temperature on Sauté mode, until the fish is opaque. 10. When done, top with the basil and serve warm.
Per Serving: Calories:198; Fat:10g, Sodium:279mg; Fiber:2g, Carbs: 17g, Sugar: 6g; Protein:9g

Mediterranean Fish Stew with Hot Sauce

Prep Time: 15 minutes | Cook Time: 12 minutes | Serves: 4

4 tablespoons olive oil
1 medium yellow onion, peeled and diced
2 cloves garlic, peeled and minced
½ teaspoon dried oregano leaves
½ teaspoon ground fennel
¼ teaspoon dried thyme leaves
1 (14.5-ounce) can diced tomatoes
1 cup seafood stock
½ cup white wine
1-pound white fish fillets, such as halibut or sea bass, cut into 2" pieces
¼ teaspoon salt
¼ teaspoon ground black pepper
½ teaspoon hot sauce

1. Insert the pot into the Cooker Base without the lid. 2. Select Sauté mode and then press the same button again and then adjust the cooking temperature to Normal. 3. When the display switches On to Hot, add and heat the oil; add the onion and cook for 4 minutes or until soft; add the garlic, oregano, fennel, thyme and cook for 30 seconds; lastly, stir in the tomatoes, seafood stock, and wine. 4. Press Cancel button to stop this cooking program. 5. Place and close the lid in right way.

6. Select Pressure Cook mode. Press Pressure Cook button again to adjust the cooking time to 3 minutes; press Pressure Level to choose High Pressure. 7. When the time is up, quickly and carefully turn the steam release handle from the Sealing position to the Venting position. 8. When released, press Cancel button to stop this cooking program. 9. Still in the Inner Pot, add fish and cook at Normal cooking temperature on Sauté for 5 minutes, until the fish is opaque. 10. When done, season with the salt and pepper; serve with the hot sauce.
Per Serving: Calories:282; Fat:15g, Sodium:456mg; Fiber:2g, Carbs: 8g, Sugar: 5g; Protein:26g

Delectable Orange Roughy Fillets

Prep Time: 15 minutes | Cook Time: 5 minutes | Serves: 2

⅜ cup dry white wine
⅜ cup water
2 (8-ounce) orange roughy fillets, rinsed and patted dry
¼ teaspoon salt
4 thin slices white onion, divided
6 sprigs fresh dill, divided
3 tablespoons unsalted butter, melted
4 teaspoons lime juice
6 Kalamata olives, pitted and chopped

1. Sprinkle the fillets with salt 2. In the Inner Pot, add the water and place the Steam Rack; place 2 onion slices on the rack and top each slice with a dill sprig. 3. Arrange the fillets to the rack, top each fillet with a dill sprig and the remaining onion slices. 4. Place and close the lid rightly. 5. Select Pressure Cook mode. Press the button again to adjust the cooking time to 5 minutes; press Pressure Level to choose High Pressure. 6. When the time is up, quickly and carefully turn the steam release handle from the Sealing position to the Venting position. 7. In a small bowl, mix up the butter, lime juice, and ½ tablespoon cooking liquid from the fillet; stir in the olives. 8. Add the sauce over the fillets and garnish with the remaining dill sprigs; enjoy.
Per Serving: Calories:337; Fat:21g, Sodium:650mg; Fiber:0g, Carbs: 1g, Sugar: 0g; Protein:37g

Herbed River Trout

Prep Time: 15 minutes | Cook Time: 3 minutes | Serves: 4

4 (½-pound) fresh river trout, rinsed and patted dry
1 teaspoon salt, divided
1 teaspoon white wine vinegar
½ cup water
½ cup minced fresh flat-leaf parsley
2 tablespoons chopped fresh oregano
1 teaspoon fresh thyme leaves
1 small shallot, peeled and minced
2 tablespoons olive oil
½ teaspoon lemon juice

1. Season the trout inside and out with ¾ teaspoon of salt. 2. In the Inner Pot, stir in the vinegar and water; place the Steam Rack and then arrange the trout to the rack. 3. Place and close the lid in right way. 4. Select Pressure Cook mode. Press the button again to adjust the cooking time to 3 minutes; press Pressure Level to choose High Pressure. 5. When the time is up, leave the steam release handle in the Sealing position. 6. Transfer the trout to a plate with a spatula, peel and discard the skin and heads. 7. In a small bowl, thoroughly mix up the parsley, oregano, thyme, shallot, olive oil, lemon juice and the remaining salt. 8. Pour the mixture over the trout and enjoy.
Per Serving: Calories:344; Fat:18g, Sodium:581mg; Fiber:0g, Carbs: 1g, Sugar: 0g; Protein:45g

Mustard Fish Fillets with Lemon Wedges

Prep Time: 15 minutes | Cook Time: 3 minutes | Serves: 4

1 cup water
4 (4-ounce) cod or other white fish fillets
2 tablespoons Dijon mustard
2 tablespoons chopped fresh dill
2 tablespoons chopped fresh chives
½ teaspoon salt
½ teaspoon ground black pepper
1 small lemon, cut into wedges

1. In the Inner Pot, add the water and place the Steam Rack. 2. Brush the fish fillets with the Dijon mustard; sprinkle each fillet with dill, chives and season with salt and pepper, then arrange them to the rack. 3. Place and close the lid in right way. 4. Select Steam mode. Press the button again to adjust the cooking time to 3 minutes; press Pressure Level to choose High Pressure. 5. When the time is up, quickly and carefully turn the steam release handle from the Sealing position to the Venting position. 6. When released, take out the fillets. 7. With the lemon wedges, serve and enjoy.
Per Serving: Calories:80; Fat:3g, Sodium:765mg; Fiber:0g, Carbs: 0g, Sugar: 0g; Protein:14g

Lemon Crab Orzo with Parmesan Cheese

Prep Time: 15 minutes | Cook Time: 5 minutes | Serves: 4

2 tablespoons light olive oil	¼ teaspoon salt
1 medium shallot, peeled and minced	¼ teaspoon ground black pepper
1 clove garlic, peeled and minced	2 cups water
¼ cup chopped fresh flat-leaf parsley	8 ounces' orzo
2 tablespoons chopped fresh basil	8 ounces' jumbo lump crabmeat
	1 tablespoon lemon juice
	¼ cup grated Parmesan cheese

1. Insert the pot into the Cooker Base without the lid. 2. Select Sauté mode and then press the same button again and then adjust the cooking temperature to Normal. 3. When the display switches On to Hot, heat the oil; add the shallot and garlic and cook for 1 minute until fragrant; stir in the parsley, basil, salt and pepper; add water and pasta. 4. Press Cancel button to stop this cooking program. 5. Place and close the lid in right way. 6. Select Pressure Cook mode. Press Pressure Cook button again to adjust the cooking time to 4 minutes; press Pressure Level to choose High Pressure. 7. When the time is up, quickly and carefully turn the steam release handle from the Sealing position to the Venting position. 8. When released, add the crab and lemon juice, stir lightly to combine. 9. Without the lid, Keep Warm the food for 10 minutes to heat the crab. 10. When done, top with the cheese and serve.
Per Serving: Calories:367; Fat:12g, Sodium:531mg; Fiber:3g, Carbs: 43g, Sugar: 1g; Protein:24g

Tuna, Ham and Pea Chowder

Prep time: 20 minutes | Cook time: 6 minutes | Serves: 5

2 tablespoons olive oil	Sea salt and black pepper, to taste
4 slices ham, chopped	1 teaspoon cayenne pepper
1 cup shallots, chopped	½ teaspoons ground bay leaf
2 cloves garlic, minced	½ teaspoons mustard powder
2 carrots, chopped	1½ cups double cream
5 cups seafood stock	1½ cups frozen green peas
1¼-pound tuna steak, diced	

1. Press the "Sauté" button two times to select "Normal" settings. 2. Heat the oil and fry the ham until crispy. 3. Then, add the shallot and garlic; continue to cook an additional 2 minutes or until tender and fragrant. 4. Add the carrot, stock, tuna, salt, black pepper, cayenne pepper, ground bay leaf, and mustard powder. 5. Put on the pressure cooker's lid and turn the steam valve to "Sealing" position. 6. Select Pressure Cook mode, and then press the "Pressure Cook" button again to select "Less" time option. 7. Use the "+/-" keys on the control panel to set the cooking time to 6 minutes. 8. Press the Pressure Level button to adjust the pressure to "High Pressure." 9. Once the cooking cycle is completed, allow the steam to release naturally. 10. When all the steam is released, remove the pressure lid from the top carefully. 11. Add the double cream and frozen peas. 12. Press the "Sauté" button two times to select "Normal" settings again and cook for a couple of minutes more or until heated through. Bon appétit!
Per Serving: Calories 422; Fat 12.9g; Sodium 414mg; Carbs 11g; Fiber 5g; Sugar 9g; Protein 31g

Curried Halibut Steaks

Prep time: 20 minutes | Cook time: 10 minutes | Serves: 4

1 tablespoon olive oil	minced
1 cup scallions, chopped	1 teaspoon ginger garlic paste
½ cup beef bone broth	1 tablespoon red curry paste
1-pound halibut steaks, rinsed and cubed	½ teaspoons ground cumin
1 cup tomato purée	1 cup coconut milk, unsweetened
1 jalapeño pepper, seeded and	Salt and black pepper, to taste

1. Press the "Sauté" button two times to select "Normal" settings 2. Now, heat the olive oil; cook the scallions until tender and fragrant. 3. Then, use the broth to deglaze the bottom of the Inner Pot. Stir in the remaining ingredients. 4. Put on the pressure cooker's lid and turn the steam valve to "Sealing" position. 5. Select Pressure Cook mode, and then press the "Pressure Cook" button again to select "Less" time option. 6. Use the "+/-" keys on the control panel to set the cooking time to 7 minutes. 7. Press the Pressure Level button to adjust the pressure to "High Pressure." 8. Once the cooking cycle is completed, quickly and carefully turn the steam release handle from Sealing position to the Venting position. 9. When all the steam is released,

remove the pressure lid from the top carefully. 10. Taste, adjust the seasonings and serve right now.
Per Serving: Calories 334; Fat 7.9g; Sodium 704mg; Carbs 6g; Fiber 3.6g; Sugar 6g; Protein 18g

Steamed Crabs in Sauce

Prep Time: 15 minutes | Cook Time: 3 minutes | Serves: 2

2 tablespoons garlic chili sauce	2 cloves garlic, peeled and minced
1 tablespoon hoisin sauce	2 small bird's eye chilies, minced
1 tablespoon minced fresh ginger	2 (2-pound) Dungeness crabs
1 teaspoon fish sauce	1 cup water

1. In a suitable bowl, thoroughly mix up the garlic chili sauce, hoisin sauce, ginger, fish sauce, garlic, and chilies; coat the crabs with mixture well and then arrange them to the Steam Rack. 2. In the Inner Pot, add the water and place the Steam Rack, then close the lid in right way 3. Select Pressure Cook mode. Press Pressure Cook button again to adjust the cooking time to 3 minutes; press Pressure Level to choose High Pressure. 4. When the time is up, quickly and carefully turn the steam release handle from the Sealing position to the Venting position. 5. When done, serve the crabs on a clean plate and enjoy.
Per Serving: Calories:128; Fat:1g, Sodium:619mg; Fiber:0g, Carbs: 1g, Sugar: 1g; Protein:25g

Shrimp in Tomato Sauce

Prep time: 20 minutes | Cook time: 5 minutes | Serves: 4

1 tablespoon butter, at room temperature	deveined
1 cup green onion, chopped	1 tablespoon tamari sauce
1 teaspoon garlic, minced	1 sprig thyme
1½-pound shrimp, peeled and	1 sprig rosemary
	2 ripe tomatoes, chopped

1. Press the "Sauté" button two times to select "Normal" settings 2. Melt the butter and cook the green onions until they have softened. 3. Now, stir in the garlic and cook an additional 30 seconds or until it is aromatic. 4. Add the rest of the above ingredients. 5. Put on the pressure cooker's lid and turn the steam valve to "Sealing" position. 6. Select Pressure Cook mode, and then press the "Pressure Cook" button again to select "Less" time option. 7. Use the "+/-" keys on the control panel to set the cooking time to 3 minutes. 8. Press the Pressure Level button to adjust the pressure to "Low Pressure." 9. Once the cooking cycle is completed, allow the steam to release naturally. 10. When all the steam is released, remove the pressure lid from the top carefully. 11. Serve over hot jasmine rice and enjoy!
Per Serving: Calories 427; Fat 10.9g; Sodium 454mg; Carbs 10g; Fiber 3.1g; Sugar 5.2g; Protein 20g

Sole Fillets with Vegetables

Prep time: 15 minutes | Cook time: 13 minutes | Serves: 4

2 tablespoons coconut oil	Salt and black pepper, to taste
1 small shallot, quartered	1-pound fennel, quartered
4 cloves garlic, sliced	1-pound sole fillets
1 cup beef stock	1 lemon, cut into wedges
1 ripe tomato, puréed	2 tablespoons fresh Italian parsley

1. Press the "Sauté" button two times to select "Normal" settings and heat the coconut oil. 2. Once hot, sauté the shallot and garlic until tender and aromatic. 3. Add the beef stock, tomato, salt, pepper, and fennel. 4. Press the Cancel button to stop this cooking program. 5. Put on the pressure cooker's lid and turn the steam valve to "Sealing" position. 6. Select Pressure Cook mode, and then press the "Pressure Cook" button again to select "Less" time option. 7. Use the "+/-" keys on the control panel to set the cooking time to 10 minutes. 8. Press the Pressure Level button to adjust the pressure to "High Pressure." 9. Once the cooking cycle is completed, quickly and carefully turn the steam release handle from Sealing position to the Venting position. 10. When all the steam is released, remove the pressure lid from the top carefully. 11. Then, remove all the vegetables with a slotted spoon and reserve, keeping them warm. 12. Add the sole fillets to the Inner Pot. 13. Choose the "Steam" mode and cook for 3 minutes at Low Pressure. 14. Once cooking is complete, quickly and carefully turn the steam release handle from Sealing position to the Venting position; carefully remove the lid. 15. Garnish the fish fillets with lemon and parsley. 16. With the reserved vegetables, serve and enjoy!
Per Serving: Calories 334; Fat 7.9g; Sodium 704mg; Carbs 6g; Fiber 3.6g; Sugar 6g; Protein 18g

Calamari with Pimentos

Prep time: 20 minutes | Cook time: 25 minutes | Serves: 4

3 Pimentos, stem and core removed
2 tablespoons olive oil
½ cup leeks, chopped
2 cloves garlic chopped
1 ½ cups stock, preferably homemade
2 tablespoons fish sauce
⅓ cup dry sherry
Seas salt and black pepper, to taste

½ teaspoon red pepper flakes, crushed
1 teaspoon dried rosemary, chopped
1 teaspoon dried thyme, chopped
1½-pound frozen calamari, thawed and drained
2 tablespoons fresh chives, chopped

1. Split your Pimentos into halves and place them over the flame. 2. Cook, turning a couple of times, until the skin is blistering and blackened. 3. Allow them to stand for 30 minutes; peel your Pimentos and chop them. 4. Press the "Sauté" button two times to select "Normal" settings to heat up your Inner Pot; add olive oil. 5. Once hot, cook the leeks until tender and fragrant, about 4 minutes. 6. Now, stir in the garlic and cook an additional 30 seconds or until just browned and aromatic. 7. Add the stock, fish sauce, dry sherry, salt, pepper, red pepper flakes, rosemary, and thyme. 8. Add the roasted Pimentos. Lastly, place the calamari on top. Pour in 3 cups of water. 9. Put on the pressure cooker's lid and turn the steam valve to "Sealing" position. 10. Select Pressure Cook mode, and then press the "Pressure Cook" button again to select "Less" time option. 11. Use the "+/-" keys on the control panel to set the cooking time to 20 minutes. 12. Press the Pressure Level button to adjust the pressure to "High Pressure." 13. Once the cooking cycle is completed, quickly and carefully turn the steam release handle from Sealing position to the Venting position. 14. When all the steam is released, remove the pressure lid from the top carefully. 15. Serve warm garnished with fresh chopped chives. Enjoy!
Per Serving: Calories 412; Fat 20g; Sodium 491mg; Carbs 9g; Fiber 3g; Sugar 8g; Protein 31g

Louisiana-Seafood Boil

Prep time: 15 minutes | Cook time: 10 minutes | Serves: 4

1 cup jasmine rice
1 tablespoon butter
1 tablespoon olive oil
½-pound chicken breasts, cubed
1-pound shrimp
2 sweet peppers, deveined and sliced
1 habanero pepper, deveined and sliced
1 onion, chopped

4 cloves garlic, minced
1 cup chicken bone broth
2 bay leaves
1 teaspoon oregano
1 teaspoon sage
1 teaspoon basil
1 teaspoon paprika
1 tablespoon fish sauce
Sea salt and black pepper, to taste
1 tablespoon cornstarch

1. Combine the rice, butter and 1 ½ cups of water in a pot and bring to a rapid boil. 2. Cover and let it simmer on low for 15 minutes. Fluff with a fork and reserve. 3. Press the "Sauté" button two times to select "Normal" settings and heat the oil. Once hot, cook the chicken breasts for 3 to 4 minutes. 4. Add the remaining ingredients, except for the cornstarch. 5. Put on the pressure cooker's lid and turn the steam valve to "Sealing" position. 6. Select Pressure Cook mode, and then press the "Pressure Cook" button again to select "Less" time option. 7. Use the "+/-" keys on the control panel to set the cooking time to 3 minutes. 8. Press the Pressure Level button to adjust the pressure to "Low Pressure." 9. Once the cooking cycle is completed, quickly and carefully turn the steam release handle from Sealing position to the Venting position. 10. When all the steam is released, remove the pressure lid from the top carefully. 11. Mix the cornstarch with 2 tablespoons of cold water. 12. Add the cornstarch slurry to the cooking liquid and stir at "Normal" cooking temperature on the "Sauté" mode until the sauce thickens. 13. Serve over hot jasmine rice. Bon appétit!
Per Serving: Calories 479; Fat 10g; Sodium 891mg; Carbs 22.9g; Fiber 4g; Sugar 4g; Protein 23g

Tilapia Fillets with Mushrooms

Prep time: 20 minutes | Cook time: 10 minutes | Serves: 3

3 tilapia fillets
½ teaspoons sea salt
Black pepper, to taste
1 teaspoon cayenne pepper
1 cup Cremini mushrooms, thinly sliced

½ cup yellow onions, sliced
2 cloves garlic, peeled and minced
2 sprigs thyme, leaves picked
2 sprigs rosemary, leaves picked
2 tablespoons avocado oil

1. Season the tilapia fillets with salt, black pepper, and cayenne pepper on all sides. 2. Place the tilapia fillets in the steaming basket fitted for your Inner Pot. 3. Place the sliced mushroom and yellow onions on top of the fillets. 4. Add the garlic, thyme, and rosemary; drizzle avocado oil over everything. 5. Add 1 ½ cups of water to the base of your Inner Pot. Add the steaming basket to the Inner Pot and Put on the pressure cooker's lid and turn the steam valve to "Sealing" position. 6. Select Pressure Cook mode, and then press the "Pressure Cook" button again to select "Less" time option. 7. Use the "+/-" keys on the control panel to set the cooking time to 8 minutes. 8. Press the Pressure Level button to adjust the pressure to "Low Pressure." 9. Once the cooking cycle is completed, quickly and carefully turn the steam release handle from Sealing position to the Venting position. 10. When all the steam is released, remove the pressure lid from the top carefully. 11. Serve immediately.
Per Serving: Calories 472; Fat 12.9g; Sodium 414mg; Carbs 11g; Fiber 5g; Sugar 9g; Protein 31g

Trout Salad

Prep time: 20 minutes | Cook time: 15 minutes | Serves: 4

2 tablespoons olive oil
1 yellow onion, chopped
2 garlic cloves, minced
1 green chili, seeded and minced
2 pieces' ocean trout fillets, deboned and skinless
1 cup water
½ cup dry vermouth

Sea salt and black pepper, to taste
½ teaspoons sweet paprika
2 ripe Roma tomatoes, diced
8-ounce dry egg noodles
2 Lebanese cucumbers, chopped
½ bunch coriander, leaves picked, roughly chopped
¼ cup lime juice

1. Press the "Sauté" button two times to select "Normal" settings 2. Now, heat the olive oil and sauté the onion until translucent. 3. Stir in the garlic and chili; continue to sauté until they are fragrant. 4. Add the fish, water, vermouth, salt, black pepper, sweet paprika, tomatoes, and noodles. 5. Put on the pressure cooker's lid and turn the steam valve to "Sealing" position. 6. Select Pressure Cook mode, and then press the "Pressure Cook" button again to select "Less" time option. 7. Use the "+/-" keys on the control panel to set the cooking time to 10 minutes. 8. Press the Pressure Level button to adjust the pressure to "Low Pressure." 9. Once the cooking cycle is completed, quickly and carefully turn the steam release handle from Sealing position to the Venting position. 10. When all the steam is released, remove the pressure lid from the top carefully. 11. Flake the fish and allow the mixture to cool completely. Add the cucumbers and coriander. 12. Drizzle fresh lime juice over the salad and serve. Bon appétit!
Per Serving: Calories 419; Fat 14g; Sodium 791mg; Carbs 8.9g; Fiber 4.6g; Sugar 8g; Protein 31g

Risotto with Sea Bass

Prep time: 15 minutes | Cook time: 8 minutes | Serves: 4

2 tablespoons butter, melted
½ cup leeks, sliced
2 garlic cloves, minced
2 cups basmati rice
1½-pound sea bass fillets, diced

2 cups vegetable broth
1 cup water
Salt, to taste
½ teaspoon black pepper
1 teaspoon fresh ginger, grated

1. Press the "Sauté" button two times to select "Normal" settings. 2. Then, melt the butter and sweat the leeks for 2 to 3 minutes. 3. Stir in the garlic; continue to sauté an additional 40 seconds. Add the remaining ingredients. 4. Put on the pressure cooker's lid and turn the steam valve to "Sealing" position. 5. Select Pressure Cook mode, and then press the "Pressure Cook" button again to select "Less" time option. 6. Use the "+/-" keys on the control panel to set the cooking time to 4 minutes. 7. Press the Pressure Level button to adjust the pressure to "Low Pressure." 8. Once the cooking cycle is completed, quickly and carefully turn the steam release handle from Sealing position to the Venting position. 9. When all the steam is released, remove the pressure lid from the top carefully. 10. Serve warm in individual bowls and enjoy!
Per Serving: Calories 449; Fat 2.9g; Sodium 511mg; Carbs 12g; Fiber 3g; Sugar 8g; Protein 27g

Chunky Tilapia Stew

Prep time: 20 minutes | Cook time: 10 minutes | Serves: 2

2 tablespoons sesame oil
1 cup scallions, chopped
2 garlic cloves, minced
⅓ cup dry vermouth
1 cup shellfish stock
2 cups water
2 ripe plum tomatoes, crushed
Sea salt, to taste
¼ teaspoon black pepper, or more

to taste
1 teaspoon hot paprika
1-pound tilapia fillets, boneless, skinless and diced
1 tablespoon fresh lime juice
1 teaspoon dried rosemary
½ teaspoons dried oregano
½ teaspoons dried basil

1. Press the "Sauté" button two times to select "Normal" settings. 2. Heat the oil and sauté the scallions and garlic until fragrant. 3. Add a splash of vermouth to deglaze the bottom of the Inner Pot. 4. Put on the pressure cooker's lid and turn the steam valve to "Sealing" position. 5. Select Pressure Cook mode, and then press the "Pressure Cook" button again to select "Less" time option. 6. Use the "+/-" keys on the control panel to set the cooking time to 5 minutes. 7. Press the Pressure Level button to adjust the pressure to "High Pressure." 8. Once the cooking cycle is completed, quickly and carefully turn the steam release handle from Sealing position to the Venting position. 9. When all the steam is released, remove the pressure lid from the top carefully. 10. Serve with some extra lime slices if desired. Bon appétit!
Per Serving: Calories 414; Fat 10.9g; Sodium 354mg; Carbs 10.5g; Fiber 4.1g; Sugar 8.2g; Protein 26g

Salmon Steaks with Kale Pesto Sauce

Prep time: 20 minutes | Cook time: 5 minutes | Serves: 4

1-pound salmon steaks
1 shallot, peeled and sliced
½ cup Kalamata olives
2 sprigs rosemary
2 tablespoons olive oil
½ teaspoons whole mixed peppercorns
Sea salt, to taste

Kale Pesto Sauce:
1 avocado
1 teaspoon garlic, crushed
2 tablespoons fresh parsley
1 cup kale
2 tablespoons fresh lemon juice
2 tablespoons olive oil

1. Prepare your Inner Pot by adding 1 ½ cups of water and a steamer basket to its bottom. 2. Place the salmon steaks in the steamer basket. 3. Add the shallots, olives, rosemary, olive oil, peppercorns, and salt. 4. Put on the pressure cooker's lid and turn the steam valve to "Sealing" position. 5. Press the "Steam" button two times to select "Less" option. 6. Use the "+/-" keys on the control panel to set the cooking time to 5 minutes. 7. Press the Pressure Level button to adjust the pressure to "High Pressure." 8. Once the cooking cycle is completed, quickly and carefully turn the steam release handle from Sealing position to the Venting position. 9. When all the steam is released, remove the pressure lid from the top carefully. 10. Add the avocado, garlic, parsley, kale, and lemon juice to your blender. 11. Then, mix on high until a loose paste forms. 12. Add the olive oil a little at a time and continue to blend. 13. Serve the fish fillets with the pesto on the side. Bon appétit!
Per Serving: Calories 424; Fat 7.9g; Sodium 704mg; Carbs 6g; Fiber 3.6g; Sugar 6g; Protein 18g

Haddock Fillets with Black Beans

Prep time: 20 minutes | Cook time: 5 minutes | Serves: 2

1 cup water
2 haddock fillets
2 teaspoons coconut butter, at room temperature
Salt and black pepper, to taste
2 sprigs thyme, chopped
¼ teaspoon caraway seeds

½ teaspoons tarragon
½ teaspoons paprika
4 tomato slices
2 tablespoons fresh cilantro, roughly chopped
1 can black beans, drained

1. Add 1 cup of water to the bottom of your Inner Pot. Add a steamer insert. 2. Brush the haddock fillets with coconut butter. Now, season the haddock fillets with salt and pepper. 3. Place the haddock fillets on top of the steamer insert. 4. Add thyme, caraway seeds, tarragon, and paprika. Place 2 tomato slices on top of each fillet. 5. Put on the pressure cooker's lid and turn the steam valve to "Sealing" position. 6. Select Pressure Cook mode, and then press the "Pressure Cook" button again to select "Less" time option. 7. Use the "+/-" keys on the control panel to set the cooking time to 3 minutes. 8. Press the Pressure Level button

to adjust the pressure to "Low Pressure." 9. Once the cooking cycle is completed, allow the steam to release naturally. 10. When all the steam is released, remove the pressure lid from the top carefully. 11. Transfer the haddock fillets to serving plates. 12. Scatter chopped cilantro over each fillet and serve garnished with black beans. Bon appétit!
Per Serving: Calories 412; Fat 20g; Sodium 491mg; Carbs 9g; Fiber 3g; Sugar 8g; Protein 31g

Prawn Dipping Sauce

Prep time: 15 minutes | Cook time: 3 minutes | Serves: 8

2 cups crabmeat, flaked
1 onion, chopped
2 cloves garlic, smashed
½ cup cream cheese, softened
½ cup mayonnaise
½ cup Parmesan cheese, grated

1½ tablespoons cornichon, finely chopped
¼ cup tomato paste
2 or so dashes of Tabasco
½ cup fresh breadcrumbs

1. Place all ingredients, except for the breadcrumbs, in a baking dish. 2. Stir until everything is well incorporated. 3. Top with breadcrumbs. 4. Put on the pressure cooker's lid and turn the steam valve to "Sealing" position. 5. Press the "Steam" button three times to select "Less" option. 6. Press the Pressure Level button to adjust the pressure to "Low Pressure." 7. Once the cooking cycle is completed, quickly and carefully turn the steam release handle from Sealing position to the Venting position. 8. When all the steam is released, remove the pressure lid from the top carefully. 9. Serve with raw vegetable sticks if desired. 10. Bon appétit!
Per Serving: Calories 449; Fat 2.9g; Sodium 511mg; Carbs 12g; Fiber 3g; Sugar 8g; Protein 27g

Baked Fish with Parmesan

Prep time: 20 minutes | Cook time: 9 minutes | Serves: 2

2 ripe tomatoes, sliced
1 teaspoon dried rosemary
1 teaspoon dried marjoram
½ teaspoons dried thyme
4 mahi-mahi fillets

2 tablespoons butter, at room temperature
Sea salt and black pepper, to taste
8 oz. Parmesan cheese, freshly grated

1. Add 1 ½ cups of water and a rack to your Inner Pot. 2. Spritz a casserole dish with a nonstick cooking spray. 3. Arrange the slices of tomatoes on the bottom of the dish. Add the herbs. 4. Place the mahi-mahi fillets on the top; drizzle the melted butter over the fish. 5. Season it with salt and black pepper. Place the baking dish on the rack. 6. Put on the pressure cooker's lid and turn the steam valve to "Sealing" position. 7. Select Pressure Cook mode, and then press the "Pressure Cook" button again to select "Less" time option. 8. Use the "+/-" keys on the control panel to set the cooking time to 9 minutes. 9. Press the Pressure Level button to adjust the pressure to "Low Pressure." 10. Once the cooking cycle is completed, quickly and carefully turn the steam release handle from Sealing position to the Venting position. 11. When all the steam is released, remove the pressure lid from the top carefully. 12. Top with parmesan and seal the lid again; allow the cheese to melt and serve.
Per Serving: Calories 489; Fat 11g; Sodium 501mg; Carbs 8.9g; Fiber 4.6g; Sugar 8g; Protein 26g

Butter Grouper

Prep time: 20 minutes | Cook time: 5 minutes | Serves: 4

4 grouper fillets
4 tablespoons butter
2 tablespoons fresh lemon juice
2 garlic cloves, smashed

½ teaspoons sweet paprika
½ teaspoons dried basil
Sea salt and black pepper, to taste

1. Add 1 ½ cups of water and steamer basket to the Inner Pot. 2. Then, place the fish fillets in the steamer basket. 3. Add the butter; drizzle with lemon juice; add the garlic, paprika, basil, salt, and black pepper. 4. Put on the pressure cooker's lid and turn the steam valve to "Sealing" position. 5. Select Pressure Cook mode, and then press the "Pressure Cook" button again to select "Less" time option. 6. Use the "+/-" keys on the control panel to set the cooking time to 4 minutes. 7. Press the Pressure Level button to adjust the pressure to "Low Pressure." 8. Once the cooking cycle is completed, quickly and carefully turn the steam release handle from Sealing position to the Venting position. 9. When all the steam is released, remove the pressure lid from the top carefully. 10. Serve immediately.
Per Serving: Calories 361; Fat 7.9g; Sodium 704mg; Carbs 6g; Fiber 3.6g; Sugar 6g; Protein 18g

Parmesan Cod with Basmati Rice

Prep time: 20 minutes | Cook time: 5 minutes | Serves: 4

2 cups basmati rice
2 cups water
1 ¼-pound cod, slice into small pieces
Salt and black pepper, to taste
1 teaspoon paprika
2 bay leaves
1 teaspoon coriander
1 teaspoon lemon thyme
2 tablespoons lemon juice
½ cup heavy cream
1 cup Parmesan cheese, freshly grated

1. Put on the pressure cooker's lid and turn the steam valve to "Sealing" position. 2. Select Pressure Cook mode, and then press the "Pressure Cook" button again to select "Less" time option. 3. Use the "+/-" keys on the control panel to set the cooking time to 4 minutes. 4. Press the Pressure Level button to adjust the pressure to "High Pressure." 5. Once the cooking cycle is completed, allow the steam to release naturally. 6. When all the steam is released, remove the pressure lid from the top carefully. 7. Press the Cancel button to stop this cooking program. 8. Press the "Sauté" button two times to select "Normal" settings. 9. Add the remaining ingredients and cook until the Parmesan has melted. 10. Serve the fish mixture over the hot basmati rice and enjoy!
Per Serving: Calories 521; Fat 7.9g; Sodium 704mg; Carbs 6g; Fiber 3.6g; Sugar 6g; Protein 18g

Red Snapper in Mushroom Sauce

Prep time: 20 minutes | Cook time: 6 minutes | Serves: 4

½ stick butter, at room temperature
2 shallots, peeled and chopped
2 garlic cloves, minced
1 cup brown mushrooms, thinly sliced
2 tablespoons coriander
1 (11-ounce) can tomatillo,
chopped
2 tablespoons tomato ketchup
1 cup chicken stock, preferably homemade
1-pound red snapper, cut into bite-sized chunks
Salt and black pepper, to taste

1. Press the "Sauté" button two times to select "Normal" settings. 2. Then, melt the butter. Once hot, cook the shallots with garlic until tender and aromatic. 3. Stir in the mushrooms; cook an additional 3 minutes or until they have softened. 4. Stir the remaining ingredients into your Inner Pot. 5. Put on the pressure cooker's lid and turn the steam valve to "Sealing" position. 6. Select Pressure Cook mode, and then press the "Pressure Cook" button again to select "Less" time option. 7. Use the "+/-" keys on the control panel to set the cooking time to 6 minutes. 8. Press the Pressure Level button to adjust the pressure to "High Pressure." 9. Once the cooking cycle is completed, quickly and carefully turn the steam release handle from Sealing position to the Venting position. 10. When all the steam is released, remove the pressure lid from the top carefully. 11. Serve over hot basmati rice if desired. Enjoy!
Per Serving: Calories 584; Fat 15g; Sodium 441mg; Carbs 17g; Fiber 4.6g; Sugar 5g; Protein 29g

Portuguese-Fish Medley

Prep time: 20 minutes | Cook time: 8 minutes | Serves: 4

1-pound fish, mixed pieces for fish soup, cut into bite-sized pieces
1 yellow onion, chopped
1 celery with leaves, chopped
2 carrots, chopped
2 cloves garlic, minced
1 green bell pepper, thinly sliced
2 tablespoons peanut oil
1 ½ cups seafood stock
⅓ cup dry vermouth
2 fresh tomatoes, puréed
1 tablespoon loosely packed saffron threads
Sea salt and black pepper, to taste
1 teaspoon Piri Piri
2 bay leaves
¼ cup fresh cilantro, roughly chopped
½ lemon, sliced

1. Simply throw all of the above ingredients, except for the cilantro and lemon, into your Inner Pot. 2. Put on the pressure cooker's lid and turn the steam valve to "Sealing" position. 3. Select Pressure Cook mode, and then press the "Pressure Cook" button again to select "Less" time option. 4. Use the "+/-" keys on the control panel to set the cooking time to 8 minutes. 5. Press the Pressure Level button to adjust the pressure to "Low Pressure." 6. Once the cooking cycle is completed, quickly and carefully turn the steam release handle from Sealing position to the Venting position. 7. When all the steam is released, remove the pressure lid from the top carefully. 8. Ladle the medley into individual bowls; serve with fresh cilantro and lemon.

Enjoy!
Per Serving: Calories 349; Fat 2.9g; Sodium 511mg; Carbs 12g; Fiber 3g; Sugar 8g; Protein 7g

Foil-Packet Fish with Aioli

Prep time: 20 minutes | Cook time: 15 minutes | Serves: 2

2 cod fish fillets
½ teaspoons seasoned salt
¼ teaspoon black pepper, or more to taste
For Aioli:
1 egg yolk
A pinch of salt
2 garlic cloves, minced
½ teaspoons mustard powder
½ teaspoons ancho chili powder
1 shallot, thinly sliced
1 lemon, cut into slices

2 teaspoons fresh lemon juice
¼ cup olive oil

1. Prepare your Inner Pot by adding 1 ½ cups of water and steamer basket to the Inner Pot. 2. Place a fish fillet in the center of each piece of foil. 3. Season with salt, pepper, mustard powder, and chili powder. 4. Top with shallots and wrap tightly. 5. Put on the pressure cooker's lid and turn the steam valve to "Sealing" position. 6. Select Pressure Cook mode, and then press the "Pressure Cook" button again to select "Less" time option. 7. Use the "+/-" keys on the control panel to set the cooking time to 10 minutes. 8. Press the Pressure Level button to adjust the pressure to "High Pressure." 9. Once the cooking cycle is completed, allow the steam to release naturally. 10. When all the steam is released, remove the pressure lid from the top carefully. 11. In your food processor, mix the egg, salt, garlic, and lemon juice. 12. With the machine running, gradually and slowly add the olive oil. 13. Garnish the warm fish fillets with lemon slices; serve with aioli on the side. Bon appétit!
Per Serving: Calories 584; Fat 15g; Sodium 441mg; Carbs 17g; Fiber 4.6g; Sugar 5g; Protein 29g

Codfish with Scallions

Prep time: 15 minutes | Cook time: 3 minutes | Serves: 3

1 lemon, sliced
½ cup water
3 fillets smoked codfish
3 teaspoons butter
3 tablespoons scallions, chopped
Sea salt and black pepper, to taste

1. Place the lemon and water in the bottom of the Inner Pot. Place the steamer rack on top. 2. Place the cod fish fillets on the steamer rack. Add the butter, scallions, salt, and black pepper. 3. Put on the pressure cooker's lid and turn the steam valve to "Sealing" position. 4. Press the "Steam" button one time to select "Less" option. 5. Press the Pressure Level button to adjust the pressure to "Low Pressure." 6. Once the cooking cycle is completed, quickly and carefully turn the steam release handle from Sealing position to the Venting position. 7. When all the steam is released, remove the pressure lid from the top carefully. 8. Serve warm and enjoy!
Per Serving: Calories 461; Fat 7.9g; Sodium 704mg; Carbs 6g; Fiber 3.6g; Sugar 6g; Protein 18g

Tuna Fillets with Onions

Prep time: 20 minutes | Cook time: 5 minutes | Serves: 2

1 cup water
A few sprigs of tarragon
1 lemon, sliced
1-pound tuna filets
1 tablespoon butter, melted
Sea salt and black pepper, to taste
1 large onion, sliced into rings

1. Put the water, herbs and lemon slices in the Inner Pot; now, place the steamer rack in the Inner Pot. 2. Lower the tuna fillets onto the rack. Add butter, salt, and pepper; top with onion slices. 3. Put on the pressure cooker's lid and turn the steam valve to "Sealing" position. 4. Press the "Steam" button two times to select "Less" option. 5. Press the Pressure Level button to adjust the pressure to "Low Pressure." 6. Once the cooking cycle is completed, quickly and carefully turn the steam release handle from Sealing position to the Venting position. 7. When all the steam is released, remove the pressure lid from the top carefully. 8. Serve immediately.
Per Serving: Calories 489; Fat 11g; Sodium 501mg; Carbs 8.9g; Fiber 4.6g; Sugar 8g; Protein 26g

Haddock Fillets with Steamed Green Beans

Prep time: 20 minutes | Cook time: 6 minutes | Serves: 4

1 lime, cut into wedges
½ cup water
4 haddock fillets
1 rosemary sprig
2 thyme sprigs

1 tablespoon fresh parsley
4 teaspoons ghee
Sea salt and black pepper, to taste
2 cloves garlic, minced
4 cups green beans

1. Place the lime wedges and water in the Inner Pot. Add a steamer rack. 2. Lower the haddock fillets onto the rack; place the rosemary, thyme, parsley, and ghee on the haddock fillets. 3. Season with salt and pepper. 4. Then, add the garlic and green beans to the Inner Pot. 5. Put on the pressure cooker's lid and turn the steam valve to "Sealing" position. 6. Press the "Steam" button one time to select "Less" option. 7. Use the "+/-" keys on the control panel to set the cooking time to 6 minutes. 8. Press the Pressure Level button to adjust the pressure to "Low Pressure." 9. Once the cooking cycle is completed, quickly and carefully turn the steam release handle from Sealing position to the Venting position. 10. When all the steam is released, remove the pressure lid from the top carefully. 11. Serve the haddock fillets with green beans on the side. 12. Bon appétit!
Per Serving: Calories 219; Fat 10g; Sodium 891mg; Carbs 22.9g; Fiber 4g; Sugar 4g; Protein 23g

Fish Tacos

Prep time: 15 minutes | Cook time: 7 minutes | Serves: 4

1 lemon, sliced
2 tablespoons olive oil
1-pound haddock fillets
½ teaspoons ground cumin
½ teaspoons onion powder
1 teaspoon garlic powder
½ teaspoons paprika
Sea salt and black pepper, to taste
1 teaspoon dried basil

1 tablespoon ancho chili powder
4 (6-inch) flour tortillas
4 tablespoons mayonnaise
4 tablespoons sour cream
2 tablespoons fresh cilantro, chopped
Add ½ cup of water, ½ of lemon slices, and a steamer rack to the bottom of the Inner Pot.

1. Press the "Sauté" button two times to select "Normal" settings and heat the olive oil until sizzling. 2. Now, sauté the haddock fillets for 1 to 2 minutes per side. 3. Season the fish fillets with all the spices and lower them onto the rack. 4. Put on the pressure cooker's lid and turn the steam valve to "Sealing" position. 5. Press the "Steam" button two times to select "Less" option. 6. Press the Pressure Level button to adjust the pressure to "Low Pressure." 7. Once the cooking cycle is completed, quickly and carefully turn the steam release handle from Sealing position to the Venting position. 8. When all the steam is released, remove the pressure lid from the top carefully. 9. Break the fish fillets into large bite-sized pieces and divide them between the tortillas. 10. Add the mayonnaise, sour cream and cilantro to each tortilla. 11. Garnish with the remaining lemon slices and enjoy!
Per Serving: Calories 397; Fat 7.9g; Sodium 704mg; Carbs 6g; Fiber 3.6g; Sugar 6g; Protein 18g

Prawns with Basmati Rice

Prep time: 20 minutes | Cook time: 5 minutes | Serves: 5

2 tablespoons olive oil
1 cup red onions, thinly sliced
2 cloves garlic, pressed
2 bell peppers, seeded and thinly sliced
1 serrano pepper, seeded and thinly sliced
2 cups basmati rice
1 (14-ounce) can tomatoes, diced
2½ cups vegetable stock

1 tablespoon tamari sauce
1 pound prawns, peeled and deveined
Sea salt and black pepper, to taste
½ teaspoons sweet paprika
1 teaspoon dried rosemary
½ teaspoons dried oregano
2 tablespoons fresh mint, roughly chopped

1. Press the "Sauté" button two times to select "Normal" settings. 2. Then, heat the oil and sauté the onions until tender and translucent. 3. Stir in the garlic; continue to sauté until aromatic. 4. Add the rest of the above ingredients, except for the mint, to the Inner Pot. 5. Put on the pressure cooker's lid and turn the steam valve to "Sealing" position. 6. Select Pressure Cook mode, and then press the "Pressure Cook" button again to select "Less" time option. 7. Use the "+/-" keys on the control panel to set the cooking time to 3 minutes. 8. Press the Pressure Level button to adjust the pressure to "Low Pressure." 9. Once the cooking cycle is completed, allow the steam to release naturally. 10. When all

the steam is released, remove the pressure lid from the top carefully. 11. Serve garnished with fresh mint leaves. Bon appétit!
Per Serving: Calories 382; Fat 10.9g; Sodium 454mg; Carbs 10g; Fiber 3.1g; Sugar 5.2g; Protein 20g

Cod Fish with Goat Cheese

Prep time: 20 minutes | Cook time: 5 minutes | Serves: 4

1-pound baby potatoes
2 tablespoons coconut oil, at room temperature
Sea salt and pepper, to taste
1½-pound cod fish fillets
½ teaspoons smoked paprika

2 tablespoons fresh Italian parsley, chopped
½ teaspoons fresh ginger, grated
2 cloves garlic, minced
1 cup goat cheese, crumbled

1. Place the potatoes in the bottom of the Inner Pot. 2. Add 1 cup of water; then, add coconut oil, salt and pepper. Place the rack over the potatoes. 3. Place the cod fish fillets on the rack. Season the fillets with paprika and parsley. 4. Put on the pressure cooker's lid and turn the steam valve to "Sealing" position. 5. Press the "Steam" button two times to select "Less" option. 6. Press the Pressure Level button to adjust the pressure to "Low Pressure." 7. Once the cooking cycle is completed, quickly and carefully turn the steam release handle from Sealing position to the Venting position. 8. When all the steam is released, remove the pressure lid from the top carefully. 9. Continue to cook the potatoes until fork tender; add the ginger and garlic and cook for 2 minutes more. 10. Top with goat cheese and serve. Bon appétit!
Per Serving: Calories 449; Fat 2.9g; Sodium 511mg; Carbs 12g; Fiber 3g; Sugar 8g; Protein 27g

Crab Dip

Prep time: 15 minutes | Cook time: 5 minutes | Serves: 10

1-pound lump crab meat
6-ounce Cottage cheese, at room temperature
½ cup Romano cheese, shredded
1 cup sour cream
Kosher salt and black pepper, to

taste
1 teaspoon smoked paprika
1½ cups Cheddar cheese, shredded
¼ cup fresh chives, chopped
2 tablespoons fresh lime juice

1. Place 1 cup of water and a metal Steam Rack in the Inner Pot. 2. Spritz a casserole dish with nonstick cooking spray. 3. Place the crab meat, Cottage cheese, Romano cheese and sour cream in the casserole dish. 4. Season with salt, black pepper, and smoked paprika. 5. Top with the Cheddar cheese. Lower the dish onto the Steam Rack. 6. Put on the pressure cooker's lid and turn the steam valve to "Sealing" position. 7. Press the "Steam" button two times to select "Less" option. 8. Press the Pressure Level button to adjust the pressure to "Low Pressure." 9. Once the cooking cycle is completed, allow the steam to release naturally. 10. When all the steam is released, remove the pressure lid from the top carefully. 11. Scatter the chopped chives over the top and add a few drizzles of lime juice. 12. Serve warm or at room temperature. Enjoy!
Per Serving: Calories 584; Fat 15g; Sodium 441mg; Carbs 17g; Fiber 4.6g; Sugar 5g; Protein 29g

Greek-Shrimp with Feta Cheese

Prep time: 20 minutes | Cook time: 2 minutes | Serves: 4

1 pound frozen shrimp
1½ tablespoons olive oil
2 gloves garlic, minced
1 teaspoon basil
½ teaspoons dry dill weed
1 teaspoon oregano
1 (26-ounce) canned diced

tomatoes
½ cup Kalamata olives
2-ounce feta cheese, crumbled
½ lemon, sliced
Chopped fresh mint leaves, for garnish

1. Add the shrimp, olive oil, garlic, basil, dill, oregano, and tomatoes to the Inner Pot. 2. Put on the pressure cooker's lid and turn the steam valve to "Sealing" position. 3. Select Pressure Cook mode, and then press the "Pressure Cook" button again to select "Less" time option. 4. Use the "+/-" keys on the control panel to set the cooking time to 2 minutes. 5. Press the Pressure Level button to adjust the pressure to "Low Pressure." 6. Once the cooking cycle is completed, allow the steam to release naturally. 7. When all the steam is released, remove the pressure lid from the top carefully. 8. Top with Kalamata olives and feta cheese. Serve garnished with lemon and mint leaves. 9. Enjoy!
Per Serving: Calories 419; Fat 14g; Sodium 791mg; Carbs 8.9g; Fiber 4.6g; Sugar 8g; Protein 31g

Creole Gumbo

Prep time: 15 minutes | Cook time: 10 minutes | Serves: 4

2 tablespoons butter, melted
1 shallot, diced
1 sweet pepper, sliced
1 jalapeno pepper, sliced
1-pound tuna, cut into 2-inch chunks
1 tablespoon Creole seasoning
2 carrots, sliced
2 celery stalks, diced

2 ripe tomatoes, pureed
¼ cup ketchup
1 bay leaf
1 cup beef broth
2 tablespoons Worcestershire sauce
1-pound raw shrimp, deveined
1 teaspoon filé powder
Sea salt and black pepper, to taste

1. Press the "Sauté" button two times to select "Normal" settings and melt the butter. 2. Once hot, cook the shallot and peppers for about 3 minutes until just tender and fragrant. 3. Add the remaining ingredients; gently stir to combine. 4. Put on the pressure cooker's lid and turn the steam valve to "Sealing" position. 5. Select Pressure Cook mode, and then press the "Pressure Cook" button again to select "Less" time option. 6. Use the "+/-" keys on the control panel to set the cooking time to 5 minutes. 7. Press the Pressure Level button to adjust the pressure to "High Pressure." 8. Once the cooking cycle is completed, quickly and carefully turn the steam release handle from Sealing position to the Venting position. 9. When all the steam is released, remove the pressure lid from the top carefully. 10. Serve in individual bowls and enjoy!
Per Serving: Calories 489; Fat 11g; Sodium 501mg; Carbs 8.9g; Fiber 4.6g; Sugar 8g; Protein 26g

Southern California Cioppino

Prep time: 15 minutes | Cook time: 30 minutes | Serves: 6

2 tablespoons coconut oil
1 onion, diced
4 garlic cloves, minced
2 celery stalks, diced
2 carrots, diced
1 sweet pepper, diced
2 (14-ounce) cans of tomatoes, crushed
1 cup clam juice
1 teaspoon oyster sauce
½ teaspoons dried parsley flakes
1 teaspoon dried rosemary

1 teaspoon dried basil
1 teaspoon paprika
1 bay leaf
Sea salt and black pepper, to taste
1-pound halibut steaks, cubed
½-pound sea scallops, rinsed and drained
1-pound shrimp, peeled and deveined
½-pound crab legs
¼ cup dry white wine

1. Press the "Sauté" button two times to select "Normal" settings to heat the coconut oil. 2. Once hot, sauté the onion, garlic, celery, carrots, and pepper for about 3 minutes or until they are just tender. 3. Add the canned tomatoes, clam juice, oyster sauce, parsley, rosemary, basil, paprika, bay leaf, salt, and black pepper to the Inner Pot. 4. Put on the pressure cooker's lid and turn the steam valve to "Sealing" position. 5. Press the "Soup/Broth" button one time to select "Normal" option. 6. Use the "+/-" keys on the control panel to set the cooking time to 30 minutes. 7. Press the Pressure Level button to adjust the pressure to "High Pressure." 8. Once the cooking cycle is completed, allow the steam to release naturally. 9. When all the steam is released, remove the pressure lid from the top carefully. 10. Add the seafood and wine. 11. Choose the "Steam" mode and cook for 3 minutes at Low Pressure. 12. Once cooking is complete, use a quick pressure release; carefully remove the lid. 13. Serve in individual bowls and enjoy!
Per Serving: Calories 412; Fat 20g; Sodium 491mg; Carbs 9g; Fiber 3g; Sugar 8g; Protein 31g

Indian Kulambu

Prep time: 20 minutes | Cook time: 2 minutes | Serves: 4

2 tablespoons butter
6 curry leaves
1 onion, chopped
2 cloves garlic, crushed
1 (1-inch) piece fresh ginger, grated
1 dried Kashmiri chili, minced
1 cup canned tomatoes, crushed

½ teaspoons turmeric powder
1 teaspoon ground coriander
½ teaspoons ground cumin
Kosher salt and black pepper, to taste
½ (14-ounce) can coconut milk
1-pound salmon fillets
1 tablespoon lemon juice

1. Press the "Sauté" button two times to select "Normal" settings and melt the butter. 2. Once hot, cook the curry leaves for about 30 seconds. 3. Stir in the onions, garlic, ginger and Kashmiri chili

and cook for 2 minutes more or until they are fragrant. 4. Add the tomatoes, turmeric, coriander, cumin, salt, and black pepper. 5. Continue to sauté for 30 seconds more. Add the coconut milk and salmon. 6. Press the Cancel button to stop this cooking program. 7. Put on the pressure cooker's lid and turn the steam valve to "Sealing" position. 8. Select Pressure Cook mode, and then press the "Pressure Cook" button again to select "Less" time option. 9. Use the "+/-" keys on the control panel to set the cooking time to 2 minutes. 10. Press the Pressure Level button to adjust the pressure to "Low Pressure." 11. Once the cooking cycle is completed, quickly and carefully turn the steam release handle from Sealing position to the Venting position. 12. When all the steam is released, remove the pressure lid from the top carefully. 13. Spoon the fish curry into individual bowls. 14. Drizzle lemon juice over the fish curry and serve. 15. Enjoy!
Per Serving: Calories 479; Fat 10g; Sodium 891mg; Carbs 22.9g; Fiber 4g; Sugar 4g; Protein 23g

Mahi-Mahi Fish with Guacamole

Prep time: 15 minutes | Cook time: 5 minutes | Serves: 4

1 cup water
4 mahi-mahi fillets
2 tablespoons olive oil
Sea salt and black pepper, to taste
½ teaspoons red pepper flakes, crushed
For Cumin Guacamole:
2 medium tomatoes, chopped
1 large avocado, peeled, pitted and mashed
2 tablespoons salsa Verde

½ cup shallots, sliced
2 tablespoons fresh lemon juice
1 teaspoon epazote
¼ cup fresh coriander, chopped
1 teaspoon dried sage

1 clove garlic, minced
Fresh juice of 1 lime
Sea salt to taste

1. Pour 1 cup of water to the base of your Inner Pot. 2. Brush the mahi-mahi fillets with olive oil; then, sprinkle with salt, black pepper, and red pepper flakes. 3. Place the mahi-mahi fillets in the steaming basket; transfer it to the Inner Pot. 4. Add the shallots on top; add the lemon juice, epazote, coriander, and sage. 5. Put on the pressure cooker's lid and turn the steam valve to "Sealing" position. 6. Select Pressure Cook mode, and then press the "Pressure Cook" button again to select "Less" time option. 7. Use the "+/-" keys on the control panel to set the cooking time to 3 minutes. 8. Press the Pressure Level button to adjust the pressure to "Low Pressure." 9. Once the cooking cycle is completed, quickly and carefully turn the steam release handle from Sealing position to the Venting position. 10. When all the steam is released, remove the pressure lid from the top carefully. 11. Next, mix all ingredients for the cumin guacamole; place in your refrigerator for at least 20 minutes. 12. Serve the mahi-mahi fillets with fresh cumin guacamole on the side. 13. Bon appétit!
Per Serving: Calories 478; Fat 7.9g; Sodium 704mg; Carbs 6g; Fiber 3.6g; Sugar 6g; Protein 18g

Sausage and Prawn Boil

Prep time: 15 minutes | Cook time: 10 minutes | Serves: 4

½-pound beef sausage, sliced
4 baby potatoes
1 cup fume (fish stock)
¼ cup butter
2 cloves garlic, minced

1 teaspoon Old Bay seasoning
¼ teaspoon Tabasco sauce
Sea salt and white pepper, to taste
1 pound prawns
1 fresh lemon, juiced

1. Place the sausage and potatoes in the Inner Pot; cover with the fish stock. 2. Put on the pressure cooker's lid and turn the steam valve to "Sealing" position. 3. Select Pressure Cook mode, and then press the "Pressure Cook" button again to select "Less" time option. 4. Use the "+/-" keys on the control panel to set the cooking time to 5 minutes. 5. Press the Pressure Level button to adjust the pressure to "High Pressure." 6. Once the cooking cycle is completed, allow the steam to release naturally. 7. When all the steam is released, remove the pressure lid from the top carefully. 8. Reserve. Clean the Inner Pot. 9. Press the "Sauté" button two times to select "Normal" settings and melt the butter. 10. Once hot, sauté the minced garlic until aromatic or about 1 minute. 11. Stir in the Old Bay seasoning, Tabasco, salt, and white pepper. Lastly, stir in the prawns. 12. Continue to simmer for 1 to 2 minutes or until the shrimp turn pink. 13. Press the "Cancel" button. 14. Add the sausages and potatoes, drizzle lemon juice over the top and serve warm.
Per Serving: Calories 422; Fat 12.9g; Sodium 414mg; Carbs 11g; Fiber 5g; Sugar 9g; Protein 31g

Fish and Vegetables

Prep time: 15 minutes | Cook time: 10 minutes | Serves: 4

12-ounce halibut steaks, cut into four pieces	Sea salt and black pepper, to taste
1 red bell pepper, sliced	1 teaspoon dried rosemary
1 green bell pepper, sliced	1 teaspoon basil
1 onion, sliced	½ teaspoons oregano
2 garlic cloves, minced	½ teaspoons paprika
1 cup cherry tomatoes, halved	4 teaspoons olive oil

1. Place 1 cup of water and a metal Steam Rack in the bottom of the Inner Pot. 2. Place 4 large sheets of heavy-duty foil on a flat surface. 3. Divide the ingredients between sheets of foil. Add a splash of water. 4. Bring the ends of the foil together; fold in the sides to seal. Place the fish packets on the Steam Rack. 5. Put on the pressure cooker's lid and turn the steam valve to "Sealing" position. 6. Press the "Steam" button one time to select "Normal" option. 7. Press the Pressure Level button to adjust the pressure to "High Pressure." 8. Once the cooking cycle is completed, quickly and carefully turn the steam release handle from Sealing position to the Venting position. 9. When all the steam is released, remove the pressure lid from the top carefully. 10. Bon appétit!
Per Serving: Calories 472; Fat 10.9g; Sodium 354mg; Carbs 10.5g; Fiber 4.1g; Sugar 8.2g; Protein 26g

Spicy Thai Prawns

Prep time: 15 minutes | Cook time: 5 minutes | Serves: 4

2 tablespoons coconut oil	2 tablespoons lime juice
1 small white onion, chopped	1 tablespoon sugar
2 cloves garlic, minced	Kosher salt and white pepper, to your liking
1½-pound prawns, deveined	
½ teaspoons red chili flakes	½ teaspoons cayenne pepper
1 bell pepper, seeded and sliced	1 teaspoon fresh ginger, ground
1 cup coconut milk	2 tablespoons fresh cilantro, chopped
2 tablespoons fish sauce	

1. Press the "Sauté" button two times to select "Normal" settings and heat the coconut oil; once hot, sauté the onion and garlic until aromatic. 2. Add the prawns, red chili flakes, bell pepper, coconut milk, fish sauce, lime juice, sugar, salt, white pepper, cayenne pepper, and ginger. 3. Put on the pressure cooker's lid and turn the steam valve to "Sealing" position. 4. Select Pressure Cook mode, and then press the "Pressure Cook" button again to select "Less" time option. 5. Use the "+/-" keys on the control panel to set the cooking time to 3 minutes. 6. Press the Pressure Level button to adjust the pressure to "Low Pressure." 7. Once the cooking cycle is completed, quickly and carefully turn the steam release handle from Sealing position to the Venting position. 8. When all the steam is released, remove the pressure lid from the top carefully. 9. Divide between serving bowls and serve garnished with fresh cilantro. Enjoy!
Per Serving: Calories 390; Fat 10.9g; Sodium 454mg; Carbs 10g; Fiber 3.1g; Sugar 5.2g; Protein 20g

Tuna and Asparagus Casserole

Prep time: 15 minutes | Cook time: 9 minutes | Serves: 4

1-pound tuna fillets	1 teaspoon paprika
1-pound asparagus, trimmed	A pinch of fresh thyme
2 ripe tomatoes, pureed	1 tablespoon dry white wine
Sea salt and black pepper, to taste	1 cup Cheddar cheese, grated

1. Place the tuna fillets in a lightly greased baking dish. 2. Add the asparagus, tomatoes, salt, black pepper, paprika, thyme, and wine. 3. Place a steamer rack inside the Inner Pot; add ½ cup of water. 4. Cut 1 sheet of heavy-duty foil and brush with cooking spray. 5. Top with the cheese. Cover with foil and lower the baking dish onto the rack. 6. Put on the pressure cooker's lid and turn the steam valve to "Sealing" position. 7. Select Pressure Cook mode, and then press the "Pressure Cook" button again to select "Less" time option. 8. Use the "+/-" keys on the control panel to set the cooking time to 9 minutes. 9. Press the Pressure Level button to adjust the pressure to "Low Pressure." 10. Once the cooking cycle is completed, quickly and carefully turn the steam release handle from Sealing position to the Venting position. 11. When all the steam is released, remove the pressure lid from the top carefully. 12. Place the baking dish on a cooling rack for a couple of minutes before slicing and serving. 13. Bon appétit!
Per Serving: Calories 361; Fat 19g; Sodium 354mg; Carbs 15g; Fiber

5.1g; Sugar 8.2g; Protein 32g

Blue Crabs with Wine and Herbs

Prep time: 15 minutes | Cook time: 5 minutes | Serves: 4

2-pound frozen blue crab	2 sprigs rosemary
½ cup water	2 sprigs thyme
½ cup dry white wine	1 lemon, cut into wedges
Sea salt and black pepper, to taste	

1. Add the frozen crab legs, water, wine, salt, black pepper, rosemary, and thyme to the Inner Pot. 2. Put on the pressure cooker's lid and turn the steam valve to "Sealing" position. 3. Select Pressure Cook mode, and then press the "Pressure Cook" button again to select "Less" time option. 4. Use the "+/-" keys on the control panel to set the cooking time to 3 minutes. 5. Press the Pressure Level button to adjust the pressure to "High Pressure." 6. Once the cooking cycle is completed, quickly and carefully turn the steam release handle from Sealing position to the Venting position. 7. When all the steam is released, remove the pressure lid from the top carefully. 8. Serve warm, garnished with fresh lemon wedges. Bon appétit!
Per Serving: Calories 478; Fat 7.9g; Sodium 704mg; Carbs 6g; Fiber 3.6g; Sugar 6g; Protein 18g

Japanese Seafood Curry

Prep time: 15 minutes | Cook time: 5 minutes | Serves: 4

2 tablespoons butter, softened	½ pound shrimps, deveined
1 onion, chopped	2 tablespoons sesame oil
2 cloves garlic, minced	1 tablespoon garam masala
1 (1-inch) pieces fresh ginger, ground	1 teaspoon curry paste
1 red chili, deseeded and minced	1 (3-inch) kombu (dried kelp)
1 pound pollack, cut into large chunks	1 package Japanese curry roux
	2 tablespoons Shoyu sauce
	2 ripe tomatoes, pureed

1. Press the "Sauté" button two times to select "Normal" settings and melt the butter. 2. Cook the onion, garlic, ginger, and red chili until just tender and fragrant. 3. Add the pollack and shrimp and continue to sauté for a couple of minutes more. 4. Add the remaining ingredients. 5. Put on the pressure cooker's lid and turn the steam valve to "Sealing" position. 6. Select Pressure Cook mode, and then press the "Pressure Cook" button again to select "Less" time option. 7. Use the "+/-" keys on the control panel to set the cooking time to 5 minutes. 8. Press the Pressure Level button to adjust the pressure to "Low Pressure." 9. Once the cooking cycle is completed, quickly and carefully turn the steam release handle from Sealing position to the Venting position. 10. When all the steam is released, remove the pressure lid from the top carefully. 11. Serve your curry over hot steamed rice. Enjoy!
Per Serving: Calories 390; Fat 7.9g; Sodium 704mg; Carbs 6g; Fiber 3.6g; Sugar 6g; Protein 18g

Haddock Curry

Prep time: 15 minutes | Cook time: 4 minutes | Serves: 2

2 tablespoons peanut oil	1 teaspoon mustard seeds
1 onion, chopped	1 teaspoon turmeric powder
2 garlic cloves, minced	1 teaspoon ground cumin
1 (1-inch) piece fresh root ginger, peeled and grated	Sea salt and black pepper
2 long red chilies, deseeded and minced	1 can reduced fat coconut milk
	1 cup chicken stock
2 tablespoons tamarind paste	1-pound haddock

1. Press the "Sauté" button two times to select "Normal" settings and heat the peanut oil. 2. once hot, sauté the onion, garlic, ginger, and chilies until aromatic. 3. Add the remaining ingredients and gently stir to combine. 4. Put on the pressure cooker's lid and turn the steam valve to "Sealing" position. 5. Select Pressure Cook mode, and then press the "Pressure Cook" button again to select "Less" time option. 6. Use the "+/-" keys on the control panel to set the cooking time to 4 minutes. 7. Press the Pressure Level button to adjust the pressure to "Low Pressure." 8. Once the cooking cycle is completed, quickly and carefully turn the steam release handle from Sealing position to the Venting position. 9. When all the steam is released, remove the pressure lid from the top carefully. 10. Divide between serving bowls and serve warm. Enjoy!
Per Serving: Calories 584; Fat 15g; Sodium 441mg; Carbs 17g; Fiber 4.6g; Sugar 5g; Protein 29g

Spinach-Stuffed Salmon

Prep time: 15 minutes | Cook time: 5 minutes | Serves: 3

3 (6-ounce) salmon fillets
Kosher salt and black pepper, to taste
½ teaspoons cayenne pepper
½ teaspoons celery seed, crushed
½ teaspoons dried basil
½ teaspoons dried marjoram

½ cup sour cream
½ cup mozzarella, shredded
1 cup frozen spinach, defrosted
2 cloves garlic, minced
1 tablespoon olive oil
1 lemon, cut into wedges

1. Add 1 cup of water and a steamer rack to the bottom of your Inner Pot. 2. Sprinkle your salmon with all spices. In a mixing bowl, thoroughly combine sour cream, mozzarella, spinach, and garlic. 3. Cut a pocket in each fillet to within ½-inch of the opposite side. 4. Stuff the pockets with the spinach/cheese mixture. Drizzle with olive oil. 5. Wrap the salmon fillets in foil and lower onto the rack. 6. Put on the pressure cooker's lid and turn the steam valve to "Sealing" position. 7. Select Pressure Cook mode, and then press the "Pressure Cook" button again to select "Less" time option. 8. Use the "+/-" keys on the control panel to set the cooking time to 4 minutes. 9. Press the Pressure Level button to adjust the pressure to "Low Pressure." 10. Once the cooking cycle is completed, quickly and carefully turn the steam release handle from Sealing position to the Venting position. 11. When all the steam is released, remove the pressure lid from the top carefully. 12. Garnish with lemon wedges and serve warm.
Per Serving: Calories 489; Fat 11g; Sodium 501mg; Carbs 8.9g; Fiber 4.6g; Sugar 8g; Protein 26g

Orange Sea Bass

Prep time: 15 minutes | Cook time: 15 minutes | Serves: 4

1 tablespoon safflower oil
1-pound sea bass
Sea salt, to taste
¼ teaspoon white pepper
2 tablespoons tamari sauce

2 cloves garlic, minced
½ teaspoons dried dill weed
1 orange, juiced
1 tablespoon honey

1. Press the "Sauté" button two times to select "Normal" settings and heat the oil. 2. Now, cook the sea bass for 1 to 2 minutes per side. Season your fish with salt and pepper. 3. Add 1 cup of water and a steamer rack to the bottom of your Inner Pot. Lower the fish onto the rack. 4. Put on the pressure cooker's lid and turn the steam valve to "Sealing" position. 5. Press the "Steam" button three times to select "Normal" option. 6. Press the Pressure Level button to adjust the pressure to "Low Pressure." 7. Once the cooking cycle is completed, quickly and carefully turn the steam release handle from Sealing position to the Venting position. 8. When all the steam is released, remove the pressure lid from the top carefully. 9. Add the remaining ingredients to the cooking liquid and stir to combine well. 10. Press the "Sauté" button two times to select "Normal" settings again and let it simmer until the sauce thickens. 11. Spoon the sauce over the reserved fish. Bon appétit!
Per Serving: Calories 334; Fat 7.9g; Sodium 704mg; Carbs 6g; Fiber 3.6g; Sugar 6g; Protein 18g

Tilapia Fillets with Peppers

Prep time: 15 minutes | Cook time: 3 minutes | Serves: 4

1 lemon, sliced
4 (6-ounce) tilapia fillets, skin on
4 teaspoons olive oil
Sea salt and white pepper, to taste
1 tablespoon fresh parsley, chopped

1 tablespoon fresh tarragon, chopped
1 red onion, sliced into rings
2 sweet peppers, julienned
4 tablespoons dry white wine

1. Place the lemon slices, 1 cup of water, and a metal Steam Rack in the bottom of the Inner Pot. 2. Place 4 large sheets of heavy-duty foil on a flat surface. 3. Divide the ingredients between the sheets of foil. 4. Bring the ends of the foil together; fold in the sides to seal. Place the fish packets on the Steam Rack. 5. Put on the pressure cooker's lid and turn the steam valve to "Sealing" position. 6. Press the "Steam" button one time to select "Less" option. 7. Press the Pressure Level button to adjust the pressure to "Low Pressure." 8. Once the cooking cycle is completed, quickly and carefully turn the steam release handle from Sealing position to the Venting position. 9. When all the steam is released, remove the pressure lid from the top carefully. 10. Bon appétit!
Per Serving: Calories 479; Fat 10g; Sodium 891mg; Carbs 22.9g; Fiber 4g; Sugar 4g; Protein 23g

Mayo Shrimp Salad

Prep time: 15 minutes | Cook time: 2 minutes | Serves: 4

1-pound shrimp, deveined and peeled
Fresh juice of 2 lemons
Salt and black pepper, to taste
1 red onion, chopped

1 stalk celery, chopped
1 tablespoon fresh dill, minced
½ cup mayonnaise
1 teaspoon Dijon mustard

1. Prepare your Inner Pot by adding 1 cup of water and steamer basket to the Inner Pot. 2. Now, add the shrimp to the steamer basket. 3. Top with lemon slices. 4. Put on the pressure cooker's lid and turn the steam valve to "Sealing" position. 5. Select Pressure Cook mode, and then press the "Pressure Cook" button again to select "Less" time option. 6. Use the "+/-" keys on the control panel to set the cooking time to 2 minutes. 7. Press the Pressure Level button to adjust the pressure to "Low Pressure." 8. Once the cooking cycle is completed, quickly and carefully turn the steam release handle from Sealing position to the Venting position. 9. When all the steam is released, remove the pressure lid from the top carefully. 10. Add the remaining ingredients and toss to combine well. 11. Serve well chilled and enjoy!
Per Serving: Calories 489; Fat 11g; Sodium 501mg; Carbs 8.9g; Fiber 4.6g; Sugar 8g; Protein 26g

Steamed Tilapia with Spinach

Prep time: 15 minutes | Cook time: 12 minutes | Serves: 4

1 cup chicken broth
2 cloves garlic, sliced
1-pound tilapia, cut into 4 pieces
1 tablespoon Worcestershire sauce

Salt and black pepper, to taste
2 tablespoons butter, melted
2 cups fresh spinach

1. Place the chicken broth and garlic in the Inner Pot. Place the Steam Rack on top. 2. Place the tilapia fillets on a sheet of foil; add Worcestershire sauce, salt, pepper, and butter. 3. Bring up all sides of the foil to create a packet around your fish. 4. Put on the pressure cooker's lid and turn the steam valve to "Sealing" position. 5. Press the "Steam" button two times to select "Normal" option. 6. Press the Pressure Level button to adjust the pressure to "Low Pressure." 7. Once the cooking cycle is completed, quickly and carefully turn the steam release handle from Sealing position to the Venting position. 8. When all the steam is released, remove the pressure lid from the top carefully. 9. Add the spinach leaves to the cooking liquid. 10. Press the Cancel button to stop this cooking program. 11. Press the "Sauté" function and let it simmer at "Less" cooking temperature for 1 to 2 minutes or until wilted. 12. Place the fish fillets on top of the wilted spinach, adjust the seasonings, and serve immediately. 13. Bon appetit!
Per Serving: Calories 419; Fat 14g; Sodium 791mg; Carbs 8.9g; Fiber 4.6g; Sugar 8g; Protein 31g

Greek-Style Fish

Prep time: 15 minutes | Cook time: 3 minutes | Serves: 4

2 tablespoons olive oil
1½-pound cod fillets
1 pound tomatoes, chopped
Sea salt and black pepper, to taste
2 sprigs rosemary, chopped
2 sprigs thyme, chopped

1 bay leaf
2 cloves garlic, smashed
½ cup Greek olives, pitted and sliced

1. Place 1 cup of water and a metal Steam Rack in the bottom of the Inner Pot. 2. Brush the sides and bottom of a casserole dish with olive oil. 3. Place the cod fillets in the greased casserole dish. 4. Add the tomatoes, salt, pepper, rosemary, thyme, bay leaf, and garlic. 5. Lower the dish onto the Steam Rack. 6. Put on the pressure cooker's lid and turn the steam valve to "Sealing" position. 7. Press the "Steam" button one time to select "Less" option. 8. Press the Pressure Level button to adjust the pressure to "Low Pressure." 9. Once the cooking cycle is completed, quickly and carefully turn the steam release handle from Sealing position to the Venting position. 10. When all the steam is released, remove the pressure lid from the top carefully. 11. Serve garnished with Greek olives and enjoy!
Per Serving: Calories 478; Fat 7.9g; Sodium 704mg; Carbs 6g; Fiber 3.6g; Sugar 6g; Protein 18g

Halibut Steaks with Wild Rice

Prep time: 15 minutes | Cook time: 60 minutes | Serves: 6

1 cup wild rice, rinsed and drained	Sea salt and ground pepper, to
1 tablespoon butter	your liking
½ teaspoons salt flakes	4 tablespoons cream cheese
½ teaspoons red pepper flakes,	4 tablespoons mayonnaise
crushed	1 teaspoon stone-ground mustard
1½-pound halibut steaks	2 cloves garlic, minced
2 tablespoons olive oil	

1. In a saucepan, bring 3 cups of water and rice to a boil. 2. Reduce the heat to simmer; cover and let it simmer for 45 to 55 minutes. 3. Add the butter, salt, and red pepper; fluff with a fork. Cover and reserve, keeping your rice warm. 4. Cut 4 sheets of aluminum foil. Place the halibut steak in each sheet of foil. 5. Add the olive oil, salt, and black pepper to the top of the fish; close each packet and seal the edges. 6. Add 1 cup of water and a steamer rack to the bottom of your Inner Pot. Lower the packets onto the rack. 7. Put on the pressure cooker's lid and turn the steam valve to "Sealing" position. 8. Press the "Steam" button one time to select "Less" option. 9. Press the Pressure Level button to adjust the pressure to "Low Pressure." 10. Once the cooking cycle is completed, allow the steam to release naturally. 11. When all the steam is released, remove the pressure lid from the top carefully. 12. Meanwhile, mix the cream cheese, mayonnaise, stone-ground mustard, and garlic until well combined. 13. Serve the steamed fish with the mayo sauce and wild rice on the side. Bon appétit!

Per Serving: Calories 482; Fat 7.9g; Sodium 704mg; Carbs 6g; Fiber 3.6g; Sugar 6g; Protein 18g

Teriyaki Fish Steaks

Prep time: 15 minutes | Cook time: 10 minutes | Serves: 4

2 tablespoons butter, melted	⅓ cup soy sauce
4 (6-ounce) salmon steaks	½ cup water
2 cloves garlic, smashed	2 tablespoons brown sugar
1 (1-inch) piece fresh ginger,	2 teaspoons wine vinegar
peeled and grated	1 tablespoon cornstarch

1. Press the "Sauté" button two times to select "Normal" settings and then melt the butter. 2. Once hot, cook the salmon steaks for 2 minutes per side. 3. Add the garlic, ginger, soy sauce, water, sugar, and vinegar. 4. Put on the pressure cooker's lid and turn the steam valve to "Sealing" position. 5. Select Pressure Cook mode, and then press the "Pressure Cook" button again to select "Less" time option. 6. Use the "+/-" keys on the control panel to set the cooking time to 5 minutes. 7. Press the Pressure Level button to adjust the pressure to "Low Pressure." 8. Once the cooking cycle is completed, quickly and carefully turn the steam release handle from Sealing position to the Venting position. 9. When all the steam is released, remove the pressure lid from the top carefully. 10. Reserve the fish steaks. 11. Mix the cornstarch with 2 tablespoons of cold water. 12. Add the slurry to the cooking liquid. Let it simmer until the sauce thickens. 13. Spoon the sauce over the fish steaks. 14. Bon appétit!

Per Serving: Calories 385; Fat 12.9g; Sodium 414mg; Carbs 11g; Fiber 5g; Sugar 9g; Protein 31g

Tuna Steaks in Lime- Sauce

Prep time: 15 minutes | Cook time: 4 minutes | Serves: 3

3 tuna steaks	¼ teaspoon smoked paprika
1 ½ tablespoons sesame oil, melted	1 cup water
½ teaspoons salt	1 tablespoon fresh cilantro, chopped
¼ teaspoon black pepper, to taste	
For the Sauce:	
1 tablespoon butter, at room	1 tablespoon fresh lime juice
temperature	1 teaspoon Worcestershire sauce

1. Brush the tuna steaks with sesame oil. 2. Season the tuna steaks with salt, black pepper, and smoked paprika. 3. Place the fish in the steaming basket; transfer it to the Inner Pot. 4. Pour 1 cup of water into the base of your Inner Pot. 5. Put on the pressure cooker's lid and turn the steam valve to "Sealing" position. 6. Select Pressure Cook mode, and then press the "Pressure Cook" button again to select "Less" time option. 7. Use the "+/-" keys on the control panel to set the cooking time to 4 minutes. 8. Press the Pressure Level button to adjust the pressure to "Low Pressure." 9. Once the cooking cycle is completed, quickly and carefully turn the steam release handle from Sealing position to the Venting position. 10. When all the steam is released, remove the pressure lid from the top carefully. 11. Meanwhile, warm the butter over medium-low heat. 12. Add the lime juice and Worcestershire sauce; remove from the heat and stir. 13. Spoon the sauce over the tuna steaks, sprinkle with fresh cilantro leaves and serve. 14. Bon appétit!

Per Serving: Calories 471; Fat 10.9g; Sodium 454mg; Carbs 10g; Fiber 3.1g; Sugar 5.2g; Protein 20g

Shrimp Scampi with Carrots

Prep time: 15 minutes | Cook time: 6 minutes | Serves: 4

1 tablespoon olive oil	½ cup cream of celery soup
2 garlic cloves, sliced	Sea salt and freshly cracked black
1 bunch scallions, chopped	pepper, to taste
2 carrots, grated	1 teaspoon cayenne pepper
1½-pound shrimp, deveined and	½ teaspoon dried basil
rinsed	1 teaspoon dried rosemary
½ cup dry white wine see	½ teaspoons dried oregano

1. Press the "Sauté" button two times to select "Normal" settings and then heat the oil. 2. Once hot, cook the garlic, scallions, and carrots for 2 to 3 minutes. 3. Add a splash of wine to deglaze the Inner Pot. 4. Add the remaining ingredients. 5. Put on the pressure cooker's lid and turn the steam valve to "Sealing" position. 6. Press the "Pressure Cook" button three times to select "Less" option. 7. Use the "+/-" keys on the control panel to set the cooking time to 3 minutes. 8. Press the Pressure Level button to adjust the pressure to "Low Pressure." 9. Once the cooking cycle is completed, allow the steam to release naturally. 10. When all the steam is released, remove the pressure lid from the top carefully. 11. Divide between serving bowls and enjoy!

Per Serving: Calories 412; Fat 20g; Sodium 491mg; Carbs 9g; Fiber 3g; Sugar 8g; Protein 31g

Fish and Couscous Pilaf

Prep time: 15 minutes | Cook time: 10 minutes | Serves: 4

2 tablespoons butter	2 ripe tomatoes, pureed
1 yellow onion, chopped	1½-pound halibut, cut into chunks
2 cups couscous	1 teaspoon coriander
2 cups water	1 teaspoon curry paste
1 cup vegetable broth	1 teaspoon ancho chili powder
1 cup coconut milk	2 bay leaves
Sea salt and black pepper, to taste	4 cardamom pods
1 teaspoon cayenne pepper	1 teaspoon garam masala
1 teaspoon dried basil	2 tablespoons almonds, slivered

1. Press the "Sauté" button two times to select "Normal" settings and melt the butter. 2. Once hot, cook the onions until tender and translucent. 3. Add the remaining ingredients, except for the slivered almonds, to the Inner Pot; stir to combine. 4. Put on the pressure cooker's lid and turn the steam valve to "Sealing" position. 5. Select Pressure Cook mode, and then press the "Pressure Cook" button again to select "Less" time option. 6. Use the "+/-" keys on the control panel to set the cooking time to 4 minutes. 7. Press the Pressure Level button to adjust the pressure to "High Pressure." 8. Once the cooking cycle is completed, quickly and carefully turn the steam release handle from Sealing position to the Venting position. 9. When all the steam is released, remove the pressure lid from the top carefully. 10. Serve garnished with almonds. 11. Bon appétit!

Per Serving: Calories 382; Fat 7.9g; Sodium 704mg; Carbs 6g; Fiber 3.6g; Sugar 6g; Protein 18g

French Fish En Papillote

Prep time: 15 minutes | Cook time: 3 minutes | Serves: 4

2 tablespoons olive oil	Sea salt and white pepper, to taste
4 (7-ounce) rainbow trout fillets	½-pound sugar snap peas, trimmed
1 tablespoon fresh chives, chopped	2 tomatillos, sliced
1 tablespoon fresh parsley, chopped	2 garlic cloves, minced

1. Place 1 cup of water and a metal rack in your Inner Pot. 2. Place all ingredients in a large sheet of foil. Fold up the sides of the foil to make a bowl-like shape. 3. Lower the fish packet onto the rack. 4. Put on the pressure cooker's lid and turn the steam valve to "Sealing" position. 5. Press the "Steam" button one time to select "Less" option. 6. Press the Pressure Level button to adjust the pressure to "Low Pressure." 7. Once the cooking cycle is completed, quickly and carefully turn the steam release handle from Sealing position to the Venting position. 8. When all the steam is released, remove the pressure lid from the top carefully. 9. Bon appetit!

Per Serving: Calories 584; Fat 15g; Sodium 441mg; Carbs 17g; Fiber 4.6g; Sugar 5g; Protein 29g

Crabs with Garlic Sauce

Prep time: 15 minutes | Cook time: 6 minutes | Serves: 5

1½-pound crabs
1 stick butter
2 cloves garlic, minced

1 teaspoon Old Bay seasoning
1 lemon, sliced

1. Place 1 cup water and a metal Steam Rack in the bottom of your Inner Pot. 2. Lower the crabs onto the Steam Rack. 3. Put on the pressure cooker's lid and turn the steam valve to "Sealing" position. 4. Press the "Steam" button two times to select "Less" option. 5. Press the Pressure Level button to adjust the pressure to "Low Pressure." 6. Once the cooking cycle is completed, quickly and carefully turn the steam release handle from Sealing position to the Venting position. 7. When all the steam is released, remove the pressure lid from the top carefully. 8. Empty the pot and keep the crab aside. 9. Press the "Sauté" button two times to select "Normal" settings and then melt butter. 10. Once hot, sauté the garlic and Old Bay seasoning for 2 to 3 minutes. 11. Add the cooked crabs and gently stir to combine. 12. Serve with lemon slices. 13. Bon appétit!
Per Serving: Calories 489; Fat 11g; Sodium 501mg; Carbs 8.9g; Fiber 4.6g; Sugar 8g; Protein 26g

Seafood Quiche with Colby Cheese

Prep time: 15 minutes | Cook time: 10 minutes | Serves: 4

6 eggs
½ cup cream cheese
½ cup Greek-style yogurt
Himalayan salt and black pepper, to taste
1 teaspoon cayenne pepper

1 teaspoon dried basil
1 teaspoon dried oregano
1-pound crab meat, chopped
½-pound raw shrimp, chopped
1 cup Colby cheese, shredded

1. In a mixing bowl, whisk the eggs with the cream cheese and yogurt. 2. Season with salt, black pepper, cayenne pepper, basil, and oregano. 3. Stir in the seafood; stir to combine and spoon the mixture into a lightly greased baking pan. 4. Lastly, top with the shredded cheese. 5. Cover with a piece of aluminum foil. 6. Put on the pressure cooker's lid and turn the steam valve to "Sealing" position. 7. Press the "Steam" button one time to select "Normal" option. 8. Press the Pressure Level button to adjust the pressure to "Low Pressure." 9. Once the cooking cycle is completed, quickly and carefully turn the steam release handle from Sealing position to the Venting position. 10. When all the steam is released, remove the pressure lid from the top carefully. 11. Bon appétit!
Per Serving: Calories 521; Fat 7.9g; Sodium 704mg; Carbs 6g; Fiber 3.6g; Sugar 6g; Protein 18g

Butter dipped Lobster Tails

Prep time: 15 minutes | Cook time: 3 minutes | Serves: 4

1½-pound lobster tails, halved
½ stick butter, at room temperature

Sea salt and black pepper, to taste
½ teaspoon red pepper flakes

1. Add a metal Steam Rack, steamer basket, and 1 cup of water in your Inner Pot. 2. Place the lobster tails, shell side down, in the prepared steamer basket. 3. Put on the pressure cooker's lid and turn the steam valve to "Sealing" position. 4. Press the "Steam" button one time to select "Less" option. 5. Press the Pressure Level button to adjust the pressure to "Low Pressure." 6. Once the cooking cycle is completed, quickly and carefully turn the steam release handle from Sealing position to the Venting position. 7. When all the steam is released, remove the pressure lid from the top carefully. 8. Empty the pot and keep the crab aside. 9. Drizzle with butter. Season with salt, black pepper, and red pepper and serve immediately. 10. Enjoy!
Per Serving: Calories 397; Fat 12.9g; Sodium 414mg; Carbs 11g; Fiber 5g; Sugar 9g; Protein 31g

Saucy Red Snapper

Prep time: 15 minutes | Cook time: 5 minutes | Serves: 4

1 tablespoon ghee, at room temperature
1 medium-sized leek, chopped
4 cloves garlic, minced
1 tablespoon capers
2 medium ripe tomatoes, chopped
1 cup chicken broth

1 red chili pepper, seeded and chopped
1 teaspoon basil
½ teaspoons oregano
½ teaspoons rosemary
3 (6-ounce) red snapper fillets
Coarse sea salt and black pepper,

to taste
1 teaspoon Fish taco seasoning

mix
1 lemon, cut into wedges

1. Press the "Sauté" button two times to select "Normal" settings and melt the ghee. 2. Once hot, sauté the leek and garlic until tender. 3. Add the remaining ingredients, except for the lemon wedges, to the Inner Pot. 4. Put on the pressure cooker's lid and turn the steam valve to "Sealing" position. 5. Select Pressure Cook mode, and then press the "Pressure Cook" button again to select "Less" time option. 6. Use the "+/-" keys on the control panel to set the cooking time to 4 minutes. 7. Press the Pressure Level button to adjust the pressure to "High Pressure." 8. Once the cooking cycle is completed, quickly and carefully turn the steam release handle from Sealing position to the Venting position. 9. When all the steam is released, remove the pressure lid from the top carefully. 10. Serve in individual bowls, garnished with lemon wedges. Enjoy!
Per Serving: Calories 472; Fat 7.9g; Sodium 704mg; Carbs 6g; Fiber 3.6g; Sugar 6g; Protein 18g

Shrimp Salad

Prep time: 15 minutes | Cook time: 3 minutes | Serves: 4

1-pound shrimp, deveined
Kosher salt and white pepper, to taste
1 onion, thinly sliced
1 sweet pepper, thinly sliced
1 jalapeno pepper, deseeded and minced

2 heaping tablespoons fresh parsley, chopped
1 head romaine lettuce, torn into pieces
4 tablespoons olive oil
1 lime, juiced and zested
1 tablespoon Dijon mustard

1. Add a metal Steam Rack and 1 cup of water to your Inner Pot. 2. Put the shrimp into the steamer basket. Lower the steamer basket onto the Steam Rack. 3. Put on the pressure cooker's lid and turn the steam valve to "Sealing" position. 4. Press the "Steam" button one time to select "Less" option. 5. Press the Pressure Level button to adjust the pressure to "Low Pressure." 6. Once the cooking cycle is completed, quickly and carefully turn the steam release handle from Sealing position to the Venting position. 7. When all the steam is released, remove the pressure lid from the top carefully. 8. Transfer steamed shrimp to a salad bowl; toss your shrimp with the remaining ingredients. 9. Serve well chilled. Bon appétit!
Per Serving: Calories 461; Fat 7.9g; Sodium 704mg; Carbs 6g; Fiber 3.6g; Sugar 6g; Protein 18g

Halibut Steaks with Tomatoes

Prep time: 15 minutes | Cook time: 5 minutes | Serves: 4

2 tablespoons Worcestershire sauce
2 tablespoons oyster sauce
½ cup dry white wine
1 tablespoon Dijon mustard
1 (1-inch) piece fresh ginger, grated

4 halibut steaks
2 teaspoons olive oil
2 tomatoes, sliced
2 spring onions, sliced
2 garlic cloves, crushed
1 cup mixed salad greens, to serve

1. In a mixing bowl, whisk Worcestershire sauce, oyster sauce, white wine, mustard, and ginger. 2. Add the fish steaks and let them marinate for 30 minutes in your refrigerator. 3. Meanwhile, Press the "Sauté" button two times to select "Normal" settings on your Inner Pot. 4. Now, heat the olive oil and sauté the tomatoes with the spring onions and garlic until they are tender. 5. Add 2 cups of water to the base of your Inner Pot. Add the metal steamer insert to the Inner Pot. 6. Now, place the halibut steaks on top of the steamer insert. 7. Put on the pressure cooker's lid and turn the steam valve to "Sealing" position. 8. Select Pressure Cook mode, and then press the "Pressure Cook" button again to select "Less" time option. 9. Use the "+/-" keys on the control panel to set the cooking time to 5 minutes. 10. Press the Pressure Level button to adjust the pressure to "Low Pressure." 11. Once the cooking cycle is completed, quickly and carefully turn the steam release handle from Sealing position to the Venting position. 12. When all the steam is released, remove the pressure lid from the top carefully. 13. Serve the warm halibut steaks with the sautéed vegetables and mixed salad greens. 14. Enjoy!
Per Serving: Calories 334; Fat 7.9g; Sodium 704mg; Carbs 6g; Fiber 3.6g; Sugar 6g; Protein 18g

Fish Paprikash

Prep time: 15 minutes | Cook time: 7 minutes | Serves: 4

2 tablespoons butter, at room temperature	Sea salt and black pepper, to taste
1 cup leeks, chopped	2 tomatoes, puréed
2 bell peppers, seeded and sliced	2 cups vegetable broth
2 garlic cloves, minced	2 cups water
2 sprigs thyme	1½-pound cod fish, cut into bite-sized chunks
1 sprig rosemary	2 tablespoons fresh cilantro, roughly chopped
1 teaspoon sweet paprika	1 cup sour cream, well-chilled
1 teaspoon hot paprika	

1. Press the "Sauté" button two times to select "Normal" settings. 2. Melt the butter and sauté the leeks until fragrant. 3. Then, stir in the peppers and garlic and continue to sauté an additional 40 seconds. 4. Add the thyme, rosemary, paprika, salt, black pepper, tomatoes, broth, water, and fish. 5. Put on the pressure cooker's lid and turn the steam valve to "Sealing" position. 6. Select Pressure Cook mode, and then press the "Pressure Cook" button again to select "Less" time option. 7. Use the "+/-" keys on the control panel to set the cooking time to 6 minutes. 8. Press the Pressure Level button to adjust the pressure to "High Pressure." 9. Once the cooking cycle is completed, quickly and carefully turn the steam release handle from Sealing position to the Venting position. 10. When all the steam is released, remove the pressure lid from the top carefully. 11. Ladle into individual bowls and serve garnished with fresh cilantro and well-chilled sour cream. 12. Bon appétit!

Per Serving: Calories 472; Fat 12.9g; Sodium 414mg; Carbs 11g; Fiber 5g; Sugar 9g; Protein 31g

Fish Mélange

Prep time: 15 minutes | Cook time: 10 minutes | Serves: 4

1 tablespoon olive oil	Sea salt, to taste
2 shallots, diced	½ teaspoons black pepper
2 garlic cloves, smashed	2 bay leaves
2 carrots, diced	1 tablespoon Creole seasoning
2 (6-ounce) cans crab, juice reserved	2 cups water
½-pound cod, cut into bite-sized chunks	1 cup double cream
	1 tablespoon lemon juice

1. Press the "Sauté" button two times to select "Normal" settings. 2. Then, heat the oil and sauté the shallots until tender. 3. Stir in the garlic and carrots; cook an additional minute or so. 4. Add the canned crab meat, cod, salt, black pepper, bay leaves, Creole seasoning, and water. 5. Put on the pressure cooker's lid and turn the steam valve to "Sealing" position. 6. Select Pressure Cook mode, and then press the "Pressure Cook" button again to select "Less" time option. 7. Use the "+/-" keys on the control panel to set the cooking time to 6 minutes. 8. Press the Pressure Level button to adjust the pressure to "High Pressure." 9. Once the cooking cycle is completed, quickly and carefully turn the steam release handle from Sealing position to the Venting position. 10. When all the steam is released, remove the pressure lid from the top carefully. 11. Lastly, stir in the double cream and lemon juice. 12. Press the "Sauté" button two times to select "Normal" settings; let it simmer until heated through. 13. Enjoy!

Per Serving: Calories 521; Fat 19g; Sodium 354mg; Carbs 15g; Fiber 5.1g; Sugar 8.2g; Protein 32g

Crab Sliders

Prep time: 15 minutes | Cook time: 3 minutes | Serves: 4

10-ounce crabmeat	1 teaspoon Old Bay seasoning
4 heaping tablespoons fresh chives, chopped	½ cup celery stalk, chopped
2 garlic cloves, minced	1 tablespoon fresh lime juice
½ cup mayonnaise	8 mini slider rolls
½ teaspoons hot sauce	2 cups Iceberg lettuce, torn into pieces

1. Add 1 cup of water, metal Steam Rack, and a steamer basket to your Inner Pot. 2. Place the crabmeat in the prepared steamer basket. 3. Put on the pressure cooker's lid and turn the steam valve to "Sealing" position. 4. Press the "Steam" button one time to select "Less" option. 5. Press the Pressure Level button to adjust the pressure to "Low Pressure." 6. Once the cooking cycle is completed, quickly and carefully turn the steam release handle from Sealing position to the Venting position. 7.

When all the steam is released, remove the pressure lid from the top carefully. 8. Add the chives, garlic, mayo, hot sauce, Old Bay seasoning, celery, and lime juice; stir to combine well. 9. Divide the mixture between slider rolls and garnish with lettuce. 10. Serve and enjoy!

Per Serving: Calories 407; Fat 19g; Sodium 354mg; Carbs 15g; Fiber 5.1g; Sugar 8.2g; Protein 32g

Sole Fillets with Pickle

Prep time: 15 minutes | Cook time: 3 minutes | Serves: 4

1½-pound sole fillets	½ cup mayonnaise
Sea salt and black pepper, to taste	1 tablespoon pickle juice
1 teaspoon paprika	2 cloves garlic, smashed

1. Sprinkle the fillets with salt, black pepper, and paprika. 2. Add 1 ½ cups of water and a steamer basket to the Inner Pot. Place the fish in the steamer basket. 3. Put on the pressure cooker's lid and turn the steam valve to "Sealing" position. 4. Select Pressure Cook mode, and then press the "Pressure Cook" button again to select "Less" time option. 5. Use the "+/-" keys on the control panel to set the cooking time to 3 minutes. 6. Press the Pressure Level button to adjust the pressure to "Low Pressure." 7. Once the cooking cycle is completed, quickly and carefully turn the steam release handle from Sealing position to the Venting position. 8. When all the steam is released, remove the pressure lid from the top carefully. 9. Then, make the sauce by mixing the mayonnaise with the pickle juice and garlic. 10. Serve the fish fillets with the well-chilled sauce on the side. 11. Bon appétit!

Per Serving: Calories 382; Fat 7.9g; Sodium 704mg; Carbs 6g; Fiber 3.6g; Sugar 6g; Protein 18g

Mussels in Scallion Sauce

Prep time: 15 minutes | Cook time: 5 minutes | Serves: 2

1 cup water	and debearded
½ cup cooking wine	2 tablespoons butter
2 garlic cloves, sliced	1 bunch scallion, chopped
1½-pound frozen mussels, cleaned	

1. Add the water, wine, and garlic to the Inner Pot. Add a metal rack to the Inner Pot. 2. Put the mussels into the steamer basket; lower the steamer basket onto the rack. 3. Put on the pressure cooker's lid and turn the steam valve to "Sealing" position. 4. Press the "Steam" button two times to select "Less" option. 5. Press the Pressure Level button to adjust the pressure to "Low Pressure." 6. Once the cooking cycle is completed, quickly and carefully turn the steam release handle from Sealing position to the Venting position. 7. When all the steam is released, remove the pressure lid from the top carefully. 8. Press the "Sauté" button two times to select "Normal" settings and add butter and scallions; 9. let it cook until the sauce is thoroughly heated and slightly thickened. 10. Press the "Cancel" button and add the mussels. 11. Serve warm. Bon appétit!

Per Serving: Calories 419; Fat 14g; Sodium 791mg; Carbs 8.9g; Fiber 4.6g; Sugar 8g; Protein 31g

Salmon on Croissants

Prep time: 15 minutes | Cook time: 3 minutes | Serves: 2

1½-pound salmon fillets	crushed
1 red onion, thinly sliced	½ teaspoons dried rosemary, only leaves crushed
¼ cup prepared horseradish, drained	½ teaspoons dried oregano
¼ cup mayonnaise	1 cup cherry tomatoes, halved
2 tablespoons sour cream	2 cups Iceberg lettuce leaves, torn into pieces
Salt and white pepper, to taste	6 croissants, split
½ teaspoons red pepper flakes,	

1. Add 1 cup of water and metal Steam Rack to the Inner Pot. 2. Lower the salmon fillets onto the Steam Rack. 3. Put on the pressure cooker's lid and turn the steam valve to "Sealing" position. 4. Press the "Steam" button two times to select "Less" option. 5. Press the Pressure Level button to adjust the pressure to "Low Pressure." 6. Once the cooking cycle is completed, quickly and carefully turn the steam release handle from Sealing position to the Venting position. 7. When all the steam is released, remove the pressure lid from the top carefully. 8. Add the remaining ingredients and stir to combine well. 9. Place in your refrigerator until ready to serve. 10. Serve on croissants and enjoy!

Per Serving: Calories 412; Fat 20g; Sodium 491mg; Carbs 9g; Fiber 3g; Sugar 8g; Protein 31g

Fish Burritos

Prep time: 15 minutes | Cook time: 10 minutes | Serves: 4

2 tablespoons olive oil	½ teaspoons ground bay leaf
4 catfish fillets	1 teaspoon dried thyme
Sea salt to taste	4 burrito-sized tortillas
⅓ teaspoon black pepper, to taste	1 cup fresh salsa
½ teaspoons cayenne pepper	1 large-sized tomato, sliced

1. Prepare your Inner Pot by adding 1 ½ cups of water and a metal rack to its bottom. 2. Place the fish fillets in the center of a foil sheet. 3. Drizzle olive oil over the fish. 4. Season with salt, black pepper, cayenne pepper, ground bay leaf and dried thyme. 5. Wrap tightly and lower it onto the rack. 6. Put on the pressure cooker's lid and turn the steam valve to "Sealing" position. 7. Select Pressure Cook mode, and then press the "Pressure Cook" button again to select "Less" time option. 8. Use the "+/-" keys on the control panel to set the cooking time to 10 minutes. 9. Press the Pressure Level button to adjust the pressure to "High Pressure." 10. Once the cooking cycle is completed, allow the steam to release naturally. 11. When all the steam is released, remove the pressure lid from the top carefully. 12. Divide the fish fillets among tortillas. 13. Top it with the salsa and tomatoes. 14. Roll each tortilla into a burrito and serve immediately.
Per Serving: Calories 380; Fat 7.9g; Sodium 704mg; Carbs 6g; Fiber 3.6g; Sugar 6g; Protein 18g

Saucy Clams

Prep time: 15 minutes | Cook time: 10 minutes | Serves: 4

½ cup bacon, smoked and cubed	½ cup clam juice
2 onions, chopped	A pinch of cayenne pepper
3 garlic cloves, minced	1 bay leaf
1 sprig thyme	5 lime juice
3 (5-ounce) cans clams, chopped	2 tablespoons fresh chives,
⅓ cup tarty white wine	roughly chopped
⅓ cup water	

1. Press the "Sauté" button two times to select "Normal" settings. 2. Add the cubed bacon. Once your bacon releases its fat, add the onions, garlic, and thyme. 3. Cook for 3 minutes more or until the onion is transparent. 4. Add the clams, white wine, water, clam juice, cayenne pepper, and bay leaf. 5. Put on the pressure cooker's lid and turn the steam valve to "Sealing" position. 6. Select Pressure Cook mode, and then press the "Pressure Cook" button again to select "Less" time option. 7. Use the "+/-" keys on the control panel to set the cooking time to 4 minutes. 8. Press the Pressure Level button to adjust the pressure to "Low Pressure." 9. Once the cooking cycle is completed, allow the steam to release naturally. 10. When all the steam is released, remove the pressure lid from the top carefully. 11. Ladle into individual bowls and serve garnished with lime slices and fresh chives. 12. Bon appétit!
Per Serving: Calories 584; Fat 15g; Sodium 441mg; Carbs 17g; Fiber 4.6g; Sugar 5g; Protein 29g

Beer-Steamed Mussels

Prep time: 15 minutes | Cook time: 5 minutes | Serves: 4

1 tablespoon olive oil	1 tablespoon fresh cilantro, chopped
½ cup scallions, chopped	
2 cloves garlic, minced	Sea salt and black pepper, to taste
2 medium-sized ripe tomatoes, puréed	2 Thai chili peppers, stemmed and split
1 (12-ounce) bottles lager beer	1 ½-pound mussels, cleaned and debearded
1 cup water	

1. Press the "Sauté" button two times to select "Normal" settings. 2. Heat the oil and cook the scallions until tender and fragrant. 3. Then, stir in the garlic and cook an additional 30 seconds or until fragrant. 4. Add the remaining ingredients. 5. Put on the pressure cooker's lid and turn the steam valve to "Sealing" position. 6. Select Pressure Cook mode, and then press the "Pressure Cook" button again to select "Less" time option. 7. Use the "+/-" keys on the control panel to set the cooking time to 3 minutes. 8. Press the Pressure Level button to

adjust the pressure to "Low Pressure." 9. Once the cooking cycle is completed, quickly and carefully turn the steam release handle from Sealing position to the Venting position. 10. When all the steam is released, remove the pressure lid from the top carefully. 11. Serve with garlic croutons. 12. Bon appétit!
Per Serving: Calories 384; Fat 7.9g; Sodium 704mg; Carbs 6g; Fiber 3.6g; Sugar 6g; Protein 18g

Spanish Paella

Prep time: 15 minutes | Cook time: 6 minutes | Serves: 5

2 tablespoons olive oil	1 cup chicken broth
2 links (6-ounce) Spanish chorizo sausage, cut into slices	1 cup water
	⅓ cup white wine
1 yellow onion, chopped	½ teaspoons curry paste
3 cloves garlic, minced	Sea salt and white pepper, to taste
2 sweet peppers, sliced	1 cup green peas, fresh or thawed
1 Chiles de Árbol, minced	¼ cup fresh parsley leaves,
1 cup Arborio rice, rinsed	roughly chopped
1½-pound shrimp, deveined	

1. Press the "Sauté" button two times to select "Normal" settings and then heat the oil until sizzling. 2. Cook the sausage for 2 minutes, stirring continuously to ensure even cooking. 3. Stir in the onions and garlic; cook for about a minute longer, stirring frequently. 4. Add the peppers, rice, shrimp, broth, water, wine, curry paste, salt, and white pepper. 5. Put on the pressure cooker's lid and turn the steam valve to "Sealing" position. 6. Select Pressure Cook mode, and then press the "Pressure Cook" button again to select "Less" time option. 7. Use the "+/-" keys on the control panel to set the cooking time to 3 minutes. 8. Press the Pressure Level button to adjust the pressure to "High Pressure." 9. Once the cooking cycle is completed, quickly and carefully turn the steam release handle from Sealing position to the Venting position. 10. When all the steam is released, remove the pressure lid from the top carefully. 11. Add the green peas and seal the lid one more time; let it sit in the residual heat until warmed through. 12. Serve garnished with fresh parsley and enjoy!
Per Serving: Calories 397; Fat 7.9g; Sodium 704mg; Carbs 6g; Fiber 3.6g; Sugar 6g; Protein 18g

Chapter 8 Chicken and Poultry Recipes

Tasty Chicken

Prep Time: 10 minutes | Cook Time: 40 minutes | Serves: 6

1 (6-pound) whole chicken	½ teaspoon garlic powder
1 teaspoon salt	1 tablespoon olive oil
½ teaspoon black pepper	1 cup water
½ teaspoon paprika	

1. Remove giblets from chicken and discard giblets. 2. Combine salt, pepper, paprika, and garlic powder in a small bowl. Rub chicken with the spice mixture. 3. After pressing the Sauté button, add oil to the Instant Pot. 4. In the Instant Pot, add the chicken and cook it for approximately a minute on each side. After removing the chicken, turn off the Instant Pot. 5. Add steam rack and water to the Instant Pot. Put the chicken on the rack's top. 6. Set the pressure release to seal position and close the lid. 7. Turn the timer to 38 minutes and press the Pressure Cook button on high. 8. Allow pressure to naturally release on seal position -once the timer beeps, then open the lid and take it off. 9. Serve chicken hot or cold.
Per Serving: Calories 254; Fat: 8g; Sodium 546mg; Carbs: 1g; Sugars: 0.03g; Protein 42g

Delicious Chicken Hawaiian

Prep Time: 5 minutes | Cook Time: 15 minutes | Serves: 4

1 pound boneless, skinless chicken breasts	1 (20-ounce) can crushed pineapple
	1 (18-ounce) bottle barbecue sauce

1. The Instant Pot should be filled with chicken, pineapple (with juice), and barbecue sauce. To blend, stir. 2. Set the pressure release to seal position and close the lid. 3. Set the timer to 15 minutes and press Pressure Cook button on high. 4. Allow pressure to naturally release on seal position once the timer beeps, then open the lid and take it off. 5. Serve.
Per Serving: Calories 721; Fat: 8g; Sodium 1904mg; Carbs: 150g; Sugars: 120g; Protein 14g

Yummy chicken

Prep Time: 10 minutes | Cook Time: 15 minutes | Serves: 4

1 pound boneless, skinless chicken breasts	1 teaspoon salt
1½ cups chicken broth	¼ teaspoon black pepper

1. In the Instant Pot, combine the chicken, broth, salt, and pepper. 2. Set the pressure release to seal position and close the lid. 3. Set the timer to 15 minutes and press the Pressure Cook button on high. 4. Allow pressure to naturally release on seal position once the timer beeps, then open the lid and take it off. 5. Chicken should be taken out of the Instant Pot and forked into shreds. Whenever a recipe calls for cooked chicken, use it.
Per Serving: Calories 340; Fat: 13g; Sodium 1200mg; Carbs: 24g; Sugars: 6g; Protein 30g

Potato and Chicken Casserole

Prep Time: 10 minutes | Cook Time: 15 minutes | Serves: 4

3 medium russet potatoes, peeled and chopped	½ teaspoon salt
1 pound boneless, skinless chicken thighs	¼ teaspoon black pepper
4 tablespoons unsalted butter	1 cup heavy whipping cream
4 tablespoons all-purpose flour	1 cup shredded Cheddar cheese
	1 cup water

1. In a 6-cup metal dish, combine the chicken and potatoes. Mix. 2. Place butter in the Instant Pot and select Sauté. 3. Melt the butter, then stir in the flour. After 2 minutes of whisking, the flour should be well mixed and browned. 4. Add salt and pepper and continue mixing for a further 30 seconds. 5. Whisk cream in gradually. Whisk for a further 2 minutes, or until the sauce is thickened and lump-free. 6. Over the chicken and potatoes, pour the sauce. Add Cheddar cheese on top. Cooking spray a piece of foil, then wrap it firmly over the bowl's rim. 7. Place steam rack inside Instant Pot and add water. To safely drop the bowl into the Instant Pot, make a foil sling. 8. Set the pressure release to seal position and close the lid. 9. Press Pressure Cook button and adjust time to 10 minutes. 10. Allow pressure to naturally release on seal position once the timer beeps, then open the lid and take it off. Utilizing a foil sling, remove the bowl's top foil before removing the pan from the Instant Pot. Serve.
Per Serving: Calories 618; Fat: 25.17g; Sodium 624mg; Carbs: 80.7g; Sugars: 8.03g; Protein 18.39g

Chicken Breast Buffalo

Prep Time: 10 minutes | Cook Time: 15 minutes | Serves: 4

¾ cup mild hot sauce	½ teaspoon cornstarch
3 tablespoons butter, melted	1 pound boneless, skinless chicken breasts
1 tablespoon Worcestershire sauce	
½ tablespoon red wine vinegar	

1. Combine hot sauce, butter, Worcestershire, vinegar, and cornstarch in the Instant Pot. 2. Turn the chicken in the Instant Pot to coat it with sauce. 3. Set the pressure release to seal position and close the lid. 4. Set the timer to 15 minutes and press the Pressure Cook button on high. 5. Allow pressure to naturally release on seal position once the timer chimes, then open the lid and take it off. 6. Serve.
Per Serving: Calories 293; Fat: 15g; Sodium 757mg; Carbs: 28.7g; Sugars: 8.03g; Protein 11.39g

Rice and Chicken with Cheese

Prep Time: 5 minutes | Cook Time: 16 minutes | Serves: 4

3 tablespoons olive oil	½ teaspoon salt
1 pound boneless, skinless chicken thighs, cut into 1" pieces	¼ teaspoon black pepper
1 cup white rice	1½ cups chicken broth
	1 cup shredded Cheddar cheese

1. Add oil to the Instant Pot and press the Sauté button. 2. Add rice and chicken. Add salt and pepper to taste. Cook for five minutes. 3. Pour in broth to clean the pot's bottom. 4. Set the pressure release to seal position and close the lid. 5. Press Pressure Cook button and adjust time to 10 minutes. 6. Allow pressure to naturally release on seal position once the timer beeps, then. 7. open the lid and take it off. 8. Mix in cheese and serve.
Per Serving: Calories 601; Fat: 23g; Sodium 967mg; Carbs: 62g; Sugars: 6g; Protein 33.39g

Chicken Sandwiches with Bacon Ranch

Prep Time: 5 minutes | Cook Time: 20 minutes | Serves: 6

½ pound bacon, chopped	1 tablespoon cornstarch
1 cup chicken broth	½ cup shredded sharp Cheddar cheese
1 (1-ounce) ranch seasoning packet	¼ cup sliced green onions
1 pound boneless, skinless chicken breasts	6 hamburger buns
1 (8-ounce) package cream cheese	

1. Click the Sauté button. 2. In the Instant Pot, add the chopped bacon and cook for 5 minutes, until browned. Place the bacon between two paper towels after removing it. Save some for subsequent garnishing. 3. To deglaze the bottom of the pot, pour broth into the Instant Pot. 4. Mix the broth with the ranch seasoning package. Add the chicken to the pot and the cream cheese on top. 5. Set the pressure release to seal position and close the lid. 6. Set the timer to 15 minutes and press Pressure Cook button. 7. Allow pressure to naturally relax for 10 minutes on seal position after the timer beeps, then quickly remove any leftover pressure on vent position. Remove the lid. 8. With two forks, remove the chicken and shred it. 9. Stir cornstarch into sauce while chicken is being removed. 10. Transfer the chicken and bacon to the pot and mix until evenly coated with the sauce. 11. Top with Cheddar, green onions, and reserved bacon. Serve on hamburger buns.
Per Serving: Calories 445; Fat: 29g; Sodium 1301mg; Carbs: 22g; Sugars: 5g; Protein 22g

Basic Chicken

Prep Time: 15 minutes | Cook Time: 20 minutes | Serves: 4

5 lbs. chicken thighs	1 tsp black peppercorns
4 cloves garlic, minced	3 bay leaves
½ cup soy sauce	½ tsp salt
½ cup white vinegar	½ tsp ground black pepper

1. Stir everything together before adding it to the Instant Pot: garlic, soy sauce, vinegar, peppercorns, bay leaves, salt, and pepper. 2. Chicken thighs are added. Chicken is coated by stirring. 3. Lock the lid by closing it. Set the cooking time to 15 minutes and choose the Pressure Cook option on high. 4. After the timer goes off, give the pressure 10 minutes to naturally release on seal position. Open the lid. 5. Bay leaves should be taken out before serving.
Per Serving: Calories 1362; Fat: 99g; Sodium 1234mg; Carbs: 11g; Sugars: 6g; Protein 96g

Fajitas with Chicken

Prep Time: 10 minutes | Cook Time: 12 minutes | Serves: 6

1 pound boneless, skinless chicken thighs, sliced
1 cup chicken broth
1 medium sweet onion, peeled and sliced
1 medium red bell pepper, seeded and sliced

1 medium green bell pepper, seeded and sliced
1 (4-ounce) can mild diced green chilies
1 (1-ounce) packet taco seasoning
2 tablespoons lime juice
6 (10") flour tortillas, warmed

1. In the Instant Pot, combine all the ingredients minus the tortillas. To blend, stir. 2. Set the pressure release to seal position and close the lid. 3. Press Pressure Cook button and adjust time to 12 minutes. 4. Allow pressure to naturally release on seal position once the timer beeps, then open the lid and take it off. 5. Serve in warmed flour tortillas.
Per Serving: Calories 372; Fat: 9g; Sodium 957mg; Carbs: 48g; Sugars: 10g; Protein 20g

Chicken Tacos in Salsa

Prep Time: 5 minutes | Cook Time: 10 minutes | Serves: 4

2 cups chunky salsa
1 cup chicken broth
1 (1-ounce) packet taco seasoning
1 pound boneless, skinless chicken

breasts
8 crunchy taco shells
2 cups shredded romaine lettuce
1 cup grated Mexican-blend cheese

1. Chunky salsa, broth, and taco seasoning should all be combined in a medium basin. Combine by whisking. Place salsa mixture in the Instant Pot. 2. Stir in the chicken breast with the Instant Pot. 3. Set the pressure release to seal position and close the lid. 4. Press Pressure Cook button and set the timer for 10 minutes on high. 5. Allow pressure to naturally release on seal position for 10 minutes after the timer beeps, then quickly remove any leftover pressure on vent position. Remove the lid. 6. To shred chicken, use two forks. 7. Serve chicken in taco shells with cheese and lettuce shavings on top.
Per Serving: Calories 570; Fat: 24g; Sodium 1944mg; Carbs: 52g; Sugars: 12g; Protein 34g

Sour and Sweet Chicken Breast

Prep Time: 10 minutes | Cook Time: 7 minutes | Serves: 6

1 cup apple cider vinegar
1 cup granulated sugar
½ cup ketchup
2 tablespoons soy sauce
1½ teaspoons garlic powder
1 teaspoon salt
1 cup cornstarch

2 pounds boneless, skinless chicken breasts, cut into 1" chunks
½ teaspoon salt
¼ teaspoon black pepper
¼ cup vegetable oil
3 large eggs, beaten

1. Mix the vinegar, sugar, ketchup, soy sauce, garlic powder, and salt in a small bowl. Place aside. 2. Fill a gallon-sized zip-top bag with cornstarch. 3. Place the chicken into the cornstarch bag after seasoning with salt and pepper. Shake the bag tightly until the chicken is uniformly covered. 4. Press the Instant Pot Sauté button. Oil is added, heated for one minute. 5. Chicken pieces should be taken out of the bag in batches and dipped into beaten eggs. 6. Shake off any extra egg, then equally layer chicken in heated oil at the bottom of the saucepan. Let cook for 30 seconds without moving. 7. Cook for another 30 seconds after flipping. 8. Take out of the pot, then proceed with the remaining chicken. 9. Pour sauce into the pot and deglaze it when the chicken has finished cooking and been taken from the Instant Pot. 10. Turn the chicken in the sauce after adding it. 11. Set the pressure release to seal position and close the lid. 12. Set the timer to 3 minutes and press Pressure Cook button on high. 13. Allow pressure to naturally release on seal position once the timer beeps, then open the lid and take it off. Serve warm.
Per Serving: Calories 562; Fat: 20g; Sodium 1254mg; Carbs: 79g; Sugars: 25g; Protein 16g

Easy Chicken Breast with Sauce

Prep Time: 5 minutes | Cook Time: 15 minutes | Serves: 4

½ cup soy sauce
½ cup rice vinegar
½ cup packed light brown sugar
1 tablespoon cornstarch

1 teaspoon minced ginger
¼ teaspoon garlic powder
1 pound boneless, skinless chicken breasts

1. Soy sauce, rice vinegar, brown sugar, cornstarch, ginger, and garlic powder should all be combined in a small basin. 2. Place chicken and sauce into Instant Pot. To blend, stir. 3. Set the pressure release to seal position and close the lid. 4. Set the timer to 15 minutes and press Pressure Cook button. 5. Allow pressure to naturally release on seal position once the timer beeps, then open the lid and take it off. 6. Serve.
Per Serving: Calories 319; Fat: 12g; Sodium 794mg; Carbs: 35g; Sugars: 12g; Protein 13g

Chicken with Honed Garlic

Prep Time: 5 minutes | Cook Time: 17 minutes | Serves: 4

1 pound boneless, skinless chicken thighs
¼ teaspoon salt
⅛ teaspoon black pepper
1 tablespoon olive oil
1 cup chicken broth

⅓ cup honey
6 cloves garlic, minced
2 tablespoons rice vinegar
1 tablespoon soy sauce
1 tablespoon cornstarch
½ cup cold water

1. Use salt and pepper to season the chicken. 2. Add oil to the Instant Pot and press the Sauté button. 3. Cook the chicken for 30 seconds on each side in the pot. 4. After removing the chicken, deglaze the pan with stock. Turn off your Instant Pot. 5. Combine honey, garlic, vinegar, and soy sauce in a small bowl. 6. Remove the chicken to the Instant Pot and cover with sauce. 7. Set the pressure release to seal position and close the lid. 8. Press Pressure Cook button and adjust time to 10 minutes. 9. Allow pressure to naturally release on seal position for 10 minutes after the timer beeps, then quickly remove any leftover pressure on vent position. Remove the lid by unlocking it. 10. Remove chicken and set aside. 11. Click the Sauté button. 12. Cornstarch and water should be whipped together in a small bowl. Bring sauce in the pot to a boil while incorporating cornstarch slurry. Let sauce boil 5 minutes. 13. Serve sauce over chicken.
Per Serving: Calories 435; Fat: 14g; Sodium 758mg; Carbs: 51g; Sugars: 29g; Protein 24g

Stir-Fried Chicken

Prep Time: 10 minutes | Cook Time: 18 minutes | Serves: 4

2 tablespoons olive oil
1 pound boneless, skinless chicken breasts, cut into 1" pieces
½ teaspoon salt
¼ teaspoon black pepper
1 medium bunch broccoli, cut into small florets
1 medium cucumber, sliced and

halved
1 medium red bell pepper, seeded and sliced
1 tablespoon minced ginger
2 cloves garlic, minced
½ cup stir-fry sauce
2 cups cooked brown rice, warmed

1. Press the Instant Pot's Sauté button. Give the oil in the Instant Pot a minute to heat up. 2. To the Instant Pot, add chicken, salt, and pepper. For about 8 minutes, while keeping the lid on, cook until the internal temperature is no longer pink. Instant Pot chicken should be removed and left aside. 3. To the Instant Pot, add broccoli, cucumber, bell pepper, and ginger. Stir-fry for about 5 minutes, or until veggies are soft. 4. After adding the garlic, simmer for another 30 seconds. 5. Remove the chicken to the Instant Pot, then add the stir-fry sauce. Mix to evenly distribute sauce. Sauce should simmer for two minutes before finishing. 6. Serve over rice after removing from heat.
Per Serving: Calories 325; Fat: 14g; Sodium 726mg; Carbs: 30g; Sugars: 8g; Protein 17g

Chicken Pesto

Prep Time: 5 minutes | Cook Time: 15 minutes | Serves: 4

1 cup water
1 pound boneless, skinless chicken breasts, cut into strips
½ cup pesto

2 Roma tomatoes, sliced
¼ teaspoon salt
⅛ teaspoon black pepper

1. Add steam rack and fill the Instant Pot with 1 cup water. 2. Combine the chicken, pesto, tomatoes, salt, and pepper in a 6-cup metal bowl. 3. To carefully drop the bowl into the Instant Pot, use a foil sling. 4. Set the pressure release to seal position and close the lid. 5. Set the timer to 15 minutes and press Pressure Cook button on high. 6. Allow pressure to naturally release on seal position once the timer beeps, then. 7. open the lid and take it off. Using a foil sling, take the pan out of the Instant Pot. 8. Serve hot.
Per Serving: Calories 365; Fat: 23g; Sodium 729mg; Carbs: 25g; Sugars: 6g; Protein 13.39g

Tasty Alfredo Chicken

Prep Time: 10 minutes | Cook Time: 13 minutes | Serves: 6

2 tablespoons olive oil
1 pound boneless, skinless chicken breasts, sliced
1 teaspoon garlic salt
½ teaspoon black pepper

4 cups chicken broth
1-pound fettuccine
8 tablespoons butter, cubed
1 cup heavy whipping cream
1 cup grated Parmesan cheese

1. On the Instant Pot, choose Sauté and then add oil. 2. Put the chicken in the pot and season with salt and pepper and garlic. Cook for 7 minutes while periodically stirring. 3. Pour in broth to clean the pot's bottom. 4. Put half-broken fettuccine in the pot. Add butter to the fettuccine. 5. Set the pressure release to seal position and close the lid. 6. Set the timer to 6 minutes and press Pressure Cook button. 7. Quickly relieve the pressure on vent position when the timer beeps, then open the lid and take it off. 8. Add the cream and Parmesan, then stir thoroughly. 9. Serve hot.
Per Serving: Calories 805; Fat: 52g; Sodium 1581mg; Carbs: 30g; Sugars: 8g; Protein 51g

Greek-style Chicken and Quinoa with Olives

Prep Time: 15 minutes | Cook Time: 10 minutes | Serves: 4

2 tablespoons olive oil
1 red onion, finely chopped
1 red bell pepper, seeded and finely chopped
1 cup Chicken Stock or store-bought low-sodium chicken stock
1½ pounds boneless, skinless chicken breast, cubed
¾ cup quinoa, rinsed well
1 teaspoon dried oregano

½ teaspoon kosher salt
½ teaspoon freshly ground black pepper
1 cup grape or cherry tomatoes, halved
½ cup pitted kalamata olives
¼ cup crumbled full-; Fat feta cheese
2 tablespoons freshly squeezed lemon juice

1. Set your Instant Pot on Sauté and adjust the temperature to More. Add the olive oil in the inner pot. 2. When the oil is heated, add bell pepper and onion. Sauté for 3 to 4 minutes or until softened, stirring from time to time. Turn off the heat. 3. Then add chicken, quinoa, oregano, black pepper, salt, and stock in the inner pot. Close the lid and turn the steam release handle to Sealing. 4. Set your Instant Pot on Pressure Cook at High and adjust the cooking time to 10 minutes. 5. When cooked, naturally release the pressure for 10 minutes, then quick release the remaining pressure. 6. Remove the lid carefully. Add olives, feta cheese, lemon juice, and tomatoes in the inner pot and stir well. 7. Serve and enjoy!
Per Serving: Calories: 454; Fat: 17g; Carbs: 28g; Sugar: 4g; Sodium: 437mg; Protein: 45g

Chicken Cajun Pasta

Prep Time: 10 minutes | Cook Time: 13 minutes | Serves: 6

2 tablespoons olive oil
1 pound boneless, skinless chicken breasts, sliced
1 tablespoon Cajun seasoning
4 cups chicken broth

1 pound penne pasta
8 tablespoons butter, cubed
1 cup heavy whipping cream
1 cup grated Parmesan cheese

1. Add oil to the Instant Pot and press the Sauté button. 2. In the Instant Pot, add the chicken and the Cajun spices. Cook for 7 minutes while periodically stirring. 3. Pour in broth to clean the pot's bottom. 4. Put spaghetti in the pot. Add butter to pasta and chicken. 5. Set the pressure release to seal position and close the lid. 6. Press Pressure Cook button and adjust time to 5 minutes. 7. Quickly relieve the pressure on vent position when the timer beeps, then open the lid and take it off. 8. Add the cream and Parmesan, then stir thoroughly. 9. Serve hot.
Per Serving: Calories 799; Fat: 47g; Sodium 1394mg; Carbs: 41g; Sugars: 4g; Protein 49g

Chicken-Pulled Sandwiches

Prep Time: 10 minutes | Cook Time: 15 minutes | Serves: 4

1 pound boneless, skinless chicken breasts
¼ teaspoon salt
⅛ teaspoon black pepper

1½ cups barbecue sauce, divided
1 cup water
4 hamburger buns

1. Put Chicken in a 6-cup metal bowl. Chicken should be salted and peppered before being brushed with a cup of barbecue sauce. 2. Fill the Instant Pot with water. Insert steam rack into the Instant Pot. 3. Carefully drop the bowl of chicken into the Instant Pot using a foil sling. 4. Set the pressure release to seal position and close the lid. 5. Set the timer to 15 minutes and press Pressure Cook button. 6. Allow pressure to naturally release for 10 minutes on seal position after the timer beeps, then quickly remove any leftover pressure on vent position. Remove the lid by unlocking it. 7. To remove the bowl of chicken, use a foil sling. 8. With two forks, shred the chicken after draining any water in the bowl. 9. Add remaining ½ cup barbecue sauce and stir to combine. 10. Serve pulled chicken on warmed hamburger buns.
Per Serving: Calories 682; Fat: 7g; Sodium 1554mg; Carbs: 67g; Sugars: 41.03g; Protein 11g

Yummy Whole Chicken

Prep Time: 15 minutes | Cook Time: 30 minutes | Serves: 4

1 medium-sized, whole chicken (3 lbs.)
2 tbsps. sugar
2 tsp kosher salt
1 tbsp. onion powder
1 tbsp. garlic powder
1 tbsp. paprika

2 tsp ground black pepper
½ tsp cayenne pepper
1 cup water or chicken broth
1 tbsp. cooking wine
2 tsp soy sauce
1 minced green onion

1. Combine the sugar, salt, onion, garlic, paprika, black pepper, and cayenne pepper in a medium bowl. 2. Put the steam rack in the Instant Pot and fill it with water to prepare it. 3. Wine and soy sauce should be added to the stew. 4. Apply the spice mixture to the chicken's whole surface. 5. Affix the cover after placing the chicken on the steam rack. 6. The cooking time should be set to 18 minutes at HIGH pressure using the Pressure Cook mode. 7. After the timer goes off, let the pressure 15 minutes to naturally release on seal position. Take your time to open the lid. Top with minced green onion and serve.
Per Serving: Calories 168; Fat: 5.17g; Sodium 1404mg; Carbs: 16.87g; Sugars: 9g; Protein 14.39g

Yummy Italian chicken

Prep Time: 5 minutes | Cook Time: 20 minutes | Serves: 4

8 boneless, skinless chicken thighs
1 tsp kosher salt
½ tsp ground black pepper
1 tbsp. olive oil
2 medium-sized, chopped carrots
1 cup stemmed and quartered cremini mushrooms
1 chopped onion
3 cloves garlic, smashed

1 tbsp. tomato paste
2 cups cherry tomatoes
½ cup pitted green olives
½ cup thinly-sliced fresh basil
¼ cup chopped fresh Italian parsley
½ teaspoon salt and pepper should be used to season the chicken thighs.

1. Select SAUTÉ. Add the oil to the pot's bottom after waiting one minute. 2. For about 5 minutes, sauté the carrots, mushrooms, onions, and ½ teaspoon salt until tender. 3. Cook for a further 30 seconds after adding the tomato paste and garlic. 4. Stir thoroughly after adding the chicken thighs, cherry tomatoes, and olives. 5. select the Pressure Cook and cook for 10 minutes at HIGH pressure. 6. Use the Quick Release when the timer runs off. Take your time to open the lid. 7. Add some parsley and fresh basil on top. Serve.
Per Serving: Calories 548; Fat: 18g; Sodium 1292mg; Carbs: 72g; Sugars: 26g; Protein 26g

Easy Chicken Thai

Prep Time: 5 minutes | Cook Time: 20 minutes | Serves: 4

2 lbs. chicken thighs, boneless and skinless
1 cup lime juice
½ cup fish sauce
¼ cup extra virgin olive oil

2 tbsps. coconut nectar
1 tsp ginger, grated
1 tsp mint, chopped
2 tsp cilantro, finely chopped

1. Mix the coconut nectar, ginger, mint, lime juice, fish sauce, olive oil, and cilantro in a medium bowl. 2. To the instant pot, add the chicken thighs. 3. On top, pour the marinade. 4. Close the lid. Choose Pressure Cook, then 10 minutes of HIGH Pressure Cooking. 5. Use a Quick Release when the timer beeps. Open the lid. Serve.
Per Serving: Calories 665; Fat: 48g; Sodium 3157mg; Carbs: 7g; Sugars: 2g; Protein 49g

Savory Enchiladas

Prep Time: 10 minutes | Cook Time: 12 minutes | Serves: 4

2 tablespoons butter
2 tablespoons all-purpose flour
1 cup chicken broth
1 cup full-fat sour cream
1 (4-ounce) can mild diced green chilies, divided

1 cup water
1½ cups shredded cooked chicken
1½ cups shredded Monterey jack cheese
4 (8") flour tortillas

1. On the Instant Pot, select Sauté and then add butter. After allowing butter to melt, mix in flour. For about 2 minutes, mix butter and flour continuously until the flour is browned and the sauce is smooth. 2. Whisk in broth gradually. With continual stirring, cook for 2 minutes. 3. Remove sauce from Instant Pot and let it cool for five minutes in a different bowl. 4. Sauce should be combined with sour cream and half of the chopped canned chilies. 5. Add one cup of water after washing the Instant Pot. To the Instant Pot, add a steam rack. 6. Four tortillas should be filled with the remaining half-can of chopped chilies, chicken, and cheese. 7. In a 7" cake pan, roll up the tortillas and put them side by side. Over the rolled-up tortillas, drizzle sauce. 8. Set the pressure release to seal position and close the lid. 9. Press Pressure Cook button and adjust time to 5 minutes. 10. Quickly release the pressure on vent position when the timer beeps, then open the lid and take it off. 11. With the help of a foil sling, remove the foil from the pan's top and serve the cake hot.
Per Serving: Calories 719; Fat: 44g; Sodium 1104mg; Carbs: 34g; Sugars: 7g; Protein 39g

Spicy Chicken Wings

Prep Time: 5 minutes | Cook Time: 15 minutes | Serves: 4

3 lbs. chicken wings
2 tbsps. olive oil
¼ cup light brown sugar
½ tsp garlic powder
½ tsp cayenne pepper

½ tsp black pepper
½ tsp paprika
½ tsp salt
1½ cups chicken broth or water

1. Use a paper towel to dry the chicken wings after rinsing them. Place inside the big basin. 2. Olive oil, sugar, cayenne pepper, black pepper, paprika, garlic powder, and salt should all be combined in a medium bowl. Mix thoroughly. 3. Apply the spice mixture to the chicken's whole surface. 4. Add the wings to the Instant Pot after adding the chicken stock. 5. Lock the lid by closing it. Choose the Pressure Cook mode, and then set the cooking duration to HIGH pressure for 10 minutes. 6. Make advantage of the Quick Release when the Pressure Cooking is finished. Take your time to open the lid. 7. Slide under the broiler for 5–6 minutes if you want a crisp skin. Serve.
Per Serving: Calories 504; Fat: 19g; Sodium 868mg; Carbs: 2.87g; Sugars: 1.03g; Protein 75g

Easy Chicken Salsa Verde

Prep Time: 5 minutes | Cook Time: 20 minutes | Serves: 6

2½ lbs. boneless chicken breasts
1 tsp smoked paprika
1 tsp cumin

1 tsp salt
2 cup (16 oz.) salsa verde

1. Salt, paprika, cumin, and chicken breasts should all be added to the Instant Pot. 2. Add the green salsa on top. 3. Lock the lid by closing it. Choose the Pressure Cook mode, and then set the cooking duration to HIGH pressure for 20 minutes. 4. Make advantage of a Quick Release when the Pressure Cooking is finished. Open the lid. Shred the meat. Serve.
Per Serving: Calories 419; Fat: 8g; Sodium 2534mg; Carbs: 17g; Sugars: 10g; Protein 68g

Sriracha Honey Chicken Breast

Prep Time: 5 minutes | Cook Time: 15 minutes | Serves: 4

4 diced chicken breasts
5 tbsps. soy sauce
2-3 tbsps. honey
¼ cup sugar

4 tbsps. cold water
1 tbsps. minced garlic
2-3 tbsps. sriracha
2 tbsps. cornstarch

1. Stir the soy sauce, honey, sugar, 2 tablespoons of water, garlic, and sriracha together in the Instant Pot. 2. Chicken breasts should be tossed in the mixture. Lock the lid by closing it. 3. Select Pressure

Cook, and then cook for 9 minutes at HIGH pressure. 4. In the meantime, mix cornstarch and 2 tablespoons of water in a small dish. 5. Use a Quick Release once the timer goes off. Carefully unlock the lid. 6. The cornstarch mixture should be added to the saucepan. 7. The SAUTÉ option should be used. Simmer the sauce while sometimes stirring until it starts to thicken. Serve.
Per Serving: Calories 639; Fat: 30g; Sodium 484mg; Carbs: 26.87g; Sugars: 20.03g; Protein 62.39g

Chicken Dinner

Prep Time: 10 minutes | Cook Time: 35 minutes | Serves: 4

2 lbs. boneless chicken thighs
¼ cup soy sauce
3 tbsps. organic ketchup
¼ cup coconut oil

¼ cup honey
2 tsp garlic powder
½ tsp black pepper
1½ tsp sea salt

1. In the Instant Pot, mix the soy sauce, ketchup, coconut oil, honey, garlic powder, pepper, and salt. 2. Toss the mixture with the chicken thighs. Lock the lid by closing it. 3. The cooking time should be set to 18 minutes at HIGH pressure using the Pressure Cook mode. 4. Use a Quick Release when the timer chimes. Take your time to open the lid. 5. Choose the SAUTÉ option, then cook the sauce for 5 minutes, or until it starts to thicken. Serve with vegetables.
Per Serving: Calories 738; Fat: 54g; Sodium 1381mg; Carbs: 24g; Sugars: 21.03g; Protein 39g

Crispy Buffalo Wings

Prep Time: 5 minutes | Cook Time: 20 minutes | Serves: 6

4 lbs. chicken wings, sectioned, frozen or fresh
½ cup cayenne pepper hot sauce
1 tbsp. Worcestershire sauce

½ cup butter
½ tsp kosher salt
1-2 tbsp. sugar, light brown
1½ cups water

For the sauce: Combine the spicy sauce, Worcestershire sauce, butter, salt, and brown sugar in a microwave-safe bowl. Microwave for 20 seconds, or until the butter is melted.
For the wings: 1. Place a steam rack inside the Instant Pot after adding the water. 2. Place the steam rack with the chicken wings on it, then shut the lid. 3. Choose Pressure Cook, then cook for 10 minutes at HIGH pressure. 4. Use a Quick Release when the timer chimes. Take your time to open the lid. 5. Turn on the broiler in the oven. 6. Transfer the chicken wings to a baking sheet with care. 7. The sauce should be brushed on top of the chicken wings. 8. Broil for 4 to 5 minutes, or until browned. 9. Broil for an additional 4-5 minutes while brushing the leftover sauce on the opposite side. Serve.
Per Serving: Calories 796; Fat: 39g; Sodium 892mg; Carbs: 5g; Sugars: 4g; Protein 100g

Yummy Stew with Lentils

Prep Time: 45 minutes | Cook Time: 20 minutes | Serves: 8

2 Tbsp. canola oil
2 large onions, thinly sliced, divided
8 plum tomatoes, chopped
2 Tbsp. minced fresh gingerroot
3 garlic cloves, minced
2 tsp. ground coriander
1½ tsp. ground cumin
¼ tsp. cayenne pepper
3 cups vegetable broth

2 cups dried lentils, rinsed
2 cups water
1 can (4 oz.) chopped green chilies
¾ cup heavy whipping cream
2 Tbsp. butter
1 tsp. cumin seeds
6 cups hot cooked basmati or jasmine rice
Optional: Sliced green onions or minced fresh cilantro

1. Choose the Instant Pot's sauté setting. Add oil. Cook and stir half of the onions in heated oil for two to three minutes, or until crisp-tender. Cook and stir for a further minute after adding the tomatoes, ginger, garlic, coriander, cumin, and cayenne. Select Cancel. Stir in the remaining onion, green chilies, lentils, broth, and water. 2. Close the pressure-release valve and lock the lid. Adjust to Pressure Cook on high for 15 minutes. Allow the pressure to drop naturally on seal position. Add the cream right before serving. Melt butter in a small pan over a medium heat. Cook and swirl the cumin seeds for 1-2 minutes, or until they turn golden brown. To the lentil mixture, add. 3. Serve alongside rice. Add chopped cilantro or green onion slices as desired.
Per Serving: Calories 1162; Fat: 111.7g; Sodium 83mg; Carbs: 63g; Sugars: 13g; Protein 15g

Chicken Sticky Sesame

Prep Time: 5 minutes | Cook Time: 30 minutes | Serves: 6

6 boneless chicken thigh fillets	4 peeled and crushed cloves garlic
5 tbsps. sweet chili sauce	1 tbsp. rice vinegar
5 tbsps. hoisin sauce	1½ tbsp. sesame seeds
1 chunk peeled, grated fresh ginger	1 tbsp. soy sauce
	½ cup chicken stock

1. Stir the chili sauce, hoisin sauce, ginger, garlic, vinegar, sesame seeds, soy sauce, and chicken stock together in a medium bowl until well blended. 2. Pour the sauce mixture over the chicken thigh fillets and add them to the Instant Pot. 3. Lock the lid by closing it. Choose Pressure Cook, then cook for 15 minutes at HIGH pressure. 4. After cooking is finished, allow the pressure to naturally release on seal position for 10 minutes. Release any remaining steam on vent position. Open the lid. 5. Serve with mashed potatoes, cooked rice, or another type of garnish.
Per Serving: Calories 782; Fat: 49.17g; Sodium 2304mg; Carbs: 44.87g; Sugars: 9g; Protein 40g

Curry chicken with Honey

Prep Time: 10 minutes | Cook Time: 30 minutes | Serves: 4

2 lbs. chicken breast or thighs	1 cup onion, chopped or ¼ cup dry minced onion
16 oz. canned coconut milk	
16 oz. canned tomato sauce	2 tbsps. curry powder
6 oz. can tomato paste	3 tbsps. honey
2 cloves garlic, minced	1 tsp salt

1. Stir together all of the ingredients in the Instant Pot, excluding the chicken. 2. Chicken is now included. Lock the lid by closing it. 3. Choose the Pressure Cook mode, and then set the cooking duration to HIGH pressure for 15 minutes. 4. Once cooking is complete, let the pressure release naturally for 15 minutes on seal position. Release any remaining steam on vent position. 5. Gently stir after lifting the cover. 6. Serve with cooked rice, potato or peas.
Per Serving: Calories 648; Fat: 38g; Sodium 1043mg; Carbs: 34g; Sugars: 25g; Protein 42g

Poultry Piccata

Prep Time: 5 minutes | Cook Time: 25 minutes | Serves: 4

4 chicken breasts skinless, boneless, 1½ to 1¾ lbs.	¼ cup fresh lemon juice
1 tbsp. olive oil	2 tbsps. butter
¼ tsp black pepper	2 tbsps. brined capers, drained
½ tsp salt	2 tbsps. flat-leaf fresh parsley, chopped
1 cup chicken broth	Cooked rice or pasta

1. Choose SAUTÉ. Add the oil to the Instant Pot's bottom after waiting two minutes. 2. Add the chicken to the saucepan, season with salt and pepper, and cook for 3 minutes on each side. 3. Put the broth in. Lock the lid by closing it. 4. Press the Cancel button. The cooking time should be set to 5 minutes at HIGH pressure on the Pressure Cook mode. 5. Once pressure cooking is complete, use a Quick Release on vent position. Open the lid. 6. Transfer the cooked chicken to a serving dish. 7. To decrease the sauce, use the SAUTÉ setting and cook for 5 minutes. 8. Juice of a fresh lemon should be added. 9. Include the butter. Stir in the parsley and capers when the butter has melted. Press the CANCEL button to stop the cooking program. 10. Pour the sauce over chicken breasts. Serve with rice or pasta.
Per Serving: Calories 182; Fat: 13.17g; Sodium 686mg; Carbs: 2.8g; Sugars: 0.53g; Protein 13.9g

Yummy curried chicken

Prep Time: 5 minutes | Cook Time: 30 minutes | Serves: 4

1 lb. chicken breast, chopped	5 oz. canned coconut cream
1 tbsps. extra virgin olive oil	6 potatoes, cut into halves
1 yellow onion, thinly sliced	½ bunch coriander, chopped
1 bag (1 oz.) chicken curry base	

1. Heat the oil in the Instant Pot using the SAUTÉ mode. 2. Chicken should be added and sautéed for 2 minutes, or until it begins to brown. 3. Stir in the onion and heat for a further minute. 4. The coconut cream and chicken curry base should be thoroughly mixed in a medium

bowl. 5. Pour into the pot, then whisk in the potatoes. Lock the lid by closing it. 6. Select the Pressure Cook and cook for 15 minutes at HIGH pressure. 7. Use the Quick Release when the timer runs off. Open the lid slowly. Top with coriander and serve.
Per Serving: Calories 652; Fat: 13.17g; Sodium 176mg; Carbs: 98.7g; Sugars: 5g; Protein 36g

Spicy Cacciatore Chicken

Prep Time: 10 minutes | Cook Time: 35 minutes | Serves: 4

4 chicken thighs, with the bone, skin removed	¼ cup diced red bell pepper
	½ cup diced onion
2 tbsps. olive oil	½ (14 oz.) can crushed tomatoes
1 tsp kosher salt	2 tbsps. chopped parsley or basil
1 tsp ground black pepper	½ tsp dried oregano
½ cup diced green bell pepper	
1 bay leaf	

1. Select SAUTÉ. Add 1 tablespoon of oil to the bottom of the pot after waiting 1 minute. 2. Add salt and pepper to the meat to season it. 3. For a few minutes on each side, brown the meat. Chicken should be taken out of the pot and placed aside. 4. Add bell peppers and onion to the saucepan with another tablespoon of oil, and cook for approximately 5 minutes, or until soft and golden. 5. In the Instant Pot, place the chicken thighs. Give the tomatoes a pour. 6. Stir thoroughly after adding the oregano and bay leaf. Put the lid on. 7. To halt the SAUTE feature, use the CANCEL button. Set the cooking duration to 25 minutes at HIGH pressure and choose the Pressure Cook mode. 8. Once cooking is complete, select CANCEL and let Naturally Release for 5 minutes on seal position, then do a Quick Release on vent position. Carefully unlock the lid. 9. Serve.
Per Serving: Calories 502; Fat: 39g; Sodium 768mg; Carbs: 4.87g; Sugars: 2.03g; Protein 32g

Potatoes with Chicken

Prep Time: 5 minutes | Cook Time: 30 minutes | Serves: 4

2 lbs. chicken thighs, skinless and boneless	¼ cup lemon juice
	2 tbsps. Italian seasoning
2 tbsps. extra virgin olive oil	2 lbs. red potatoes, peeled and cut into quarters
¾ cup chicken stock	
3 tbsps. Dijon mustard	1 tsp salt
1 tsp ground black pepper	

1. Heat the oil in the Instant Pot using the SAUTÉ mode. 2. Add a half teaspoon of salt and a half teaspoon of pepper to the chicken thighs. 3. The chicken should be added to the Instant Pot, where it should be cooked for 3 minutes on each side. 4. Combine the stock, mustard, lemon juice, and Italian seasoning in a medium bowl. 5. Over the chicken, pour the mixture. 6. Add the potatoes along with the ½ teaspoon each of salt and pepper. Stir. 7. Select the Pressure Cook and set the cooking duration for 15 minutes at HIGH pressure. 8. After cooking is finished, allow the pressure to naturally release for 5 minutes on seal position. Quickly expel any lingering steam on vent position. Open the lid. Serve.
Per Serving: Calories 729; Fat: 42g; Sodium 1367mg; Carbs: 43g; Sugars: 4g; Protein 43g

Nachos with Chicken

Prep Time: 10 minutes | Cook Time: 35 minutes | Serves: 6

2 lbs. chicken thighs, boneless, skinless	mix
	⅔ cup mild red salsa
1 tbsps. olive oil	⅓ cup mild Herdez salsa verde
1 package (1 oz.) taco seasoning	

1. Heat the oil in the Instant Pot using the SAUTÉ mode. 2. Chicken thighs are then added, and the meat is well browned for a few minutes on each side. 3. Mix the salsa and taco seasoning in a medium basin. 4. Stir thoroughly after adding the ingredients to the saucepan. Lock the lid by closing it. 5. Before selecting the Pressure Cook and setting the cooking duration for 15 minutes at HIGH pressure, hit the CANCEL button to reset the cooking procedure. 6. Once the food has finished cooking, utilize a Natural Release for ten minutes before y releasing any leftover pressure on vent position. Open the pot's lid. Shred the meat. Serve with tortilla chips.
Per Serving: Calories 374; Fat: 28g; Sodium 317mg; Carbs: 2.87g; Sugars: 1.03g; Protein 2 5.39g

Adobo Chicken Drumstick

Prep Time: 10 minutes | Cook Time: 30 minutes | Serves: 4

4 chicken drumsticks	⅓ cup soy sauce
½ tsp kosher salt	¼ cup sugar
1 tsp ground black pepper	1 onion, chopped
2 tbsps. olive oil	5 cloves garlic, crushed
¼ cup white vinegar	2 bay leaves

1. Heat SAUTÉ on a high setting. Add the oil to the pot's bottom after waiting one minute. 2. Add ½ teaspoon pepper and salt to the legs' seasoning. 3. In the Instant Pot, add the chicken drumsticks and cook for 4 minutes on each side. 4. Include the bay leaves, vinegar, soy sauce, sugar, onion, garlic, and ½ teaspoon of pepper. 5. Lock the lid by closing it. Choose Pressure Cook, then cook for 10 minutes at HIGH pressure. 6. Use the Quick Release when the timer runs off. Open the lid slowly. 7. To reduce the sauce, use the SAUTÉ setting and simmer for 10 minutes. Press the CANCEL button to stop the cooking program. 8. Remove the bay leaves. Serve.
Per Serving: Calories 376; Fat: 22.17g; Sodium 754mg; Carbs: 16.87g; Sugars: 11.03g; Protein 25.39g

Easy Puttanesca Chicken

Prep Time: 15 minutes | Cook Time: 30 minutes | Serves: 4

6 chicken thighs, skin on	6 oz. pitted black olives
2 tbsps. olive oil	1 tbsp. capers, rinsed and drained
1 cup water	1 tbsp. fresh basil, chopped
14 oz. canned chopped tomatoes	1 tsp kosher salt
2 cloves garlic, crushed	1 tsp ground black pepper
½ tsp red chili flakes or to taste	

1. Heat the oil in the Instant Pot using the SAUTÉ mode. 2. Cook the chicken thighs for 4-6 minutes with the skin side down. 3. Transfer the chicken to a bowl. 4. The Instant Pot should be filled with water, tomatoes, garlic, chili flakes, black olives, capers, fresh basil, salt, and pepper. Stir well before simmering. 5. Put the chicken back in the pot. Lock the lid by closing it. 6. Selecting the Pressure Cook option and setting the cooking duration for 16 minutes at HIGH pressure. 7. After the timer goes off, wait 10 minutes for the pressure to naturally dissipate on seal position before quickly releasing any leftover pressure on vent position. Open the pot's lid. Serve.
Per Serving: Calories 522; Fat: 41g; Sodium 1104mg; Carbs: 4.87g; Sugars: 1g; Protein 33g

Congee with Chicken

Prep Time: 5 minutes | Cook Time: 60 minutes | Serves: 6

6 chicken drumsticks	Salt to taste
7 cups water	½ cup scallions, chopped
1 cup Jasmine rice	2 tbsps. sesame oil, optional
1 tbsp. fresh ginger	Well-rinse the rice.

1. To the Instant Pot, add the chicken, rice, water, and ginger. Good stirring. 2. Lock the lid by closing it. Set the cooking duration to 25 minutes at HIGH pressure and choose the Pressure Cook mode. 3. After cooking is finished, choose CANCEL and wait 10 minutes for the pressure to naturally release on seal position. Release any remaining steam on vent position. Open the lid. 4. Discard the bones after removing the chicken from the saucepan and shredding the flesh. 5. Refill the pot with the chicken flesh. 6. Choose SAUTÉ and simmer for about 10 minutes, stirring periodically, or until thickened. Top with scallions and sesame oil. Serve.
Per Serving: Calories 215; Fat: 20g; Sodium 146mg; Carbs: 10g; Sugars: 1.03g; Protein 26g

BBQ drumsticks of chicken

Prep Time: 5 minutes | Cook Time: 30 minutes | Serves: 6

6 chicken drumsticks	½ cup + 2 tbsps. water
1 tbsp. olive oil	½ cup sugar-free barbecue sauce
1 onion, chopped	1½ tbsp. arrowroot
1 tsp garlic, minced	

1. Heat the oil in the Instant Pot using the SAUTÉ mode. 2. The onion should be added and sautéed for about 3 minutes, or until tender. 3. Cook for a further 30 seconds after adding the garlic. 4. Stir thoroughly after adding ½ cup of water and barbeque sauce. 5.

Chicken drumsticks should be added to the stew. Lock the lid by closing it. 6. To restart the cooking program, press the CANCEL button. Choose Pressure Cook, then cook for 10 minutes at HIGH pressure. 7. Use the Quick Release when the timer runs off. Open the lid slowly. 8. The remaining water and arrowroot should be blended in a cup. Add to the pot. 9. Choose SAUTÉ, and simmer for 5 minutes over high heat, or until the sauce has thickened. Serve the drumsticks with the sauce.
Per Serving: Calories 245; Fat: 14.17g; Sodium 147mg; Carbs: 3.87g; Sugars: 1.03g; Protein 23g

Chicken and Tomato Drumsticks

Prep Time: 10 minutes | Cook Time: 30 minutes | Serves: 6

6 chicken drumsticks (24 oz.), skin removed, on the bone	½ tsp ground black pepper
	1 tsp olive oil
1 tbsp. apple cider vinegar	1½ cups tomato sauce
1 tsp oregano, dried	1 jalapeno, seeded, cut in halves
½ tsp salt	¼ cup cilantro, chopped

1. Combine the apple cider vinegar, oregano, salt, and pepper in a medium bowl. 2. Fill the bowl with the marinade, then add the chicken. If preferred, let the chicken to marinate for a few hours. 3. Heat up the oil in your instant pot while it is in SAUTÉ mode. 4. Chicken should be lowered into the saucepan and seared for 5-8 minutes, until beautifully browned. 5. Add the cilantro, tomato sauce, and half of the jalapenos. Lock the lid by closing it. 6. Selecting the Pressure Cook option and setting the cooking duration for 20 minutes at HIGH pressure. 7. Once pressure cooking is complete, use a Quick Release on seal position. Open the lid. Serve with the remaining cilantro and jalapeno.
Per Serving: Calories 290; Fat: 13g; Sodium 1246mg; Carbs: 14g; Sugars: 7g; Protein 25g

Chicken Wings with Honey

Prep Time: 5 minutes | Cook Time: 30 minutes | Serves: 4

2 lbs. chicken wings	1 small lime, juiced
3 tbsps. honey	½ tsp sea salt
2 tbsps. soy sauce	½ cup water

1. Soy sauce, lime juice, honey, and salt should all be combined in a bowl. 2. Use a paper towel to dry the chicken wings after rinsing them. 3. Shake a Ziploc bag a few times after adding the chicken wings and honey mixture inside. After that, chill for 60 minutes. 4. The chicken wings with marinade should be added to the Instant Pot along with the water. 5. Lock the lid by closing it. Choose the Pressure Cook mode, and then set the cooking duration to HIGH pressure for 15 minutes. 6. After the timer goes off, give the pressure 10 minutes to naturally release on seal position. Open the lid. 7. Choose SAUTÉ and keep cooking until the sauce becomes thick. Serve. If desired, season with some more herbs or spices.
Per Serving: Calories 360; Fat: 9g; Sodium 596mg; Carbs: 16g; Sugars: 14g; Protein 50g

Cheesy Chicken

Prep Time: 10 minutes | Cook Time: 25 minutes | Serves: 6

1 lb. chicken breasts, boneless and skinless	1 package (1 oz.) dry ranch seasoning
1 can (10 oz.) rotel tomato, undrained	1½ tsp chili powder
	1½ tsp cumin
1 can (15 oz.) corn, undrained	8 oz. cream cheese
1 can (15 oz.) black beans, drained and rinsed	¼ cup parsley

1. In the Instant Pot, combine all the ingredients with the exception of the cheese. 2. Lock the lid by closing it. Choose Pressure Cook, then cook for 20 minutes at HIGH pressure. 3. Release the pressure when the timer sounds. After 10 minutes of naturally releasing steam on seal position, quickly release any leftover steam on vent position. Open the lid. 4. Shred the chicken and place it on a platter. 5. Stir thoroughly after adding the cheese to the saucepan. Once the cheese has melted, cover the pan and let it stand for 5 minutes. 6. Return the chicken to the pot after lifting the cover. To blend, stir. Top with parsley and serve.
Per Serving: Calories 322; Fat: 18g; Sodium 504mg; Carbs: 20.87g; Sugars: 5g; Protein 21.39g

Tasty Chicken Teriyaki

Prep Time: 10 minutes | Cook Time: 20 minutes | Serves: 4

2 lbs. chicken breasts, skinless and boneless
⅔ cup teriyaki sauce
1 tbsp. honey
½ cup chicken stock
½ tsp salt
½ tsp ground black pepper
A handful green onions, chopped

1. Using SAUTÉ on the Instant Pot. 2. Stir in the honey and teriyaki sauce, then boil for one minute. 3. Chicken, stock, salt, and pepper should be added. Good stirring. Lock the lid by closing it. 4. The cooking time should be set to 12 minutes at HIGH pressure on the Pressure Cook. 5. When the food is done cooking, choose CANCEL and allow the pressure naturally release for 5 minutes on seal position. Quickly expel any residual steam on vent position. 6. Shred the chicken and place it on a platter. 7. Return the shredded chicken to the pot after removing ½ cup of the cooking liquid. Add green onions and stir. Serve.
Per Serving: Calories 462; Fat: 21g; Sodium 1335mg; Carbs: 13g; Sugars: 11g; Protein 51g

Delicious Chicken Buffalo

Prep Time: 5 minutes | Cook Time: 20 minutes | Serves: 4

2 lbs. chicken breasts, skinless, boneless and cut into thin strips
1 small yellow onion, chopped
½ cup celery, chopped
½ cup buffalo sauce
½ cup chicken stock
¼ cup bleu cheese, crumbled

1. To the Instant Pot, add the chicken breasts, celery, onion, buffalo sauce, and stock. 2. Close the lid. Choose Pressure Cook, then cook for 12 minutes at HIGH pressure. 3. Allow the pressure to naturally release for five minutes after the timer has finished on seal position, then quickly remove any leftover pressure on vent position. Take your time to open the lid. 4. ⅔ cup of cooking liquid should be drained. 5. Stir thoroughly after adding the crumbled bleu cheese to the pot. Serve.
Per Serving: Calories 494; Fat: 23g; Sodium 621mg; Carbs: 17g; Sugars: 13g; Protein 50g

Yummy Chicken Crack

Prep Time: 10 minutes | Cook Time: 30 minutes | Serves: 4

2 lbs. chicken breast, boneless
8 oz. cream cheese
1 (1 oz.) packet ranch seasoning
1 cup water
3 tbsps. cornstarch
4 oz. cheddar cheese, shredded
6-8 bacon slices, cooked

1. Cream cheese and chicken breasts should be added to the Instant Pot. 2. Use ranch seasoning to season. Pour in a cup of water. 3. Lock the lid by closing it. Choose Pressure Cook, and then cook for 25 minutes at HIGH pressure. 4. Use a Quick Release in the vent position when the timer runs off. Open the lid. 5. Shred the chicken and place it on a platter. 6. Choose SAUTÉ and incorporate the cornstarch. Good stirring. 7. Stir in the bacon, cheese, and shredded chicken to the saucepan. Cook for three minutes. 8. To end the cooking program, use the CANCEL button. Allow the pressure to release naturally. Close the lid and let the dish sit for a few minutes before serving.
Per Serving: Calories 829; Fat: 58.17g; Sodium 1226mg; Carbs: 13g; Sugars: 4g; Protein 61g

Easy Chicken Pina Colada

Prep Time: 10 minutes | Cook Time: 30 minutes | Serves: 4

2 lbs. chicken thighs cut into 1-inch pieces
½ cup coconut cream, full fat
2 tbsps. soy sauce
1 cup pineapple chunks, fresh or frozen
1 tsp cinnamon
⅛ tsp salt
½ cup green onion, chopped
1 tsp arrowroot starch
1 tbsp. water

1. Stir to mix all the ingredients in the Instant Pot, excluding the green onion. 2. Lock the lid by closing it. Set the cooking time to 15 minutes and choose the Pressure Cook option. 3. Allow the pressure to naturally relax on seal position for 10 minutes after the timer goes off before quickly release any leftover pressure. Open the lid slowly. 4. Place the chicken in a bowl for serving. 5. Combine the arrowroot starch and water in a cup. Mix thoroughly. 6. Press the SAUTÉ button

on the instant pot, add the contents, and heat while occasionally stirring until the sauce starts to thicken. Serve the chicken with green onion and sauce.
Per Serving: Calories 939; Fat: 62g; Sodium 2004mg; Carbs: 51g; Sugars: 14g; Protein 44g

Citrus Chicken

Prep Time: 10 minutes | Cook Time: 20 minutes | Serves:4

4 chicken breasts
¼ cup water
¾ cup orange juice
¾ cup barbecue sauce
2 tbsps. soy sauce
1 tbsp. cornstarch + 2 tbsps. water
2 tbsps. green onions, chopped

1. To the Instant Pot, add the chicken breasts, 14 cup of water, orange juice, barbecue sauce, and soy sauce. Good stirring. 2. Lock the lid by closing it. Set the cooking time to 15 minutes and choose the Pressure Cook option. 3. Use a Quick Release on the vent position when the pressure cooking is finished. Open the lid by slowly unlocking it. 4. Combine the cornstarch and two tablespoons of water in a cup. 5. Add the cornstarch slurry to the pot and choose SAUTÉ as the cooking mode. 6. 5 minutes should pass while simmering for the sauce to thicken. Add green onions and serve.
Per Serving: Calories 638; Fat: 28g; Sodium 854mg; Carbs: 29g; Sugars: 23g; Protein 61g

Diced Chicken Breast

Prep Time: 10 minutes | Cook Time: 20 minutes | Serves: 4

1.5-2 lbs. boneless chicken breasts
½ tsp ground black pepper
½ tsp garlic salt
½ cup chicken broth

1. Black pepper and salt should be used to season the chicken on both sides. 2. Pour the chicken stock over the chicken breasts in the Instant Pot. 3. Lock the lid by closing it. Choose Pressure Cook, then cook for 8 minutes at HIGH pressure. 4. Once the food has finished cooking, utilize a Natural Release for ten minutes on seal position before quickly release any leftover pressure on vent position. 5. With two forks, remove the chicken from the pot and shred it. Serve.
Per Serving: Calories 392; Fat: 20g; Sodium 249mg; Carbs: 0.87g; Sugars: 0.03g; Protein 48g

Chicken Marinara with Shredded Pieces

Prep Time: 10 minutes | Cook Time: 30 minutes | Serves: 6

4 lbs. chicken breasts
½ cup chicken broth
½ tsp black pepper
1 tsp salt
2 cups marinara sauce

1. Stir thoroughly before adding the chicken breasts, stock, pepper, and salt to the Instant Pot. 2. Lock the lid by closing it. Choose Pressure Cook, then cook for 20 minutes at HIGH pressure. 3. Once pressure cooking is complete, use a Quick Release on vent position. Open the lid by slowly unlocking it. 4. In the pot, shred the chicken. 5. Choose SAUTÉ as your setting. Sauté for 5 minutes after adding the marinara sauce. Serve with cooked rice, potato, peas or green salad.
Per Serving: Calories 577; Fat: 29g; Sodium 1271mg; Carbs: 6g; Sugars: 3g; Protein 68.39g

Potatoes and BBQ Chicken

Prep Time: 10 minutes | Cook Time: 20 minutes | Serves: 4

2 lbs. chicken (breasts or thighs)
½ cup water
3 large potatoes, unpeeled and quartered
1 cup BBQ sauce
1 tbsp. Italian seasoning
1 tbsp. minced garlic
1 large onion, sliced

1. To the Instant Pot, add the chicken, water, potatoes, BBQ sauce, Italian seasoning, garlic, and onion. Good stirring. 2. Lock the lid by closing it. Choose Pressure Cook, then cook for 15 minutes at HIGH pressure. 3. Once pressure cooking is complete, use a Quick Release on vent position. Open the lid by slowly unlocking it. 4. Shred the chicken and place it on a platter. Chicken shreds should be added back to the pot. 5. Stir well until the sauce is evenly distributed. Serve.
Per Serving: Calories 509; Fat: 6g; Sodium 802mg; Carbs: 58g; Sugars: 6g; Protein 53g

Lemon Mustard Potatoes with Chicken

Prep Time: 10 minutes | Cook Time: 30 minutes | Serves: 8

2 lbs. chicken thighs
2 tbsps. olive oil
3 lbs. red potatoes, peeled and quartered
2 tbsps. Italian seasoning

3 tbsps. Dijon mustard
¾ cup chicken broth
¼ cup lemon juice
1 tsp salt
1 tsp ground black pepper

1. Heat the oil in the Instant Pot using the SAUTÉ mode. 2. Cook the chicken thighs in the saucepan for two to three minutes, or until they begin to brown. 3. Potatoes, Italian spice, and Dijon mustard should all be added. Cook for minutes while periodically stirring. 4. Stir after adding the broth and lemon juice to the saucepan. 5. Add salt and pepper to taste. Lock the lid by closing it. 6. To restart the cooking program, press the CANCEL button. Choose the Pressure Cook option, and then enter 15 minutes for the cooking duration. 7. Release the pressure naturally on seal position for 10 minutes when the timer chimes. Quickly expel any leftover steam on vent position. Take your time to open the lid. Serve.
Per Serving: Calories 448; Fat: 24.17g; Sodium 724mg; Carbs: 30g; Sugars: 2.03g; Protein 27g

Chicken Apricot

Prep Time: 5 minutes | Cook Time: 25 minutes | Serves: 6

2½ lbs. chicken thighs, skinless
1 tbsp. vegetable oil
1 tsp kosher salt
1 tsp ground black pepper
3 cloves garlic, minced
1 large onion, chopped
⅛ tsp allspice powder

½ cup chicken broth
8 oz. canned apricots
1 lb. canned tomatoes, diced
1 tbsp. fresh ginger, grated
½ tsp cinnamon, ground
Fresh parsley, chopped (optional)

1. Heat up the oil in your instant pot while it is in SAUTÉ mode. 2. Chicken thighs should be salted and peppered. 3. To the Instant Pot, add the chicken, onion, and garlic. 4. Add the allspice powder and simmer for a further five minutes, or until well browned. 5. The broth is poured. To the saucepan, add the tomatoes, fresh ginger, cinnamon, and apricots. Good stirring. Lock the lid by closing it. 6. To restart the cooking program, press the CANCEL button. Choose the Pressure Cook option, and then enter 12 minutes of HIGH pressure cooking. 7. Use a Quick Release when the timer chimes. Take your time to open the lid. Transfer the dish to a serving bowl, top with parsley and serve.
Per Serving: Calories 535; Fat: 35.17g; Sodium 719mg; Carbs: 15.87g; Sugars: 10.3g; Protein 37g

Chicken in Cream with Bacon

Prep Time: 5 minutes | Cook Time: 30 minutes | Serves: 4

2 lbs. chicken breasts, skinless and boneless
2 slices bacon, chopped
1 cup chicken stock

1 oz. ranch seasoning
4 oz. cream cheese
Green onions, chopped for serving

1. Add the bacon to the Instant Pot and choose the SAUTÉ option. 2. For four to five minutes, sauté the bacon. 3. Add the stock, ranch dressing, and chicken. Good stirring. 4. Lock the lid by closing it. Choose Pressure Cook, then cook for 12 minutes at HIGH pressure. 5. Allow the pressure to naturally release for five minutes on seal position after the timer goes off, then quickly release any leftover steam on vent position. Take your time to open the lid. 6. Shred the chicken and place it on a platter. 7. Take out ⅔ cup of the cooking liquid. After adding the cheese, choose SAUTÉ and let the food simmer for an additional 3 minutes. 8. Stir in the chicken one more. To halt the cooking program, choose CANCEL. Add green onions, stir and serve.
Per Serving: Calories 814; Fat: 40g; Sodium 1018mg; Carbs: 5g; Sugars: 1g; Protein 99g

Chicken Cajun with Rice

Prep Time: 15 minutes | Cook Time: 30 minutes | Serves: 6

1 tbsp. olive oil
1 onion, diced
3 cloves garlic, minced
1 lb. chicken breasts, sliced
2 cups chicken broth
1 tbsp. tomato paste

1½ cups white rice, rinsed
1 bell pepper, chopped
Cajun spices:
¼ tsp cayenne pepper
2 tsp dried thyme
1 tbsp. paprika

1. Heat the oil in the Instant Pot using the SAUTÉ mode. 2. Once aromatic, add the onion and garlic. 3. Stir thoroughly after adding the chicken breasts and Cajun seasonings. additional three minutes of sautéing. 4. Add the tomato paste and broth to the pot. To make the tomato paste dissolve, stir. 5. Stir in the bell pepper and rice. Lock the lid by closing it. 6. To restart the cooking program, press the CANCEL button. Choose the Pressure Cook mode, and then set the cooking duration to HIGH pressure for 20 minutes. 7. After cooking is finished, allow the pressure to naturally release for 10 minutes on seal position. Release any remaining steam quickly on vent position. Serve.
Per Serving: Calories 699; Fat: 22g; Sodium 576mg; Carbs: 63g; Sugars: 2g; Protein 55g

Chicken Tacos Mojo

Prep Time: 5 minutes | Cook Time: 20 minutes | Serves: 4

4 skinless, boneless chicken
For the Mojo:
¼ cup olive oil
⅔ cup fresh lime juice
⅔ cup orange juice
8 cloves garlic, minced
1 tbsp. grated orange peel
1 tbsp. dried oregano
To serve:
8 – 12 mission organic corn tortillas
½ cup red onion, finely diced

breasts

2 tsp ground cumin
2 tsp Kosher salt
¼ tsp ground black pepper
¼ cup chopped fresh cilantro + more for garnishing

1 avocado, sliced

1. To the Instant Pot, add the chicken breasts. 2. Mix the ingredients for the mojo in a bowl with a whisk. 3. Lock the lid by closing it. Choose the Pressure Cook option, and then enter 20 minutes for the cooking duration. 4. After cooking is finished, choose CANCEL and wait 10 minutes for the pressure to naturally release on seal position. Open the pot's lid. 5. Shred the chicken and place it on a platter. Stir the meat back into the pot. 6. Turn on the broiler in the oven. Add the sauce and the shredded chicken on a baking sheet. 7. For 5 to 8 minutes, or until the chicken's edges are browned and crispy, place under the broiler. Top with cilantro. Serve in tacos with chopped onion and sliced avocado.
Per Serving: Calories 146; Fat: 13g; Sodium 1168mg; Carbs: 11g; Sugars: 4g; Protein 2g

Tandoori Chicken Roast

Prep Time: 10 minutes | Cook Time: 20 minutes | Serves: 6

6 chicken thighs, bone in
½ cup plain yogurt
1-2 tbsp. tandoori paste
1 tbsp. lemon juice

1 tsp kosher salt
1 tsp ground black pepper
½ cup water

1. Combine the yoghurt, lemon juice, and tandoori paste in a large basin. 2. Fill the bowl with the marinade, then add the chicken. 3. Refrigerate the marinade for at least 6 hours. 4. Salt and pepper the chicken as desired. 5. In the Instant Pot, combine the chicken, marinade, and water. 6. Lock the lid by closing it. Choose Pressure Cook for 10 minutes at HIGH pressure. 7. Allow the pressure to naturally release for five minutes on seal position after the timer goes off, then quickly release any leftover steam on vent position. Take your time to open the lid. 8. Cook for 3 to 5 minutes, or until browned on sauté function. Serve.
Per Serving: Calories 471; Fat: 32.17g; Sodium 554mg; Carbs: 2.87g; Sugars: 1.03g; Protein 32g

Tasty Chicken Salsa

Prep Time: 10 minutes | Cook Time: 30 minutes | Serves: 4

2 lb. chicken breasts, skinless and boneless
1 tsp kosher salt
1 tsp ground black pepper

A pinch of oregano
2 tsp cumin
2 cups chunky salsa, or your preference

1. Salt and pepper the chicken breasts before adding them to the Instant Pot. 2. Stir thoroughly after adding the oregano, cumin, and salsa. 3. Lock the lid by closing it. Choose the Pressure Cook option, and then enter 25 minutes for the cooking duration. 4. Use a Quick Release on the vent position as soon as the timer beeps. Take your time to open the lid. 5. Shred the chicken after removing it. 6. The shredded chicken may be added to corn tortillas with avocado, cilantro, and a squeeze of lime juice for a fast supper or used in casseroles.
Per Serving: Calories 396; Fat: 21g; Sodium 704mg; Carbs: 0.87g; Sugars: 0.03g; Protein 47.39g

Tasty Coca-Cola Chicken

Prep Time: 15 minutes | Cook Time: 30 minutes | Serves: 4

4 chicken drumsticks
2 tbsps. olive oil
Salt and ground black pepper to taste

1 large finely onion, chopped
1 small chopped chili
1 tbsp. balsamic vinegar
500ml Coca Cola

1. Heat SAUTÉ. Add the oil to the pot's bottom after waiting one minute. 2. Chicken drumsticks should be salted and peppered to taste. 3. In the Instant Pot, add the drumsticks and cook for 4 minutes on each side, or until beautifully browned. 4. Chicken should be taken out of the pot. Add the onions and cook them for a few minutes, until they are tender. 5. Stir after adding the Coca-Cola, vinegar, and chili. 6. Place the drumsticks back in the Instant Pot. Lock the lid by closing it. 7. To restart the cooking program, press the CANCEL button. Choose the Pressure 8. Cook mode, and then set the cooking duration to HIGH pressure for 10 minutes. 9. After cooking is finished, allow the pressure to naturally release for 10 minutes on seal position. Release any remaining steam quickly on vent position. Open the lid. Serve.
Per Serving: Calories 292; Fat: 18g; Sodium 141mg; Carbs: 5.87g; Sugars: 2.03g; Protein 24g

Hunter Style Chicken Drumstick

Prep Time: 15 minutes | Cook Time: 35 minutes | Serves: 6

8 chicken drumsticks, bone in
1 yellow onion, chopped
1 cup chicken stock
1 tsp garlic powder
28 oz. canned tomatoes and juice, crushed

1 tsp oregano, dried
1 bay leaf
1 tsp kosher salt
½ cup black olives, pitted and sliced

1. Select SAUTÉ in the Instant Pot. 2. When the onion is transparent, add it and simmer for an additional 6 to 7 minutes. 3. Stir thoroughly after adding the stock, garlic powder, tomatoes, oregano, bay leaf, and salt. 4. Stir after adding the chicken to the pot. Close the lid. 5. To restart the cooking program, press the CANCEL button. Choose the Pressure Cook option, and then enter a 15-minute HIGH pressure cooking duration. 6. After the timer goes off, wait 10 minutes for the pressure to naturally dissipate on seal position before manually release any leftover pressure on vent psition. Open the pot's lid. 7. Get rid of the bay leaf. Place the meal on plates, sprinkle with the olives, and then serve.
Per Serving: Calories 598; Fat: 22g; Sodium 844mg; Carbs: 6g; Sugars: 4g; Protein 65g

Olive and Lemon Chicken

Prep Time: 10 minutes | Cook Time: 20 minutes | Serves: 4

4 chicken breasts, skinless and boneless
½ cup butter
½ tsp cumin
1 tsp salt

½ tsp ground black pepper
Juice of 1 lemon
1 cup chicken broth
1 can pitted green olives

1. Choose SAUTÉ to start the Instant Pot heating up. Add the butter and let it melt once it is heated. 2. Chicken breasts are seasoned with salt, pepper, and cumin. 3. Place the breasts in the saucepan and brown them well for 3–5 minutes on each side. 4. Stir thoroughly after adding the lemon juice, broth, and olives. Lock the lid by closing it. 5. To restart the cooking program, press the CANCEL button. Choose the Pressure Cook option, and then set the cooking duration to HIGH pressure for 10 minutes. 6. Once the food has finished cooking, use a Natural Release for five minutes on seal position before quickly release any leftover pressure on vent position. Open the lid. Serve.
Per Serving: Calories 804; Fat: 54g; Sodium 1203mg; Carbs: 2g; Sugars: 1.03g; Protein 73g

Limy Chicken

Prep Time: 10 minutes | Cook Time: 25 minutes | Serves: 4

2 lbs. chicken breasts, bones removed
¾ cup chicken broth or water
Juice of 2 medium limes
1½ tsp chili powder
1 tsp cumin

1 tsp onion powder
6 cloves garlic, minced
½ tsp liquid smoke
1 tsp kosher salt
1 tsp ground black pepper

1. Place all of the ingredients in the Instant Pot and stir just enough to combine everything. 2. Lock the lid by closing it. Choose Pressure Cook and cook for 10 minutes at HIGH pressure. 3. Release the pressure when the timer sounds. After 10 minutes of naturally occurring release on seal position, quickly release any leftover steam on vent position. Open the lid slowly. 4. Shred the chicken after removing it. Serve with the remaining juice in Instant Pot.
Per Serving: Calories 413; Fat: 21g; Sodium 905mg; Carbs: 5g; Sugars: 1g; Protein 48g

Potato and Chickpea Curry

Prep Time: 25 minutes | Cook Time: 5 minutes | Serves: 6

1 Tbsp. canola oil
1 medium onion, chopped
2 garlic cloves, minced
2 tsp. minced fresh gingerroot
2 tsp. ground coriander
1 tsp. garam masala
1 tsp. chili powder
½ tsp. salt
½ tsp. ground cumin
¼ tsp. ground turmeric
2 ½ cups vegetable stock

2 cans (15 oz. each) chickpeas or garbanzo beans, rinsed and drained
1 can (15 oz.) crushed tomatoes
1 large baking potato, peeled and cut into ¾-in. cubes
1 Tbsp. lime juice
Chopped fresh cilantro
Hot cooked rice
Optional: Sliced red onion and lime wedges

1. Set Instant pot to the sauté setting. Add oil and adjust for medium heat. Onion should be cooked and stirred for 2-4 minutes once the oil is heated. Add the dry spices, ginger, and garlic; simmer and stir for one minute. To the Instant pot, add stock. Stirring to release browned parts from the pan, cook for 30 seconds. Select Cancel. Toss in the potatoes, tomatoes, and chickpeas. 2. Close the pressure-release valve and lock the lid. Adjust to Pressure Cook on high for 3 minutes. Allow any leftover pressure to naturally relax for ten minutes on seal position before quickly release it on vent position. 3. Add the lime juice and cilantro, and stir. Serve with lime wedges, red onion, and rice, if preferred.
Per Serving: Calories 989; Fat: 95.17g; Sodium 554mg; Carbs: 34g; Sugars: 6.88g; Protein 8g

Easy Poached Salmon

Prep Time: 10 minutes | Cook Time: 5 minutes | Serves: 4

2 cups water
1 cup white wine
1 medium onion, sliced
1 celery rib, sliced
1 medium carrot, sliced
2 Tbsp. lemon juice
3 fresh thyme sprigs

1 fresh rosemary sprig
1 bay leaf
½ tsp. salt
¼ tsp. pepper
4 salmon fillets (1¼ in. thick and 6 oz. each)
Lemon wedges

1. Add the first 11 ingredients in Instant pot then add salmon. Close the pressure-release valve and lock the lid. Select Pressure Cook on high for 3 minutes. Rapidly release pressure on vent position. when implanted the fish, a thermometers should register at least 290°F/145°C. 2. Take the fish out of the pot. With lemon wedges, serve warm or cold.
Per Serving: Calories 390; Fat: 18g; Sodium 1303mg; Carbs: 2.87g; Sugars: 1.03g; Protein 52g

Alaskan Wild Cod

Prep Time: 5 minutes | Cook Time: 10 minutes | Serves:2

1 large fillet wild Alaskan Cod
1 cup cherry tomatoes, chopped
Salt and ground black pepper to

taste
2 tbsps. butter

1. Place the tomatoes in the Instant Pot. 2. Then, add the fish. 3. Add salt and pepper to taste. 4. Lock the lid by closing it. Choose Pressure Cook, then cook for 8 minutes at HIGH pressure. 5. Use a Quick Release on vent position when the timer chimes. Take your time to open the lid. 6. The fish fillet should be covered with butter. After covering it, leave the dish alone for one minute. Serve.
Per Serving: Calories 782; Fat: 23g; Sodium 884mg; Carbs: 23.87g; Sugars: 11.03g; Protein 18.39g

Delicious Manchester Stew

Prep Time: 25 minutes | Cook Time: 5 minutes | Serves: 6

2 tbsp. olive oil
2 medium onions, chopped
2 garlic cloves, minced
1 tsp. dried oregano
1 cup dry red wine
1 lb. small red potatoes, quartered
1 can (16 oz.) kidney beans, rinsed and drained
½ lb. sliced fresh mushrooms
2 medium leeks (white portion

only), sliced
1 cup fresh baby carrots
2 ½ cups water
1 can (14½ oz.) no-salt-added diced tomatoes
1 tsp. dried thyme
½ tsp. salt
¼ tsp. pepper
Fresh basil leaves

1. Choose the Instant Pot's sauté setting. add oil Onions should be cooked and stirred for two to three minutes after the oil is heated. Cook and stir for another minute after adding the garlic and oregano. Stir in the wine. Bring to a boil; simmer for 3 to 4 minutes, or until liquid is reduced by half. Select Cancel. 2. Add carrots, potatoes, beans, mushrooms, leeks, and beans. Add salt, pepper, tomatoes, water, and thyme while stirring. Close the pressure-release valve and lock the lid. Set to Pressure Cook for 3 minutes on high. Allow any leftover pressure to naturally relax on seal position for ten minutes before quick-releasing it on vent position. Add basil leaves on top.
Per Serving: Calories 201; Fat: 8g; Sodium 244mg; Carbs: 28.7g; Sugars: 8g; Protein 6g

Mussels Steamed with Pepper

Prep Time: 30 minutes | Cook Time: 5 minutes | Serves: 4

2 lbs. fresh mussels, scrubbed and beards removed
2 Tbsp. olive oil
1 jalapeno pepper, seeded and chopped
3 garlic cloves, minced
1 bottle (8 oz.) clam juice
½ cup white wine or additional clam juice

⅓ cup chopped sweet red pepper
3 green onions, sliced
½ tsp. dried oregano
1 bay leaf
2 Tbsp. minced fresh parsley
¼ tsp. salt
¼ tsp. pepper
French bread baguette, sliced, optional

1. Tap the mussels and throw away those that don't shut. Place aside. Set Instant pot to the sauté setting. Add oil and adjust for medium heat. Cook and stir the chopped jalapeño for 2 to 3 minutes, or until it is crisp-tender. Add the garlic and simmer for another minute. Select Cancel. Add the mussels, wine, clam juice, red pepper, green onions, oregano, and bay leaf after stirring. Close the pressure-release valve and lock the lid. Adjust to Pressure Cook on high 2 minutes. Rapidly release pressure on vent position. 2. Throw away the bay leaf and any closed mussels. Add parsley, salt, and pepper to taste. Serve with pieces of baguette, if preferred.
Per Serving: Calories 265; Fat: 12g; Sodium 804mg; Carbs: 10g; Sugars: 1g; Protein 27g

Bulgur and Spice Trade Beans

Prep Time: 30 minutes | Cook Time: 15 minutes | Serves: 10

3 Tbsp. canola oil, divided
1½ cups bulgur
2 medium onions, chopped
1 medium sweet red pepper, chopped
5 garlic cloves, minced
1 Tbsp. ground cumin
1 Tbsp. paprika
2 tsp. ground ginger
1 tsp. pepper
½ tsp. ground cinnamon

½ tsp. cayenne pepper
1 carton (32 oz.) vegetable broth
2 Tbsp. soy sauce
1 can (28 oz.) crushed tomatoes
1 can (14½ oz.) diced tomatoes, undrained
1 can (15 oz.) garbanzo beans or chickpeas, rinsed and drained
½ cup golden raisins
2 Tbsp. brown sugar
Minced fresh cilantro, optional

1. Set Instant pot to the sauté setting. Add 1 Tbsp. oil and adjust for medium heat. Cook and stir bulgur for two to three minutes once the oil is heated. Remove from pot. 2. In the Instant pot, heat the final 2 tablespoons of oil. Cook and stir red pepper and onions for 2-3 minutes, or until they are crisp-tender. After adding the spices, simmer for another minute. Select Cancel. To the pot, add broth, soy sauce, and bulgur. 3. Close the pressure-release valve and lock the lid. Make adjustments for 12 minutes of low Pressure Cook. Rapidly release pressure on vent position. Select Cancel. Choose the sauté option and lower the heat. Add the tomatoes, beans, raisins, and brown sugar; cook, stirring periodically, for approximately 10 minutes, until the

sauce is slightly thickened and well cooked. If desired, sprinkle with the minced cilantro.
Per Serving: Calories 178; Fat: 6g; Sodium 263mg; Carbs: 28.7g; Sugars: 13g; Protein 5g

Healthy Cod

Prep Time: 5 minutes | Cook Time: 20 minutes | Serves: 4

1½ lbs. fresh (or frozen) cod fillets
3 tbsps. butter
1 onion, sliced
1 can diced tomatoes

1 lemon juice, freshly squeezed
Salt and ground black pepper to taste

1. Choose SAUTÉ on the Instant Pot. 2. Add the butter and let it melt once it is heated. 3. Add the salt, pepper, onion, tomatoes, and lemon juice. Stir well and cook for 9 minutes. 4. Fish fillets should be added to the pot and well covered in sauce. 5. To stop the SAUTE feature, hit the CANCEL button. Then, choose the Pressure Cook setting, and set the cooking duration to 3 minutes (or 5 minutes for frozen), at HIGH pressure. 6. Make advantage of a Quick Release on vent position when the pressure cooking is finished. Open the lid by slowly unlocking it. Serve the fish with sauce.
Per Serving: Calories 304; Fat: 15.17g; Sodium 234mg; Carbs: 40.87g; Sugars: 35g; Protein 5g

Halibut Poached in Tomato

Prep Time: 15 minutes | Cook Time: 5 minutes | Serves: 4

1 Tbsp. olive oil
2 poblano peppers, finely chopped
1 small onion, finely chopped
1 can (14½ oz.) fire-roasted diced tomatoes, undrained
1 can (14½ oz.) no-salt-added diced tomatoes, undrained
½ cup water

¼ cup chopped pitted green olives
3 garlic cloves, minced
¼ tsp. pepper
⅛ tsp. salt
4 halibut fillets (4 oz. each)
⅓ cup chopped fresh cilantro
4 lemon wedges
Crusty whole grain bread, optional

1. Select sauté setting on Instant pot. Add oil and adjust for medium heat. Poblano peppers and onion should be cooked and stirred in heated oil for 2 to 3 minutes, or until crisp-tender. Select Cancel. Add salt, pepper, olives, garlic, and tomatoes after stirring. Put fillets on top. 2. Close the pressure-release valve and lock the lid. Adjust to Pressure Cook on high for 3 minutes. Rapidly release pressure on vent position. when inserted the fish, a thermometers should read at least 290°F/145°C. 3. Put some cilantro on top. Serve with bread, if preferred, and lemon wedges.
Per Serving: Calories 343; Fat: 20g; Sodium 637mg; Carbs: 23g; Sugars: 9g; Protein 22g

Delicious Fish Stew

Prep Time: 25 minutes | Cook Time: 5 minutes | Serves: 8

1 lb. potatoes (about 2 medium), peeled and finely chopped
1 can (14½ oz.) diced tomatoes, undrained
1 can (10½ oz.) condensed cream of celery soup, undiluted
1 pkg. (10 oz.) frozen corn, thawed
1½ cups frozen lima beans, thawed
1½ cups vegetable or chicken broth
1 large onion, finely chopped
1 celery rib, finely chopped
1 medium carrot, finely chopped

½ cup white wine or additional vegetable broth
4 garlic cloves, minced
1 bay leaf
1 tsp. lemon-pepper seasoning
1 tsp. dried parsley flakes
1 tsp. dried rosemary, crushed
½ tsp. salt
1 lb. cod fillets, cut into 1-in. pieces
1 can (12 oz.) fat-free evaporated milk

1. In an Instant Pot, combine the first 16 ingredients; add the cod on top. Close the pressure-release valve and lock the lid. Adjust to pressure-cook on high for 2 minutes. 2. Allow the pressure to drop naturally on seal position. Remove the bay leaf. Milk is heated thoroughly by stirring in.
Per Serving: Calories 360; Fat: 13g; Sodium 744mg; Carbs: 40g; Sugars: 60g; Protein 21g

Peppers Stuffed

Prep Time: 15 minutes | Cook Time: 5 minutes | Serves: 4

4 medium sweet red peppers	½ cup frozen corn
1 can (15 oz.) black beans, rinsed and drained	⅓ cup uncooked converted long grain rice
1 cup shredded pepper jack cheese	1¼ tsp. chili powder
¾ cup salsa	½ tsp. ground cumin
1 small onion, chopped	Reduced-fat sour cream, optional

1. In the Instant Pot, add a steam rack and one cup of water. 2. Remove the peppers' tops and throw them away. Fill peppers with a mixture of beans, cheese, salsa, onion, corn, rice, chili powder, and cumin. peppers on the rack. 3. Close the pressure-release valve and lock the lid. Adjust to pressure-cook on high for 5 minutes. Allow the pressure to drop naturally on seal position. Serve with sour cream, if preferred.
Per Serving: Calories 265; Fat: 10g; Sodium 547mg; Carbs: 32g; Sugars: 9g; Protein 11g

Yummy Squid

Prep Time: 10 minutes | Cook Time: 25 minutes | Serves: 4

1 lb. squid	1 tsp salt
1 tsp onion powder	1 tsp white pepper
2 tbsps. starch	1 tbsp. lemon juice
1 tbsp. garlic, minced	3 tbsps. fish sauce
1 tbsp. chives	2 tbsps. butter
¼ tsp chili pepper, chopped	

1.Cut up the squid. 2. Mix the onion powder, starch, garlic, chives, chili pepper, salt, and white pepper in a large bowl. Mix thoroughly. 3. Squid is added to the spice mixture. Gently stir. 4. Stir in the fish sauce and lemon juice to season the mixture. For 10 minutes, set the mixture aside. 5. By choosing SAUTÉ, the Instant Pot will be preheated. Add the butter and let it melt once it is heated. 6. Add the squid mixture to the pot and secure the lid. 7. Select the Pressure Cook setting and cook for 13 minutes. Allow the pressure to release naturally on seal position. 8. Uncover the pot and serve when the cooking is finished.
Per Serving: Calories 170; Fat: 7g; Sodium 733mg; Carbs: 6g; Sugars: 1g; Protein 18.39g

Steam Fish

Prep Time: 5 minutes | Cook Time: 25 minutes | Serves: 4

4 white fish fillet	1 tbsp. olive oil
1 cup water	1 clove garlic, minced
1 lb. cherry tomatoes cut into halves	½ tsp thyme, dried
1 cup olives, pitted and chopped	Salt and ground black pepper to taste

1. Put the steam rack in the Instant Pot after adding water to the pot to prepare it. 2. Fish fillets should be placed in the rack. 3. Then add the tomatoes and olives on top. Olive oil, garlic, thyme, salt, and pepper should be added. 4. Lock the lid by closing it. Choose Pressure Cook, then cook for 10 minutes at LOW pressure. 5. When the food is done cooking, choose Cancel and let the pressure naturally release for 10 minutes on seal position. Open the lid. Serve the fish with tomatoes mix.
Per Serving: Calories 287; Fat: 10g; Sodium 312mg; Carbs: 20g; Sugars: 14g; Protein 28g

Fish and Vegetables from Asia

Prep Time: 10 minutes | Cook Time: 30 minutes | Serves: 4

2 fillets white fish	¼ long red chili, sliced
1 cup water	1 tbsp. honey
½ lb. frozen vegetables of your choice	2 tbsps. soy sauce
1 clove garlic, minced	Salt and ground black pepper to taste
2 tsp grated ginger	

1. Add water to instant pot. 2. Place a steam rack on top of the water that has been added to the Instant Pot. 3. In the pan, place the veggies. 4. The pan should be placed on the steam rack. 5. Garlic, ginger, red chili, honey, soy sauce, salt, and pepper should all be combined in a bowl. Good stirring. 6. Add the fillets and thoroughly coat them with the mixture in the basin. 7. On top of the veggies, arrange the fish fillets. Lock the lid by closing it. 8. Set the cooking duration to 15 minutes by pressing the STEAM button. 9. After cooking is finished, choose Cancel and wait 10 minutes for the pressure to naturally release on seal position. Quickly expel any lingering steam on vent position. Open the pot's lid. Serve.
Per Serving: Calories 603; Fat: 60g; Sodium 154mg; Carbs: 6g; Sugars: 5g; Protein 14g

Sauce of Clam

Prep Time: 10 minutes | Cook Time: 5 minutes | Serves: 4 cups

4 Tbsp. butter	¾ tsp. dried oregano
2 Tbsp. olive oil	½ tsp. garlic salt
½ cup finely chopped onion	¼ tsp. white pepper
8 oz. fresh mushrooms, chopped	¼ tsp. Italian seasoning
2 garlic cloves, minced	¼ tsp. black pepper
2 cans (10 oz. each) whole baby clams	2 Tbsp. chopped fresh parsley
½ cup water	Hot cooked pasta
¼ cup sherry	Grated Parmesan cheese, additional
2 tsp. lemon juice	lemon juice, minced parsley
1 bay leaf	optional

1. Select sauté setting on Instant pot. Add butter and oil after adjusting for medium heat. When heated, sauté onion for two minutes while stirring. Cook for another minute after adding the garlic and mushrooms. Select Cancel. 2. Chop clams coarsely after draining liquid from them. To the Instant Pot, add the clams, the conserved clam liquid, and the remaining 9 ingredients. Close the pressure-release valve and lock the lid. Adjust to Pressure Cook on high 2 minutes. Rapidly releasing pressure on vent position. 3. Remove the bay leaf and add the parsley. accompanied by spaghetti. Serve with more lemon juice, parsley, and grated Parmesan cheese, if preferred.
Per Serving: Calories 425; Fat: 19g; Sodium 685mg; Carbs: 63g; Sugars: 7g; Protein 7g

Special Fish

Prep Time: 10 minutes | Cook Time: 30 minutes | Serves: 4

4 salmon fillets	½ tbsp. coriander
12 oz. squid	1 tbsp. kosher salt
5 cups water	1 tsp ground black pepper
¼ cup soy sauce	1 tsp chili flakes
¼ tsp thyme	1 clove garlic, sliced
½ cup fresh dill	

1. Choose Sauté in the Instant Pot. 2. Add the water, soy sauce, thyme, fresh dill, coriander, salt, black pepper, and chili flakes to the Instant Pot. Mix thoroughly. 3. The mixture should be sautéed for 15 minutes with the lid on. 4. Slice the squid and fish into 1 to 2 inch chunks. 5. Remove all of the ingredients from the pot, excluding the liquid, when the time is up. 6. Fish, squid, and garlic are added. Continue light stirring. 7. Lock the lid by closing it. Choose Pressure Cook, then cook for 10 minutes at HIGH pressure. 8. Use the Quick Release on vent position when the timer runs off. Open the lid slowly. 9. Serve with cooked rice noodles.
Per Serving: Calories 512; Fat: 22g; Sodium 3131mg; Carbs: 7g; Sugars: 3g; Protein 66g

Lemon-Dill Fish

Prep Time: 5 minutes | Cook Time: 10 minutes | Serves: 2

2 cod fillets	¼ tsp garlic powder
1 cup water	2 sprigs fresh dill
Salt and ground black pepper to taste	4 slices lemon
	2 tbsps. butter

1. Put the steam rack in the Instant Pot and fill it with water to prepare it. 2. Cod fillets should be placed on the steam rack. Add some garlic powder, salt, and pepper. 3. Put one dill sprig, two lemon slices, and one tablespoon of butter in that order on each fillet. 4. Lock the lid by closing it. Choose Pressure Cook, then cook for 5 minutes at HIGH pressure. 5. Make advantage of a Quick Release on vent position when the pressure cooking is finished. Open the lid by slowly unlocking it. Serve.
Per Serving: Calories 382; Fat: 27g; Sodium 513mg; Carbs: 16g; Sugars: 4g; Protein 20g

Tilapia, Steamed

Prep Time: 5 minutes | Cook Time: 15 minutes | Serves: 4

1 lb. tilapia fillets
1 cup water
½ cup green commercial chutney

1. Place a steam rack inside the Instant Pot after filling it with water to prepare it. 2. Fish should be positioned in the center of a huge parchment paper square. 3. All of the fillets should receive some of the green chutney. 4. To create a package, tightly roll the paper's edges together. Put inside of steamer basket. 5. Lock the lid by closing it. Choose Pressure Cook, then cook for 10 minutes at HIGH pressure. 6. Use a Quick Release when the timer beeps on vent position. Open the pot's lid. Serve.
Per Serving: Calories 112; Fat: 2g; Sodium 68mg; Carbs: 1.87g; Sugars: 1.03g; Protein 23g

Coconut Milk Crabs

Prep Time: 5 minutes | Cook Time: 10 minutes | Serves: 4

1 lb. crabs, halved
1 tbsp. olive oil
1 onion, chopped
3 cloves garlic, minced
1 can coconut milk
1 thumb-size ginger, sliced
1 lemongrass stalk
Salt and ground black pepper to taste

1. By choosing SAUTÉ, the Instant Pot will be preheated. Oil is added, then heated. 2. Sauté for two minutes after adding the onion. 3. Add the garlic and cook for a further minute. 4. Crabs, coconut milk, ginger, lemongrass stem, salt, and pepper should also be added. 5. To stop the SAUTÉ feature, use the CANCEL key. 6. Lock the lid by closing it. Choose Pressure Cook, and then cook for 6 minutes at HIGH pressure. 7. Use the Quick Release on vent position when the timer runs off. Open the lid slowly. Serve.
Per Serving: Calories 238; Fat: 12g; Sodium 438mg; Carbs: 7g; Sugars: 2g; Protein 24g

Fish with Orange Sauce

Prep Time: 5 minutes | Cook Time: 10 minutes | Serves: 4

4 cod fillets, boneless
A small ginger piece, grated
1 cup white wine
Juice from 1 orange
Salt and ground black pepper to taste.
4 spring onions, chopped

1. Mix thoroughly before adding the ginger, wine, and orange juice to the Instant Pot. 2. On top, put a steam rack. 3. Cod fillets should be placed in the basket. Add salt and pepper to taste. 4. Lock the lid by closing it. Choose Pressure Cook, then cook for 7 minutes at HIGH pressure. 5. Use the Quick Release on vent position when the timer runs off. Open the lid slowly. 6. Add green onions and sauce to the fish before serving.
Per Serving: Calories 260; Fat: 15g; Sodium 434mg; Carbs: 10g; Sugars: 2g; Protein 20g

Tilapia Almond

Prep Time: 5 minutes | Cook Time: 10 minutes | Serves: 4

4 tilapia fillets
1 cup water
1 tsp olive oil
¼ tsp lemon pepper
2 tbsps. Dijon mustard
⅔ cup sliced almonds

1. Place the steam rack on top of the water after adding it to the Instant Pot. 2. Mix the oil, lemon pepper, and Dijon mustard together in a bowl. 3. Apply the mixture like a brush to the fish fillets. 4. To coat all sides, add the fillets to the almond. 5. Suspend from the steam rack. Lock the lid by closing it. 6. Choose Pressure Cook, then cook for 5 minutes at HIGH pressure. 7. Use the Quick Release on vent position when the timer runs off. Open the lid slowly. Serve.
Per Serving: Calories 127; Fat: 3.17g; Sodium 147mg; Carbs: 0.87g; Sugars: 0.03g; Protein 23g

Haddock Cheddar

Prep Time: 5 minutes | Cook Time: 10 minutes | Serves: 2

1 lb. fresh or frozen haddock fillets
1 tbsp. butter
1 tbsp. flour
¼ tsp salt
Ground black pepper to taste
½ cup milk

1 cup parmesan cheese, grated
1 cup water

1. Choose SAUTÉ to start the Instant Pot heating up. Melt the butter before adding it. 2. Stir thoroughly after adding the flour, salt, and pepper. For one minute, sauté. 3. Pour the milk in slowly and whisk occasionally for 3 to 5 minutes, or until the sauce is thick and smooth. 4. When adding the cheese, whisk the mixture. 5. To stop the SAUTÉ feature, use the CANCEL key. 6. Combine the sauce and fish fillets in a pan. Use foil to securely enclose. 7. With water, clean the inside pot. 8. Place a steam rack inside the pot after adding a cup of water to it. 9. The pan should be placed on the steam rack. 10. Choose Pressure Cook for 5 minutes at HIGH pressure. 11. Make advantage of a Quick Release on vent position when the pressure cooking is finished. Open the lid by slowly unlocking it. Serve.
Per Serving: Calories 496; Fat: 27g; Sodium 1829mg; Carbs: 24g; Sugars: 9g; Protein 38g

Shell oysters

Prep Time: 5 minutes | Cook Time: 10 minutes | Serves: 6

36 in-shell oysters
1 cup water
Salt and ground black pepper to
taste
6 tbsps. butter, melted

1. Clearly clean the oysters.2. Oysters, water, salt, and pepper should all be added to the Instant Pot. 3. Close the lid. The cooking time should be set to 3 minutes at HIGH pressure on the Pressure Cook setting. 4. Use a Quick Release on vent position when the timer beeps. Carefully unlock the lid. 5. Serve with melted butter.
Per Serving: Calories 137; Fat: 12g; Sodium 146mg; Carbs: 3g; Sugars: 1g; Protein 3g

Delicious Crab Legs

Prep Time: 5 minutes | Cook Time: 10 minutes | Serves: 4

4 lbs. king crab legs, broken in half
1 cup water
¼ cup butter
3 lemon wedges

1. Place a steam rack inside the Instant Pot after adding the water. 2. Crab legs should be placed on the rack. 3. Lock the lid by closing it. Choose Pressure Cook, then cook for 3 minutes at HIGH pressure. 4. Use the Quick Release on vent position when the timer runs off. Open the lid slowly. 5. Place the legs in a serving basin together with the lemon wedges and melted butter. Serve.
Per Serving: Calories 482; Fat: 14.17g; Sodium 3998mg; Carbs: 0.87g; Sugars: 0.03g; Protein 83.9g

Lobster Claws

Prep Time: 5 minutes | Cook Time: 20 minutes | Serves: 4

4 lobster tails, cut in half
1 cup water
½ cup white wine
½ cup butter, melted

1. Add a steam rack to the Instant Pot after adding the water and wine. 2. Put the basket with the lobster tails inside. 3. Select the Pressure Cook setting and set the cooking time for 5 minutes at LOW pressure. 4. Once the food has finished cooking, utilize a Natural Release for ten minutes on seal position before quickly release any leftover pressure on vent position. Open the lid. 5. Place the serving bowl with the legs in it. Add melted butter and serve.
Per Serving: Calories 321; Fat: 24g; Sodium 820mg; Carbs: 0.8g; Sugars: 0.06g; Protein 25g

Octopus Boiled

Prep Time: 5 minutes | Cook Time: 25 minutes | Serves:6

2½ lbs. whole octopus, cleaned and sliced
1 cup water
3 tbsps. lemon juice, freshly squeezed
Salt and ground black pepper to taste

1. Add water and lemon juice to the Instant Pot. 2. Salt and pepper it, then add the octopus. 3. Lock the lid by closing it. Choose Pressure Cook, and then cook for 15 minutes at HIGH pressure. 4. Use the Quick Release on vent position when the timer runs off. Open the lid slowly. 5. Return the food to the pot and simmer for an additional five minutes if necessary. Serve.
Per Serving: Calories 208; Fat: 6g; Sodium 1692mg; Carbs: 2.87g; Sugars: 2.03g; Protein 36g

Squid Mediterranean

Prep Time: 5 minutes | Cook Time: 20 minutes | Serves: 4

2 lbs. squid, chopped
2 tbsps. olive oil
Salt and ground black pepper to taste
1 cup red wine
3 stalks of celery, chopped

1 can (28 oz.) crushed tomatoes
1 red onion, sliced
3 cloves garlic, chopped
3 sprigs fresh rosemary
½ cup Italian parsley, chopped

1. Combine the squid, olive oil, salt, and pepper in a bowl. 2. To the cooking pot, add the wine, tomatoes, onion, garlic, rosemary, and celery. 3. In the pot, place steam rack. 4. Squid should be placed in the steam rack. 5. Lock the lid by closing it. Choose Pressure Cook for four minutes at HIGH pressure. 6. After the timer goes off, wait 10 minutes for the pressure to drop naturally on seal position before quickly release any leftover steam on vent position. Open the lid. Top with fresh parsley and serve.
Per Serving: Calories 319; Fat: 10g; Sodium 318mg; Carbs: 18g; Sugars: 6g; Protein 38g

Simple Scallops

Prep Time: 5 minutes | Cook Time: 10 minutes | Serves:2

1 lb. sea scallops, shells removed
1 cup water
1 tbsp. olive oil
3 tbsps. maple syrup

½ cup soy sauce
½ tsp ground ginger
½ tsp garlic powder
½ tsp salt

1. Put the steam rack in the Instant Pot and fill it with water to prepare it. 2. Scallops, olive oil, maple syrup, soy sauce, ginger, garlic powder, and salt are placed in a baking dish that is 6-7 inches in diameter. 3. The pan should be placed on the steam rack. 4. The cooking time should be set at 6 minutes using the STEAM setting. 5. Use a Quick Release on vent position when the timer chimes. Carefully unlock the lid.
Per Serving: Calories 319; Fat: 14g; Sodium 534mg; Carbs: 18g; Sugars: 15g; Protein 28g

Yummy Seafood Gumbo

Prep Time: 5 minutes | Cook Time: 20 minutes | Serves: 4

12 oz. sea bass filets cut into 2" chunks
1 lb. medium to large raw shrimp, deveined
Salt and ground black pepper to taste
1½ tbsp. Cajun or creole seasoning
1½ tbsp. ghee or avocado oil

1 yellow onion, diced
2 celery ribs, diced
¾ cups bone broth
14 oz. diced tomatoes
⅛ cup tomato paste
2 bay leaves
1 bell pepper, diced

1. Salt, pepper, and half of the Cajun or Creole spice should be applied to the fillets' both sides. 2. By choosing SAUTÉ, the Instant Pot will be preheated. Heat the oil or ghee before adding it. 3. Cook the fish for 2 minutes on each side in the pot. 4. From the saucepan, remove the fillets. Celery, onions, and any extra Cajun or Creole flavor should be added. 5. For 2 minutes, sauté until aromatic. 6. Add the fish that has been cooked, the shrimp, the bell pepper, the tomato paste, and the broth. 7. Once the cooking program has been reset by pressing the CANCEL button, click the Pressure Cook button to set the cooking time to 5 minutes at HIGH pressure. 8. Make advantage of a Quick Release on vent position when the pressure cooking is finished. Open the lid by slowly unlocking it. Serve.
Per Serving: Calories 407; Fat: 20g; Sodium 1275mg; Carbs: 21g; Sugars: 7g; Protein 35g

Seafood Plov with Cranberries

Prep Time: 10 minutes | Cook Time: 20 minutes | Serves: 4

1 package (16 oz.) frozen seafood blend
2-3 tbsps. butter
1 onion, large-sized, chopped
1 bell pepper, red or yellow, sliced
3 big carrots, shredded

1½ cups basmati rice, organic
½ cup dried cranberries
Salt and ground black pepper to taste
3 cups water
1 lemon, sliced (optional)

1. Choose SAUTÉ to start the Instant Pot heating up. 2. Add the butter and let it melt once it is heated. 3. Include the carrots, bell pepper, and onion. Sauté while occasionally stirring for 5-7 minutes. 4. Stir thoroughly after adding the fish mixture, rice, and cranberries. 5. To taste, add salt and pepper to the food. 6. Add some water. Lock the lid by closing it. 7. Choose Pressure Cook and set time for 10 minutes. 8. Naturally release the pressure on vent position for 10 minutes after the timer beeps. Open the pot's lid. 9. You may drizzle the meal with fresh lemon juice if you'd like. Serve.
Per Serving: Calories 403; Fat: 20g; Sodium 165mg; Carbs: 60g; Sugars: 31g; Protein 10g

Yummy Seafood

Prep Time: 10 minutes | Cook Time: 25 minutes | Serves: 6

2 cups chopped white fish and scallops
2 cups mussels and shrimp
4 tbsps. olive oil
1 onion, diced
1 red bell pepper, diced

1 green bell pepper, diced
2 cups rice
A few saffron threads
2 cups fish stock
Salt and ground black pepper to taste

1. Heat up the oil in your instant pot while it is in SAUTÉ mode. 2. For 4 minutes, add the onion and bell peppers and sauté. 3. Stir in the rice, fish, and saffron. Cook for a further 2 minutes. 4. Add the fish stock and stir while adding salt and pepper. 5. Then add the shellfish. 6. To stop the SAUTÉ feature, use the CANCEL key. 7. Lock the lid by closing it. Choose Pressure Cook, and then cook for 6 minutes at HIGH pressure. 8. After cooking is finished, choose CANCEL and wait 10 minutes for the pressure to naturally release on seal position. Release any remaining steam quickly on vent position. Open the pot's lid. Stir the dish and let sit for 5 minutes. Serve.
Per Serving: Calories 906; Fat: 85g; Sodium 211mg; Carbs: 12g; Sugars: 6g; Protein 20g

Simple Grits and Shrimp

Prep Time: 10 minutes | Cook Time: 30 minutes | Serves: 2

3 uncooked bacon slices, chopped
2 shallots, chopped
¼ green bell pepper, chopped
¼ cup chopped celery
1 garlic clove, minced
Splash dry white wine or stock
½ cup fresh or canned diced tomatoes
⅓ cup Chicken Stock
1 tablespoon freshly squeezed lemon juice

Kosher salt
Freshly ground black pepper
½ cup dry grits
1 cup milk
1 cup water
½ pound uncooked shrimp, tails removed, peeled and deveined
1 tablespoon butter
¾ cup shredded Cheddar cheese
2 tablespoons heavy cream

1. Set the Instant pot to the sauté setting. Add the bacon to the pot when the indicator says "hot" and cook for 5 to 6 minutes, or until crispy. Transfer to a plate covered with paper towels to drain. Don't drain the pot. In the bacon fat in the pot, add the shallots, bell pepper, and celery. Sauté for two to three minutes, stirring regularly. 2. Add the garlic and then press the Cancel button. For one minute, sauté. 3. Pouring wine into the pot while scraping off the browned pieces from the bottom will deglaze it. Add the chopped tomatoes, stock, and lemon juice after allowing the liquid to reduce for 1 to 2 minutes while stirring regularly. Salt and pepper are added after stirring. The tomato sauce should be poured into a big basin, covered, and put aside. Clean the cooking pot, pat it dry, and put it back in the pot. 4. Grits, milk, and water should be combined in a medium glass or metal heatproof bowl along with salt and pepper. The grits dish should be placed on top of a steam rack or egg rack in the pot. 5. Select Pressure Cook, cook the food for 10 minutes on high pressure, then let the pressure naturally drop for around 10 minutes on seal position. Then use a Quick Release on vent position. After taking off the cover, carefully take the grits bowl from the cooking pot and set it aside. 6. Place the shrimp in the pot, then whisk in the tomato sauce. Replace the lid and cook the shrimp for 7 to 8 minutes in the residual heat, tossing once or twice to ensure equal cooking on both sides. 7. While waiting, use a fork to fluff the grits and whisk in the butter and cheese. To keep the bowl warm, cover it with plastic wrap. 8. Stir in the cream and let it warm through when the shrimp is almost done cooking. 9. The shrimp and tomato sauce should be added on top of the divided grits in two dishes. Add the chopped bacon on top, garnish with scallions, and serve with spicy sauce.
Per Serving: Calories 538; Fat: 32g; Sodium 1375mg; Carbs: 27g; Sugars: 22g; Protein 34g

Shrimp Scampi

Prep Time: 10 minutes | Cook Time: 10 minutes | Serves: 2

6 ounces linguine
1 tablespoon oil
1 tablespoon butter
1 shallot, chopped
1 tablespoon minced garlic
Pinch red pepper flakes, plus more for seasoning (optional)
¼ cup white wine

¼ cup Chicken Stock
1 tablespoon freshly squeezed lemon juice
¾ pound thawed frozen raw jumbo shrimp, tails removed, peeled and deveined
Kosher salt
Freshly ground black pepper

1. While the other ingredients are cooking in the Instant Pot, prepare the pasta according to the package's instructions. Transfer the pasta to a serving bowl, cover it, and put it aside after draining but before rinsing. 2. Set the Instant pot to the sauté setting. Add the oil and butter and stir until they melt. Sauté for 2 minutes after adding the shallot, garlic, and red pepper flakes. 3. Pour the wine into the pot to deglaze it, scraping off any browned pieces with a wooden spoon and adding them to the liquid as you go. Cook for one minute, then cut in half. Select Cancel. 4. Include the shrimp, lemon juice, and stock. Close the lid. Select Pressure Cook on high for 5 minutes. Remove the lid after quickly release the pressure in the pot. Select Cancel. 5. Add the parsley after seasoning with salt, pepper, and more red pepper flakes (if preferred). Pour into the pasta serving bowl and stir. Serve alongside pieces of stale bread.
Per Serving: Calories 596; Fat: 14g; Sodium 1404mg; Carbs: 46g; Sugars: 15g; Protein 68.39g

Shrimp Cajun Boil

Prep Time: 5 minutes | Cook Time: 10 minutes | Serves: 2

1 cup water
½ pound red potatoes, halved
1 medium sweet onion, chopped
2 ears of corn, shucked and broken in half
½ pound fully cooked kielbasa sausage, cut into 2-inch slices

2 tablespoons Old Bay seasoning, plus more for seasoning
2 tablespoons crab boil seasoning (optional)
½ teaspoon kosher salt
1-pound peel-on large raw shrimp, deveined

1. Combine the water, potatoes, onion, corn, kielbasa, 2 tablespoons of Old Bay, salt, and crab boil spice (if using) in the Instant pot. 2. Secure the lid and cook on Pressure Cook and high pressure for 4 minutes, then quickly release the pressure in the pot on vent position and remove the lid. Select Cancel. 3. Add the shrimp, cover loosely, and simmer for 3 to 4 minutes in the residual heat. Old Bay and additional salt are used to season. Drain water into a big colander. 4. Serve in sizable, shallow dishes along with some lemon wedges, melted butter, and crusty bread for dipping.
Per Serving: Calories 982; Fat: 40.17g; Sodium 799mg; Carbs: 46g; Sugars: 11g; Protein 11g

Paella Shrimp

Prep Time: 10 minutes | Cook Time: 10 minutes | Serves:2

2 tablespoons oil
½ onion, chopped
2 garlic cloves, minced
Kosher salt
Freshly ground black pepper
1 teaspoon paprika
¼ teaspoon red pepper flakes
Pinch saffron threads

¼ cup white wine
½ cup basmati rice
1 (14-ounce) can diced tomatoes and chilies, with their juices
½ cup Chicken Stock
½ pound peel-on large raw shrimp, deveined

1. Set the Instant pot to the sauté setting. Add the oil when the display says "hot." Add the onion and cook for 3 minutes, or until tender. For one minute, stir regularly while cooking the garlic. Add the paprika, red pepper flakes, and saffron after seasoning with salt and pepper, and mix to incorporate. 2. Pour the wine into the pot to deglaze it while scraping the browned pieces from the bottom. Rice should be stirred in before the stock, tomatoes, chilies, and their juices are added. Make sure the rice is well coated by stirring. 3. Secure the lid and cook on high pressure for 5 minutes on Pressure Cook option, then quickly release the pressure in the pot on vent position and remove the lid. After pressing Cancel, choose sauté. 4. Stir the shrimp into the rice, cover the pot with the lid loosely, and cook for 3 to 5 minutes, or until pink. Serve with chopped fresh cilantro and lime wedges.
Per Serving: Calories 439; Fat: 12g; Sodium 704mg; Carbs: 50g; Sugars: 17g; Protein 28.9g

White Wine and Mussels

Prep Time: 5 minutes | Cook Time: 10 minutes | Serves: 4

3 lbs. mussels, cleaned and debearded
6 tbsps. butter

4 shallots, chopped
1 cup white wine
1½ cups chicken stock

1. Select SAUTÉ and add the butter to the Instant Pot. 2. The shallots should be added after the butter has melted and sautéed for 2 minutes. 3. Add the wine, stir, and simmer for an additional 30 seconds. 4. Stir thoroughly after adding the stock and mussels. Lock the lid by closing it. 5. After selecting the Pressure Cook option and setting the cooking duration to 3 minutes at HIGH pressure. 6. Once pressure cooking is complete, use a Quick Release on vent position. Open the lid. Remove unopened mussels and serve.
Per Serving: Calories 488; Fat: 26g; Sodium 1404mg; Carbs: 18g; Sugars: 2g; Protein 43g

Gumbo Seafood

Prep Time: 30 minutes | Cook Time: 30 minutes | Serves: 2

3 tablespoons oil, divided
½ pound andouille sausage, cut into ½-inch slices
1 small onion, diced
1 celery stalk, diced
1 cup diced green bell pepper
3 garlic cloves, minced
2 tablespoons butter
3 tablespoons all-purpose flour
3 cups Chicken Stock (here)
1 cup sliced okra
2 tablespoons tomato paste

1 tablespoon Creole seasoning, plus more for seasoning (optional)
¼ teaspoon cayenne pepper, plus more for seasoning (optional)
Kosher salt
Freshly ground black pepper
1 medium tomato, diced
½ pound raw medium shrimp, tail-on, peeled and deveined
¼ pound lump crabmeat, picked over
Gumbo filé powder (optional)

1. Set the Instant pot to the sauté setting. Add two teaspoons of oil. Add the sausage, onion, celery, bell pepper, and sauté for 6 to 8 minutes, or until browned. Add the garlic and stir for one minute. Put the mixture on a dish and reserve. 2. Melt the butter in the pot with the remaining 1 tablespoon of oil. Flour should be added and whisked in. Cook the roux until it reaches a medium to dark brown color for 12 to 15 minutes, continually whisking to prevent burning. 3. Add the liquid, tomato paste, okra, sausage combination, creole spice, and cayenne pepper after stirring. To taste, add salt and black pepper to the food. Add the tomato. 4. Secure the lid and cook on Pressure Cook and high pressure for 4 minutes, then quickly release the pressure in the pot on vent position and remove the lid. choose sauté. If necessary, add extra cayenne pepper or Creole spice after tasting the dish and adjusting the flavors. 5. Add the crabmeat on top after stirring in the shrimp, and simmer for 4 to 5 minutes, or until the shrimp are pink. Mix in the gumbo filé powder (if using). 6. Serve with white rice and a sprinkle of scallions.
Per Serving: Calories 1020; Fat: 67g; Sodium 1404mg; Carbs: 34g; Sugars: 9.9g; Protein 70g

Sesame Teriyaki Chicken Thighs and Rice

Prep Time: 5 minutes | Cook Time: 15 minutes | Serves: 1

2 (8-ounce) boneless, skinless chicken thighs
½ cup teriyaki sauce
½ cup uncooked long-grain white

rice
½ cup water
½ tablespoon sesame seeds
½ tablespoon chopped green onion

1. Place the chicken thighs in the inner pot and pour the teriyaki sauce over the chicken. Place a trivet on the chicken. 2. Combine together water and rice in a suitable cake pan. Transfer onto the trivet. 3. Then close the lid and turn the steam release handle to Sealing position. 4. Set the Instant Pot on Pressure Cook at High and adjust the time to 10 minutes. 5. When cooked, naturally release the pressure about 5 minutes. 6. Remove the lid. Transfer the pan from the Instant Pot. Using a fork, fluff the rice. 7. Transfer the chicken on the rice and keep warm. 8. Sauté the remaining teriyaki sauce in the Instant Pot about 5 minutes until thicken. 9. Then pour the thickened teriyaki sauce over the chicken and rice. 10. Sprinkle the sesame seeds and onion on the top of the chicken and rice. 11. Serve and treat yourself now!
Per Serving: Calories: 704; Fat: 12g; Sodium: 5,605mg; Carbs: 98g; Sugar: 21g; Protein: 43g

Yummy Cioppino

Prep Time: 15 minutes | Cook Time: 30 minutes | Serves: 2

2 tablespoons butter
1 tablespoon oil
1 shallot, thinly sliced
½ small fennel bulb, thinly sliced
2 garlic cloves, minced
½ teaspoon red pepper flakes, plus more for seasoning (optional)
½ teaspoon dried oregano
Pinch kosher salt
1 (14-ounce) can diced tomatoes with their juices

¾ cup canned clam juice
1 cup white wine
Freshly ground black pepper
½ pound mussels, rinsed, scrubbed, and debearded
½ pound manila clams, scrubbed
½ pound flaky white fish, such as cod or flounder
½ pound medium shrimp, tail-on, peeled and deveined

1. Set the Instant pot to the sauté setting. Melt the butter into the oil. Sauté the fennel and shallot together for 2 minutes or until tender. Cook for one minute after adding the oregano, garlic, and ½ teaspoon of red pepper flakes. 2. Add wine, clam juice, tomatoes and their liquids, and stir. Add salt and pepper to taste. After sealing the valve and cooking for 10 minutes at high pressure, let the pressure decrease naturally for around 10 minutes. Remove the cover by releasing the top vent. Select Cancel. 3. Choose sauté. When the clams and mussels start to open, add them to the pot and simmer them for 5 to 6 minutes with the lid off. Cook the fish and shrimp through for 3 to 4 minutes after adding them to the pot. Any mussels or clams that don't open should be discarded. Red pepper flakes and extra salt should be added after tasting (if desired). 4. Divide the cioppino between two big dishes and garnish with toasted crusty bread, lemon wedges, and chopped parsley.
Per Serving: Calories 733; Fat: 25g; Sodium 404mg; Carbs: 36g; Sugars: 13g; Protein 72g

Seamed Cod with Vegetables

Prep Time: 15 minutes | Cook Time: 10 minutes | Serves: 2

2 (6-ounce) cod fillets
Kosher salt
Freshly ground black pepper
2 tablespoons melted butter
2 tablespoons freshly squeezed lemon juice, divided
1 garlic clove, minced

1 cup cherry tomatoes
1 zucchini or yellow summer squash, cut into thick slices
1 cup whole Brussels sprouts
2 thyme sprigs or ½ teaspoon dried thyme

1. Place the steam rack in the bottom of the Instant pot after adding ½ cup of water. 2. Fish should be salted and peppered. Combine the butter, the garlic, and one tablespoon of the lemon juice in a small bowl. Place aside. 3. Add the tomatoes, zucchini, and Brussels sprouts to the steam rack. After adding salt and pepper, sprinkle the remaining 1 tablespoon of lemon juice over the dish. 4. On top of the veggies, arrange the fish fillets. Brush the fish with the garlic-lemon butter, then turn it over and continue. Any remaining butter should be drizzled over the veggies. Add the thyme sprigs on top. 5. Secure the pot lid. Select Pressure Cook and cook on high pressure for 2 to 4 minutes, depending on the thickness of the fish, then quickly release the pressure in the pot on vent position and remove the lid. 6. Along with cooked rice or couscous, lemon wedges, and the fish on top of the veggies, serve.
Per Serving: Calories 271; Fat: 12g; Sodium 514mg; Carbs: 17g; Sugars: 3.03g; Protein 25g

Easy Clam Chowders

Prep Time: 25 minutes | Cook Time: 20 minutes | Serves: 2

4 uncooked bacon slices, chopped
2 tablespoons butter
1 small onion, diced
1 garlic clove, minced
¼ cup white wine
1 cup clam juice
1 cup Chicken Stock or water
1 large Russet potato, cubed (2 cups)
2 thyme sprigs or ¼ teaspoon dried thyme

½ teaspoon red pepper flakes (optional)
Kosher salt
Freshly ground black or white pepper
1 tablespoon cornstarch
3 (6.5-ounce) cans clams, whole, chopped, or minced, or 1½ pounds fresh clams in the shell
1 cup heavy cream
½ cup whole milk

1. Set the Instant pot to the sauté setting. Add the bacon to the pan when it says heated and cook for approximately 5 minutes, or until just beginning to crisp up. Transfer to a plate covered with paper towels to drain. Don't drain the pot. 2. Melt butter in the pot of bacon fat. Add the onion and garlic, and sauté for 3 to 4 minutes, or until tender. 3. By adding the wine and scraping off the browned pieces from the bottom, you will deglaze the saucepan. Once the liquid has reduced by half, choose Cancel. 4. Add salt and pepper, along with the clam juice, stock, potato, thyme, and red pepper flakes (if using). Good stirring 5. After five minutes of high pressure cooking, quickly release the pressure in the pot on vent position and take the cover off. Select Cancel. 6. Take out the thyme leaves. Carefully mash some or all of the potato cubes with a potato masher. choose sauté. 2 tablespoons of the chowder should be combined with the cornstarch and whisked until smooth in a small bowl. 7. Add the clams, cream, and milk to the pot while stirring in the cornstarch mixture. Before serving, let simmer for about 5 minutes.
Per Serving: Calories 722; Fat: 37g; Sodium 999mg; Carbs: 63g; Sugars: 13g; Protein 29g

Mussels Fra Diavolo

Prep Time: 15 minutes | Cook Time: 10 minutes | Serves: 2

6 ounces linguine
1 tablespoon oil, plus more for the pasta
½ large onion, chopped
3 garlic cloves, minced
2 tablespoons red pepper flakes
½ cup dry white wine
1 (14-ounce) can fire-roasted

crushed tomatoes with their juices
4 ounces canned clam juice
Kosher salt
Freshly ground black pepper
1 pound fresh mussels, rinsed, scrubbed, and debearded
⅓ cup fresh chopped basil

1. The pasta should be prepared as directed on the packaging. Drain and combine with a little oil. 2. Sort the mussels and throw away those that have shells that have fractured or aren't completely closed. 3. Set the Instant Pot to sauté mode. Add 1 tablespoon of oil. Add the onion and cook for 2 minutes, or until soft. Add the garlic and red pepper flakes, and cook for about a minute, or until fragrant. 4. Pour the wine into the saucepan to deglaze it while scraping the browned pieces from the bottom. Cook the wine for 1 to 2 minutes, or until it has been cut in half. 5. Stir thoroughly before adding the tomatoes, together with their juices, and the clam juice. Add salt and pepper to taste. Stir in the mussels after letting the liquid quickly boil. 6. Secure the lid and cook on Pressure Cook and high pressure for 3 minutes, then quickly release the pressure in the pot on vent position and remove the lid. Select Cancel. 7. Add the chopped basil and stir. As needed, add additional salt and pepper to the dish. 8. Place the mussels and sauce on top of the spaghetti once you've divided it up into bowls. Serve with crusty bread and lime wedges.
Per Serving: Calories 631; Fat: 15.17g; Sodium 804mg; Carbs: 15g; Sugars: 6g; Protein 45g

Fish Tacos from California

Prep Time: 15 minutes | Cook Time: 15 minutes | Serves: 2

For The Mango Salsa
1 cup mango, diced
¼ cup red onion, diced
½ avocado, chopped
For The Fish
1 teaspoon kosher salt, divided
½ teaspoon ground cumin
½ teaspoon paprika
½ teaspoon garlic powder
¼ teaspoon cayenne pepper

1 jalapeño pepper, stemmed, seeded and diced
1 tablespoon lime juice

12 ounces flaky white fish (cod, snapper, or mahi-mahi), cut into fingers
Juice of ½ lime, divided

1. In a small bowl, combine the cayenne pepper, cumin, paprika, garlic powder, and ½ tsp salt. 2. Fold the two oblong parchment paper pieces so there is about 1 inch of space on either side of the Instant Pot, then cut two of them. Onto a work surface, transfer. 3. On one side of a sheet of parchment paper, place half of the fish. Before applying the spice mixture to the fish, drizzle some lime juice over it. The parchment package should be sealed and covered with a sizable piece of aluminum foil. To make another package, repeat the procedure with the remaining fish. 4. The steam rack should be put at the bottom of the pot after adding 1 cup of water. 5. Secure the lid. Select Pressure Cook and cook on high pressure for 8 minutes, then quickly release the pressure in the pot on vent position and remove the lid. 6. Open the packets carefully (the steam will be hot!), take the fish from the packages, and place it in a medium dish after moving the packets to a work surface using tongs. With a fork, flake the fish, then combine it with the remaining lime juice. 7. Serve with the mango salsa, shredded cabbage, cilantro, and lime wedges wrapped in warmed flour or corn tortillas.
Per Serving: Calories 777; Fat: 16g; Sodium 786mg; Carbs: 57g; Sugars: 13g; Protein 102g

Poached Red Snapper with Salsa

Prep Time: 5 minutes | Cook Time: 10 minutes | Serves: 2

2 (6-ounce) snapper fillets
1 teaspoon kosher salt
½ teaspoon freshly ground black pepper

1½ cups fresh salsa
¼ cup pale lager beer or water
½ lime

1. In the Instant Pot's base, place the steam rack. 2. Salt and pepper should be used to season the fish. Place the fish on the rack, then cover with the salsa and beer. Over the fish and salsa, squeeze some lime juice. 3. Secure the pot lid. Select Pressure Cook and cook on high pressure for 3 to 4 minutes, depending on the thickness of the fish, then quickly release the pressure in the pot and remove the lid. 4. Over rice, quinoa, or steamed veggies, dish out the poached snapper. Serve with lime wedges and top with more salsa and chopped cilantro.
Per Serving: Calories 292; Fat: 3g; Sodium 604mg; Carbs: 8g; Sugars: 3g; Protein 46g

Delicious Chicken Drumsticks with Sweet Chili Sauce

Prep Time: 5 minutes | Cook Time: 18 minutes | Serves: 1

1 cup water
4 (4-ounce) chicken drumsticks

¾ cup sweet chili sauce
1 tablespoon chopped green onion

1. Add the chicken drumsticks on a trivet. Pour water in the inner pot and place the trivet. 2. Close the lid and turn the steam release knob to Sealing position. 3. Set your Instant Pot on Pressure Cook at High and adjust the cooking time to 10 minutes for fresh chicken legs and 12 minutes for frozen chicken legs. 4. When cooked, quickly release the pressure, turning the knob from Sealing to the Venting position. 5. Line foil over a baking sheet and preheat an oven broiler to high. 6. Transfer the cooked chicken on the baking pan and brush chili sauce on the chicken. Broil for 4 minutes. 7. Again brush the other side and broil for 4 minutes or until browned and fluffy. 8. Transfer to a serving plate and baste with your favorite sauce. 9. Sprinkle green onion or your favorite seasoning blend on top to serve. 10. Enjoy!
Per Serving: Calories: 1,090; Fat: 29g; Sodium: 3,116mg; Carbs: 102g; Sugar: 84g; Protein: 88g

Teriyaki Salad with Salmon

Prep Time: 10 minutes | Cook Time: 20 minutes | Serves: 2

¼ cup sesame oil
¼ cup soy sauce
¼ cup lime juice
2 tablespoons honey
2 tablespoons fish sauce
1 tablespoon sesame seeds
1 teaspoon grated peeled fresh ginger

1 teaspoon minced garlic
Grated zest of 1 lime
1 scallion, chopped, plus more for serving
2 (4- to 6-ounce) skinless or skin-on salmon fillets
2 teaspoons cornstarch

1. Combine the sesame oil, soy sauce, lime juice, honey, fish sauce, sesame seeds, ginger, garlic, lime zest, scallion, and salmon in a gallon-size zip-top bag. Shake the bag carefully after sealing. For one to two hours, marinade the fish in the refrigerator. 2. Pick the sauté option. Transfer the salmon to a platter after removing it from the marinade. Pour the marinade from the bag into the pot when the display says "heated" and come to a simmer. Select Cancel. 3. Bring the fish to a boil (skin-side up, if using skin-on fillets). Over the fish, spoon the marinade. 4. Secure the lid. Select Pressure Cook and cook on high pressure for 4 minutes, then quickly release the pressure in the pot on vent position and remove the lid. Press Cancel. 5. The fish should be carefully moved to a fresh dish using a spatula. Whenever necessary, remove the skin. Transfer 2 teaspoons of the warm teriyaki liquid from the pot to a small bowl. Pour it back into the saucepan after whisking in the cornstarch. Choose sauté and cook the liquid, stirring often, for 8 to 10 minutes, or until it thickens to the consistency of a glaze. 6. To serve, split the salad greens between two plates and combine with the shredded cabbage and carrots, sliced bell pepper, edamame, mandarin orange slices, and slivered almonds. Place a salmon fillet on top of each. 7. Brush or spoon the teriyaki sauce over the fish and salad.
Per Serving: Calories 608; Fat: 41g; Sodium 666mg; Carbs: 26g; Sugars: 10.3g; Protein 39g

Lobster Tails with Lemon-Butter Sauce

Prep Time: 5 minutes | Cook Time: 10 minutes | Serves: 2

1 cup Chicken Stock (here) or water
1 teaspoon Old Bay seasoning
2 (about 1-pound) fresh Maine lobster tails

Juice of 1 lemon, divided
½ cup butter, melted
½ tablespoon minced garlic
½ lemon, cut into wedges

1. Put the Steam rack in the bottom of your Instant pot and add the stock and Old Bay. Place each lobster tail shell-side down, meat-side up on the rack. Sprinkle the lobster with the juice of half a lemon. 2. Select Pressure Cook. Cook for 3 minutes under high pressure with the lid securely on the pot. Remove the lid after quickly releasing the pressure in the pot on vent position. 3. In the meantime, fill a large bowl with cold water. To prevent overcooking, move the lobster tails to the ice bath right away using tongs. Allow it cool for a minute or two. 4. Mix the butter, the remaining lemon juice, and the garlic in a small bowl. 5. Put the lobster tails on a chopping board that has been covered with a dish towel. Using kitchen shears or a big knife, butterfly the lobster tail by making a cut through the middle of the underside of the tail, with the flesh side facing up. 6. Lemon wedges and the lemon-butter sauce are served alongside for dipping.
Per Serving: Calories 572; Fat: 48g; Sodium 404mg; Carbs: 7g; Sugars: 1.03g; Protein 32g

Fresh Casserole Tuna

Prep Time: 15 minutes | Cook Time: 30 minutes | Serves: 2

2 teaspoons butter, plus more for greasing
1 shallot, chopped
1 celery stalk, chopped
½ cup sliced cremini mushrooms
1 garlic clove, minced
1 cup Chicken Stock
1½ cups water
1½ cups egg noodles
Kosher salt

Freshly ground black pepper
2 tablespoons heavy cream
1 tablespoon Dijon mustard
1 tablespoon freshly squeezed lemon juice
1 (5-ounce) can tuna, drained and broken up
½ cup shredded Cheddar cheese
½ cup panko bread crumbs
4 lemon wedges

1. Set aside a small casserole dish after butter-coating it. 2. Set the Instant pot to the sauté setting. Add the 2 tablespoons of butter and let it melt. Sauté the mushrooms, shallot, and celery for 3 minutes or until tender. Sauté for one minute after adding the garlic. 3. Noodles, water, and stock are added. Add salt and pepper to taste. Select Pressure Cook. After two minutes of high pressure cooking with the lid securely in place, quickly release the pressure in the pot on vent position and take off the lid. 4. Return the solids to the cooking pot after carefully pouring the contents of the pot through a colander or fine-mesh strainer to drain the excess liquid. 5. Add the tuna, cream, mustard, lemon juice, and salt and pepper to taste. Add the ingredients to the casserole dish that has been prepared. Add the panko and cheese shavings on top. 6. Use the Pressure Cook option to cook in the pot for 12 to 15 minutes at Low setting until the panko is lightly toasted and crunchy and the cheese has melted. With the lemon wedges, serve.
Per Serving: Calories 736; Fat: 25.17g; Sodium 1404mg; Carbs: 60g; Sugars: 23g; Protein 74g

Garlic Turkey Sweet Potato Hash

Prep Time: 10 minutes | Cook Time: 17 minutes | Serves: 4

1½ tablespoons avocado oil
1 medium yellow onion, peeled and diced
2 cloves garlic, minced
1 medium sweet potato, cut into

cubes (peeling not necessary)
½ pound lean ground turkey
½ teaspoon salt
1 teaspoon Italian seasoning blend

1. Set your Instant Pot on Sauté and adjust the temperature to More. 2. Add the oil in the inner pot and heat for 1 minute. 3. Then add onion and cook about 5 minutes or until transparent. Add garlic and cook for 30 seconds more. 4. Add the turkey, Italian seasoning, salt, and sweet potato in the inner pot and cook for another 5 minutes. 5. Turn off the heat and close the lid. 6. Set your Instant Pot on Pressure Cook at High and adjust the cooking time to 5 minutes. 7. When cooked, quick release the pressure until the float valve drops. 8. Carefully remove the lid and spoon onto serving plates. 9. Serve and enjoy!
Per Serving: Calories: 172; Fat: 9g; Sodium: 348mg; Carbs: 10g; Sugar: 3g; Protein: 12g

Barbecue Chicken and Veggies Bowl

Prep Time: 5 minutes | Cook Time: 20 minutes | Serves: 1

1 tablespoon olive oil
2 (4-ounce) boneless, skinless chicken thighs
1 teaspoon barbecue dry rub
¾ cup chicken broth
¼ cup uncooked long-grain white rice
¼ cup drained and rinsed canned black beans
¼ cup corn

2 tablespoons shredded Cheddar cheese
2 tablespoons barbecue sauce
½ cup shredded lettuce
¼ cup diced avocado
2 tablespoons diced cherry tomatoes
1 tablespoon diced red onion
1 tablespoon chopped cilantro
½ medium lime

1. Rub well the dry rub over the chicken. 2. Set your Instant Pot on Sauté and adjust the temperature level at More. 3. Wait for 10 seconds and add oil on the inner pot. 4. Place the seasoned chicken in the inner pot and cook about 8 minutes or until both sides are browned. Halfway through cooking, turn the chicken to the other side. 5. When cooked, remove the inner pot from the Instant Pot and turn off the heat. 6. Pour broth in the inner pot and scrape all the browned bits off the pot to deglaze. 7. Stir together corn, beans, and rice in the inner pot. Return the inner pot to the cooker base. 8. Then close the lid and turn the steam release handle to Sealing position. 9. Set your Instant Pot on Pressure cook at High and adjust the cooking time to 10 minutes. 10. When cooked, naturally release the pressure about 5 minutes. 11. Remove the lid and scoop the cooked chicken meal into a serving bowl. 12. Sprinkle barbecue sauce, lettuce, tomatoes, onion, lime, Cheddar, and lime on top. 13. Serve and enjoy!
Per Serving: Calories: 832; Fat: 36g; Sodium: 1,590mg; Carbs: 78g; Sugar: 16g; Protein: 42g

Quick Balsamic Chicken

Prep Time: 15 minutes | Cook Time: 20 minutes | Serves: 4

¼ cup Chicken Stock or store-bought low-sodium chicken stock
2 tablespoons balsamic vinegar
4 garlic cloves, minced
1½ pounds chicken tenderloins
1-pound baby red potatoes

8 carrots, peeled and cut into thirds
½ teaspoon cornstarch
¼ teaspoon kosher salt
¼ teaspoon freshly ground black pepper

1. Combine together the vinegar, garlic, and the stock in the inner pot. Then add the chicken, carrots, and potatoes in the pot. 2. Close the lid and turn the steam release handle to Sealing. 3. Set your Instant Pot on Pressure Cook at High and adjust the cooking time to 8 minutes. 4. When cooked, naturally release the pressure about 10 minutes and then quickly release the remaining pressure. 5. Remove the lid carefully and remove the chicken and vegetables to a serving bowl. Reserve the soup behind. 6. Set the Instant Pot on Sauté and adjust the temperature to More. 7. Whisk the cornstarch in the inner pot and simmer for 2 to 3 minutes or until the sauce is thickened. 8. To season, add salt and pepper. 9. Then carefully spoon the sauce over the chicken and vegetables. 10. Serve and enjoy!
Per Serving: Calories: 336; Fat: 3g; Carbs: 32g; Sugar: 8g; Sodium: 265mg; Protein: 43g

Fresh Coconut Curry Seafood

Prep Time: 10 minutes | Cook Time: 10 minutes | Serves: 2

2 teaspoons oil
5 to 6 curry leaves or kaffir lime leaves, plus more for garnish
½ onion, sliced
1 green Chile (preferably serrano or jalapeño), stemmed, seeded, and sliced
2 garlic cloves, minced
½ tablespoon grated peeled fresh ginger
2 tablespoons curry powder

1 cup unsweetened coconut milk
¾ cup cherry tomatoes
¼ cup chopped fresh cilantro
½ pound fresh or thawed frozen tilapia fillets, cut into bite-size pieces
Kosher salt
1 tablespoon freshly squeezed lime juice
¼ pound raw medium shrimp, peeled and deveined

1. Set the Instant pot to the sauté setting. Add the oil. Add the curry leaves and cook for 1 minute. Next, add the onion, Chile, garlic, and ginger and cook for an additional 30 seconds, or until the onion is tender. 2. Sauté for 30 seconds after adding the curry powder. As you deglaze the pan and scrape out any browned pieces from the bottom, add the coconut milk and thoroughly combine. Simmer for between 30 and 60 seconds. 3. Tomatoes, cilantro, and fish pieces should be added. To carefully coat the fish, stir. 4. Depending on how thick the fish pieces are, fast-release the pressure in the pot on vent position and remove the lid after cooking on high pressure for 2 to 3 minutes. Select Cancel. 5. Add the lime juice after adding salt to taste. Add the shrimp, stir, and loosely cover the pot with the lid. The shrimp should cook for 3 to 4 minutes, or until pink, in the residual heat. Serve in bowls with cooked jasmine rice, lime wedges, and coconut shavings. Add more curry leaves as a garnish.
Per Serving: Calories 522; Fat: 36g; Sodium 404mg; Carbs: 28g; Sugars: 10g; Protein 38g

Sweet and Spicy Pineapple Chicken

Prep Time: 7 minutes | Cook Time: 9 minutes | Serves: 1

1 tablespoon olive oil
1 cup diced chicken breast in 1" cubes
⅛ teaspoon garlic powder
⅛ teaspoon salt
⅛ teaspoon ground black pepper
1/16 teaspoon ground ginger
⅛ teaspoon crushed red pepper flakes

¾ cup diced red bell pepper in 1 ½" pieces
⅓ cup pineapple chunks
¼ cup chicken broth
1 tablespoon soy sauce
¼ cup pineapple juice
1 tablespoon sweet chili sauce
½ tablespoon cold water
½ tablespoon cornstarch

1. Season the chicken with salt, black pepper, red pepper flakes, and ginger in a small bowl. 2. Set your Instant Pot on Sauté and adjust the temperature to More. 3. After 10 seconds, add oil. 4. Add the season chicken in the heated oil and sear each side of the chicken about 3 minutes or until browned without stirring. 5. Turn off the heat and add pineapple chunks, soy sauce, broth, pineapple juice, bell pepper, and chili sauce. Scrape all the browned bits off the pot to deglaze. 6. Close the lid and turn the steam release handle to Sealing position. 7. Set your Instant Pot on Pressure Cook at High and adjust the cooking time to 3 minutes. 8. When cooked, quickly release the pressure by turning the handle from Sealing to Venting. 9. Remove the lid and set the Instant Pot on Sauté and temperature at More. 10. Whisk water and cornstarch together in a cup. 11. Then drizzle the mixture slowly and stir in the inner pot. 12. Cook in the inner pot for about 3 minutes or until thickened. 13. Serve on a serving plate and enjoy!
Per Serving: Calories: 544; Fat: 17g; Sodium: 4,372mg; Carbs: 31g; Sugar: 20g; Protein: 58g

Chicken and Rice Bowl with Cilantro

Prep Time: 5 minutes | Cook Time: 5 minutes | Serves: 4

1 cup jasmine rice
1 (13.66-ounce) can unsweetened full-; Fat coconut milk
½ cup chicken stock
1¼ pounds boneless, skinless chicken breasts, cut into 1" cubes

1 teaspoon salt
½ teaspoon ground cumin
¼ teaspoon ground ginger
Juice from 1 medium lime
½ cup chopped cilantro leaves and stems

1. In the inner pot, add coconut milk, chicken, cumin, salt, ginger, stock, and rice and stir until well combined. Close the lid and turn the steam release handle to Sealing. 2. Set your Instant Pot on Pressure Cook at High and adjust the cooking time to 5 minutes. 3. When cooked, naturally release the pressure for 10 minutes and then quick release the remaining pressure. 4. Carefully remove the lid and add the lime juice and stir to mix well. 5. Divide the soup into four bowls and sprinkle with cilantro. 6. Serve and enjoy!
Per Serving: Calories: 527; Fat: 22g; Sodium: 702mg; Carbs: 38g; Sugar: 1g; Protein: 38g

Lemon Whole "Roasted" Chicken

Prep Time: 5 minutes | Cook Time: 28 minutes | Serves: 6

¾ cup water
1 medium lemon
1 (4-pound) whole chicken

1 tablespoon salt
2 teaspoons black pepper

1. In the inner pot, pour water. Cut the lemon into two. 2. Squeeze out juice from the lemon half and add salt and pepper to season. 3. Stuff the chicken with the rest half lemon. 4. Arrange the chicken in the inner pot with breast-side down. Close the lid. 5. Set your Instant Pot on Pressure Cook at High and adjust the cooking time to 28 minutes. 6. When cooked, naturally release the pressure. 7. Carefully remove the lid and then the chicken. On a cutting board, cut the cooled chicken into your desired size. 8. Serve and enjoy!
Per Serving: Calories: 341; Fat: 20g; Sodium: 1,249mg; Carbs: 1g; Sugar: 0g; Protein: 32g

Lemony Chicken Thighs and Rice

Prep Time: 5 minutes | Cook Time: 25 minutes | Serves: 1

1 tablespoon olive oil	½ cup uncooked long-grain white rice
1 tablespoon butter	
2 (4-ounce) boneless, skinless chicken thighs	1 teaspoon Italian seasoning
	1 teaspoon minced garlic
1 teaspoon ground lemon pepper	¼ teaspoon salt
Juice and zest of 1 medium lemon	⅛ teaspoon ground black pepper
1 cup chicken broth	1 tablespoon chopped parsley

1. Using lemon pepper, season all sides of the chicken thighs. 2. Set your Instant Pot on Sauté and adjust the temperature to More. 3. After 10 seconds, add oil and butter in the inner pot. Put the seasoned chicken inside and cook both sides for about 10 minutes to brown. 4. When cooked, turn off the machine and remove the inner pot from the cooker base. Add the lemon zest and juice in the inner pot, and then pour the broth. Scrape the browned bits off the inner pot to deglaze the pot. 5. Then add Italian seasoning, garlic, pepper, rice, and salt in the inner pot. 6. Return the inner pot back to the cooker base and close the lid. Then turn the steam release handle to the Sealing position. 7. Set the Instant Pot on Pressure Cook at High and adjust time to 10 minutes. 8. When cooked, naturally release the pressure about 5 minutes and then remove the lid. 9. Transfer the chicken and rice into a bowl and top with the chopped parsley. 10. Serve with a side of steamed broccoli or roasted vegetables.
Per Serving: Calories: 796; Fat: 34g; Sodium: 1,593mg; Carbs: 79g; Sugar: 2g; Protein: 36g

Ranch Chicken Lettuce Wraps

Prep Time: 5 minutes | Cook Time: 15 minutes | Serves: 1

1 (8-ounce) boneless, skinless chicken breast, thinly sliced	½ tablespoon chopped green onion
	2–4 leaves romaine lettuce
1 cup water	2 tablespoons shredded carrot
1/16 teaspoon salt	2 tablespoons crispy chow Mein noodles
1/16 teaspoon ground black pepper	
1 teaspoon dry ranch seasoning	2 tablespoons sweetened dried cranberries
3 tablespoons buffalo sauce	
1 tablespoon melted butter	2 tablespoons ranch dressing

1. With salt and pepper, season the chicken breast. 2. Then place the chicken thighs and water in the inner pot. 3. Close the pressure lid and turn the steam pressure knob to Sealing position. 4. Set your Instant Pot on Pressure Cook mode at High and adjust time to 10 minutes. 5. When cooked, naturally release the pressure about 5 minutes and remove the lid. 6. Transfer the cooked chicken in a small bowl and drip over with 1 tablespoon of cooking liquid. Shred the chicken with 2 forks. 7. Mix together with buffalo sauce, green onion, butter, and dry ranch seasoning. 8. Line a serving plate with the lettuce leaves. Evenly divide the chicken mixture onto the lettuce leaves and then add chow Mein noodles, ranch dressing, cranberries, and carrot over the chicken mixture. 9. Serve and enjoy!
Per Serving: Calories: 565; Fat: 30g; Sodium: 2,498mg; Carbs: 26g; Sugar: 13g; Protein: 48g

Lime Chicken Fajitas

Prep Time: 7 minutes | Cook Time: 8 minutes | Serves: 1

1 tablespoon olive oil	flakes
½ teaspoon chili powder	1 cup diced chicken breast in 1" cubes
½ teaspoon salt	
½ teaspoon dried oregano	2 cups frozen bell pepper mix
¼ teaspoon garlic powder	⅓ cup water
¼ teaspoon ground cumin	1 tablespoon soy sauce
⅛ teaspoon crushed red pepper	1 tablespoon lime juice

1. Set your Instant Pot on Sauté and adjust the temperature to More. 2. After 10 seconds, add oil in the inner pot. 3. Mix together salt, oregano, cumin, garlic powder, red pepper flakes, and chili powder in a small bowl. 4. Transfer half of the mixture to a second small bowl and reserve the rest half. Set aside. 5. Toss the chicken in the mixture and coat well. 6. Place the seasoned chicken in the heated inner pot and sear each side about 3 minutes or until browned without stirring. 7. Turn off the heat and add water, soy sauce, the reserved seasoning mixture, lime juice, and bell pepper in the inner pot. Scrape all the browned bits off the pot to deglaze. 8. Close the lid and turn the steam release handle to Sealing position. 9. Set your Instant Pot on Pressure Cook at High and adjust the cooking time to 2 minutes. 10. When

cooked, quickly release the pressure turning the handle from Sealing to Venting. Remove the lid. 11. Transfer chicken and peppers to a serving plate with a tong. Serve and enjoy!
Per Serving: Calories: 476; Fat: 17g; Sodium: 2,194mg; Carbs: 17g; Sugar: 8g; Protein: 56g

Chicken and Quinoa Bowl with Mushrooms

Prep Time: 15 minutes | Cook Time: 5 minutes | Serves: 6

1 tablespoon avocado oil	2 (8-ounce) packages sliced white mushrooms
1 small yellow onion, diced	
6 cloves garlic, minced	3 cups chicken stock
1½ pounds boneless, skinless chicken thighs, cut into bite-sized pieces	1½ cups quinoa, rinsed well
	1 cup nondairy Greek-style yogurt

1. Set your Instant Pot on Sauté and adjust the temperature to More. 2. Add oil in the inner pot and heat for 1 minute. 3. Add onion and sauté about 5 minutes or until soften. Then add garlic and sauté for 30 seconds. 4. Turn off the heat. Add the mushrooms, quinoa, stock, yogurt, and chicken in the inner pot. Stir well. Close the lid and turn the steam release handle to Sealing. 5. Set your Instant Pot on Pressure Cook at High and adjust the cooking time to 3 minutes. 6. When cooked, quick release the pressure until the float valve drops. 7. Carefully remove the lid and spoon the chicken mixture onto a serving plate. 8. Serve and enjoy!
Per Serving: Calories: 397; Fat: 10g; Sodium: 294mg; Carbs: 37g; Sugar: 5g; Protein: 37g

Barbecue Chicken Salad with Berries

Prep Time: 10 minutes | Cook Time: 15 minutes | Serves: 1

1 (8-ounce) boneless, skinless chicken breast	fried onion
	2 tablespoons sweetened dried cranberries
1 cup water	
1 teaspoon barbecue dry rub	2 tablespoons corn
3 tablespoons barbecue sauce	1 ½ tablespoons shredded smoked Gouda cheese
1 ½ cups chopped romaine lettuce	
2 tablespoons drained and rinsed canned black beans	1 tablespoon bacon bits
	¼ cup sliced avocado
2 tablespoons sliced strawberries	2 tablespoons ranch dressing
1 ½ tablespoons packaged French	

1. In the inner pot, add chicken, water, and dry rub. 2. Close the lid and turn the steam release knob to Sealing position. 3. When cooked, naturally release the pressure and remove the lid. 4. Transfer the cooked chicken to a small bowl and add 1 tablespoon of cooking liquid. 5. Shred the chicken with 2 forks. 6. Mix in barbecue sauce thoroughly and cool slightly. 7. Meanwhile, toss together the beans, strawberries, French fried onions, corn, cranberries, Gouda, avocado, lettuce, and bacon bits in a medium bowl. 8. Arrange the shredded chicken on the top and sprinkle with ranch dressing. 9. Serve and enjoy!
Per Serving: Calories: 771; Fat: 35g; Sodium: 1,651mg; Carbs: 56g; Sugar: 32g; Protein: 60g

Savory Brown Butter Chicken Thighs

Prep Time: 5 minutes | Cook Time: 27 minutes | Serves: 1

2 tablespoons butter	½ teaspoon Italian seasoning
2 (6-ounce) bone-in chicken thighs	½ teaspoon salt
½ teaspoon garlic powder	½ teaspoon ground black pepper
1 teaspoon minced garlic	
½ cup chicken broth	

1. Season both sides of the chicken with Italian seasoning, salt, pepper, and garlic powder. 2. Set your Instant Pot on Sauté and adjust the temperature to More. 3. After 10 seconds, add butter in the inner pot and Sauté for about 5 minutes or until browned. 4. Place the chicken in the pot, skin side down, and cook for 5 minutes with stirring. 5. When cooked, remove the chicken to a plate. 6. In the inner pot, add broth and the minced garlic. Turn off the heat and scrape all the browned bits off the pot to deglaze. 7. Close the lid and turn the steam release handle to Sealing position. 8. Set your Instant Pot to Pressure Cook at High and adjust time to 12 minutes. 9. When cooked, naturally release the pressure about 5 minutes and remove the lid. 10. Serve on a serving plate and enjoy!
Per Serving: Calories: 1,074; Fat: 79g; Sodium: 1,938mg; Fiber: 0g; Carbs: 4g; Sugar: 1g; Protein: 65g

Chicken and Broccoli with Honey-Sesame Sauce

Prep Time: 2 minutes | Cook Time: 10 minutes | Serves: 1

¼ cup water
2 tablespoons honey
1 ½ tablespoons brown sugar
1 tablespoon soy sauce
1 tablespoon ketchup
½ tablespoon sriracha sauce
½ tablespoon sesame oil

½ teaspoon minced garlic
1 cup diced chicken breast in 1" pieces
1 ½ cups broccoli florets
½ teaspoon sesame seeds
1 cup cooked white rice

1. Whisk water, brown sugar, ketchup, oil, garlic, honey, and sriracha together in a small bowl. 2. Add the chicken to the inner pot and pour sauce over the chicken. 3. Close the lid and turn the steam release handle to Sealing. 4. Set your Instant Pot on Pressure Cook at High and adjust the cooking time to 2 minutes. 5. When cooked, quickly release the pressure by turning the handle from Sealing to Venting. 6. Remove the lid and set your Instant Pot on Sauté and adjust the temperature to More. 7. Place broccoli to the chicken and mix into sauce. Sauté for 6 to 8 minutes or until the broccoli is completely cooked and sauce is thickened and sticky. 8. Serve over rice with sesame seeds on top. Enjoy!
Per Serving: Calories: 830; Fat: 12g; Sodium: 1,336mg; Carbs: 116g; Sugar: 62g; Protein: 61g

Teriyaki Chicken Rice Bowl

Prep Time: 5 minutes | Cook Time: 15 minutes | Serves: 1

Tzatziki Sauce
4 ½ tablespoons unsweetened plain Greek-style yogurt
3 tablespoons grated cucumber; liquid squeezed out
1 teaspoon lemon juice
Chicken Bowl
1 tablespoon olive oil
1 tablespoon butter
Juice and zest of 1 medium lemon
1 cup chicken broth
½ cup uncooked long-grain white rice
Topping
2 tablespoons diced tomato
2 tablespoons diced red bell pepper
2 tablespoons crumbled feta cheese
2 tablespoons diced red onion

⅛ teaspoon salt
1/16 teaspoon ground black pepper
¼ teaspoon dried dill
⅛ teaspoon minced garlic
1 teaspoon olive oil

1 teaspoon dried oregano
1 teaspoon minced garlic
¼ teaspoon salt
⅛ teaspoon ground black pepper
1 cup chopped chicken breast
1 teaspoon ground lemon pepper

2 tablespoons diced cucumber
2 tablespoons chopped Kalamata olives

1. Combine all the sauce ingredients in a small jar or bowl and chill in refrigerator until ready to serve to make the Tzatziki sauce. 2. In the Instant Pot, add butter, oil, lime zest, lemon juice, rice, broth, salt, oregano, garlic, and black pepper and stir to combine to make the chicken bowl. 3. Toss the chicken with lemon pepper in a small bowl and then evenly spread the chicken over rice. 4. Close the lid and turn the steam release handle to Sealing position. 5. Set your Instant Pot on Pressure Cook at High and adjust cooking time to 10 minutes. 6. When cooked, naturally release the pressure about 5 minutes. Remove the lid. 7. Transfer the chicken and rice onto a serving bowl, and arrange bell pepper, feta cheese, cucumber, onion, olives, and tomato on the top. 8. Serve with the Tzatziki Sauce and enjoy!
Per Serving: Calories: 849; Fat: 44g; Sodium: 2,442mg; Carbs: 40g; Sugar: 7g; Protein: 64g

Enticing Bruschetta Chicken

Prep Time: 5 minutes | Cook Time: 15 minutes | Serves: 1

Chicken
1 cup water
1 (8-ounce) boneless, skinless chicken breast
⅛ teaspoon salt
Bruschetta
⅓ cup diced tomatoes
½ tablespoon olive oil
¼ teaspoon balsamic glaze
¼ teaspoon minced garlic
1 teaspoon chopped fresh basil

⅛ teaspoon ground black pepper
¼ teaspoon Italian seasoning
2 (1-ounce) slices fresh mozzarella cheese

1/16 teaspoon crushed red pepper flakes
1/16 teaspoon ground black pepper
1/16 teaspoon salt

1. In the inner pot, pour water and then place the trivet. 2. Rub the chicken with black pepper, Italian seasoning, and salt to season. Then place the seasoned chicken on the trivet. 3. Close the lid and turn the steam release handle to Sealing position. 4. Set your Instant Pot on Pressure Cook at High and adjust time to 15 minutes. 5. Meanwhile, to make the bruschetta, mix together the Bruschetta ingredients in a small bowl and then let it chill in refrigerator until ready to serve. 6. When cooked, naturally release the pressure about 5 minutes. Remove the lid and arrange mozzarella slices over the chicken. Close the lid and let it stand for 5 minutes or until the cheese has slightly melted. 7. When done, transfer to a serving plate and serve with Bruschetta on the top. 8. Enjoy!
Per Serving: Calories: 472; Fat: 22g; Sodium: 1,020mg; Carbs: 8g; Sugar: 4g; Protein: 60g

Turkey Carrot Taco Lettuce Boats

Prep Time: 10 minutes | Cook Time: 24 minutes | Serves: 4

1 tablespoon avocado oil
1 medium onion, peeled and diced
2 large carrots, peeled and diced
2 medium stalks celery, ends removed and diced
2 cloves garlic, minced
1-pound lean ground turkey
1 teaspoon chili powder

1 teaspoon paprika
1 teaspoon cumin
½ teaspoon salt
¼ teaspoon black pepper
1 cup chipotle salsa
12 large romaine leaves
1 medium avocado, peeled, pitted, and sliced

1. Set your Instant Pot on Sauté and adjust the temperature to More. 2. Add the oil in the inner pot and heat 1 minute. Then add onion, celery, garlic, and carrots and cook about 5 minutes or until soften. 3. Add the turkey in the inner pot and cook about 3 minutes or until browned. 4. Stir in paprika, salt, cumin, chili powder, salsa, and pepper until well combined. 5. Turn off the heat and close the lid. 6. Set your Instant Pot on Pressure Cook at High and adjust the cooking time to 15 minutes. 7. When cooked, quick release the pressure until float valve drops. 8. Carefully remove the lid and spoon the taco meat into a romaine lettuce leaf. 9. Then top with the avocado slices as you like. 10. Serve and enjoy!
Per Serving: Calories: 339; Fat: 18g; Sodium: 900mg; Carbs: 18g; Sugar: 8g; Protein: 27g

Chicken Pasta with Parmesan Cheese

Prep Time: 5 minutes | Cook Time: 16 minutes | Serves: 1

1 tablespoon olive oil
1 tablespoon butter
1 cup diced chicken breast
1 teaspoon Cajun seasoning
1 cup chopped bell pepper, any color
½ tablespoon dried onion flakes
¾ cup chicken broth
½ cup heavy cream

1 tablespoon white wine
½ teaspoon minced garlic
½ tablespoon soy sauce
4 ounces uncooked linguine, broken in half
¾ cup diced tomatoes
1 tablespoon shredded Parmesan cheese

1. Toss the Cajun seasoning over the chicken in a medium bowl. 2. Set your Instant Pot on Sauté and adjust the temperature level to More. 3. After 10 seconds, add oil and butter in the inner pot. 4. When the butter has melted, add the chicken in the inner pot and sear the chicken for 5 minutes, flipping from time to time to evenly cook the chicken. 5. When cooked, remove the chicken. Place bell pepper and Sauté for 3 minutes. 6. Transfer the bell pepper to a small bowl and set aside. 7. Pour broth, wine, cream, and soy sauce with onion flakes and scrape all the browned bits off the pot to deglaze. 8. Turn off the heat and line noodles in a crisscross shape over the liquid to reduce clumping. 9. Pour the chicken together with the soup and pepper over the noodles. Add in the tomato. Do not stir the mixture. 10. Close the lid and turn the steam release handle to Sealing position. 11. Set your Instant Pot on Pressure Cook at High and adjust the cooking time to 8 minutes. 12. When cooked, quick release the pressure turning the handle from Sealing to Venting. 13. Remove the lid and stir. You can sauté for several minutes to thicken the sauce stirring from time to time if the sauce is too thin for your taste. 14. Transfer to a serving plate and top with Parmesan cheese. 15. Serve and enjoy!
Per Serving: Calories: 1,449; Fat: 72g; Sodium: 1,620mg; Carbs: 107g; Sugar: 18g; Protein: 75g

Mayonnaise Chicken Salad

Prep Time: 15 minutes | Cook Time: 10 minutes | Serves: 1

1 cup water
1 (8-ounce) boneless, skinless chicken breast
⅛ teaspoon salt
⅛ teaspoon ground black pepper
4 ½ tablespoons mayonnaise
¼ teaspoon dried dill
⅛ teaspoon garlic powder
¼ teaspoon dried onion flakes
⅛ teaspoon dried basil
⅛ teaspoon seasoned salt
1 ½ tablespoons finely diced celery
8 grapes, quartered (about ¼ cup)
1 tablespoon cashew halves

1. Rub the chicken with salt and pepper to season. 2. Pour water inside the inner pot and then place the chicken inside. 3. Close the lid and turn the steam release knob to Sealing position. 4. Set your Instant Pot on Pressure Cook at high and adjust the cooking time to 10 minutes. 5. When cooked, naturally release the pressure about 10 minutes. 6. Remove the lid and transfer the chicken to a small bowl. 7. Dice the chicken into small pieces and cool in the refrigerator to get ready for serving. 8. Combine dill, onion flakes, basil, mayonnaise, garlic powder, seasoned salt, grapes, cashews, and celery in a separate bowl. 9. Mix together with the chicken slices and transfer to a serving plate. 10. Serve immediately or cool in the refrigerator to keep fresh.
Per Serving: Calories: 750; Fat: 55g; Sodium: 1,181mg; Carbs: 11g; Sugar: 7g; Protein: 51g

Asian Noodle Bowls with Almonds

Prep Time: 10 minutes | Cook Time: 3 minutes | Serves: 1

½ cup reduced sodium tamari
2 tablespoons rice vinegar
2 tablespoons almond butter
2 tablespoons erythritol
2 cups chicken broth
1 pound boneless, skinless chicken breast, cut into bite-sized pieces
2 large carrots, peeled and thickly sliced (½") on the diagonal
8 ounces uncooked brown rice noodles
¼ cup sliced scallions
4 tablespoons chopped almonds

1. In the inner pot, add vinegar, erythritol, chicken pieces, carrots, broth, and almond butter. Sprinkle the noodles on the top. 2. Close the lid and turn the steam release handle to Sealing position. 3. Set your Instant Pot on Pressure Cook at High and adjust the cooking time to 3 minutes. 4. When cooked, quick release the pressure until the float valve drops. 5. Remove the lid and stir carefully the ingredients. 6. Divide the meal into four serving bowls. 7. Sprinkle the slices scallions and chopped almonds on the top to serve.
Per Serving: Calories: 482; Fat: 11g; Sodium: 1,392mg; Carbs: 62g; Sugar: 6g; Protein: 36g

Curried Chicken Tikka Masala

Prep Time: 15 minutes | Cook Time: 15 minutes | Serves: 4

1-pound boneless, skinless chicken breast, cubed
1 cup tomato puree
¼ cup water
1 yellow onion, chopped
4 garlic cloves, minced
1 (1-inch) knob fresh ginger,
grated
1 tablespoon garam masala
¼ teaspoon kosher salt
¼ cup Homemade Yogurt or store-bought plain whole-milk yogurt
1 cup frozen peas

1. Combine the tomato sauce, onion, water, garlic, garam masala, salt, and chicken in the inner pot and close the lid. 2. Set your Instant Pot on Pressure Cook at High and adjust the cooking time to 13 minutes. 3. When cooked, naturally release the pressure about 10 minutes, and then quickly release the remaining pressure. 4. Remove the lid carefully. Add peas and yogurt and stir well. 5. Let it sit for 1 to 2 minutes or until the peas are thoroughly warmed. 6. Serve and enjoy!
Per Serving: Calories: 189; Fat: 3g; Carbs: 12g; Sugar: 6g; Sodium: 187mg; Protein: 29g

Homemade Chicken and Vegetables

Prep Time: 5 minutes | Cook Time: 15 minutes | Serves: 4

2 large bone-in chicken breasts (about 2 pounds)
1 teaspoon kosher salt, divided
½ teaspoon black pepper, divided
½ cup chicken stock
6 large carrots
8 medium whole new potatoes

1. To season, rub the chicken breasts with ½ teaspoon salt and ¼

teaspoon pepper. 2. In the inner pot, pour the stock and soak the chicken breasts in. 3. Arrange the potatoes and carrots over the chicken and add the rest of the salt and pepper to add taste. Close the lid and turn the steam release handle to Sealing. 4. Set your Instant Pot on Pressure Cook at High and adjust the cooking time to 15 minutes. 5. When cooked, naturally release the pressure and carefully remove the lid. 6. Serve on a serving plate and spoon the soup over. 7. Enjoy!
Per Serving: Calories: 398; Fat: 5g; Sodium: 822mg; Carbs: 24g; Sugar: 6g; Protein: 58g

Baked Chicken and Veggies

Prep Time: 5 minutes | Cook Time: 5 minutes | Serves: 4

4 cups riced cauliflower
8 ounces white mushrooms, chopped
8 ounces shiitake mushrooms, stems removed and chopped
8 ounces oyster mushrooms, chopped
1½ pounds boneless, skinless
chicken breasts, cut into bite-sized pieces
¼ cup chicken stock
1 tablespoon minced garlic
1 teaspoon salt
1 teaspoon dried thyme
Juice from 1 large lemon

1. In the inner pot, add the mushrooms, chicken, and cauliflower. 2. Whisk the garlic, stock, salt, thyme, and lemon juice in a small bowl. 3. Pour the mixture over the chicken and vegetables and stir well. 4. Close the lid and turn the steam release handle to Sealing. 5. Set your Instant Pot on Pressure Cook at High and adjust the cooking time to 5 minutes. 6. When cooked, naturally release the pressure until the float valve drops. 7. Remove the lid. 8. Stir the mixture well. Serve and enjoy!
Per Serving: Calories: 432; Fat: 4g; Sodium: 428mg; Carbs: 54g; Sugar: 5g; Protein: 50g

Classic Chicken Alfredo

Prep Time: 5 minutes | Cook Time: 17 minutes | Serves: 1

1 tablespoon butter
¼ cup chicken broth
1 cup heavy cream
½ teaspoon minced garlic
4 ounces uncooked fettuccine, broken in half
1 cup diced chicken breast
¼ teaspoon salt
⅛ teaspoon ground black pepper
1 cup broccoli florets
¼ cup shredded Parmesan cheese

1. Add broth, garlic, butter, and cream in the inner pot. To reduce clumping, layer the noodles in a crisscross shape over the liquid. 2. Place the chicken over the noodles and season with salt and pepper. 3. Set your Instant Pot on Pressure Cook at High and adjust the cooking time to 7 minutes. 4. When cooked, quick release the pressure, turning from Sealing to Venting. 5. Remove the lid and stir for a while. Arrange the broccoli and close the lid. 6. Cook the broccoli for 8 to 10 minutes or until cooked completely. 7. Sprinkle Parmesan cheese on the top and stir well. 8. Serve and enjoy!
Per Serving: Calories: 1,732; Fat: 104g; Sodium: 1,379mg; Fiber: 6g; Carbs: 99g; Sugar: 12g; Protein: 81g

Dijon Avocado Chicken Salad

Prep Time: 10 minutes | Cook Time: 6 minutes | Serves: 4

1 pound boneless, skinless chicken breasts
½ cup chicken stock
1½ medium avocados, peeled, pitted, and mashed (1 cup mashed)
1 medium stalk celery, ends removed and diced
1 scallion, thinly sliced
1 tablespoon lemon juice
1 tablespoon chopped fresh parsley
½ teaspoon dried dill weed
2 teaspoons Dijon mustard
½ teaspoon kosher salt
¼ teaspoon freshly ground black pepper

1. In the inner pot, pour the chicken stock and soak the chicken breasts in. 2. Close the lid and turn the steam release handle to Sealing. 3. Set your Instant Pot on Pressure Cook at High and adjust the cooking time to 6 minutes. 4. When cooked, naturally release the pressure and carefully remove the lid. 5. Transfer the chicken breasts onto a cutting board and let it cool completely. 6. Then cut the chicken into your desired size. 7. In a medium bowl, add the chopped chicken and the rest of the ingredients and stir until well tossed. 8. Serve and enjoy!
Per Serving: Calories: 230; Fat: 9g; Sodium: 421mg; Carbs: 6g; Sugar: 1g; Protein: 27g

Chili Chicken Thighs and Rice

Prep Time: 5 minutes | Cook Time: 22 minutes | Serves: 1

½ tablespoon olive oil
1 teaspoon dried cilantro
¼ teaspoon chili powder
¼ teaspoon ground cumin
¼ teaspoon salt
¼ teaspoon garlic powder

2 (6–8-ounce) bone-in chicken thighs
½ cup uncooked long-grain white rice
½ cup chicken broth
1 medium lime, quartered

1. Combine together chili powder, salt, cumin, cilantro, and garlic powder in a small bowl. 2. Season each side of the chicken with ½ teaspoon of the mixture and reserve the remaining seasoning. 3. Set your Instant Pot on Sauté and adjust the temperature to More. 4. After 10 seconds, add oil in the inner pot and let it heat up until shiny. 5. Add the seasoned chicken in the inner pot, skin side down and sauté for 5 minutes or until the skin is golden and crispy. 6. Then add the reserved mixture, broth, rice, and ¾ lime to the chicken. 7. Turn off the heat and scrape all the browned bits off the pot to deglaze. 8. Close the lid and turn the steam release handle to Sealing position. 9. Set your Instant Pot on Pressure Cook at High and adjust the cooking time to 12 minutes. 10. When cooked, naturally release the pressure about 5 minutes. 11. Remove the lid and transfer to a serving bowl and serve with the remaining lime on the top. Enjoy!
Per Serving: Calories: 1,261; Fat: 65g; Sodium: 1,378mg; Carbs: 77g; Sugar: 1g; Protein: 71g

Avocado Chicken Salad with Strawberries

Prep Time: 10 minutes | Cook Time: 6 minutes | Serves: 4

1-pound boneless, skinless chicken breasts
½ cup chicken stock
13 large strawberries, hulled, divided
2 tablespoons extra-virgin olive oil
2 tablespoons fresh lemon juice
¼ teaspoon ground ginger

⅛ teaspoon white pepper
8 cups baby spinach
1 medium avocado, peeled, pitted, and cut into slices
⅓ cup sliced almonds
½ teaspoon salt
¼ teaspoon freshly ground black pepper

1. In the inner pot, add the chicken breasts and stock. 2. Close the lid and turn the steam release handle to Sealing. 3. Set your Instant Pot on Pressure Cook at High and adjust the cooking time to 6 minutes. 4. Place the hulled strawberries, lemon juice, ginger, white pepper, and oil in a blender and blend together until smooth. Set aside. 5. When cooked, naturally release the pressure until the float valve drops. 6. Carefully remove the lid and transfer the chicken onto a cutting board. 7. When cooled completely, cut the chicken into your desired size. 8. Add the avocado slices, almonds, strawberry slices, the chicken slices, and the baby spinach in a large serving bowl. 9. Drizzle the salad dressing over the chicken and fruit mixture. 10. Season with salt and pepper and toss well. 11. Serve and enjoy!
Per Serving: Calories: 333; Fat: 18g; Sodium: 392mg; Carbs: 12g; Sugar: 4g; Protein: 33g

Balsamic Chicken Cacciatore

Prep Time: 15 minutes | Cook Time: 12 minutes | Serves: 6

6 bone-in chicken thighs, with skin
¼ teaspoon kosher salt
¼ teaspoon freshly ground black pepper
2 tablespoons olive oil
1 (28-ounce) can crushed tomatoes
2 green bell peppers, seeded and diced

1 pint cremini mushrooms, halved lengthwise
½ cup pitted black olives
1 yellow onion, diced
1 teaspoon dried oregano
2 garlic cloves, minced
1 teaspoon balsamic vinegar

1. Toss the chicken with black pepper and salt to season. 2. Set your Instant Pot on Sauté and adjust the temperature to More. 3. After 10 seconds, pour olive oil in the inner pot. 4. When the oil has heated, place the chicken in the pot, with skin-side down. 5. Cook without stirring for 5 to 8 minutes or until the skin is golden brown. 6. Turn the chicken to skin-side up and turn off the heat. 7. Add bell peppers, onion, olives, garlic, oregano, balsamic vinegar, and tomatoes in the inner pot and close the lid. 8. Set your Instant Pot to Pressure Cook at High and adjust the cooking time to 12 minutes. 9. When cooked, naturally release the pressure about 10 minutes and quickly release the remaining pressure. 10. Transfer carefully the lid. 11. Serve and enjoy!
Per Serving: Calories: 520; Fat: 38g; Carbs: 10g; Sugar: 5g; Sodium: 446mg; Protein: 34g

Kale Chicken Salad

Prep Time: 20 minutes | Cook Time: 6 minutes | Serves: 4

1-pound boneless, skinless chicken breast
½ cup chicken stock
2 bunches kale (about 12 ounces total), deveined and finely chopped
1 medium red bell pepper, seeded and diced
1 cup diced carrot
3 cups chopped cabbage

¼ cup pure sesame oil
¼ cup almond butter
¼ cup raw honey
Juice from 2 medium limes
1 tablespoon reduced sodium tamari
¼ teaspoon minced garlic
⅓ cup sesame seeds

1. In the inner pot, pour the stock and soak the chicken breast in. 2. Close the lid and turn the steam release handle to Sealing. 3. Set your Instant Pot on Pressure Cook at High and adjust the cooking time to 6 minutes. 4. When cooked, naturally release the pressure. 5. Carefully remove the lid. Transfer the chicken onto a cutting board. When it is completely cool, cut into your desired size. 6. Mix together the bell pepper, cabbage, carrots, chopped chicken, and kale in a large bowl. 7. Blend the almond butter, lime juice, garlic, tamari, and oil in a blender until smooth. 8. Then pour the almond butter mixture over the chicken mixture to make the salad. Toss well. 9. Sprinkle sesame seeds on the top and lightly toss. 10. Serve and enjoy!
Per Serving: Calories: 561; Fat: 30g; Sodium: 332mg; Carbs: 41g; Sugar: 25g; Protein: 36g

Turkey with Butternut Squash and Carrots

Prep Time: 15 minutes | Cook Time: 40 minutes | Serves: 4

1½ pounds turkey tenderloin
2 teaspoons olive oil, divided
½ teaspoon poultry seasoning
½ teaspoon kosher salt
¼ teaspoon freshly ground black

pepper
2 cups cubed butternut squash
4 celery stalks, sliced
4 carrots, peeled and sliced

1. Rub the 1 teaspoon of olive oil over the turkey. Then season with salt, pepper, and the poultry seasoning. Set the mixture aside. 2. On a piece of aluminum foil, add celery, carrots, and the squash. Foil the sides up together like a boat to contain the vegetables. Do not cover the top. 3. Drizzle the remaining olive oil over the vegetables and set aside. 4. In the inner pot, pour 1 cup of water. Place a trivet in the inner pot. Arrange the turkey on the trivet and then close the lid. 5. Turn the steam release handle to Sealing position. 6. Set your Instant Pot on Pressure Cook at High and adjust the cooking time to 20 minutes. 7. When cooked, quick release the pressure. 8. Remove the lid carefully and put the foil boat of vegetables directly on the turkey. 9. Close the lid and turn the steam release handle to Sealing position. 10. Set your Instant Pot on Pressure Cook at High and adjust the cooking time to 20 minutes. 11. When cooked, naturally release the pressure about 10 minutes, then quick release the remaining pressure. 12. Remove the lid carefully. Then transfer the foil boat of vegetables and set aside for serving. 13. Remove the turkey onto a cutting board and cut into your desired slices. 14. Serve alongside the vegetables and enjoy!
Per Serving: Calories: 281; Fat: 7g; Carbs: 16g; Sugar: 5g; Sodium: 367mg; Protein: 41g

Spiced Chicken and Carrots

Prep Time: 15 minutes | Cook Time: 15 minutes | Serves: 4

1 teaspoon dried thyme
¼ teaspoon ground ginger
¼ teaspoon ground allspice
1 teaspoon kosher salt
½ teaspoon black pepper
2 large bone-in chicken breasts

(about 2 pounds)
½ cup chicken stock
2 medium onions, peeled and cut in fourths
4 medium carrots

1. Mix together ginger, ground allspice, ginger, salt, thyme, and pepper in a small bowl. 2. Season the chicken breasts with half of the spice mixture. 3. In the inner pot, add the chicken stock and then place the chicken breasts. 4. Top the chicken with onions and carrots and add the remaining spice mixture. 5. Close the lid and turn the steam release handle to Sealing position. 6. Set your Instant Pot on Pressure Cook at High and adjust the cooking time to 15 minutes. 7. When cooked, naturally release the pressure. 8. Carefully remove the chicken and vegetables over rice or lentils to serve.
Per Serving: Calories: 337; Fat: 5g; Sodium: 755mg; Carbs: 12g; Sugar: 5g; Protein: 56g

Tuscan Chicken with Tomatoes and Kale

Prep Time: 5 minutes | Cook Time: 14 minutes | Serves: 1

1 tablespoon olive oil
1 cup diced chicken breast in 1"
cubes
¼ teaspoon Italian seasoning
⅛ teaspoon garlic powder
⅛ teaspoon salt
⅛ teaspoon ground black pepper
½ teaspoon dried onion flakes

½ cup chicken broth
¼ teaspoon soy sauce
1 tablespoon chopped sun-dried
tomatoes
½ cup sliced packed kale
¼ cup heavy cream
¼ cup shredded Parmesan cheese

1. Set your Instant Pot on Sauté and adjust the temperature level to More. 2. After 10 seconds, add oil. 3. Place the chicken in a small bowl. Then add garlic powder, pepper, salt, and Italian seasoning to coat the chicken. 4. Place the chicken in the inner pot and sear each side for about 3 minutes or until browned without stirring. 5. Turn off the heat and then add soy sauce, tomatoes, broth, and onion flakes. Scrape all the browned bits off the pot to deglaze. 6. Close the lid and turn the steam release handle to Sealing position. 7. Set your Instant Pot on Pressure Cook at High and adjust the cooking time to 3 minutes. 8. When cooked, quickly release the pressure turning the handle from Sealing to Venting. 9. Remove the lid. Add kale and stir. Close the lid and let it stand in the Instant Pot for about 5 minutes or until wilt down. 10. Then remove the lid. Add cream and Parmesan and stir well. 11. Transfer onto a serving plate and enjoy!
Per Serving: Calories: 704; Fat: 43g; Sodium: 1,300mg; Carbs: 7g; Sugar: 4g; Protein: 62g

Flavorful Turkey Lettuce Wraps

Prep Time: 15 minutes | Cook Time: 15 minutes | Serves: 4

1 tablespoon olive oil
1 yellow onion, diced
2 garlic cloves, minced
1-pound lean (93 percent) ground
turkey
⅓ cup water
2 tablespoons honey
2 tablespoons coconut aminos or

tamari
1 tablespoon rice vinegar
1 (1-inch) knob fresh ginger, grated
1 (8-ounce) can water chestnuts,
drained and diced
2 scallions, white and light green
parts, thinly sliced
1 head butter lettuce

1. Set your Instant Pot on Sauté and adjust the temperature to More. 2. Add the olive oil in the inner pot. 3. When the oil has heated, add the garlic and onion and cook for 2 to 3 minutes or until softened, stirring from time to time. Turn off the heat. 4. Then add water, coconut aminos, honey, vinegar, ginger, and ground turkey in the inner pot and stir well to break up the turkey. 5. Close the lid and turn the steam release handle to Sealing position. 6. Set your Instant Pot on Pressure Cook at High and adjust the cooking time to 5 minutes. 7. When cooked, naturally release the pressure for 10 minutes and quick release the remaining pressure. 8. Remove the lid carefully. Then add water, scallions, and chestnuts and stir well. 9. If the sauce is too thin, simmer the sauce about 3 to 4 minutes to thicken. 10. Wrap the turkey mixture with lettuce to serve. Enjoy!
Per Serving: Calories: 355; Fat: 13g; Carbs: 35g; Sugar: 10g; Sodium: 488mg; Protein: 25g

Tasty Lemon Chicken Thighs

Prep Time: 10 minutes | Cook Time: 11 minutes | Serves: 4

1 tablespoon avocado oil
1½ pounds boneless, skinless
chicken thighs
1 small onion, peeled and diced
1 tablespoon minced garlic

Juice and zest from 1 large lemon
1 tablespoon Italian seasoning
blend
⅓ cup chicken stock
1 tablespoon arrowroot powder

1. Set your Instant Pot on Sauté and adjust the temperature to Normal. 2. Add oil onto the inner pot and heat for 2 minutes. 3. When the oil has heated, add the chicken thighs in the inner pot and cook each side for 2 minutes or until brown. 4. When cooked, remove the chicken thighs from the inner pot and set aside. 5. Sauté the onion in the inner pot for 2 minutes or until transparent. 6. Add garlic and cook for 30 seconds more. 7. Add the lemon zest, lemon juice, and Italian seasoning in the inner pot. To deglaze, scrape up all the brown bites off the pot. Turn off the heat. 8. Place the chicken thighs in the stock and close the lid. 9. Set your Instant Pot on Pressure Cook at High and adjust the cooking time to 7 minutes. 10. When cooked, naturally release the pressure until the float valve drops. 11. Remove the lid and transfer the chicken to a serving bowl. 12. Add the arrowroot powder

in the sauce and stir well. 13. Pour the thickened sauce over the chicken thighs. 14. Serve and enjoy!
Per Serving: Calories: 262; Fat: 10g; Sodium: 190mg; Carbs: 6g; Sugar: 1g; Protein: 34g

Lemon Turkey Breast with Shallot

Prep Time: 10 minutes | Cook Time: 17 minutes | Serves: 4

1 (1½-pound) boneless, skinless
turkey breast
2 tablespoons avocado oil, divided
Zest from ½ large lemon
½ medium shallot, peeled and

minced
1 large clove garlic, minced
½ teaspoon kosher salt
¼ teaspoon black pepper

1. Using a towel, pat dry the turkey breast. Then cut the turkey breast into two. 2. Rub the 1 tablespoon of oil over the turkey breast. 3. Mix together the shallot, minced garlic, pepper, salt, and lemon zest in a small bowl. 4. Rub the turkey breast with mixture to season. 5. Set the Instant Pot on Sauté and adjust the temperature to More. 6. Add the remaining oil in the inner pot and heat about 2 minutes. 7. Add the turkey breast and sear each side about 3 minutes. Turn off the heat. 8. Set your Instant Pot on Pressure Cook at High and adjust the cooking time to 10 minutes. 9. When cooked, naturally release the pressure and carefully remove the lid. 10. Transfer the turkey breast onto a cutting board. When it is completely cool, cut into your desired slice. 11. Serve and enjoy!
Per Serving: Calories: 250; Fat: 9g; Sodium: 445mg; Carbs: 1g; Sugar: 0g; Protein: 40g

Chicken Fajitas with Cilantro

Prep Time: 15 minutes | Cook Time: 0 minutes | Serves: 4

2 red or yellow bell peppers,
seeded and sliced
1 red onion, sliced
1 teaspoon olive oil
½ teaspoon chili powder

¼ teaspoon kosher salt
1¼ pounds boneless, skinless
chicken breast, thinly sliced
12 cassava flour or corn tortillas

Combine onion, olive oil, bell pepper, salt, and chili powder
Per Serving: Calories: 367; Fat: 7g; Carbs: 38g; Sugar: 4g; Sodium: 187mg; Protein: 37g

Chicken Tikka Masala

Prep time: 10 minutes | Cook time: 20 minutes | Serves: 4

2 tablespoons butter
1 small onion, chopped
3 garlic cloves, minced
1 (1-inch) piece ginger, peeled and
grated
2 teaspoons ground cumin
2 teaspoons paprika
1 teaspoon ground turmeric
Big pinch cayenne
1 tablespoon sugar

1 (15-ounce) can diced or crushed
tomatoes with juice
4 medium boneless, skinless
chicken breasts
½ cup chicken broth
Kosher salt
Black pepper
¼ cup heavy cream
Juice of 1 lemon

1. Press the "Sauté" Button, two times to select "More" settings. Add the butter. 2. When the butter sizzles, add the onion, garlic, and ginger and stir. Cook for 3 to 4 minutes, stirring, until the onion is translucent. 3. Select Cancel and add the cumin, paprika, turmeric, and cayenne and stir, scraping the bottom. 4. Add the sugar and tomatoes with juice, stir, then add the chicken and broth. 5. Nestle the chicken in the mixture and season with salt and pepper. 6. Put on the pressure cooker's lid and turn the steam valve to "Sealing" position. 7. Select Pressure Cook mode, and then press the "Pressure Cook" button again to select "Less" time option. 8. Use the "+/-" keys on the control panel to set the cooking time to 7 minutes. 9. Press the Pressure Level button to adjust the pressure to "High Pressure." 10. Once the cooking cycle is completed, quickly and carefully turn the steam release handle from Sealing position to the Venting position. 11. When all the steam is released, remove the pressure lid from the top carefully. 12. Carefully remove the chicken and chop. 13. Press Cancel button. 14. Press the "Sauté" Button two times to select "normal" settings and simmer for 4 to 5 minutes until the liquid is reduced. 15. While simmering, add the cream and return the chicken to the pot. 16. Add the lemon juice and stir. Season as needed. 17. Serve and enjoy.
Per Serving: Calories 372; Fat 20g; Sodium 891mg; Carbs 29g; Fiber 3g; Sugar 8g; Protein 27g

Coconut Chicken and Vegetables Bowl

Prep Time: 15 minutes | Cook Time: 11 minutes | Serves: 4

1 tablespoon coconut oil	full-; Fat coconut milk
1 small yellow onion, peeled and diced	1 cup chicken broth
2 heaping cups large cauliflower florets	Juice from 1 medium lime
1½ pounds boneless, skinless chicken breasts, cut into 1½" chunks	1 teaspoon kosher salt
1 (13.66-ounce) can unsweetened	1 teaspoon ground cumin
	½ teaspoon ground ginger
	2 cups baby spinach leaves

1. Set your Instant Pot on Sauté and adjust the temperature to Normal. 2. Add the coconut oil in the inner pot, heat until the oil melts. 3. Then sauté the onion in the pot for 5 minutes, or until soften. 4. Stir in chicken, cauliflower, broth, coconut milk, lime juice, cumin, salt, and ginger until combined well. 5. Close the lid and turn the steam release handle to Sealing. 6. Set your Instant Pot on Pressure Cook at High and adjust the cooking time to 6 minutes. 7. When cooked, naturally release the pressure until the float valve drops. 8. Then remove the lid and add spinach in the inner pot. 9. Stir until wilted. 10. Serve and enjoy!
Per Serving: Calories: 457; Fat: 26g; Sodium: 931mg; Carbs: 9g; Sugar: 2g; Protein: 43g

Chicken and Fresh Green Beans

Prep Time: 5 minutes | Cook Time: 7 minutes | Serves: 1

1 slice uncooked thick-cut bacon, chopped	½ tablespoon dried onion flakes
⅓ cup diced mushrooms	½ teaspoon minced garlic
1 cup diced chicken breast	¼ cup chicken broth
¼ teaspoon seasoned salt	1 teaspoon soy sauce
½ teaspoon Italian seasoning	5 ounces fresh green beans, trimmed

1. Set your Instant Pot to Sauté and adjust the temperature level to More. 2. Sauté the bacon in the inner pot for about 5 minutes or until crispy. 3. Then place onion flakes, soy sauce, chicken, salt, broth, garlic, Italian seasoning, and mushrooms in the inner pot. Turn off the heat and deglaze the pot by scraping the bottom of the pot with a wooden spoon. 4. Then stir in green beans. 5. Close the lid and turn the steam release handle to Sealing position. 6. Set your Instant Pot on Pressure Cook at High and adjust the cooking time to 2 minutes. 7. When cooked, naturally release the pressure about 5 minutes. 8. Remove the lid and serve on a serving bowl. 9. Enjoy!
Per Serving: Calories: 442; Fat: 12g; Sodium: 1,019mg; Carbs: 14g; Sugar: 6g; Protein: 63g

Mushroom and Chicken Sausage Risotto

Prep time: 10 minutes | Cook time: 25 minutes | Serves: 4

2 tablespoons canola oil	Kosher salt
12-ounce fully cooked chicken sausage, cut into ¼-inch slices	Black pepper
3 tablespoons butter	1 tablespoon soy sauce
1 pound mushrooms (cremini, shiitake, oyster, or a mix), thinly sliced	½ cup dry white wine or red wine
1 medium yellow onion, chopped	4 cups good-quality chicken broth, preferably homemade (try the recipe here)
3 garlic cloves, minced	2 cups Arborio or Calrose rice
3 thyme sprigs, leaves only, plus more leaves for garnish	¼ cup finely grated Parmesan cheese

1. Press the "Sauté" Button, two times to select "More" settings. Add the oil. 2. Once hot, add the sausage and cook, stirring, for 5 minutes, until browned. Remove the sausage. 3. Reduce the heat to Normal. Melt the butter, then add the mushrooms and onion. 4. Cook, stirring, for 6 minutes until the onion is translucent and the mushrooms are cooked. 5. Add the garlic and cook for 1 minute more. Add the thyme and season with salt and pepper. 6. Add the soy sauce and wine. Cook, scraping up any brown bits off the bottom of the pot, for about 3 minutes, or until the alcohol smell has gone. 7. Add the broth and rice and stir. Press Cancel to stop this cooking program. 8. Put on the pressure cooker's lid and turn the steam valve to "Sealing" position. 9. Select Pressure Cook mode, and then press the "Pressure Cook" button again to select "Less" time option. 10. Use the "+/-" keys on the control panel to set the cooking time to 6 minutes. 11. Press the Pressure Level button to adjust the pressure to "High Pressure." 12. Once the cooking cycle is completed, quickly and carefully turn the steam release handle from Sealing position to the Venting position. 13. When all the steam is released, remove the pressure lid from the top carefully and stir. 14.

If the risotto is too soupy, press the "Sauté" button two times to select "Normal" mode and cook, uncovered, for a few minutes. 15. Add the sausage and Parmesan. 16. Serve topped with thyme leaves.
Per Serving: Calories 289; Fat 14g; Sodium 791mg; Carbs 18.9g; Fiber 4.6g; Sugar 8g; Protein 6g

Dijon Chicken Tenders

Prep Time: 5 minutes | Cook Time: 7 minutes | Serves: 4

1-pound chicken tenders	1 tablespoon avocado oil
1 tablespoon fresh thyme leaves	1 cup chicken stock
½ teaspoon salt	¼ cup Dijon mustard
¼ teaspoon black pepper	¼ cup raw honey

1. Using a towel, pat dry the chicken tender and rub with salt, pepper, and thyme to season. 2. Set your Instant Pot on Sauté and adjust the temperature to More. 3. Add the oil in the inner pot and heat for 2 minutes. 4. Add the chicken tenders and sear each side for 1 minute or until brown. Turn off the heat. 5. Carefully remove the chicken tenders and set aside. 6. Pour the stock in the inner pot and scrape up all the browned bits off the pot. 7. Place the steam rack with handles in the inner pot and arrange the chicken tender on top. 8. Close the lid and turn the steam release handle to Sealing. 9. Set your Instant Pot on Pressure Cook at High and adjust the cooking time to 3 minutes. 10. Combine the Dijon mustard and honey together in a small mixing bowl to make the honey mustard sauce. 11. When cooked, naturally release the pressure and carefully remove the lid. 12. Drizzle the honey mustard sauce over the chicken tenders. 13. Serve and enjoy!
Per Serving: Calories: 223; Fat: 5g; Sodium: 778mg; Carbs: 19g; Sugar: 18g; Protein: 22g

Savory Chicken Breasts with Veggies

Prep Time: 10 minutes | Cook Time: 18 minutes | Serves: 4

2 tablespoons avocado oil	1½ teaspoons dried thyme
1-pound sliced baby bella mushrooms	½ cup chicken stock
1½ teaspoons salt, divided	1½ pounds boneless, skinless chicken breasts
2 cloves garlic, minced	
8 cups chopped green cabbage	

1. Set your Instant Pot on Sauté and adjust the temperature to More. 2. Add oil in the inner pot and heat about 1 minute. 3. Add the ¼ teaspoon salt and mushrooms in the inner pot and cook about 10 minutes or until their liquid evaporated. 4. Then add garlic and cook for 10 seconds more. Turn off the heat and close the lid. 5. Stir ¼ teaspoon salt, stock, thyme, and cabbage in the inner pot until well combined. 6. Close the lid and turn the steam release handle to Sealing. 7. Set your Instant Pot on Pressure Cook at High and adjust the cooking time to 6 minutes. 8. When cooked, naturally release the pressure for 10 minutes and quick release the remaining pressure. 9. Carefully remove the lid. 10. Serve on serving plates and drizzle the soup over.
Per Serving: Calories: 337; Fat: 10g; Sodium: 1,023mg; Carbs: 14g; Sugar: 2g; Protein: 44g

Chicken Wings

Prep time: 10 minutes | Cook time: 20 minutes | Serves: 4-5

3-pound chicken wings	Kosher salt
1 cup water	2 cups wing sauce

1. Add the chicken wings and water to the Inner Pot and season with salt. 2. Put on the pressure cooker's lid and turn the steam valve to "Sealing" position. 3. Select Pressure Cook mode, and then press the "Pressure Cook" button again to select "Less" time option. 4. Use the "+/-" keys on the control panel to set the cooking time to 10 minutes. 5. Press the Pressure Level button to adjust the pressure to "High Pressure." 6. Once the cooking cycle is completed, allow the steam to release naturally for 10 minutes, then turn the steam release handle to the Venting position. 7. When all the steam is released, remove the pressure lid from the top carefully. 8. Remove the wings to a cooling rack to drain. 9. In a large bowl, toss the wings in the sauce. 10. Place on a baking sheet and broil for about 5 minutes in your preheated oven, until crispy. Flip the wings and repeat. 11. Place the cooling rack with the wings on a baking sheet and refrigerate for 1 hour. 12. Heat the oil to 385°F/195°C in your oven. Once hot, carefully lower 7 or 8 wings into the oil and fry for 3 minutes until crispy. Remove and place back on the rack. Repeat with the remaining wings. 13. Toss the wings in the sauce and serve immediately.
Per Serving: Calories 372; Fat 20g; Sodium 891mg; Carbs 29g; Fiber 3g; Sugar 8g; Protein 7g

Chicken and Green Beans with Basil

Prep Time: 15 minutes | Cook Time: 10 minutes | Serves: 4

2 teaspoons olive oil	½ cup water
1½ pounds ground chicken	1 tablespoon coconut aminos or
1 red bell pepper, seeded and	tamari
sliced	1 tablespoon gluten-free fish sauce
1 shallot, finely chopped	½ pound fresh green beans
1 tablespoon all-natural Chile	1 cup whole fresh basil leaves
pepper paste	

1. Set your Instant Pot on Sauté and adjust the temperature to More. 2. Add olive oil in the inner pot. When the oil is heated, add the chicken and cook for 2 to 3 minutes or until brown. Stir from time to time to break up the chicken. Turn off the heat. 3. Sit in shallot, chile pepper paste, coconut aminos, fish sauce, water, and bell pepper to combine. 4. Close the lid and turn the steam release handle to Sealing position. 5. Set your Instant Pot on Pressure Cook at High and adjust the temperature to 2 minutes. Press Keep Warm. 6. When cooked, quick release the pressure. 7. Remove the lid carefully and add the green beans. 8. Let it sit in the pot for 5 minutes or until the green beans are steamed. 9. Remove the lid. Add basil in the pot and stir well. 10. Serve and enjoy!
Per Serving: Calories: 298; Fat: 16g; Carbs: 7g; Sugar: 4g; Sodium: 513mg; Protein: 32g

Thyme Turkey Breast

Prep Time: 10 minutes | Cook Time: 18 minutes | Serves: 4

1½ pounds boneless, skinless	½ teaspoon kosher salt
turkey breast	½ teaspoon thyme
2 tablespoons avocado oil, divided	¼ teaspoon garlic salt
1 teaspoon sweet paprika	¼ teaspoon black pepper
1 teaspoon Italian seasoning blend	

1. Using a towel, pat dry the turkey breast. Then cut the turkey breast into two. 2. Rub 1 tablespoon of oil over the turkey breast. 3. Mix together Italian seasoning, thyme, kosher salt, garlic salt, pepper, and paprika in a small bowl. 4. Toss the chicken well with the mixture to season. 5. Set your Instant Pot on Sauté and adjust the temperature to More. Add the remaining oil and heat about 2 minutes. 6. Add the seasoned turkey breast and sear each side about 3 minutes. 7. Turn off the heat and transfer the turkey onto a serving plate. 8. Then pour 1 cup of water in the inner pot and scrape up all the brown bits off the pot with a spatula. 9. Place the steam rack with handles in the inner pot and top the turkey breast on the rack. 10. Close the lid and turn the steam release handle to Sealing. 11. When cooked, naturally release the pressure until the float valve drops. 12. Carefully remove onto a cutting board. When the meat is cool, cut into your desired slices. 13. Serve and enjoy!
Per Serving: Calories: 248; Fat: 9g; Sodium: 568mg; Carbs: 0g; Sugar: 0g; Protein: 40g

Tasty Turkey and Greens Meatloaf

Prep Time: 15 minutes | Cook Time: 25 minutes | Serves: 4

1 tablespoon avocado oil	1-pound lean ground turkey
1 small onion, peeled and diced	¼ cup almond flour
2 cloves garlic, minced	1 large egg
3 cups mixed baby greens, finely	¾ teaspoon salt
chopped	½ teaspoon black pepper

1. Set your Instant Pot on Sauté and adjust the temperature to More. 2. Add oil in the inner pot and heat 1 minute. 3. Add the onion and sauté about 3 minutes or until soften. Add the garlic and greens and cook for 1 more minute. Turn off the heat. 4. Combine the flour, salt, egg, pepper, and turkey in a medium bowl. 5. Then stir the onion and greens mixture in the turkey mixture until well combined. 6. Rinse out the pot and pour in 2 cups of water. 7. Fold a large piece of foil in half and bend the edge upward to make an aluminum foil sling. 8. Make a rectangular loaf from the turkey mixture and place onto the aluminum sling. 9. Transfer the sling onto the steam rack with handles and lower into the pot. Close the lid. 10. Set the Instant Pot on Pressure Cook at High and adjust the cooking time to 20 minutes. 11. When cooked, quick release the pressure until the float valve drops. 12. Carefully remove the lid and transfer the meatloaf onto a cutting board. 13. When the meatloaf is completely cool, cut into your desired slices. 14. Serve and enjoy!
Per Serving: Calories: 271; Fat: 17g; Sodium: 406mg; Carbs: 5g; Sugar: 1g; Protein: 25g

Jerk Chicken with Mustard

Prep Time: 15 minutes | Cook Time: 22 minutes | Serves: 8

1 large onion, peeled and cut into	1 teaspoon black pepper
8 pieces	2 tablespoons red wine vinegar
1 tablespoon peeled and chopped	2 tablespoons coconut aminos
fresh ginger	2 cloves garlic, minced
3 small hot chili peppers, deveined	½ cup chicken stock
and deseeded	4 pounds boneless, skinless
½ teaspoon ground allspice	chicken breasts cut in 1" pieces
2 tablespoons dry mustard	

1. In a food processor, combine the onion, ginger, chili peppers, allspice, black pepper, red wine vinegar, coconut aminos, minced garlic, and chicken stock together. 2. Place the chicken in the inner pot and drizzle over with the sauce. Stir well. 3. Close the lid and turn the steam release handle to Sealing. 4. Set your Instant Pot on Pressure Cook at High and adjust the cooking time to 12 minutes. 5. When cooked, quick release the pressure. 6. Transfer the chicken onto a baking sheet lined with parchment paper or a silicone baking mat. 7. If you want it golden-browned, set your broiler to high and broil for 6 to 10 minutes or until the chicken is nicely browned, flipping once. 8. Pour the sauce over the chicken. 9. Serve and enjoy!
Per Serving: Calories: 306; Fat: 5g; Sodium: 210mg; Carbs: 6g; Sugar: 2g; Protein: 52g

Chicken Dumplings

Prep time: 10 minutes | Cook time: 30 minutes | Serves: 8

For the chicken and broth

4 tablespoons butter	3 carrots, peeled and chopped
8 medium bone-in, skin-on	2 onions, chopped
chicken thighs	3½ cups chicken broth, preferably
Kosher salt	homemade (try the recipe here)
Black pepper	½ cup whole milk or half-and-half
½ cup all-purpose flour	2 tablespoons cornstarch
4 celery stalks, chopped	

For the dumplings

1¾ cups all-purpose flour	¼ teaspoon black pepper
¼ cup cornmeal	1 cup whole milk or half-and-half
1 tablespoon baking powder	3 tablespoons melted butter
½ teaspoon kosher salt	

1. Press the "Sauté" Button, two times to select "More" settings. 2. Add the butter. Season the chicken with salt and pepper and dredge in the flour, shaking off the excess. 3. Once the butter is sizzling and the pot is hot, add half of the chicken in one layer. 4. Brown on one side for 3 or 4 minutes, without moving, and flip and brown on the other side. 5. Remove and repeat with the remaining chicken. Set aside. 6. Add the celery, carrots, and onions to the pot. Sauté for 3 minutes, scraping the bottom of the pot. 7. Press Cancel button to stop this cooking program. 8. Add the chicken and broth. Season with salt and pepper. 9. Put on the pressure cooker's lid and turn the steam valve to "Sealing" position. 10. Select Pressure Cook mode, and then press the "Pressure Cook" button again to select "Less" time option. 11. Use the "+/-" keys on the control panel to set the cooking time to 11 minutes. 12. Press the Pressure Level button to adjust the pressure to "High Pressure." 13. Once the cooking cycle is completed, allow the steam to release naturally. 14. When all the steam is released, remove the pressure lid from the top carefully. 15. While the chicken is cooking, make the dumplings. 16. Mix together the flour, cornmeal, baking powder, salt, and pepper in a medium bowl. 17. Add the milk or half-and-half and melted butter, and stir just until incorporated (don't over-mix). Set aside. 18. Once cooking is complete, use a quick release. Remove the chicken and set aside. 19. Add the milk to the broth in the pot, mix, and season with salt and pepper. 20. In a small bowl, combine ½ cup of hot broth with the cornstarch and whisk well to combine. 21. Add back to the pot and stir. 22. Press the "Sauté" Button, two times to select "Normal" settings. 23. Once simmering, scoop heaping tablespoons of the dumpling mixture and drop them into the pot. 24. Reduce Sauté heat to low and cook for 12 to 15 minutes, loosely covered with the top without locking it, until the dumplings have doubled in size. 25. Meanwhile, bone the chicken, remove and discard the skin, and shred the meat. 26. Add back to the pot and serve in bowls.
Per Serving: Calories 334; Fat 7.9g; Sodium 704mg; Carbs 6g; Fiber 3.6g; Sugar 6g; Protein 18g

Chicken Enchiladas

Prep time: 10 minutes | Cook time: 35 minutes | Serves: 4

3 medium boneless, skinless chicken breasts	2 (10-ounce) cans green enchilada sauce
Kosher salt	½ cup sour cream, plus more for serving
Black pepper	
1 cup chicken broth or water	10 to 12 corn tortillas
2 garlic cloves, minced	2 cups Monterey Jack cheese
½ onion, sliced	

1. Season the chicken with salt and pepper and place it in the Inner Pot, along with the broth, garlic, and onion. 2. Put on the pressure cooker's lid and turn the steam valve to "Sealing" position. 3. Select Pressure Cook mode, and then press the "Pressure Cook" button again to select "Less" time option. 4. Use the "+/-" keys on the control panel to set the cooking time to 7 minutes. 5. Press the Pressure Level button to adjust the pressure to "High Pressure." 6. Once the cooking cycle is completed, allow the steam to release naturally. 7. When all the steam is released, remove the pressure lid from the top carefully. 8. Heat your oven to 375°F/190°C in advance. 9. Remove the chicken, shred it, and combine in a large bowl with ½ cup of enchilada sauce and the sour cream. Season with salt and pepper. 10. Spread another ½ cup of enchilada sauce into a 9-by-13-inch baking dish. 11. Warm the tortillas slightly in the oven, on the stove, or in the microwave to make them pliable. 12. Fill each with 2 to 3 tablespoons of the chicken mixture and a sprinkle of cheese. 13. Roll into cigar shapes and place, side-by-side and seam-side down, into the baking dish. 14. Top with the remaining sauce and cheese. Cover with foil. 15. Bake for 15 minutes. Remove the foil and bake for 5 to 10 minutes more, until the cheese is melted. 16. Serve hot.
Per Serving: Calories 382; Fat 7.9g; Sodium 704mg; Carbs 6g; Fiber 3.6g; Sugar 6g; Protein 18g

Chicken Pot Pie

Prep time: 10 minutes | Cook time: 25 minutes | Serves: 4-5

1 frozen puff pastry sheet	chicken breasts
1 tablespoon olive oil	1½ cups chicken broth
1 small onion, chopped	1 teaspoon kosher salt
2 medium carrots, peeled and chopped	2 tablespoons all-purpose flour
2 celery stalks, chopped	2 tablespoons cold butter
2 medium potatoes, cut into ¾-inch cubes	½ cup heavy cream or whole milk
3 medium bone-in, skin-on	1 cup frozen peas
	Black pepper

1. Thaw the puff pastry sheet on the counter for 30 minutes. 2. Press the "Sauté" Button, two times to select "Normal" settings and add the oil. 3. Add the onion, carrots, and celery. Stir and cook for 3 minutes. 4. Add the potatoes, chicken, broth, and salt. 5. Put on the pressure cooker's lid and turn the steam valve to "Sealing" position. 6. Select Pressure Cook mode, and then press the "Pressure Cook" button again to select "Less" time option. 7. Use the "+/-" keys on the control panel to set the cooking time to 7 minutes. 8. Press the Pressure Level button to adjust the pressure to "High Pressure." 9. Meanwhile, once the pastry sheet is pliable but still cold, lay it out on a baking sheet and cut into 4 even squares or rectangles. Bake for 15 minutes. 10. Remove the chicken and, once cool enough to handle, pull off the meat and discard the skin and bones. 11. Cut the meat into cubes. 12. Once the cooking cycle of Instant Pot is completed, allow the steam to release naturally. 13. When all the steam is released, press Cancel button and remove the pressure lid from the top carefully. 14. Press the "Sauté" Button, two times to select "Normal" settings 15. In a small bowl, combine the flour and butter into a smooth paste. 16. Add the paste to the simmering broth along with the cream or milk and peas. 17. Cook, stirring, until the paste has dissolved, 3 to 5 minutes. Add the chicken and season with salt and pepper. 18. To serve, spoon the stew into bowls and top with the puff pastry.
Per Serving: Calories 489; Fat 11g; Sodium 501mg; Carbs 8.9g; Fiber 4.6g; Sugar 8g; Protein 26g

Chicken with Potatoes and Peas

Prep time: 10 minutes | Cook time: 15 minutes | Serves: 4

4 small or 3 large bone-in, skin-on chicken breasts	1 teaspoon dried oregano
Kosher salt	Pinch red pepper flakes
Black pepper	1-pound large fingerling potatoes, washed and pricked with a knife
4 tablespoons olive oil, plus extra for garnish	2 cups chicken broth
3 garlic cloves, minced	1 cup frozen peas
1 fresh rosemary sprig, chopped (leaves only)	1 lemon
	½ cup olives

1. Season the chicken with salt and pepper. 2. In a large bowl, coat the chicken with 2 tablespoons of olive oil, the garlic, rosemary, oregano, and red pepper flakes. 3. Marinate for at least 30 minutes in the refrigerator. 4. Press the "Sauté" Button, two times to select "More" settings. 5. Add the remaining 2 tablespoons of olive oil and coat the bottom of the pot. 6. Add the chicken, skin-side down (reserving any marinade), and cook without moving for about 5 minutes, until the skin is crispy. 7. Remove the chicken and select Cancel. Add the potatoes and broth. 8. Place the chicken on top, skin-side up, and pour the reserved marinade on top. Season with salt and pepper. 9. Put on the pressure cooker's lid and turn the steam valve to "Sealing" position. 10. Select Pressure Cook mode, and then press the "Pressure Cook" button again to select "Less" time option. 11. Use the "+/-" keys on the control panel to set the cooking time to 7 minutes. 12. Press the Pressure Level button to adjust the pressure to "High Pressure." 13. Once the cooking cycle is completed, allow the steam to release naturally for 10 minutes, then turn the steam release handle to the Venting position. 14. When all the steam is released, remove the pressure lid from the top carefully. 15. Remove the chicken. Stir in the peas and cook until warmed. 16. Serve the potatoes and peas topped with the chicken. 17. Just before serving, add a squeeze of lemon, a drizzle of olive oil, and the olives.
Per Serving: Calories 221; Fat 7.9g; Sodium 704mg; Carbs 6g; Fiber 3.6g; Sugar 6g; Protein 18g

Chapter 9 Stock and Sauce Recipes

Homemade Marinara Sauce

Prep Time: 5 minutes | Cook Time: 24 minutes | Serves: 4 cups

1 tablespoon olive oil
1 yellow onion, finely chopped
5 garlic cloves, minced
3 pounds plum tomatoes, quartered
½ cup Vegetable Broth or store-
bought low-sodium vegetable broth
2 tablespoons double concentrated tomato paste

1. Insert the inner pot into the cooker base. Connect the power cord to a 120 V power source. The cooker goes to Standby mode and the display indicates OFF. Press Sauté to select the program and then press it again to choose the Normal temperature option 2. Pour the olive oil into the Inner Pot and heat it. When the oil is hot, add the onion and garlic. Cook for 3 to 4 minutes, stirring now and then, until softened. Press Cancel. 3. Add the tomatoes, broth, and tomato paste. Cover the lid and lock it 4. Select the Pressure Cook on the panel. Press the button again to choose Less option. Press Pressure Level to choose High pressure. 5. When the cook time is complete, quickly and carefully turn the steam release handle from Sealing position to the Venting position. 6. Open the lid carefully and stir, pressing down on any large pieces of tomato to break them down. For a smoother sauce, use an immersion blender to blend to your desired consistency. Refrigerate the marinara sauce for up to 1 week or freeze it for up to 3 months.
Per Serving: Calories: 29; Fat: 1g; Carbs: 5g; Fiber: 1g; Sugar: 3g; Sodium: 6mg; Protein: 1g

Perfect Vegan Tikka Masala Sauce

Prep Time: 15 minutes | Cook Time: 15 minutes | Serves: 4

2 teaspoons olive oil
1 onion, chopped
4 cloves garlic, chopped
1 (1-inch) piece fresh ginger, peeled and grated
1 bird's eye chili, minced
1 bell pepper, seeded and chopped
Sea salt and ground black pepper,
to taste
1 teaspoon cayenne pepper
1 teaspoon coriander powder
½ teaspoon turmeric powder
1 teaspoon Garam Masala
2 ripe tomatoes, pureed
1 cup vegetable broth
1 cup plain coconut yogurt

1. Insert the inner pot into the cooker base. 2. Press Sauté to select the program and press it again to choose Normal option. Add the oil and sauté the onion for about 3 minutes or until tender and fragrant. 3. Now, add the garlic, ginger and peppers; continue to sauté an additional minute or until they are aromatic. 4. Add the spices, tomatoes, and broth. 5. Put the lid in place and lock it. Select the Pressure Cook on the panel. Press the button again to choose Less option; use the "+/-" button to adjust the cooking time to 11 minutes. Press Pressure Level to choose High pressure. 6. Once cooking is complete, leave the steam release handle in the Sealing position for 10 minutes. Open the lid carefully. 7. Afterwards, add the coconut yogurt to the inner pot and stir to combine. 8. Serve with chickpeas or roasted vegetables.
Per Serving: Calories 206; Fat 17.3g; Sodium 195mg; Carbs 12.4g; Fiber 1g; Sugars 6.5g; Protein 4g

Delicious Chicken Broth

Prep Time: 15 minutes | Cook Time: 40 minutes | Serves: 10 cups

2½ pounds bone-in, skin-on chicken parts
1 onion, peeled and quartered
1 celery stalk, cut into 2-inch pieces
1 carrot, peeled and cut into 2-inch pieces
½ teaspoon whole black peppercorns
1 bay leaf
10 cups water

1. Put the chicken, onion, celery, carrots, peppercorns, and bay leaf in the pressure cooker pot, then add some water to make sure the water does not exceed your pot's maximum fill line. 2. Put the lid in place and lock it. Press the button again to choose Normal option; use the "+" button to adjust the cooking time to 40 minutes. Press Pressure Level to choose High pressure. 3. Leave the steam release handle in the Sealing position for about 30 minutes and then tap or lightly shake the pot before removing the lid. 4. Put a colander over a bowl and dump in the food pot. Remove the solids. 5. Let the Broth sit for about 30 minutes, then skim and remove the layer of; Fat on the surface. Put into the refrigerator to cool. Portion into glass jars or plastic freezer bags to refrigerate or freeze.
Per Serving: Calories: 35; Fat: 1g; Sodium: 54mg; Carbs: 1g; Sugar: 5g; Fiber: 0g; Protein: 5g

Perfect French Brown Stock

Prep Time: 15 minutes | Cook Time: 2 hours | Serves: 10

3 pounds meaty pork bones
2 carrots, chopped
1 celery stalk, chopped
2 brown onions, quartered
1 tablespoon olive oil

1. Add all ingredients to the inner pot of your Inner Pot. 2. Put the lid in place and lock it. Select the Soup/Broth on the panel. Press the button again to adjust the cooking time to 120 minutes. Press Pressure Level to choose Low pressure. 3. Once cooking is complete, leave the steam release handle in the Sealing position for 10 minutes. Open the lid carefully. 4. Remove the bones and vegetables using a metal spoon with holes and discard. Pour the liquid through the sieve into the bowl. 5. Use immediately or store in your refrigerator.
Per Serving: Calories 13; Fat 2.3g; Sodium 95mg; Carbs 2.4g; Fiber 1g; Sugars 1.5g; Protein 1.4g

Fresh and Delicious Berry Compote

Prep Time: 5 minutes | Cook Time: 1 minutes | Serves: 2 cups

1-pound fresh blueberries, raspberries, blackberries, and/or sliced strawberries
¼ cup sugar
1 teaspoon grated lemon zest
2 tablespoons fresh lemon juice

1. Put the berries in the pressure cooker pot and sprinkle the sugar evenly over them. Let the food sit for 10 minutes. 2. Stir in the lemon zest and juice. 3. Put the lid in place and lock it, Select the Pressure Cook on the panel. Press the button Again to choose Less option; use the "-" button to adjust the cooking time to 1 minutes. Press Pressure Level to choose High pressure. 4. When the cooking time ends, leave the steam release handle in the Sealing position for 10 minutes and then quickly and carefully turn the steam release handle from Sealing position to the Venting position. 5. Remove the lid and stir the compote. Once cooled, it can be used immediately as a breakfast or dessert topping, or in a jar in the refrigerator if you plan to serve it later.
Per Serving: Calories: 57; Fat: 0g; Sodium: 1mg; Carbs: 15g; Sugar: 1g; Fiber: 1g; Protein: 1g

Basic and Delicious Beans

Prep Time: 5 minutes | Cook Time: 35 minutes | Serves: 6 cups

1-pound dried beans
4 cups vegetable broth or store-bought low-sodium vegetable broth, or water
2 bay leaves
2 teaspoons olive oil
½ teaspoon kosher salt

1. Combine the dried beans, broth, bay leaves, olive oil, and salt in the Inner Pot. Cover the lid and lock it 2. Select the Pressure Cook on the panel. Press the button again to choose Normal option. Press Pressure Level to choose High pressure. 3. Leave the steam release handle in the Sealing position for 15 minutes after cooking has completed, then turn the steam release handle to the Venting position. 4. Open the lid carefully and remove the bay leaves.
Per Serving: Calories: 133; Fat: 1g; Carbs: 23g; Fiber: 6g; Sugar: 1g; Sodium: 55mg; Protein: 9g

Turkey Stock

Prep time: 20 minutes | Cook time: 45 minutes | Serves: 6

1 bag turkey giblet
6 cups water
1 stalk celery, cut in half
1 carrot, cut into chunks
1 onion, quartered
1 bay leaf
1 teaspoon whole black peppercorns

1. Put all of the ingredients into the Instant Pot. 2. Put on the pressure cooker's lid and turn the steam valve to "Sealing" position. 3. Set the Instant Pot to Pressure Cook. 4. Use the "+/-" keys on the control panel to set the cooking time to 45 minutes. 5. Press the Pressure Level button to adjust the pressure to "High". 6. Once the cooking cycle is completed, allow the steam to release naturally for 10 minutes and then release the remaining pressure manually. 7. When all the steam is released, remove the pressure lid from the top carefully. 8. Strain the stock and pour into jars. Store in the refrigerator or freeze.
Per Serving: Calories 42; Fat 11g; Sodium 91mg; Carbs 4g; Fiber 3g; Sugar 8g; Protein 3g

Homemade Beef Bone Broth

Prep Time: 15 minutes | Cook Time: 2 hours 50 minutes | Serves: 8

3 pounds frozen beef bones
2 onions, halved
2 stalks celery, chopped
2 carrots, chopped
4 cloves garlic, whole

2 bay leaves
2 tablespoons apple cider vinegar
1 teaspoon sea salt
1 teaspoon black pepper
8 cups water

1. Preheat your oven to 390°F/200°C. Line a baking sheet with aluminum foil. 2. Place the beef bones, onions, celery, carrots, and garlic on the baking pan. Roast for 40 to 45 minutes. 3. Transfer the roasted beef bones and vegetables to the inner pot of your Inner Pot. Add the bay leaves, apple cider vinegar, sea salt, pepper, and boiling water to the inner pot. 4. Put the lid in place and lock it. Select the Pressure Cook on the panel. Press the button again to choose More option; use the "+/-" button to adjust the cooking time to 120 minutes. Press Pressure Level to choose High pressure. 5. Once cooking is complete, leave the steam release handle in the Sealing position for 20 minutes. Open the lid carefully. 6. Remove the beef bones and vegetables and discard. Pour the broth through a strainer. 7. Enjoy,
Per Serving: Calories 65; Fat 2.4g; Sodium 200mg; Carbs 6.7g; Fiber 1g; Sugars 1.5g; Protein 6.4g

Homemade Shrimp Stock

Prep Time: 15 minutes | Cook Time: 30 minutes | Serves: 8

Shrimp shells from 3 pounds shrimp
8 cups water
½ cup cilantro, chopped
2 celery stalks, diced
4 cloves garlic

1 onion, quartered
1 teaspoon mixed peppercorns
1 tablespoon sea salt
2 bay leaves
4 tablespoons olive oil

1. Add all ingredients to the inner pot. 2. Put the lid in place and lock it. Select the Soup/Broth on the panel. Press the button again to choose Less option and use the "+/-" buttons to adjust the cooking time to 30 minutes. Press Pressure Level to choose High pressure. 3. Once cooking is complete, leave the steam release handle in the Sealing position. Open the lid carefully. 4. Strain the shrimp shells and vegetables using a colander.
Per Serving: Calories 69; Fat 6.3g; Sodium 255mg; Carbs 1.4g; Fiber 1g; Sugars 0.5g; Protein 0.4g

Seafood Soup Stock

Prep time: 20 minutes | Cook time: 30 minutes | Serves: 8

Shells and heads from ½ lb. prawns
8 cups water
4 onions, quartered

4 carrots, cut into chunks
3 cloves garlic, sliced
2 bay leaves
1 teaspoon whole black peppercorns

1. Put all of the ingredients into the Instant Pot. 2. Put on the pressure cooker's lid and turn the steam valve to "Sealing" position. 3. Set the Instant Pot to Pressure Cook. 4. Press the Pressure Level button to adjust the pressure to "High". 5. Use the "+/-" keys on the control panel to set the cooking time to 30 minutes. 6. Once the cooking cycle is completed, allow the steam to release naturally for 15 minutes and then release the remaining pressure manually. 7. When all the steam is released, remove the pressure lid from the top carefully. 8. Strain the stock and pour into jars. Store in the refrigerator or freeze.
Per Serving: Calories 89; Fat 11g; Sodium 51mg; Carbs 8.9g; Fiber 4.6g; Sugar 8g; Protein 26g

Perfect Sicilian-Style Meat Sauce

Prep Time: 15 minutes | Cook Time: 40 minutes | Serves: 10

2 tablespoons olive oil
2 ½ pounds pork butt
1 onion, chopped
4 garlic cloves, pressed
¼ cup Malvasia wine, or other Sicilian wine
2 fresh tomatoes, pureed
5 ounces tomato paste
2 bay leaves

2 tablespoons fresh cilantro, chopped
1 teaspoon dried basil
1 teaspoon dried rosemary
½ teaspoon cayenne pepper
½ teaspoon black pepper, freshly cracked
½ teaspoon salt
1 cup chicken broth

1. Insert the inner pot into the cooker base. 2. Press Sauté to select the program and press it again to choose Normal option, then add and heat the oil. When the oil starts to sizzle, cook the pork until no longer pink. 3. Add the onion and garlic and continue to cook for a few minutes more or until they are tender. Add a splash of wine to deglaze the pot. 4. Stir in the other ingredients. 5. Put the lid in place and lock it. Select the Meat/Stew on the panel. Press the button again to choose Normal option. Press Pressure Level to choose High pressure. 6. Once cooking is complete, leave the steam release handle in the Sealing position for 15 minutes. Open the lid carefully. 7. Next, remove the meat from the inner pot; shred the meat, removing the bones. Return the meat to your sauce.
Per Serving: Calories 378; Fat 24.3g; Sodium 127mg; Carbs 4.4g; Fiber 1g; Sugars 1.1g; Protein 34g

Homemade Spanish Chorizo Sauce

Prep Time: 10 minutes | Cook Time: 10 minutes | Serves: 4

1 tablespoon olive oil
1-pound Chorizo sausage, sliced
1 onion, chopped
1 teaspoon garlic, minced
1 sweet pepper, seeded and finely chopped
1 habanero pepper, seeded and minced
2 tablespoons sugar

1 teaspoon dried basil
1 teaspoon dried rosemary
1 teaspoon red pepper flakes
Sea salt and freshly ground black pepper, to taste
1 (28-ounce) can diced tomatoes, with juice
1 cup chicken broth

1. Insert the inner pot into the cooker base. Connect the power cord to a 120 V power source. The cooker goes to Standby mode and the display indicates OFF. 2. Press Sauté to select the program and press it again to choose Normal option, then add and heat the oil. When the oil starts to sizzle, cook the Chorizo until no longer pink; crumble it with a wooden spatula. 3. Add the onion, garlic, and peppers and cook for a minute or so. Add a splash of chicken broth to deglaze the pan. 4. Stir in the remaining ingredients. 5. Put the lid in place and lock it. Select the Pressure Cook on the panel. Press the button again to choose Less option; use the "-" button to adjust the cooking time to 6 minutes. 6. Press Pressure Level to choose High pressure. Once cooking is complete, leave the steam release handle in the Sealing position for 10 minutes; Open the lid carefully. 7. Serve and enjoy.
Per Serving: Calories 385; Fat 24.3g; Sodium 124mg; Carbs 20.4g; Fiber 1g; Sugars 11.5g; Protein 21.4g

Simple Vegetable Broth

Prep Time: 5 minutes | Cook Time: 40 minutes | Serves: 10 cups

About 8 cups mixed vegetable scraps

10 cups water

1. Put the vegetable scraps into the pressure cooker pot, then add some water to make sure the water does not exceed your pot's maximum fill line. 2. Put the lid in place and lock it. Select the Pressure Cook on the panel. Press the button again to choose Less option; use the "-" button to adjust the cooking time to 40 minutes. Press Pressure Level to choose High pressure. It will take 23 to 28 minutes for the pot to come to pressure before the cooking time begins. 3. Leave the steam release handle in the Sealing position for 5 minutes and then quickly and carefully turn the steam release handle from Sealing position to the Venting position. (which will take an additional 3 to 4 minutes). 4. Set a colander over a large bowl and pour in the contents of the pot. Remove the solids. 5. Let the Broth sit for about 20 minutes before putting it to the fridge to cool. Portion into glass jars or plastic freezer bags to refrigerate or freeze.
Per Serving: Calories: 20; Fat: 0g; Sodium: 42mg; Carbs: 2g; Sugar: 5g; Fiber: 0g; Protein: 2g

Delicious Court Bouillon

Prep Time: 15 minutes | Cook Time: 30 minutes | Serves: 8

1 tablespoon salt
1 teaspoon mixed peppercorns
1 cup white wine
2 onions, sliced
2 celery ribs, sliced
2 carrots, sliced

2 bay leaves
2 sprig fresh rosemary
A bunch of fresh parsley
1 lemon, sliced
2 tablespoons olive oil

1. Add all ingredients to the inner pot of your Inner Pot. Add cold water until the inner pot is ⅔ full. 2. Put the lid in place and lock it. Select the Soup/Broth on the panel. Press the button again to choose Normal option. Press Pressure Level to choose High pressure. 3. Once cooking is complete, leave the steam release handle in the Sealing position. 10 minutes. Open the lid carefully. 4. Remove the vegetables.
Per Serving: Calories 55; Fat 3.3g; Sodium 205mg; Carbs 0.4g; Fiber 1g; Sugars 1.5g; Protein 0.6g

Homemade Sugar-Free Ketchup

Prep Time: 5 minutes | Cook Time: 20 minutes | Serves: 12

1 (28-ounce) can crushed tomatoes
1 yellow onion, quartered
4 pitted dates
¼ cup apple cider vinegar
¼ teaspoon paprika
¼ teaspoon garlic powder
¼ teaspoon kosher salt

1. In the Inner Pot, combine the tomatoes, onion, dates, vinegar, paprika, garlic powder, and salt. Cover the lid and lock it 2. Select the Pressure Cook on the panel. Press the button again to choose Less option; use the "+/-" button to adjust the cooking time to 5 minutes. Press Pressure Level to choose High pressure. 3. When the cook time is complete, quickly and carefully turn the steam release handle from the Sealing position to the Venting position. Press Cancel. 4. Open the lid carefully and remove the onion. Insert the inner pot into the cooker base. 5. Press Sauté to select the program and press again to choose Less option. Simmer for 15 minutes, stirring now and then, until thickened. 6. Transfer the ketchup to an airtight container and refrigerate it for up to 2 weeks.
Per Serving: Calories: 33; Fat: 0g; Carbs: 8g; Fiber: 2g; Sugar: 5g; Sodium: 150mg; Protein: 1g

Herb Stock

Prep time: 20 minutes | Cook time: 15 minutes | Serves: 8

4 cups water
3 bay leaves
2 cloves garlic, crushed
1 teaspoon whole black peppercorns
A handful of rosemary
2 sprigs parsley
½ teaspoon salt

1. Put all of the ingredients, except salt, into the Instant Pot. 2. Put on the pressure cooker's lid and turn the steam valve to "Sealing" position. 3. Set the Instant Pot to Pressure Cook. 4. Press the Pressure Level button to adjust the pressure to "High". 5. Use the "+/-" keys on the control panel to set the cooking time to 15 minutes. 6. Once the cooking cycle is completed, allow the steam to release naturally for 10 minutes and then release the remaining steam manually. 7. When all the steam is released, remove the pressure lid from the top carefully. 8. Season with salt to taste. 9. Strain the stock and pour into jars. Store in the refrigerator or freeze.
Per Serving: Calories 84; Fat 5g; Sodium 41mg; Carbs 7g; Fiber 7.6g; Sugar 5g; Protein 2g

White Chicken Stock

Prep Time: 20 minutes | Cook Time: 40 minutes | Serves: 10

2 pounds chicken white meat
1 white onion, quartered
1 leek, white parts
2 parsnips, sliced thickly
1 celery rib, sliced thickly
2 bay leaves
2 stalks flat-leaf parsley
½ teaspoon dried dill weed
1 teaspoon mixed peppercorns

1. Add all ingredients to the inner pot. 2. Put the lid in place and lock it. Select the Soup/Broth on the panel. Press the button again to choose Normal option and use the "+/-" buttons to adjust the cooking time to 40 minutes. Press Pressure Level to choose High pressure. 3. Once cooking is complete, leave the steam release handle in the Sealing position for 20 minutes; open the lid carefully. 4. Remove the vegetables and bones; save the chicken meat for later use.
Per Serving: Calories 53; Fat 1g; Sodium 95mg; Carbs 1.4g; Fiber 1g; Sugars 1.5g; Protein 1.4g

Simple Chicken Ragù

Prep Time: 10 minutes | Cook Time: 10 minutes | Serves: 4

2 tablespoons olive oil
1-pound ground chicken
1 onion, chopped
2 cloves garlic, minced
¼ cup dry red wine
1 stalk celery, chopped
1 bell pepper, chopped
1 teaspoon fresh basil, chopped
1 teaspoon fresh rosemary, chopped
1 teaspoon cayenne pepper
Salt and fresh ground pepper to taste
2 cups tomato sauce
1 cup chicken bone broth

1. Insert the inner pot into the cooker base. 2. Press Sauté to select the program and press it again to choose Normal option, then add and heat the oil. When the oil starts to sizzle, cook the ground chicken until no longer pink; crumble it with a wooden spatula. 3. Add the onion and garlic to the browned chicken; let it cook for a minute or so. Add a splash of wine to deglaze the pan. 4. Stir in the remaining ingredients. 5. Put the lid in place and lock it. Select the Pressure Cook on the panel. Press the button again to choose Less option; use the "-" button to adjust the cooking time to 6 minutes. Press Pressure Level to choose High pressure. 6. Once cooking is complete, leave the steam release handle in the Sealing position for 10 minutes; Open the lid carefully. 7. Serve and enjoy.
Per Serving: Calories 431; Fat 18g; Sodium 152mg; Carbs 33.4g; Fiber 1g; Sugars 17.5g; Protein 27g

Perfect Chicken and Herb Broth

Prep Time: 15 minutes | Cook Time: 2 hours| Serves: 10

Chicken bones from 3 pounds roast chicken
1 parsnip
1 celery
2 tablespoons fresh parsley
1 tablespoon fresh thyme
2 tablespoons fresh coriander
1 teaspoon fresh dill
2 tablespoons cider vinegar
1 teaspoon sea salt
1 teaspoon ground black pepper

1. Place all ingredients in the Inner Pot. Add cold water until the pot is ⅔ full. 2. Put the lid in place and lock it. Select the Soup/Broth on the panel. Press the button again to adjust the cooking time to 120 minutes. Press Pressure Level to choose Low pressure. 3. Once cooking is complete, leave the steam release handle in the Sealing position for 10 minutes; Open the lid carefully. 4. Remove the bones and vegetables using a metal spoon with holes and discard. Pour the liquid through the sieve into the bowl. 5. Use immediately or store in your refrigerator.
Per Serving: Calories 69; Fat 3g; Sodium 255mg; Carbs 8.4g; Fiber 1g; Sugars 1g; Protein 1g

Delicious Roasted Vegetable Stock

Prep Time: 10 minutes | Cook Time: 65 minutes | Serves: 10

4 carrots, cut into 2-inch pieces
4 medium celery ribs, cut into 2-inch pieces
2 onions, peeled and quartered
2 sprigs fresh rosemary
2 sprigs fresh thyme
3 tablespoons olive oil
Kosher salt and black peppercorns, to taste
1 cup dry white wine
10 cups water

1. Start by preheating your oven to 400°F/200°C. Grease a large roasting pan with cooking spray 2. Place carrots, celery, onions and herbs in prepared baking pan. Roast for 35 minutes, tossing halfway through the cooking time, until the vegetables are tender. 3. Transfer the vegetables to the inner pot. Put the remaining ingredients into the Inner Pot. 4. Put the lid in place and lock it. Select the Soup/Broth on the panel. Press the button again to choose Normal option. Press Pressure Level to choose High pressure. 5. Once cooking is complete, leave the steam release handle in the Sealing position for 10 minutes; Open the lid carefully. 6. Strain the broth through a fine-mesh sieve and remove the solids. 7. Let it cool completely before storing.
Per Serving: Calories 56; Fat 1.3g; Sodium 195mg; Carbs 4.4g; Fiber 1g; Sugars 3.5g; Protein 0.4g

Simple Salted Caramel Sauce

Prep Time: 10 minutes | Cook Time: 5 minutes | Serves:6

½ cup water
1 ⅓ cups granulated sugar
4 tablespoons butter, cut into small pieces
½ cup heavy whipping cream
½ teaspoon coarse sea salt
1 teaspoon vanilla
A pinch of cardamom

1. Insert the inner pot into the cooker base. 2. Press Sauté to select the program and press it again to choose Normal option. Cook the sugar and water, stirring frequently, until the sugar has dissolved. 3. Let the mixture boiling until it turns an amber color. 4. Add the butter followed by the rest of the ingredients. 5. Allow your sauce to cool. It will thicken up once it's cooled in your refrigerator.
Per Serving: Calories 191; Fat 11.3g; Sodium 170mg; Carbs 22.4g; Fiber 1g; Sugars 22.5g; Protein 0.3g

Homemade Pork Stock

2 pounds pork bones
4 celery stalks, cut into large chunks
4 carrots, cut into large chunks
1 onion, quartered

3 garlic cloves, smashed
2 bay leaves
Sea salt and black peppercorns, to taste
10 cups water, divided in half

1. Preheat your oven to 400°F/200°C. Coat a roasting pan with a piece of aluminum foil; brush with a little oil. 2. Arrange pork bones and vegetables on prepared baking sheet. Bake in preheated oven for 25 to 30 minutes. 3. Transfer the roasted pork bones and vegetables to the inner pot of your Inner Pot. Now, stir in the bay leaves, salt, black peppercorns, and water. 4. Put the lid in place and lock it. Select the Pressure Cook on the panel. Press the button again to choose Less option; use the "+/-" button to adjust the cooking time to 25 minutes. Press Pressure Level to choose High pressure. 5. Once cooking is complete, quickly and carefully turn the steam release handle from Sealing position to the Venting position. Open the lid carefully. 6. Strain the stock and remove the solids. 7. Keep in your refrigerator or freezer if desired.
Per Serving: Calories 91; Fat 4.3g; Sodium 157mg; Carbs 3.3g; Fiber 1g; Sugars 1.5g; Protein 9.9g

Delicious Herby Tomato Sauce

2 (28-ounce) cans tomatoes, crushed
3 tablespoons olive oil
3 cloves garlic, minced
½ teaspoon dried rosemary
½ teaspoon dried basil
½ tablespoon dried oregano

1 onion, quartered
Kosher salt and freshly ground black pepper, to taste
1 teaspoon tamari sauce
2 tablespoons fresh parsley leaves, finely chopped

1. Reserve 1 cup of the crushed tomatoes. 2. Insert the inner pot into the cooker base. 3. Press Sauté to select the program and press it again to choose Normal option, then add and heat olive oil. Once hot, cook the garlic for a minute or so or until it is fragrant but not browned. 4. Now, stir in the rosemary, basil, and oregano; continue to sauté for 30 seconds more. Stir in the tomatoes, onion, salt, and pepper. 5. Put the lid in place and lock it. Select the Soup/Broth on the panel. Press the button again to choose Normal option; use the "+/-" button to adjust the cooking time to 40 minutes. Press Pressure Level to choose High pressure. 6. Once cooking is complete, quickly and carefully turn the steam release handle from Sealing position to the Venting position. Open the lid carefully. 7. Add the reserved tomatoes, tamari sauce and parsley to your tomato sauce.
Per Serving: Calories 115; Fat 7.3g; Sodium 168mg; Carbs5.4g; Fiber 1g; Sugars 3.5g; Protein 2.4g

Perfect Mixed Berry Sauce

2 cups frozen blueberries, thawed
2 cups frozen raspberries, thawed
2 cups frozen strawberries, thawed
½ cup granulated sugar
1 teaspoon cornstarch

1 cup water
2 tablespoons orange juice
½ cup cream cheese, at room temperature

1. Add the berries, sugar, and cornstarch, and water to the Inner Pot; stir to combine. 2. Put the lid in place and lock it. Select the Pressure Cook on the panel. Press the button again to choose Less option; use the "-" button to adjust the cooking time to 10 minutes. Press Pressure Level to choose High pressure. 3. Once cooking is complete, leave the steam release handle in the Sealing position for 10 minutes. Open the lid carefully. 4. Stir in the orange juice and cream cheese; stir to combine and serve with waffles or pancakes.
Per Serving: Calories 117; Fat 3g; Sodium 115mg; Carbs 22.4g; Fiber 1g; Sugars 1.5g; Protein 17.4g

Simple Cranberry Sauce

1 ½ pounds fresh cranberries, rinsed
2 blood oranges, juiced

1 tablespoon blood orange zest
¾ cup sugar
¼ cup golden cane syrup

2-3 cloves
1 cinnamon stick

1 teaspoon vanilla extract

1. Add the cranberries to the inner pot of your Inner Pot. 2. Put the remaining ingredients into the Inner Pot to the inner pot; stir to combine well. 3. Put the lid in place and lock it. Select the Pressure Cook on the panel. Press the button again to choose Less option; use the "+/-" button to adjust the cooking time to 3 minutes. Press Pressure Level to choose High pressure. 4. Once cooking is complete, leave the steam release handle in the Sealing position for 10 minutes; Open the lid carefully. 5. Let it cool. Serve your sauce chilled or at room temperature.
Per Serving: Calories 125; Fat 13g; Sodium 254mg; Carbs 24.4g; Fiber 1g; Sugars 3.5g; Protein 0.4g

Homemade Beef Bolognese Pasta Sauce

2 tablespoons olive oil
1-pound ground beef
1 onion, chopped
1 teaspoon fresh garlic, minced
Sea salt and ground black pepper, to taste
1 teaspoon brown sugar
½ teaspoon dried sage

1 teaspoon dried oregano
1 teaspoon dried basil
½ teaspoon cayenne pepper, or to taste
2 cups beef broth
2 ripe tomatoes, pureed
2 tablespoons tomato ketchup

1. Insert the inner pot into the cooker base. 2. Press Sauté to select the program and press it again to choose Normal option, then add and heat the oil. When the oil starts to sizzle, cook the ground beef until no longer pink; crumble it with a wooden spatula. 3. Add the onion and garlic and continue to cook for a few minutes more or until they are tender and fragrant. Add a splash of beef broth to deglaze the pot. 4. Stir in the remaining ingredients; stir to combine well. 5. Put the lid in place and lock it. Select the Pressure Cook on the panel. Press the button again to choose Less option; use the "-" button to adjust the cooking time to 6 minutes. Press Pressure Level to choose High pressure. Once cooking is complete, leave the steam release handle in the Sealing position. Open the lid carefully. 6. Serve over pasta if desired.
Per Serving: Calories 358; Fat 20.3g; Sodium 522mg; Carbs 8.4g; Fiber 1g; Sugars 4.5g; Protein 24.4g

Homemade Fish Stock

2 pounds meaty bones and heads of halibut, washed
2 lemongrass stalks, chopped
2 carrots, chopped
1 parsnip, chopped

1 onion, quartered
2 sprigs rosemary
2 sprigs thyme
2 tablespoons olive oil

1. Place all ingredients in the inner pot. Add cold water until the pot is ⅔ full. 2. Put the lid in place and lock it. Select the Soup/Broth on the panel. Press the button again to choose Normal option and use the "+/-" buttons to adjust the cooking time to 40 minutes. Press Pressure Level to choose High pressure. 3. Once cooking is complete, leave the steam release handle in the Sealing position. Open the lid carefully. 4. Strain the vegetables and fish. 5. Serve and enjoy.
Per Serving: Calories 63; Fat 3g; Sodium 155mg; Carbs 4.9g; Fiber 1g; Sugars 1.5g; Protein 1.4g

Perfect Applesauce with Dates

6 Honeycrisp apples, peeled, cored and chopped
1 cup water
1 tablespoon fresh lemon juice

¼ teaspoon ground cloves
½ teaspoon cinnamon powder
10 dates, pitted and chopped

1. Add all ingredients to the inner pot; stir to combine. 2. Put the lid in place and lock it. Select the Pressure Cook on the panel. Press the button again to choose Less option; use the "+/-" button to adjust the cooking time to 10 minutes. Press Pressure Level to choose High pressure. 3. Once cooking is complete, leave the steam release handle in the Sealing position for 10 minutes. Open the lid carefully. 4. Mash the apple mixture to the desired consistency. Serve warm or cold.
Per Serving: Calories 97; Fat 12.3g; Sodium 255mg; Carbs 24.4g; Fiber 1g; Sugars 11.5g; Protein 2.4g

Homemade Eggplant Light Sauce with Wine

Prep Time: 5 minutes | Cook Time: 10 minutes | Serves: 6

2 tablespoons olive oil
1-pound eggplants, sliced
4 garlic cloves, minced
2 tomatoes, chopped
1 cup white wine
1 teaspoon oregano
½ teaspoon rosemary

1 teaspoon basil
Sea salt and ground black pepper, to taste
2 tablespoons tahini (sesame butter)
½ cup Romano cheese, freshly grated

1. Insert the inner pot into the cooker base without the lid. 2. Press Sauté to select the program and press it again to choose Normal option, then add and heat the olive oil. Then, cook the eggplant slices until they are charred at the bottom. Work with batches. 3. Add the garlic, tomatoes, wine, and spices. 4. Put the lid in place and lock it. Select the Bean/Chili Cook on the panel. Press the button again to choose Less option; use the "-" button to adjust the cooking time to 3 minutes. Press Pressure Level to choose High pressure. 5. Once cooking is complete, quickly and carefully turn the steam release handle from Sealing position to the Venting position; open the lid carefully. 6. Press the Cancel button to stop this cooking program. 7. Press Sauté to select the program again and press it again to choose Normal option, then add to thicken the cooking liquid. Add the tahini paste and stir to combine. 8. Top with Romano cheese and serve.
Per Serving: Calories 147; Fat 10.3g; Sodium 118mg; Carbs 9.4g; Fiber 1g; Sugars 4.5g; Protein 5.4g

Cheese and Bacon Sauce

Prep Time: 5 minutes | Cook Time: 10 minutes | Serves: 10

4 ounces bacon, diced
1 onion, chopped
1 red chili pepper, seeded and minced
2 cloves garlic, pressed
2 ripe tomatoes, chopped
½ teaspoon ground cumin

½ teaspoon turmeric powder
Kosher salt and ground black pepper, to taste
1 cup vegetable broth
10 ounces Cottage cheese, at room temperature
1 cup Pepper Jack cheese, grated

1. Insert the inner pot into the cooker base. 2. Press Sauté to select the program and press it again to choose Normal option, then add to preheat your Inner Pot. Then, cook the bacon for 2 to 3 minutes. Reserve. 3. Add the onion and pepper to the inner pot and continue to cook until they are fragrant. Stir in the garlic and continue to sauté for 30 seconds more. 4. Now, add the tomatoes, spices, and broth. 5. Put the lid in place and lock it. Select the Pressure Cook on the panel. Press the button again to choose Less option; use the "-" button to adjust the cooking time to 5 minutes. Press Pressure Level to choose High pressure. 6. Once cooking is complete, quickly and carefully turn the steam release handle from the Sealing position to the Venting position. Open the lid carefully. 7. Finally, add the cheese. Cover again and let sit in residual heat until cheese is melted. 8. Ladle into a nice serving bowl, top with the reserved bacon, and serve.
Per Serving: Calories 135; Fat 9.5g; Sodium 154mg; Carbs 8.4g; Fiber 1g; Sugars 2.5g; Protein 8.4g

Homemade Black Bean Sauce in Mexican Style

Prep Time: 5 minutes | Cook Time: 30 minutes | Serves: 8

2 tablespoons olive oil
1 brown onion, chopped
3 garlic cloves, chopped
1 jalapeño pepper, seeded and minced
1 teaspoon dried Mexican oregano
½ teaspoon ground cumin

Sea salt and ground black pepper, to taste
1 ½ cups black beans, rinsed, drained
1 ½ cups chicken broth
¼ cup fresh cilantro, chopped
½ cup Pico de Gallo

1. Insert the inner pot into the cooker base. 2. Press Sauté to select the program and press it again to choose Normal option, then add and heat the olive oil until sizzling. Once hot, cook the onion for 3 to 4 minutes or until tender and fragrant. 3. After that, stir in the garlic; continue sautéing an additional 30 to 40 seconds. 4. Add the jalapeño pepper, oregano, cumin, salt, black pepper, beans, and broth to the inner pot. 5. Put the lid in place and lock it. Select the Bean/Chili Cook on the panel. Press the button again to choose Less option; press Pressure Level to choose High pressure. Once cooking is complete, quickly and carefully turn the steam release handle from Sealing position to the Venting position. Open the lid carefully. 5. Then, mash your beans with potato masher or use your blender. 6. Serve garnished with cilantro and Pico de Gallo.
Per Serving: Calories 181; Fat 4.3g; Sodium 121mg; Carbs 27.4g; Fiber 1g; Sugars 3.5g; Protein 9.4g

Spinach and Artichoke Dipping Sauce

Prep Time: 5 minutes | Cook Time: 10 minutes | Serves: 8

2 tablespoons butter
1 onion, chopped
2 cloves garlic, minced
10 ounces artichoke hearts
1 cup chicken broth
Sea salt and freshly ground black

pepper, to taste
1 teaspoon red pepper flakes
1 pound fresh or frozen spinach leaves
9 ounces cream cheese
1 cup goat cheese, crumbled

1. Insert the inner pot into the cooker base. 2. Press Sauté to select the program and press it again to choose Normal option, then add and melt the butter. Sauté the onion and garlic until just tender and fragrant. 3. Then, add the artichoke hearts, broth, salt, black pepper, and red pepper flakes. 4. Press the Cancel button to stop this cooking program. 5. Put the lid in place and lock it. Select the Pressure Cook on the panel. Press the button again to choose Less option; use the "-" button to adjust the cooking time to 5 minutes. Press Pressure Level to choose High pressure. 6. Once cooking is complete, quickly and carefully turn the steam release handle from Sealing position to the Venting position. Open the lid carefully. 7. Add the spinach and cheese to the inner pot; seal the lid and let it sit in the residual heat until thoroughly warmed.
Per Serving: Calories 222; Fat 17g; Sodium 275mg; Carbs 8.4g; Fiber 1g; Sugars 2.5g; Protein 9.4g

Simple Carolina-Style Sticky Barbecue Sauce

Prep Time: 10 minutes | Cook Time: 10 minutes | Serves: 8

2 tablespoons butter
1 shallot, chopped
2 cloves garlic, minced
2 cups tomato sauce
½ cup cider vinegar
2 tablespoons coconut sugar
⅓ cup molasses
2 tablespoons Worcestershire

sauce
1 teaspoon yellow mustard
1 teaspoon hot sauce
Kosher salt and ground black pepper
½ teaspoon paprika
1 cup vegetable broth

1. Insert the inner pot into the cooker base. 2. Press Sauté to select the program and press it again to choose Normal option, then add and melt the butter. Sauté the shallot for 4 minutes until tender and translucent. Add the garlic and cook for a further 30 seconds. 3. Stir in the remaining ingredients. 4. Put the lid in place and lock it. Select the Pressure Cook on the panel. Press the button again to choose Less option; use the "+/-" button to adjust the cooking time to 5 minutes. Press Pressure Level to choose High pressure. 5. Once cooking is complete, leave the steam release handle in the Sealing position for 5 minutes; Open the lid carefully.
Per Serving: Calories 215; Fat 4.4g; Sodium 225mg; Carbs 37.4g; Fiber 1g; Sugars 37.5g; Protein 37.4g

Delicious Hot Sauce

Prep Time: 10 minutes | Cook Time: 30 minutes | Serves: 10

1 tablespoon butter, melted
1 banana shallot, chopped
1 teaspoon garlic, minced
5 jalapeño peppers, seeded and chopped
5 serrano peppers, seeded and chopped

2 tomatoes, chopped
1 cup white vinegar
1 cup water
2 tablespoons white sugar
Sea salt and ground black pepper, to taste

1. Insert the inner pot into the cooker base. 2. Press Sauté to select the program and press it again to choose Normal option, then add and melt the butter. Once hot, cook the shallot for 3 to 4 minute or until it is tender and fragrant. 3. Now, add the garlic and continue to cook an additional 30 seconds or until aromatic. 4. Put the remaining ingredients into the Inner Pot. 5. Put the lid in place and lock it. Select the Pressure Cook on the panel. Press the button again to choose Normal option; use the "-" button to adjust the cooking time to 25 minutes. Press Pressure Level to choose High pressure. 6. Once cooking is complete, leave the steam release handle in the Sealing position for 10 minutes. Open the lid carefully. 7. Let it cool. Serve your sauce hot or at room temperature.
Per Serving: Calories 33; Fat 1.3g; Sodium 195mg; Carbs 4.4g; Fiber 1g; Sugars 3.5g; Protein 0.4g

Yummy Zesty Pear Sauce

Prep Time: 15 minutes | Cook Time: 10 minutes | Serves: 8

1 ½ pounds cup pears, cored, peeled and chopped
2 teaspoons freshly squeezed lemon juice
½ cup sugar
1 teaspoon ground cinnamon
½ teaspoon ground cardamom
1 teaspoon vanilla essence

1. Add all ingredients to the inner pot; stir to combine. 2. Put the lid in place and lock it. Select the Pressure Cook on the panel. Press the button again to choose Less option; use the "-" button to adjust the cooking time to 10 minutes. Press Pressure Level to choose High pressure. 3. Once cooking is complete, leave the steam release handle in the Sealing position for10 minutes. Open the lid carefully. 4. Mash the pear mixture to the desired consistency. 5. Serve at room temperature or cold.
Per Serving: Calories 73; Fat 1.3g; Sodium 195mg; Carbs 4.4g; Fiber 1g; Sugars 3.5g; Protein 0.4g

Easy Salsa

Prep Time: 15 minutes | Cook Time: 25 minutes | Serves: 8

2 onions, chopped
2 garlic cloves, pressed
2 ripe tomatoes, crushed
12 ounces canned tomato paste
2 sweet peppers, chopped
2 chili peppers, chopped
½ cup rice vinegar
2 tablespoons brown sugar
Sea salt and red pepper, to taste
1 teaspoon dried Mexican oregano

1. Put all ingredients into the inner pot of your Inner Pot. 2. Put the lid in place and lock it. Select the Pressure Cook on the panel. Press the button again to choose Less option; use the "+" button to adjust the cooking time to 25 minutes. Press Pressure Level to choose High pressure. 3. Once cooking is complete, leave the steam release handle in the Sealing position for 10 minutes. Open the lid carefully. 4. Allow your salsa to cool completely; store in your refrigerator or freezer.
Per Serving: Calories 83; Fat 0.3g; Sodium 241mg; Carbs 18.4g; Fiber 1g; Sugars 10.5g; Protein 3.4g

Simple Marinara Sauce

Prep Time: 10 minutes | Cook Time: 45 minutes | Serves: 8

4 tablespoons olive oil
4 garlic cloves, minced
4 tablespoons tomato paste
1 (28-ounce) can crushed tomatoes with juice
1 cup water
Sea salt to taste
2 tablespoons fresh basil, minced
1 tablespoon fresh parsley, minced

1. Insert the inner pot into the cooker base without the lid. 2. Press Sauté to select the program and press it again to choose Normal option, then add and heat olive oil. Once hot, cook the garlic for a minute or so or until it is fragrant but not browned. 3. Now, stir in the remaining ingredients. 4. Put the lid in place and lock it. Select the Soup/Broth on the panel. Press the button Again to choose Normal option; use the "+" button to adjust the cooking time to 40 minutes. Press Pressure Level to choose High pressure. 5. Once cooking is complete, quickly and carefully turn the steam release handle from the Sealing position to the Venting position. Open the lid carefully. 6. Serve and enjoy.
Per Serving: Calories 86; Fat 7g; Sodium 220mg; Carbs 5.4g; Fiber 1g; Sugars 3.5g; Protein 1.4g.

Homemade Ketchup

Prep time: 20 minutes | Cook time: 15 minutes | Serves: 8

2 tablespoons olive oil
1 medium onion, finely chopped
4 garlic cloves, smashed
1 (28-ounce) can whole tomatoes with juice
½ cup red wine vinegar
1 tablespoon tomato paste
1 teaspoon Worcestershire sauce
⅓ cup packed brown sugar
½ teaspoon paprika
¼ teaspoon white pepper
⅛ teaspoon ground allspice
Pinch kosher salt

1. Press the "Sauté" button twice to select "Normal" mode. 2. Once hot, add the oil followed by the onion. 3. Cook for 3 minutes until the onion is starting to turn translucent. Add the garlic and sauté 1 minute more. 4. Add the tomatoes with juice, crushing the tomatoes with your hand as you add them. 5. Add the vinegar, tomato paste, Worcestershire sauce, brown sugar, paprika, white pepper, and allspice

and bring to a simmer. Add a pinch of salt. 6. Put on the pressure cooker's lid and turn the steam valve to "Sealing" position. 7. Set the Instant Pot to Pressure Cook. 8. Use the "+/-" keys on the control panel to set the cooking time to 15 minutes. 9. Press the Pressure Level button to adjust the pressure to "High". 10. Once the cooking cycle is completed, allow the steam to release naturally. 11. When all the steam is released, remove the pressure lid from the top carefully. 12. Remove the lid and stir. Taste for seasoning. 13. Press the "Sauté" button twice to select "Normal" mode and cook, for 15 to 20 minutes. 14. Use an immersion blender to blend until smooth, or blend in a food processor. 15. Let it cool and store it in the refrigerator for up to 1 month or the freezer for several months.
Per Serving: Calories 84; Fat 15g; Sodium 441mg; Carbs 17g; Fiber 4.6g; Sugar 5g; Protein 29g

Raspberry Ginger Coulis

Prep Time: 10 minutes | Cook Time: 5 minutes | Serves: 6

1 (12-ounce) bag fresh or frozen raspberries
1 cup brown sugar
1 cup water
½ cup fresh orange juice
1 tablespoon fresh ginger root, peeled and finely grated
Zest from 1 organic orange, finely grated

1. Add all the ingredients to the inner pot of your Inner Pot. 2. Put the lid in place and lock it. Select the Pressure Cook on the panel. Press the button again to choose Less option; use the "-" button to adjust the cooking time to 3 minutes. Press Pressure Level to choose High pressure. 3. Once cooking is complete, leave the steam release handle in the Sealing position for 10 minutes. Open the lid carefully. 4. Let it cool. Serve your sauce chilled or at room temperature.
Per Serving: Calories 134; Fat 0.3g; Sodium 145mg; Carbs 34.4g; Fiber 1g; Sugars 30.5g; Protein 0.5g

Chicken Onion Stock

Prep time: 20 minutes | Cook time: 60 minutes | Serves: 8

2-pound chicken bones and parts
1 yellow onion, quartered
1 large garlic clove, smashed
1 carrot, cut into large chunks
1 bay leaf
½ teaspoon kosher salt
1 teaspoon whole black peppercorns
8 cups water

1. Add the chicken, onion, garlic, carrot, bay leaf, salt, and peppercorns to the pot. Pour the water over. 2. Put on the pressure cooker's lid and turn the steam valve to "Sealing" position. 3. Set the Instant Pot to Pressure Cook. 4. Press the Pressure Level button to adjust the pressure to "High". 5. Use the "+/-" keys on the control panel to set the cooking time to 60 minutes. 6. Once the cooking cycle is completed, allow the steam to release naturally. 7. When all the steam is released, remove the pressure lid from the top carefully. 8. Carefully strain the broth through a fine-mesh strainer or cheesecloth. 9. Store the stock in the refrigerator for a few days or freeze for up to 3 months.
Per Serving: Calories 19; Fat 14g; Sodium 91mg; Carbs 8.9g; Fiber 4.6g; Sugar 8g; Protein 3g

Vegetable Stock

Prep time: 20 minutes | Cook time: 60minutes | Serves: 8

2 onions, quartered
2 celery stalks, quartered
2 carrots, cut into large chunks
10 button mushrooms
4 garlic cloves, smashed
1 small bunch fresh parsley
1 bay leaf
8 cups water
Kosher salt

1. Add the onions, celery, carrots, mushrooms, garlic, parsley, bay leaf, and water to the Instant Pot. 2. Put on the pressure cooker's lid and turn the steam valve to "Sealing" position. 3. Set the Instant Pot to Pressure Cook. 4. Press the Pressure Level button to adjust the pressure to "High". 5. Use the "+/-" keys on the control panel to set the cooking time to 60 minutes. 6. Once the cooking cycle is completed, allow the steam to release naturally. 7. When all the steam is released, remove the pressure lid from the top carefully. 8. Carefully strain the stock using a fine-mesh strainer or cheesecloth. Season with salt. 9. Store the stock in the refrigerator for a few days or freeze for up to 3 months.
Per Serving: Calories 54; Fat 7.9g; Sodium 704mg; Carbs 6g; Fiber 3.6g; Sugar 6g; Protein 18g

Beef Bone Broth

Prep time: 20 minutes | Cook time: 1 hr. 30 minutes | Serves: 8

2½-pound beef bones, including short ribs, knuckles, oxtails, and more
1 teaspoon olive oil
1 yellow onion, quartered
2 celery stalks, quartered

1 carrot, cut into large chunks
1 bay leaf
2 teaspoons apple cider vinegar
1 tablespoon fish sauce
8 cups water

1. Preheat the oven to 400°F/200°C. 2. Toss the bones with the oil on a baking sheet and roast for 30 minutes. 3. Once cool enough to handle, add the bones, onion, celery, carrot, bay leaf, vinegar, fish sauce, and water to the Instant Pot. 4. Put on the pressure cooker's lid and turn the steam valve to "Sealing" position. 5. Set the Instant Pot to Pressure Cook. 6. Use the "+/-" keys on the control panel to set the cooking time to 1 hour 30 minutes. 7. Press the Pressure Level button to adjust the pressure to "High". 8. Once the cooking cycle is completed, allow the steam to release naturally. 9. When all the steam is released, remove the pressure lid from the top carefully. 10. Skim any fat off the top of the stock, if desired. 11. Carefully strain the broth using a fine-mesh strainer or cheesecloth. 12. Store the broth in the refrigerator for a few days or freeze for up to 3 months.
Per Serving: Calories 79; Fat 10g; Sodium 891mg; Carbs 22.9g; Fiber 4g; Sugar 4g; Protein 33g

Spicy Chicken Bone Broth

Prep time: 20 minutes | Cook time: 1 hr. 30 minutes | Serves: 8

2½-pound mixed chicken bones and feet
1 yellow onion, quartered
1 celery stalk, quartered
1 carrot, cut into large chunks
1 (1½-inch) piece ginger, peeled

and cut into ¼-inch slices
1 teaspoon whole black peppercorns
1 tablespoon fish sauce
1 teaspoon apple cider vinegar
8 cups water

1. Add the bones, onion, celery, carrot, ginger, peppercorns, fish sauce, vinegar, and water to the Instant Pot. 2. Put on the pressure cooker's lid and turn the steam valve to "Sealing" position. 3. Set the Instant Pot to Pressure Cook. 4. Press the Pressure Level button to adjust the pressure to "High". 5. Use the "+/-" keys on the control panel to set the cooking time to 1 hour 30 minutes. 6. Once the cooking cycle is completed, allow the steam to release naturally. 7. When all the steam is released, remove the pressure lid from the top carefully. 8. Skim any fat off the top of the stock, if desired. Carefully strain the broth using a fine-mesh strainer or cheesecloth. 9. Store the broth in the refrigerator for a few days or freeze for up to 3 months.
Per Serving: Calories 78; Fat 19g; Sodium 354mg; Carbs 15g; Fiber 5.1g; Sugar 8.2g; Protein 32g

Sweet and Tangy Barbecue Sauce

Prep time: 20 minutes | Cook time: 15 minutes | Serves: 8

4 tablespoons butter
1 small onion, finely chopped
3 garlic cloves, minced
1 cup tomato sauce
½ cup ketchup
½ cup apple cider vinegar

½ cup brown sugar
3 tablespoons molasses
1 tablespoon Dijon mustard
1 teaspoon liquid smoke
¼ teaspoon cayenne
¼ teaspoon black pepper

1. Press the "Sauté" button two times to select "Normal" mode 2. Once hot, add the butter and let it melt. Add the onion and cook for 3 minutes until it is starting to turn translucent. Add the garlic and sauté 1 minute more. 3. Add the tomato sauce, ketchup, vinegar, brown sugar, molasses, mustard, liquid smoke, cayenne, and pepper. 4. Put on the pressure cooker's lid and turn the steam valve to "Sealing" position. 5. Set the Instant Pot to Pressure Cook. 6. Use the "+/-" keys on the control panel to set the cooking time to 15 minutes. 7. Press the Pressure Level button to adjust the pressure to "High". 8. Once the cooking cycle is completed, allow the steam to release naturally. 9. When all the steam is released, remove the pressure lid from the top carefully. 10. Stir and taste for seasoning. If a thicker sauce is desired. 11. Press the "Sauté" button two times to select "Normal" mode and cook, stirring occasionally, for 10 to 15 minutes. 12. Let it cool and store it in the refrigerator for up to 2 weeks or the freezer for several months.
Per Serving: Calories 32; Fat 10.9g; Sodium 354mg; Carbs 10.5g; Fiber 4.1g; Sugar 8.2g; Protein 26g

Mango-Apple Chutney

Prep time: 20 minutes | Cook time: 11 minutes | Serves: 8

1 tablespoon canola oil
1 large red onion, finely chopped
1 heaping tablespoon grated fresh ginger
1 red Thai chile, cut into a few pieces
2 large mangos, peeled and diced
2 apples, cored, partially peeled, and diced

1 red bell pepper, diced
½ cup golden raisins
1¼ cups sugar
½ cup apple cider vinegar
1 teaspoon kosher salt
1½ teaspoons curry powder
½ teaspoon ground cinnamon
1 tablespoon lemon juice

1. Press the "Sauté" button twice to select "Normal" mode. Add the oil. 2. Once hot, add the onion and sauté for 3 minutes. Add the ginger and chile, and cook for 1 minute. 3. Add the mangos, apples, bell pepper, raisins, sugar, vinegar, salt, curry powder, and cinnamon. 4. Put on the pressure cooker's lid and turn the steam valve to "Sealing" position. 5. Set the Instant Pot to Pressure Cook. 6. Press the Pressure Level button to adjust the pressure to "High".
7. Use the "+/-" keys on the control panel to set the cooking time to 7 minutes. 8. Once the cooking cycle is completed, allow the steam to release naturally. 9. When all the steam is released, remove the pressure lid from the top carefully. 10. Press the "Sauté" button two times to select "Normal" mode and simmer for 10 minutes. 11. Add the lemon juice and stir. 12. Store in airtight containers in the refrigerator for up to a month or in the freezer for up to a year.
Per Serving: Calories 49; Fat 2.9g; Sodium 511mg; Carbs 12g; Fiber 3g; Sugar 8g; Protein 28g

Puttanesca Sauce

Prep time: 20 minutes | Cook time: 20 minutes | Serves: 8

2 tablespoons olive oil
1 small onion, finely chopped
4 garlic cloves, minced
1 (28-ounce) can whole tomatoes with juice
½ cup chopped pitted Kalamata olives

4 anchovy fillets, drained and minced
1 tablespoon tomato paste
1 tablespoon drained capers
¼ teaspoon red pepper flakes
Kosher salt
Black pepper

1. Press the "Sauté" button two times to select "Normal" mode 2. Once hot, add the oil followed by the onion. Sauté for 3 minutes, then add the garlic. Sauté 1 minute more. 3. Add the tomatoes with juice, squishing each one with your hand as it goes into the pot. 4. Add the olives, anchovies, tomato paste, capers, and red pepper flakes. Season with salt and pepper. 5. Put on the pressure cooker's lid and turn the steam valve to "Sealing" position. 6. Set the Instant Pot to Pressure Cook. 7. Press the Pressure Level button to adjust the pressure to "High". 8. Use the "+/-" keys on the control panel to set the cooking time to 20 minutes. 9. Once the cooking cycle is completed, allow the steam to release naturally. 10. When all the steam is released, remove the pressure lid from the top carefully. 11. If a thicker sauce is desired, press the "Sauté" button twice to select "Normal" mode and simmer for 5 minutes. Serve over pasta.
Per Serving: Calories 41; Fat 10.9g; Sodium 454mg; Carbs 10g; Fiber 3.1g; Sugar 5.2g; Protein 05g

Homemade Gravy Sauce

Prep Time: 15 minutes | Cook Time: 5 minutes | Serves: 6

3 cups pan juices
⅓ cup cornstarch
⅓ cup cold water

Salt and ground black pepper, to taste
½ teaspoon cayenne pepper

1. Insert the inner pot into the cooker base. 2. Press Sauté to select the program to and press it again to choose Normal option; cook the pan juices for about 3 minutes, bringing it to a boil. Stir cornstarch with cold water until cornstarch dissolves; then stir cornstarch slurry into pot juices. Add the salt, black pepper, and cayenne pepper; continue cooking on the lowest setting until your sauce has reduced slightly and the flavors have concentrated. 3. Serve and enjoy.
Per Serving: Calories 80; Fat 0.3g; Sodium 254mg; Carbs 21.4g; Fiber 1g; Sugars 13.5g; Protein 0.2g

Broccoli Pesto

Prep time: 20 minutes | Cook time: 3 minutes | Serves: 8

1 bunch broccoli (about 1 pound), cut into florets (reserve stems for vegetable stock)
3 cups water
⅓ cup toasted walnuts
3 garlic cloves, minced

1 packed cup fresh basil leaves
¼ cup olive oil
2 tablespoons lemon juice
¼ cup grated Parmesan cheese
Kosher salt
Black pepper

1. Add the broccoli and water to the Instant Pot. 2. Put on the pressure cooker's lid and turn the steam valve to "Sealing" position. 3. Set the Instant Pot to Pressure Cook. 4. Press the Pressure Level button to adjust the pressure to "High". 5. Use the "+/-" keys on the control panel to set the cooking time to 3 minutes. 6. Once the cooking cycle is completed, quick-release pressure. 7. When all the steam is released, remove the pressure lid from the top carefully. 8. Meanwhile, combine the walnuts and garlic in a food processor. 9. Pulse several times until crumbly, but before the walnuts turn to butter. 10. Remove the broccoli and rinse with cold water. 11. Drain well and add to the food processor, along with the basil, oil, and lemon juice. 12. Pulse until well mixed. Add ¼ cup of cooking liquid and the Parmesan, and season with salt and pepper. 13. Process until smooth. Add more cooking liquid as needed.
Per Serving: Calories 49; Fat 11g; Sodium 501mg; Carbs 8.9g; Fiber 4.6g; Sugar 8g; Protein 26g

Mushroom Broth

Prep time: 20 minutes | Cook time: 15 minutes | Serves: 8

4-ounce dried mushrooms, soaked and rinsed
8 cups water
½ cup carrots, chopped
½ cup celery, chopped

1 onion, quartered
4 cloves garlic, crushed
4 bay leaves
Salt and black pepper to taste.

1. Put all of the ingredients into the Instant Pot. 2. Put on the pressure cooker's lid and turn the steam valve to "Sealing" position. 3. Set the Instant Pot to Pressure Cook. 4. Press the Pressure Level button to adjust the pressure to "High". 5. Use the "+/-" keys on the control panel to set the cooking time to 15 minutes. 6. Once the cooking cycle is completed, quick-release pressure. 7. When all the steam is released, remove the pressure lid from the top carefully. 8. Season with salt and pepper to taste. 9. Strain the broth and pour into jars. Store in the refrigerator or freeze.
Per Serving: Calories 34; Fat 12.9g; Sodium 44mg; Carbs 11g; Fiber 5g; Sugar 9g; Protein 31g

Cinnamon Applesauce

Prep time: 20 minutes | Cook time: 4 minutes | Serves: 8

10 to 12 medium apples, peeled, cored, and diced
½ cup apple cider, apple juice, or water

1 cinnamon stick, broken in half
Up to ¼ cup honey
1 tablespoon lemon juice

1. Add the apples, cider or juice or water, and both halves of the cinnamon stick to the Instant Pot. 2. Put on the pressure cooker's lid and turn the steam valve to "Sealing" position. 3. Set the Instant Pot to Pressure Cook. 4. Press the Pressure Level button to adjust the pressure to "Low". 5. Use the "+/-" keys on the control panel to set the cooking time to 4 minutes. 6. Once the cooking cycle is completed, allow the steam to release naturally. 7. When all the steam is released, remove the pressure lid from the top carefully. 8. Stir and remove the cinnamon stick halves. If the applesauce isn't sweet enough, add honey. 9. Serve.
Per Serving: Calories 84; Fat 5g; Sodium 41mg; Carbs 7g; Fiber 7.6g; Sugar 5g; Protein 2g

Onion Gravy

Prep time: 20 minutes | Cook time: 10 minutes | Serves: 8

3 tablespoons butter
1 large sweet onion, finely chopped
2 cups chicken broth (try the recipe here)
2 fresh thyme sprigs

1 bay leaf
2 tablespoons all-purpose flour
Kosher salt
Black pepper

1. Press the "Sauté" button twice to select "Normal" mode. 2. Once hot, add 1 tablespoon of butter followed by the onion. 3. Sauté for 6 minutes, until translucent and starting to brown. 4. Add the broth, thyme, and bay leaf. 5. Put on the pressure cooker's lid and turn the steam valve to "Sealing" position. 6. Set the Instant Pot to Pressure Cook. 7. Press the Pressure Level button to adjust the pressure to "High". 8. Use the "+/-" keys on the control panel to set the cooking time to 10 minutes. 9. Once the cooking cycle is completed, allow the steam to release naturally. 10. When all the steam is released, remove the pressure lid from the top carefully. 11. Press the "Sauté" button twice to select "Normal" mode. 12. In a small bowl, knead together the remaining 2 tablespoons of butter with the flour until a pasty ball forms. 13. Add to the simmering broth and stir until the paste is dissolved and the gravy is thick, about 5 minutes. 14. Season with salt and pepper as desired.
Per Serving: Calories 33; Fat 7.9g; Sodium 704mg; Carbs 6g; Fiber 3.6g; Sugar 6g; Protein 18g

Cranberry Sauce

Prep time: 20 minutes | Cook time: 15 minutes | Serves: 8

4 cups washed cranberries, fresh or frozen
1 (1-inch) piece ginger, peeled and cut into ⅛-inch slices

½ cup orange juice
Zest from ½ orange
Juice and zest from ½ lemon
1 cup sugar

1. Add the cranberries, ginger, orange juice, orange zest, lemon juice, lemon zest, and sugar to the Instant Pot. 2. Put on the pressure cooker's lid and turn the steam valve to "Sealing" position. 3. Set the Instant Pot to Pressure Cook. 4. Press the Pressure Level button to adjust the pressure to "Low". 5. Use the "+/-" keys on the control panel to set the cooking time to 15 minutes. 6. Once the cooking cycle is completed, allow the steam to release naturally. 7. When all the steam is released, remove the pressure lid from the top carefully. 8. Let cool and remove the ginger if desired. 9. Store the sauce in the refrigerator for up to 3 weeks.
Per Serving: Calories 51; Fat 12.9g; Sodium 414mg; Carbs 11g; Fiber 5g; Sugar 9g; Protein 31g

Apple Butter

Prep time: 20 minutes | Cook time: 30 minutes | Serves: 8

4-pound apples, peeled, cored, and roughly chopped
½ cup apple cider
1 tablespoon lemon juice

1 cup brown sugar
1 teaspoon ground cinnamon
Pinch ground cloves or nutmeg
Pinch kosher salt

1. Add the apples and cider to the Instant Pot. 2. Put on the pressure cooker's lid and turn the steam valve to "Sealing" position. 3. Set the Instant Pot to Pressure Cook. 4. Use the "+/-" keys on the control panel to set the cooking time to 30 minutes. 5. Press the Pressure Level button to adjust the pressure to "High". 6. Once the cooking cycle is completed, allow the steam to release naturally. 7. When all the steam is released, remove the pressure lid from the top carefully. 8. Add the lemon juice, brown sugar, cinnamon, cloves or nutmeg, and salt and stir. 9. Press the "Sauté" button two times to select "Normal" mode and cook for about 30 minutes. 10. Store in an airtight container in the refrigerator for up to a week or in the freezer for up to 3 months.
Per Serving: Calories 79; Fat 10g; Sodium 891mg; Carbs 22.9g; Fiber 4g; Sugar 4g; Protein 33g

Chicken Feet Stock

Prep time: 20 minutes | Cook time: 60 minutes | Serves: 8

1½-pound chicken feet, cleaned and rinsed
8 cups water
2 carrots, cut into chunks

1 onion, quartered
2 stalks celery, cut in half
1 teaspoon black peppercorns
1 bay leaf

1. Put all of the ingredients into the Instant Pot. 2. Put on the pressure cooker's lid and turn the steam valve to "Sealing" position. 3. Set the Instant Pot to Pressure Cook. 4. Press the Pressure Level button to adjust the pressure to "High". 5. Use the "+/-" keys on the control panel to set the cooking time to 60 minutes. 6. Once the cooking cycle is completed, allow the steam to release naturally for 10 minutes and then release the remaining steam manually. 7. When all the steam is released, remove the pressure lid from the top carefully. 8. Strain the stock and pour into jars. Store in the refrigerator or freeze.
Per Serving: Calories 44; Fat 2.2g; Sodium 811mg; Carbs 12g; Fiber 3g; Sugar 8g; Protein 8g

Marinara Sauce

Prep time: 20 minutes | Cook time: 30 minutes | Serves: 8

2 tablespoons olive oil
1 medium onion, grated
1 large carrot, peeled and grated
5 garlic cloves, grated
1 (28-ounce) can crushed tomatoes

with juice
½ teaspoon dried oregano
Pinch sugar
Kosher salt
Black pepper

1. Press the "Sauté" button twice to select "Normal" mode. 2. Once hot, add the oil followed by the onion and carrot. 3. Sauté for 2 minutes until the onion is translucent. Add the garlic and cook for 30 seconds. 4. Add the tomatoes with juice and stir. Add the oregano. 5. Put on the pressure cooker's lid and turn the steam valve to "Sealing" position. 6. Set the Instant Pot to Pressure Cook. 7. Use the "+/-" keys on the control panel to set the cooking time to 30 minutes. 8. Press the Pressure Level button to adjust the pressure to "High". 9. Once the cooking cycle is completed, allow the steam to release naturally. 10. When all the steam is released, remove the pressure lid from the top carefully. 11. Stir and taste for seasoning. Add the sugar, and season with salt and pepper as desired. 12. Store for up to a week in the refrigerator or freezer for several months.
Per Serving: Calories 42; Fat 19g; Sodium 354mg; Carbs 15g; Fiber 5.1g; Sugar 8.2g; Protein 2g

Orange and Lemon Marmalade

Prep time: 20 minutes | Cook time: 14 minutes | Serves: 8

1½-pound sweet oranges
8 oz. lemons, such as Meyer lemons

1 cup water
3-pound sugar

1. Cut the oranges and lemons into ⅛-inch slices. 2. Discard the end pieces that are all peel or pith, and remove the seeds and set aside for use later. Cut the slices into 4 or 5 pieces. 3. Add the fruit and water to the Instant Pot. 4. Put on the pressure cooker's lid and turn the steam valve to "Sealing" position. 5. Set the Instant Pot to Pressure Cook. 6. Use the "+/-" keys on the control panel to set the cooking time to 14 minutes. 7. Press the Pressure Level button to adjust the pressure to "Low". 8. Once the cooking cycle is completed, allow the steam to release naturally. 9. When all the steam is released, remove the pressure lid from the top carefully. 10. Add the sugar and stir until dissolved. 11. Place the seeds in a tea bag or gauze packet, cinch, and place in the mixture. Taste for sweetness. 12. Press the "Sauté" button two times to select "More" mode and boil for about 5 minutes. 13. Pour into clean jars and let them sit at room temperature until totally cooled. 14. Store in jars in the refrigerator for up to 3 weeks or the freezer for several months.
Per Serving: Calories 19; Fat 14g; Sodium 791mg; Carbs 8.9g; Fiber 4.6g; Sugar 8g; Protein 3g

Triple-Berry Jam

Prep time: 20 minutes | Cook time: 11 minutes | Serves: 8

8-ounce fresh strawberries, hulled and halved
8-ounce fresh blueberries
8-ounce fresh raspberries

1 cup sugar
2 teaspoons lemon juice
1 teaspoon grated lemon zest
Up to ¼ cup honey

1. Add the strawberries, blueberries, raspberries, and sugar to the Instant Pot and stir. 2. Let it sit for at least 15 minutes or up to 1 hour. 3. Press the "Sauté" button twice to select "Normal" mode and bring the mixture to a boil for 3 minutes. 4. Put on the pressure cooker's lid and turn the steam valve to "Sealing" position. 5. Set the Instant Pot to Pressure Cook. 6. Use the "+/-" keys on the control panel to set the cooking time to 8 minutes. 7. Press the Pressure Level button to adjust the pressure to "High". 8. Once the cooking cycle is completed, allow the steam to release naturally. 9. When all the steam is released, remove the pressure lid from the top carefully. 10. Remove the lid and Press the "Sauté" button two times to select "Normal" mode. 11. Add the lemon juice and zest. Carefully taste the jam and add honey if needed. 12. Boil for 3 to 4 minutes, stirring frequently, or until the gel point is reached. 13. Select Cancel. Mash the jam if a smoother texture is desired. 14. Carefully transfer to lidded containers, close, and let them cool. 15. The jam could be kept in the refrigerator for up to 3 weeks or the freezer for at least 6 months.
Per Serving: Calories 42; Fat 11g; Sodium 91mg; Carbs 4g; Fiber 3g; Sugar 8g; Protein 3g

Vegetable Broth

Prep time: 20 minutes | Cook time: 40 minutes | Serves: 8

2 medium onions, halved
2 celery stalks with leaves, roughly chopped
2 large carrots, scrubbed and roughly chopped
8-ounce white button or cremini

mushrooms, whole
12 cups water
1 head garlic, halved crosswise
1 bunch parsley stems
2 bay leaves
5 to 7 whole black peppercorns

1. Press the "Sauté" button two time on the Instant pot to select "Normal" settings. 2. Sauté the onions, celery, carrots, and mushrooms for 3 to 5 minutes. 3. Add the water, garlic, parsley, bay leaves, and peppercorns. 4. Put on the pressure cooker's lid and turn the steam valve to "Sealing" position. 5. Set the Instant Pot to Pressure Cook. 6. Use the "+/-" keys on the control panel to set the cooking time to 40 minutes. 7. Press the Pressure Level button to adjust the pressure to "High". 8. Once the cooking cycle is completed, quick-release pressure. 9. When all the steam is released, remove the pressure lid from the top carefully. 10. When the cook time is complete, quick-release the pressure and carefully remove the lid. 11. Strain the broth through a fine-mesh sieve into a large bowl and discard the solids. 12. Store the broth in a covered container in the fridge for up to 4 days or in the freezer for up to 6 months.
Per Serving: Calories 61; Fat 7.9g; Sodium 704mg; Carbs 6g; Fiber 3.6g; Sugar 6g; Protein 18g

Oil-Free Marinara Sauce

Prep time: 20 minutes | Cook time: 12 minutes | Serves: 8

1 medium onion, diced
4 tablespoons water, as needed
4 garlic cloves, minced
1 tablespoon dried basil
1 tablespoon dried oregano
¼ to 1 teaspoon red pepper flakes

2 (28-ounce) cans no-salt-added crushed tomatoes
½ cup Easy Vegetable Broth or no-salt-added vegetable broth
Black pepper
Salt

1. Press the "Sauté" button twice on the Instant pot to select "Normal" settings. 2. Sauté the onion for 1 to 2 minutes, until slightly browned, adding water as needed to prevent sticking. 3. Add the garlic, basil, oregano, and red pepper flakes to taste and stir for 30 seconds, until fragrant. 4. Stir in the tomatoes and broth, scraping up any browned bits from the bottom of the pot. 5. Season to taste with black pepper and salt. 6. Put on the pressure cooker's lid and turn the steam valve to "Sealing" position. 7. Set the Instant Pot to Pressure Cook. 8. Use the "+/-" keys on the control panel to set the cooking time to 12 minutes. 9. Press the Pressure Level button to adjust the pressure to "High". 10. Once the cooking cycle is completed, allow the steam to release naturally. 11. When all the steam is released, remove the pressure lid from the top carefully. 12. Store in a covered container in the fridge for up to 4 weeks or in the freezer for up to 3 months.
Per Serving: Calories 54; Fat 10.9g; Sodium 354mg; Carbs 10.5g; Fiber 4.1g; Sugar 8.2g; Protein 26g

Bolognese Sauce

Prep time: 20 minutes | Cook time: 15 minutes | Serves: 4

½ tablespoon unsalted butter
2 teaspoons garlic, minced
1 carrot, chopped
1 stalk celery, chopped
1 lb. ground beef
1 can pasta sauce

1 tablespoon sugar
½ teaspoon kosher salt
¼ teaspoon black pepper
¼ teaspoon basil, dried
¼ cup half and half cream
⅛ cup parsley, chopped

1. Press the "Sauté" button two times to select "Normal" mode. Once hot, add the butter and melt it. 2. Add the garlic and sauté for 30 seconds. 3. Add the carrots and celery and sauté for 6-8 minutes, or until soft. 4. Add the ground beef and sauté for another 4-5 minutes until browned, stirring occasionally. 5. Add the pasta sauce, sugar, salt, pepper, and basil. Stir well. 6. Put on the pressure cooker's lid and turn the steam valve to "Sealing" position. 7. Set the Instant Pot to Pressure Cook. 8. Press the Pressure Level button to adjust the pressure to "High". 9. Use the "+/-" keys on the control panel to set the cooking time to 15 minutes. 10. Once the cooking cycle is completed, allow the steam to release naturally for 10 minutes, and then release the remaining pressure manually. 11. When all the steam is released, remove the pressure lid from the top carefully. 12. Add the half and half to the pot. Stir to combine. 13. Top with parsley and serve.
Per Serving: Calories 42; Fat 11g; Sodium 91mg; Carbs 4g; Fiber 3g; Sugar 8g; Protein 3g

Fresh Tomato Ketchup

Prep time: 20 minutes | Cook time: 15 minutes | Serves: 8

2-pound plum tomatoes, roughly chopped
5 pitted dates
6 tablespoons distilled white vinegar
1 tablespoon gluten-free vegan Worcestershire sauce
1 tablespoon paprika
1 teaspoon onion powder

1 teaspoon salt
½ teaspoon mustard powder
¼ teaspoon celery seed
¼ teaspoon garlic powder
Pinch of ground cloves
2 tablespoons water
1 tablespoon arrowroot powder or cornstarch

1. In your Instant Pot, combine the tomatoes, dates, vinegar, Worcestershire sauce, paprika, onion powder, salt, mustard powder, celery seed, garlic powder, and cloves. 2. Using a potato masher, mash the tomatoes until they have released much of their liquid. 3. Put on the pressure cooker's lid and turn the steam valve to "Sealing" position. 4. Set the Instant Pot to Pressure Cook. 5. Use the "+/-" keys on the control panel to set the cooking time to 5 minutes. 6. Press the Pressure Level button to adjust the pressure to "High". 7. Once the cooking cycle is completed, quick-release pressure. 8. When all the steam is released, remove the pressure lid from the top carefully. 9. Select the Sauté function and simmer about 10 minutes, until reduced, stirring often. 10. In a small bowl, whisk together the water and arrowroot and add to the simmering ketchup for 2 to 4 minutes. 11. Strain the ketchup through a fine-mesh sieve. 12. Store in the fridge for up to 6 months in a covered container.
Per Serving: Calories 84; Fat 5g; Sodium 41mg; Carbs 7g; Fiber 7.6g; Sugar 5g; Protein 2g

Maple Barbecue Sauce

Prep time: 20 minutes | Cook time: 6 minutes | Serves: 8

2 tablespoons minced onion
2 garlic cloves, minced
1 teaspoon smoked paprika
1 teaspoon ground allspice
1 cup water
1 (15-ounce) can no-salt-added

tomato sauce
¼ cup maple syrup
2 tablespoons stone-ground mustard
2 tablespoons apple cider vinegar
½ teaspoon salt

1. Press the "Sauté" button twice on the Instant pot to select "Normal" settings. Sauté the onion for 2 minutes. 2. Add the garlic, paprika, and allspice and stir for 30 seconds, until fragrant. 3. Stir in the water, scraping up any browned bits from the bottom of the pot. 4. Add the tomato sauce, maple syrup, mustard, vinegar, and salt. Whisk to combine. 5. Put on the pressure cooker's lid and turn the steam valve to "Sealing" position. 6. Set the Instant Pot to Pressure Cook. 7. Press the Pressure Level button to adjust the pressure to "High". 8. Use the "+/-" keys on the control panel to set the cooking time to 4 minutes. 9. Once the cooking cycle is completed, quick-release pressure. 10. When all the steam is released, remove the pressure lid from the top carefully. 11. Store in the refrigerator for up to 4 weeks in a covered container.
Per Serving: Calories 34; Fat 9g; Sodium 354mg; Carbs 5g; Fiber 5.1g; Sugar 8.2g; Protein 2g

Nut-Free Cheese Sauce

Prep time: 20 minutes | Cook time: 7 minutes | Serves: 8

3 medium yellow potatoes, cut into 1-inch chunks
1 large carrot, cut into 1-inch chunks
2 cups water
¼ cup nutritional yeast

2 tablespoons lemon juice
2 teaspoons chickpea miso paste
½ teaspoon onion powder
½ teaspoon garlic powder
½ teaspoon mustard powder
¼ teaspoon ground turmeric

1. In your Instant Pot, combine the potatoes, carrot, and water. 2. Put on the pressure cooker's lid and turn the steam valve to "Sealing" position. 3. Set the Instant Pot to Pressure Cook. 4. Press the Pressure Level button to adjust the pressure to "High". 5. Use the "+/-" keys on the control panel to set the cooking time to 7 minutes. 6. Once the cooking cycle is completed, allow the steam to release naturally for 10 minutes and then quick-release the remaining pressure. 7. When all the steam is released, remove the pressure lid from the top carefully. 8. Using a slotted spoon, remove the potatoes and carrots to a blender, then add ½ cup of the cooking water along with the nutritional yeast, lemon juice, miso, onion powder, garlic powder, mustard powder, and

turmeric. 9. Blend until smooth and creamy, adding more cooking water as necessary to thin. 10. Store in the fridge for up to 4 days in a covered container.
Per Serving: Calories 32; Fat 9g; Sodium 34mg; Carbs 2g; Fiber 5.1g; Sugar 2g; Protein 2g

Applesauce

Prep time: 20 minutes | Cook time: 4 minutes | Serves: 8

3-pound apples, cored, cut into large chunks

⅓ cup water
1 tablespoon lemon juice

1. In your Instant Pot, combine the apples, water, and lemon juice. 2. Put on the pressure cooker's lid and turn the steam valve to "Sealing" position. 3. Set the Instant Pot to Pressure Cook. 4. Press the Pressure Level button to adjust the pressure to "High". 5. Use the "+/-" keys on the control panel to set the cooking time to 4 minutes. 6. Once the cooking cycle is completed, allow the steam to release naturally for 10 minutes and then quick-release the remaining pressure. 7. When all the steam is released, remove the pressure lid from the top carefully. 8. Using a potato masher, mash the apples to your desired chunkiness. 9. Using a pair of tongs or a fork, transfer the apple peels to a deep, narrow container and blend using an immersion blender. 10. Return to the pot and stir to combine. Store in the fridge for up to 4 weeks in a covered container.
Per Serving: Calories 34; Fat 19g; Sodium 354mg; Carbs 25g; Fiber 5.1g; Sugar 8.2g; Protein 2g

Fish Stock

Prep time: 20 minutes | Cook time: 45 minutes | Serves: 10

2 salmon heads, large-sized, cut into quarters
1 tablespoon olive oil
2 lemongrass stalks, roughly chopped
1 cup carrots, roughly chopped

1 cup celery, roughly chopped
2 cloves garlic, sliced
Handful fresh thyme, including stems
Water as needed

1. Wash the fish heads and pat them dry. 2. Press the "Sauté" button two times to select "Normal" mode. Add and heat the oil. 3. Add the salmon heads and lightly sear the fish on both sides. 4. Put all of the ingredients into the Instant Pot and pour the water to cover mix. 5. Put on the pressure cooker's lid and turn the steam valve to "Sealing" position. 6. Set your Instant Pot to Soup/Broth. 7. Use the "+/-" keys on the control panel to set the cooking time to 45 minutes. 8. Press the Pressure Level button to adjust the pressure to "High". 9. Once the cooking cycle is completed, allow the steam to release naturally for 15 minutes and then release the remaining pressure manually. 10. When all the steam is released, remove the pressure lid from the top carefully. 11. Strain the stock and pour into jars. Store in the refrigerator or freeze.
Per Serving: Calories 72; Fat 9g; Sodium 354mg; Carbs 2g; Fiber 5.1g; Sugar 8.2g; Protein 2g

Bone Broth

Prep time: 20 minutes | Cook time: 120 minutes | Serves: 8

2-3-pound bones (2-3-pound beef, lamb, pork, or 1 carcass of chicken)
½ onion
3 carrots, cut into large chunks
2 stalks celery, cut into large

chunks
Fresh herbs
1 teaspoon sea salt
1-2 tablespoon apple cider vinegar
Water as needed

1. Add the bones to the Instant Pot. Add all of the veggies, herbs, salt and vinegar. 2. Pour in the water to fill the pot 2/3 full. 3. Put on the pressure cooker's lid and turn the steam valve to "Sealing" position. 4. Press the "Soup" button one time to select "Less" option. 5. Use the "+/-" keys on the control panel to set the cooking time to 120 minutes. 6. Once the cooking cycle is completed, allow the steam to release naturally. 7. When all the steam is released, remove the pressure lid from the top carefully. 8. Strain the broth and pour into jars. Store in the refrigerator or freeze.
Per Serving: Calories 79; Fat 10g; Sodium 891mg; Carbs 2.9g; Fiber 4g; Sugar 4g; Protein 3g

Pork Broth

Prep time: 20 minutes | Cook time: 60 minutes | Serves: 8

3-pound pork bones	1 bay leaf
8 cups water	2 cloves garlic, sliced
3 large carrots, cut into large chunks	1 tablespoon apple cider vinegar
3 large stalks celery, cut into large chunks	1 teaspoon whole peppercorns
	Salt to taste

1. Dump all of the ingredients into the Instant Pot and give it a little stir to mix everything evenly. 2. Put on the pressure cooker's lid and turn the steam valve to "Sealing" position. 3. Set the Instant Pot to Pressure Cook. 4. Use the "+/-" keys on the control panel to set the cooking time to 60 minutes. 5. Press the Pressure Level button to adjust the pressure to "High". 6. Once the cooking cycle is completed, allow the steam to release naturally. 7. When all the steam is released, remove the pressure lid from the top carefully. 8. Strain the broth and pour into jars. Store in the refrigerator or freeze.
Per Serving: Calories 61; Fat 7.9g; Sodium 704mg; Carbs 6g; Fiber 3.6g; Sugar 6g; Protein 18g

Chicken Stock

Prep time: 20 minutes | Cook time: 60 minutes | Serves: 8

1 chicken carcass	2 bay leaves
10 cups water	2 tablespoons apple cider vinegar
1 onion, quartered	1 sprig thyme
2 large carrots, cut into chunks	Salt to taste
12 whole pieces' peppercorns	

1. Put all of the ingredients into the Instant Pot. 2. Put on the pressure cooker's lid and turn the steam valve to "Sealing" position. 3. Set the Instant Pot to Pressure Cook. 4. Press the Pressure Level button to adjust the pressure to "High". 5. Use the "+/-" keys on the control panel to set the cooking time to 60 minutes. 6. Once the cooking cycle is completed, allow the steam to release naturally. 7. When all the steam is released, remove the pressure lid from the top carefully. 8. Season with salt to taste. Strain the stock and pour into jars. 9. Store in the refrigerator or freeze.
Per Serving: Calories 84; Fat 5g; Sodium 41mg; Carbs 7g; Fiber 7.6g; Sugar 5g; Protein 2g

Cranberry Apple Sauce

Prep time: 20 minutes | Cook time: 5 minutes | Serves: 2

1-2 apples, peeled, cored, and then cut into chunks	1 teaspoon cinnamon
10-ounce cranberries, frozen or fresh, preferably organic	½ cup maple syrup or honey
	¼ cup lemon juice
	¼ teaspoon sea salt

1. Combine all of the ingredients in the Instant Pot. 2. Put on the pressure cooker's lid and turn the steam valve to "Sealing" position. 3. Set the Instant Pot to Pressure Cook. 4. Use the "+/-" keys on the control panel to set the cooking time to 1 minute. 5. Press the Pressure Level button to adjust the pressure to "High". 6. Once the cooking cycle is completed, allow the steam to release naturally for 15 minutes and then release the remaining pressure manually. 7. When all the steam is released, remove the pressure lid from the top carefully. 8. Using a wooden spoon, mash the fruit a bit. 9. Press the "Sauté" button twice to select "Normal" mode and simmer for 1-2 minutes to evaporate some water, stirring occasionally. 10. Once the sauce begins to thicken, press the CANCEL key to stop the SAUTÉ function. 11. Pour into clean jars and refrigerate.
Per Serving: Calories 82; Fat 10.9g; Sodium 454mg; Carbs 10g; Fiber 3.1g; Sugar 5.2g; Protein 05g

Vegan Alfredo Sauce

Prep time: 20 minutes | Cook time: 3 minutes | Serves: 8

1½ tablespoons olive oil	2 cups asparagus
10 cloves garlic, minced	6 cups vegetable broth
¾ cup raw cashews	½ teaspoon salt
6 cups cauliflower florets	

1. Press the "Sauté" button twice to select "Normal" mode. and heat the oil. 2. Add the garlic and sauté for 1-2 minutes, until fragrant. 3. Add the cashews, cauliflower, asparagus, and broth. Press Cancel to stop heating. 4. Put on the pressure cooker's lid and turn the steam valve to "Sealing" position. 5. Set the Instant Pot to Pressure Cook. 6. Press the Pressure Level button to adjust the pressure to "High". 7. Use the "+/-" keys on the control panel to set the cooking time to 3 minutes. 8. Once the cooking cycle is completed, quick-release steam. 9. When all the steam is released, remove the pressure lid from the top carefully. 10. Transfer to a blender. Season with salt and blend until smooth. 11. Serve with pasta or brow rice.
Per Serving: Calories 84; Fat 5g; Sodium 41mg; Carbs 7g; Fiber 7.6g; Sugar 5g; Protein 2g

Chili Sauce

Prep time: 15 minutes | Cook time: 8 minutes | Serves: 4

4 medium-sized Ancho chili peppers	1½ teaspoons sugar
½ teaspoon cumin, ground	1½ cups water
½ teaspoon dried oregano, ground	2 tablespoon apple cider vinegar
2 teaspoons kosher salt	2 cloves garlic, crushed
	2 tablespoons heavy cream

1. Cut the peppers in half and remove the stems and seeds. Chop into small pieces. 2. Add the peppers, cumin, oregano, salt, and sugar to the Instant Pot. 3. Pour in the water and stir well. 4. Put on the pressure cooker's lid and turn the steam valve to "Sealing" position. 5. Set the Instant Pot to Pressure Cook. 6. Use the "+/-" keys on the control panel to set the cooking time to 8 minutes. 7. Press the Pressure Level button to adjust the pressure to "High". 8. Once the cooking cycle is completed, allow the steam to release naturally for 10 minutes and then release the remaining pressure manually. 9. When all the steam is released, remove the pressure lid from the top carefully. 10. Transfer the mixture to a food processor. 11. Add the vinegar, garlic, and heavy cream. Pulse until smooth and creamy. 12. Serve.
Per Serving: Calories 78; Fat 7.9g; Sodium 704mg; Carbs 6g; Fiber 3.6g; Sugar 6g; Protein 18g

Hot Pepper Sauce

Prep time: 20 minutes | Cook time: 2 minutes | Serves: 8

12 to 16-ounce fresh hot red peppers, stems removed, halved	¼ cup apple cider vinegar
1 cup distilled white vinegar	3 garlic cloves, smashed

1. In your Instant Pot, stir together the peppers, white vinegar, cider vinegar, and garlic. 2. Put on the pressure cooker's lid and turn the steam valve to "Sealing" position. 3. Set the Instant Pot to Pressure Cook. 4. Use the "+/-" keys on the control panel to set the cooking time to 2 minutes. 5. Press the Pressure Level button to adjust the pressure to "High". 6. Once the cooking cycle is completed, allow the steam to release naturally. 7. When all the steam is released, remove the pressure lid from the top carefully. 8. Using an immersion blender, food processor, or blender, blend the sauce until smooth. 9. Strain through a fine-mesh sieve and store in glass bottles or jars at room temperature for up to 6 months.
Per Serving: Calories 78; Fat 10.9g; Sodium 454mg; Carbs 10g; Fiber 3.1g; Sugar 5.2g; Protein 05g

Mushroom Gravy Sauce

Prep time: 20 minutes | Cook time: 3 minutes | Serves: 8

2 tablespoon butter	2 tablespoon flour
¼ cup shallots, chopped	¼ cup half and half
1 package button mushrooms, sliced	Salt to taste
2 cups beef broth	½ teaspoon black pepper

1. Press the "Sauté" button twice to select "Normal" mode 2. Once hot, add the butter and melt it. 3. Add the shallots and mushrooms. Cook until fragrant. 4. Whisk in the broth and flour. Whisk until smooth. 5. Simmer the mixture for 5 minutes. 6. Pour in half and half, stir well. Season with salt and pepper. 7. Put on the pressure cooker's lid and turn the steam valve to "Sealing" position. 8. Set the Instant Pot to Pressure Cook. 9. Use the "+/-" keys on the control panel to set the cooking time to 3 minutes. 10. Press the Pressure Level button to adjust the pressure to "High". 11. Once the cooking cycle is completed, allow the steam to release naturally for 10 minutes and then release the remaining pressure manually. 12. When all the steam is released, remove the pressure lid from the top carefully. 13. Serve.
Per Serving: Calories 72; Fat 10g; Sodium 891mg; Carbs 22.9g; Fiber 4g; Sugar 4g; Protein 3g

Tomato Basil Sauce

Prep time: 20 minutes | Cook time: 15 minutes | Serves: 4

1 tablespoon olive oil
3 cloves garlic, minced
2½-pound Roma tomatoes, diced

½ cup chopped basil
¼ cup vegetable broth
Salt to taste

1. Press the "Sauté" button twice to select "Normal" mode on the Instant Pot and heat the oil. 2. Add the garlic and sauté for 1 minute. 3. Add the tomatoes, basil, and broth. Mix well. 4. Put on the pressure cooker's lid and turn the steam valve to "Sealing" position. 5. Set the Instant Pot to Pressure Cook. 6. Use the "+/-" keys on the control panel to set the cooking time to 10 minutes. 7. Press the Pressure Level button to adjust the pressure to "High". 8. Once the cooking cycle is completed, quick-release steam. 9. When all the steam is released, remove the pressure lid from the top carefully. 10. Press the "Sauté" button twice to select "Normal" mode again and cook for 5 minutes more. Turn off heat. 11. Using an immersion blender, blend until smooth. 12. Taste and season with salt if necessary. Serve.
Per Serving: Calories 79; Fat 10g; Sodium 891mg; Carbs 22.9g; Fiber 4g; Sugar 4g; Protein 3g

Homemade Salsa

Prep time: 20 minutes | Cook time: 30 minutes | Serves: 8

6 cups fresh tomatoes, diced, peeled and seeded
1½ green bell peppers, diced
2 yellow onions, diced
1 cup jalapeno peppers, seeded and chopped

1½ cans (6-ounce) tomato paste
¼ cup vinegar
1½ tablespoon sugar
½ tablespoon kosher salt
1 tablespoon garlic powder
1 tablespoon cayenne pepper

1. Put all of the ingredients into the Instant Pot. Stir well to combine. 2. Put on the pressure cooker's lid and turn the steam valve to "Sealing" position. 3. Set the Instant Pot to Pressure Cook. 4. Press the Pressure Level button to adjust the pressure to "High". 5. Use the "+/-" keys on the control panel to set the cooking time to 30 minutes. 6. Once the cooking cycle is completed, allow the steam to release naturally for 10 minutes and then release the remaining pressure manually. 7. When all the steam is released, remove the pressure lid from the top carefully. 8. Serve warm or cool.
Per Serving: Calories 34; Fat 10.9g; Sodium 354mg; Carbs 10.5g; Fiber 4.1g; Sugar 8.2g; Protein 26g

Strawberry Compote

Prep time: 20 minutes | Cook time: 4 minutes | Serves: 8

4 cups frozen strawberries
¼ cup sugar

1 tablespoon lemon juice

1. In your Instant Pot, combine the strawberries, sugar, and lemon juice. Stir to coat the berries. 2. Put on the pressure cooker's lid and turn the steam valve to "Sealing" position. 3. Set the Instant Pot to Pressure Cook. 4. Press the Pressure Level button to adjust the pressure to "High". 5. Use the "+/-" keys on the control panel to set the cooking time to 4 minutes. 6. Once the cooking cycle is completed, allow the steam to release naturally for 10 minutes and then quick-release the remaining pressure. 7. When all the steam is released, remove the pressure lid from the top carefully. 8. Using a potato masher, mash the berries until they are broken down completely. 9. Pour into a container and chill. The compote will thicken as it cools. 10. Store in the fridge for up to 4 weeks in a covered container.
Per Serving: Calories 42; Fat 11g; Sodium 91mg; Carbs 4g; Fiber 3g; Sugar 8g; Protein 3g

Caramel Sauce

Prep time: 20 minutes | Cook time: 15 minutes | Serves: 4

1 cup sugar
⅓ cup water
3 tablespoon coconut oil

⅓ cup condensed coconut milk
1 teaspoon vanilla extract

1. Press the "Sauté" button twice to select "Normal" mode. 2. In the Instant Pot, combine the sugar and water. Cook for 12 minutes. 3. Add the coconut oil, milk, and vanilla. Stir well. 4. Cook, stirring occasionally, until the mixture is smooth. 5. Press the CANCEL key to stop the SAUTÉ function. 6. Transfer to a heatproof container. 7. Let it cool and serve.
Per Serving: Calories 7; Fat 10g; Sodium 891mg; Carbs 22.9g; Fiber 4g; Sugar 4g; Protein 3g

White Sauce

Prep time: 15 minutes | Cook time: 3 minutes | Serves: 8

12-ounce cauliflower florets
2 tablespoons almond milk
¼ teaspoon garlic salt

½ cup water
¼ teaspoon pepper

1. In the Instant Pot, combine the cauliflower florets, garlic salt, pepper, and water. 2. Put on the pressure cooker's lid and turn the steam valve to "Sealing" position. 3. Set the Instant Pot to Pressure Cook. 4. Use the "+/-" keys on the control panel to set the cooking time to 3 minutes. 5. Press the Pressure Level button to adjust the pressure to "High". 6. Once the cooking cycle is completed, quick-release the steam. 7. When all the steam is released, remove the pressure lid from the top carefully. 8. Using an immersion blender, blend until smooth. 9. Pour in the almond milk and mix well. 10. Serve.
Per Serving: Calories 84; Fat 5g; Sodium 41mg; Carbs 7g; Fiber 7.6g; Sugar 5g; Protein 2g

Strawberry Applesauce

Prep time: 15 minutes | Cook time: 5 minutes | Serves: 6

8 peeled apples, cored and sliced
3 cups strawberries, hulled and chopped

2 tablespoons lemon juice
¼ teaspoon cinnamon powder
2 tablespoons sugar

1. Combine all of the ingredients in the Instant Pot and stir to mix. 2. Put on the pressure cooker's lid and turn the steam valve to "Sealing" position. 3. Set the Instant Pot to Pressure Cook. 4. Press the Pressure Level button to adjust the pressure to "High". 5. Use the "+/-" keys on the control panel to set the cooking time to 5 minutes. 6. Once the cooking cycle is completed, allow the steam to release naturally for 15 minutes and then release the remaining pressure manually. 7. When all the steam is released, remove the pressure lid from the top carefully. 8. Use a potato masher to mash the mixture and get the consistency you like.
Per Serving: Calories 32; Fat 2.9g; Sodium 41mg; Carbs 11g; Fiber 5g; Sugar 9g; Protein 31g

Tabasco Sauce

Prep time: 20 minutes | Cook time: 1 minutes | Serves: 8

18-ounce fresh hot peppers or any kind, stems removed, chopped

3 teaspoon smoked or plain salt
1¾ cups apple cider

1. Combine all of the ingredients in the Instant Pot. 2. Put on the pressure cooker's lid and turn the steam valve to "Sealing" position. 3. Set the Instant Pot to Pressure Cook. 4. Press the Pressure Level button to adjust the pressure to "High". 5. Use the "+/-" keys on the control panel to set the cooking time to 1 minute. 6. Once the cooking cycle is completed, allow the steam to release naturally for 15 minutes and then release the remaining pressure manually. 7. When all the steam is released, remove the pressure lid from the top carefully. 8. Using an immersion blender, puree the mixture. 9. Pour into clean and sterilized bottles and refrigerate.
Per Serving: Calories 51; Fat 10.9g; Sodium 354mg; Carbs 10.5g; Fiber 4.1g; Sugar 8.2g; Protein 6g

Chapter 10 Meat Mains Recipes

Chops of Pork

Prep Time: 15 minutes | Cook Time: 5 minutes | Serves: 4

½ cup all-purpose flour, divided
½ tsp. ground mustard
½ tsp. garlic-pepper blend
¼ tsp. seasoned salt
4 boneless pork loin chops (4 oz.

each)
2 Tbsp. canola oil
1 can (14½ oz.) chicken broth, divided

1. ¼ cup flour, mustard, garlic pepper, and seasoned salt should be combined in a small bowl. Shake off excess after each addition of 1 pork chop and toss to coat. 2. Use the sauté or browning mode. Add canola oil. Brown the pork in batches once the oil is heated. To pot, add 1½ cups of broth. Cook for 30 seconds, stirring to loosen browned bits from pan. 3. Secure the lid and close the pressure-release valve. Adjust to Pressure Cook on high for 3 minutes. Rapidly release pressure on vent position. Pork should register a temperature of at least 145°F/60°C on a thermometer. Select Cancel. Remove pork to serving plate and keep warm. 4. Stir remaining ¼ cup flour and ¼ cup broth into Instant Pot after thoroughly combining in a small bowl. Choose the sauté option. Simmer for 1-2 minutes while stirring often to achieve thickening. Serve with pork.
Per Serving: Calories 257; Fat: 14g; Sodium 774mg; Carbs: 8g; Sugars: 3.03g; Protein 23g

Ragout of Mushroom Pork

Prep Time: 20 minutes | Cook Time: 10 minutes | Serves: 2

1 pork tenderloin (¾ lb.)
⅛ tsp. salt
⅛ tsp. pepper
1½ cups sliced fresh mushrooms
¾ cup canned crushed tomatoes
¾ cup reduced-sodium chicken broth, divided

⅓ cup sliced onion
1 Tbsp. chopped sun-dried tomatoes (not packed in oil)
1¼ tsp. dried savory
1 Tbsp. cornstarch
1½ cups hot cooked egg noodles

1. Salt and pepper the pork, then chop it in half. Put the ingredients in pot. Add savory, onion, sun-dried tomatoes, mushrooms, tomatoes, and ½ cup broth to the top. 2. Close the pressure-release valve and lock the lid. Set to Pressure Cook for 6 minutes on high. Rapidly release pressure on vent position. Pork should register a temperature of at least 145°F/60°C on a thermometer. Select Cancel. 3. To keep warm, remove the meat. Stir the cornstarch and remaining broth into the Instant Pot after thoroughly blending them in a small dish. Choose the sauté option. Simmer for 1-2 minutes while stirring often to achieve thickening. Sliced pork is served with noodles and sauce.
Per Serving: Calories 387; Fat: 8g; Sodium 404mg; Carbs: 37g; Sugars: 8g; Protein 43g

Chops of Pork and Acorn Squash

Prep Time: 15 minutes | Cook Time: 5 minutes | Serves: 6

6 boneless pork loin chops (4 oz. each)
2 medium acorn squash, halved lengthwise, seeded and sliced
½ cup packed brown sugar
½ cup reduced-sodium chicken

broth
2 Tbsp. butter, melted
1 Tbsp. orange juice
¾ tsp. salt
¾ tsp. browning sauce, optional
½ tsp. grated orange zest

Squash and pork chops should be placed in pot. Pour over squash before combining the remaining ingredients in a small dish. Close the pressure-release valve and lock the lid. Set to Pressure Cook for 4 minutes on high. Rapidly release pressure on vent position. Pork should register a temperature of at least 145°F/60°C on a thermometer.
Per Serving: Calories 350; Fat: 11g; Sodium 777mg; Carbs: 42.87g; Sugars: 23g; Protein 824g

Tasty Pork and Squash Ragu

Prep Time: 20 minutes | Cook Time: 15 minutes | Serves: 10

2 cans (14½ oz. each) stewed tomatoes, undrained
1 pkg. (12 oz.) frozen cooked winter squash, thawed
1 large sweet onion, cut into ½-in. pieces
1 medium sweet red pepper, cut into ½-in. pieces

¾ cup reduced-sodium chicken broth
1 ½ tsp. crushed red pepper flakes
2 lbs. boneless country-style pork ribs
1 tsp. salt
¼ tsp. garlic powder
¼ tsp. pepper

Hot cooked pasta
Shaved Parmesan cheese, optional

1. In Instant pot, combine the first six ingredients. Place ribs in Instant Pot after seasoning with salt, pepper, and garlic powder. Close the pressure-release valve and lock the lid. Adjust to Pressure Cook on high for 15 minutes. Allow any leftover pressure to naturally relax for ten minutes on seal position before quick-release it on vent position. 2. Take off the lid and stir the meat to break it up. accompanied by spaghetti. Add Parmesan cheese on top.
Per Serving: Calories 196; Fat: 8g; Sodium 804mg; Carbs: 13g; Sugars: 6g; Protein 18.39g

Pork with Apple and Curry

Prep Time: 15 minutes | Cook Time: 10 minutes | Serves: 8

2 lbs. boneless pork loin roast, cut into 1-in. cubes
1 small onion, chopped
½ cup orange juice
1 Tbsp. curry powder
1 tsp. chicken bouillon granules
1 garlic clove, minced
½ tsp. salt
½ tsp. ground ginger

¼ tsp. ground cinnamon
1 medium apple, peeled and chopped
2 tbsp. cornstarch
2 tbsp. cold water
Hot cooked rice, optional
¼ cup raisins
¼ cup sweetened shredded coconut, toasted

1. Combine the first nine ingredients in an instant pot. Close the pressure-release valve and lock the lid. Set to Pressure Cook for 3 minutes on high. Release the pressure quickly on vent position. Pork should register a temperature of at least 145°F/60°C on a thermometer. Select Cancel. 2. To the Instant Pot, add apple. Cornstarch and water should be blended in a small bowl before adding to the Instant Pot. Choose the sauté option and lower the heat. Cook for 3 to 5 minutes, stirring often, until thickened and apple is soft. 3. You can add rice if you'd like. Add some coconut and raisins as garnish.
Per Serving: Calories 174; Fat: 6g; Sodium 404mg; Carbs: 8g; Sugars: 4g; Protein 22g

Beef Stew

Prep Time: 5 minutes | Cook Time: 60 minutes | Serves: 4

3 pounds beef stew meat or chuck cubes
Kosher salt and black pepper, to season beef (1–2 teaspoons of each)
3 tablespoons extra-virgin olive oil
5 tablespoons salted butter, divided
1 large yellow onion, diced
1-pound baby bella mushrooms, sliced
3 cloves garlic, minced or pressed
¼ cup dry white wine (like a sauvignon blanc)
1 tablespoon Dijon mustard

1 teaspoon seasoned salt
1½ cups beef broth
1 teaspoon dried thyme
4 tablespoons cornstarch
1 packet dry onion soup/dip mix
1 cup sour cream
1 (5.2-ounce) package Boursin spread (any flavor) or 4 ounces cream cheese, cut into chunky cubes
1 (12-ounce) package wide egg noodles, prepared separately according to package directions

1. Black pepper and kosher salt should be thoroughly rubbed into the meat.
2. Hit Sauté after adding 2 tablespoons of butter and olive oil to the Instant Pot. After adding butter melt it, sauté the beef for two to three minutes in melte4d butter, until it is gently browned on both sides. With a slotted spoon, remove the meat and set it aside. 3. The onion should start to soften after 2 minutes of cooking in the saucepan with the remaining 3 tablespoons of butter and the onion. For three more minutes, add the mushrooms. After one more minute, add the garlic. After adding the white wine and scraping off any browned pieces from the pan's bottom, add the Dijon mustard and seasoned salt and mix thoroughly. 4. Place the meat chunks in the sauce, then add the beef broth and thyme. 5. Put the lid on tightly, turn the valve to the seal position, and then press Pressure Cook. Cook for 20 minutes at high pressure. After finishing, let a fast release on vent position after a 10-minute natural release on seal position. 6. Construct a slurry by mixing 4 tablespoons of cold water with the cornstarch in the meantime. Place aside. 7. Press Sauté. Stir the cornstarch slurry in after bringing the saucepan to a simmer. Before switching the pot to the Keep Warm setting, add the package of onion soup and allow it to boil for 30 seconds. 8. Stir in the sour cream and Boursin (or cream cheese) until combined after the bubbles have mostly disappeared. 9. Serve over egg noodles.
Per Serving: Calories 1397; Fat: 41g; Sodium 2589mg; Carbs: 170g; Sugars: 4g; Protein 99g

Sugar-Cherry Pork Chops

Prep Time: 15 minutes | Cook Time: 5 minutes | Serves: 4

1 cup fresh or frozen pitted tart cherries, thawed	1 tsp. seasoned salt
1 cup reduced-sodium chicken broth	½ tsp. pepper
¼ cup chopped sweet onion	4 boneless pork loin chops (5 oz. each)
2 Tbsp. honey	1 tbsp. cornstarch
	1 tbsp. cold water

1. Combine the first six ingredients in an Instant Pot, then add the pork chops. Close the pressure-release valve and lock the lid. Set to Pressure Cook for 3 minutes on high. Rapidly release pressure on vent position. Pork should register a temperature of at least 145°F/60°C on a thermometer. Select Cancel. 2. Transfer the pork to a serving dish and keep it heated. Cornstarch and water should be smoothly combined in a small bowl before being added to the Instant Pot. Choose the sauté option and lower the heat. Simmer for 1-2 minutes while stirring often to achieve thickening. Serve alongside pork.
Per Serving: Calories 260; Fat: 8g; Sodium 664mg; Carbs: 17g; Sugars: 14g; Protein 29g

Roasted Teriyaki Pork

Prep Time: 10 minutes | Cook Time: 30 minutes | Serves: 10

¾ cup unsweetened apple juice	⅛ tsp. pepper
2 Tbsp. sugar	1 boneless pork loin roast (about 3 lbs.), halved
2 Tbsp. reduced-sodium soy sauce	8 tsp. cornstarch
1 Tbsp. white vinegar	3 Tbsp. cold water
1 tsp. ground ginger	
¼ tsp. garlic powder	

1. In the Instant Pot, combine the first 7 ingredients. Add roast and turn to coat. Close the pressure-release valve and lock the lid. Adapt to pressure-cook for 25 minutes on high. Allow any leftover pressure to naturally relax for ten minutes on seal position before quick-releasing it on vent position. Pork should register a temperature of at least 145°F/60°C on a thermometer. Select Cancel. 2. Transfer the pork to a serving dish and keep warm. Stir the cornstarch and water together until thoroughly combined before adding to the Instant pot. Choose the sauté option and lower the heat. Simmer for 1-2 minutes while stirring often to achieve thickening. With the meat, serve.
Per Serving: Calories 198; Fat: 6g; Sodium 999mg; Carbs: 7g; Sugars: 4g; Protein 27g

Tasty Satay Pork with Rice Noodles

Prep Time: 20 minutes | Cook Time: 5 minutes | Serves: 6

1½ lbs. boneless pork loin chops, cut into 2-in. pieces	½ tsp. hot pepper sauce
¼ tsp. pepper	1 can (14½ oz.) reduced-sodium chicken broth, divided
1 medium onion, halved and sliced	3 tbsp. cornstarch
⅓ cup creamy peanut butter	9 oz. uncooked thick rice noodles
¼ cup reduced-sodium soy sauce	Optional: Minced fresh cilantro and chopped peanuts
½ tsp. onion powder	
½ tsp. garlic powder	

1. Add pepper to the meat. Place in Instant pot; add onion. Combine peanut butter, soy sauce, onion, garlic, and pepper sauce in a small bowl. Add 1½ cups broth gradually. Add over onion. 2. Close the pressure-release valve and lock the lid. Set to Pressure Cook for 3 minutes on high. Rapidly release pressure on vent position. Pork should register a temperature of at least 145°F/60°C on a thermometer. Select Cancel. Keep warm after removing the pork chops from the Instant Pot. 3. Stir remaining ¼ cup of the broth and cornstarch together in a small dish before adding to the pot. Choose the sauté option and lower the heat. Simmer for 1-2 minutes while stirring often to achieve thickening. Sauté the meat until done. 4. Rice noodles should be prepared as directed on the box while waiting. With the pork combination, serve.
Per Serving: Calories 427; Fat: 14g; Sodium 444mg; Carbs: 44g; Sugars: 3g; Protein 29g

Easy Pork Tacos With Mango Salsa

Prep Time: 25 minutes | Cook Time: 5 minutes | Serves: 12

2 tbsp. white vinegar	1 small red onion, coarsely chopped
2 tbsp. lime juice	3 tbsp. chili powder
3 cups cubed fresh pineapple	

2 chipotle peppers in adobo sauce	cubes
2 tsp. ground cumin	¼ cup chopped fresh cilantro
1½ tsp. salt	1 jar (16 oz.) mango salsa
½ tsp. pepper	24 corn tortillas (6 in.), warmed
1 bottle (12 oz.) dark Mexican beer	Optional toppings: Cubed fresh pineapple, cubed avocado and queso fresco
3 lbs. pork tenderloin, cut into 1-in.	

1. Blend the first nine ingredients until smooth; add the beer there after. Pork and pineapple combination should be combined in pot. Close the pressure-release valve and lock the lid. Set to Pressure Cook for 3 minutes on high. Rapidly release pressure on vent position. Pork should register a temperature of at least 145°F/60°C on a thermometer. Stir to disperse the pork. 2. Salsa will now have cilantro. Serve the pork mixture in tortillas using a slotted spoon; top with salsa and other ingredients as desired.
Per Serving: Calories 282; Fat: 6g; Sodium 695mg; Carbs: 30g; Sugars: 5.03g; Protein 26.39g

Pork with Apples

Prep Time: 20 minutes | Cook Time: 35 minutes | Serves: 10

1 boneless pork loin roast (3 to 4 lbs.)	apple juice
2 tbsp. all-purpose flour	2 medium onions, halved and thinly sliced
1 tbsp. herbes de Provence	1 cup beef stock
1½ tsp. salt	2 bay leaves
¾ tsp. pepper	2 large tart apples, peeled and chopped
2 tbsp. olive oil	1 cup pitted dried plums
1 cup apple cider or unsweetened	

1. Halve the roast. Rub pork with a mixture of flour, herbes de Provence, salt, and pepper. Use the sauté option. Add 1 tbsp. oil and adjust for medium heat. Cook a roast half on all sides in heated oil. Repeat with the remaining pork and oil after removal. 2. To the Pot, add cider. Stirring to release browned parts from the pan, cook for 1 minute. Select Cancel. Roast after adding onions, stock, and bay leaves. 3. Close the pressure-release valve and lock the lid. Set to Pressure Cook for 25 minutes on high. Allow any leftover pressure to naturally relax for ten minutes on seal position before quick-release it on vent position. Pork should register a temperature of at least 145°F/60°C on a thermometer. Select Cancel. Discard the bay leaves and transfer the roast and onions to a serving plate while covering with foil. 4. Select sauté setting and adjust for low heat. Add apples and plums; simmer, uncovered, until the apples are tender, 6-8 minutes, stirring occasionally. Serve with roast.
Per Serving: Calories 286; Fat: 9.17g; Sodium 554mg; Carbs: 22g; Sugars: 13g; Protein 28.39g

Pulled Pork in Hawaii

Prep Time: 15 minutes | Cook Time: 95 minutes | Serves: 10

1 (5-pound) bone-in pork butt or shoulder	1 teaspoon ground cumin
Dry Rub	Sauce
½ teaspoon ground ginger	1 (8-ounce) can crushed pineapple
½ teaspoon celery seed	¼ cup soy sauce
½ teaspoon cayenne pepper	¼ cup tomato sauce
1 teaspoon garlic powder	¼ cup pure maple syrup
1 teaspoon sea salt	1 tablespoon rice wine
1 teaspoon onion powder	3 cloves garlic, peeled and halved
	1 tablespoon grated fresh ginger

1. paper towels, dry the pork butt and set it aside. 2. Mix the ingredients for the dry rub in a small dish. Rub the pork on all sides with the rub. Covered refrigeration is recommended for up to overnight. 3. In a small saucepan, combine the ingredients for the sauce. Up to a boil. Once the sauce has reduced by a quarter and begun to thicken, turn the heat down and let it simmer for 10 minutes. Allow to cool for five minutes. Pulse till smooth in a food processor after adding. 4. Put the pork butt in the Instant Pot and cover it with sauce. Lock the lid. 5. Set the timer to 85 minutes and press the Pressure Cook button. When the timer sounds, open the lid after allowing the pressure to release naturally until the float valve lowers. Make sure the pork can be easily pulled apart. If not, select Sauté and cook without a lid for an extra ten minutes. 6. Pull the pork apart with two forks while the meat is still in the Instant Pot. Get rid of the bone. In the Instant Pot, stir the sauce and the meat. Use a slotted spoon for serving.
Per Serving: Calories 872; Fat: 36.17g; Sodium 504mg; Carbs: 85g; Sugars: 83g; Protein 48.39g

Drunken Chuck Roast

Prep Time: 15 minutes | Cook Time: 65 minutes | Serves: 8

2 tablespoons Dijon mustard	1 cup beef broth
1 teaspoon sea salt	2 teaspoons Worcestershire sauce
½ teaspoon ground black pepper	1 medium yellow onion, peeled
1 teaspoon smoked paprika	and diced
1 (3-pound) boneless chuck roast	2 large carrots, peeled and diced
1 tablespoon olive oil	1 small stalk celery, diced
1 (12-ounce) bottle dark lager	2 cups sliced mushrooms
2 tablespoons tomato paste	

1. Combine the mustard, paprika, salt, and pepper in a small bowl. The mustard mixture should be applied to the meat on both sides. 2. Select Sauté. Heat oil. Meat needs roughly 5 minutes to be seared on both sides. Remove and keep the meat. 3. Pour in the beer and use the Instant Pot to deglaze it by swirling and scraping any browned pieces from the bottom and sides. 4. The tomato paste is whisked in. Refill the saucepan with the stock, Worcestershire sauce, onion, carrots, celery, and mushrooms before adding the meat back in. Lock lid. 5. Set the timer to 60 minutes by pressing the Pressure Cook button. When the timer sounds, open the lid after allowing the pressure to naturally dissipate on seal position until the float valve lowers. 6. Put the meat on a serving dish after removal. Allow to rest for five minutes. Slice. If desired, use an immersion blender to purée the juices in the Instant Pot. Pour juices over the sliced meat. Serve warm.

Per Serving: Calories 264; Fat: 12g; Sodium 824mg; Carbs: 2.87g; Sugars: 2g; Protein 33g

Taco Filling Made with Grilled Flank Steak

Prep Time: 10 minutes | Cook Time: 45 minutes | Serves: 4

¼ cup ketchup	¼ teaspoon ground black pepper
¼ cup apricot preserves	1 (2-pound) flank steak
⅛ cup honey	2 tablespoons avocado oil, divided
⅛ cup apple cider vinegar	1 large sweet onion, peeled and
¼ cup soy sauce	sliced
⅛ teaspoon cayenne pepper	1½ cups beef broth
1 teaspoon ground mustard	

1. In a small bowl, combine ketchup, preserves, honey, vinegar, soy sauce, cayenne pepper, mustard, and pepper. Spread mixture on all sides of the flank steak. 2. Press the Sauté button on Instant Pot. Heat 1 tablespoon oil. Sear meat on each side for approximately 5 minutes. Remove the meat and set aside. Add remaining 1 tablespoon oil and onions. Sauté onions for 3–5 minutes until translucent. 3. Add beef broth. Set meat and all of the sauce on the layer of onions. Lock lid. 4. Press the Pressure Cook button and adjust time to 35 minutes. When timer beeps, let pressure release naturally on seal position until float valve drops and then unlock lid. 5. Transfer the meat to a serving platter. Thinly slice against the grain and serve immediately.

Per Serving: Calories 267; Fat: 12g; Sodium 408mg; Carbs: 28.7g; Sugars: 23g; Protein 11g

Pork Chops with Sauerkraut

Prep Time: 15 minutes | Cook Time: 30 minutes | Serves: 4

2 tablespoons olive oil	1 clove garlic, peeled and minced
4 (1"-thick) bone-in pork loin	1 (12-ounce) bottle lager
chops	4 medium red potatoes, peeled and
1 teaspoon sea salt	quartered
½ teaspoon ground black pepper	2 medium red apples, peeled,
4 slices bacon, diced	cored, and quartered
1 stalk celery, finely chopped	1 (1-pound) bag high-quality
3 large carrots, peeled and sliced	sauerkraut, rinsed and drained
1 large onion, peeled and diced	1 tablespoon caraway seeds

1. On the Instant Pot, click the Sauté button. Olive oil is warmed. Salt and pepper are used to season pork chops. Pork chops should be seared in batches for 1–2 minutes each side. Set aside the pork. 2. To the Instant Pot, add bacon, celery, carrots, and onion. Stir-fry the onions for 3 to 5 minutes, or until they are transparent. Cook for another minute after adding the garlic. Pour in the beer and whisk continuously while you deglaze the Instant Pot. Cook without a lid for five minutes. 3. Add the sauerkraut, apples, and potatoes. Add some caraway seeds. To avoid crowding the meat, slightly lean the pork chops against the pot's sides. Lock lid. 4. Set the timer to 15 minutes and press the Pressure Cook button. Allow pressure to naturally relax for five minutes on seal position after the timer beeps. Release any

further pressure quickly on vent position until the float valve lowers, and then open the lid. 5. Put the apples, potatoes, sauerkraut, and pork chops on a serving platter.

Per Serving: Calories 823; Fat: 35.17g; Sodium 866mg; Carbs: 76g; Sugars: 16g; Protein 51g

Yummy Fajitas

Prep Time: 15 minutes | Cook Time: 45 minutes | Serves: 6

⅛ cup avocado oil	1 (2-pound) skirt steak
¼ cup coconut aminos	1 small onion, peeled and diced
1 tablespoon fish sauce	1 medium green bell pepper,
1 teaspoon ground cumin	seeded and diced
1 teaspoon chili powder	1 medium red bell pepper, seeded
2 tablespoons tomato paste	and diced
½ teaspoon sea salt	1 cup beef broth

1. Oil, coconut aminos, fish sauce, cumin, chili powder, tomato paste, and salt should all be combined in a small dish. On the beef's four sides, evenly distribute ¾ of the mixture. Set aside more sauce. 2. On the Instant Pot, click the Sauté button. Add the skirt steak and sear for about 5 minutes on each side. Remove and save the meat. Add the onion, peppers, and saved sauce to the Instant Pot. Sauté for 3–5 minutes until onions are translucent. 3. Include beef broth. Place the meat over the onion and pepper layer. Lock lid. 4. Press the Pressure Cook button and cook for the 35 minutes that are set as the default. When the timer sounds, open the lid after allowing the pressure to gradually subside until the float valve lowers. 5. Using a slotted spoon, remove the meat and vegetables to a serving platter. Thinly slice the skirt steak against the grain. Serve.

Per Serving: Calories 402; Fat: 10.17g; Sodium 704mg; Carbs: 9g; Sugars: 6.03g; Protein 23.39g

Pork Chops in Balsamic Sauce

Prep Time: 10 minutes | Cook Time: 15 minutes | Serves:2

2 (1"-thick) bone-in pork chops	1 medium sweet onion, peeled and
1 teaspoon sea salt	sliced
1 teaspoon ground black pepper	3 pears, peeled, cored, and diced
¼ cup balsamic vinegar	large
¼ cup chicken broth	5 dried figs, stems removed and
1 tablespoon dried mint	halved
2 tablespoons avocado oil	

1. With a paper towel, pat the pork chops dry. Then, liberally sprinkle salt and pepper on both sides. Place aside. 2. Mix the vinegar, broth, and mint in a small bowl. Place aside. 3. On the Instant Pot, click the Sauté button. heating oil Cook pork chops on both sides for five minutes. Remove and save the chops. 4. By adding vinegar mixture and scraping the brown particles from the Instant Pot's sides and bottom, you may deglaze the appliance. The pears and figs are arranged on top of the layered onions in the saucepan. Put the pork chops there. Lock lid. 5. To set the time to 3 minutes, press the Steam button. Allow the pressure to naturally relax for 10 minutes on seal position after the timer chimes. Quick-release any additional pressure on vent position until the float valve drops and then unlock lid. 6. By using a slotted spoon, transfer pork, onions, figs, and pears to a serving platter. Serve warm.

Per Serving: Calories 835; Fat: 34g; Sodium 1404mg; Carbs: 85g; Sugars: 67g; Protein 50g

Rice with Red Beans

Prep Time: 20 minutes | Cook Time: 45 minutes | Serves: 6

3 cups water	1 tsp. ground cumin
2 smoked ham hocks (about 1 lb.)	1 medium tomato, chopped
1 cup dried red beans	1 medium green pepper, chopped
1 medium onion, chopped	1 tsp. salt
1½ tsp. minced garlic	4 cups hot cooked rice

1. In Instant Pot, combine the first six ingredients. Close the pressure-release valve and lock the lid. Adapt to Pressure Cook for 35 minutes on high. 2. Allow the pressure to drop naturally. Select Cancel. Remove the ham hocks and let them cool. Take the flesh off the bones. Remove meat from Instant Pot, cut finely, and add back in bones. Add salt, green pepper, and tomato to the mixture. Choose the sauté option and lower the heat. For 8 to 10 minutes, simmer while stirring often until the pepper is soft. Serve alongside rice.

Per Serving: Calories 216; Fat: 2g; Sodium 404mg; Carbs: 49g; Sugars: 3g; Protein 12g

Baby Back Pork Ribs

Prep Time: 40 minutes | Cook Time: 30 minutes | Serves:6

2 racks (about 3 pounds) baby
back pork ribs
1 teaspoon instant coffee crystals
1 teaspoon sea salt
½ teaspoon chili powder
½ teaspoon ground cumin
½ teaspoon cayenne pepper
½ teaspoon ground mustard
½ teaspoon garlic powder

½ teaspoon onion powder
¼ teaspoon ground coriander
¼ cup pure maple syrup
¼ cup soy sauce
1 tablespoon apple cider vinegar
2 tablespoons tomato paste
1 tablespoon olive oil
1 medium onion, peeled and large
diced

1. Section the ribs into two pieces. Coffee, salt, chili powder, cumin, cayenne pepper, mustard, garlic powder, onion powder, and coriander should all be combined in a small bowl. Rub this mixture into the rib regions with your palms. Covered refrigeration is recommended for up to 24 hours. 2. Combine tomato paste, apple cider vinegar, soy sauce, and maple syrup in a small mixing bowl. 3. On the Instant Pot, click the Sauté button. Olive oil is warmed. When the onions are transparent, add them and sauté for 3 to 5 minutes. Add the mixture of maple syrup. Add a couple ribs at a time, coating them with sauce carefully with tongs. The meaty side should be facing outside when you arrange the ribs standing erect. Lock lid. 4. Set the timer to 25 minutes and press the Pressure Cook button on high. When the timer beeps, let pressure release naturally on seal position until float valve drops and then unlock lid. Serve warm.
Per Serving: Calories 197; Fat: 8g; Sodium 605mg; Carbs: 16g; Sugars: 12g; Protein 15g

Simple and Quick Meatloaf

Prep Time: 10 minutes | Cook Time: 35 minutes | Serves: 6

1-pound ground beef
1-pound ground pork
4 large eggs
1 cup panko bread crumbs
1 large shallot, finely diced
¼ cup seeded and finely diced red
bell pepper
½ cup tomato sauce

1 tablespoon Italian seasoning
½ teaspoon smoked paprika
½ teaspoon garlic powder
½ teaspoon celery seed
1 teaspoon sea salt
½ teaspoon ground black pepper
1 cup beef broth

1. With the exception of the broth, mix all the ingredients in a big basin using your hands. 2. Place meatloaf onto a 7-cup glass dish by shaping the mixture into a ball and flattening the top. 3. Fill the Instant Pot with beef broth. Place the steam rack. Put a glass dish on top of the rack. Lock lid. 4. Press the Pressure Cook button and cook for the 35 minutes on high. Allow pressure to naturally relax for 10 minutes on seal position after the timer chimes. Release any further pressure quickly on vent position until the float valve lowers, and then open the lid. 5. Take the meatloaf out of the Instant Pot and let it cool for 10 minutes at room temperature. Pour any liquid or rendered fat into a glass bowl that has been tilted over a sink. Slice and serve.
Per Serving: Calories 525; Fat: 30g; Sodium 967mg; Carbs: 9g; Sugars: 3g; Protein 51g

Best Pot Roast

Prep Time: 15 minutes | Cook Time: 20 minutes | Serves: 4

2 teaspoons black pepper
1½ teaspoons kosher salt
1½ teaspoons seasoned salt
1½ teaspoons dried parsley
1 teaspoon dried thyme
1 teaspoon dried rosemary
1 teaspoon onion powder
1 teaspoon garlic powder
1 (3-pound) chuck roast
3 tablespoons extra-virgin olive oil
1 tablespoon salted butter
2 medium yellow onions, sliced

into thick wedges
3 cloves garlic, sliced
2 tablespoons Worcestershire
sauce
1 cup dry red wine (like a cabernet)
6–8 ounces portobello mushrooms,
sliced
2 cups beef broth
8 ounces fresh baby carrots
1-pound baby white potatoes
3 tablespoons cornstarch
1 packet beef gravy mix

1. Rub the roast with the mixture of pepper, kosher salt, seasoned salt, parsley, thyme, rosemary, onion powder, and garlic powder. 2. Press Sauté on the Instant Pot and change the setting to High. Pour the oil into the pan and heat it for three minutes. Then, without moving the roast, sear each side for around one to two minutes. Roast should be taken out of the saucepan and placed aside. 3. Put the butter in the Instant Pot without removing the inner pot, and as it melts, use

a wooden spoon to scrape up any spices that may have fallen to the bottom. While continuing to stir and scrape off any browned parts, add the onions and simmer for 2 minutes. Rub the roast with the mixture of pepper, kosher salt, seasoned salt, parsley, thyme, rosemary, onion powder, and garlic powder. 4. Press Sauté on the Instant Pot and change the setting to High. Pour the oil into the pan and heat it for three minutes. Then, without moving the roast, sear each side for around one to two minutes. Roast should be taken out of the pot and placed aside. 5. Put the butter in the Instant Pot, and as it melts, use a wooden spoon to scrape up any spices that may have fallen to the bottom. While continuing to stir and scrape off any browned parts, add the onions and simmer for 2 minutes. When done, use a natural release for 15 minutes on seal position, and then quickly release on vent position. 6. In the meanwhile, combine the cornstarch with 3 tablespoons of cold water to produce a slurry, and put it aside. 7. After the vegetables in the foil-wrapped pot have completed cooking, remove them and set them aside. Remove the steam rack and the roast with care, then set the meat aside on a chopping board. 8. Press Keep Warm/Cancel and then Sauté and adjust to High level, bring the sauce to simmer. Unwrap the vegetables, add the cornstarch slurry, and gravy package to the sauce. After 30 seconds of simmering, switch the pot to the Keep Warm position. 9. Slice the pot roast into strips that are around ¼-inch-thick, cutting against the grain (or make thicker or bite-size cuts if you wish). Add them to the sauce after that (still on the Keep Warm setting). Don't forget to add any last strands of meat off the cutting board, give everything one more swirl, and then serve.
Per Serving: Calories 809; Fat: 26g; Sodium 4449mg; Carbs: 43g; Sugars: 6g; Protein 93g

Peppers Hoagies with Italian Sausage

Prep Time: 15 minutes | Cook Time: 20 minutes | Serves: 6

2 tablespoons olive oil, divided
1 pound sweet Italian sausage
links, uncooked, divided
1 large onion, peeled and sliced
1 small red bell pepper, seeded and
sliced
1 small green bell pepper, seeded
and sliced
1 small yellow bell pepper, seeded
and sliced

4 cloves garlic, minced
½ cup chicken broth
1 (15-ounce) can diced stewed
tomatoes, including juice
¼ cup chopped fresh basil
2 tablespoons fresh oregano leaves
1 teaspoon cayenne pepper
1 teaspoon sea salt
½ teaspoon ground black pepper
6 hoagie rolls

1. On the Instant Pot, click the Sauté button. 1 tablespoon olive oil is heated. For about 4-5 minutes, add half of the sausage links and brown them on both sides. Take out and place aside. Add the remaining sausages and 1 tablespoon of olive oil. For a further 4-5 minutes, brown all sides. Take out of the Instant Pot, then leave it aside. 2. Stir-fry the bell peppers and onions in the Instant Pot for 3 to 5 minutes, or until the onions are transparent. Include garlic cook for one more minute. By adding broth and scraping the Instant Pot's sides and bottom, you may deglaze it. Tomatoes, basil, oregano, cayenne, salt, and pepper should be added. Lock lid. 3. Set the timer to 5 minutes and press the Pressure Cook button. Quickly release the pressure on vent position once the timer sounds. Then unlock the lid. 4. Using a slotted spoon, transfer pot ingredients to a serving platter. Slice sausages. Serve on hoagie rolls.
Per Serving: Calories 344; Fat: 14g; Sodium 1200mg; Carbs: 32g; Sugars: 7g; Protein 22g

Pork Tenderloin with Cherry and Rosemary

Prep Time: 5 minutes | Cook Time: 30 minutes | Serves: 6

2 tablespoons avocado oil
2 (3-pound) pork tenderloins,
halved
½ cup balsamic vinegar
¼ cup olive oil

¼ cup cherry preserves
½ teaspoon sea salt
¼ teaspoon ground black pepper
¼ cup finely chopped fresh rosemary
4 garlic cloves, minced

1. On the Instant Pot, click the Sauté button. Heating oil Brown the pork for two minutes on each side (4 sides total). 2. Pour the other ingredients over the meat after combining them in a small bowl. Lid locked. 3. Set the time to 20 minutes and press the Pressure Cook button. Allow the pressure to naturally relax for five minutes on seal position after the timer chimes. Release any further pressure quickly on vent position until the float valve lowers, and then open the lid. 4. Tenderloin should be moved to a chopping board. Allow to rest for five minutes. Slice into medallions and serve.
Per Serving: Calories 624; Fat: 25.17g; Sodium 390mg; Carbs: 5.87g; Sugars: 4.03g; Protein 87g

Short Ribs with Sauce

Prep Time: 10 minutes | Cook Time: 25 minutes | Serves: 6

½ cup soy sauce
½ cup pure maple syrup
½ cup rice wine
1 tablespoon sesame oil
1 teaspoon white pepper
½ teaspoon ground ginger

½ teaspoon garlic powder
½ teaspoon gochujang
3 pounds beef short ribs
1 cup beef broth
2 green onions, sliced
1 tablespoon toasted sesame seeds

1. Soy sauce, maple syrup, rice wine, sesame oil, white pepper, ground ginger, garlic powder, and gochujang should all be combined in a small bowl. Rub this mixture into the rib regions with your palms. Place covered in the refrigerator for up to overnight. 2. Fill the Instant Pot with beef broth. Place the steam rack. The meaty side should be facing outside when you arrange the ribs standing erect. Lock lid. 3. Set the timer to 25 minutes and press the Pressure Cook button. Allow pressure to naturally release on seal position when the timer beeps until the float valve lowers, and then open the lid. 4. Place the ribs on a serving plate and top with sesame seeds and green onions.
Per Serving: Calories 526; Fat: 27g; Sodium 545mg; Carbs: 24g; Sugars: 20g; Protein 47g

Wraps with Carnitas Lettuce

Prep Time: 10 minutes | Cook Time: 60 minutes | Serves: 6

1 tablespoon unsweetened cocoa powder
2 teaspoons salt
1 teaspoon cayenne pepper
2 teaspoons ground oregano
1 teaspoon white pepper
1 teaspoon garlic powder
1 teaspoon onion salt
1 teaspoon ground cumin
½ teaspoon ground coriander

1 (3-pound) pork shoulder
2 tablespoons olive oil
2–3 cups water
1 head butter lettuce, washed and dried
1 small jalapeño, sliced
¼ cup julienned radishes
1 medium avocado, diced
2 small Roma tomatoes, diced
2 limes, cut into wedges

1. Cocoa powder, salt, cayenne pepper, oregano, white pepper, garlic powder, onion salt, cumin, and coriander should all be combined in a small basin. Rub spice into the pork shoulder and place in the refrigerator overnight. 2. On the Instant Pot, click the Sauté button. Include 2 teaspoons of oil. About 8 to 10 minutes, sear the roast on all sides, making sure that they are completely browned. Add 2 to 3 cups of water, or enough to almost cover the meat. Lock lid. 3. Set the time to 45 minutes and press the Pressure Cook button. Allow pressure to naturally relax for 10 minutes on seal position after the timer chimes. Release any further pressure quickly on vent position until the float valve lowers, and then open the lid. 4. Place the meat on a plate. Shred the meat with two forks. Save for ½ cup, discard the entire cooking liquid. Remove the meat to the Instant Pot. Press the Sauté button and stir-fry meat for 4–5 minutes creating some crispy edges. 5. Serve with lettuce leaves, jalapeño slices, radishes, avocado, tomatoes, and lime wedges.
Per Serving: Calories 717; Fat: 50g; Sodium 916mg; Carbs: 8.7g; Sugars: 2.03g; Protein 59g

Yummy meatballs

Prep Time: 15 minutes | Cook Time: 30 minutes | Serves: 4

½-pound ground beef
½-pound ground pork
2 large eggs
1 tablespoon Italian seasoning
1 teaspoon garlic powder
1 teaspoon celery seed
½ teaspoon onion powder

½ teaspoon smoked paprika
½ cup old-fashioned oats
2 tablespoons plus 2 cups marinara sauce, divided
3 tablespoons avocado oil, divided
2 cups water

1. Beef, pork, eggs, Italian seasoning, celery seed, onion powder, smoked paprika, oats, and 2 tablespoons marinara sauce should all be combined in a medium bowl. Form into 20 meatballs. Place aside. 2. Heat 2 tablespoons of oil in the Instant Pot by pressing the Sauté button. 10 meatballs should be placed around the pot's edge. The meatballs need around 4 minutes to be seared on both sides. Remove and reserve the first batch. The remaining meatballs should be seared after adding a further tablespoon of oil. Delete the meatballs. 3. Extra juice and oil from the Instant Pot should be discarded. In a 7-cup glass dish, put seared meatballs. Add the last 2 cups of marinara sauce on top. 4. Fill the Instant Pot with water. Add the steam rack. Place the glass dish on top of the steam rack. Lock lid. 5. Set the time to 20 minutes and press the Pressure Cook button. Allow the pressure to naturally relax for 10 minutes on seal position after the timer chimes. Release any further pressure quickly on vent position until the float valve lowers, and then open the lid. 6. Transfer meatballs to a serving dish.
Per Serving: Calories 518; Fat: 33g; Sodium 278mg; Carbs: 20g; Sugars: 8g; Protein 35g

Mongolian beef

Prep Time: 10 minutes | Cook Time: 15 minutes | Serves: 4

1 tablespoon sesame oil
1 (2-pound) skirt steak, sliced into thin strips
¼ cup coconut aminos
½ cup pure maple syrup
1" knob of fresh gingerroot, peeled

and grated
4 cloves garlic, minced
½ cup plus 2 tablespoons water, divided
2 tablespoons arrowroot powder

1. On the Instant Pot, click the Sauté button. Cook steak strips in hot oil for two to three minutes, or until just barely browned on all sides. 2. Mix the coconut aminos, maple syrup, ginger, garlic, and ½ cup water in a medium bowl. Pour over the meat and swirl to remove any browned particles from the Instant Pot's bottom and sides. Lid locked. 3. Select Pressure Cook and set the timer to 10 minutes. Quickly release pressure on vent position until the float valve lowers when the timer sounds, and then open the lid. 4. To make a slurry, combine arrowroot and 2 tablespoons water in a small bowl and whisk until combined. Add this to the meat mixture and stir. Press the Sauté and Adjust buttons to lower the temperature to Less, then boil the dish without a lid for 5 minutes to thicken the sauce. 5. Ladle mixture into bowls and serve.
Per Serving: Calories 612; Fat: 26g; Sodium 947mg; Carbs: 32.87g; Sugars: 24g; Protein 63g

Brisket Jews

Prep Time: 5 minutes | Cook Time: 120 minutes | Serves: 4

1 (4- or 5-pound) beef brisket (don't trim the fat prior to cooking)
Kosher salt
1½ cups water
1½ cups ketchup

¾ cup dark-brown sugar
¾ cup white vinegar
1 clove garlic, minced or pressed
4 yellow onions, coarsely chopped
3 tablespoons cornstarch

1. To fit the brisket inside your Instant Pot, cut it in half against the grain. Kosher salt should be applied all over the brisket. 2. On the Instant Pot, hit Sauté. When it says Hot, sear the brisket for 2 minutes on each side, or until browned, working with one piece at a time. Hit Cancel when finished, transfer the brisket to a platter, and then wash and dry the liner pot. 3. In a mixing basin, combine the water, ketchup, brown sugar, vinegar, and garlic to make the sauce. 4. With one half of the brisket, fat-side up, put on top of the steam rack, and top with about half the onions and sauce. The second half of the brisket should then be layered on top of the onions in a crisscross pattern. The rest of the onions and sauce should be spread over the brisket. 5. Move the valve to the seal position, fasten the lid, and press Pressure Cook, if you want it extremely soft (shredding apart), cook it on High pressure for 75 minutes; if you want it a bit harder, cook it for 65 minutes. When finished, use a quick-release on vent position after a 20-minute natural release on seal position. 6. Transferring the brisket halves to a carving board should be done very gently. It will shred apart if you decide to cut it into strips before it has finished cooling. While you wait, you may gently trim away any extra fat and throw it away. 7. The cornstarch should be combined with 3 tablespoons of cold water to make a slurry, which should then be left aside while the brisket cools. 8. To simmer the sauce, press Keep Warm/Cancel, then Sauté. Stir quickly after adding the slurry, then let it simmer for 30 seconds before switching the pot to the Keep Warm position. As the brisket cools, the sauce will get thicker. 9. After the brisket has cooled, slice it into pieces or strips by cutting against the grain. 10. Return the meat slices to the Instant Pot with care and give them 5 to 10 minutes to marinade in the sauce so that it will keep its tenderness until you're ready to serve.
Per Serving: Calories 761; Fat: 43g; Sodium 3592mg; Carbs: 56.87g; Sugars: 42.03g; Protein 35g

Wraps with Cubano Sloppy Joe

Prep Time: 10 minutes | Cook Time: 10 minutes | Serves: 8

1-pound ground pork
½ medium onion, peeled and diced
¼ cup chicken broth
1 tablespoon fresh lime juice
1 tablespoon fresh orange juice
1 teaspoon garlic powder
1 teaspoon dried oregano
1 teaspoon cayenne pepper

2 teaspoons ground cumin
1 teaspoon sea salt
1 teaspoon ground black pepper
8 slices Swiss cheese
8 (8") flour tortillas
8 slices ham
24 dill pickle slices
8 teaspoons yellow mustard

1. On the Instant Pot, click the Sauté button. Pork should no longer be pink after 5 minutes of stirring with onions. 2. Deglaze the Instant Pot by adding chicken stock and scraping any browned residue from the sides and bottom. Add the lime juice, orange juice, cayenne pepper, cumin, oregano, garlic powder, and salt and pepper after stirring. Lock lid. 3. Set the timer to 5 minutes and press the Pressure Cook button. When the timer sounds, open the lid after allowing the pressure to naturally dissipate on seal position until the float valve lowers. 4. Place a Swiss cheese slice on a flour tortilla before assembling the tortillas. Each tortilla should have a piece of ham and three slices of pickles. One teaspoon of yellow mustard should be placed down the middle. ⅛ of the Instant Pot's ground pork mixture should be added down the center using a slotted spoon. Flip the tortilla's edges toward the center after folding the bottom 2-3" of the tortilla upward. For the remaining tortillas, repeat. Serve right away.
Per Serving: Calories 463; Fat: 24g; Sodium 1237mg; Carbs: 28.7g; Sugars: 2g; Protein 32g

Stuffed Peppers from Mexico

Prep Time: 10 minutes | Cook Time: 20 minutes | Serves: 4

4 large red bell peppers
¼-pound chorizo, loose or cut from casings
½-pound ground pork
1 medium onion, peeled and diced
1 small Roma tomato, diced
1 tablespoon tomato paste
½ cup corn kernels (cut from the

cob is preferred)
1 large egg
1 teaspoon ground cumin
1 teaspoon sea salt
1 teaspoon garlic powder
½ cup vegetable broth
½ cup shredded Cheddar cheese

1. Bell pepper tops should be removed as near to the tops as feasible. Hollow out the seeds and discard them. Make a few tiny holes in the peppers' bottoms to let the fat leak out. 2. Combine the other ingredients in a medium bowl, leaving out the cheese and broth. Put the same quantity of the mixture into each bell pepper. 3. Place the steam rack inside the Instant Pot, then add the broth. On the rack, arrange the peppers upright. Lock lid. 4. Set the time to 15 minutes and press the Pressure Cook button. Allow the pressure to naturally release on seal position when the timer beeps until the float valve lowers, and then open the lid. The cheese should melt after 3 minutes of simmering in the Instant Pot after pressing the Sauté button. 5. Peppers should be placed on a dish and served warm.
Per Serving: Calories 601; Fat: 52.17g; Sodium 1022mg; Carbs: 14g; Sugars: 5g; Protein 24g

Swiss Steak with Potato

Prep Time: 10 minutes | Cook Time: 35 minutes | Serves: 6

2½ (1"-thick) pounds beef round steak
1 teaspoon sea salt
½ teaspoon ground black pepper
2 tablespoons olive oil, divided
1 medium yellow onion, peeled and diced
2 stalks celery, diced
1 large green bell pepper, seeded

and diced
1 cup tomato juice
1 cup beef broth
6 large carrots, peeled and cut into 1" pieces
6 medium Yukon gold potatoes, diced large
4 teaspoons butter

1. The round steak should be divided into six serving-sized pieces after being salt and peppered on both sides. 2. On the Instant Pot, click the Sauté button. 1 tablespoon oil is heated. 3 pieces of beef should be added, and each should be seared for 3 minutes. Repeat with the remaining 1 tablespoon oil and the remaining 3 pieces of pork, then transfer to a dish. 3. Add the onion, celery, and green pepper on top of the final three pieces of browned beef in the Instant Pot. Place the remaining 3 pieces of beef on top and cover with tomato juice and broth. On top of the meat, arrange the potatoes and carrots. Lock lid.

4. Set the time to 20 minutes and press the Pressure Cook button. Quickly release pressure on vent position until the float valve lowers when the timer sounds, and then open the lid. 5. Place the meat, potatoes, and carrots on a serving plate. Cover up to stay warm. 6. Remove any fatty particles from the juices still in the Instant Pot. To simmer the juices without a cover for 5 minutes, press the Sauté button, adjust button, and reduce temperature to Low. 7. One spoonful of butter at a time, whisk in. Serve the finished gravy beside the meat at the table. Serve immediately.
Per Serving: Calories 1415; Fat: 38g; Sodium 1023mg; Carbs: 74g; Sugars: 8g; Protein 184g

Potatoes and Meatloaf

Prep Time: 10 minutes | Cook Time: 75 minutes | Serves: 4

The Meatloaf
2 pounds ground meat (I use a mix of beef, pork, and veal)
1 cup breadcrumbs
½ cup grated Parmesan cheese
½ cup whole milk
2 large eggs, lightly beaten
9 cloves garlic, minced or pressed
The Mashed Potatoes
3 pounds mixed baby white and red potatoes, rinsed, skins on, and quartered
1½ cups chicken broth
5 cloves of garlic
4 tablespoons (½ stick) salted butter
½ cup heavy cream or half-and-half
The Glaze
½ cup ketchup
¼ cup barbecue sauce
2 tablespoons brown sugar (light or dark)

½ yellow onion, grated
2 tablespoons ketchup
2 tablespoons barbecue sauce
2 tablespoons dried parsley
1 tablespoon seasoned salt
2 teaspoons black pepper
2 teaspoons dried oregano

1 (5.2-ounce) package Boursin spread (any flavor) or 4 ounces cream cheese, cut into chunky cubes
1 teaspoon kosher salt
1 teaspoon black pepper
1 teaspoon garlic powder
½ teaspoon Italian seasoning
¼ cup chives, sliced

1 tablespoon yellow mustard
1 tablespoon honey
1 tablespoon balsamic glaze
1 teaspoon Worcestershire sauce

1. Mix the meatloaf ingredients by hand in a large bowl until they come together (like a giant meatball). 2. The meatloaf mixture should be packed tightly into a 6-cup Bundt pan that will fit inside your Instant Pot and has been coated with nonstick cooking spray. In order for the steam to escape through the center of the Bundt pan, spray a piece of aluminum foil with nonstick spray and cover the pan with it. Place aside. 3. In the Instant Pot, combine the potatoes, chicken stock, and garlic. Place the potatoes and garlic on the rack, then place the Bundt pan on top of the steam rack. Put the lid on tightly, turn the valve to the seal position, and press Pressure Cook for 35 minutes at High Pressure. Quickly release on vent position once finished. 4. In a dish, thoroughly combine all the ingredients for the meatloaf glaze; put away while the meatloaf cooks. 5. Remove the Bundt pan with care from the pot. The meatloaf should be carefully held in place with a spatula or cloth so that it doesn't fall out as you pour off any extra drippings. 6. If you wish to caramelize the meatloaf: A baking sheet should be lined with foil sprayed with nonstick cooking spray. Using oven mitts to securely keep the foil and Bundt pan together, place the foil-lined baking sheet over the Bundt pan and swiftly turn the meatloaf out onto the foil. If it disintegrates a bit, you may just press it back together. The meatloaf should be covered with the meatloaf glaze and placed in a Pressure Cook on high for 5 to 10 minutes, or until the glaze has caramelized. 7. To the mashed potatoes in the meantime, add the butter, cream, Boursin (or cream cheese), kosher salt, black pepper, garlic powder, Italian seasoning, and chives after mashing the potatoes to the appropriate consistency. 8. The meatloaf should be gently transferred to a serving plate after being removed from the Bundt pan (or the oven, if you caramelized it). Apply a meatloaf glaze using a brush. For aesthetic purposes, arrange part of the mashed potatoes in the middle of the ring; the remaining portions should go in a serving dish.
Per Serving: Calories 1596; Fat: 87g; Sodium 6605mg; Carbs: 145g; Sugars: 37g; Protein 61g

Tasty Barbeque Ribs

Prep Time: 5 minutes | Cook Time: 80 minutes | Serves: 4

2–6 pounds (up to 3 full racks) of St. Louis or baby back ribs (pork loin back ribs), unseasoned	1 cup apple cider vinegar
	¼ cup liquid smoke (either hickory or mesquite is fine)
1 (64-ounce) bottle of apple juice	Barbecue sauce (a few cups' worth)

1. Take the ribs and coil them so they fit in the Instant Pot lined against the edge of the pot. Add into pot. 2. Add the liquid smoke, vinegar, and apple juice. 3. Set valve to the seal position, close the lid, and press Pressure Cook for 5-6 pounds/1.5-2 racks of ribs, cook under high pressure for 30 minutes (25 minutes for 2-4 pounds/1 rack). 4. When finished, quickly release the pressure on vent position after a 5-minute natural release on seal position. 5. Delicately transfer the ribs to a baking sheet covered with nonstick foil after carefully removing them from the saucepan since they will be quite tender (bone side down). After the ribs are taken out of the saucepan, discard the fluids. 6. Apply plenty of barbecue sauce to the ribs' tops using a basting brush. Put a lot of it on to make them attractive and saucy. 7. Grab lots of napkins, chop up the ribs after removing them from the pot, and enjoy!

Per Serving: Calories 567; Fat: 10g; Sodium 191mg; Carbs: 51g; Sugars: 43g; Protein 63g

Corned Beef with Cabbage

Prep Time: 5 minutes | Cook Time: 120 minutes | Serves: 4

1 medium yellow onion, cut into quarters	1 pound Idaho or russet potatoes, peeled and cut into 1-inch cubes
3 cloves garlic, minced or pressed	4 large carrots, peeled and cut into 1½-inch lengths
2–4-pound corned beef brisket, with spice/seasoning pack included in the packaging	1 head of cabbage, hard bottom removed and cut into 6 wedges
12 ounces Guinness or beef broth	

1. Steam rack should be placed inside Instant Pot. On the rack, set the onion and garlic. 2. The corned beef brisket should be taken out of the packaging, the spice packet should be saved, and the meat should be well rinsed under cool water to remove the salty brine. 3. On top of the onion and garlic, lay the corned beef, fat side up. On top of the brisket and all around it in the saucepan, evenly distribute the spice packet's contents. Carefully pour the beer in to avoid washing the brisket's seasonings away. 4. Put the lid on tightly, turn the valve to the seal position, and press Pressure Cook for 70 minutes at High Pressure. After finishing, let a natural release of 15 minutes on seal position before doing a fast release on vent position. 5. Just the corned beef should be moved to a casserole dish; remove the rack. Two cups of the liquid should be kept aside, leaving the remaining liquid in the saucepan. Brush the spices off the brisket with a paper towel or clean hands (they may be more challenging to remove once it has cooled). 6. To the Instant Pot, add the potatoes, carrots, and cabbage. It won't matter whether it looks to fit snugly; nothing to worry about. 7. Secure the lid, turn the valve to the seal position, then select Pressure Cook on High Pressure for 3 minutes. 8. Slice the corned beef against the grain in the meantime. 9. The brisket in the casserole dish should be covered with the 2 cups of liquid that have been saved. Use aluminum foil to protect. 10. When the vegetables have finished cooking, quickly release the steam on vent position, then add them to the casserole dish. Before serving, you may ladle any leftover liquid over the meat to keep it moist and tasty.

Per Serving: Calories 658; Fat: 34g; Sodium 2967mg; Carbs: 48.7g; Sugars: 10.3g; Protein 39g

Sesame Beef

Prep Time: 5 minutes | Cook Time: 50 minutes | Serves: 4

2 tablespoons sesame oil	¼ cup low-sodium soy sauce
1 medium yellow onion, diced	3 tablespoons cornstarch
3 cloves garlic, minced	½ cup honey
2–3 pounds flank steak, sliced into ¼-inch strips	2 tablespoons hoisin sauce
¾ cup orange juice	1½ tablespoons orange zest
¾ cup beef broth	Sesame seeds, for serving
½ cup light- or dark-brown sugar	Scallions, sliced, for serving

1. Press Sauté while putting the Instant Pot after adding the sesame oil. After heating the oil for three minutes, add the onion and stir-fry it for another three minutes to soften it. Add the garlic and cook for a further minute. 2. Add the steak and cook for about 2 minutes, until gently charred all over. 3. Stir in the beef broth, brown sugar, orange

juice, and soy sauce. Lock the lid in place, turn the valve to the seal position, then cook for 12 minutes at high pressure using the Pressure Cook. Allow a 10-minute natural release on seal position once you're finished, then execute a rapid release on vent position. 4. In the meanwhile, combine the cornstarch with 3 tablespoons of cold water to create a slurry. 5. Honey and hoisin sauce should be combined. To simmer the sauce, choose Sauté and adjust and set it to the High setting after pressing Keep Warm/Cancel. The cornstarch slurry and zest should be added as soon as the sauce begins to simmer. The sauce should simmer for 30 seconds before the pot should be placed to the Keep Warm position. 6. Serve with scallions and/or sesame seeds on top.

Per Serving: Calories 656; Fat: 18g; Sodium 889mg; Carbs: 70g; Sugars: 54g; Protein 51g

Yummy Pork

Prep Time: 5 minutes | Cook Time: 90 minutes | Serves: 4

1 tablespoon light- or dark-brown sugar	(you can also use country-style ribs)
1 tablespoon onion powder	1 tablespoon liquid smoke
1 tablespoon garlic powder	1 large Spanish (or yellow) onion, quartered
1½ teaspoons paprika	2 cups Coca-Cola or Dr Pepper
1½ teaspoons ground cumin	1 cup barbecue sauce (use your favorite)
1 teaspoon salt	
1 teaspoon black pepper	
3–4-pound boneless pork shoulder or butt, cut into 1-pound segments	Potato rolls or hamburger buns, for serving

1. Combine the sugar, paprika, cumin, onion powder, garlic powder, salt, and pepper in a large bowl. 2. Apply liquid smoke on the pork, then roll it in the spice bowl to coat. Place aside. 3. Round sides down, add the onion wedges to the Instant Pot. Place the pig slices on top of the onion, then add the soda. 4. Put the lid on tightly, turn the valve to the seal position, and press Pressure Cook for 60 minutes at High Pressure. Allow a 10-minute natural release on seal position once you're finished, then a rapid release on vent position. 5. Add the onion and pork to a mixing bowl. Out of the pot's juices, set aside ¼ cup and throw away the remainder. 6. Shred the pork and onion with a pair of forks or a hand mixer, and mix in the reserved juices and barbecue sauce before serving with some slaw in rolls or buns.

Per Serving: Calories 1106; Fat: 61g; Sodium 1577mg; Carbs: 44g; Sugars: 28g; Protein 88g

Meatballs from Sweden

Prep Time: 5 minutes | Cook Time: 40 minutes | Serves: 4

The Meatballs

1-pound ground beef (the less lean, the better)	2 tablespoons dried parsley flakes
½ pound ground pork	1½ teaspoons seasoned salt
⅓ cup whole milk	1½ teaspoons onion powder
⅓ cup plain breadcrumbs	½ teaspoon white pepper
1 large egg, lightly beaten	¼ teaspoon black pepper
3 cloves garlic, minced	¼ teaspoon allspice
	2 cups beef broth

The Sauce

2 tablespoons cornstarch	1 packet beef gravy mix
5 tablespoons salted butter	1 teaspoon Dijon mustard
½ cup heavy cream	

1. To make the meatballs, combine all of the ingredients in a large mixing basin (apart from the broth) using clean hands. Approximately 24 meatballs, each approximately the size of a Ping-Pong ball, should be formed. 2. To the pot, add the steam rack. The meatballs should be carefully placed on top of the soup in the saucepan after adding the stock and adding the meatballs. Put the lid on tightly, turn the valve to the seal position, and then set the timer for 10 minutes on High Pressure Cook. When finished, give a fast release on vent position after a 5-minute natural release on seal position. 3. Put the meatballs on a platter and reserve. Remove the steam rack, but keep the Instant Pot's broth in place. Mix 2 tablespoons of cold water with the cornstarch and leave aside. 4. Press Keep Warm/Cancel, then press Sauté. Bring to a boil after stirring in the butter, cream, gravy mix, and mustard. Stir the cornstarch slurry in as soon as the sauce starts to boil. After 10 seconds of simmering, turn the pot off. 5. Reintroduce the meatballs to the sauce, toss, and then serve.

Per Serving: Calories 897; Fat: 60g; Sodium 1247mg; Carbs: 12.87g; Sugars: 4g; Protein 76g

Short Ribs with Spice

Prep Time: 5 minutes | Cook Time: 90 minutes | Serves: 4

1 cup beef broth
¾ cup dry red wine (like a cabernet)
½ cup hoisin sauce
3 cloves garlic, minced or pressed
1 teaspoon ground allspice
1 teaspoon cinnamon
1 teaspoon Chinese five spice powder (optional)

5–6 pounds bone-in short ribs
Kosher salt and black pepper, to season ribs (about 1½ teaspoons of each)
1 large Spanish (or yellow) onion, quartered
¼ cup cornstarch
½ cup honey

1. Mix the beef broth, red wine, hoisin sauce, garlic, allspice, cinnamon, and five spice powder in a bowl to make the sauce (if using). Place aside. 2. Sprinkle kosher salt and black pepper all over the short ribs in a light coating. 3. Hit Sauté and then adjust it such that More or High is selected. Working in batches, cook the short ribs for 2 minutes before searing them for 1 minute on each side. 4. About a half cup of the sauce should be added to the saucepan. Stir while doing so to scrape out any browned pieces. To turn the pot off after the bottom is clean, press Keep Warm/Cancel. 5. All of the short ribs should be placed on top of the onion wedges with the rounded side up. The remaining sauce should then be poured on top. 6. Put the lid on tightly, turn the valve to the seal position, choose Keep Warm/Cancel, then select Pressure Cook on high. 45 minutes of high pressure cooking. When finished, let a rapid release on vent position after a 15-minute natural release on seal position. 7. In the meantime, create a slurry by mixing the cornstarch with ¼ cup cold water. 8. Place the ribs in a serving plate after carefully removing them from the saucepan (they will be delicate and likely to come apart). Hit Sauté and adjust the temperature to High then bring the sauce to a bubble. Stir immediately after adding the honey and the cornstarch slurry. Before clicking Keep Warm/Cancel to turn the pot off, let it boil for 30 seconds. Wait for five minutes. 9. Pour the sauce over the short ribs and serve with some bread to sop up the extra sauce.
Per Serving: Calories 1260; Fat: 55.17g; Sodium 1174mg; Carbs: 62.87g; Sugars: 45.03g; Protein 129g

Dill Pork Tenderloin with Dijon

Prep Time: 5 minutes | Cook Time: 40 minutes | Serves: 4

2 pounds pork tenderloin
2 cups chicken broth
½ cup Dijon mustard, divided
4 tablespoons (½ stick) salted butter

4 tablespoons cornstarch
Juice of 1 lemon
½ cup fresh dill, chopped, plus more for garnish

1. Cut the pork into discs or medallions that are 1 inch thick. 2. Stirring is required after adding the broth and ¼ cup of mustard to the Instant Pot. Place the butter on top before adding the meat. 3. Move the valve to the seal position, fasten the lid, and press Pressure Cook for 8 minutes on high pressure. When finished, let pressure a 10-minute natural release on seal position before releasing quickly on vent position. 4. Create a slurry by combining 4 tablespoons of cold water with the cornstarch in the meantime. 5. Transfer the cooked pork to a serving plate and let it aside after the pot has finished cooking. 6. Choose Sauté and adjust the Instant Pot so that the High setting is selected. Bring to a simmer after adding the remaining ¼ cup of mustard and lemon juice. 7. As soon as it starts to bubble, whisk in the cornstarch slurry right away, then let it simmer for about a minute until it starts to thicken. After hitting Keep Warm/Cancel, turn off the pot and let it sit for around 5 minutes or until the sauce is thick enough for you. 8. Pour the sauce over the pork after adding the dill, then top with more dill.
Per Serving: Calories 634; Fat: 24g; Sodium 1030mg; Carbs: 11g; Sugars: 1.03g; Protein 86g

Homemade Hungarian Goulash

Prep Time: 5 minutes | Cook Time: 75 minutes | Serves: 4

4 tablespoons (½ stick) salted butter, divided
1 large Spanish (or yellow) onion, cut lengthwise into thin slices
2 tablespoons paprika
1 teaspoon caraway seeds
3 pounds beef stew meat or chuck cubes

½ cup dry red wine (like a pinot noir)
1½ cups beef broth
2 cups baby carrots
1 (14.5-ounce) can diced tomatoes
¼ cup ketchup
3 tablespoons dark-brown sugar
1 tablespoon white vinegar

1 tablespoon seasoned salt
1 teaspoon black pepper
3 tablespoons cornstarch

1 (12-ounce) package egg noodles, prepared separately, cooked according to package directions

1. 1 tablespoons of butter should be added to the Instant Pot. Select Sauté. The onion should be added after the butter has melted and sauté for 3 minutes, or until it starts to soften. 2. Stirring often will prevent the paprika from sticking to the bottom of the pot as you add it, along with the caraway seeds and the last 2 tablespoons of butter. 3. When the meat is gently charred but not totally done, add it to the pan and cook it for 2–3 minutes while continually stirring. 4. Add the wine and scrape any brown pieces that may have become trapped to the bottom of the saucepan for 1 minute to deglaze it. Stir in the other ingredients, excluding the cornstarch and egg noodles. 5. Put the lid on tightly, turn the valve to the seal position, and then select Pressure Cook. Cook for 30 minutes on high. After finishing, let a fast release on vent position after a 10-minute natural release on seal position. 6. Make a slurry by combining 3 tablespoons of cold water with the cornstarch in the meanwhile. Place aside. 7. Once the lid has been removed, select Sauté, and adjust, making sure the High option is selected. When the sauce starts to boil, add the cornstarch slurry right away, then let it simmer for a minute to thicken. 8. Serve over egg noodles.
Per Serving: Calories 756; Fat: 24g; Sodium 2504mg; Carbs: 52.87g; Sugars: 9g; Protein 81g

Yummy Meat Pie

Prep Time: 5 minutes | Cook Time: 45 minutes | Serves: 4

The Meat
¼ cup extra-virgin olive oil
1 large yellow onion, diced
3 cloves garlic, minced
1½ pounds ground meat (I like ground lamb or a veal, pork, and beef mix)
½ cup dry red wine (like a cabernet)

1 teaspoon seasoned salt
1 teaspoon Italian seasoning
¼ teaspoon nutmeg
1 (10-ounce) box frozen mixed peas and carrots
4 tablespoons tomato paste, divided

The potatoes
1½ pounds baby potatoes (any color you like), skin on
3 tablespoons salted butter
¼ cup heavy cream or half-and-half

Half package (3 ounces) of Boursin spread (any flavor) or 2 ounces cream cheese, cut into chunky cubes
½ teaspoon garlic salt
1 teaspoon black pepper

1. Press Sauté on the Instant Pot and change the setting to High. Add the oil and heat for 3 minutes. Add the onion and cook for an additional 3 minutes, or until the onion is tender. Add the garlic and cook for a further minute. 2. Then add the wine, seasoned salt, Italian seasoning, and nutmeg and bring to a boil, scraping up any browned pieces from the bottom of the pot as you go. Add the beef and sauté for 2 minutes, until starting to brown. Cook for a further minute after stirring in 2 tablespoons of tomato paste and adding the peas and carrots. 3. Scoop the beef mixture with a mixing spoon into a round 112-quart oven-safe casserole dish that will fit inside your Instant Pot. 4. Scrape the bottom of the Instant Pot after adding 1 cup of water to let any meat scraps rise to the surface. Keep the water in; it's necessary to create pressure. The casserole dish should be set on the rack, which is in the pot. Add the entire baby potatoes on top of the meat. 5. To cook for 12 minutes under high pressure, secure the lid, select Pressure Cook. Quickly let go on vent position once finished. 6. Move the potatoes to a basin with care, then mash them until the appropriate consistency is achieved. Black pepper, garlic salt, Boursin (or cream cheese), and butter should all be combined. 7. Carefully remove the casserole dish from the rack and Instant Pot using oven mitts. Skim off excess juices by pressing the back of a mixing spoon against the top of the meat and letting the spoon fill; discard. About 5 spoonful should do the trick. Stir in the remaining 2 tablespoons of tomato paste, layer the mashed potatoes on top, and serve.
Per Serving: Calories 734; Fat: 37g; Sodium 1030mg; Carbs: 57g; Sugars: 5g; Protein 43.9g

Biryani De Beef

Prep Time: 10 minutes | Cook Time: 25 minutes | Serves: 6

1 tablespoon ghee
1 small onion, peeled and sliced
1-pound top round, cut into strips
1 tablespoon minced fresh gingerroot
2 cloves garlic, peeled and minced
½ teaspoon ground cloves
1 cup plain yogurt
1 (28-ounce) can whole stewed tomatoes, including juice
2 cups cooked basmati rice

½ teaspoon ground cardamom
½ teaspoon ground coriander
½ teaspoon ground black pepper
½ teaspoon ground cinnamon
½ teaspoon ground cumin
1 teaspoon salt

1. On the Instant Pot, click the Sauté button. Burn ghee. Sauté the onion for three to five minutes, or until transparent. Rice is the only ingredient left to add to the Instant Pot. Lid closed. 2. Select Pressure Cook and set the timer to 10 minutes. Quickly release the pressure on vent position until the float valve lowers when the timer whistles, and then open the lid. 3. Press the Sauté, adjust, and less temperature, then simmer the food, covered, for about 10 minutes, or until most of the liquid has evaporated. Serve over cooked basmati rice.
Per Serving: Calories 303; Fat: 12.17g; Sodium 628mg; Carbs: 28.7g; Sugars: 6g; Protein 30g

Parmesan Sausage & Peppers

Prep Time: 5 minutes | Cook Time: 45 minutes | Serves: 4

3 tablespoons extra-virgin olive oil
2 tablespoons (¼ stick) salted butter
2 Vidalia (sweet) onions, cut into strands
2 green bell peppers, cut lengthwise into slices
2 red bell peppers, cut lengthwise into slices
6 cloves garlic, minced or pressed
2 pounds Italian sausage links (sweet and/or hot), sliced into

disks ½ inch thick
½ cup dry white wine (like a chardonnay)
1 teaspoon oregano
1 teaspoon Italian seasoning
1 cup grated Parmesan cheese
1 (5.2-ounce) package Boursin spread (any flavor) or 4 ounces cream cheese, cut into chunky cubes

1. Hit Sauté after it add the butter and olive oil to the Instant Pot. Add the onion and peppers when the butter has melted. The onion should be sautéed for 10 minutes, or until tender and starting to brown. Cook for another minute after adding the garlic. 2. Sausage will cook for two to three minutes, until it begins to faintly brown. If the insides are still raw, don't worry; pressure cooking will fix that. 3. Sauté for a further one to two minutes, until simmering and aromatic, before adding the wine, oregano, and Italian seasoning. 4. Select Pressure Cook on high and secure the lid. Cook for 5 minutes at high pressure. Quickly let pressure go on vent position once finished. 5. Once melted and creamy, stir in the Parmesan and Boursin (or cream cheese). 6. Serve the dish as a hero, over white or brown rice, pasta, or with crusty bread to sop up the sauce.
Per Serving: Calories 658; Fat: 40g; Sodium 2186mg; Carbs: 27g; Sugars: 11g; Protein 49g

Chapter 11 Vegetable and Side Recipes

Delicious Cauliflower Queso

Prep Time: 5 minutes | Cook Time: 5 minutes | Serves: 2

1 head cauliflower cut into about 4 cups florets	diced tomatoes, divided
2 cups water	½ cup nutritional yeast
1½ cups carrots, chopped into ½-inch-thick round pieces	1 tablespoon white miso paste
½ cup raw cashews	2 teaspoons gluten-free chili powder
1 (15-ounce) can no-salt-added	1 red bell pepper, diced
	4 scallions, white and green parts, diced

1. In your inner pot, combine the cauliflower, water, carrots, and cashews. Lock the lid and turn the steam release handle to Sealing. 2. Select the Pressure Cook on the panel. Press the button again to choose Less option; use the "-" button to adjust the cooking time to 5 minutes. Press Pressure Level to choose High pressure. 3. After cooking has completed, quickly and carefully turn the steam release from Sealing position to the Venting position and uncover the lid carefully. 4. Drain and pour the mixture into a blender or food processor. Add the liquid from the can of tomatoes and put the drained tomatoes aside. Add the nutritional yeast, miso, and chili powder and stir well until it is very smooth. 5. Transfer to a medium bowl before stirring in the drained tomatoes, bell pepper, and scallions. 6. Serve right away. 7. If you haven't eaten up the dish, you can put the leftovers in a covered container and put them in the refrigerator for up to 4 days.
Per Serving: Calories: 77; Fat: 4g; Carbs: 10g; Fiber: 3g; Sugar: 4g; Sodium: 114mg; Protein: 3g

Homemade Smoky "Baked" Beans

Prep Time: 15 minutes | Cook Time: 6 minutes | Serves: 4-6

2 cups dried great Northern beans, picked over and soaked overnight or quick-soaked	Salt and freshly ground black pepper
1 medium yellow onion, chopped	¼ cup ketchup
½ cup chopped dry-cured Spanish chorizo (2½ ounces; optional)	¼ cup lightly packed brown sugar
	3 tablespoons molasses
	2 tablespoons cider vinegar

1. Drain the beans and place them in the pot. Add 2¾ cups water (just enough to cover the beans), the onion, chorizo, 1 teaspoon salt, and several grinds of pepper. 2. Lock on the lid. Select the Pressure Cook on the panel. Press the button again to choose Less option; use the "-" button to adjust the cooking time to 6 minutes. Press Pressure Level to choose High pressure. Make sure the steam valve is in the "Sealing" position. 3. When the cooking time is up, leave the steam release handle in the Sealing position for about 20 minutes. Ladle off 1 cup of the cooking liquid and discard. 4. In a small bowl, mix the remaining ingredients and add to the beans. 5. Insert the inner pot into the cooker base. 6. Press Sauté to select the program and then press it again to choose the Normal heat. Simmer and stir constantly for 5 minutes, until the sauce has thickened, 5 minutes. 7. Press Cancel. 8. Season with salt and pepper and serve.
Per Serving: Calories 351; Fat 22g; Sodium 502mg; Carbs 15.2g; Sugar 1.1g; Fiber 0.7g; Protein 6.4g

Savory Mushroom Polenta

Prep Time: 10 minutes | Cook Time: 21 minutes | Serves: 6

1 medium onion, diced	3 tablespoons tomato paste
1⅓ cups Easy Vegetable Broth or no-salt-added vegetable broth, divided, plus more as needed	2 teaspoons dried thyme
	1 teaspoon balsamic vinegar
	Freshly ground black pepper
2 garlic cloves, minced	3 cups water
8 ounces white button mushrooms, sliced	1 cup polenta or coarsely ground cornmeal
8 ounces cremini mushrooms, sliced	1 cup milk

1. Insert the Inner Pot into the Cooker Base without the lid. 2. Select Sauté mode and then press the same button again and then adjust the cooking temperature to Normal. 3. When the display switches On to Hot, add the onion and cook for 3 to 5 minutes until translucent, adding water to prevent sticking; add the garlic and cook for 30 seconds until fragrant; add the mushroom and cook for 5 minutes or until softened; stir in the tomato paste, vinegar, thyme, pepper and ⅓ cup of the broth, cook for 3 minutes and scrape the browned bits from the bottom. 4. When done, transfer the mushroom mixture to a prepared bowl; rinse and then dry the Inner Pot. 5. Insert the Inner Pot into the Cooker Base again without the lid. 6. Select Sauté mode and then press the same button again and then adjust the cooking

temperature to Normal. 7. When the display switches On to Hot, add the polenta, milk, water and the remaining broth and stir constantly for 5 minutes, until the mixture starts to simmer. 8. Press the Cancel button and lock the lid. 9. Select the Pressure Cook mode and press the button again to adjust the cooking time to 10 minutes; press the Pressure Level button to choose High Pressure. 10. When the time is up, quickly and carefully turn the steam release handle from the Sealing position to the Venting position. 11. Uncover the lid and serve the food on a plate, then top with the mushroom mixture. 12. Enjoy!
Per Serving: Calories: 221; Fat: 2g; Carbs: 43g; Fiber: 4g; Sugar: 7g; Sodium: 47mg; Protein: 9g

Homemade Jalapeño Popper Dip

Prep Time: 10 minutes | Cook Time: 30 minutes | Serves: 2

2 jalapeño peppers, divided	¼ cup milk
½ pound dried great northern beans, rinsed and sorted	2 garlic cloves, crushed
½ medium onion, roughly chopped	2 tablespoons nutritional yeast
4 cups water, divided	1 tablespoon chickpea miso paste
½ cup cashews	1 tablespoon apple cider vinegar

1. Slice 1 of the jalapeños in half lengthwise and remove the seeds. 2. In your Inner Pot, combine the halved pepper, beans, onion, and 3 cups of the water. Lock the lid and turn the steam release handle to Sealing. 3. Select the Pressure Cook on the panel. Press the button again to choose Normal option; use the "-" button to adjust the cooking time to 30 minutes. Press Pressure Level to choose High pressure. 4. Boil the remaining 1 cup of water and pour in a large bowl over cashews; soak for at least 30 minutes. Drain the soaking liquid before adding the cashews. 5. After cooking has completed, leave the steam release handle in the Sealing position for 10 minutes after cooking has completed, then turn the steam release handle to the Venting position; quick-release any remaining pressure and uncover the lid carefully. 6. Remove the jalapeño from the pot and then chop it. Finely chop the remaining raw jalapeño and remove the seed. Put both peppers aside. 7. Drain the beans and onion, then combine them in a blender with the cashews, milk, garlic, nutritional yeast, miso, and vinegar. Blend all of them until the mixture is creamy. Spoon into a medium mixing bowl and stir in the jalapeños. 8. Serve right away.
Per Serving: Calories: 314; Fat: 9g; Carbs: 44g; Fiber: 13g; Sugar: 4g; Sodium: 177mg; Protein: 17g

Fresh Steamed Artichokes with Lemon-Dijon Dipping Sauce

Prep Time: 10 minutes | Cook Time: 15 minutes | Serves: 4

4 (10-ounce) whole artichokes, rinsed and drained	2½ tablespoons fresh lemon juice
½ cup (1 stick) unsalted butter, at room temperature	1 tablespoon Dijon mustard
2 garlic cloves, chopped	Salt and freshly ground black pepper

1. Trim the artichoke stems to within 1 inch of the base. Place the Steam Rack in the pot and add 1½ cups warm water. Place the artichokes stem-side down on the rack. 2. Select the Pressure Cook on the panel. Press the button again to choose Less option; use the "-" button to adjust the cooking time to 10 minutes. Press Pressure Level to choose High pressure. Make sure the steam valve is in the "Sealing" position. 3. When the cooking time is up, quickly and carefully turn the steam release handle from Sealing position to the Venting position. 4. To test for doneness, pull a leaf from near the center of an artichoke and scrape the tender bottom of the leaf off with your teeth; the flesh should come away easily. If they're not done, lock on the lid and cook under High pressure for a minute or so more. 5. Transfer the artichokes to serving plates with tongs, cover loosely. Remove the rack from the pot and remove the cooking water. 6. Press the Cancel button to stop this cooking program. 7. Insert the inner pot into the cooker base without the lid. 8. Press Sauté to select the program and press it again to choose More option. Add the butter and garlic to the pot and cook for 1 minute until the garlic is sizzling and fragrant. 9. Press Cancel. 10. Whisk in the lemon juice and mustard. Add some salt and pepper to season as you like. 11. Pour the butter mixture into dipping bowls and serve with the artichokes.
Per Serving: Calories 336; Fat 17.3g; Sodium 281mg; Carbs 8.1g; Fiber 5.3g; Sugars 17.7g; Protein 3.3g

Steamed Corn with Parsley

Prep Time: 10 minutes | Cook Time: 6 minutes | Serves: 4

4 cups water
4 ears corn, shucked and halved
½ teaspoon canola oil
1 tablespoon finely grated Parmesan cheese

Kosher salt
Freshly ground black pepper
⅛ teaspoon paprika
1 tablespoon finely chopped fresh parsley

1. In the Inner Pot, add the water and corn. 2. Place and lock the lid. 3. Select the Pressure Cook mode and press the button again to adjust the cooking time to 2 minutes; press the Pressure Level button to choose High Pressure. 4. When the time is up, quickly and carefully turn the steam release handle from the Sealing position to the Venting position. 5. Uncover the lid and transfer the corn to a prepared plate lined with paper towel, then carefully pour the hot water and dry the pot. 6. Without the lid, select Sauté mode and then press the same button again and then adjust the cooking temperature to Normal. 7. When the display switches On to Hot, add and heat the oil; add the corn and quickly toss with the oil, cook for 4 minutes without moving the corn or until charred, then rotate the corn and repeat twice until a few sided are charred. 8. Press the Cancel button to stop this cooking program, then transfer the corn to a platter, sprinkle with half of the Parmesan and season with the salt, pepper and a sprinkle of paprika on all sides. 9. Garnish with the parsley and enjoy.
Per Serving: Calories 254; Fat 28 g; Sodium 346mg; Carbs 12.3 g; Sugar 1g; Fiber 0.7g; Protein 24.3 g

Steamed Garlic Edamame

Prep Time: 10 minutes | Cook Time: 10 minutes | Serves: 4

1 cup water
2 cups fresh or frozen edamame, in their pods
1 teaspoon sesame oil or extra-

virgin olive oil
3 large garlic cloves, minced
1 tablespoon soy sauce
Sea salt

1. In the Inner Pot, add the water and place the Steam Rack; put the edamame on the rack. 2. Place and lock the lid. 3. Select the Steam mode and press the button again to adjust the cooking time to 3 minutes; press the Pressure Level button to choose High Pressure. 4. While cooking, heat the oil in a suitable skillet over medium heat, once hot, add the garlic and cook for 1 to 2 minutes until cooked but not brown; add the soy sauce and then turn off the heat. 5. When the time is up, quickly and carefully turn the steam release handle from the Sealing position to the Venting position. 6. Uncover the lid and serve the edamame in a prepared bowl, toss with the garlic mixture. 7. Season with salt and enjoy.
Per Serving: Calories 249; Fat 13g; Sodium 556mg; Carbs 10g; Sugar 1.1g; Fiber 0.7g; Protein 31g

Steamed Artichokes Dip

Prep Time: 10 minutes | Cook Time: 15 minutes | Serves: 4

2 large artichokes
1 lemon, halved
1 cup water

3 tablespoons mayonnaise
1 teaspoon Dijon mustard
Pinch smoked paprika

1. Discard the damaged outer leaves of the artichokes, trim the bottoms flat and trim the tough ends of the leaves, then rub with 1 lemon half. 2. In the Inner Pot, add the water and place the Steam Rack; put the artichokes on the rack with the bloom facing up. 3. Place and lock the lid. 4. Select the Pressure Cook mode and press the button again to adjust the cooking time to 10 to 15 minutes (depending on the size of the artichokes, you can also cook a few minutes more); press the Pressure Level button to choose High Pressure. 5. While cooking, in a suitable bowl, thoroughly mix up the mayonnaise, mustard, paprika, and a generous squeeze of lemon juice. 6. When the time is up, leave the steam release handle from the Sealing position. 7. Uncover the lid, serve and enjoy the artichokes warm with the dipping sauce on the side.
Per Serving: Calories 344; Fat 14.9g; Sodium 227mg; Carbs 14g; Fiber 1g; Sugars 1.4g; Protein 25.7g

Bok Choy with Sesame Seeds

Prep Time: 10 minutes | Cook Time: 4 minutes | Serves: 4

1 cup water
1 medium head bok choy, leaves separated
1 teaspoon soy sauce

½ teaspoon sesame oil
2 teaspoons sesame seeds
Kosher salt
Freshly ground black pepper

1. In the Inner Pot, add the water and place the Steam Rack; put the bok choy on the rack with the thickest leaves facing down. 2. Place and lock the lid. 3. Select the Pressure Cook mode and press the button again to adjust the cooking time to 4 minutes; press the Pressure Level button to choose High Pressure. 4. When the time is up, quickly and carefully turn the steam release handle from the Sealing position to the Venting position. 5. Uncover the lid and carefully remove the bok choy to a prepared bowl, toss with the soy sauce, sesame oil, sesame seeds and season with the salt and pepper. 6. Enjoy.
Per Serving: Calories 36; Fat 17.3g; Sodium 281mg; Carbs 8.1g; Fiber 5.3g; Sugars 17.7g; Protein 32.3g

Lemon Beet Hummus

Prep Time: 10 minutes | Cook Time: 45 minutes | Serves: 6

3 cups water
1 cup dried chickpeas, rinsed and sorted
1 medium beet, peeled and quartered
½ cup tahini

2 tablespoons freshly squeezed lemon juice
4 garlic cloves, crushed
Salt (optional)

1. In the Inner Pot, add the chickpeas, beets and stir in water. 2. Place and lock the lid. 3. Select the Pressure Cook mode and press the button again to adjust the cooking time to 45 minutes; press the Pressure Level button to choose High Pressure. 4. While cooking, add the lemon juice, garlic and salt to the blender, do not blend. 5. When the time is up, leave the steam release handle from the Sealing position for 10 minutes, then turn it to the Venting position. 6. Uncover the lid and carefully transfer the chickpeas and beets to the blender, then blend well. 7. Chill until cool before serving; if the dip needs to be thinner, you can add the remaining liquid in the pot as needed.
Per Serving: Calories: 382; Fat: 19g; Carbs: 41g; Fiber: 10g; Sugar: 7g; Sodium: 63mg; Protein: 16g

Egg Salad

Prep Time: 10 minutes | Cook Time: 7 minutes | Serves: 4

1 cup water
6 eggs
⅓ cup finely diced celery
¼ cup high-quality or homemade mayonnaise
2 teaspoons minced fresh parsley

1 teaspoon Dijon or wholegrain mustard
1 teaspoon freshly squeezed lemon juice
Kosher salt
Freshly ground black pepper

1. In the Inner Pot, add the water and place the Steam Rack; put the eggs on the rack. 2. Place and lock the lid. 3. Select the Pressure Cook mode and press the button again to adjust the cooking time to 7 minutes; press the Pressure Level button to choose Low Pressure. 4. While cooking, thoroughly mix up the celery, mayonnaise, parsley, mustard, lemon juice, pepper and a sprinkle in a suitable bowl. 5. When the time is up, quickly and carefully turn the steam release handle from the Sealing position to the Venting position. 6. Uncover the lid and let the eggs cool for 30 seconds before rinsing them under the cold water. 7. In a prepared bowl, peel the eggs; use a fork to mash them for the desired consistency and mix with the mayonnaise mixture. 8. You can refrigerate this dish in an airtight container for up to 3 days.
Per Serving: Calories 305; Fat 15g; Sodium 548mg; Carbs 12g; Sugar 1.2g; Fiber 0.7g; Protein 29g

Dandelion Greens

Prep time: 15 minutes | Cook time: 1 minutes | Serves: 8

4-pound dandelion greens, stalks cut and, and greens washed
½ cup water
¼ cup olive oil

¼ cup lemon juice
½ teaspoon salt
½ teaspoon black pepper

1. Add dandelion greens and water to the Instant Pot. 2. Put on the pressure cooker's lid and turn the steam valve to "Sealing" position. 3. Set the Instant Pot to Pressure Cook. 4. Press the Pressure Level button to adjust the pressure to "Low". 5. Use the "+/-" keys on the control panel to set the cooking time to 1 minute. 6. Once the cooking cycle is completed, allow the steam to release quickly. 7. When all the steam is released, remove the pressure lid from the top carefully. 8. Combine olive oil, lemon juice, salt, and pepper in a small bowl. 9. Pour over greens and toss to coat.
Per Serving: Calories 305; Fat 12.9g; Sodium 754mg; Carbs 21g; Fiber 6.1g; Sugar 4.2g; Protein 11g

Fingerling Potatoes in Broth

Prep Time: 10 minutes | Cook Time: 17 minutes | Serves: 4

2 tablespoons butter
1½ pounds small fingerling potatoes, each pricked twice with a small knife
½ cup vegetable or chicken broth
Kosher salt
Freshly ground black pepper
1 fresh rosemary sprig (leaves only), minced

1. Insert the Inner Pot into the Cooker Base without the lid. 2. Select Sauté mode and then press the same button again and then adjust the cooking temperature to More. 3. When the display switches On to Hot, add and melt the butter; add the potatoes and stir regularly for 10 minutes to coat well, or until the skins start to get crispy and the butter is browned; pour in the broth. 4. Press the Cancel button and lock the lid. 5. Select the Pressure Cook mode and press the button again to adjust the cooking time to 7 minutes; press the Pressure Level button to choose High Pressure. 6. When the time is up, leave the steam release handle in the Sealing position for 10 minutes, then turn it to the Venting position. 7. Uncover the lid and serve the food on a plate. 8. Season with salt, pepper and top with the rosemary and enjoy.
Per Serving: Calories 344; Fat 14.9g; Sodium 227mg; Carbs 12g; Fiber 1.2g; Sugars 1g; Protein 27g

Delicious Corn Pudding

Prep Time: 10 minutes | Cook Time: 30 minutes | Serves: 4

2 tablespoons butter
2 shallots, finely chopped
1 cup fresh corn, cut off the cob
¾ cup whole milk
¼ cup sour cream
3 tablespoons cornmeal
1 tablespoon sugar
2 eggs, beaten
½ teaspoon kosher salt
¼ teaspoon freshly ground black pepper
1½ cups water

1. In a suitable bowl, mix up the corn, milk, sour cream, cornmeal, sugar, eggs, salt, and pepper. 2. Insert the Inner Pot into the Cooker Base without the lid. 3. Select Sauté mode and then press the same button again and then adjust the cooking temperature to More. 4. When the display switches On to Hot, add and melt the butter; add the shallots and press the Cancel button, cook the shallots until the sizzling stops. 5. Add the butter and shallots to the corn mixture and stir well. 6. Oil a suitable round baking dish with the butter and pour the mixture into it, cover with foil. 7. Add the water to the pot and place the Steam Rack, then arrange the baking dish to the rack; place and lock the lid. 8. Select the Pressure Cook mode and press the button again to adjust the cooking time to 30 minutes; press the Pressure Level button to choose Low Pressure. 9. When the time is up, quickly and carefully turn the steam release handle from the Sealing position to the Venting position. 10. Uncover the lid and remove the dish, let it cool a few minutes before serving.
Per Serving: Calories 236; Fat 13.9g; Sodium 451mg; Carbs 13.2g; Fiber 1.2g; Sugars 1.4g; Protein 14.3g

Faux Gratin Potatoes in Broth

Prep Time: 10 minutes | Cook Time: 50 minutes | Serves: 4

2 tablespoons butter
2 medium garlic cloves, sliced
2 pounds Yukon Gold potatoes, peeled and cut into ¼-inch-thick slices
Salt and freshly ground black pepper
⅔ cup store-bought vegetable or chicken broth
1½ cups grated cheese of your choice (cheddar, Gruyère, or Swiss; 6 ounces)
¼ cup heavy cream, warmed

1. Insert the Inner Pot into the Cooker Base without the lid. 2. Select Sauté mode and then press the same button again and then adjust the cooking temperature to Normal. 3. When the display switches On to Hot, add and melt the butter; add the garlic and stir constantly for 45 seconds until fragrant 4. Press the Cancel button to stop this cooking program. 5. Still in the pot, add the potatoes, 1 teaspoon of salt and several grinds of pepper, then stir to coat the potatoes with the garlic mixture; pour in the broth and then lock the lid. 6. Select the Pressure Cook mode and press the button again to adjust the cooking time to 9 minutes; press the Pressure Level button to choose Low Pressure. 7. When the time is up, leave turn the steam release handle in the Sealing position for 1 minute, then turn it to the Venting position. 8. Preheat your oven with the suitable oven rack in it. 9. In the suitable baking dish, pour the potato mixture and use the spatula to gently fold in 1 cup of cheese and cream; top with the ½ cup of cheese and broil for 3 to 5 minutes until browned and bubbly. 10. When done, serve and enjoy.

Per Serving: Calories 236; Fat 13.9g; Sodium 451mg; Carbs 13.2g; Fiber 1.2g; Sugars 1.4g; Protein 14.3g

Honey Cayenne Carrots

Prep Time: 10 minutes | Cook Time: 2 minutes | Serves: 4

1 cup water
5 to 6 large carrots, peeled and cut into 1-inch chunks (about 3 cups)
1 tablespoon butter
¼ teaspoon ground cumin
¼ teaspoon cayenne
Kosher salt
Freshly ground black pepper
2 teaspoons honey

1. In the Inner Pot, add the water and place the Steam Rack; put the carrots on the rack. 2. Place and lock the lid. 3. Select the Steam mode and press the button again to adjust the cooking time to 2 minutes; press the Pressure Level button to choose High Pressure. 4. When the time is up, quickly and carefully turn the steam release handle from the Sealing position to the Venting position. 5. Uncover the lid and carefully take out the carrots and rack; pour the hot cooking water, clean and dry the pot. 6. Insert the Inner Pot into the Cooker Base without the lid. 7. Select Sauté mode and then press the same button again and then adjust the cooking temperature to Normal. 8. When the display switches On to Hot, add and melt the butter; put the carrots back to pot and stir until well coated; stir in the cumin, cayenne, salt and pepper. 9. Lastly, add the honey and press the Cancel button. 10. Stir until fully coated before serving.
Per Serving: Calories 344; Fat 14.9g; Sodium 227mg; Carbs 14g; Fiber 1g; Sugars 1.4g; Protein 25.7g

Butternut Squash and Parsnips

Prep Time: 10 minutes | Cook Time: 10 minutes | Serves: 4

2 tablespoons butter
1½ cups peeled butternut squash, cut into 1-inch cubes
1 cup peeled parsnips, cut into 1-inch cubes
1 cup peeled turnips, cut into 1-inch cubes
¾ cup vegetable or chicken broth
⅛ teaspoon sugar
¼ teaspoon baking soda
Kosher salt
Freshly ground black pepper
1 teaspoon finely chopped fresh rosemary

1. Insert the Inner Pot into the Cooker Base without the lid. 2. Select Sauté mode and then press the same button again and then adjust the cooking temperature to Normal. 3. When the display switches On to Hot, add and melt the butter; add the butternut squash cubes and stir regularly for 4 minutes; stir in the parsnips, turnips, broth, sugar, baking soda, salt and pepper. 4. Press the Cancel button and then lock the lid. 5. Select the Pressure Cook mode and press the button again to adjust the cooking time to 6 minutes; press the Pressure Level button to choose High Pressure. 6. When the time is up, quickly and carefully turn the steam release handle from the Sealing position to the Venting position. 7. Uncover the lid and drain off most of the liquid. 8. With the rosemary, serve and enjoy.
Per Serving: Calories 236; Fat 13.9g; Sodium 451mg; Carbs 13.2g; Fiber 1.2g; Sugars 1.4g; Protein 14.3g

Butter Mashed Potatoes

Prep Time: 10 minutes | Cook Time: 10 minutes | Serves: 8

4 pounds Yukon Gold potatoes, peeled and quartered
3 cups water
1 teaspoon kosher salt, plus more for seasoning
5 tablespoons butter
½ cup whole milk
1 cup sour cream
¼ cup drained prepared horseradish
Freshly ground black pepper

1. In the Inner Pot, add the potatoes, water and salt. 2. Place and lock the lid. 3. Select the Pressure Cook mode and press the button again to adjust the cooking time to 10 minutes; press the Pressure Level button to choose High Pressure. 4. While cooking, heat the butter and milk in a small saucepan over low heat until start to be very warm. 5. When the time is up, quickly and carefully turn the steam release handle from the Sealing position to the Venting position. 6. Uncover the lid and drain off the cooking liquid, reserving ½ cup. 7. Mash the potatoes with a masher until fluffy and all lumps are gone; add the sour cream, horseradish, warm milk and butter; season with the pepper and then mix them to combine well. 8. Serve and enjoy. 9. You can add the cooking liquid as needed if the potatoes are too thick.
Per Serving: Calories 351; Fat 22g; Sodium 502mg; Carbs 15.2g; Sugar 1.1g; Fiber 0.7g; Protein 6.4g

Lemon Beets with Goat Cheese

Prep Time: 10 minutes | Cook Time: 20 minutes | Serves: 4

1 cup water
4 medium beets
½ cup crumbled goat cheese
Juice of ½ lemon

Extra-virgin olive oil
Kosher salt
Freshly ground black pepper

1. Trim the beets in the sink after cleaning them. 2. In the Inner Pot, add the water and place the Steam Rack; put the beets on the rack. 3. Place and lock the lid. 4. Select the Pressure Cook mode and press the button again to adjust the cooking time to 20 minutes (you can cook for 5 minutes more if the beets don't reach the needed doneness); press the Pressure Level button to choose High Pressure. 5. When the time is up, quickly and carefully turn the steam release handle from the Sealing position to the Venting position. 6. Uncover the lid and carefully take out the beets and rack. 7. Cool the beets under cold water in the sink, then slide the skins off and slice them on a plate board. 8. Serve the beet slices on a prepared plate, top them with the goat cheese, lemon juice, a drizzle of olive oil and season with salt and pepper. 9. Enjoy.
Per Serving: Calories 285; Fat 9.8g; Sodium 639mg; Carbs 11.1g; Fiber 1.2g; Sugars 5.1g; Protein 27.8g

Creamy Parmesan Polenta

Prep Time: 10 minutes | Cook Time: 39 minutes | Serves: 4

2 tablespoons olive oil
2 medium garlic cloves, thinly sliced
4 cups store-bought chicken or vegetable broth, warmed

1 bay leaf
Salt and freshly ground black pepper
1 cup polenta (not quick-cooking)
½ cup grated Parmesan cheese

1. Insert the Inner Pot into the Cooker Base without the lid. 2.Select Sauté mode and then press the same button again and then adjust the cooking temperature to Normal. 3.When the display switches On to Hot, add and heat the oil; add the garlic and stir constantly for 30 seconds until fragrant; add the broth, bay leaf and ½ teaspoon of salt, when the liquid starts to simmer, gradually whisk in the polenta. 4.Press the Cancel button to stop this cooking program and lock the lid. 5.Select the Pressure Cook mode and press the button again to adjust the cooking time to 9 minutes; press the Pressure Level button to choose Low Pressure. 6.When the time is up, leave turn the steam release handle in the Sealing position for 10 minutes, then turn it to the Venting position. 7.Uncover the lid, wait for seconds until the food is thicken, then whisk in the cheese and season with the salt and pepper; discard the bay leaf. 8.Serve. 9.For solid polenta to pan-fry or broil, transfer the polenta to a container and refrigerate without covering for at least 2 hours. 10.For pan-fry, cut into cubes and pan-fry in a non-stick skillet with a few tablespoons of olive oil over medium heat for 10 minutes, flipping halfway through, until golden brown. 11. For broil, spread squares of polenta on a baking sheet lined with foil; drizzle with oil, sprinkle with a little Parmesan cheese, and broil 4 inches for 6 minutes from the broiler element until the cheese is bubbly.
Per Serving: Calories 305; Fat 15g; Sodium 548mg; Carbs 12g; Sugar 1.2g; Fiber 0.7g; Protein 2g

Corn on the Cob

Prep Time: 10 minutes | Cook Time: 2 minutes | Serves: 4

For The Corn
4 ears corn, shucked
For Mexican Corn on The Cob
⅓ cup mayonnaise
¼ cup finely chopped fresh cilantro
2 teaspoons ground New Mexican
For Maple-Barbecue Corn on The Cob
4 tablespoons (½ stick) room-temperature butter
2 tablespoons maple syrup
For Hot Wings–Style Corn On The Cob
4 tablespoons (½ stick) butter, at room temperature
2 tablespoons hot sauce
For French Corn On The Cob
½ cup soft herb and garlic cheese spread (such as Boursin), at room temperature

chile powder
½ cup crumbled aged Cotija or feta cheese

4 teaspoons thick barbecue sauce
Garlic salt

4 teaspoons honey
½ cup crumbled blue cheese
1¼ teaspoons celery salt

2 tablespoons finely chopped fresh chives
Freshly ground black pepper

1. In the Inner Pot, add 1½ cups of warm water and place the Steam Rack; put the corn on the rack. 2. Place and lock the lid. 3. Select the Pressure Cook mode and press the button again to adjust the cooking time to 2 minutes; press the Pressure Level button to choose High Pressure. 4. When the time is up, quickly and carefully turn the steam release handle from the Sealing position to the Venting position. 5. To make the Mexican Corn: Spread the mayonnaise on the corn, sprinkle with the cilantro, cheese and chili powder. 6. To make the Maple-Barbecue Corn: Mix up the butter, maple syrup, BBQ sauce in a suitable bowl and then spread on the corn; sprinkle with the garlic salt before serving. 7. To make the Hot Wings-Style Corn: Mix up the butter, hot sauce and honey in a suitable bowl, then spread on the corn; roll the cobs in the blue cheese and sprinkle with the celery salt. 8. To make the French Corn: Spread the cheese all over the cobs, roll in the chives and season with pepper.
Per Serving: Calories 285; Fat 9.8g; Sodium 639mg; Carbs 11.1g; Fiber 1.2g; Sugars 5.1g; Protein 7.8g

Butter Potatoes Mash

Prep Time: 10 minutes | Cook Time: 10 minutes | Serves: 6

4 medium russet potatoes (2 pounds), peeled and quartered
Salt
1 medium (8-ounce) bunch lacinato kale, tough center rib discarded, leaves chopped

4 tablespoons (½ stick) unsalted butter, at room temperature
4 green onions, thinly sliced
¼ to ½ cup whole milk or heavy cream

1. In the Inner Pot, add 1 cup of water and add the potatoes; sprinkle with ½ teaspoon of salt; top the potatoes with the kale. 2. Place and lock the lid. 3. Select the Pressure Cook mode and press the button again to adjust the cooking time to 8 minutes; press the Pressure Level button to choose High Pressure. 4. When the time is up, quickly and carefully turn the steam release handle from the Sealing position to the Venting position. 5. Uncover the lid, transfer the potatoes and kale to the colander in the sink and cool them for a few minutes; let the steam evaporate will make the potatoes fluffier when you mash them. 6. While cooling, insert the Inner Pot into the Cooker Base without the lid. 7. Select Sauté mode and then press the same button again and then adjust the cooking temperature to Normal. 8. When the display switches On to Hot, add and melt the butter; add the green onions and cook for 1 minutes until tender; add the milk or cream and cook for 1 minute to bring to a simmer. 9. When done, press the Cancel button to stop this cooking program, then transfer the cooled potatoes and kale back to the pot. 10. Use a potato masher to mash the potatoes until mostly smooth. 11. Season with salt and pepper before serving.
Per Serving: Calories 344; Fat 14.9g; Sodium 227mg; Carbs 14g; Fiber 1g; Sugars 1.4g; Protein 2.7g

Tasty Indian-Style Spaghetti Squash

Prep Time: 10 minutes | Cook Time: 15 minutes | Serves: 4

1 medium (2½-pound) spaghetti squash, halved lengthwise and seeded
3 tablespoons unsalted butter or ghee
1½ teaspoons brown mustard seeds

1 teaspoon cumin seeds
3 medium garlic cloves, chopped
1 medium tomato, chopped
Salt and freshly ground black pepper

1. Place a trivet in the bottom of the pot and add 1½ cups cold water. Place the squash halves cut-side up in the pot. Lock on the lid, select the Pressure Cook on the panel. Press the button again to choose Less option; use the "-" button to adjust the cooking time to 8 minutes. Press Pressure Level to choose High pressure. Make sure the steam valve is in the "Sealing" position. 2. When the cooking time is up, quickly and carefully turn the steam release handle from Sealing position to the Venting position. 3. Transfer the squash to a cutting board. Drag a fork crosswise over the squash to scrape out the flesh into strands; remove the skins. Place the squash in a large serving bowl and cover with foil. 4. Insert the inner pot into the cooker base. 5. Remove the steaming water, dry out the pot, and return it to the appliance. Press Sauté to select the program and then adjust to Normal heat. Add the butter and when the butter has melted, add the mustard seeds and cumin seeds and cook, stirring frequently, until the seeds begin to pop, 1 minute. Add the garlic and tomato and cook until fragrant, 1 minute. 6. Press the Cancel button. 7. Pour the butter mixture over the squash. Add some salt and pepper to taste and mix well with tongs.
Per Serving: Calories 344; Fat 14.9g; Sodium 227mg; Carbs 14g; Fiber 1g; Sugars 1.4g; Protein 2.7g

Bacon Potatoes

Prep Time: 10 minutes | Cook Time: 15 minutes | Serves: 6

8 ounces applewood-smoked bacon, chopped
½ cup store-bought chicken broth, or homemade
6 tablespoons white wine vinegar
2½ tablespoons grainy mustard
2 tablespoons packed light brown sugar

2 teaspoons caraway seeds
½ teaspoon salt, plus more for seasoning
3 pounds small red potatoes, unpeeled, cut into ¾-inch chunks
½ cup finely chopped sweet onion (such as Walla Walla or Vidalia)
Freshly ground black pepper

1. Insert the Inner Pot into the Cooker Base without the lid. 2. Select Sauté mode and then press the same button again and then adjust the cooking temperature to Normal. 3. When the display switches On to Hot, add the bacon and stir constantly for 8 minutes until crisp and browned, then transfer the bacon to the plate lined with a paper towel. 4. Reserve 2 tablespoons of the drippings in a small bowl for the dressing and discard the remaining drippings. 5. Press the Cancel button to stop this cooking program. 6. Still in the Inner Pot, stir in the broth, vinegar, mustard, brown sugar, caraway seeds and ½ teaspoon salt; place the Steam Rack and put the potatoes on it. 7. Place and lock the lid. 8. Select the Pressure Cook mode and press the button again to adjust the cooking time to 7 minutes; press the Pressure Level button to choose High Pressure. 9. When the time is up, quickly and carefully turn the steam release handle from the Sealing position to the Venting position. 10. Uncover the lid, transfer the potatoes to a suitable bowl; take out the rack, pour the cooking liquid and reserved bacon drippings over the potatoes. 11. After adding the onion and seasoning with the salt and several grinds of pepper, gently use a spatula to toss them to combine well. Enjoy.
Per Serving: Calories 336; Fat 17.3g; Sodium 281mg; Carbs 8.1g; Fiber 5.3g; Sugars 17.7g; Protein 2.3g

Garlic Baby Potatoes with Herbs

Prep Time: 10 minutes | Cook Time: 7 minutes | Serves: 6

2 pounds baby red-skinned potatoes
1 cup water
3 tablespoons plant-based butter, melted, or extra-virgin olive oil

1 teaspoon garlic powder
1 teaspoon dried thyme
1 teaspoon dried rosemary, crushed
1 teaspoon salt
Freshly ground black pepper

1. Use a fork to pierce the potatoes. 2. In the Inner Pot, add the potatoes and water. 3. Place and lock the lid. 4. Select the Pressure Cook mode and press the button again to adjust the cooking time to 7 minutes; press the Pressure Level button to choose High Pressure. 5. When the time is up, quickly and carefully turn the steam release handle from the Sealing position to the Venting position. 6. Press the Cancel button and uncover the lid; drain the water and select the Sauté mode, press it again to choose Normal option. 7. Add the olive oil or butter, garlic powder, thyme, rosemary, salt and pepper in the pot, then cook the mixture for 3 to 4 minutes until the potatoes are slightly browned. 8. When done, serve and enjoy.
Per Serving: Calories: 251; Fat: 10g; Carbs: 37g; Fiber: 4g; Sugar: 3g; Sodium: 623mg; Protein: 4g

Mini Corn on the Cob

Prep Time: 10 minutes | Cook Time: 6 minutes | Serves: 6

1 cup water
4 to 6 frozen mini corncobs
1 (14-ounce) package silken tofu, drained
1 tablespoon freshly squeezed lemon juice

1 tablespoon apple cider vinegar
1 teaspoon ground cumin
Salt (optional)
1 lime, cut into wedges
1 tablespoon no-salt-added gluten-free chili powder

1. In the Inner Pot, add the water and place the Steam Rack; put the corn on the rack. 2. Place and lock the lid. 3. Select the Pressure Cook mode and press the button again to adjust the cooking time to 6 minutes; press the Pressure Level button to choose High Pressure. 4. While cooking, blend the tofu, lemon juice, vinegar, cumin and salt well in a blender; set aside for later use. 5. When the time is up, quickly and carefully turn the steam release handle from the Sealing position to the Venting position. 6. Uncover the lid, rub each cob with a lime wedge and then slather it with a generous amount of crema; sprinkle ¼ to ½ teaspoon chili powder on each cob. 7. Serve and enjoy. 8. You can refrigerate the leftovers in an airtight container for up to 4 days.
Per Serving: Calories: 103; Fat: 4g; Carbs: 12g; Fiber: 2g; Sugar: 2g; Sodium: 68mg; Protein: 8g

Simple Zucchini Ratatouille

Prep Time: 10 minutes | Cook Time: 15 minutes | Serves: 4

1 tablespoon extra-virgin olive oil, plus extra for serving
1 medium yellow onion, finely chopped
1 large red bell pepper, finely chopped
2 garlic cloves, minced
4 medium zucchini, chopped into bite-size pieces

¼ cup dry white wine
2 large tomatoes, seeded and diced, or 2 handfuls large cherry tomatoes, halved
1 bay leaf
3 fresh thyme sprigs
Kosher salt
Freshly ground black pepper
2 tablespoons torn fresh basil

1. Insert the Inner Pot into the Cooker Base without the lid. 2. Select Sauté mode and then press the same button again and then adjust the cooking temperature to More. 3. When the display switches On to Hot, add the oil, onion, bell pepper, garlic in order and stir regularly for 2 minutes until the vegetables start to brown; add the zucchini and cook for 3 minutes until it starts to brown; stir in the wine and then scrape the brown bits from the bottom of the pot. 4. Press the Cancel button to stop this cooking program, add the tomatoes, bay leaf, thyme, salt and pepper, then place and lock the lid. 5. Select the Pressure Cook mode and press the button again to adjust the cooking time to 3 minutes; press the Pressure Level button to choose High Pressure. 6. When the time is up, quickly and carefully turn the steam release handle from the Sealing position to the Venting position. 7. Uncover the lid. To reduce the liquid, resume cooking the food for 2 to 3 minutes on Sauté mode at More temperature. 8. When done, remove and discard the bay leaf; wait for a few minutes before serving and topping with the fresh basil and a drizzle of olive oil.
Per Serving: Calories 285; Fat 9.8g; Sodium 639mg; Carbs 11.1g; Fiber 1.2g; Sugars 5.1g; Protein 27.8g

Cinnamon Sweet Potatoes

Prep Time: 10 minutes | Cook Time: 15-23 minutes | Serves: 6

1 cup water
6 medium sweet potatoes, pricked a few times with a fork
4 tablespoons butter, cubed

½ cup brown sugar
¼ cup all-purpose flour
½ teaspoon ground cinnamon
Pinch kosher salt

1. In the Inner Pot, add the water and place the Steam Rack; put the sweet potatoes on the rack. 2. Place and lock the lid. 3. Select the Pressure Cook mode and press the button again to adjust the cooking time to 12 to 18 minutes (depending on the size of the sweet potatoes); press the Pressure Level button to choose High Pressure. 4. While cooking, in a suitable bowl, thoroughly mix up the butter, brown sugar, flour, cinnamon and salt, until a well-combined but crumbly mixture is formed. 5. When the time is up, leave the steam release handle from the Sealing position for 10 minutes, then turn it to the Venting position. 6. Preheat your oven and prepare a suitable baking sheet. 7. Transfer the sweet potatoes to the baking sheet, slice each in half lengthwise and lay side by side with cut-side up; sprinkle each half with 1 heaping tablespoon of the sugar mixture and broil for 3 to 5 minutes until lightly crispy. 8. When done, serve and enjoy.
Per Serving: Calories 285; Fat 9.8g; Sodium 639mg; Carbs 11.1g; Fiber 1.2g; Sugars 5.1g; Protein 7.8g

Braised Cabbage in Broth

Prep Time: 10 minutes | Cook Time: 8 minutes | Serves: 6

3 bacon slices
1 tablespoon butter
1 small head green cabbage, cored, quartered, and cut into ½-inch

strips
1 cup vegetable or chicken broth
Kosher salt
Freshly ground pepper

1. Insert the Inner Pot into the Cooker Base without the lid. 2. Select Sauté mode and then press the same button again and then adjust the cooking temperature to Normal. 3. When the display switches On to Hot, add the bacon and cook for 5 minutes, flipping halfway through, then remove the bacon and cut into pieces; add and melt the butter; stir in the cabbage, bacon, broth, salt and pepper. 4. Press the Cancel button and lock the lid. 5. Select the Pressure Cook mode and press the button again to adjust the cooking time to 3 minutes; press the Pressure Level button to choose High Pressure. 6. When the time is up, quickly and carefully turn the steam release handle from the Sealing position to the Venting position. 7. Uncover the lid and enjoy.
Per Serving: Calories: 70; Fat: 2g; Sodium: 263mg; Carbs: 7g; Sugar: 3g; Protein: 4g

Delicious Smoky Collard Greens or Kale

Prep Time: 15 minutes | Cook Time: 15 minutes | Serves: 4

3 slices thick-cut pepper bacon, chopped
1 small yellow onion, chopped
3 medium garlic cloves, chopped
¾ cup store-bought chicken or vegetable broth, or homemade (page 227 or 226)
2 large (9-ounce) bunches collard

greens or kale, tough center stems discarded, leaves torn
2 tablespoons cider vinegar or red wine vinegar
1 teaspoon smoked paprika
Salt and freshly ground black pepper

1. Insert the inner pot into the cooker base. 2. Press Sauté to select the program and adjust to Normal heat. Add the bacon and onion and cook, stirring now and then, until the bacon is browned, 8 minutes. Add the garlic and sauté until fragrant, 45 seconds. 3. Press. Cancel. 4. Add the broth and scrape up the browned bits on the bottom of the pot. Add the greens, vinegar, paprika, ½ teaspoon salt, and several grinds of pepper and toss with tongs to coat the greens with the liquid. Lock on the lid, select the Pressure Cook on the panel. Press the button again to choose Less option; use the "-" button to adjust the cooking time to 5 minutes. Press Pressure Level to choose High pressure. Make sure the steam valve is in the "Sealing" position. 5. When the cooking time is up, leave the steam release handle in the Sealing position for 10 minutes and then quickly and carefully turn the steam release handle from Sealing position to the Venting position. Add some salt and pepper to season as you like. 6. Serve the greens immediately.
Per Serving: Calories 285; Fat 9.8g; Sodium 639mg; Carbs 11.1g; Fiber 1.2g; Sugars 5.1g; Protein 2.8g

Parmesan Spaghetti Squash

Prep Time: 10 minutes | Cook Time: 11 minutes | Serves: 4

1 (2- to 4-pound) spaghetti squash, halved crosswise
1 cup water
⅓ cup pine nuts
2 tablespoons extra-virgin olive oil
3 garlic cloves, minced

Juice of ½ lemon
⅓ cup grated Parmesan cheese
Kosher salt
Freshly ground black pepper
2 tablespoons chopped fresh basil leaves

1. Set half of each squash aside. Scoop out all the seeds and sticky fibrous innards with a spoon, making the two halves hollow. 2. In the Inner Pot, add the water and set the squash inside with the cut-side up. 3. Place and lock the lid. 4. Select the Pressure Cook mode and press the button again to adjust the cooking time to 7 minutes; press the Pressure Level button to choose High Pressure. 5. While cooking, cook the pine nuts for 3 minutes in a sauté pan over medium-high heat until toasted, tossing every 30 seconds; when done, remove and set aside for later use. 6. Still in the sauté pan, heat the oil and cook the garlic for 1 minutes, until cooked but not brown; when done, turn off the heat. 7. When the time is up, quickly and carefully turn the steam release handle from the Sealing position to the Venting position. 8. Uncover the lid, take out the squash and drain any collected water. 9. Separate the strands from the peel with a fork, keeping the strands as long as possible. 10. In a suitable bowl, toss the strands with the lemon juice, most of the Parmesan, cooked oil and garlic mixture; season the strands with salt and pepper, and top them with the toasted pine nuts, more Parmesan and basil. 11. Serve.
Per Serving: Calories 305; Fat 15g; Sodium 548mg; Carbs 12g; Sugar 1.2g; Fiber 0.7g; Protein 29g

Long-Grain Rice in Tomato Sauce

Prep Time: 10 minutes | Cook Time: 13 minutes | Serves: 4

2 tablespoons olive oil
1 small onion, finely chopped
1 cup chopped green bell pepper
1½ cups long-grain rice, rinsed

and drained
2 tablespoons taco seasoning
⅔ cup V8 tomato juice (1 small 5.5-ounce can)

1. Insert the Inner Pot into the Cooker Base without the lid. 2. Select Sauté mode and then press the same button again and then adjust the cooking temperature to Normal. 3. When the display switches On to Hot, add and heat the oil; add the onion, bell pepper and stir constantly for 4 minutes until tender. 4. Press the Cancel button to stop this cooking program. 5. Stir in the rice and taco seasoning and coat the rice with the vegetables and oil. 6. Place and lock the lid. 7. Select the Pressure Cook mode and press the button again to adjust the cooking time to 4 minutes; press the Pressure Level button to choose High Pressure. 8. When the

time is up, leave turn the steam release handle in the Sealing position for 5 minutes, then turn it to the Venting position. 9. Uncover the lid and use a fork to fluff the rice. 10. Serve and enjoy.
Per Serving: Calories 348; Fat 8.92g; Sodium 361mg; Carbs 60.16g; Fiber 4.2g; Sugar 3.39g; Protein 6.44g

Homemade Sweet-and-Sour Red Cabbage

Prep Time: 10 minutes | Cook Time: 10 minutes | Serves: 6

1 medium (2-pound) red cabbage
2 tablespoons olive oil
½ medium red onion, sliced
1½ teaspoons caraway seeds
½ teaspoon baking soda

3 tablespoons red wine vinegar
1 tablespoon brown sugar
Salt and freshly ground black pepper

1. Cut the cabbage into quarters. Cut out the hard, white core at the base of each quarter and discard. Shred the cabbage into ¼-inch-wide strips. Set aside. 2. Insert the inner pot into the cooker base without the lid. 3. Press Sauté to select the program and then press it again to choose the Less temperature options. Put the oil in the pot, when the oil is hot, add the onion, caraway seeds, and baking soda and cook until tender, 4 minutes. Add the vinegar and brown sugar and sauté. 4. Add the cabbage, ½ teaspoon salt, and several grinds of black pepper and toss to coat. 5. Lock on the lid, select the Pressure Cook on the panel. Press the button again to choose Less option; use the "-" button to adjust the cooking time to 5 minutes. Press Pressure Level to choose High pressure. Make sure the steam valve is in the "Sealing" position. 6. When the cooking time is up, quickly and carefully turn the steam release handle from Sealing position to the Venting position. Season with salt and pepper, and serve.
Per Serving: Calories 249; Fat 13g; Sodium 556mg; Carbs 10g; Sugar 1.1g; Fiber 0.7g; Protein 1g

Spicy Corn On the Cob

Prep time: 15 minutes | Cook time: 2 minutes | Serves: 4

2 tablespoons olive oil
¼ teaspoon smoked paprika
¼ teaspoon ground cumin
¼ teaspoon black pepper
⅛ teaspoon cayenne pepper

1 cup water
4 large ears corn, husk and silks removed
½ teaspoon flaky sea salt

1. In a small bowl, whisk together olive oil, paprika, cumin, black pepper, and cayenne pepper. Set aside. 2. Place the rack in the Instant Pot, pour in water, and place corn on the rack. 3. Put on the pressure cooker's lid and turn the steam valve to "Sealing" position. 4. Set the Instant Pot to Pressure Cook. 5. Use the "+/-" keys on the control panel to set the cooking time to 2 minutes. 6. Press the Pressure Level button to adjust the pressure to "Low". 7. Once the cooking cycle is completed, allow the steam to release naturally. 8. When all the steam is released, remove the pressure lid from the top carefully. 9. Carefully transfer corn to a platter and brush with spiced olive oil. 10. Serve immediately with sea salt.
Per Serving: Calories 242; Fat 11g; Sodium 91mg; Carbs 14g; Fiber 3g; Sugar 8g; Protein 13g

Gingered Sweet Potatoes

Prep time: 15 minutes | Cook time: 10 minutes | Serves: 6

2½-pound sweet potatoes, peeled and chopped
2 cups water
1 tablespoon minced fresh ginger

½ teaspoon salt
1 tablespoon maple syrup
1 tablespoon unsalted butter
¼ cup whole milk

1. Place sweet potatoes and water in the Instant Pot. 2. Put on the pressure cooker's lid and turn the steam valve to "Sealing" position. 3. Set the Instant Pot to Pressure Cook. 4. Use the "+/-" keys on the control panel to set the cooking time to 10 minutes. 5. Press the Pressure Level button to adjust the pressure to "Low". 6. Once the cooking cycle is completed, allow the steam to release naturally. 7. When all the steam is released, remove the pressure lid from the top carefully. 8. Drain water from the Instant Pot. Add ginger, salt, maple syrup, butter, and milk to sweet potatoes. 9. Using an immersion blender, cream the potatoes until desired consistency is reached. 10. Serve warm.
Per Serving: Calories 419; Fat 14g; Sodium 791mg; Carbs 8.9g; Fiber 4.6g; Sugar 8g; Protein 3g

California Basmati Rice

Prep Time: 10 minutes | Cook Time: 6 minutes | Serves: 4

2 tablespoons canola oil
3 medium garlic cloves, finely chopped
1 tablespoon finely chopped fresh ginger
1½ cups California basmati rice (such as Lundberg brand), rinsed
and drained
1½ teaspoons garam masala or curry powder
½ teaspoon ground turmeric
Salt
1 cup frozen peas

1. Insert the Inner Pot into the Cooker Base without the lid. 2. Select Sauté mode and then press the same button again and then adjust the cooking temperature to Normal. 3. When the display switches On to Hot, add and heat the oil; add the ginger, garlic and stir constantly for 45 seconds until fragrant. 4. Press the Cancel button to stop this cooking program. 5. Still in the Inner Pot, add the rice, garam marsala and turmeric, 1½ cups of water and ¾ teaspoon of salt, stir to coat, then top the rice with the peas. 6. Place and lock the lid. 7. Select the Pressure Cook mode and press the button again to adjust the cooking time to 6 minutes; press the Pressure Level button to choose High Pressure. 8. When the time is up, leave turn the steam release handle in the Sealing position for 10 minutes, then turn it to the Venting position. 9. Uncover the lid and use a fork to fluff the rice. 10. Serve and enjoy.
Per Serving: Calories 225; Fat 16.47g; Sodium 43mg; Carbs 26.26g; Fiber 11g; Sugar 0.48g; Protein 7.23g

Homemade Baba Ghanoush

Prep Time: 5 minutes | Cook Time: 12 minutes | Serves: 2

¼ to ½ cup Easy Vegetable Broth or no-salt-added vegetable broth, divided
1 medium eggplant, peeled and sliced into 1-inch-thick rounds
1 cup water
3 garlic cloves, unpeeled
2 tablespoons freshly squeezed lemon juice
2 tablespoons tahini
1 tablespoon white miso paste
½ teaspoon ground cumin, plus more for garnish

1. Insert the Inner Pot into the Cooker Base without the lid. 2. Press Sauté to select the program and then press it again to choose the Normal temperature option. 3. Pour in 2 tablespoons of the broth. Arrange some slices of eggplant in one layer on the bottom of the pot. Sauté for 2 minutes, and then flip. Pour in more broth when needed. 2 minutes later, pile the first batch of eggplant on one side of the Inner Pot and add the remaining eggplant. Sauté on each side for 2 minutes, adding broth as needed. 4. Add the water and garlic, then lock the lid and set the steam valve to Sealing. Select the Pressure Cook on the panel. Press the button again to choose Less option; use the "-" button to adjust the cooking time to 3 minutes. Press Pressure Level to choose High pressure. 5. After cooking has completed, quickly and carefully turn the steam release handle from the Sealing position to the Venting position and uncover the lid carefully. 6. Remove the garlic and take off the outer peel with a pair of tongs. In a blender, combine the garlic, eggplant, lemon juice, tahini, miso, and cumin. Blend until smooth. 7. Serve warm or cover, refrigerate, and serve cold. 8. If you haven't eaten up the dish, you can put the leftovers in a covered container and put them in the refrigerator for up to 4 days.
Per Serving: Calories: 62; Fat: 3g; Carbs: 8g; Fiber: 3g; Sugar: 4g; Sodium: 110mg; Protein: 2g

Delicious Scalloped Potatoes

Prep Time: 15 minutes | Cook Time: 27 minutes | Serves: 2

1 cup milk
½ cup Easy Vegetable Broth or no-salt-added vegetable broth
2 scallions, white and green parts, chopped
2 tablespoons nutritional yeast
1 tablespoon arrowroot powder
1 teaspoon garlic powder
1 teaspoon minced fresh rosemary
1 teaspoon mustard powder
Freshly ground black pepper
Salt (optional)
1½ pounds russet potatoes (4 or 5 medium), peeled
1 cup water

1. Whisk together the milk, broth, scallions, nutritional yeast, arrowroot powder, garlic powder, rosemary, and mustard powder in a large bowl. Add some pepper and salt as you like. 2. Slice the potatoes thinly and finely with a Mandoline, the slicing blade on a food processor, or the slicing side of a box grater. 3. Arrange a 1-inch layer of potatoes in an ovenproof baking plate, and then add some sauce to cover the potatoes. Continue layering until all the potatoes

are submerged under the sauce in the dish. 4. Add the water into the inner pot and insert a trivet on which the dish is placed. Lock and seal the lid. Select the Pressure Cook on the panel. Press the button again to choose Less option; use the "+" button to adjust the cooking time to 27 minutes. Press Pressure Level to choose High pressure. 5. After cooking has completed, quickly and carefully turn the steam release handle from the Sealing position to the Venting position and uncover the lid carefully and the dish. 6. Serve right away.
Per Serving: Calories: 172; Fat: 1g; Carbs: 36g; Fiber: 3g; Sugar: 3g; Sodium: 54mg; Protein: 6g

Tasty Brussels Sprouts with Sweet Dijon Vinaigrette

Prep Time: 5 minutes | Cook Time: 1 minutes | Serves: 2

1-pound fresh Brussels sprouts
1 cup water
2 garlic cloves, smashed
3 tablespoons apple cider vinegar
2 tablespoons Dijon mustard
1 tablespoon maple syrup
Freshly ground black pepper

1. In your inner pot, combine the Brussels sprouts, water, and garlic. Lock the lid and turn the steam release handle to Sealing. 2. Select the Pressure Cook on the panel. Press the button again to choose Less option; use the "-" button to adjust the cooking time to 1 minute. Press Pressure Level to choose High pressure. 3. While cooking, whisk together the vinegar, mustard, and maple syrup in a small bowl. 4. After cooking has completed, quickly and carefully turn the steam release handle from the Sealing position to the Venting position and uncover the lid carefully. 5. Drain the water and mince the garlic. Add the dressing to the sprouts and garlic and toss to coat. Add some pepper to season and serve right away.
Per Serving: Calories: 71; Fat: 1g; Carbs: 15g; Fiber: 5g; Sugar: 6g; Sodium: 116mg; Protein: 4g

Sweet Acorn Squash in Sriracha Hot Sauce

Prep Time: 10 minutes | Cook Time: 5 minutes | Serves: 4

2 tablespoons butter, at room temperature
2 tablespoons packed brown sugar
1 teaspoon to 1 tablespoon Sriracha hot sauce
1 medium (2-pound) acorn squash,
halved and seeded
Salt and freshly ground black pepper
½ cup chopped toasted pecans, for garnish (optional)

1. In a small bowl, mix up the butter, brown sugar and the Sriracha. 2. Use a fork to prick the inside of the squash halves, season with the salt and pepper, then smear the mixture in the bowl all over the inside of the squash. 3. In the Inner Pot, add 1½ cups of water and place the Steam Rack; carefully transfer the squash to the rack with the cut-side facing up. 4. Select the Pressure Cook mode and press the button again to adjust the cooking time to 5 minutes; press the Pressure Level button to choose High Pressure. 5. When the time is up, leave the steam release handle from the Sealing position for 10 minutes, then turn it to the Venting position. 6. Uncover the lid, serve the squash on a prepared plate, making sure not to spill the liquid in the center. 7. Cut each half into 2 wedges and you can serve with the pecans.
Per Serving: Calories 254; Fat 28 g; Sodium 346mg; Carbs 12.3 g; Sugar 1g; Fiber 0.7g; Protein 4.3 g

Boiled Cabbage

Prep time: 15 minutes | Cook time: 5 minutes | Serves: 6

1 large head green cabbage, cored and chopped
3 cups vegetable broth
1 teaspoon salt
½ teaspoon black pepper

1. Place the cabbage, broth, salt, and pepper in the inner pot. 2. Put on the pressure cooker's lid and turn the steam valve to "Sealing" position. 3. Set the Instant Pot to Pressure Cook. 4. Press the Pressure Level button to adjust the pressure to "Low". 5. Use the "+/-" keys on the control panel to set the cooking time to 5 minutes. 6. Once the cooking cycle is completed, allow the steam to release naturally. 7. When all the steam is released, remove the pressure lid from the top carefully. 8. Serve the cabbage with a little of the cooking liquid.
Per Serving: Calories 199; Fat 5g; Sodium 41mg; Carbs 7g; Fiber 7.6g; Sugar 5g; Protein 2g

Healthy Broccoli with Lemon Garlic Dressing

Prep Time: 5 minutes | Cook Time: 10 minutes | Serves: 4

4 medium garlic cloves, unpeeled, left whole
1-pound broccoli, cut into 1- to 1½-inch florets, stems thinly sliced
2 tablespoons fresh lemon juice

1 teaspoon Dijon mustard
¼ cup olive oil
Salt and freshly ground black pepper

1. Place 1 cup warm water and the garlic in the pot. Set a steamer basket in the pot and place the broccoli in it. 2. Lock on the lid, select the Pressure Cook on the panel. Press the button again to choose Less option; use the "- button to adjust the cooking time to 10 minutes. Press Pressure Level to choose High pressure. Make sure the steam valve is in the "Sealing" position. 3. When the cooking time is up, quickly and carefully turn the steam release handle from Sealing position to the Venting position. Transfer the broccoli to a large serving bowl. Remove the steaming basket from the pot. 4. Transfer the garlic to a cutting board, remove the peels, and chop the cloves. Dump the garlic, lemon juice, and mustard into a medium bowl and combine them. Gradually whisk in the oil. 5. Season the broccoli and season with salt and pepper.
Per Serving: Calories 285; Fat 9.8g; Sodium 639mg; Carbs 11.1g; Fiber 1.2g; Sugars 5.1g; Protein 2.8g

Creamed Spinach with Nutmeg

Prep Time: 10 minutes | Cook Time: 10 minutes | Serves: 6

½ medium onion, diced
4 garlic cloves, minced
1 (16-ounce) package frozen chopped spinach
1¾ cups milk, divided
1 cup water
¾ cup raw cashews

1 tablespoon freshly squeezed lemon juice
1 teaspoon chickpea miso paste
½ teaspoon ground or freshly grated nutmeg
Freshly ground black pepper

1. Insert the Inner Pot into the Cooker Base without the lid. 2. Select Sauté mode and then press the same button again and then adjust the cooking temperature to Normal. 3. When the display switches On to Hot, add the onion and cook for 3 to 5 minutes until translucent, adding water to prevent sticking; add the garlic and cook for 30 seconds or until fragrant. 4. Press the Cancel button; add the spinach and 1¼ cups of the milk, then lock the lid. 5. Select the Pressure Cook mode and press the button again to adjust the cooking time to 5 minutes; press the Pressure Level button to choose High Pressure. 6. While cooking, in a suitable bowl, add the cashews and the enough boiled water over them, let the cashews soak for at least 30 minutes; then drain them. 7. Blend the drained cashews, lemon juice, miso, nutmeg, pepper and the remaining milk in a blender, until smooth. 8. When the time is up, leave the steam release handle from the Sealing position for 5 minutes, then turn it to the Venting position. 9. Uncover the lid combine the food with the cashews mixture. 10. Serve and enjoy.
Per Serving: Calories: 237; Fat: 14g; Carbs: 19g; Fiber: 5g; Sugar: 6g; Sodium: 193mg; Protein: 13g

Red Pepper Eggplant Dip

Prep Time: 10 minutes | Cook Time: 15 minutes | Serves: 6

5 tablespoons extra-virgin olive oil, divided
2 pounds eggplant, at least half peeled but leaving some skin, and cut into 1-inch chunks
4 garlic cloves, minced
1 cup water

1 teaspoon kosher salt
¾ cup roasted red peppers, chopped
3 tablespoons freshly squeezed lemon juice
1 tablespoon tahini
1 teaspoon ground cumin
Freshly ground black pepper

1. Insert the Inner Pot into the Cooker Base without the lid. 2. Select Sauté mode and then press the same button again and then adjust the cooking temperature to Normal. 3. When the display switches On to Hot, add 3 tablespoons of oil and heat; add half of the eggplant and brown one side for 4 to 5 minutes; remove and add 1 tablespoon of oil, garlic and the remaining eggplant and cook for 1 minutes. 4. Put the first batch of eggplant back to the pot, add the salt and water, then lock the lid. 5. Select the Pressure Cook mode and press the button again to adjust the cooking time to 3 minutes; press the Pressure Level button

to choose High Pressure. 6. When the time is up, quickly and carefully turn the steam release handle from the Sealing position to the Venting position. 7. Uncover the lid, stir in the roasted red peppers and then wait for 5 minutes. 8. Drain out the cooking liquid, add the remaining oil, lemon juice, tahini, cumin and lastly season with the pepper. 9. Blend the mixture in an immersion blender until smooth, serve with bread or pita for dipping.
Per Serving: Calories 336; Fat 17.3g; Sodium 281mg; Carbs 8.1g; Fiber 5.3g; Sugars 17.7g; Protein 32.3g

Greek-Style Peas

Prep time: 15 minutes | Cook time: 9 minutes | Serves: 4

3 tablespoons olive oil
1 large russet potato, peeled and cut into ½" pieces
1 medium white onion, peeled and diced
1 medium carrot, peeled and diced
3 medium tomatoes, seeded and

diced
1 clove garlic, peeled and minced
1 pound fresh or frozen green peas
¼ cup chopped fresh dill
¼ teaspoon salt
¼ teaspoon black pepper
⅓ cup crumbled feta cheese

1. Press the "Sauté" button two time to select "Normal" temperature setting on the Instant Pot and heat oil. 2. Add potato, onion, and carrot, and cook until onion and carrot are tender, about 8 minutes. 3. Add tomatoes and garlic, and cook until garlic is fragrant, about 1 minute. Add peas. 4. Put on the pressure cooker's lid and turn the steam valve to "Sealing" position. 5. Set the Instant Pot to Pressure Cook. 6. Use the "+/-" keys on the control panel to set the cooking time to 1 minute. 7. Press the Pressure Level button to adjust the pressure to "Low". 8. Once the cooking cycle is completed, allow the steam to release quickly. 9. When all the steam is released, remove the pressure lid from the top carefully. 10. Stir in dill, salt, and pepper. Top with feta and serve hot.
Per Serving: Calories 242; Fat 11g; Sodium 91mg; Carbs 4g; Fiber 3g; Sugar 8g; Protein 3g

Stuffed Acorn Squash

Prep time: 15 minutes | Cook time: 25 minutes | Serves: 2

1 cup water
1 (1-pound) acorn squash, halved and seeded
2 tablespoons olive oil
½ medium white onion, peeled and sliced
1 stalk celery, sliced
2 cloves garlic, peeled and chopped
1 tablespoon chopped fresh sage
1 tablespoon chopped fresh flat-leaf parsley

1 teaspoon chopped fresh rosemary
1 teaspoon fresh thyme leaves
¼ teaspoon salt
¼ teaspoon black pepper
½ cup wild rice
¾ cup vegetable stock
¼ cup chopped toasted walnuts
¼ cup golden raisins
¼ cup dried cranberries
¼ cup crumbled goat cheese

1. Place the rack in the Instant Pot and add water. 2. Place squash halves on the rack. 3. Put on the pressure cooker's lid and turn the steam valve to "Sealing" position. 4. Set the Instant Pot to Pressure Cook. 5. Use the "+/-" keys on the control panel to set the cooking time to 10 minutes. 6. Press the Pressure Level button to adjust the pressure to "Low". 7. Once the cooking cycle is completed, allow the steam to release naturally for 10 minutes and then quick-release the remaining pressure. 8. Insert a paring knife into the squash to check for doneness. Once it pierces easily, it is cooked. Then transfer the squash to a platter and cover with foil to keep warm. 9. Wash and dry the inner pot. Set your Instant Pot to Sauté on "Normal" temperature setting. Heat oil. 10. Add garlic, sage, parsley, rosemary, and thyme. Then cook until fragrant, about 30 seconds. 11. Add salt and pepper and stir well to season. Then add wild rice and stock. Press the Cancel button. 12. Close the lid and turn the handle to "Sealing" position. 13. Set your Instant Pot to Pressure Cook. 14. Use the "+/-" keys on the control panel to set the cooking time to 25 minutes. 15. Press the Pressure Level button to adjust the pressure to "Low". 16. Once the cooking cycle is completed, quick-release the pressure. 17. When all the steam is released, remove the pressure lid from the top carefully. 18. Add walnuts, raisins, and cranberries, and stir well. 19. Close lid and let stand on the Keep Warm setting for 10 minutes. 20. Spoon mixture into acorn squash halves and top with goat cheese. 21. Serve warm.
Per Serving: Calories 305; Fat 12.9g; Sodium 754mg; Carbs 21g; Fiber 6.1g; Sugar 4.2g; Protein 11g

Braised Eggplant

Prep time: 15 minutes | Cook time: 25 minutes | Serves: 4

2 large eggplants, cut into 1" pieces
1¾ teaspoons salt
3 tablespoons olive oil
1 medium yellow onion, peeled and diced
3 cloves garlic, peeled and minced

2 cups diced fresh tomatoes
1 cup water
1 tablespoon dried oregano
½ teaspoon black pepper
2 tablespoons minced fresh basil

1. Place eggplant in a colander and sprinkle with 1½ teaspoons salt. 2. Place colander over a plate. Let stand 30 minutes to drain. 3. Press the "Sauté" button twice to select "Normal" temperature setting on the Instant Pot and heat 2 tablespoons oil. 4. Add onion and cook until soft, about 5 minutes. Add garlic and cook until fragrant, about 30 seconds. 5. Add tomatoes and water. Press the Cancel button. Rinse eggplant well and drain. Add to pot. 6. Put on the pressure cooker's lid and turn the steam valve to "Sealing" position. 7. Set the Instant Pot to Pressure Cook. 8. Use the "+/-" keys on the control panel to set the cooking time to 8 minutes. 9. Press the Pressure Level button to adjust the pressure to "Low". 10. Once the cooking cycle is completed, allow the steam to release quickly. 11. When all the steam is released, remove the pressure lid from the top carefully. 12. Add oregano, pepper, and remaining ¼ teaspoon salt. 13. Add remaining 1 tablespoon oil to pot and stir well. 14. Press the "Sauté" button twice to select "Normal" temperature setting and simmer for 15 minutes to thicken. 15. Add basil and serve hot.
Per Serving: Calories 334; Fat 7.9g; Sodium 704mg; Carbs 6g; Fiber 3.6g; Sugar 6g; Protein 18g

Roasted Spaghetti Squash

Prep time: 15 minutes | Cook time: 10 minutes | Serves: 4

1 bulb garlic, top sliced off
3 tablespoons olive oil
1 (3-pound) spaghetti squash
1 cup water

½ teaspoon salt
½ teaspoon black pepper
¼ cup chopped fresh flat-leaf parsley
¼ cup grated Parmesan cheese

1. At 400°F/200°C, preheat your oven. 2. Place garlic bulb on a sheet of aluminum foil. Drizzle with 1 tablespoon oil. 3. Wrap bulb tightly and roast directly on the oven rack for 30–40 minutes, or until bulb is tender. 4. Unwrap and let bulb rest while you prepare squash. 5. Slice spaghetti squash in half lengthwise. Scoop out seeds with a spoon and discard. 6. Place the rack in the Instant Pot, add water, and place spaghetti squash on rack. 7. Put on the pressure cooker's lid and turn the steam valve to "Sealing" position. 8. Set the Instant Pot to Pressure Cook. 9. Press the Pressure Level button to adjust the pressure to "Low". 10. Use the "+/-" keys on the control panel to set the cooking time to 7 minutes. 11. Once the cooking cycle is completed, allow the steam to release naturally. 12. When all the steam is released, remove the pressure lid from the top carefully. 13. Clean and dry pot. Press the "Sauté" button twice to select "Normal" temperature setting and heat remaining 2 tablespoons of oil. 14. Squeeze garlic into pot and cook for 30 seconds, then add squash, salt, and pepper and cook until squash is thoroughly coated in the garlic. 15. Transfer to a serving bowl and top with parsley and cheese. 16. Serve immediately.
Per Serving: Calories 442; Fat 11g; Sodium 91mg; Carbs 14g; Fiber 3g; Sugar 8g; Protein 13g

Tomato Basil Soup

Prep time: 15 minutes | Cook time: 12 minutes | Serves: 4

1 tablespoon olive oil
1 small onion, peeled and diced
1 stalk celery, sliced
8 medium heirloom tomatoes, seeded and quartered

¼ cup julienned fresh basil
½ teaspoon salt
3 cups low-sodium chicken broth
1 cup heavy cream
1 teaspoon black pepper

1. Press the "Sauté" button twice to select "Normal" temperature setting on the Instant Pot and heat oil. 2. Add onion and celery and cook until translucent, about 5 minutes. 3. Add tomatoes and cook for 3 minutes, or until tomatoes are tender and start to break down. 4. Add basil, salt, and broth. Press the Cancel button. 5. Put on the pressure cooker's lid and turn the steam valve to "Sealing" position. 6. Set the Instant Pot to Pressure Cook. 7. Use the "+/-" keys on the control panel to set the cooking time to 7 minutes. 8. Press the Pressure Level button to adjust the pressure to "Low". 9. Once the cooking cycle is completed, allow the steam to release naturally. 10. When all the steam is released, remove the pressure lid from the top carefully. 11. Add

cream and pepper. Purée soup with an immersion blender, or purée in batches in a blender. 12. Ladle into bowls and serve warm.
Per Serving: Calories 472; Fat 7.9g; Sodium 704mg; Carbs 6g; Fiber 3.6g; Sugar 6g; Protein 18g

Artichokes Provençal

Prep time: 15 minutes | Cook time: 7 minutes | Serves: 4

4 large artichokes
1 medium lemon, cut in half
2 tablespoons olive oil
½ medium white onion, peeled and sliced
4 cloves garlic, peeled and chopped
2 tablespoons chopped fresh oregano
2 tablespoons chopped fresh basil

2 sprigs fresh thyme
2 medium tomatoes, seeded and chopped
¼ cup chopped Kalamata olives
¼ cup red wine
¼ cup water
¼ teaspoon salt
¼ teaspoon black pepper

1. Run artichokes under running water, making sure water runs between leaves to flush out any debris. 2. Slice off top ⅓ of artichoke, trim stem, and pull away any tough outer leaves. 3. Rub all cut surfaces with lemon. 4. Press the "Sauté" button twice to select "Normal" temperature setting on the Instant Pot and heat oil. 5. Add onion and cook until just tender, about 2 minutes. Add garlic, oregano, basil, and thyme, and cook until fragrant, about 30 seconds. 6. Add tomatoes and olives and gently mix, then add wine and water and cook for 30 seconds. 7. Press the Cancel button, then add artichokes cut side down to the Instant Pot. 8. Put on the pressure cooker's lid and turn the steam valve to "Sealing" position. 9. Set the Instant Pot to Pressure Cook. 10. Use the "+/-" keys on the control panel to set the cooking time to 5 minutes. 11. Press the Pressure Level button to adjust the pressure to "Low". 12. Once the cooking cycle is completed, allow the steam to release quickly. 13. When all the steam is released, remove the pressure lid from the top carefully. 14. Pour sauce over top, then season with salt and pepper. Serve warm.
Per Serving: Calories 272; Fat 10g; Sodium 891mg; Carbs 22.9g; Fiber 4g; Sugar 4g; Protein 3g

Garlic Green Beans

Prep time: 15 minutes | Cook time: 5 minutes | Serves: 4

12-ounce green beans, ends trimmed
4 cloves garlic, minced
1 tablespoon avocado oil

½ teaspoon salt
1 cup water

1. Place the green beans in a medium bowl and toss with the garlic, oil, and salt. 2. Transfer this mixture to the steamer basket. 3. Pour 1 cup water into the inner pot and place the steam rack inside. 4. Place the steamer basket with the green beans on top of the steam rack. 5. Put on the pressure cooker's lid and turn the steam valve to "Sealing" position. 6. Set the Instant Pot to Pressure Cook. 7. Use the "+/-" keys on the control panel to set the cooking time to 5 minutes. 8. Press the Pressure Level button to adjust the pressure to "Low". 9. Once the cooking cycle is completed, allow the steam to release naturally. 10. When all the steam is released, remove the pressure lid from the top carefully. 11. Transfer to a bowl for serving.
Per Serving: Calories 199; Fat 5g; Sodium 41mg; Carbs 7g; Fiber 7.6g; Sugar 5g; Protein 2g

Lemony Steamed Asparagus

Prep time: 15 minutes | Cook time: 1 minutes | Serves: 4-6

1-pound asparagus, woody ends removed

Juice from ½ large lemon
¼ teaspoon kosher salt

1. Add ½ cup water to the inner pot and add the steam rack. 2. Add the asparagus to the steamer basket and place the basket on top of the rack. 3. Put on the pressure cooker's lid and turn the steam valve to "Sealing" position. 4. Set the Instant Pot on "Steam". 5. Use the "+/-" keys on the control panel to set the cooking time to 1 minute. 6. Press the Pressure Level button to adjust the pressure to "Low". 7. Once the cooking cycle is completed, quick-release pressure. 8. When all the steam is released, remove the pressure lid from the top carefully. 9. Transfer the asparagus to a plate and top with lemon juice and salt.
Per Serving: Calories 44; Fat 2.2g; Sodium 811mg; Carbs 12g; Fiber 3g; Sugar 8g; Protein 8g

Hearty Minestrone Soup

Prep time: 15 minutes | Cook time: 20 minutes | Serves: 4

2 cups dried Great Northern beans, soaked overnight and drained
1 cup orzo
2 large carrots, peeled and diced
1 bunch Swiss chard, ribs removed and roughly chopped
1 medium zucchini, trimmed and diced
2 stalks celery, diced
1 medium onion, peeled and diced

1 teaspoon minced garlic
1 tablespoon Italian seasoning
1 teaspoon salt
½ teaspoon black pepper
2 bay leaves
1 (15-ounce) can diced tomatoes, including juice
4 cups vegetable broth
1 cup tomato juice

1. Place all ingredients in the Instant Pot and stir to combine. 2. Put on the pressure cooker's lid and turn the steam valve to "Sealing" position. 3. Set the Instant Pot to Pressure Cook. 4. Use the "+/-" keys on the control panel to set the cooking time to 20 minutes. 5. Press the Pressure Level button to adjust the pressure to "Low". 6. Once the cooking cycle is completed, allow the steam to release naturally for 10 minutes and then quick-release the remaining pressure. 7. When all the steam is released, remove the pressure lid from the top carefully. Remove and discard bay leaves. 8. Ladle into bowls and serve warm.
Per Serving: Calories 384; Fat 5g; Sodium 41mg; Carbs 7g; Fiber 7.6g; Sugar 5g; Protein 2g

Spaghetti Squash with Mushrooms

Prep time: 15 minutes | Cook time: 15 minutes | Serves: 4

1 (3-pound) spaghetti squash
1 cup water
2 tablespoons olive oil
4 cups sliced button mushrooms
2 cloves garlic, peeled and minced
1 tablespoon chopped fresh oregano

1 tablespoon chopped fresh basil
¼ teaspoon crushed red pepper flakes
1 cup marinara sauce
½ cup shredded Parmesan cheese

1. Slice spaghetti squash in half lengthwise. Scoop out seeds with a spoon and discard. 2. Place the rack in the Instant Pot, add water, and place spaghetti squash on rack. 3. Put on the pressure cooker's lid and turn the steam valve to "Sealing" position. 4. Set the Instant Pot to Pressure Cook. 5. Use the "+/-" keys on the control panel to set the cooking time to 7 minutes. 6. Press the Pressure Level button to adjust the pressure to "Low". 7. Once the cooking cycle is completed, allow the steam to release quickly. 8. When all the steam is released, remove the pressure lid from the top carefully. 9. Wash and dry pot. Press the "Sauté" button two time to select "Normal" temperature setting and heat oil. 10. Add mushrooms and cook until tender and any juices have evaporated, about 8 minutes. 11. Add garlic and cook until fragrant, about 30 seconds. 12. Add spaghetti squash to pot and toss to mix. Add oregano, basil, red pepper flakes, and marinara sauce and toss to coat. 13. Press the Cancel button. Top with cheese and close the lid. Let stand 5 minutes until cheese melts. Serve hot.
Per Serving: Calories 305; Fat 10.9g; Sodium 454mg; Carbs 10g; Fiber 3.1g; Sugar 5.2g; Protein 05g

Artichoke Soup

Prep time: 15 minutes | Cook time: 30 minutes | Serves: 8

18 large fresh artichokes, trimmed, halved, and chokes removed
1 medium lemon, halved
6 tablespoons lemon juice
2 tablespoons olive oil
6 medium leeks, trimmed, cut lengthwise, and sliced

¾ teaspoon salt
½ teaspoon pepper
3 large potatoes, peeled and quartered
10 cups vegetable stock
½ cup low-fat plain Greek yogurt
½ cup chopped fresh chives

1. Rinse artichokes under running water, making sure water runs between leaves to flush out any debris. 2. Rub all cut surfaces with lemon. In a large bowl, combine artichokes, enough water to cover them, and 3 tablespoons lemon juice. Set aside. 3. Press the "Sauté" button two time to select "Normal" temperature setting on the Instant Pot and heat oil. 4. Add leeks, ½ teaspoon salt, and ¼ teaspoon pepper. Cook for 10 minutes or until leeks are softened. 5. Drain artichokes and add to leeks along with potatoes and stock. Add remaining ¼ teaspoon each salt and pepper. 6. Put on the pressure cooker's lid and turn the steam valve to "Sealing" position. 7. Set the Instant Pot to Pressure Cook. 8. Use the "+/-" keys on the control panel to set the cooking time to 20 minutes. 9. Press the Pressure Level

button to adjust the pressure to "Low". 10. Once the cooking cycle is completed, allow the steam to release naturally. 11. When all the steam is released, remove the pressure lid from the top carefully. 12. Using an immersion blender, or in batches in a regular blender, purée the soup until smooth. Stir in remaining 3 tablespoons lemon juice. 13. Serve soup with a dollop of yogurt and a sprinkle of chives.
Per Serving: Calories 361; Fat 19g; Sodium 354mg; Carbs 25g; Fiber 5.1g; Sugar 8.2g; Protein 2g

Green Beans with Tomatoes and Potatoes

Prep time: 15 minutes | Cook time: 4 minutes | Serves: 8

1 pound small new potatoes
1 cup water
1 teaspoon salt
2-pound fresh green beans, trimmed
2 medium tomatoes, seeded and diced

2 tablespoons olive oil
1 tablespoon red wine vinegar
1 clove garlic, peeled and minced
½ teaspoon dry mustard powder
¼ teaspoon smoked paprika
¼ teaspoon black pepper

1. Place potatoes in a steamer basket. 2. Place the rack in the Instant Pot, add water, and then top with the steamer basket. 3. Put on the pressure cooker's lid and turn the steam valve to "Sealing" position. 4. Set the Instant Pot to Pressure Cook. 5. Use the "+/-" keys on the control panel to set the cooking time to 4 minutes. 6. Press the Pressure Level button to adjust the pressure to "Low". 7. Once the cooking cycle is completed, allow the steam to release quickly. 8. When all the steam is released, remove the pressure lid from the top carefully. 9. Add salt, green beans, and tomatoes to the Instant Pot. 10. Transfer mixture to a serving platter or large bowl. 11. In a small bowl, whisk oil, vinegar, garlic, mustard, paprika, and pepper. Pour dressing over vegetables and gently toss to coat. 12. Serve hot.
Per Serving: Calories 489; Fat 11g; Sodium 501mg; Carbs 8.9g; Fiber 4.6g; Sugar 8g; Protein 26g

Purple Cabbage Salad

Prep time: 15 minutes | Cook time: 2 minutes | Serves: 8

½ cup dry quinoa
1 (10-ounce) bag frozen shelled edamame
1 cup vegetable broth
¼ cup reduced sodium tamari
¼ cup natural almond butter

3 tablespoons toasted sesame seed oil
½ teaspoon pure stevia powder
1 head purple cabbage, cored and chopped

1. Place the quinoa, edamame, and broth in the inner pot of your Instant Pot. 2. Put on the pressure cooker's lid and turn the steam valve to "Sealing" position. 3. Set the Instant Pot to Pressure Cook. 4. Use the "+/-" keys on the control panel to set the cooking time to 2 minutes. 5. Press the Pressure Level button to adjust the pressure to "Low". 6. Once the cooking cycle is completed, quick-release pressure. 7. When all the steam is released, remove the pressure lid from the top carefully. 8. Meanwhile, in a small bowl, whisk together the tamari, almond butter, sesame seed oil, and stevia. Set aside. 9. Use a fork to fluff the quinoa, and then transfer the mixture to a large bowl. 10. Allow the quinoa and edamame to cool, and then add the purple cabbage to the bowl and toss to combine. 11. Add the dressing and toss again until everything is evenly coated. 12. Serve.
Per Serving: Calories 242; Fat 11g; Sodium 91mg; Carbs 14g; Fiber 3g; Sugar 8g; Protein 13g

Steamed Cauliflower

Prep time: 15 minutes | Cook time: 2 minutes | Serves: 6

1 large head cauliflower, cored and   cut into large florets

1. Pour 2 cups water into the inner pot of the Instant Pot. Place a steam rack inside. 2. Place the cauliflower florets inside a steamer basket and place the basket on the steam rack. 3. Put on the pressure cooker's lid and turn the steam valve to "Sealing" position. 4. Set the Instant Pot on "Steam". 5. Use the "+/-" keys on the control panel to set the cooking time to 2 minutes. 6. Press the Pressure Level button to adjust the pressure to "Low". 7. Once the cooking cycle is completed, allow the steam to release naturally. 8. When all the steam is released, remove the pressure lid from the top carefully. 9. Carefully remove the steamer basket and serve.
Per Serving: Calories 378; Fat 19g; Sodium 354mg; Carbs 25g; Fiber 5.1g; Sugar 8.2g; Protein 2g

Cabbage Soup

Prep time: 15 minutes | Cook time: 20 minutes | Serves: 8

2 tablespoons olive oil	1 (15-ounce) can white navy
3 medium onions, peeled and chopped	beans, drained
1 large carrot, peeled, quartered, and sliced	1½ cups low-sodium vegetable cocktail beverage
1 stalk celery, chopped	7 cups low-sodium vegetable stock
3 bay leaves	1 dried chili pepper
1 teaspoon smoked paprika	2 medium zucchini, trimmed, halved lengthwise, and thinly sliced
3 cups sliced white cabbage	
1 teaspoon fresh thyme leaves	1 teaspoon salt
3 cloves garlic, peeled and minced	½ teaspoon black pepper
½ cup chopped roasted red pepper	

1. Press the "Sauté" button two time to select "Normal" temperature setting on the Instant Pot and heat oil. 2. Add onions, carrot, celery, and bay leaves. Cook for 7–10 minutes or until vegetables are soft. 3. Add paprika, cabbage, thyme, garlic, roasted red pepper, and beans. 4. Stir to combine and cook for 2 minutes. Add vegetable cocktail beverage, stock, and chili pepper. 5. Put on the pressure cooker's lid and turn the steam valve to "Sealing" position. 6. Set the Instant Pot to Pressure Cook. 7. Use the "+/-" keys on the control panel to set the cooking time to 20 minutes. 8. Press the Pressure Level button to adjust the pressure to "Low". 9. Once the cooking cycle is completed, allow the steam to release quickly. 10. When all the steam is released, remove the pressure lid from the top carefully. 11. Remove and discard bay leaves. 12. Add zucchini, close lid, and let stand on the Keep Warm setting for 15 minutes. 13. Season with salt and pepper. 14. Serve hot.
Per Serving: Calories 374; Fat 5g; Sodium 41mg; Carbs 7g; Fiber 7.6g; Sugar 5g; Protein 2g

Eggplant Caponata

Prep time: 15 minutes | Cook time: 5 minutes | Serves: 8

¼ cup olive oil	2 cloves garlic, peeled and minced
¼ cup white wine	1 (15-ounce) can diced tomatoes
2 tablespoons red wine vinegar	3 stalks celery, diced
1 teaspoon ground cinnamon	½ cup chopped oil-cured olives
1 large eggplant, peeled and diced	½ cup golden raisins
1 medium onion, peeled and diced	2 tablespoons capers, rinsed and drained
1 medium green bell pepper, seeded and diced	
1 medium red bell pepper, seeded and diced	½ teaspoon salt
	½ teaspoon black pepper

1. Place all ingredients in the Instant Pot. Stir well to mix. 2. Put on the pressure cooker's lid and turn the steam valve to "Sealing" position. 3. Set the Instant Pot to Pressure Cook. 4. Use the "+/-" keys on the control panel to set the cooking time to 5 minutes. 5. Press the Pressure Level button to adjust the pressure to "Low". 6. Once the cooking cycle is completed, allow the steam to release quickly. 7. When all the steam is released, remove the pressure lid from the top carefully. 8. Serve warm.
Per Serving: Calories 478; Fat 7.9g; Sodium 704mg; Carbs 6g; Fiber 3.6g; Sugar 6g; Protein 18g

Pureed Cauliflower Soup

Prep time: 15 minutes | Cook time: 21 minutes | Serves: 6

2 tablespoons olive oil	4 cups cauliflower florets
1 medium onion, peeled and chopped	2 cups vegetable stock
1 stalk celery, chopped	½ cup half-and-half
1 medium carrot, peeled and chopped	¼ cup low-fat plain Greek yogurt
3 sprigs fresh thyme	2 tablespoons chopped fresh chives

1. Press the "Sauté" button twice to select "Normal" temperature setting on the Instant Pot and heat oil. 2. Add onion, celery, and carrot. Cook until just tender, about 6 minutes. 3. Add thyme, cauliflower, and stock. Stir well, then press the Cancel button. 4. Put on the pressure cooker's lid and turn the steam valve to "Sealing" position. 5. Set the Instant Pot to Pressure Cook. 6. Use the "+/-" keys on the control panel to set the cooking time to 5 minutes. 7. Press the Pressure Level button to adjust the pressure to "Low". 8. Once the cooking cycle is completed, allow the steam to release naturally. 9. When all the steam is released, remove the pressure lid from the top carefully. 10. Open lid, remove and discard thyme stems, and with an immersion blender,

purée soup until smooth. 11. Stir in half-and-half and yogurt. Garnish with chives and serve immediately.
Per Serving: Calories 484; Fat 5g; Sodium 41mg; Carbs 7g; Fiber 7.6g; Sugar 5g; Protein 2g

Zucchini Pomodoro

Prep time: 15 minutes | Cook time: 6 minutes | Serves: 4-6

1 tablespoon vegetable oil	1 tablespoon Italian seasoning
1 large onion, peeled and diced	½ teaspoon salt
3 cloves garlic, peeled and minced	½ teaspoon black pepper
1 (28-ounce) can diced tomatoes, including juice	2 medium zucchini, trimmed and spiralized
½ cup water	

1. Press the "Sauté" button twice to select "Normal" temperature setting on the Instant Pot and heat oil. 2. Add onion and cook until translucent, about 5 minutes. Add garlic and cook for an additional 30 seconds. 3. Add tomatoes, water, Italian seasoning, salt, and pepper. Add zucchini and toss to combine. 4. Put on the pressure cooker's lid and turn the steam valve to "Sealing" position. 5. Set the Instant Pot to Pressure Cook. 6. Use the "+/-" keys on the control panel to set the cooking time to 1 minute. 7. Press the Pressure Level button to adjust the pressure to "Low". 8. Once the cooking cycle is completed, allow the steam to release naturally for 5 minutes and then quick-release the remaining pressure. 9. When all the steam is released, remove the pressure lid from the top carefully. 10. Transfer zucchini to four bowls. 11. Press the Sauté button, then adjust the temperature setting to Less, and simmer sauce in the Instant Pot uncovered for 5 minutes. 12. Ladle over zucchini and serve immediately.
Per Serving: Calories 272; Fat 10g; Sodium 891mg; Carbs 22.9g; Fiber 4g; Sugar 4g; Protein 3g

Burgundy Mushrooms

Prep time: 15 minutes | Cook time: 20 minutes | Serves: 8

¼ cup olive oil	1 teaspoon dried thyme
3 cloves garlic, peeled and halved	1 tablespoon Dijon mustard
16-ounce whole white mushrooms	1 teaspoon ground celery seed
16-ounce whole baby bella mushrooms	½ teaspoon black pepper
	3 cups beef broth
1½ cups dry red wine	2 slices bacon
1 teaspoon Worcestershire sauce	

1. Press the "Sauté" button twice to select "Normal" temperature setting on the Instant Pot and heat oil. 2. Add garlic and mushrooms, and cook until mushrooms start to get tender, about 3 minutes. 3. Add wine and simmer for 3 minutes. 4. Add Worcestershire sauce, thyme, mustard, celery seed, pepper, broth, and bacon to pot. 5. Put on the pressure cooker's lid and turn the steam valve to "Sealing" position. 6. Set the Instant Pot to Pressure Cook. 7. Press the Pressure Level button to adjust the pressure to "Low". 8. Use the "+/-" keys on the control panel to set the cooking time to 20 minutes. 9. Once the cooking cycle is completed, allow the steam to release naturally. 10. When all the steam is released, remove the pressure lid from the top carefully. 11. Remove and discard bacon and garlic halves. Transfer mushrooms to a serving bowl. 12. Serve warm.
Per Serving: Calories 484; Fat 5g; Sodium 41mg; Carbs 7g; Fiber 7.6g; Sugar 5g; Protein 2g

Cheesy Brussels Sprouts and Carrots

Prep time: 15 minutes | Cook time: 10 minutes | Serves: 4

1 pound Brussels sprouts, tough ends removed and cut in half	2 tablespoons lemon juice
	½ cup nutritional yeast
1-pound baby carrots	¼ teaspoon salt
1 cup chicken stock	

1. Add the Brussels sprouts, carrots, stock, lemon juice, nutritional yeast, and salt to the inner pot of your Instant Pot. Stir well to combine. 2. Put on the pressure cooker's lid and turn the steam valve to "Sealing" position. 3. Set the Instant Pot to Pressure Cook. 4. Use the "+/-" keys on the control panel to set the cooking time to 10 minutes. 5. Press the Pressure Level button to adjust the pressure to "Low". 6. Once the cooking cycle is completed, quick-release pressure. 7. When all the steam is released, remove the pressure lid from the top carefully. 8. Transfer the vegetables and sauce to a bowl and serve.
Per Serving: Calories 382; Fat 19g; Sodium 354mg; Carbs 25g; Fiber 5.1g; Sugar 8.2g; Protein 2g

Wild Mushroom Soup

Prep time: 15 minutes | Cook time: 10 minutes | Serves: 8

3 tablespoons olive oil
1 stalk celery, diced
1 medium carrot, peeled and diced
½ medium yellow onion, peeled and diced
1 clove garlic, peeled and minced
1 (8-ounce) container hen of the woods mushrooms, sliced
1 (8-ounce) container porcini or

chanterelle mushrooms, sliced
2 cups sliced shiitake mushrooms
2 tablespoons dry sherry
4 cups vegetable broth
2 cups water
1 tablespoon chopped fresh tarragon
½ teaspoon salt
½ teaspoon black pepper

1. Press the "Sauté" button twice to select "Normal" temperature setting on the Instant Pot and heat oil. 2. Add celery, carrot, and onion. Cook, stirring often, until softened, about 5 minutes. 3. Add garlic and cook 30 seconds until fragrant, then add mushrooms and cook for 5 minutes. 4. Add sherry, broth, water, tarragon, salt, and pepper to pot, and stir well. Press the Cancel button. 5. Put on the pressure cooker's lid and turn the steam valve to "Sealing" position. 6. Set the Instant Pot to Pressure Cook. 7. Use the "+/-" keys on the control panel to set the cooking time to 5 minutes. 8. Press the Pressure Level button to adjust the pressure to "Low". 9. Once the cooking cycle is completed, allow the steam to release naturally. 10. When all the steam is released, remove the pressure lid from the top carefully. 11. Serve hot.
Per Serving: Calories 199; Fat 5g; Sodium 41mg; Carbs 7g; Fiber 7.6g; Sugar 5g; Protein 2g

Herbed Potato Salad

Prep time: 15 minutes | Cook time: 25 minutes | Serves: 10

¼ cup olive oil
3 tablespoons red wine vinegar
¼ cup chopped fresh flat-leaf parsley
2 tablespoons chopped fresh dill
2 tablespoons chopped fresh chives
1 clove garlic, peeled and minced

½ teaspoon dry mustard powder
¼ teaspoon black pepper
2-pound baby Yukon Gold potatoes
1 cup water
1 teaspoon salt

1. Whisk together oil, vinegar, parsley, dill, chives, garlic, mustard, and pepper in a small bowl. Set aside. 2. Place potatoes in a steamer basket. 3. Place the rack in the Instant Pot, add water and salt, then top with the steamer basket. 4. Put on the pressure cooker's lid and turn the steam valve to "Sealing" position. 5. Set the Instant Pot to Pressure Cook. 6. Press the Pressure Level button to adjust the pressure to "Low". 7. Use the "+/-" keys on the control panel to set the cooking time to 4 minutes. 8. Once the cooking cycle is completed, allow the steam to quick-release pressure. 9. When all the steam is released, remove the pressure lid from the top carefully. 10. Transfer hot potatoes to a serving bowl. Pour dressing over potatoes and gently toss to coat. 11. Serve warm or at room temperature.
Per Serving: Calories 382; Fat 7.9g; Sodium 704mg; Carbs 6g; Fiber 3.6g; Sugar 6g; Protein 18g

Ratatouille

Prep time: 15 minutes | Cook time: 25 minutes | Serves: 8

1 medium eggplant, cut into 1" pieces
2 teaspoons salt
4 tablespoons olive oil
1 medium white onion, peeled and chopped
1 medium green bell pepper, seeded and chopped
1 medium red bell pepper, seeded and chopped

1 medium zucchini, trimmed and chopped
1 medium yellow squash, chopped
4 cloves garlic, peeled and minced
4 large tomatoes, cut into 1" pieces
2 teaspoons Italian seasoning
¼ teaspoon crushed red pepper flakes
6 fresh basil leaves, thinly sliced

1. Place eggplant in a colander and sprinkle evenly with salt. 2. Let stand 30 minutes, then rinse and dry eggplant. Set aside. 3. Press the "Sauté" button twice to select "Normal" temperature setting on the Instant Pot and heat 1 tablespoon oil. 4. Add onion and bell peppers. Cook, stirring often, until vegetables are just tender, about 5 minutes. 5. Transfer to a large bowl and set aside. 6. Add 1 tablespoon oil to pot and heat for 30 seconds, then add zucchini and squash. 7. Cook, stirring constantly, until vegetables are tender, about 5 minutes. 8. Add garlic and cook until fragrant, about 30 seconds. Transfer to bowl with onion and peppers. 9. Add 1 tablespoon oil to pot and heat for 30 seconds. 10. Add eggplant and cook, stirring constantly, until eggplant is golden brown, about 8 minutes. 11. Add tomatoes and cook until they are tender and releasing juice, about 4

minutes. 12. Return reserved vegetables to pot and stir in Italian seasoning and red pepper flakes. 13. Put on the pressure cooker's lid and turn the steam valve to "Sealing" position. 14. Set the Instant Pot to Pressure Cook. 15. Use the "+/-" keys on the control panel to set the cooking time to 5 minutes. 16. Press the Pressure Level button to adjust the pressure to "Low". 17. Once the cooking cycle is completed, quick-release the steam. 18. When all the steam is released, remove the pressure lid from the top carefully. 19. Serve topped with basil and remaining 1 tablespoon oil.
Per Serving: Calories 334; Fat 10.9g; Sodium 354mg; Carbs 10.5g; Fiber 4.1g; Sugar 8.2g; Protein 6g

Steamed Broccoli

Prep time: 5 minutes | Cook time: 1 minutes | Serves: 6

6 cups broccoli florets

1. Pour 1½ cups water into the inner pot of the Instant Pot. Place a steam rack inside. 2. Place the broccoli florets inside a steamer basket and place the basket on the steam rack. 3. Put on the pressure cooker's lid and turn the steam valve to "Sealing" position. 4. Set the Instant Pot on "Steam". 5. Use the "+/-" keys on the control panel to set the cooking time to 1 minute. 6. Press the Pressure Level button to adjust the pressure to "Low". 7. Once the cooking cycle is completed, quick-release the pressure. 8. When all the steam is released, remove the pressure lid from the top carefully. 9. Remove the steamer basket and serve.
Per Serving: Calories 305; Fat 10.9g; Sodium 454mg; Carbs 10g; Fiber 3.1g; Sugar 5.2g; Protein 05g

Steamed Cauliflower with Herbs

Prep time: 15 minutes | Cook time: 10 minutes | Serves: 6

1 head cauliflower, cut into florets (about 6 cups)
1 cup water
4 tablespoons olive oil
1 clove garlic, peeled and minced
2 tablespoons chopped fresh

oregano
1 teaspoon chopped fresh thyme leaves
1 teaspoon chopped fresh sage
¼ teaspoon salt
¼ teaspoon black pepper

1. Place cauliflower florets in a steamer basket. 2. Place the rack in the Instant Pot, add water, then top with the steamer basket. 3. Put on the pressure cooker's lid and turn the steam valve to "Sealing" position. 4. Set the Instant Pot to Pressure Cook. 5. Press the Pressure Level button to adjust the pressure to "Low". 6. Use the "+/-" keys on the control panel to set the cooking time to 10 minute. 7. Once the cooking cycle is completed, quick-release the steam. 8. When all the steam is released, remove the pressure lid from the top carefully. 9. While cauliflower cooks, prepare the dressing. 10. Whisk together olive oil, garlic, oregano, thyme, sage, salt, and pepper. 11. Carefully transfer cauliflower to a serving bowl and immediately pour dressing over cauliflower. 12. Carefully toss to coat. Let stand for 5 minutes. Serve hot.
Per Serving: Calories 272; Fat 10g; Sodium 891mg; Carbs 22.9g; Fiber 4g; Sugar 4g; Protein 3g

Maple Dill Carrots

Prep time: 15 minutes | Cook time: 5 minutes | Serves: 6

1 pound carrots, peeled and cut into quarters, or whole baby carrots
1 tablespoon minced fresh dill
1 tablespoon maple syrup

1 tablespoon ghee
½ teaspoon salt
½ cup water

1. Place all ingredients in the Instant Pot. 2. Put on the pressure cooker's lid and turn the steam valve to "Sealing" position. 3. Set the Instant Pot to Pressure Cook. 4. Use the "+/-" keys on the control panel to set the cooking time to 5 minutes. 5. Press the Pressure Level button to adjust the pressure to "Low". 6. Once the cooking cycle is completed, let the steam release naturally for 5 minutes and then quick-release the remaining pressure. 7. When all the steam is released, remove the pressure lid from the top carefully. 8. Transfer to a serving dish and serve warm.
Per Serving: Calories 472; Fat 10.9g; Sodium 354mg; Carbs 10.5g; Fiber 4.1g; Sugar 8.2g; Protein 6g

Vegetable Cheese Sauce

Prep time: 15 minutes | Cook time: 6 minutes | Serves: 6

1 small yellow onion, peeled and chopped	2¼ cups vegetable broth
1 medium zucchini, peeled and sliced	¼ teaspoon paprika
	1 medium sweet potato, peeled and chopped
6 cloves garlic, chopped	½ cup nutritional yeast

1. Place the onion, zucchini, garlic, and ¼ cup broth into the inner pot. 2. Press the "Sauté" button two time to select "Normal" mode and let the vegetables sauté until soft, 5 minutes. 3. Add the remaining 2 cups broth, paprika, and sweet potato. 4. Put on the pressure cooker's lid and turn the steam valve to "Sealing" position. 5. Set the Instant Pot to Pressure Cook. 6. Press the Pressure Level button to adjust the pressure to "Low". 7. Use the "+/-" keys on the control panel to set the cooking time to 6 minutes. 8. Once the cooking cycle is completed, quick-release the pressure. 9. When all the steam is released, remove the pressure lid from the top carefully. 10. Allow to cool for a few minutes and then transfer the mixture to a large blender. 11. Add the nutritional yeast to the blender with the other ingredients and blend on high until smooth. 12. Serve warm as a topping for the vegetables of your choice.
Per Serving: Calories 521; Fat 7.9g; Sodium 704mg; Carbs 6g; Fiber 3.6g; Sugar 6g; Protein 18g

Saucy Brussels Sprouts and Carrots

Prep time: 15 minutes | Cook time: 13 minutes | Serves: 4

1 tablespoon coconut oil	and cut into 1" chunks
12-ounce Brussels sprouts, tough ends removed and cut in half	¼ cup fresh lime juice
	¼ cup apple cider vinegar
12-ounce carrots (about 4 medium), peeled, ends removed,	½ cup coconut aminos
	¼ cup almond butter

1. Press the "Sauté" button twice to select "Normal" mode and melt the oil in the inner pot. 2. Add the Brussels sprouts and carrots and sauté until browned, about 5–7 minutes. 3. While the vegetables are browning, make the sauce. 4. In a small bowl, whisk together the lime juice, vinegar, coconut aminos, and almond butter. 5. Pour the sauce over the vegetables and press the Cancel button. 6. Put on the pressure cooker's lid and turn the steam valve to "Sealing" position. 7. Set the Instant Pot to Pressure Cook. 8. Press the Pressure Level button to adjust the pressure to "Low". 9. Use the "+/-" keys on the control panel to set the cooking time to 6 minutes. 10. Once the cooking cycle is completed, allow the steam to release quickly. 11. When all the steam is released, remove the pressure lid from the top carefully. 12. Serve.
Per Serving: Calories 272; Fat 10g; Sodium 891mg; Carbs 22.9g; Fiber 4g; Sugar 4g; Protein 3g

Spinach Salad with Quinoa

Prep time: 15 minutes | Cook time: 6 minutes | Serves: 6

¼ cup olive oil	diced
2 tablespoons fresh lemon juice	1 large carrot, peeled and diced
¼ teaspoon pure stevia powder	1 medium stalk celery, ends removed and sliced
1 teaspoon Dijon mustard	
¼ teaspoon salt	½ cup dry quinoa
⅛ teaspoon black pepper	1 cup vegetable broth
1 tablespoon avocado oil	10-ounce baby spinach leaves
1 small yellow onion, peeled and	

1. In a small bowl, whisk together the olive oil, lemon juice, stevia, mustard, salt, and pepper. Set aside. 2. Add the avocado oil to the inner pot of the Instant Pot and press the Sauté button. 3. Allow the oil to heat 1 minute and then add the onion, carrot, and celery. 4. Cook the vegetables until they are softened, about 5 minutes. 5. Rinse the quinoa in a fine-mesh strainer under water until the water runs clear. 6. Add the quinoa to the inner pot and stir to combine with the vegetables. Press the Cancel button. 7. Add the vegetable broth to the inner pot. 8. Put on the pressure cooker's lid and turn the steam valve to "Sealing" position. 9. Set the Instant Pot to Pressure Cook. 10. Use the "+/-" keys on the control panel to set the cooking time to 6 minutes. 11. Press the Pressure Level button to adjust the pressure to "Low". 12. Once the cooking cycle is completed, quick-release pressure. 13. When all the steam is released, remove the pressure lid from the top carefully. 14. Place the spinach leaves in a large bowl and top with

the quinoa mixture. 15. Drizzle with the dressing and toss to combine. Serve warm.
Per Serving: Calories 371; Fat 10.9g; Sodium 454mg; Carbs 10g; Fiber 3.1g; Sugar 5.2g; Protein 05g

Simple Spaghetti Squash

Prep time: 15 minutes | Cook time: 25 minutes | Serves: 4

1 medium spaghetti squash	⅛ teaspoon salt
2 tablespoons olive oil	⅛ teaspoon black pepper

1. Place 1½ cups water in the inner pot of your Instant Pot. Place the steam rack inside. 2. Wash squash with soap and water and dry it. 3. Place the whole uncut squash on top of the steam rack inside the inner pot. 4. Put on the pressure cooker's lid and turn the steam valve to "Sealing" position. 5. Set the Instant Pot to Pressure Cook. 6. Use the "+/-" keys on the control panel to set the cooking time to 25 minutes. 7. Press the Pressure Level button to adjust the pressure to "Low". 8. Once the cooking cycle is completed, quick-release the pressure. 9. When all the steam is released, remove the pressure lid from the top carefully. 10. Allow the squash to cool, and then carefully remove it from the pot. 11. Use a sharp knife to cut the squash in half lengthwise. 12. Spoon out the seeds and discard. Use a fork to scrape out the squash strands into a medium bowl. 13. Drizzle with the oil, add the salt and pepper, and serve.
Per Serving: Calories 382; Fat 19g; Sodium 354mg; Carbs 25g; Fiber 5.1g; Sugar 8.2g; Protein 2g

Lemony Cauliflower Rice

Prep time: 15 minutes | Cook time: 7 minutes | Serves: 4

1 tablespoon avocado oil	4 cups riced cauliflower
1 small yellow onion, peeled and diced	Juice from 1 small lemon
	½ teaspoon salt
1 teaspoon minced garlic	¼ teaspoon black pepper

1. Press the Sauté button, add the oil to the pot, and heat 1 minute. 2. Add the onion and sauté 5 minutes. 3. Add the garlic and sauté 1 more minute. Press the Cancel button. 4. Add the cauliflower rice, lemon juice, salt, and pepper and stir to combine. 5. Put on the pressure cooker's lid and turn the steam valve to "Sealing" position. 6. Set the Instant Pot to Pressure Cook. 7. Press the Pressure Level button to adjust the pressure to "Low". 8. Use the "+/-" keys on the control panel to set the cooking time to 1 minute. 9. Once the cooking cycle is completed, quick-release pressure. 10. When all the steam is released, remove the pressure lid from the top carefully. 11. Serve.
Per Serving: Calories 334; Fat 7.9g; Sodium 704mg; Carbs 6g; Fiber 3.6g; Sugar 6g; Protein 18g

Curried Mustard Greens

Prep time: 15 minutes | Cook time: 10 minutes | Serves: 6

1 tablespoon avocado oil	½ teaspoon salt
1 medium white onion, peeled and chopped	¼ teaspoon black pepper
	2 cups vegetable broth
1 tablespoon peeled and chopped ginger	½ cup coconut cream
	1 large bunch mustard greens
3 cloves garlic, minced	(about 1 pound), tough stems
2 tablespoons curry powder	removed and roughly chopped

1. Add the oil to the inner pot. 2. Press the "Sauté" button two time to select "Normal" mode and heat the oil 2 minutes. 3. Add the onion and sauté until softened, about 5 minutes. 4. Add the ginger, garlic, curry, salt, and pepper and sauté 1 more minute. 5. Stir in the vegetable broth and coconut cream until combined and then allow it to come to a boil, about 2–3 minutes more. 6. Stir in the mustard greens until everything is well combined. 7. Put on the pressure cooker's lid and turn the steam valve to "Sealing" position. 8. Set the Instant Pot to Pressure Cook. 9. Press the Pressure Level button to adjust the pressure to "Low". 10. Use the "+/-" keys on the control panel to set the cooking time to 1 minute. 11. Once the cooking cycle is completed, quick-release pressure. 12. When all the steam is released, remove the pressure lid from the top carefully. 13. Transfer to a bowl and serve.
Per Serving: Calories 272; Fat 10g; Sodium 891mg; Carbs 22.9g; Fiber 4g; Sugar 4g; Protein 3g

Lemon Garlic Red Chard

Prep time: 15 minutes | Cook time: 7 minutes | Serves: 4

1 tablespoon avocado oil
1 small yellow onion, peeled and diced
1 bunch red chard, leaves and stems chopped

3 cloves garlic, minced
¾ teaspoon salt
Juice from ½ medium lemon
1 teaspoon lemon zest

1. Add the oil to the inner pot of the Instant Pot and allow it to heat 1 minute. 2. Add the onion and chard stems and sauté 5 minutes. 3. Add the garlic and sauté another 30 seconds. 4. Add the chard leaves, salt, and lemon juice and stir to combine. Press the Cancel button. 5. Put on the pressure cooker's lid and turn the steam valve to "Sealing" position. 6. Set the Instant Pot to Pressure Cook. 7. Press the Pressure Level button to adjust the pressure to "Low". 8. Use the "+/-" keys on the control panel to set the cooking time to 1 minute. 9. Once the cooking cycle is completed, quick-release pressure. 10. When all the steam is released, remove the pressure lid from the top carefully. 11. Spoon the chard mixture into a serving bowl and top with lemon zest.
Per Serving: Calories 203; Fat 12.9g; Sodium 754mg; Carbs 21g; Fiber 6.1g; Sugar 4.2g; Protein 11g

Ginger Broccoli and Carrots

Prep time: 15 minutes | Cook time: 5 minutes | Serves: 6

1 tablespoon avocado oil
1" fresh ginger, peeled and thinly sliced
1 clove garlic, minced
2 broccoli crowns, stems removed and cut into large florets

2 large carrots, peeled and thinly sliced
½ teaspoon kosher salt
Juice from ½ large lemon
¼ cup water

1. Add the oil to the inner pot. 2. Press the "Sauté" button twice to select "Normal" mode and heat oil 2 minutes. 3. Add the ginger and garlic and sauté 1 minute. 4. Add the broccoli, carrots, and salt and stir to combine. Press the Cancel button. 5. Add the lemon juice and water and use a wooden spoon to scrape up any brown bits. 6. Put on the pressure cooker's lid and turn the steam valve to "Sealing" position. 7. Set the Instant Pot to Pressure Cook. 8. Press the Pressure Level button to adjust the pressure to "Low". 9. Use the "+/-" keys on the control panel to set the cooking time to 2 minutes. 10. Once the cooking cycle is completed, quick-release pressure. 11. When all the steam is released, remove the pressure lid from the top carefully. 12. Serve immediately.
Per Serving: Calories 419; Fat 14g; Sodium 791mg; Carbs 28.9g; Fiber 4.6g; Sugar 8g; Protein 3g

Great Pâté with Lentils and Walnuts

Prep Time: 10 minutes | Cook Time: 3-5 minutes | Serves: 2

¾ cup walnuts
2 cups water
1 cup green or brown lentils
½ medium onion, roughly chopped
1 bay leaf
2 garlic cloves, minced

2 tablespoons freshly squeezed lemon juice
1 tablespoon white miso paste
1 tablespoon apple cider vinegar
Freshly ground black pepper

1. Insert the inner pot into the cooker base. Connect the power cord to a 120 V power source. The cooker goes to Standby mode and the display indicates OFF. 2. Press Sauté to select the program and then press it again to choose the Normal temperature option. 3. Pour in the walnuts and sauté for 3 to 5 minutes, stirring now and then, until slightly darker in color and the oils begin to release. Remove from the inner pot and set aside. 4. In your inner pot, combine the water, lentils, onion, and bay leaf. Lock the lid and turn the steam release handle to Sealing. Select the Pressure Cook on the panel. Press the button again to choose Less option; use the "-" button to adjust the cooking time to 10 minutes. Press Pressure Level to choose High pressure. 5. After cooking has completed, leave the steam release handle in the Sealing position for 10 minutes after cooking has completed, then turn the steam release handle to the Venting position; quick-release any remaining pressure and uncover the lid carefully. 6. Discard the bay leaf; blend the lentils, onion, garlic, lemon juice, miso, vinegar, and pepper in a blender until creamy. 7. Serve immediately or serve as a warm dip.
Per Serving: Calories: 331; Fat: 15g; Carbs: 37g; Fiber: 7g; Sugar: 3g; Sodium: 163mg; Protein: 16g

Chapter 12 Dessert Recipes

Cheese Pumpkin with Spices

Prep Time: 5 minutes | Cook Time: 45 minutes | Serves: 10

Crust

2 tbsp. (28g) grass-fed butter or ghee, melted, plus more butter for pan	1 cup (100g) superfine blanched almond flour
2 tbsp. (19g) maple sugar	

Cheesecake

16 oz. (455g) cream cheese, softened	½ tsp ground cloves
1 cup (245g) pure pumpkin puree	½ tsp ground allspice
2 large eggs, at room temperature	¼ tsp sea salt
½ cup (76g) maple sugar	1 cup (237ml) water
1 tbsp. (8g) cassava flour	Homemade whipped cream or coconut whipped cream, for garnish (optional)
1 tsp pure vanilla extract	
Zest of 1 orange	
2 tsp (5g) ground cinnamon	Ground cinnamon, for garnish (optional)
½ tsp ground ginger	

1. Get the crust ready. Butter an Instant Pot-compatible 6- or 7-inch (15- or 18.5-cm) round springform pan. Place aside. 2. All the crust ingredients should be combined in a bowl and well mixed with clean hands. Pour the mixture into the prepared springform pan, pressing it down to create a dense bottom crust. Don't let the pan's sides fill up too much. Place the pan in the freezer for 15 minutes to cold. 3. Get the cheesecake ready. Cream cheese, pumpkin, eggs, maple sugar, cassava flour, vanilla, orange zest, cinnamon, ginger, cloves, allspice, and salt should all be combined in a blender. Process slowly until everything is well-blended and smooth. Incorporate the frozen crust with the cheesecake filling. 4. Place the steam rack into the Instant Pot after adding the water. Place the springform pan carefully on the rack and cover with a glass casserole lid. Put the steam vent in the sealed position and fasten the lid. 45 minutes of high pressure are set by pressing Pressure Cook. 5. Open the lid when the timer goes off. 15 minutes should be given for the Instant Pot's natural pressure release. Perform a fast release while holding an oven mitt. Allow any remaining steam to escape until the float valve lowers, and then carefully lift the lid. 6. Lift the rack and springform pan out of the Instant Pot with care after removing the cover. Employ oven mitts. With the glass top still on, let the cheesecake to cool to room temperature. Remove the lid once it has cooled completely, being careful not to drop any moisture onto the cheesecake's top. When you're ready to take the cheesecake from the pan, gently run a knife over the edges to release them. Return the lid on the cheesecake after thoroughly wiping away all of the dampness. Transfer to the refrigerator and refrigerate for at least 6 hours, ideally overnight. 7. Serve cold. If you choose, top the dish with homemade whipped cream, coconut whipped cream, or cinnamon powder.

Per Serving: Calories 415; Fat: 32g; Sodium 409mg; Carbs: 23g; Sugars: 10g; Protein 11g

Cheesecake and Cookies

Prep Time: 5 minutes | Cook Time: 25 minutes | Serves: 4

Crust

2 cups (180g) finely ground chocolate sandwich cookies, preferably Oreos	Pinch of salt
	3 tbsps. (43g) unsalted butter, melted
1 tbsp. (13g) sugar	

Cheesecake

16 oz. (455g) cream cheese, softened	1 tsp pure vanilla extract
1⅓ cups (268g) sugar	2 large eggs
1 tbsp. (5.6g) finely ground chocolate sandwich cookies, preferably Oreos	½ cup (120ml) heavy cream
	1 cup (237ml) water

1. Prepare the crust. Combine the cookie crumbs, sugar, salt, and butter in a medium bowl. In a round, leak-proof springform pan measuring 7 inches (18.5 cm), press the mixture into the bottom. 2. Prepare the cheesecake. Cream the cream cheese and sugar in the paddle-equipped bowl of an electric stand mixer until it is light and fluffy. Scrape the sides clean. 3. Vanilla and cookie crumbs should be added. Assemble by combining. Once mixed, add each egg one at a time, scraping the bowl as necessary. Incorporate the heavy cream. 4. Over the springform pan's shell, pour the cheese mixture. 5. Place the steam rack into the Instant Pot after adding the water. The springform pan should be put on the rack. 6. Secure the lid with the steam vent in the sealed position. Select Pressure Cook. Adjust the time to 25 minutes. 7. Allow the pressure to naturally release on seal position as the timer goes off. 8. Remove the springform pan from the pot when the float valve opens. Before cutting, place the cake in the refrigerator

to cool for the night.

Per Serving: Calories 448; Fat: 60g; Sodium 834mg; Carbs: 62.87g; Sugars: 43g; Protein 13g

Bread Pudding with Pomegranates

Prep Time: 5 minutes | Cook Time: 15 minutes | Serves: 4

1 cup (237ml) whole milk	2 large eggs, beaten
1 cup (237ml) heavy cream	½ loaf challah bread, cut into 2" (5-cm) cubes
2 tbsps. (30g) unsalted butter, melted, plus more for pan	½ cup (87g) pomegranate arils, divided
1 tsp pure vanilla extract	1 cup (237ml) water
⅓ cup (67g) plus 1 tsp granulated sugar, plus more for sprinkling	Confectioners' sugar
Pinch of salt	

1. Combine the milk, cream, melted butter, vanilla, sugar, salt, and eggs in a large basin. until smooth, whisk. Challah cubes should be added to the basin. Mix until the bread is well covered. Three-quarters of the pomegranate arils should be added after letting the bread soak in the liquid for a few minutes. 2. a 7" (18.5 cm) heatproof dish with butter. To the prepared bowl, add the challah mixture. Top the challah mixture with the rest of the pomegranate seeds. Add little sugar granules. 3. Place the steam rack into the Instant Pot after adding the water. Put the pudding bowl on the rack's middle. 4. Put the steam valve in the seal position and fasten the lid. Push Pressure Cook on high. Adjust the time until the display reads "15 minutes." 5. When the timer sounds, quickly release the pressure on vent position. Remove the lid and carefully remove the bowl. Lightly dust with confectioners' sugar.

Per Serving: Calories 265; Fat: 19g; Sodium 70mg; Carbs: 18g; Sugars: 14g; Protein 5g

Delicious Dulce De Leche

Prep Time: 5 minutes | Cook Time: 30 minutes | Serves: 1 cup

1½ cups water plus 3 tablespoons warm water	One 14-ounce can full-fat sweetened condensed milk
½ teaspoon baking soda	

1. Fill the Instant Pot with 1 ½ cups of water. In the pot, place the steam rack. In a 2-quart, high-sided, round soufflé dish, combine the baking soda with the remaining 3 tablespoons warm water. Until smooth, whisk in the condensed milk. Lock the lid and place this bowl on the steam rack. 2. Select Pressure Cook on high. Set time to 30 minutes. 3. After the time has done cooking, switch it off and wait for around 15 minutes for the pressure to naturally release on seal position. Open the lid. Use an immersion blender inside the insert to make the dulce de leche sauce extremely smooth, or whisk until smooth. Place the sauce in a small bowl and refrigerate for one to two hours. For up to 5 days, cover and refrigerate; before serving, reheat tiny amounts in the microwave to help them soften.

Per Serving: Calories 865; Fat: 40g; Sodium 344mg; Carbs: 65g; Sugars: 14g; Protein 68.39g

Yummy Vanilla Custard

Prep Time: 5 minutes | Cook Time: 8 minutes | Serves: 4

4 large eggs	½ teaspoon vanilla extract
2 cups whole milk	¼ teaspoon table salt
3 tablespoons granulated white sugar	1½ cups water

1. In a large bowl, combine the eggs, milk, sugar, vanilla, and salt and whisk until very creamy. Distribute this mixture equally among four pressure- and heat-safe One-cup ramekins. A little piece of aluminum foil should be placed over each ramekin. 2. Fill the instant pot with water. Add a steam rack to the pot. Then place ramekins on the rack (probably 3 on the rack and then one balanced in the middle on the edges of the three below). Close the lid. 3. Select Pressure Cook on high. Set time to 8 minutes. 4. After the time has done cooking, switch it off and wait for around 15 minutes for the pressure to naturally release on seal position. Open the lid. The heated covered ramekins should be moved to a wire rack, uncovered, and allowed to cool for 15 minutes. Serve warm or cover once more and store in the refrigerator for up to 4 days or at least two hours.

Per Serving: Calories 190; Fat: 8g; Sodium 209mg; Carbs: 22.87g; Sugars: 21.03g; Protein 6g

Pumpkin Cheesecake

Prep Time: 5 minutes | Cook Time: 35 minutes | Serves: 4

1 cup (237ml) water
Nonstick cooking spray, for pan
1½ cups (183g) granola
4 tbsps. (55g) unsalted butter, melted
2 (8-oz [225-g]) packages cream cheese, softened
½ cup (100g) sugar
2 large eggs
½ cup (123g) pure pumpkin puree
1½ tsp (3g) pumpkin pie spice
½ tsp pure vanilla extract

1. Pour the water into the Instant Pot and insert the steam rack. 2. Nonstick cooking spray should be used to coat a 7-inch (18.5-cm) cheesecake pan with a removable bottom. Grind the granola into big crumbs in a food processor or strong blender. Combine the granola crumbs and melted butter, and then firmly press the mixture into the pan's bottom. 3. Cream cheese and sugar should be combined in a medium basin and beaten until smooth. Add the eggs one at a time, mixing well after each addition. Blend in the vanilla, pumpkin pie spice, and pumpkin puree after adding them. 4. After adding the batter to the cheesecake pan, wrap it with aluminum foil. Sling some foil. Carefully set the pan on the rack using the sling. 5. Put the steam vent in the seal position and fasten the lid. As soon as you press manual, set the timer to 30 minutes. Verify that high pressure is beneath the display light. 6. Allow the pressure to naturally drop on seal position for 15 minutes after the timer goes off, then quickly release the pressure on vent position and gently remove the lid. Use the sling to carefully remove the cheesecake, and then allow it to cool completely on a wire rack (gently dab any condensation from the top of cheesecake before cooling). At least four hours to chill.
Per Serving: Calories 491; Fat: 32g; Sodium 153mg; Carbs: 40g; Sugars: 23g; Protein 10g

A Chocolate Cake without Flour

Prep Time: 5 minutes | Cook Time: 35 minutes | Serves: 6

5 oz. (140g) high-quality unsweetened chocolate
6 tbsps. (85g) unsalted butter
1 tbsp. (15ml) pure vanilla or chocolate extract
1 cup (200g) sugar
4 large eggs, whisked
½ cup (55g) unsweetened cocoa powder
Nonstick cooking spray, for pan
1 cup (237ml) water
½ cup (65g) raspberries, for serving (optional)

1. Melt the chocolate and butter together in a microwave or double boiler, then allow to cool. 2. Once the chocolate liquid is smooth, add the vanilla, sugar, eggs, and cocoa powder. 3. Spray some nonstick cooking spray in a 6-inch (15-cm) springform pan lightly. Use a 6- to 7-inch (15- to 18.5-cm) round cake pan as an alternative, but make a sling out of foil to make removing the cake easier. After pouring the batter into the pan, wrap it with foil. 4. Place the cake pan on top of the steam rack after adding water to the Instant Pot. 5. Put the steam valve in the seal position and fasten the lid. 35 minutes on high pressure with the Pressure Cook option. 6. Use a Quick Release on vent position. Remove the lid, then use potholders to remove the cake pan. 7. Chill for 1 to 2 hours before removing from the pan and slicing. Serve chilled or at room temperature with berries (if using).
Per Serving: Calories 422; Fat: 35.17g; Sodium 15mg; Carbs: 26.87g; Sugars: 21g; Protein 3g

Grain-Free Banana Bread

Prep Time: 5 minutes | Cook Time: 35 minutes | Serves: 6

1½ cups (150g) blanched almond flour
2 tbsps. (14g) coconut flour
2 tsp (5g) ground cinnamon
Pinch of ground nutmeg
¾ tsp baking soda
½ tsp sea salt
Nonstick cooking spray, for dish or pan
¼ cup (60ml) melted coconut oil
2 medium very ripe bananas, mashed
2 large eggs
2 tbsps. (30ml) pure maple syrup
1 tsp pure vanilla extract
½ cup (88g) chocolate chips

1. Almond flour, coconut flour, cinnamon, nutmeg, baking soda, and salt should all be combined in a small basin. 2. Bananas, eggs, maple syrup, vanilla, and coconut oil should be combined in a large bowl using an electric mixer on low speed until largely smooth. When all dry pockets have been eliminated, fold in the flour mixture and continue beating. Add the chocolate chunks and stir. 3. Use nonstick cooking spray to coat a 6- to 7-inch (15- to 18.5-cm) springform pan or a 7-inch (18.5-cm) heatproof round glass dish. Once the batter has

been added to the dish, it should be covered with foil. 4. Place the steam rack into the Instant Pot after adding the water. The dish should be put on the rack. 5. Ensure that the lid is sealed. Select Pressure Cook on high pressure for 35 minutes. 6. Use a Quick Release on seal position. Carefully remove the dish from the Instant Pot, using pot holders. Allow the banana bread to completely cool before slicing.
Per Serving: Calories 418; Fat: 31g; Sodium 400mg; Carbs: 30g; Sugars: 18g; Protein 9g

Glazed Doughnut and Apple Crisp

Prep Time: 5 minutes | Cook Time: 10 minutes | Serves: 6

6 Honeycrisp apples, partially peeled
½ cup (115g) brown sugar, divided
1 tsp ground cinnamon
½ tsp pure vanilla extract
1 cup (237ml) water
½ cup (40g) old-fashioned rolled
oats
3 tbsps. (43g) unsalted butter
¼ cup (30g) all-purpose flour
3 leftover glazed doughnuts, cut into 1" (2.5-cm) pieces
Vanilla ice cream, for topping

1. To avoid the seeds, cut each apple into four wedges (discard the seeds). You should have 8 pieces if you cut those wedges in half. In the Instant Pot, add the apples, ¼ cup (58g) of the brown sugar, the cinnamon, vanilla, and water. 2. Put the steam valve in the seal position and fasten the lid. Choose Pressure Cook on high. Adjust the time using the plus and minus buttons until the display says "1 minute." 3. Release the pressure immediately on vent position once the timer beeps. Take off the lid. 4. Combine the remaining brown sugar, oats, butter, and flour in a small bowl. 5. Doughnuts and apple mixture should be combined. 6. Press sauté. Use your hands to crumble the oat mixture over the apple mixture. Let the crisp bubble away for 2 minutes. 7. Press Cancel. Let the crisp cool for 5 minutes before spooning into bowls and topping with vanilla ice cream.
Per Serving: Calories 337; Fat: 10g; Sodium 81mg; Carbs: 63g; Sugars: 42g; Protein 3g

Yummy Cup Pudding

Prep Time: 5 minutes | Cook Time: 10 minutes | Serves: 5

1½ cups (355ml) heavy cream
½ cup (120ml) milk
¾ cup (131g) chocolate chips or chopped chocolate
2 large eggs
¼ cup (60ml) pure maple syrup or honey
1½ tbsp. (11g) unsweetened cocoa powder
2 tbsps. (28g) grass-fed butter, ghee or coconut oil, melted, divided
1 tbsp. (15ml) pure vanilla extract
½ tsp organic orange extract
½ tsp ground cinnamon
⅛ tsp ground cayenne
⅛ tsp sea salt
1 tsp grass-fed bovine gelatin
1 cup (237ml) water
Homemade whipped cream, for garnish (optional)
Shaved or chopped organic stone-ground Mexican chocolate, for garnish (optional)

1. Warm the cream, milk, and chocolate in a small saucepan over low heat while stirring until smooth. Turn off the heat and leave the pot alone. 2. Eggs, your preferred sweetener, cocoa powder, melted fat of your choice, vanilla, orange essence, cinnamon, cayenne, and salt should all be put in a blender. Process slowly for 30 seconds to completely combine. Remove the vent cap from the blender while it's running, add the chocolate mixture, followed by the gelatin, and blend for an additional 30 seconds to integrate completely. 3. Fill five half-pints (250ml) glass jars with the custard mixture evenly, allowing at least a 12-inch (1.3-cm) headroom at the top. Jars are covered and sealed with lids. 4. Place the steam rack inside your Instant Pot after adding the water. 5. Put the rack on top of the five jars. They ought should fit the Instant Pot just right. Fix the cover in the sealed position. Press Pressure Cook, then set the timer for 5 minutes on LOW pressure. 6. When the timer beeps, select Cancel or keep warm. Perform a fast release on vent position while holding an oven mitt. Carefully open the lid after the steam valve stops and the float valve drops. 7. Carefully take out the jars and take off their lids using an oven mitt or tongs. After thoroughly stirring the ingredients to make it smooth, let each pudding cup cool to room temperature. Transfer them to the refrigerator to set after they have cooled. For the most realistic solid texture, refrigerate them for at least 6 hours, preferably overnight. 8. Serve chilled as is or garnished, if desired, with homemade whipped cream and/or shaved or chopped organic stone-ground Mexican chocolate.
Per Serving: Calories 250; Fat: 17g; Sodium 99mg; Carbs: 16g; Sugars: 12g; Protein 3g

Applesauce with Pear and Sweet Potato

Prep Time: 5 minutes | Cook Time: 10 minutes | Serves: 6

5 Honeycrisp apples, cored and chopped
1 sweet potato, peeled and chopped
1 Bartlett pear, cored and chopped

Pinch of salt
1 cup (237ml) water
½ tsp cinnamon
1 tbsp. (15ml) pure maple syrup

1. Mix all the ingredients thoroughly before adding them to the Instant Pot. 2. Put the steam valve in the seal position and fasten the lid. Choose Pressure Cook on high. Adjust the time using the plus and minus buttons until the display says "10 minutes." 3. Release the pressure immediately on vent position once the timer beeps. Then, using an immersion blender, purée the mixture until it is smooth.
Per Serving: Calories 109; Fat: 1g; Sodium 3mg; Carbs: 28.7g; Sugars: 20g; Protein 1g

Lemon Curd with Honey

Prep Time: 5 minutes | Cook Time: 10 minutes | Serves: 2

4 large eggs
⅓ cup (80ml) honey
Zest of 3 lemons
½ cup (120ml) fresh lemon juice

7 tbsps. (99g) grass-fed butter, melted and cooled
1 cup (237ml) water

1. The eggs, honey, lemon zest, lemon juice, and melted butter should all be combined in a blender. Blend them on low speed for 30 seconds, or until well combined. 2. The 1 ½-quart (1.5-L) casserole dish that fits inside the Instant Pot should be filled with the lemon mixture. The casserole dish should then be covered with the glass lid. If the casserole dish you're using doesn't have a glass lid, you may line the top with unbleached parchment paper, then cover it with foil and fasten it around the sides. 3. Place the steam rack into the Instant Pot after adding the water. Place the covered casserole dish carefully on the rack. 4. Close the lid. For 5 minutes, press Pressure Cook while setting the pressure to high. 5. When the timer beeps, select Cancel or keep warm. 15 minutes should be given for the Instant Pot's pressure release naturally on seal position. Perform a fast release while holding an oven mitt. Allow any remaining steam to release on vent position then open the lid. 6. Carefully remove the casserole dish from the Instant Pot using an oven mitt, then remove the glass cover. Pour the curd into your preferred half-pint (250ml) glass jars, ramekins, or single glass airtight container after whisking it continuously until the mixture is perfectly smooth, or just leave it in the casserole dish. Refrigerate the lemon curd so that it can solidify. 7. Let chill for a minimum of 5 hours, or until fully chilled. Serve chilled.
Per Serving: Calories 309; Fat: 9g; Sodium 22mg; Carbs: 56g; Sugars: 50g; Protein 6g

Spiced Apple-Cranberry Cider

Prep Time: 5 minutes | Cook Time: 10 minutes | Serves: 1.5L

6 apples, peeled, cored and quartered
2½ cups (590ml) filtered water, plus more as needed
3 cups (300g) frozen or fresh cranberries
Zest and juice of 2 medium oranges
⅓ cup (80ml) honey or pure maple

syrup
1 (1" [2.5-cm]) piece fresh ginger, peeled and sliced
3 cinnamon sticks
13 whole cloves
Vanilla ice cream, for serving (optional)

1. Apples and water should be put in a powerful blender and processed until completely smooth and liquefied. 2. Through a fine-mesh filter, add the apple juice to the Instant Pot. 3. Cranberries, orange zest and juice, ginger, cinnamon sticks, and cloves should all be included. Add extra filtered water until the liquid level reaches the "5 cup" mark on the Instant Pot's inside. 4. Press sauté to start boiling the ingredients. Press Cancel to stop the Instant Pot once the cider begins to boil. 5. Close the lid. For 10 minutes, press Pressure Cook at high pressure. 6. When the timer beeps, select Cancel or keep warm. 15 minutes should be given for the Instant Pot's natural pressure release on seal position. Perform a fast release while holding an oven mitt. Allow any remaining steam to escape on vent position until the float valve lowers, and then carefully lift the lid. 7. Into a very big bowl or a sizable heatproof pitcher, very gently spoon or pour the extremely hot spiced cider using an oven mitt. If extra straining is required to get rid of all the fruit pulp, do so. 8. Serve right away in your preferred cup and top with a dollop of vanilla ice cream for an added touch of luxury (if using).

Per Serving: Calories 180; Fat: 1g; Sodium 19mg; Carbs: 44g; Sugars: 34g; Protein 1g

Yummy Brownies

Prep Time: 5 minutes | Cook Time: 35 minutes | Serves: 6

1 cup (245g) pure pumpkin puree
¼ cup (65g) almond butter
2 large eggs
1 tbsp. (30ml) pure vanilla extract
1 cup (225g) coconut sugar
½ cup (50g) almond flour
½ cup (55g) unsweetened cocoa

powder
½ tsp baking powder
½ tsp sea salt
½ cup (88g) chocolate chips
Nonstick cooking spray, for pan
2 cups (475ml) water

1. Use an electric mixer to thoroughly combine the pumpkin, almond butter, eggs, vanilla, and coconut sugar in a medium bowl. 2. Mix the almond flour, baking powder, salt, and cocoa powder in a separate basin. When there are no dry pockets left, add the dry ingredients to the wet components and continue beating. Add the chocolate chunks and stir. 3. Apply nonstick cooking spray to a 7-inch (18.5-cm) round springform or cake pan to prepare it. Smooth the batter after pouring it into the pan (it should be thick). After wrapping the pan in foil, cover it with a paper towel. This will aid in preventing moisture buildup. 4. Place the steam rack into the Instant Pot after adding the water. On the rack, put the pan. Affix the lid. 35 minutes on high pressure with the Pressure Cook option. 5. For at least 15 minutes, use a natural release on seal position, and then let out any leftover steam on vent position. Pot holders are used to lift the pan after removing the cover. 6. The brownies should cool for at least 15 minutes before being taken out of the pan.
Per Serving: Calories 282; Fat: 18g; Sodium 276mg; Carbs: 26g; Sugars: 17g; Protein 10g

Filled Apples

Prep Time: 5 minutes | Cook Time: 5 minutes | Serves: 4

4 medium Honeycrisp apples
⅓ cup (37g) crushed pecans
⅓ cup (75g) coconut sugar or dark brown sugar
½ cup (75g) raisins
2 tsp (5g) ground cinnamon

Pinch of sea salt
4 tbsp. (55g) butter, cut into 4 equal pieces
¾ cup (160ml) water
2 cups (280g) vanilla ice cream (optional)

1. Each apple should have a core that is removed from the top, leaving approximately ¼ inch (6 mm) of the apple around the edges and at the bottom. 2. Mix the nuts, coconut sugar, raisins, cinnamon, and salt in a medium bowl. Each apple's cavity should be filled with the mixture. Add a piece of butter on top. 3. Fill the Instant Pot with water. Alongside one another, add enough apples to fill the pot's cavity. 4. Put the steam valve in the seal position and fasten the lid. Choose Pressure Cook, then cook for 3 minutes at high pressure. 5. Use a fast release on vent position, then use tongs to remove the apples. 6. With vanilla ice cream, serve warm (if using).
Per Serving: Calories 288; Fat: 17g; Sodium 94mg; Carbs: 35g; Sugars: 27g; Protein 1g

Fresh Mango-Coconut Custard

Prep Time: 5 minutes | Cook Time: 25 minutes | Serves: 4

2 cups chopped fresh or frozen mango
½ (13.5-ounce) can full-fat coconut milk (about ¾ cup)

2 tablespoons cornstarch or arrowroot powder
Unrefined sugar, for sprinkling (optional)

1. Mango, coconut milk, and cornstarch should be blended or processed into a smooth paste. The mixture should go into 4 heat-resistant ramekins. If desired, add a little sugar on the top of each. 2. Place the steam rack and a cup or two of water in the Instant Pot's bottom. Stack the ramekins if necessary as you lower them onto the rack (3 on the bottom, 1 on top). Select High Pressure Cook, set the timer for 10 minutes, secure the lid and make sure the pressure valve is sealed. 3. After the cooking period is through, wait 10 minutes for the pressure to naturally release on seal position. 4. After the last bit of pressure has dissipated, carefully unlock and take off the lid. Let cool for a few minutes before carefully lifting out the ramekins with oven mitts or tongs. 5. Let the custards cool to room temperature, or refrigerate until cooled and set.
Per Serving: Calories 122; Fat: 7g; Sodium 5mg; Carbs: 18g; Sugars: 12g; Protein 1g

Crisp Pear and Cranberry

Prep Time: 5 minutes | Cook Time: 5 minutes | Serves: 6

3 large Anjou pears, peeled, cored and diced
1 cup (100g) fresh cranberries
1 tbsp. (13g) granulated sugar
2 tsp (5g) ground cinnamon
½ tsp ground nutmeg
½ cup (120ml) water
1 tbsp. (15ml) pure maple syrup
6 tbsps. (90g) unsalted butter, melted

1 cup (80g) old-fashioned rolled oats
⅓ cup (75g) dark brown sugar
¼ cup (30g) all-purpose flour
½ tsp sea salt
½ cup (50g) pecans, toasted (optional)
Vanilla ice cream, for serving (optional)

1. Combine the pears and cranberries in the Instant Pot, then top with the sugar. Sprinkle with cinnamon and nutmeg after let it settle for a few minutes. Add the maple syrup and water over top. 2. Oats, brown sugar, flour, salt, and melted butter should all be combined in a medium basin. 3. In the Instant Pot, spoon the mixture over the fruit. 4. Put the steam valve in the seal position and fasten the lid. Choose Pressure Cook, and then cook for 5 minutes at high pressure. Utilize a rapid release on vent position after timer beeps. 5. Serve hot after spooning into separate dishes. Add pecans and vanilla ice cream on top (if using).
Per Serving: Calories 336; Fat: 15.17g; Sodium 220mg; Carbs: 52.87g; Sugars: 27g; Protein 5g

Brownie Pudding

Prep Time: 5 minutes | Cook Time: 12 minutes | Serves: 4

6 ounces semi-sweet chocolate, chopped; or 6 ounces semi-sweet morsels (about 1 cup)
½ ounce unsweetened chocolate, chopped (half of a 1-ounce square of standard baking chocolate, or about 1½ tablespoons chopped

unsweetened chocolate)
1 cup whole milk
½ cup heavy cream
4 large egg yolks
Up to 2 teaspoons vanilla extract
¼ teaspoon salt
1½ cups water

1. Put both kinds of chocolate in a large dish that can withstand heat. Place aside. 2. Add the milk and cream to a medium bowl that can withstand the microwave. Heat for one to two minutes on high until steaming. After adding the chocolate to the boiling milk mixture, steep for one minute. Until melted and smooth, stir. while whisking intermittently, let cool for five minutes. 3. Salt, vanilla, and egg yolks should all be well mixed in. Divide this mixture into four 1-cup ramekins that can withstand pressure and heat. Wrap each in aluminum foil securely. Fill the Instant Pot with water. The ramekins should be stacked on the steam rack with three on the bottom and one in the center, on their edges, on top of the pot. Close lid. 4. Select Pressure Cook on high. Set time to 8 minutes. 5. After the time has done cooking, switch it off and wait for around 20 minutes for the pressure to naturally release on seal position. Open the pot's lid by unlatching it. The heated covered ramekins should be moved to a wire rack, uncovered, and allowed to cool for 15 minutes. Serve warm or cover once more and store in the refrigerator for up to 4 days or at least 2 hours until cooled.
Per Serving: Calories 399; Fat: 26g; Sodium 197mg; Carbs: 37g; Sugars: 32g; Protein 6g

Yummy Pudding Butterscotch

Prep Time: 5 minutes | Cook Time: 15 minutes | Serves: 4

3 tablespoons butter
½ cup packed dark brown sugar
1½ cups whole milk
½ cup heavy cream

6 large egg yolks
¼ teaspoon vanilla extract
⅛ teaspoon salt
1½ cups water

1. Select sauté. 2. Butter should be melted in a 6- or 8-quart pot. For about three minutes, boil the mixture while continuously bubbling after smoothing out the brown sugar. Add the milk and cream and stir until the sugar mixture smooths out and melts once more. Pour the contents of the hot insert into a nearby big basin after turning off the SAUTÉ function. 15 minutes to cool. Return the insert to the machine after cleaning and drying it in the interim. 3. Blend the milk mixture by whisking in the egg yolks, vanilla, and salt. Distribute this mixture equally into four 1-cup ramekins that can withstand pressure and heat. Wrap them all with aluminum foil. 4. Fill the instant pot with water. Put steam rack in pot. Stack the ramekins on the rack. Close lid. 5. Select Pressure Cook on high. Set time to 10 minutes. 6. After

the machine has done cooking, switch it off and wait for around 20 minutes for the pressure to naturally release on seal position. Open the lid. The heated covered ramekins should be moved to a wire rack, uncovered, and allowed to cool for 15 minutes. Serve hot or cover once more and store in the fridge for at least two hours or up to four days.
Per Serving: Calories 342; Fat: 23g; Sodium 206mg; Carbs: 25.87g; Sugars: 24g; Protein 7g

Yummy Pudding

Prep Time: 5 minutes | Cook Time: 7 minutes | Serves: 4

3 cups whole, low-fat, or fat-free milk
½ cup granulated white sugar
½ cup instant tapioca
1 teaspoon vanilla extract

¼ teaspoon table salt
1½ cups water
1 large egg, at room temperature
1 large egg yolk, at room temperature

1. In a 2-quart, high-sided, round, pressure- and heat-safe soufflé dish, whisk the milk, sugar, tapioca, vanilla, and salt until the sugar dissolves. Never cover. 2. Fill the Instant Pot with water. Put steam rack in pot. Close lid. 3. Select Pressure Cook on high. Set time to 5 minutes. 4. After the time has done cooking, switch it off and wait for around 20 minutes for the pressure to naturally return to normal. Open the cooker by releasing the lid clasp. In the baking dish, whisk the heated liquid until it is smooth, scraping up any clumps of tapioca that may have formed there. 5. In a medium dish, combine the egg and egg yolk and whisk to combine. When all of the hot milk mixture has been added, continue whisking in tiny amounts of the hot tapioca custard into the eggs. After chilling for two hours, serve immediately, or cover and keep in the refrigerator for up to four days.
Per Serving: Calories 265; Fat: 13g; Sodium 232mg; Carbs: 29g; Sugars: 12.03g; Protein 7g

Cake Made of Bananas

Prep Time: 5 minutes | Cook Time: 25 minutes | Serves: 8

⅔ cup sliced almonds
⅔ cup graham cracker crumbs
½ cup plus 2 tablespoons granulated white sugar
3 tablespoons butter, melted and cooled, plus additional butter for greasing the pan
1-pound regular cream cheese

1 small very ripe banana
⅓ cup packaged, dehydrated, crisp, unsweetened, unsalted banana chips
2 large eggs
1 tablespoon all-purpose flour
½ teaspoon almond extract
1½ cups water

1. Butter a 7-inch round springform pan well on the inside. In a medium bowl, combine the melted butter, 2 tablespoons sugar, almond slices, and graham cracker crumbs. Stir to combine well. To create a crust, press this mixture firmly into the bottom and halfway up the edges of the pan. 2. In a food processor, combine the remaining ½ cup sugar, cream cheese, banana, and banana chips (if using), cover, and process for approximately a minute or until smooth. One at a time, add the eggs and process each one until smooth. Add the flour and almond extract after opening the machine and cleaning the interior. Process while covered until smooth. Fill the prepared crust in the pan with this mixture. Do not cover the pan with foil. 3. Fill the Instant Pot with water. In the cooker, place the steam rack. Make a sling out of aluminum foil, place the full springform pan on it, and then drop it into the pot using the sling. To prevent the sling's ends from coming in contact with the cheesecake mixture in the pan, fold them down. Lock lid. 4. Select Pressure Cook on high for 25 minutes. 5. After the time has done cooking, switch it off and wait for around 20 minutes for the pressure to naturally return to normal. Open the lid. The heated springform pan may be moved to a wire rack using the sling. After 15 minutes of cooling, refrigerate for one hour. For at least another hour or up to two days, cover and keep the food in the fridge. 6. To serve, remove the cake from the pan and slice it with a small knife. To remove the cake from the pan, unlatch the sides and pry it open. If desired, slice the cake from the pan's bottom with a long, thin knife before transferring the cheesecake to a serving tray with a big metal spatula.
Per Serving: Calories 282; Fat: 22g; Sodium 291mg; Carbs: 16g; Sugars: 11g; Protein 5g

Pudding of Rice

Prep Time: 5 minutes | Cook Time: 17 minutes | Serves: 6

1 tablespoon butter	Up to 2 teaspoons vanilla extract
¾ cup raw white Arborio rice	¼ teaspoon table salt
One 12-ounce can whole or low-fat evaporated milk (1½ cups)	1 large egg, at room temperature
½ cup water	1 large egg yolk, at room temperature
½ cup granulated white sugar	⅓ cup heavy cream

1. Select sauté function. 2. Melt the butter in Instant Pot. For approximately a minute, while continually stirring, add the rice, cooking it until the tips of the grains become translucent. Add the salt, water, vanilla, sugar, and evaporated milk and stir until the sugar dissolves. Lock the lid on the pot and deactivate SAUTÉ. 3. Select Pressure Cook on high and set time to 10 minutes. 4. After the time has done cooking, switch it off and wait for around 15 minutes for the pressure to naturally release on seal position. Open the lid. Repeatedly stir the rice mixture. 5. In a big bowl, combine the cream, egg, and egg yolk and whisk to combine well. Once the mixture is smooth, stir the remaining rice mixture in the pot along with about 1 cup of the leftover rice mixture on sauté function. After 5 minutes, either serve warm or spoon into a large, clean dish and chill for about an hour. The pudding may be stored in the fridge for up to two days when covered.
Per Serving: Calories 270; Fat: 21.17g; Sodium 481mg; Carbs: 19g; Sugars: 5g; Protein 8g

Fresh Mango with Sweet Coconut Rice

Prep Time: 5 minutes | Cook Time: 17 minutes | Serves: 6

One 14-ounce can full-fat coconut milk or coconut cream (but not cream of coconut)	3½ cups water
½ cup granulated white sugar	1½ cups raw, sweet, glutinous white rice
½ teaspoon vanilla extract	3 medium ripe mangos, peeled, pitted, and cut into bite-size chunks
½ teaspoon table salt	

1. Select sauté function. 2. In Instant pot, combine the coconut milk, sugar, vanilla, and salt. Cook for approximately 4 minutes, stirring often, until bubbling. Scrape all of the coconut mixture into a large basin and turn off the SAUTÉ feature before removing the heated insert from the appliance. Place aside. 3. Place the steam rack inside the pot after adding 1½ cups of water. In a 2-quart, high-sided, round soufflé dish, combine the rice with the remaining 2 cups water. Place this dish on the rack and tighten the pot's lid. 4. Select Pressure Cook on high for 12 minutes. 5. Quickly release the pressure on vent position. Then wait 10 minutes, open the pot. The heated dish should be taken from the rack. 6. Combine the cooked rice with all except ⅓ cup of the coconut milk mixture. Warm rice is served in bowls with mango slices scattered on top. The leftover coconut milk mixture is drizzled over the servings as desired.
Per Serving: Calories 367; Fat: 16.17g; Sodium 254mg; Carbs: 35g; Sugars: 6g; Protein 23g

Fired-Up Sugar Flan

Prep Time: 5 minutes | Cook Time: 17 minutes | Serves: 4

½ plus ⅓ cup granulated white sugar	1¼ cups heavy cream
1½ cups plus 3 tablespoons water	¾ cup whole milk
3 large eggs	2 teaspoons vanilla extract
	⅛ teaspoon table salt

1. In instant pot on sauté, melt the ½ cup sugar and 3 tablespoons water until amber or even somewhat darker. Stir regularly until the sugar melts, then let it sit undisturbed for 4 to 6 minutes, depending on the color you want. Four 1-cup ramekins, ideally Pyrex custard cups, that are heat- and pressure-safe should be filled evenly with the boiling sugar syrup. To slightly coat the sides of the cups, turn them this way and that while holding them with hot pads or oven mitts. Cool for 15 minutes at room temperature. 2. In a medium bowl, combine the eggs, cream, milk, vanilla, salt, and the remaining ⅓ cup sugar. Whisk the ingredients well to combine. Divide this mixture evenly into the covered custard cups. 3. Add the final 1½ cups of water to the Instant Pot. Place the steam rack inside the pot, then arrange the custard cups—possibly three below and one perched in the middle on the rims on the rack. Close the lid. 4. Select Pressure Cook on high and set time to 10 minutes. 5. After the time has done cooking, switch it off and wait for around 20 minutes for the pressure to naturally release on seal

position. Open the lid. The hot custard cups should be moved to a wire rack, unveiled, and allowed to cool for ten minutes. Next, place them in the refrigerator to chill for an hour. For at least one further hour or up to three days, cover and keep chilling. To release the custard and sugar sauce from within, flip one upside down on a serving platter and shake it a little.
Per Serving: Calories 266; Fat: 18g; Sodium 120mg; Carbs: 20g; Sugars: 19g; Protein 4g

Traditional Cheesecake

Prep Time: 5 minutes | Cook Time: 25 minutes | Serves: 8

1¼ cups graham cracker crumbs	2 teaspoons finely grated lemon zest
5 tablespoons butter, melted, cooled, and additional butter for greasing the pan	1 tablespoon fresh lemon juice
1-pound regular cream cheese	½ teaspoon vanilla extract
½ cup granulated white sugar	¼ teaspoon table salt (optional)
2 large eggs	1½ tablespoons all-purpose flour
¼ cup regular sour cream	1½ cups water

1. Butter a 7-inch round springform pan well on the inside. Mix the graham cracker crumbs with the melted butter in a medium bowl. Next, spread this mixture into the prepared pan. To create a crust, press this mixture firmly into the bottom and halfway up the edges of the pan. 2. Combine cream cheese and sugar in a food processor; cover the machine and pulse for approximately a minute, or until smooth. One at a time, add the eggs and process each one until smooth. Open the appliance, clean the interior, and then add the sour cream. Process while covered until smooth. 3. Include the salt, vanilla, lemon juice, and zest of one lemon (if using). Repeat the process until it is smooth, then pause the machine and clean the interior. Pour the mixture into the prepared crust in the pan (it will rise above the crust on the side). Do not cover the pan. 4. Fill the Instant Pot with water. Set up the steam rack. Make a sling out of aluminum foil, place the full springform pan on it, and then drop it into the pot using the sling. To prevent the sling's ends from coming in contact with the pan's batter, fold them down. Put the pot's lid on securely. 5. Select Pressure Cook on high for 25 minutes. 6. After the time has done cooking, switch it off and wait for around 20 minutes for the pressure to naturally return to normal. Open the lid. The heated springform pan may be moved to a wire rack using the sling. After 15 minutes of cooling, refrigerate for one hour. For at least another hour or up to two days, cover and keep the food in the fridge. 7. To serve, remove the pan and slice the cake with a small knife. To remove the cake from the pan, unlatch the sides and pry it open. If desired, slice the cake from the pan's bottom with a long, thin knife before transferring the cheesecake to a serving tray with a big metal spatula.
Per Serving: Calories 302; Fat: 28g; Sodium 397mg; Carbs: 7g; Sugars: 4g; Protein 6g

Pears in Buttery Caramel

Prep Time: 5 minutes | Cook Time: 15 minutes | Serves: 4

½ cup (1 stick) butter, cut into four or five pieces	½ cup unsweetened apple juice or cider
⅔ cup packed light brown sugar	4 large firm ripe pears, peeled, cored, and each cut into 4 to 6 wedges
1 teaspoon ground cinnamon	2 teaspoons cornstarch
¼ teaspoon grated nutmeg	2 teaspoons water
¼ teaspoon baking soda	
¼ teaspoon table salt	

1. Select sauté function. 2. In the Instant Pot, combine the butter, brown sugar, cinnamon, nutmeg, baking soda, and salt. Stir until the butter is melted. After thoroughly incorporating the apple juice, add the pears and mix once more. Lock the lid on the pot and turn off SAUTÉ function. 3. Select Pressure Cook on high for 6 minutes. 4. When the machine has finished cooking, turn it off and let its pressure return to normal naturally on seal position, about 15 minutes. Unlatch the lid. 5. Select Sauté function. 6. Stir the cornstarch and water in a small bowl until completely smooth while the sauce comes to a boil. Add this slurry to the sauce and pears. For approximately a minute, stir continually until the mixture somewhat thickens. Remove the heated insert from the machine and turn off the SAUTÉ function. 5 to 10 minutes should pass before serving.
Per Serving: Calories 244; Fat: 23g; Sodium 422mg; Carbs: 7g; Sugars: 3g; Protein 1g

Baked Kugel

Prep Time: 5 minutes | Cook Time: 25 minutes | Serves: 6

6 ounces wide egg noodles (3 cups)
1½ quarts (6 cups) water
2 large eggs
6 tablespoons granulated white sugar
6 tablespoons regular or low-fat sour cream
6 tablespoons regular or low-fat

cream cheese
¼ cup regular or low-fat evaporated milk
2 tablespoons butter, melted and cooled, plus more butter as needed
½ teaspoon ground cinnamon
½ teaspoon vanilla extract
¼ teaspoon table salt
¼ cup raisins

1. Put the noodles into the Instant Pot and pour in the water. Close lid. 2. Select Pressure Cook on high for 4 minutes. 3. To restore the pot's pressure to normal, use the quick-release technique. Open the lid. Noodles should be removed from the hot insert and placed in a colander in the sink. Clean the insert, then put it back in the pot. The noodles should cool for ten minutes, sometimes being tossed to prevent sticking. 4. In the meantime, grease a 7-inch round springform pan. In a blender, combine the eggs, sugar, sour cream, cream cheese, evaporated milk, melted butter, cinnamon, vanilla, and salt. Cover the container and mix until well combined, pausing the blender at least once to scrape the inside. 5. Pour the egg mixture into a large bowl, then combine it with the noodles and raisins. This mixture should be poured and scraped into the springform pan that has been prepared (if not tightly). Wrap with aluminum foil firmly. 6. Place the steam rack inside the pot after adding 1½ cups of water. The covered springform pan should be placed on a sling made of aluminum foil. Lower the pan onto the rack using the sling and tuck the ends of the sling into the pot. Close lid. 7. Select Pressure Cook on high for 20 minutes. 8. After the time has done cooking, switch it off and wait for around 20 minutes for the pressure to naturally return to normal. Open the lid. To remove the heated springform pan from the pot, use the foil sling. After 10 minutes, place on a wire rack to cool. Remove the springform pan by unlatching the ring. Slice into wedges and serve warm after another 5 minutes of cooling, or let cool to room temperature, cover in plastic wrap, and keep in the fridge for up to 3 days.
Per Serving: Calories 191; Fat: 10g; Sodium 277mg; Carbs: 18g; Sugars: 10g; Protein 4.39g

Sour Cream Cheesecake with Chocolate

Prep Time: 5 minutes | Cook Time: 25 minutes | Serves: 8

1¼ cups graham cracker crumbs
5 tablespoons butter, melted and cooled, plus additional butter for greasing the pan
1-pound regular cream cheese
¾ cup granulated white sugar
2 large eggs, at room temperature

1 large egg yolk, at room temperature
¾ cup regular sour cream
12 ounces bittersweet chocolate, melted and cooled
2 tablespoons unsweetened cocoa powder
1½ cups water

1. Butter a 7-inch round springform pan well on the inside. In a medium bowl, combine the graham cracker crumbs and melted butter. Then, transfer the mixture to the prepared pan. To create a crust, press this mixture firmly into the bottom and halfway up the edges of the pan. 2. Combine the cream cheese and sugar in a food processor; cover the machine and pulse for approximately a minute, or until smooth. One at a time, add the eggs and process each one until smooth. When everything is smooth, add the egg yolk. Open the appliance, clean the interior, and then add the sour cream. Once again, process under cover until smooth. 3. Include the cocoa powder and the melted and cooled chocolate. Pour this mixture into the prepared crust in the pan (it will rise above the crust on the sides). 4. Fill instant pot with water. In the pot, place the steam rack. Create a sling out of aluminum foil, place the full but uncovered springform pan on it, and then drop the pan into the pot using the sling. To prevent the sling's ends from coming in contact with the cheesecake mixture in the pan, fold them down. Put the pot's lid on securely. 5. Select Pressure Cook on high for 25 minutes. 6. After the time has done cooking, switch it off and wait for around 20 minutes for the pressure to naturally return to normal. Open the lid. The heated springform pan may be moved to a wire rack using the sling. After 15 minutes of cooling, refrigerate for one hour. For at least another hour or up to two days, cover and keep the food in the fridge. 7. To serve, remove the pan and slice the cake with a small knife. To remove the cake from the pan, unlatch the sides and pry it open. If desired, slice the cake from the pan's bottom with a long, thin knife before transferring the cheesecake to a serving tray with a big metal spatula.
Per Serving: Calories 464; Fat: 32g; Sodium 366mg; Carbs: 36g; Sugars: 25g; Protein 8.39g

Cake with Lemon Sponge

Prep Time: 5 minutes | Cook Time: 25 minutes | Serves: 8

1½ cups water
Flour-and-fat baking spray
⅔ cup granulated white sugar
1 large egg, at room temperature
1 large egg white, at room temperature
5½ tablespoons butter, melted and cooled to room temperature
¼ cup regular sour cream (do not

use low-fat or fat-free)
¼ cup fresh lemon juice
1 teaspoon vanilla extract
½ teaspoon lemon extract
1 cup all-purpose flour
½ teaspoon baking powder
½ teaspoon baking soda
¼ teaspoon table salt

1. In Instant pot, pour the water. Insert a steam rack that is pressure- and heat-safe in the pot. Spray baking spray liberally into a 7-inch Bundt pan, making sure to get the fat and flour into every nook and cranny. Create a sling out of aluminum foil, then place the pan in the center of it. 2. In a food processor, combine the sugar, egg, egg white, melted butter, sour cream, lemon juice, and vanilla and lemon extracts. Process while covered until smooth. Stop the device and clean it inside out. Salt, baking soda, baking powder, and flour should all be added. until smooth, process. 3. Spoon and stir this mixture into the pan that has been ready. Lower the pan into the pot using the sling. Fold the ends of the sling down to fit inside without touching the batter. Lay a large paper towel over the top of the Bundt pan. Lock the lid. 4. Select Pressure Cook on high for 25 minutes. 5. After the time has done cooking, switch it off and wait for around 20 minutes for the pressure to naturally return to normal. Open the pot's lid by unlatching it. Take the paper towel off. Transfer the heated Bundt pan to a wire cooling rack using the sling. When the cake has cooled for five minutes, flip the pan onto a cutting board to release it. Before cutting into wedges to serve, transfer it from the board to the cooling rack and let it cool for at least another 15 minutes.
Per Serving: Calories 190; Fat: 12g; Sodium 230mg; Carbs: 12.87g; Sugars: 16.03g; Protein 3.39g

Cheesecake with Eggnog

Prep Time: 5 minutes | Cook Time: 25 minutes | Serves: 8

1½ cups vanilla wafer cookie crumbs
¼ cup (½ stick) butter, melted and cooled, plus additional butter for greasing the pan
2 tablespoons confectioners' sugar
1-pound regular cream cheese
½ cup granulated white sugar
1 large egg, at room temperature

3 large egg yolks, at room temperature
3 tablespoons brandy
3 tablespoons heavy cream
2 tablespoons all-purpose flour
½ teaspoon grated nutmeg
¼ teaspoon salt (optional)
1½ cups water

1. Butter a 7-inch round springform pan well on the inside. In a medium bowl, combine the cookie crumbs, melted butter, and confectioners' sugar until well-combined. Pour into the prepared pan. To create a crust, press this mixture firmly into the bottom and halfway up the edges of the pan. 2. Combine the cream cheese and sugar in a food processor; cover the machine and pulse for approximately a minute, or until smooth. Process the egg until smooth after adding it. The egg yolks are then added, one at a time, and processed before being added to the mixture. 3. Remove the machine's cover, clean the interior, and then pour in the brandy and cream. Process while covered until smooth. Add salt, nutmeg, and flour (if using). Process once more until seamless. Pour this mixture into the prepared crust in the pan. Do not cover the pan with foil. 4. Fill the Instant Pot with water. In the pot, place the steam rack. Make a sling out of aluminum foil, place the full springform pan on it, and then drop it into the pot using the sling. To prevent the sling's ends from coming in contact with the cheesecake mixture in the pan, fold them down. Lock lid. 5. Select Pressure Cook on high for 25 minutes. 6. After the time has done cooking, switch it off and wait for around 20 minutes for the pressure to naturally return to normal. Open the lid. The heated springform pan may be moved to a wire rack using the sling. After 15 minutes of cooling, refrigerate for one hour. For at least another hour or up to two days, cover and keep the food in the fridge. 7. To serve, remove the cake from the pan and slice it with a small knife. To remove the cake from the pan, unlatch the sides and pry it open. Using a spatula, remove the cheesecake from the pan and, if preferred, slice the cake off the pan's base.
Per Serving: Calories 374; Fat: 31g; Sodium 432mg; Carbs: 18g; Sugars: 11g; Protein 6.39g

Crème Caramel (Purin)

Prep time: 20 minutes | Cook time: 9 minutes | Serves: 1

4 tablespoons sugar
1 cup plus 2 tablespoons and 1 teaspoon water
½ cup whole milk
1 large egg yolk

½ teaspoon vanilla extract
1 tablespoon sweetened whipped cream
1 maraschino cherry

1. To a small saucepan over medium heat, add 3 tablespoons sugar and 2 tablespoons water. 2. Tilt the pot and swirl to combine the mixture—do not stir—and cook about 6 minutes until dark amber in color and caramelized. 3. Remove from heat and carefully add 1 teaspoon water to the caramel to thin. 4. Quickly and carefully pour the hot caramel into an 8-ounce ramekin and set aside. 5. In a separate small saucepan over medium heat, heat milk until steaming, then remove from heat. 6. In a small bowl, whisk egg yolk and remaining 1 tablespoon sugar until creamy. 7. Slowly pour hot milk mixture into egg yolk mixture while constantly whisking. 8. Whisk in vanilla, then pour mixture over caramel in the ramekin and cover with foil. 9. Pour remaining 1 cup water into Instant Pot and add the trivet. Place ramekin on trivet. 10. Put on the pressure cooker's lid and turn the steam valve to "Sealing" position. 11. Set the Instant Pot to Pressure Cook. Use the "+/-" keys on the control panel to set the cooking time to 9 minutes. 12. Press the Pressure Level button to adjust the pressure to "Low". 13. Once the cooking cycle is completed, allow the steam to release naturally. 14. When all the steam is released, remove the pressure lid from the top carefully. 15. Carefully remove ramekin from the Instant Pot and let cool to room temperature. 16. Then refrigerate 6–8 hours or overnight. 17. When ready to serve, slide a wet knife around the edges of custard, then invert onto a plate. 18. Serve with whipped cream and cherry.
Per Serving: Calories 272; Fat 10g; Sodium 891mg; Carbs 22.9g; Fiber 4g; Sugar 4g; Protein 3g

Cakes with Date Nuts

Prep Time: 5 minutes | Cook Time: 35 minutes | Serves: 4

½ cup chopped baking dates
½ teaspoon baking soda
⅓ cup boiling water
1 large egg, at room temperature
¼ cup whole or low-fat milk (do not use fat-free)
3 tablespoons butter, melted and cooled, plus more for greasing the ramekins and the foil
2 tablespoons bourbon, whiskey, or rum

⅔ cup all-purpose flour
¼ cup finely chopped walnuts
1 teaspoon baking powder
½ teaspoon ground dried ginger
½ teaspoon ground cinnamon
1¼ cups plus ½ teaspoon granulated white sugar
½ teaspoon table salt
2 cups water
1 cup heavy cream
1 teaspoon vanilla extract

1. In a small dish, evenly combine the baking soda and dates for baking. After adding the boiling water, stir briefly to allow the mixture to cool to room temperature (approximately 30 minutes). Meanwhile, liberally butter the inside of four 1-cup ramekins that are both heat- and pressure-safe. 2. In a large bowl, stir together the egg, milk, melted butter, and bourbon for about 2 minutes, until the mixture is homogenous and smooth. Add the flour, walnuts, baking soda, ginger, cinnamon, ½ teaspoon sugar, and ¼ teaspoon salt. Whisk until combined. Mix thoroughly after adding the date mixture. Divide this batter among the four ramekins that have been ready. 3. Use the greased side of four little pieces of aluminum foil to close the ramekins. 1 ½ cups of water should be added to the Instant Pot. Set steam rack inside the pot. Stack the four filled ramekins on the rack, using three for the first layer and balancing the remaining in the center on the edges of the three below. Close lid. 4. Select Pressure Cook on high for 35 minutes. 5. Make the caramel sauce in the interim: In a medium saucepan over medium heat, stir the remaining 1 ¼ cups sugar, the remaining ½ cup water, and the remaining ¼ teaspoon salt until the sugar melts. It will take 5 to 6 minutes of undisturbed cooking for the mixture to turn amber. As low as you can, lower the heat. Whisk in the cream and vanilla while being careful since the mixture may bubble up. Whisk continuously until smooth. After turning off the heat, let the pan cool for up to two hours at room temperature while whisking every so often. 6. After the appliance has done cooking, switch it off and wait for around 20 minutes for the pressure to naturally return to normal. After removing the foil lids, place the heated ramekins to a wire rack. Invert the ramekins onto serving plates when they have cooled for 5 minutes. Gently tap and shake the ramekins to release the cakes within. Warm the caramel sauce and drizzle some over each.

Per Serving: Calories 388; Fat: 24g; Sodium 559mg; Carbs: 37g; Sugars: 16g; Protein 5g

Bread Pudding with Blueberries

Prep Time: 5 minutes | Cook Time: 26 minutes | Serves: 6

Butter for greasing the baking dish and foil
1½ cups water
4 large eggs, at room temperature
2 cups whole or low-fat milk (do not use fat-free)
½ cup granulated white sugar

1 teaspoon vanilla extract
¼ teaspoon table salt
8 ounces white bread, preferably country-style bread, cut into 1-inch squares (do not remove the crusts)
1 cup fresh blueberries

1. Butter a 2-quart, high-sided, round soufflé dish liberally on the interior. Fill the Instant Pot with water. Place steam rack into pot. Additionally, create a foil sling and place the greased baking dish in the middle of it. 2. In a large bowl, whisk the eggs until they are smooth. Salt, milk, vanilla, and sugar should all be whisked in until the sugar dissolves. The bread cubes should be well covered in the egg mixture after being stirred with a rubber spatula. Add the blueberries and gently fold them in until they are dispersed throughout. 3. Pour and heap this mixture onto the baking dish that has been prepared. Cover the baking dish completely with aluminum foil, greased side down, and seal the edges. Use the sling to pick up and lower the baking dish onto the rack. Lock the lid on the pot. 4. Select Pressure Cook on high for 26 minutes. 5. After the time has done cooking, switch it off and wait for around 20 minutes for the pressure to naturally return to normal. Open the lid. Transfer the heated baking dish to a wire rack using the sling. After ten minutes, remove the top and let it cool. Serve in dishes with generous spoonful.
Per Serving: Calories 232; Fat: 7g; Sodium 329mg; Carbs: 32.87g; Sugars: 16.03g; Protein 9g

Cake with Orange And Pecans

Prep Time: 5 minutes | Cook Time: 35 minutes | Serves: 6

⅓ cup orange marmalade
½ cup (1 stick) cool butter, cut into chunks, plus additional for greasing the pan and the foil
¼ cup granulated white sugar
¼ cup packed light brown sugar
2 large eggs, at room temperature

3 tablespoons Triple Sec or Grand Marnier
1 tablespoon vanilla extract
¾ cup finely ground pecans
½ cup all-purpose flour
¼ teaspoon table salt
1½ cups water

1. Butter a 2-quart, high-sided, round soufflé dish liberally on the interior. The marmalade should cover the whole bottom of this plate. 2. In a large basin, beat the butter, white, and brown sugars for about 5 minutes at medium speed with an electric mixer. One at a time, beat in the eggs, making sure the first is well absorbed before continuing. 3. Wipe the bowl's inside clean. Grand Marnier and vanilla should be well mixed in. Beat the flour, salt, and crushed pecans into the mixture on low speed just until combined. Smooth the top of the batter before pouring it into the prepared pan. Use a piece of aluminum foil with butter on one side to cover the dish, butter side up. Tightly seal this foil over the baking dish. 4. Pour the water into Instant pot. Set steam rack in the pot. Make a foil sling, set the baking dish on it, and use the sling to lower the dish onto the trivet. Fold down the ends of the sling and lock the lid on the pot. 5. Select Pressure Cook on high for 35 minutes. 6. After the time has done cooking, switch it off and wait for around 20 minutes for the pressure to naturally return to normal. Open the lid. Transfer the heated baking dish to a wire rack using the sling. Remove the lid and allow the food to cool for five minutes. To remove the cake, carefully run a flatware knife along the dish's inside edge. Over the baking pan, place a big plate or cake stand. Turn everything upside down, then shake and hit the baking dish to loosen the cake. After approximately an hour, serve warm or cool to room temperature. For around three hours, the cake can be left unattended at room temperature.
Per Serving: Calories 885; Fat: 64g; Sodium 1204mg; Carbs: 40g; Sugars: 15g; Protein 35.39g

Raspberry Curd with Lemon Juice

Prep Time: 5 minutes | Cook Time: 5 minutes | Serves: 2

12 oz. (340g) fresh raspberries	1 tsp lemon zest
¾ cup (150g) sugar	2 large egg yolks
2 tbsps. (30ml) fresh lemon juice	2 tbsps. (28g) unsalted butter

1. Combine the raspberries, sugar, lemon juice, and zest in the Instant Pot. 2. Put the steam valve in the sealed position and fasten the lid. Choose Pressure Cook, then cook for 1 minute at high pressure. 3. For at least 10 minutes, use a natural release on seal position. Let off any lingering steam on vent position. 4. Take off the lid. Blend the ingredients with an immersion blender or in a blender, then pulse until it's smooth. If it has been taken out, put the mixture back in and choose sauté. 5. Egg yolks should be whisked together in a small dish in the meanwhile. Add them gradually to the raspberry mixture. Stir the mixture continuously until it boils, then choose Cancel. Include the butter. 6. Transfer to a glass or other airtight, heatproof container and let cool to room temperature. Refrigerate until the curd is completely set. Serve chilled. 7. Store this recipe in the fridge for up to 2 weeks.
Per Serving: Calories 363; Fat: 13g; Sodium 16mg; Carbs: 60g; Sugars: 44g; Protein 5g

Homemade Poached Pears in White Wine

Prep Time: 5 minutes | Cook Time: 15 minutes | Serves: 4

2 cups water	1 (1-inch) piece fresh ginger,
1 cup dry white wine	peeled and sliced
1 cup apple juice, apple cider,	1 or 2 cinnamon sticks
other pure fruit juice	1 teaspoon green cardamom pods
2 tablespoons pure maple syrup or	(optional)
unrefined sugar	4 to 6 pears

1. Combine the water, wine, apple juice, maple syrup, ginger, cinnamon, and cardamom in the instant pot (if using). To blend, stir. 2. Add the pears next. (The pears can be kept whole, peeled, and the bottoms cut off so they stand straight in the saucepan. Alternatively, split them in half, remove the core, and place cut-side up in the pot.) Select High Pressure Cook, set the timer for 3 minutes, lock the lid and check that the pressure valve is sealed. 3. Quickly release the pressure on vent position when the cooking period is through, taking cautious not to touch your fingers or face near the steam release. 4. After the last bit of pressure has dissipated, carefully unlock and take off the lid.
Per Serving: Calories 134; Fat: 6g; Sodium 445mg; Carbs: 14g; Sugars: 12g; Protein 6.39g

Apple Maple Cake

Prep Time: 5 minutes | Cook Time: 35 minutes | Serves: 6

1 cup all-purpose flour	McIntosh apples, peeled, cored, and
1 teaspoon baking powder	thinly sliced
1 teaspoon ground cinnamon	1½ cups water
9 tablespoons (1 stick plus 1	½ cup granulated white sugar
tablespoon) butter, plus more for	2 large eggs, at room temperature
greasing the pan	2 teaspoons vanilla extract
¼ cup maple syrup	3 tablespoons whole milk
2 medium baking apples, preferably	

1 Whisk the flour, baking powder, and cinnamon in a medium bowl. Set aside. Generously butter the inside of one 2-quart, high-sided, round soufflé dish. 2. Press sauté. 3. In the Instant Pot, melt two tablespoons of the butter. When the maple syrup is heated, add it and stir. Cook the apples for approximately 5 minutes, stirring frequently, until tender. Fill the baking dish with the whole contents of the heated insert, smoothing the apple mixture into an equal layer. 4. After drying and cleaning, put the insert back into the machine. Fill the pot with water. Place the steam rack inside that is heat- and pressure-safe. 5. In a large bowl, whisk the remaining 7 tablespoons butter and sugar for about 4 minutes on medium speed with an electric mixer. One at a time, beat in the eggs, ensuring sure the first is well mixed in before adding the second. Add the vanilla extract after lowering the mixer's speed. Just until combined, add the flour mixture. When adding the milk, beat it in well. Over the apples in the prepared pan, pour this batter. Wrap with aluminum foil firmly. 6. Construct a foil sling. Place the trivet on top of the baking dish after setting it on the sling. Before locking the lid onto the pot, fold the ends of the sling down so they don't contact the batter. 7. Select Pressure Cook on high for 35

minutes. 8. After the time has done cooking, switch it off and wait for around 20 minutes for the pressure to naturally return to normal. Open the lid. Transfer the heated baking dish to a wire rack using the sling. Remove the lid and allow the food to cool for five minutes. To remove the cake, carefully run a flatware knife along the dish's inner edge. Over the baking pan, place a big plate or cake stand. Turn everything upside down before tapping and jiggling the baking dish to loosen the cake and allow the apple "sauce" to flow over it. After 15 minutes of cooling, serve warm.
Per Serving: Calories 352; Fat: 22g; Sodium 140mg; Carbs: 36g; Sugars: 16g; Protein 3.9g

Cakes Made of Chocolate

Prep Time: 5 minutes | Cook Time: 12 minutes | Serves: 4

½ cup (1 stick) butter, cut into	3 large eggs, at room temperature
small chunks, plus more for	1 large egg yolk, at room temperature
greasing the ramekins	6 tablespoons all-purpose flour
8 ounces bittersweet chocolate,	¼ teaspoon table salt
preferably 70% cocoa solids, chopped	1½ cups water
1 cup confectioners' sugar	

1. In a large dish that can go in the microwave, combine the butter and chocolate. 10 second intervals on high, stirring thoroughly between each, until little over half the butter has melted. Take out of the microwave and whisk continuously until smooth. 2. After 20 minutes, stir the chocolate mixture regularly while it cools to room temperature. Meanwhile, liberally butter the inside of four 1-cup ramekins that are both heat- and pressure-safe. 3. Smoothly combine the confectioners' sugar with the chocolate mixture. Before adding the second egg, fully integrate the first one by stirring it in. The egg yolk should be thoroughly mixed in before adding the flour and salt. Divide this mixture equally among the ramekins that have been ready. Ramekins must not be covered. 4. Pour the water in Instant pot. Set steam rack in the pot, then stack the four ramekins on the rack, placing three on the bottom layer and one on the top, balanced on the three below. Close lid. 5. Select Pressure Cook on high for 10 minutes. 6. After the time has done cooking, switch it off and wait for around 20 minutes for the pressure to naturally return to normal. Open the lid. To cool for 15 minutes, move the heated ramekins to a wire rack. Serve them warm or in their ramekins while covered and chilled in the refrigerator for up to a day.
Per Serving: Calories 556; Fat: 28g; Sodium 379mg; Carbs: 72g; Sugars: 52g; Protein 5g

Chocolate Cheesecake with Coconut

Prep time: 10 minutes | Cook Time: 1 hour | Serves: 10

1 ½ cups vanilla sugar cookies,	½ stick butter, melted
crumbled	
For the Filling:	
22 ounces' cream cheese, room	½ teaspoon pure anise extract
temperature	¼ teaspoon freshly grated nutmeg
¾ cup granulated sugar	6 ounces' semisweet chocolate
1 ½ tablespoons cornstarch	chips
2 eggs, room temperature	3 ounces sweetened shredded
⅓ cup sour cream	coconut
½ teaspoon coconut extract	

1. Brush a suitable baking pan in the Instant Pot and cover a baking paper over the bottom. 2. Combine the crumbled cookies with the melted butter thoroughly and then press the crust into the prepared pan. Transfer the pan into your freezer. 3. Using a mixer, beat the cream cheese at low speed. Add sugar and cornstarch in the cheese and stir well at low speed until uniform and smooth. 4. Fold in the eggs, one at a time. Beat again with the mixer. 5. Then add the sour cream, coconut extract, anise extract, and nutmeg in the mixture and stir with the mixer. 6. Microwave the chocolate chips about 1 minute, stirring once or twice while cooking. 7. Add the melted chocolate to the cheesecake batter and then sprinkle with the shredded coconut. Stir until well combined. 8. Drizzle the chocolate mixture over the crust. 9. Pour 1 cup of water in the inner pot and place the trivet. 10. Lower the baking pan onto the trivet and then close the lid. Then turn the steam release handle to the Sealing position. 11. Set the Instant Pot on Pressure Cook at High and adjust time to 40 minutes. 12. Once cooked, naturally release for 15 minutes. Carefully remove the lid. 13. Cool the cheesecake completely and then slice. 14. Serve and enjoy!
Per Serving: Calories:444; Fat 34.1g; Sodium 242mg; Carbs 30.5g; Fiber 0.9g; Sugars 24.5g; Protein 6.2g

Cake with Key Lime Soufflé

Prep Time: 5 minutes | Cook Time: 25 minutes | Serves: 6

Butter for greasing the pan and foil
1½ cups water
3 large eggs, separated and at room temperature
¾ cup granulated white sugar
1 cup regular cultured buttermilk
1 tablespoon finely grated lime

zest, preferably from key limes
4½ tablespoons bottled or fresh key lime juice (from 3 to 4 key limes)
2 teaspoons vanilla extract
½ teaspoon table salt
6 tablespoons all-purpose flour

1. Butter a 2-quart, high-sided, round soufflé dish liberally on the interior. Fill a 6- or 8-quart pot with water. Place a trivet inside the pot that is both pressure- and heat-safe. 2. In a medium bowl, whip the egg whites with an electric mixer on high speed for about 3 minutes, or until soft peaks form when a spatula is inserted into the mixture. For approximately two minutes, or until the mixture is thick and can form silky peaks that keep their shape on a spatula, add 14 cup of sugar in a slow, steady stream. 3. Wash the beaters and dry them. The egg yolks and remaining ½ cup sugar should be beaten for about 4 minutes, or until thick and pale yellow. After cleaning the interior of the bowl, beat the buttermilk, lime juice, lime zest, and vanilla until creamy. Remove the beaters and scrape the surface. 4. Stir the flour into the egg yolk mixture with a rubber spatula until just moistened. Gently fold the egg whites in until they are combined but not quite dissolved. The batter ought to have white flecks in it. 5. Spoon the batter into the baking dish as carefully as possible. Aluminum foil should be lightly greased before being used to loosely encase the cake, buttered side down. Create a foil sling, place the baking dish in the middle of the sling, and then lower the sling onto the rack to place the baking dish. Fold down the ends of the sling so they don't touch the batter, then lock the lid onto the pot. 6. Select Pressure Cook on high for 20 minutes. 7. After the time has done cooking, switch it off and wait for around 20 minutes for the pressure to naturally return to normal. Open the lid. Transfer the heated baking dish to a wire rack using the sling. Remove the lid and allow the food to cool for at least 10 or even up to an hour. Serve in bowls or on small plates with large spoonful.
Per Serving: Calories 140; Fat: 7g; Sodium 281mg; Carbs: 13g; Sugars: 5g; Protein 4.39g

Easy Maple-Sweetened Applesauce

Prep Time: 10 minutes | Cook Time: 20 minutes | Serves: 3 cups

2 pounds apples (6 medium), peeled if desired, cored, and quartered (see tip)
1 cup water, plus more as needed
¼ cup unrefined sugar or pure

maple syrup, plus more as needed
¼ cup freshly squeezed lemon juice (from 2 lemons)
⅛ teaspoon ground nutmeg (optional)

1. Apples and water should be combined in the Instant pot. Select High Pressure Cook, set the timer for 4 minutes, then lock the lid and check that the pressure valve is sealed. 2. After the cooking period is through, quickly release the pressure on vent position. Avoid getting your fingers or face too close to the steam release. 3. After the lid has been properly unlocked and removed, release the remaining pressure. Allow to cool for a while. Add the nutmeg, sugar, and lemon juice (if using). The sauce may be puréed in the saucepan itself with an immersion blender or transferred to a countertop blender. If the sauce needs to be sweeter, you can add additional sugar or maple syrup as well as extra water.
Per Serving: Calories 231; Fat: 1g; Sodium 8mg; Carbs: 60g; Sugars: 47g; Protein 1g

Simple Mango-Peach Crumble

Prep Time: 10 minutes | Cook Time: 21 minutes | Serves: 6

3 cups chopped fresh or frozen peaches
3 cups chopped fresh or frozen mangos
4 tablespoons unrefined sugar or pure maple syrup, divided

1 cup gluten-free rolled oats
½ cup shredded coconut, sweetened or unsweetened
2 tablespoons coconut oil or vegan margarine

1. Mix the peaches, mangos, and 2 tablespoons of sugar in a 6- to 7-inch round baking dish. 2. Combine the remaining 2 tablespoons of sugar, the coconut, the coconut oil, and the oats in a food processor. until well-combined, pulse (You'll need less coconut oil if you use maple syrup. If the mixture isn't staying together, start with simply

the syrup and add oil as needed.) The fruit combination should be covered with the oat mixture. Use aluminum foil to cover the dish. 3. Add a steam rack and a cup or two of water to the Instant Pot. Lower pan into rack using silicone aid handles or a foil sling. Select High Pressure Cook, set the timer for 6 minutes, secure the lid and check that the pressure valve is closed. 4. Quickly release the pressure on vent position when the cooking period is through, taking cautious not to touch your face or fingers to the steam release. 5. After the lid has been gently unlocked and removed, release the remaining pressure. Before gently removing the dish with oven gloves or tongs, let it to cool for a few minutes. 6. Scoop out portions to serve.
Per Serving: Calories 278; Fat: 5g; Sodium 33mg; Carbs: 62.87g; Sugars: 48.03g; Protein 4g

Fresh Lemony Blueberry Butter

Prep time: 10 minutes | Cook Time: 2 minutes | Serves: 10

2 pounds' fresh blueberries
1-pound granulated sugar
½ teaspoon vanilla extract

1 tablespoon freshly grated lemon zest
¼ cup fresh lemon juice

1. In the inner pot, add the sugar, vanilla, and blueberries. 2. Close the lid and turn the steam release handle to Sealing position. 3. Set the Instant Pot on Pressure Cook at High and adjust time to 2 minutes. 4. When cooked, naturally release the pressure about 15 minutes and then remove the lid carefully. 5. Add the lemon zest and lemon juice and stir well. 6. To store, puree in a food processor and strain and push the mixture through a sieve. 7. Serve and enjoy!
Per Serving: Calories:224; Fat 0.4g; Sodium 2mg; Carbs 58.8g; Fiber 2.3g; Sugars 54.6g; Protein 0.8g

Honey-Yogurt Compote

Prep time: 10 minutes | Cook Time: 2 minutes | Serves: 4

1 cup rhubarb
1 cup plums
1 cup apples
1 cup pears
1 teaspoon ground ginger

1 vanilla bean
1 cinnamon stick
½ cup caster sugar
1 cup Greek yoghurt
4 tablespoons honey

1. In the inner pot, add gingers, vanilla, caster sugar, cinnamon, and the fruits. 2. Close the lid and turn the steam release handle to Sealing position. 3. Set the Instant Pot on Pressure Cook at High and adjust time to 2 minutes. 4. When cooked, naturally release the pressure about 10 minutes and then remove the lid carefully. 5. Meanwhile, whisk the yogurt with honey. 6. Transfer the compote in individual bowls and drizzle with a dollop of honeyed Greek yogurt. Serve and enjoy!
Per Serving: Calories:225; Fat 0.3g; Sodium 3mg; Carbs 59.8g; Fiber 3.5g; Sugars 54.1g; Protein 0.8g

Simple Lemon Custard Pie

Prep time: 10 minutes | Cook Time:30 minutes | Serves: 6

½ cup coconut oil or vegan margarine, melted, plus more for preparing the pan
¾ cup coconut flour
½ cup plus 2 tablespoons unrefined sugar, divided

1 (13.5-ounce) can full-fat coconut milk
½ cup freshly squeezed lemon juice (from 4 lemons)
¼ cup cornstarch or arrowroot powder

1. Use coconut oil to grease a 6-inch springform pan or pie plate. 2. Combine the coconut flour, coconut oil, and 2 tablespoons of sugar in a small bowl. Into the prepared pan, press the crust. 3. Mix the remaining ½ cup sugar, cornstarch, lemon juice, and coconut milk in a medium bowl until the starch is dissolved. Over the crust, pour this mixture. Wrap aluminum foil around the pan. 4. Add a cup or two of water to the saucepan and add the steam rack. Lower the pan onto the rack using a silicone assist handle or a foil sling. Select High Pressure Cook, set the timer for 15 minutes, secure the lid and make sure the pressure valve is sealed. 5. Quickly release the pressure on vent position when the cooking period is through, taking cautious not to touch your face or fingers to the steam release. 6. After the pressure has completely subsided, carefully unlock and take off the lid. After a brief cooling period, carefully remove the pan using oven gloves or tongs. 7. Refrigerate the pie until it has cooled and set, or let it cool to room temperature.
Per Serving: Calories 362; Fat: 34g; Sodium 44mg; Carbs: 15g; Sugars: 11g; Protein 2.39g

Cups of Pumpkin Pie

Prep Time: 5 minutes | Cook Time: 20 minutes | Serves: 4

1 cup canned pumpkin purée
1 cup nondairy milk
6 tablespoons unrefined sugar or pure maple syrup (less if using sweetened milk), plus more for

sprinkling
¼ cup spelt flour or all-purpose flour
½ teaspoon pumpkin pie spice
Pinch salt

1. Mix the pumpkin, milk, sugar, flour, pumpkin pie spice, and salt in a medium basin. The mixture should go into 4 heat-resistant ramekins. If you'd like, add a little more sugar on the top of each. 2. Add two cups of water to the instant pot and add the steam rack. Stack the ramekins if necessary before placing them on the rack (3 on the bottom, 1 on top). Select High Pressure, set the timer for 6 minutes, secure the lid and check that the pressure valve is shut. 3. Quickly release the pressure on vent position when the cooking period is through, taking cautious not to touch your fingers or face near the steam release. 4. After the last bit of pressure has dissipated, carefully unlock and take off the lid. Let cool for a few minutes before carefully lifting out the ramekins with oven mitts or tongs. 5. Let cool for at least 10 minutes before serving.
Per Serving: Calories 314; Fat: 16g; Sodium 104mg; Carbs: 33g; Sugars: 21.03g; Protein 11.39g

Cake with Blueberries

Prep Time: 10 minutes | Cook Time:30 minutes | Serves: 6

Coconut oil or vegan margarine, for preparing the pan
1¼ cups soft pitted Medjool dates, divided
1 cup gluten-free rolled oats
2 cups cashews

1 cup fresh blueberries
3 tablespoons freshly squeezed lemon juice or lime juice
¾ cups water
Pinch salt

1. Use coconut oil to grease a 6-inch springform pan or pie plate. 2. Combine the oats and 1 cup of dates in a food processor. Pulse them until a sticky mixture forms. Incorporate this into the pan as is. 3. Add the remaining ¼ cup of dates, cashews, blueberries, lemon juice, water, and a dash of salt to a high-speed blender. Blend on high speed for approximately a minute, scraping down the edges a few times, until the mixture is smooth and creamy. Over the crust, pour this mixture. Wrap aluminum foil around the pan. 4. Add a cup or two more of water to the instant pot and add the steam rack. Lower the pan onto the rack using a silicone assist handle or a foil sling. Select High Pressure Cook, set the timer for 6 minutes, secure the lid and check that the pressure valve is shut. 5. After the allotted cooking time has passed, allow the pressure to naturally relax on seal position for 10 minutes. 6. After the pressure has completely subsided, carefully unlock and take off the lid. After a brief cooling period, carefully remove the pan using oven mitts. 7. Let the cake cool to room temperature, or refrigerate until cooled and set.
Per Serving: Calories 100; Fat: 2g; Sodium 4mg; Carbs: 24.87g; Sugars: 12g; Protein 3g

Sweet Brownies

Prep Time: 10 minutes | Cook Time: 20 minutes | Serves: 3

3 ounces dairy-free dark chocolate
1 tablespoon coconut oil or vegan margarine
½ cup applesauce

2 tablespoons unrefined sugar
⅓cup all-purpose flour
½ teaspoon baking powder
Pinch salt

1. Add a cup or two of water to the instant pot after placing the steam rack inside Instant Pot. Select sauté. 2. Combine the chocolate and coconut oil in a large heat-resistant glass or ceramic dish. As you would with a double boiler, place the bowl on top of the rack. Once the chocolate has melted, stop cooking and stir occasionally. 3. Combine the sugar and applesauce with the chocolate mixture. Just till mixed, add the flour, baking powder, and salt. Fill three heat-resistant ramekins with the batter. Put them in a heat-resistant dish, then wrap it with aluminum foil. Lower the dish onto the rack using a silicone assist handle or a foil sling. Select High Pressure Cook, set the timer for 5 minutes, lock the lid and check that the pressure valve is sealed. 4. Quickly release the pressure on vent position when the cooking period is through, taking care not to touch your fingers or face near the steam release. 5. After the lid has been gently unlocked and removed, release the remaining pressure. After a short period of cooling, carefully remove the dish or ramekins using oven gloves or tongs. Before

serving, let it to cool for a little while longer.
Per Serving: Calories 131; Fat: 4g; Sodium 21mg; Carbs: 12.8g; Sugars: 9.03g; Protein 2g

Strawberry-Rhubarb Crumble Pie

Prep Time: 10 minutes | Cook Time: 25 minutes | Serves: 6

3 tablespoons coconut oil or vegan margarine, plus more for preparing the pan
1½ cups gluten-free rolled oats
1 cup walnuts

4 tablespoons unrefined sugar or pure maple syrup, divided
2 cups fresh strawberries, chopped
1 cup chopped rhubarb

1. Use coconut oil to grease a 6- to 7-inch springform pan or pie plate. 2. Combine the oats, walnuts, coconut oil, and 2 tablespoons of sugar in a food processor. until well-combined, pulse (You'll need less coconut oil if you use maple syrup. If the mixture isn't staying together, start out with only the syrup and add oil if necessary.) In the bottom of the pan that has been prepared, press two-thirds of the mixture. 3. Combine the strawberries, rhubarb, and 2 tablespoons of the remaining sugar in a medium bowl. On top of the crust, spoon the fruit mixture. Over the fruit, distribute the final third of the crust mixture. Wrap aluminum foil around the pan. 4. Add a cup or two of water to the instant pot and add the steam rack. Lower the pan onto the rack using a silicone assist handle or a foil sling. Select High Pressure Cook, set the timer for 6 minutes, secure the lid and check that the pressure valve is shut. 5. Quickly release the pressure on vent position when the cooking period is through, being cautious not to touch your fingers or face near the steam release. 6. After the pressure has completely subsided, carefully unlock and take off the lid. After a brief cooling period, carefully remove the pan using oven gloves or tongs. 7. Let cool before slicing and serving for at least 10 minutes. Remove the rim of the springform pan you used for simpler slicing.
Per Serving: Calories 292; Fat: 16g; Sodium 6mg; Carbs: 42g; Sugars: 22g; Protein 6g

Bread Pudding with Apricots

Prep time: 10 minutes | Cook Time: 15 minutes | Serves: 6

4 cups Italian bread, cubed
½ cup granulated sugar
2 tablespoons molasses
½ cup dried apricots, soaked and chopped
2 tablespoons coconut oil
1 teaspoon vanilla paste

A pinch of grated nutmeg
A pinch of salt
1 teaspoon cinnamon, ground
½ teaspoon star anise, ground
2 cups milk
4 eggs, whisked
1 ⅓ cups heavy cream

1. In the inner pot, pour 1 ½ cups of water and place the trivet over the water. 2. Spritz the nonstick cooking spray inside a baking dish. Then divide the bread cubes in the greased baking dish. 3. Combine together the remaining ingredients in a mixing bowl. Then sprinkle the mixture over the bread cubes. 4. Cover the baking dish with a foil sheet. 5. Close the lid and turn the steam release handle to Sealing position. 6. Set the Instant Pot to Porridge at High and adjust time to 15 minutes. When cooked, quick-release the pressure and remove the lid carefully. 8. Serve and enjoy!
Per Serving: Calories:358; Fat 19.8g; Sodium 236mg; Carbs 38.5g; Fiber 1g; Sugars 25.7g; Protein 8.9g

Avocado Chocolate Delight

Prep time: 10 minutes | Cook Time: 15 minutes | Serves: 8

⅓ cup avocado, mashed
2 plantains
1 ½ tablespoons butter, softened
¼ cup agave syrup
4 tablespoons cocoa powder

½ cup coconut flakes
1 teaspoon baking soda
½ teaspoon vanilla paste
1 teaspoon star anise, ground
⅛ teaspoon cream of tartar

1. In the inner pot, pour a cup of water and arrange a trivet in the inner pot. 2. Brush the melted butter over a baking pan. 3. In a blender, mix all the ingredients to make a batter. 4. Then arrange the batter to the baking pan. 5. Close the lid and turn the steam release handle to Sealing position. 6. Set the Instant Pot to Porridge at High and timer for 15 minutes. 7. When cooked, add some fresh or dried fruit as you needed. 8. Serve and enjoy!
Per Serving: Calories:142; Fat 5.6g; Sodium 185mg; Carbs 25.5Fiber 2.7g; Sugars 7.1g; Protein 1.4g

Rice Pudding with Raisin

Prep time: 10 minutes | Cook Time: 3 minutes | Serves: 4

1 ½ cups basmati rice
3 cups coconut milk
1 teaspoon rosewater
A pinch of coarse salt
¼ teaspoon saffron, crushed

4 tablespoons unsalted pistachios, minced
½ cup jaggery
½ cup raisins

1. In the inner pot, add the basmati rice, coconut milk, rosewater, salt, saffron, pistachios, and jaggery and stir well. 2. Close the lid and then turn the steam release handle to Sealing position. 3. Set the Instant Pot to Soup at High and adjust time to 3 minutes. 4. When cooked, naturally release the pressure and then carefully remove the lid. 5. Sprinkle the raisins on the top and serve.
Per Serving: Calories:362; Fat 21.8g; Sodium 60mg; Carbs 40.2g; Fiber 2.8g; Sugars 8.7g; Protein 4.8g

Crispy Peach and Raisin

Prep time: 10 minutes | Cook Time: 10 minutes | Serves: 6

6 peaches, pitted and chopped
½ teaspoon ground cardamom
1 teaspoon ground cinnamon
1 teaspoon vanilla extract
⅓ cup orange juice
2 tablespoons honey
4 tablespoons raisins

4 tablespoons butter
1 cup rolled oats
4 tablespoons all-purpose flour
⅓ cup brown sugar
A pinch of grated nutmeg
A pinch of salt

1. In the inner pot, spread the peaches on the bottom. Then add cardamom, vanilla, and cinnamon and drizzle on the top with honey, raisins, and orange juice. 2. Whisk together the oats, flour, nutmeg, brown sugar, salt, and butter in a mixing bowl. 3. Close the lid and turn the steam release handle to Sealing position. 4. Set the Instant Pot on Pressure Cook at High and adjust time to 10 minutes. 5. When cooked, naturally release the pressure about 10 minutes and then carefully remove the lid. 6. Serve and enjoy!
Per Serving: Calories:278; Fat 9.1g; Sodium 86mg; Carbs 47.7g; Fiber 4.3g; Sugars 32.6g; Protein 4.2g

Cherry and Almond Crisp Pie with Cinnamon

Prep time: 10 minutes | Cook Time: 10 minutes | Serves: 4

1-pound sweet cherries, pitted
1 teaspoon ground cinnamon
⅓ teaspoon ground cardamom
1 teaspoon pure vanilla extract
⅓ cup water
⅓ cup honey

½ stick butter, at room temperature
1 cup rolled oats
2 tablespoons all-purpose flour
¼ cup almonds, slivered
A pinch of salt
A pinch of grated nutmeg

1. In the inner pot, place the cherries and then top with cinnamon, vanilla, and cardamom. Then pour in water and honey. 2. Combine the oats, butter, and flour in a separate mixing bowl and then sprinkle on the top of the cherry mixture with almond and nutmeg evenly. 3. Close the lid and turn the steam release handle to Sealing position. 4. Set the Instant Pot on Pressure Cook at High and adjust time to 10 minutes. 5. When cooked, naturally release the steam and then carefully remove the lid. 6. Serve and enjoy!
Per Serving: Calories:449; Fat 15.9g; Sodium 144mg; Carbs 73.9g; Fiber 4g; Sugars 23.8g; Protein 5g

Coconut Mini Cheesecakes with Almond

Prep time: 10 minutes | Cook Time: 25 minutes | Serves: 4

½ cup almonds
½ cup sunflower kernels
6 dates, chopped

16 ounces' coconut milk
¾ cup coconut yogurt

1. Grease 4 ramekins with nonstick cooking spray. 2. In a blender, blend the almonds, dates, and sunflower kernels until sticky. 3. Divide the mixture into the prepared ramekins and press well. 4. Combine the yogurt and coconut milk thoroughly in a mixing bowl. Then pour the liquid mixture in the ramekins and cover with a foil sheet. 5. In the inner pot, pour 1 cup of water and place the trivet. Lower the ramekins onto the trivet. 6. Close the lid and turn the steam release handle to

Sealing position. 7. Set the Instant Pot on Pressure Cook at High and adjust time to 25 minutes. 8. When cooked, naturally release the pressure about 15 minutes and remove the lid carefully. 9. Serve and enjoy!
Per Serving: Calories:423; Fat 36.9g; Sodium 50mg; Carbs 22.2g; Fiber 5.7g; Sugars 15g; Protein 7.8g

Creamy Rum Cheesecake

Prep time: 10 minutes | Cook Time: 20 minutes | Serves: 6

14 ounces full-; Fat cream cheese
3 eggs, whisked
½ teaspoon vanilla extract
1 teaspoon rum extract
½ cup agave syrup
¼ teaspoon cardamom
¼ teaspoon ground cinnamon

Butter-Rum Sauce:
½ cup granulated sugar
½ stick butter
½ cup whipping cream
1 tablespoon dark rum
⅓ teaspoon nutmeg

1. In a blender or food processor, combine together the eggs, cream cheese, rum extract, cardamom, cinnamon, agave syrup, cream cheese, and vanilla to make the batter. 2. Remove the batter to a baking pan and then use a sheet of foil to cover. 3. Pour 1 ½ cups of water in the inner pot and a metal trivet to the Instant Pot. Lower the pan onto the trivet. 4. Secure the lid and turn the steam release handle to Sealing position. 5. Set the Instant Pot on Soup/Broth at High and adjust the time to 20 minutes. 6. When cooked, naturally release the pressure and then carefully remove the lid. 7. In a sauté pan over moderate heat, melt the sugar with butter. 8. Then add rum, nutmeg, and the whipping cream in the pan. 9. To serve, top the cooled cheesecake with the warm sauce. Enjoy!
Per Serving: Calories:342; Fat 13.9g; Sodium 468mg; Carbs 43.3g Fiber 0.1g; Sugars 17.2g; Protein 12.6g

Double-Chocolate and Peanut Fudge

Prep time: 10 minutes | Cook Time: 5 minutes | Serves: 6

8 ounces' semisweet chocolate, chopped
2 ounces' milk chocolate, chopped
⅓ cup applesauce
1 egg, beaten
½ teaspoon vanilla extract

½ teaspoon almond extract
¼ teaspoon ground cinnamon
⅓ cup peanut butter
A pinch of coarse salt
¼ cup arrowroot powder

1. In the inner pot, pour 1½ cups of water and then place a metal trivet. 2. Set the Instant pot on "Sauté" at Normal and melt the chocolate in a heatproof bowl over the simmering water. Turn off the heat. 3. Combine the egg, vanilla, almond extract, cinnamon, salt, peanut butter and applesauce in a mixing bowl. 4. Stir in the arrowroot powder in the mixture. Then fold in the melted chocolate and mix well. 5. Spritz the nonstick cooking spray inside the 6 heatproof ramekins and then divide the batter in the ramekins. Cover with foil and then transfer in the inner pot on the trivet. 6. Close the lid and turn the steam release handle to the Sealing position. 7. Set the Instant Pot on Pressure Cook at High and adjust time to 5 minutes. 8. When cooked, quick-release the pressure and then carefully remove the lid. 9. Allow the dessert to cool on a wire rack. Serve and enjoy!
Per Serving: Calories:333; Fat 22.1g; Sodium 128mg; Carbs 34g; Fiber 3.6g; Sugars 28.3g; Protein 6.8g

Chocolate Mug Cakes with Mango

Prep time: 10 minutes | Cook Time: 10 minutes | Serves: 2

½ cup coconut flour
2 eggs
2 tablespoons honey
1 teaspoon vanilla

¼ teaspoon grated nutmeg
1 tablespoon cocoa powder
1 medium-sized mango, peeled and diced

1. Lightly grease two mugs. Add the eggs, vanilla, cocoa powder, nutmeg, coconut flour, and honey and combine together. 2. In the inner pot, pour 1 cup of water and then place the trivet. Lower the mugs onto the trivet. 3. Close the lid and turn the steam release handle to Sealing position. 4. Set the Instant Pot on Pressure Cook at High and adjust time to 10 minutes. 5. When cooked, quick-release the pressure and then remove the lid carefully. 6. Sprinkle the diced mango on the top. Serve chilled.
Per Serving: Calories:205; Fat 5.5g; Sodium 64mg; Carbs 34.4g; Fiber 3.7g; Sugars 29.3g; Protein 7.3g

Traditional Apple Cake

Prep time: 10 minutes | Cook Time: 55 minutes | Serves: 8

4 apples, peeled, cored and chopped
½ teaspoon ground cloves
½ teaspoon ground cardamom
1 teaspoon ground cinnamon
3 tablespoons sugar
1 ⅓ cups flour

1 teaspoon baking powder
A pinch of salt
1 stick butter, melted
½ cup honey
2 tablespoons orange juice
½ teaspoon vanilla paste

1. Lightly brush a cake pan with oil and set it aside. 2. Toss the ground cloves, cardamom, sugar, and cinnamon over the apples. 3. Combine together the baking powder, salt, and flour in a mixing bowl. 4. In a separate bowl, add orange juice, vanilla paste, honey, and butter and combine well. 5. Stir in together with the wet ingredients to make the batter. 6. Then spoon half to the prepared baking pan. 7. On top of the batter, spread half of the apples. Then add the remaining batter on the apple chunks. Place the rest apple chunks on the top. 8. Use paper towel to cover the cake pan. 9. In the inner pot, pour 1 cup of water and place trivet. Lower the cake pan onto the trivet. 10. Close the lid and turn the steam release handle to Sealing position. Set the Instant Pot on Pressure Cook at High and adjust time to 55 minutes. 11. When cooked, naturally release the pressure and then remove the lid carefully. 12. Allow the cake to cool on a rack and sit for about 15 minutes. 13. Slice into your desired size and serve.
Per Serving: Calories:427; Fat 15.9g; Sodium 140mg; Carbs 72.5g; Fiber 4.8g; Sugars 45.2g; Protein 3.6g

Carrot and Almond Pudding

Prep time: 10 minutes | Cook Time: 10 minutes | Serves: 4

1 ½ cups jasmine rice
1 ½ cups milk
½ cup water
2 large-sized carrots, shredded
¼ teaspoon kosher salt
⅓ cup granulated sugar
2 eggs, beaten

⅓ cup almonds, ground
¼ cup dried figs, chopped
½ teaspoon pure almond extract
½ teaspoon vanilla extract
⅓ teaspoon ground cardamom
½ teaspoon ground star anise

1. In the inner pot, add carrots, salt, and jasmine rice and pour water and milk. Stir until well combined. 2. Close the lid and turn the steam release handle to Sealing position. 3. Set the Instant Pot on Pressure Cook at High and adjust time to 10 minutes. 4. When cooked, naturally release the pressure and carefully remove the lid. 5. Set the Instant Pot to Sauté at Less and then add eggs, almonds, and sugar. Stir well. 6. Cook to bring a boil and then turn off the heat. 7. Add the rest ingredients in the inner pot and stir well. The pudding will thicken as it sits. 8. Serve and enjoy!
Per Serving: Calories:249; Fat 4.8g; Sodium 138mg; Carbs 45.6g; Fiber 3.4g; Sugars 15.7g; Protein 6.4g

Creamy Carrot Soufflé

Prep time: 10 minutes | Cook Time: 45 minutes | Serves: 6

1 ½ pounds carrots, trimmed and cut into chunks
¾ cup sugar
1 teaspoon baking powder
1 teaspoon vanilla paste
¼ teaspoon ground cardamom

½ teaspoon ground cinnamon
3 tablespoons flour
3 eggs
⅓ cup cream cheese room temperature
1 stick butter, softened

1. In the inner pot, pour 1 cup of water and place a steamer basket on the bottom. Then spread the carrots in the steamer basket. 2. Close the lid and turn the steam release handle to Sealing position. 3. Set the Instant Pot on Steam at High and adjust time to 10 minutes. 4. When cooked, quick-release the pressure and remove the lid carefully. 5. In a food processor, stir together sugar, baking powder, vanilla, cardamom, cinnamon, flour, and the mashed carrot until creamy and smooth. 6. Fold in eggs one at a time and mix well. Then add butter and the cream cheese and stir well. 7. Lightly grease a baking pan. Then spoon the carrot batter inside the baking dish. 8. Transfer to the steamer basket. Close the lid and turn the steamer release handle to Sealing position. 9. Set the Instant Pot on Pressure Cook at High and adjust time to 35 minutes. 10. When cooked, naturally release the pressure about 10 minutes and then remove the lid carefully. 11. Serve and Enjoy!
Per Serving: Calories:353; Fat 21.6g; Sodium 240mg; Carbs 40.2g; Fiber 3g; Sugars 30.6g; Protein 2.9g

Chocolate Pumpkin Puddings with Cinnamon

Prep time: 10 minutes | Cook Time: 25 minutes | Serves: 4

½ cup half-and-half
1 cup pumpkin puree
⅓ cup Turbinado sugar
1 egg plus 1 egg yolk, beaten
⅓ teaspoon crystallized ginger
½ teaspoon ground cinnamon

¼ teaspoon ground nutmeg
A pinch of table salt
For the Chocolate Ganache:
½ cup chocolate chips
¼ cup double cream

1. Pour the water in the inner pot and place the trivet. 2. Grease the four ramekins with butter and set them aside. 3. Combine the half-and-half with the pumpkin puree and sugar in the mixing bowl. 4. Then fold gently in the eggs and mix well. Divide evenly the mixture into the greased ramekins and put on the trivet side by side. 5. Close the lid and turn the steam release handle to Sealing position. 6. Set the Instant Pot on Pressure Cook at High and adjust the time to 25 minutes. 7. When cooked, quick-release the pressure and remove the lid carefully. 8. Allow the pudding to cool about 2 hours. Meanwhile, microwave the chocolate until melt to make the chocolate ganache about 30 seconds. Then stir and microwave for another 15 seconds. 9. Stir in the double cream until well combined. 10. Pour the chocolate ganache over the pumpkin puddings and use a table knife to spread, letting the cream run over sides. 11. Cool in the refrigerator. Serve and enjoy!
Per Serving: Calories:269; Fat 14.4g; Sodium 99mg; Carbs 31.4g; Fiber 2.7g; Sugars 24.9g; Protein 4.9g

Rice Pudding with Cherry and Vanilla

Prep Time: 5 minutes | Cook Time: 1 hour and 5 minutes | Serves: 6

1 cup short-grain brown rice
1¾ cups nondairy milk, plus more as needed
1½ cups water
4 tablespoons unrefined sugar or pure maple syrup (use 2 tablespoons if you use a sweetened

milk), plus more as needed
1 teaspoon vanilla extract (use ½ teaspoon if you use vanilla milk)
Pinch of salt
¼ cup dried cherries or ½ cup fresh or frozen pitted cherries

1. Combine the rice, milk, water, sugar, vanilla, and salt in an Instant Pot. Select High Pressure Cook, set the timer for 30 minutes, lock the lid and check that the pressure valve is secured. 2. After the cooking period has over, allow the pressure to naturally relax on seal position for 20 minutes. 3. After the lid has been properly unlocked and removed, release the remaining pressure. Add the cherries after stirring, then loosely replace the cover for about 10 minutes. Serve with appropriate amounts of additional milk or sugar.
Per Serving: Calories 131; Fat: 1g; Sodium 2mg; Carbs: 29g; Sugars: 2.03g; Protein 2g

Walnut Monkey Bread

Prep time: 10 minutes | Cook Time: 25 minutes | Serves: 6

12 frozen egg dinner rolls, thawed
¼ cup brown sugar
1 teaspoon ground cinnamon
¼ cup walnuts, ground

¼ cup coconut oil, melted
⅓ cup powdered sugar
1 tablespoon coconut milk

1. In the inner pot, pour 1 cup of water and place trivet. Then spritz cooking spray over a Bundt pan. Set aside. 2. Cut each dinner roll in half. 3. Combine thoroughly the brown sugar, cinnamon, and walnuts in a mixing bowl. 4. In a separate bowl, add the melted coconut oil. Sink the rolls halves in the coconut oil and roll them in the brown sugar mixture to coat. 5. Spread the rolls in the prepared Bundt pan. Use a piece of aluminum foil over the pan and allow it to rise overnight at room temperature. 6. Then transfer to the trivet. 7. Close the lid and turn the steam release handle to Sealing position. 8. Set the Instant Pot on Pressure Cook at High and adjust time to 25 minutes. 9. When cooked, naturally release the pressure about 10 minutes and then remove the lid carefully. 10. Remove the bread onto serving plates. 11. Whisk the coconut milk and powdered sugar in a mixing bowl until smooth. 12. Then top with the mixture to glaze over the top and sides of the bread. 13. Serve and enjoy!
Per Serving: Calories:306; Fat 14.8g; Sodium 302mg; Carbs 41.5g; Fiber 2.6g; Sugars 14.5g; Protein 5.3g

Classic Chocolate Pots de Crème

Prep time: 10 minutes | Cook Time: 7 minutes | Serves: 4

½ cup granulated sugar
⅓ cup cocoa powder
2 tablespoons carob powder
⅔ cup whipping cream
1 cup coconut milk
1 teaspoon vanilla

½ teaspoon hazelnut extract
5 eggs, well-beaten
¼ teaspoon nutmeg, preferably
freshly grated
A pinch of coarse salt

1. Melt the sugar, milk, vanilla, hazelnut extract, cocoa powder, carob powder, and cream in a sauté pan over medium-low heat. 2. Whisk together until everything is well combined and melted. 3. Fold in the eggs and mix well. Then season with salt and nutmeg. 4. Divide the mixture among jars. 5. In the inner pot, pour 1 cup of water and place the trivet. 6. Close the lid and turn the steam release handle to Sealing position. 7. Set the Instant Pot on Pressure Cook at High and adjust time to 7 minutes. 8. When cooked, quick-release the pressure and then remove the lid carefully. 9. Cool in the refrigerator about 4 hours. Serve and enjoy!
Per Serving: Calories:311; Fat 21g; Sodium 113mg; Carbs 27.6g; Fiber 2.7g; Sugars 21.7g; Protein 7.5g

Maple Rice Pudding with Cranberry

Prep time: 10 minutes | Cook Time: 3 minutes | Serves: 4

1 cup white rice
1 ½ cups water
A pinch of salt
2 cups milk
⅓ cup maple syrup

2 eggs, beaten
1 teaspoon vanilla extract
¼ teaspoon cardamom
A pinch of grated nutmeg
½ cup dried cranberries

1. In the inner pot, add the salt, rice, and water. 2. Close the lid and turn the steam release handle to Sealing position. 3. Set the Instant Pot on Pressure Cook at High and adjust time to 3 minutes. 4. When cooked, naturally release the pressure and then carefully remove the lid. 5. Then stir in the maple syrup, eggs, vanilla extract, cardamom, nutmeg, and milk in the inner pot until well combined. 6. Set the Instant Pot to Sauté at Normal. Cook and stir from time to time until the pudding begins to boil. 7. Then turn off the heat. Add the dried cranberries and stir well. 8. Cool the pudding to let it thicken. Serve and enjoy!
Per Serving: Calories:341; Fat 5.1g; Sodium 135mg; Carbs 62.3g; Fiber 1.2g; Sugars 22g; Protein 10.1g

Lemony Mixed Berry Jam

Prep time: 10 minutes | Cook Time: 7 minutes | Serves: 10

2 ½ pounds fresh mixed berries
1 ¼ cups granulated sugar

2 tablespoons fresh lemon juice
3 tablespoons cornstarch

1. In the inner pot, add the sugar, lemon juice, and the fresh mixed berries. 2. Close the lid and turn the steam release handle to Sealing position. 3. Set the Instant Pot on Pressure Cook at High and adjust time to 2 minutes. 4. When cooked, naturally release the pressure about 15 minutes and remove the lid carefully. 5. Whisk the cornstarch with 3 tablespoons of water and stir well. 6. Set the Instant Pot on Sauté at More. Cook to bring the mixture to a rolling boil. Boil for about 5 minutes to thicken the jam, stirring frequently. 7. Serve and enjoy!
Per Serving: Calories:168; Fat 0.4g; Sodium 1mg; Carbs 41g; Fiber 4.1g; Sugars 33.2g; Protein 0.8g

Honey Butter Cake

Prep time: 10 minutes | Cook Time: 15 minutes | Serves: 6

1 cup butter cookies, crumbled
3 tablespoons butter, melted
1 egg
2 egg yolks
½ cup lemon juice

1 (14-ounce) can sweetened
condensed milk
3 tablespoons honey
½ cup heavy cream
¼ cup sugar

1. In the inner pot, pour 1 cup of water and place the trivet. Spritz nonstick cooking spray over a baking pan. 2. Combine together butter and cookies. Then press the crust in the prepared baking pan. 3. Using a hand mixer, combine the lemon juice, condensed milk, and honey. 4. Drizzle the mixture on the top of the crust. Transfer the baking pan onto the trivet and cover with foil sheet. 5. Close the lid and turn the steam release handle to Sealing position. 6. Set the Instant Pot on

Pressure Cook at High and adjust time to 15 minutes. 7. When cooked, naturally release the pressure about 15 minutes and then remove the lid carefully. 8. Whip together the heavy cream with sugar until the crema gets stiff. 9. Frost the cake and serve chilled.
Per Serving: Calories:488; Fat 22.3g; Sodium 223mg; Carbs 66.6g; Fiber 0.8g; Sugars 60.8g; Protein 8.9g

Buttery Banana Bread

Prep time: 10 minutes | Cook Time: 45 minutes | Serves: 8

1 stick butter, melted
2 eggs
1 teaspoon vanilla extract
¾ cup sugar

1 teaspoon baking soda
2 bananas, mashed
1 ½ cups all-purpose flour
½ cup coconut flaked

1. In a mixing bowl, add all the ingredients and stir well to make the batter. 2. In the inner pot, pour 1 cup of water and place the trivet on the bottom. 3. Grease lightly a baking pan with nonstick cooking oil. 4. Then place the batter into the greased pan and then transfer to the trivet. 5. Close the lid and turn the steam release handle to Sealing position. 6. Set the Instant Pot on Pressure Cook at High and adjust time to 45 minutes. 7. When cooked, quick-release the pressure and then remove the lid carefully. 8. Cool the banana bread and then slice into your desired size. Serve and enjoy!
Per Serving: Calories:305; Fat 13.2g; Sodium 258mg; Carbs 43.9g; Fiber 1.5g; Sugars 22.9g; Protein 4.3g

Blood Orange Cake

Prep time: 10 minutes | Cook Time: 40 minutes | Serves: 8

Nonstick cooking spray
3 teaspoons granulated sugar
3 blood oranges, peeled and cut
into slices
1 egg plus 1 egg yolk, beaten
1 cup sugar
1 stick butter, at room temperature
⅓ cup plain 2% yogurt

½ teaspoon ground cloves
¼ teaspoon ground cardamom
¼ teaspoon ginger flavoring
2 tablespoons fresh orange juice
1 ⅓ cups cake flour
1 ½ teaspoons baking powder
A pinch of table salt

1. Spritz nonstick cooking spray over a baking pan. 2. In the inner pot, spread the orange slices at the bottom. 3. Whisk the eggs in a mixing bowl until frothy. Then mix in sugar and then stir in butter. 4. Then add yogurt, fresh orange juice, ginger flavoring, cardamom, and cloves. 5. Combine together salt, baking powder, and the flour. 6. Then stir together the wet egg mixture with the flour mixture to make the batter. Pour the batter over the orange slices. 7. In the inner pot, pour 1 cup of water and place a metal trivet at the bottom. Then transfer the baking pan onto the trivet. 8. Close the lid and turn the steam release handle to Sealing position. 9. Then set the Instant Pot on Soup at High and adjust time to 40 minutes. 10. When cooked, quick-release the pressure and carefully remove the lid. 11. Place a platter on the cake and invert the baking pan, lifting it to reveal the oranges on top. 12. Serve and enjoy!
Per Serving: Calories:284; Fat 11.8g; Sodium 110mg; Carbs 42.2g; Fiber 2.3g; Sugars 23.7g; Protein 3.6g

Coffee Cake with Cinnamon

Prep time: 10 minutes | Cook Time: 25 minutes | Serves: 10

2 (16.3-ounce) cans refrigerated
biscuits
¾ cup granulated sugar
1 tablespoon ground cinnamon
¼ teaspoon nutmeg, preferably

freshly grated
½ cup raisins, if desired
¾ cup butter, melted
½ cup firmly packed brown sugar

1. In the inner pot, pour 1 cup of water and place the trivet. 2. Grease lightly cooking spray over the 12-cup fluted tube pan. 3. Mix the granulated sugar, nutmeg, and cinnamon in a food bag. 4. Divide the dough into biscuits and then cut into quarters. Transfer to the food bag and coat well on all sides. 5. Add into the pan and sprinkle with raisins among the biscuit pieces. 6. Whisk the melted butter with brown sugar in a small mixing bowl. Then pour the butter mixture over the biscuit. 7. Close the lid and turn the steam release handle to Sealing position. 8. Set the Instant Pot on Pressure Cook at High and adjust time to 25 minutes. 9. When cooked, naturally release the pressure about 10 minutes and then remove the lid carefully. 10. Transfer to a serving plate. Serve warm and enjoy!
Per Serving: Calories:507; Fat 18.7g; Sodium 1442mg; Carbs 79.6g; Fiber 2.4g; Sugars 33.9g; Protein 7.6g

Coconut Butternut Squash Pudding

Prep time: 10 minutes | Cook Time: 10 minutes | Serves: 6

2 pounds' butternut squash, peeled, seeded, and diced
1 cup coconut cream
½ cup maple syrup
A pinch of kosher salt
1 teaspoon pumpkin pie spice mix
6 tablespoons almond milk

1. In the inner pot, pour 1 cup of water and place a metal rack on the bottom. Place the squash in a steamer basket. Then transfer to the rack. 2. Close the lid and secure. 3. Set the Instant Pot on Steam at High and adjust time to 10 minutes. 4. When cooked, quick-release the pressure and remove the lid carefully. 5. Add the remaining ingredients in the cooked squash and stir well with a potato masher. 6. Then sauté at Normal about 4 minutes or until everything is heated completely. 7. Serve and enjoy!
Per Serving: Calories:289; Fat 12.2g; Sodium 182mg; Carbs 45.5g; Fiber 3.9g; Sugars 26.3g; Protein 3.4g

Chocolate Mini Crepes with Cinnamon

Prep time: 10 minutes | Cook Time: 25 minutes | Serves: 6

½ cup all-purpose flour
½ cup rice flour
1 ½ teaspoons baking powder
1 teaspoon vanilla paste
¼ teaspoon ground cinnamon
A pinch of salt
2 tablespoons granulated sugar
2 eggs, whisked
1 cup milk
¼ cup coconut oil
1 cup chocolate syrup

1. In the inner pot, pour 1 cup of water and place a metal rack at the bottom. 2. Lightly grease a mini muffin tin with shortening of choice. 3. Add the flour, vanilla, salt, cinnamon, eggs, sugar, milk, coconut oil, and baking powder in a mixing bowl and mix until completely combined and smooth. 4. Transfer the batter into the muffin tin and lower it onto the rack. 5. Close the lid and turn the steam release handle to Sealing position. 6. Set the Instant Pot on Pressure Cook at High and adjust time to 25 minutes. 7. When cooked, naturally release the pressure about 10 minutes and remove the lid carefully. 8. Drizzle chocolate syrup over the mini crepe and enjoy!
Per Serving: Calories:362; Fat 12.2g; Sodium 104mg; Carbs 57.8g; Fiber 2g; Sugars 30.8g; Protein 6.1g

Simple Almond Cheesecake

Prep time: 10 minutes | Cook Time: 25 minutes | Serves: 8

1 cup cookies, crushed
3 tablespoons coconut oil, melted
18 ounces' cream cheese
1 cup granulated sugar
2 eggs
⅓ cup sour cream
¼ teaspoon grated nutmeg
½ teaspoon pure vanilla extract
½ cup almonds, slivered

1. In the inner pot, pour 1 cup of water and place the trivet. 2. Lightly grease a baking pan with nonstick cooking spray. 3. Then mix the coconut oil and cookies to make a sticky crust. Then press into the greased baking pan. 4. In a mixing bowl, combine together the sugar, eggs, nutmeg, vanilla extract, sour cream, and cream cheese. 5. Pour the mixture over the crust and use a foil sheet to cover. 6. Transfer the baking pan onto the trivet. 7. Close the lid and turn the steam release handle to Sealing position. 8. Set the Instant Pot on Pressure Cook at High and adjust time to 25 minutes. 9. When cooked, naturally release the pressure for 15 minutes and then remove the lid carefully. 10. Sprinkle on the top with slivered almonds. Serve and enjoy!
Per Serving: Calories:476; Fat 34.5g; Sodium 273mg; Carbs 36.6g; Fiber 1g; Sugars 28.8g; Protein 8.5g

Creamy Cupcakes

Prep time: 10 minutes | Cook Time: 25 minutes | Serves: 4

1 cup cake flour
1 ½ teaspoons baking powder
A pinch of salt
¼ teaspoon ground cardamom
¼ teaspoon ground cinnamon
1 teaspoon vanilla extract
1 egg
½ cup honey
¼ almond milk
4 ounces' cream cheese
⅓ cup powdered sugar
1 cup heavy cream, cold

1. Combine the baking powder, cardamom, cinnamon, vanilla, flour, and salt in a mixing bowl. 2. Add in the egg, milk, and honey and then mix well. Then spoon the batter into silicone cupcake liners and use foil sheet to cover. 3. In the inner pot, pour 1 cup of water and place the trivet. Then transfer the cupcakes to the trivet. 4. Close the lid and turn the steam release handle to Sealing position. 5. Set the Instant Pot on Pressure Cook at High and adjust time to 25 minutes. 6. When cooked, naturally release the pressure about 10 minutes and then remove the lid carefully. 7. Meanwhile, mix the remaining ingredients to make frost. 8. Frost the cupcakes and serve.
Per Serving: Calories:509; Fat 22.6g; Sodium 162mg; Carbs 72.1g; Fiber 1.1g; Sugars 45.4g; Protein 7.6g

Chocolate Lava Cakes

Prep time: 10 minutes | Cook Time: 15 minutes | Serves: 6

½ stick butter
1 cup sugar
2 eggs
3 tablespoons coconut milk
1 teaspoon vanilla
1 ½ cups self-rising flour
2 tablespoons cocoa powder
1 tablespoon carob powder
4 ounces' bittersweet chocolate
4 ounces' semisweet chocolate

1. In the inner pot, pour 1 cup of water and place the trivet. 2. Add butter inside the custard cups and set them aside. 3. Beat the butter and sugar until creamy and then fold with eggs, one at a time. Then mix well. 4. Mix in the milk and vanilla. Then add cocoa powder, carob powder, and the flour and stir well. 5. Fold in chocolate and stir until well combined. 6. Divide into the prepared custard cups. Transfer to the trivet. 7. Close the lid and turn the steam release handle to Sealing position. 8. Set the Instant Pot on Pressure Cook at High and adjust time to 15 minutes. 9. When cooked, naturally release the pressure about 10 minutes and then remove the lid carefully. 10. Serve and enjoy!
Per Serving: Calories:542; Fat 22.7g; Sodium 94mg; Carbs 82g; Fiber 3.3g; Sugars 53.9g; Protein 7.9g

Stuffed Apples with Walnuts

Prep time: 10 minutes | Cook Time: 15 minutes | Serves: 4

4 baking apples
⅓ cup granulated sugar
½ teaspoon cardamom
½ teaspoon cinnamon
⅓ cup walnuts, chopped
4 tablespoons currants
2 tablespoons coconut oil

1. In the inner pot, pour 1 ½ cups of water and place a metal rack at the bottom. 2. Core the apples and scoop out a bit of the flesh with a melon baller. Add in the remaining ingredients and mix together. Divide into the cored apples. 3. Close the lid and secure. 4. Set the Instant Pot on Steam at High and adjust time to 15 minutes. 5. When cooked, quick-release the pressure and remove the lid carefully. 6. Serve with ice cream as you like. Serve and enjoy!
Per Serving: Calories:307; Fat 13.4g; Sodium 2mg; Carbs 49.9g; Fiber 6.6g; Sugars 40.5g; Protein 3.3g

Gooey Chocolate Chip Cookie Sundae

Prep time: 5 minutes | Cook time: 20 minutes | Serves: 1

1½ tablespoons butter, melted
1 tablespoon brown sugar
1 tablespoon granulated sugar
1 large egg yolk
½ teaspoon vanilla extract
⅓ cup all-purpose flour
⅛ teaspoon baking soda
1/16 teaspoon salt
1 tablespoon mini semisweet chocolate chips
1 cup water
¼ cup vanilla bean ice cream
1 tablespoon chopped pecans
1 tablespoon chocolate syrup

1. Grease an 8-ounce ramekin. Set aside. 2. In a small bowl, combine butter with brown sugar and granulated sugar until dissolved. 3. Add egg yolk and vanilla and mix until smooth. 4. Add flour, baking soda, and salt; combine to make a dough. Mix in chocolate chips. 5. Scrape dough into prepared ramekin and press into the bottom of the ramekin. Cover with foil. 6. Pour water into Instant Pot and add the trivet. Place ramekin on trivet. 7. Put on the pressure cooker's lid and turn the steam valve to "Sealing" position. 8. Set your Instant Pot on Pressure Cook. Use the "+/-" keys on the control panel to set the cooking time to 20 minutes. 9. Press the Pressure Level button to adjust the pressure to "Low". 10. Once the cooking cycle is completed, allow the steam to release naturally. 11. When all the steam is released, remove the pressure lid from the top carefully. 12. Carefully remove ramekin from the pot. Remove foil and cool 3–5 minutes. 13. Top warm cookie with ice cream, pecans, and chocolate syrup. Serve immediately.
Per Serving: Calories 489; Fat 11g; Sodium 501mg; Carbs 8.9g; Fiber 4.6g; Sugar 8g; Protein 26g

Yummy Dulce de Leche

Prep time: 10 minutes | Cook Time: 20 minutes | Serves: 2

1 can (14-ounce) sweetened   condensed milk

1. In the inner pot, place the trivet and a steamer basket on the bottom. Put the can of milk in the steamer basket. 2. Then pour water in until the can is covered. 3. Close the lid and turn the steam release handle to Sealing position. 4. Set the Instant Pot on Pressure Cook at High and adjust time to 20 minutes. 5. When cooked, naturally release the pressure and remove the lid carefully. 6. Serve and enjoy!
Per Serving: Calories:491; Fat 13.3g; Sodium 194mg; Carbs 83.2g; Fiber 0g; Sugars 83.2g; Protein 12.1g

Honey-Glazed Apples

Prep time: 10 minutes | Cook Time: 2 minutes | Serves: 4

4 apples   ½ teaspoon ground cloves
1 teaspoon ground cinnamon   2 tablespoons honey

1. In the inner pot, add all the ingredients and then pour ⅓ cup of water. 2. Close the lid and turn the steam release handle to Sealing position. 3. Set the Instant Pot on Pressure Cook at High and adjust time to 2 minutes. 4. When cooked, quick-release the pressure and carefully remove the lid. 5. Divide into serving bowls. Enjoy!
Per Serving: Calories:150; Fat 0.5g; Sodium 3mg; Carbs 40.1g; Fiber 5.8g; Sugars 31.8g; Protein 0.7g

Citrusy Berries Compote

Prep time: 10 minutes | Cook Time: 2 minutes | Serves: 4

1-pound blueberries   1 tablespoon orange juice
½ pound blackberries   ¼ teaspoon ground cloves
½ pound strawberries   1 vanilla bean
½ cup brown sugar

1. In the inner pot, add all the berries. 2. Then add sugar and set aside for 15 minutes. Add ground cloves, vanilla bean, and orange juice. 3. Close the lid and turn the steam release handle to Sealing position. 4. Set the Instant Pot on Pressure Cook at High and adjust time to 2 minutes. 5. When cooked, naturally release the pressure about 10 minutes and then remove the lid carefully. 6. Let it cool to thicken Serve and enjoy!
Per Serving: Calories:178; Fat 0.9g; Sodium 7mg; Carbs 44.5g; Fiber 6.9g; Sugars 34.7g; Protein 2.1g

Simple Mexican Horchata

Prep time: 10 minutes | Cook Time: 5 minutes | Serves: 8

20 ounces' rice milk, unsweetened   5 tablespoons agave syrup
8 ounces' almond milk,   1 cinnamon stick
unsweetened   1 vanilla bean

1. In the inner pot, add all the ingredients and combine well. 2. Close the lid and turn the steam release handle to Sealing position. 3. Set the Instant Pot on Pressure Cook at High and adjust time to 5 minutes. 4. When cooked, naturally release the pressure about 10 minutes and then carefully remove the lid. 5. Sprinkle the ground cinnamon to garnish as you desire. 6. Serve and enjoy!
Per Serving: Calories:140; Fat 7.3g; Sodium 38mg; Carbs 19.3g; Fiber 0.6g; Sugars 1g; Protein 0.8g

Nuts Cheesecake

Prep time: 10 minutes | Cook Time: 25 minutes | Serves: 10

4 tablespoons granulated sugar   1 teaspoon vanilla extract
4 tablespoons butter   1 tablespoon lemon zest
10 large graham crackers,   1 tablespoon arrowroot powder
crumbled   ½ cup golden caster sugar
3 tablespoons almonds, ground   3 eggs
⅓ teaspoon cinnamon   1 cup creme fraiche
12 ounces Philadelphia cheese   2 tablespoons golden caster sugar

1. In the inner pot, pour 1 cup of water and place a metal trivet. 2. Spritz nonstick cooking spray over a baking pan. 3. Add in 4 tablespoons of granulated sugar, almonds, cinnamon, crackers, and butter and combine into a sticky crust. Then press the crust in the baking pan. 4. Combine the vanilla extract, arrowroot powder, ½ cup

of golden caster sugar, eggs, lemon zest, and the Philadelphia cheese. 5. Pour the filling mixture over the crust and cover with a piece of foil. 6. Transfer the baking pan onto the trivet. 7. Close the lid and turn the steam release to Sealing position. 8. Set the Instant Pot on Pressure Cook at High and adjust time to 25 minutes. 9. When cooked, naturally release the pressure about 15 minutes and then remove the lid carefully. 10. Beat together the creme fraiche with 2 tablespoons of golden caster sugar. 11. Then spread over the cheesecake evenly. 12. Cover with foil and chill in the refrigerator. Serve and enjoy!
Per Serving: Calories:385; Fat 23.1g; Sodium 410mg; Carbs 37.1g; Fiber 0.9g; Sugars 27.3g; Protein 9.3g

Classic Agua de Jamaica

Prep time: 10 minutes | Cook Time: 5 minutes | Serves: 4

4 cups water   ½ teaspoon fresh ginger, peeled
½ cup dried hibiscus flowers   and minced
½ cup brown sugar   2 tablespoons lime juice

1. In the inner pot, add water, the dried hibiscus flowers, brown sugar, and fresh ginger and combine well. 2. Close the lid and turn the steam release handle to Sealing position. 3. Set the Instant Pot on Pressure Cook at High and adjust time to 5 minutes. 4. When cooked, naturally release the pressure about 10 minutes and then remove the lid carefully. 5. Pour in the lime juice and stir well 6. Allow it to cool. Serve and enjoy!
Per Serving: Calories:70; Fat 0g; Sodium 12mg; Carbs 17.9g; Fiber 0g; Sugars 17.6g; Protein 0g

Yummy Arroz Con Leche

Prep time: 10 minutes | Cook Time: 10 minutes | Serves: 4

1 cup white pearl rice   ¼ teaspoon grated nutmeg
1 cup water   1 teaspoon vanilla extract
A pinch of salt   1 teaspoon cinnamon
2 ¼ cups milk   Peel of ½ lemon
½ cup sugar

1. In the inner pot, add ice, water, and salt. 2. Close the lid and turn the steam release handle to Sealing position. 3. Set the Instant Pot on Pressure Cook at Low and adjust time to 10 minutes. 4. When cooked, naturally release the pressure about 10 minutes and then carefully remove the lid. 5. Set the Instant Pot on Sauté at Normal. Cook until the pudding starts to boil, stirring continuously. 6. Turn off the heat. Serve and enjoy!
Per Serving: Calories:228; Fat 3g; Sodium 105mg; Carbs 45.8g; Fiber 0.3g; Sugars 31.4g; Protein 5.6g

Mango Sticky Rice

Prep time: 15 minutes | Cook time: 5 minutes | Serves: 4-6

Sticky Rice
½ cup uncooked jasmine rice   coconut milk
¾ cup canned unsweetened full-fat   ⅛ teaspoon salt
Coconut Sauce
½ cup canned unsweetened full-fat   1/16 teaspoon salt
coconut milk   ½ tablespoon cornstarch
4 teaspoons sugar   ½ tablespoon cold water
For Serving
½ cup ripe mango slices, chilled   ½ teaspoon toasted sesame seeds

1. To the Instant Pot, add all Sticky Rice ingredients. 2. Put on the pressure cooker's lid and turn the steam valve to "Sealing" position. 3. Set the Instant Pot to Pressure Cook. Use the "+/-" keys on the control panel to set the cooking time to 3 minutes. 4. Press the Pressure Level button to adjust the pressure to "Low". 5. Once the cooking cycle is completed, allow the steam to release naturally. 6. When all the steam is released, remove the pressure lid from the top carefully. 7. While the rice is cooking, make the Coconut Sauce. 8. In a small saucepan over medium heat, combine coconut milk, sugar, and salt. 9. In a small bowl, mix together cornstarch and cold water to make a slurry. 10. When coconut milk mixture comes to a boil, whisk in the slurry about 1–2 minutes until thickened. 11. Remove from heat and allow to cool to room temperature. 12. Add ¼ cup Coconut Sauce to the rice in the Instant Pot and stir to combine. 13. Replace the lid and let cool 10 minutes. 14. To serve, spoon rice into a bowl and arrange mango slices over rice. 15. Pour remaining coconut sauce over the top and sprinkle with sesame seeds. Serve.
Per Serving: Calories: 489; Fat 11g; Sodium 501mg; Carbs 28.9g; Fiber 4.6g; Sugar 8g; Protein 6g

Aranygaluska Cake

Prep time: 10 minutes | Cook Time: 25 minutes | Serves: 8

1 cup granulated sugar	16 ounces refrigerated buttermilk
4 ounces' walnuts, ground	biscuits
1 tablespoon grated lemon peel	2 tablespoons cream cheese, at
4 tablespoons butter, at room	room temperature
temperature	½ cup powdered sugar
1 tablespoon fresh lemon juice	1 teaspoon vanilla extract

1. In the inner pot, pour 1 cup of water and place the trivet. 2. Mix the walnuts, lemon peel, and granulated sugar. 3. In another shallow bowl, mix the lemon juice and melted butter. 4. Cut the biscuits in half. Dip the biscuits in the butter mixture. Roll in the walnut/sugar mixture. 5. Transfer onto a loaf pan. 6. Close the lid and turn the steam release handle to Sealing position. 7. Set the Instant Pot on Pressure Cook at High and adjust time to 25 minutes. 8. When cooked, naturally release the pressure about 5 minutes and then remove the lid carefully. 9. Meanwhile, whip together the powdered sugar, cream cheese, and vanilla extract. 10. Drizzle the mixture over the hot cake. Serve and enjoy!
Per Serving: Calories:418; Fat 17.6g; Sodium 757mg; Carbs 61.2g; Fiber 1.9g; Sugars 36.6g; Protein 7.5g

Spiced Apple Cider

Prep time: 10 minutes | Cook Time: 50 minutes | Serves: 6

6 apples, cored and diced	1 teaspoon whole cloves
¾ cup brown sugar	1 small naval orange
2 cinnamon sticks	4 tablespoons rum
1 vanilla bean	4 cups water

1. In the inner pot, add all the ingredients. 2. Close the lid and turn the steam release handle to Sealing position. 3. Set the Instant Pot on Pressure Cook at High and adjust time to 50 minutes. 4. When cooked, quick-release the pressure and then remove the lid carefully. 5. Using a fork or potato masher, mash the apples and pour over a mesh strainer. 6. Serve and enjoy!
Per Serving: Calories:215; Fat 0.5g; Sodium 13mg; Carbs 50.7g; Fiber 5.9g; Sugars 42.3g; Protein 0.8g

Amazing Hot Mulled Apple Cider

Prep time: 10 minutes | Cook Time: 1 hour 30 minutes | Serves: 8

8 cups apple cider	1 teaspoon whole cloves
1 (1-inch piece) fresh ginger,	1 teaspoon allspice berries
peeled and sliced	1 orange, sliced into thin rounds
2 cinnamon sticks	½ cups brandy
2 vanilla beans	

1. In the inner pot, add apple cider, fresh ginger, cinnamon, vanilla beans, whole cloves, all spice berries, and orange rounds. 2. Close the lid and turn steam release handle to Venting position. 3. Set the Instant Pot on Slow Cook at Less and adjust time to 1 hour 30 minutes. 4. Strain the cider mixture and stir in the brandy. Serve and enjoy!
Per Serving: Calories:132; Fat 0.4g; Sodium 8mg; Carbs 32g; Fiber 0.9g; Sugars 29.2g; Protein 0.4g

Classical German Pancake

Prep time: 10 minutes | Cook Time: 30 minutes | Serves: 4

4 tablespoons butter, melted	½ teaspoon cinnamon powder
5 eggs	½ teaspoon vanilla extract
1 ¼ cups milk	1 cup canned blueberries with
1 cup all-purpose flour	syrup
¼ teaspoon kosher salt	

1. In the inner pot, pour 1 cup of water and place the trivet. Line the parchment paper over the bottom of a spring-form pan. 2. Then grease the melted butter in the bottom and sides. 3. Add in the milk, flour, salt, vanilla, cinnamon, and eggs and mix well to make the batter. Then spoon the batter into the greased pan. Transfer to the trivet. 4. Close the lid and turn the steam release handle to Sealing position. 5. Set the Instant Pot on Pressure Cook at High and adjust time to 30 minutes. 6. When cooked, quick-release the pressure and then remove the lid carefully. 7. Garnish with fresh blueberries. Serve and enjoy!
Per Serving: Calories:354; Fat 19g; Sodium 343mg; Carbs 33.4g; Fiber 1.7g; Sugars 7.7g; Protein 13.1g

Enticing Caramel Croissant Pudding

Prep time: 10 minutes | Cook Time: 25 minutes | Serves: 6

6 stale croissants, cut into chunks	3 tablespoons rum
1 cup granulated sugar	¼ teaspoon ground cinnamon
4 tablespoons water	3 eggs, whisked
1 cup milk	Lightly grease a casserole dish.
1 cup heavy cream	

1. In the inner pot, pour 1 cup of water and place the trivet. Place the croissants in the greased dish. 2. Set the Instant Pot on Sauté at Less. Cook the granulated sugar and water until brown. 3. Then add the heavy cream and milk. Cook until completely heated. Add the cinnamon, eggs, and rum and stir well. 4. Close the lid and turn the steam release handle to Sealing position. 5. Set the Instant Pot on Pressure Cook at High and adjust time to 25 minutes. 6. When cooked, naturally release the pressure about 10 minutes and then remove the lid carefully. 7. Serve and enjoy!
Per Serving: Calories:493; Fat 17.4g; Sodium 324mg; Carbs 62.1g; Fiber 1.6g; Sugars 41.4g; Protein 9.2g

Citrusy Cranberry Spritzer

Prep time: 10 minutes | Cook Time: 15 minutes | Serves: 8

12 ounces' fresh cranberries	2 cups pulp-free orange juice
½ cup granulated sugar	1 cup water

1. In the inner pot, add all the ingredients. 2. Close the lid and turn the steam release handle to Sealing position. 3. Set the Instant Pot on Pressure Cook at High and adjust time to 15 minutes. 4. When cooked, naturally release the pressure about 15 minutes and then remove the lid carefully. 5. Serve in eight glasses and add club soda. Enjoy!
Per Serving: Calories:98; Fat 0.1g; Sodium 1mg; Carbs 22.8g; Fiber 1.7g; Sugars 19.3g; Protein 0.4g

Pumpkin Pie Bites

Prep time: 5 minutes | Cook time: 20 minutes | Serves: 1

¼ cup pumpkin puree	1/16 teaspoon salt
3 tablespoons sugar	1 cup water
¼ cup heavy cream	2 tablespoons sweetened whipped
1 large egg	cream
¼ teaspoon pumpkin pie spice	

1. Grease three cups of a silicone egg bites mold. Set aside. 2. In a small bowl, whisk together pumpkin, sugar, heavy cream, egg, pumpkin pie spice, and salt until combined. 3. Equally divide the mixture among prepared egg bite mold cups. Cover tightly with foil. 4. Pour water into Instant Pot and add the trivet. 5. Place mold on trivet. Alternatively, place the mold on a silicone sling and lower into the Instant Pot. 6. Put on the pressure cooker's lid and turn the steam valve to "Sealing" position. 7. Set the Instant Pot to Pressure Cook. 8. Use the "+/-" keys on the control panel to set the timer to 20 minutes. 9. Press the Pressure Level button to adjust the pressure to "Low". 10. Once the cooking cycle is completed, allow the steam to release naturally. 11. When all the steam is released, remove the pressure lid from the top carefully. 12. Allow pie bites to cool to room temperature, then refrigerate 4–8 hours until set. 13. Remove foil, invert pie bites onto a plate, and enjoy with whipped cream.
Per Serving: Calories 334; Fat 10.9g; Sodium 454mg; Carbs 10g; Fiber 3.1g; Sugar 5.2g; Protein 05g

Peanut Butter Chocolate Fudge

Prep time: 10 minutes | Cook Time: 15 minutes | Serves: 12

16-ounce canned condensed milk	8 ounces' bittersweet chocolate
2 tablespoons peanut butter	chips
½ teaspoon ground cardamom	8 ounces' semisweet chocolate
½ teaspoon ground cinnamon	chips
1 teaspoon vanilla extract	

1. Line a piece of foil at the bottom of a baking sheet. 2. In the inner pot, combine peanut butter, milk, cinnamon, vanilla, and cardamom until well incorporated. 3. Set the Instant Pot on Sauté at Less. 4. Cook until completely warmed. Fold in the chocolate chips and stir well. 5. Transfer onto the prepared baking sheet and chill in the refrigerator until solid. 6. Cut into squares and serve. Bon appétit!
Per Serving: Calories:333; Fat 15.6g; Sodium 75mg; Carbs 44.5g; Fiber 1.9g; Sugars 39.9g; Protein 5.1g

Rican Pudding

Prep time: 10 minutes | Cook Time: 25 minutes | Serves: 8

1 pound Puerto Rican sweet bread, torn into pieces	1 cup brown sugar
1 cup water	4 cups coconut milk
1 teaspoon cinnamon powder	2 tablespoons rum
½ teaspoon ground cloves	4 eggs, beaten
1 teaspoon vanilla essence	A pinch of salt
	½ stick butter, melted

1. In the inner pot, pour 1 cup of water and place a metal trivet at the bottom. 2. Lightly grease a casserole dish and place the sweet bread pieces inside. 3. Mix the rest ingredients in a mixing bowl until well combined. Pour over the bread pieces. Set it aside and let it stand for 20 minutes. Spread the mixture evenly over the bread. 4. Close the lid and turn the steam release handle to Sealing position. 5. Set the Instant Pot on Pressure Cook at High and adjust time to 25 minutes. 6. When cooked, naturally release the pressure about 10 minutes and remove the lid carefully. 7. Serve and enjoy!
Per Serving: Calories:467; Fat 36.6g; Sodium 305mg; Carbs 32.8g; Fiber 2.7g; Sugars 28.8g; Protein 5.6g

Berry Almond Crisp

Prep time: 15 minutes | Cook time: 25 minutes | Serves: 4-6

¾ cup frozen berry mix	1/16 teaspoon ground cinnamon
½ teaspoon almond extract	1/16 teaspoon nutmeg
2 tablespoons granulated sugar	1½ tablespoons all-purpose flour
½ tablespoon cornstarch	1½ tablespoons rolled oats
1 tablespoon cold butter, cut up	1 cup water
1 tablespoon brown sugar	¼ cup vanilla ice cream

1. In a small bowl, toss together berries, almond extract, granulated sugar, and cornstarch. 2. Pour into an 8-ounce ramekin. 3. In a separate small bowl, using a fork, combine butter, brown sugar, cinnamon, nutmeg, flour, and oats until mixture resembles large crumbs. 4. Crumble over berry mixture and cover with foil. 5. Pour water into Instant Pot and add the trivet. Place ramekin on trivet. 6. Put on the pressure cooker's lid and turn the steam valve to "Sealing" position. 7. Set the Instant Pot to Pressure Cook. Use the "+/-" keys on the control panel to set the cooking time to 25 minutes. 8. Press the Pressure Level button to adjust the pressure to "Low". 9. Once the cooking cycle is completed, allow the steam to release naturally. 10. When all the steam is released, remove the pressure lid from the top carefully. 11. Carefully remove ramekin from the Instant Pot, then remove foil and let cool 5 minutes. 12. Top with ice cream and serve immediately.
Per Serving: Calories 199; Fat 5g; Sodium 41mg; Carbs 7g; Fiber 7.6g; Sugar 5g; Protein 2g

Romantic Pots de Crème

Prep time: 10 minutes | Cook Time: 6 minutes | Serves: 6

2 cups double cream	1 teaspoon instant coffee
½ cup whole milk	A pinch of pink salt
4 egg yolks	9 ounces' chocolate chips
⅓ cup sugar	

1. In the inner pot, pour 1 cup of water and place the trivet. 2. Add cream and milk in a saucepan and simmer. 3. Then combine sugar, instant coffee, salt, and egg yolks thoroughly. Whisk in the how cream mixture slowly and gently. 4. Blend together with chocolate chips. Then pour into mason jars. Transfer to the trivet. 5. Close the lid and turn the steam release handle to Sealing position. 6. Set the Instant Pot on Pressure Cook at High and adjust time to 6 minutes. 7. When cooked, naturally release the pressure and then remove the lid carefully. 8. Serve and enjoy!
Per Serving: Calories 455; Fat 31.1g; Sodium 62mg; Carbs 38.8g; Fiber 1.5g; Sugars 34.2g; Protein 6.5g

Chocolate Pudding with Apricots

Prep time: 10 minutes | Cook Time: 30 minutes | Serves: 10

4 ounces instant pudding mix	½ cup peanut butter
3 cups milk	1 ½ cups chocolate chips
1 package vanilla cake mix	½ cup dried apricots, chopped

1. Lightly grease the inner pot. 2. Combine together the milk and pudding mix in a mixing bowl. Then pour into the inner pot. 3. Follow the cake mix instruction to prepare the vanilla cake mix. Gradually add in the peanut butter. Then place the batter over the pudding. 4. Close the lid and turn the steam release handle to Sealing position. 5. Set the Instant Pot on Pressure Cook at High and adjust time to 30 minutes. 6. When cooked, naturally release the pressure about 10 minutes and then remove the lid carefully. 7. Top with chocolate chips and dried apricots. Close the lid and stand for 10 to 15 minutes or until the chocolate melts. 8. Serve and enjoy!
Per Serving: Calories:408; Fat 15.5g; Sodium 981mg; Carbs 60.5g; Fiber 3.5g; Sugars 20.2g; Protein 7.7g

Traditional Chewy Brownies

Prep time: 10 minutes | Cook Time: 20 minutes | Serves: 12

½ cup walnut butter	½ cardamom powder
½ cup sunflower seed butter	½ teaspoon cinnamon powder
1 cup coconut sugar	½ teaspoon baking soda
½ cup cocoa powder	1 teaspoon vanilla extract
2 eggs	½ cup dark chocolate, cut into chunks
A pinch of grated nutmeg	
A pinch of salt	

1. In the inner pot, pour 1 cup of water and place a metal trivet at the bottom. 2. Spritz cooking spray over a baking pan. 3. Add all ingredients except the chocolate in a mixing bowl and mix well to make a thick batter 4. Spoon onto the greased pan and then sprinkle over with the chocolate chunks. Press gently into the batter. Transfer to the trivet. 5. Close the lid and turn the steam release handle to Sealing position. 6. Set the Instant Pot on Pressure Cook at High and adjust time to 20 minutes. 7. When cooked, naturally release the pressure about 10 minutes and then remove the lid carefully. 8. Allow the brownies to cool on a rack and slice into your desired size. 9. Serve and enjoy!
Per Serving: Calories:82; Fat 1.2g; Sodium 75mg; Carbs 18.8g; Fiber 1.1g; Sugars 16.8g; Protein 1.6g

Cinnamon Pear Pie with Pecans

Prep time: 10 minutes | Cook Time: 25 minutes | Serves: 8

2 cans (12-ounce) refrigerated cinnamon rolls	½ teaspoon cinnamon
	2 tablespoons butter
¼ cup all-purpose flour	⅓ cup pecans, chopped
¼ cup packed brown sugar	5 pears, cored and sliced

1. Add all the ingredients except the pears in a large mixing bowl and mix together to make the dough. 2. Make 8 rolls from the dough and press the rolls into a lightly greased pie plate. Place the pear slices on the prepared cinnamon roll crust. Then spoon the streusel onto the pear slices. 3. In the inner pot, pour 1 cup of water and place a metal rack on the bottom. Transfer the pie plate on the rack. 4. Close the lid and turn the steam release handle to Sealing position. 5. Set the Instant Pot on Pressure Cook at High and adjust time to 25 minutes. 6. When cooked, naturally release about 5 minutes and remove the lid carefully. 7. Serve and enjoy!
Per Serving: Calories:185; Fat 8.4g; Sodium 23mg; Carbs 34.2g; Fiber 5.2g; Sugars 22.2g; Protein 1.9g

Chai White Hot Chocolate

Prep time: 10 minutes | Cook Time: 6 minutes | Serves: 5

4 cups whole milk	1 teaspoon vanilla extract
⅓ cup almond butter	A pinch of sea salt
4 tablespoons honey	A pinch of grated nutmeg
2 tablespoons Masala Chai Syrup	2 tablespoons gelatin

1. In the inner pot, add the almond butter, milk, Masala Chai Syrup, honey, sea salt, vanilla extract, sea salt, and grated nutmeg. 2. Close the lid and turn the steam release handle to Sealing position. 3. Set the Instant Pot on Pressure Cook at Low and adjust time to 6 minutes. 4. When cooked, quick-release the pressure and then remove the lid carefully. 5. Using an immersion blender, add the gelatin and mix well until the chocolate is smooth. 6. Serve and enjoy!
Per Serving: Calories:187; Fat 7g; Sodium 131mg; Carbs 23g; Fiber 0.2g; Sugars 24.3g; Protein 9g

Cinnamon-Vanilla Rice Pudding

Prep time: 20 minutes | Cook time: 8 minutes | Serves: 1

½ cup uncooked long-grain white rice
1 cup water
1/16 teaspoon salt
2 ½ tablespoons sugar
1 cup whole milk

1 large egg
½ tablespoon butter
½ tablespoon vanilla extract
2 tablespoons heavy cream
⅛ teaspoon ground cinnamon

1. To the Instant Pot, add rice, water, and salt. 2. Put on the pressure cooker's lid and turn the steam valve to "Sealing" position. 3. Set the Instant Pot to Pressure Cook. Use the "+/-" keys on the control panel to set the cooking time to 3 minutes. 4. Press the Pressure Level button to adjust the pressure to "Low". 5. Once the cooking cycle is completed, allow the steam to release naturally. 6. When all the steam is released, remove the pressure lid from the top carefully. 7. Fluff rice, then add sugar and stir to dissolve. 8. Press Sauté button and adjust to Less. Whisk in ½ cup milk and bring to a low simmer. 9. In a liquid measuring cup, measure remaining ½ cup milk and whisk together with egg until completely combined. 10. While whisking, pour egg mixture into the pot until completely incorporated. 11. Whisk about 5 minutes until thickened. Press Cancel button to turn off the heat. 12. Stir in butter, vanilla, and cream. Scoop into a bowl and serve with a sprinkle of cinnamon.
Per Serving: Calories 199; Fat 5g; Sodium 41mg; Carbs 7g; Fiber 7.6g; Sugar 5g; Protein 2g

Polynesian Hazelnut Cake

Prep time: 10 minutes | Cook Time: 25 minutes | Serves: 8

1 cup granulated sugar
4 tablespoons hazelnuts, ground
10 refrigerated biscuits
1 stick butter, melted
4 ounces' cream cheese, at room

temperature
¼ cup powdered sugar
2 tablespoons apple juice
1 teaspoon vanilla extract

1. In the inner pot, pour 1 cup of water and place the trivet. Using cooking spray, lightly grease a suitable fluted tube pan. 2. Mix 1 cup of granulated sugar and ground hazelnuts in a shallow bowl. 3. Cut the biscuits into half and then dip with melted butter. Roll in the hazelnut/sugar mixture and then arrange in the fluted tube pan. 4. Close the lid and turn the steam release handle to Sealing position. 5. Set the Instant Pot on Pressure Cook at High and adjust time to 25 minutes. 6. When cooked, naturally release the pressure about 5 minutes and then remove the lid carefully. 7. Meanwhile, whip together the cream cheese with vanilla extract, apple juice, and the powdered sugar. 8. Then pour over the hot cake. Serve and enjoy!
Per Serving: Calories:382; Fat 19.3g; Sodium 507mg; Carbs 51.1g; Fiber 0.9g; Sugars 37g; Protein 3.6g

Honey Stewed Dried Fruits

Prep time: 10 minutes | Cook Time: 2 minutes | Serves: 8

½ cup dried figs
1 cup dried apricots
½ cup sultana raisins
1 cup prunes, pitted
1 cup almonds
1 cup sugar

1 cinnamon stick
1 vanilla bean
½ teaspoon whole cloves
½ teaspoon whole star anise
2 cups water
2 tablespoons Greek honey

1. In the inner pot, add all the ingredients. 2. Close the lid and turn the steam release handle to Sealing position. 3. Set the Instant Pot on Pressure Cook at High and adjust time to 2 minutes. 4. When cooked, naturally release the pressure about 10 minutes and then remove the lid carefully. 5. Pour Greek yogurt or ice cream on the top as you desire. 6. Serve and enjoy!
Per Serving: Calories:260; Fat 6.3g; Sodium 4mg; Carbs 52.9g; Fiber 4.7g; Sugars 42.8g; Protein 3.7g

Stuffed Baked Apple À La Mode

Prep time: 15 minutes | Cook time: 7 minutes | Serves: 1

1 medium Honeycrisp apple
1 tablespoon brown sugar
1 tablespoon butter
½ teaspoon ground cinnamon
1 tablespoon chopped pecans

1 tablespoon sweetened dried cranberries
1 cup water
¼ cup vanilla ice cream

1. Core apple and scrape out center to create a cavity in the middle about 1" in diameter. 2. In a small bowl, mix together brown sugar, butter, cinnamon, pecans, and cranberries into a paste. 3. Scoop paste into apple and cover the top with a small piece of foil. 4. Pour water into Instant Pot and add the trivet. Place apple on trivet. 5. Put on the pressure cooker's lid and turn the steam valve to "Sealing" position. 6. Set the Instant Pot to Pressure Cook. 7. Press the Pressure Level button to adjust the pressure to "Low". 8. Use the "+/-" keys on the control panel to set the cooking time to 7 minutes. 9. Once the cooking cycle is completed, allow the steam to release naturally. 10. When all the steam is released, remove the pressure lid from the top carefully. 11. Using tongs, carefully remove apple from the Instant Pot and transfer to a bowl. Let cool 5 minutes. 12. Top with ice cream and serve immediately.
Per Serving: Calories 334; Fat 10.9g; Sodium 354mg; Carbs 25g; Fiber 4.1g; Sugar 8.2g; Protein 6g

Vanilla Crème Brulee

Prep time: 20 minutes | Cook time: 8 minutes | Serves: 1

½ cup heavy cream
½ teaspoon vanilla bean paste
2 large egg yolks

2 tablespoons sugar
1 cup water
3 whole raspberries

1. In a small saucepan over medium-high heat, combine cream and vanilla bean paste until steaming. Do not boil and then remove from heat. 2. In a small bowl, whisk egg yolks and 1 tablespoon sugar until light and smooth. 3. While whisking, slowly pour hot cream into egg yolks and whisk to combine. 4. Pour cream mixture through a fine-mesh strainer into an 8-ounce ramekin. Cover with foil. 5. Pour water into Instant Pot and add the trivet. Place ramekin on trivet. 6. Put on the pressure cooker's lid and turn the steam valve to "Sealing" position. 7. Set the Instant Pot to Pressure Cook. Use the "+/-" keys on the control panel to set the cooking time to 8 minutes. 8. Press the Pressure Level button to adjust the pressure to "Low". 9. Once the cooking cycle is completed, allow the steam to release naturally. 10. When all the steam is released, remove the pressure lid from the top carefully. 11. Remove ramekin to cooling rack. Let cool and then refrigerate 6–8 hours. 12. To serve, remove foil. Sprinkle remaining 1 tablespoon sugar over the top of the crème Brûlée. 13. Using a kitchen torch, quickly torch the sugar in small circles until sugar is completely caramelized. 14. Cool 1 minute, then top with raspberries and serve.
Per Serving: Calories 334; Fat 10.9g; Sodium 354mg; Carbs 25g; Fiber 4.1g; Sugar 8.2g; Protein 11g

Conclusion

The Instant Pot appliance has two programs: Pressure cooking and Non-pressure cooking. Pressure cook, steam, rice, porridge, bean/chili, meat/stew, and soup/stock are included in pressure cooking. In non-pressure cooking, sauté, slow cook, and yogurt are included. It comes with a cooker base, inner pot, stealing ring, and steam-release valve, float valve, condensation collector, and pressure lid. This cookbook is filled with delicious pressure cooking and non-pressure cooking recipes. It is a wonderful appliance because you can cook food in very little time. You didn't need to purchase separate appliances. You can select your favorite recipe, adjust the pressure level, cooking time, and temperatures, put ingredients, close the lid, and press the start/stop button to start cooking. It has user-friendly operating buttons. The cleaning process is pretty simple. The install and removal process of accessories are super easy. Thank you for reading this book.
Stay safe and happy cooking!!!

Appendix 1 Measurement Conversion Chart

WEIGHT EQUIVALENTS

US STANDARD	METRIC (APPROXIMATE)
1 ounce	28 g
2 ounces	57 g
5 ounces	142 g
10 ounces	284 g
15 ounces	425 g
16 ounces (1 pound)	455 g
1.5pounds	680 g
2pounds	907 g

VOLUME EQUIVALENTS (LIQUID)

US STANDARD	US STANDARD (OUNCES)	METRIC (APPROXIMATE)
2 tablespoons	1 fl.oz	30 mL
¼ cup	2 fl.oz	60 mL
½ cup	4 fl.oz	120 mL
1 cup	8 fl.oz	240 mL
1½ cup	12 fl.oz	355 mL
2 cups or 1 pint	16 fl.oz	475 mL
4 cups or 1 quart	32 fl.oz	1 L
1 gallon	128 fl.oz	4 L

VOLUME EQUIVALENTS (DRY)

US STANDARD	METRIC (APPROXIMATE)
⅛ teaspoon	0.5 mL
¼ teaspoon	1 mL
½ teaspoon	2 mL
¾ teaspoon	4 mL
1 teaspoon	5 mL
1 tablespoon	15 mL
¼ cup	59 mL
½ cup	118 mL
¾ cup	177 mL
1 cup	235 mL
2 cups	475 mL
3 cups	700 mL
4 cups	1 L

TEMPERATURES EQUIVALENTS

FAHRENHEIT (F)	CELSIUS (C) (APPROXIMATE)
225 ℉	107℃
250 ℉	120℃
275 ℉	135℃
300 ℉	150℃
325 ℉	160℃
350 ℉	180℃
375 ℉	190℃
400 ℉	205℃
425 ℉	220℃
450 ℉	235℃
475 ℉	245℃
500 ℉	260℃

Appendix 2 Recipes Index

Printed in Great Britain
by Amazon